For Dick

An American with an Iranian soul !

Love
Layla
February 2017

THE FALL
OF
HEAVEN

HENRY HOLT AND COMPANY
NEW YORK

THE FALL
OF
HEAVEN

The Pahlavis and the Final Days of Imperial Iran

Andrew Scott Cooper

Henry Holt and Company, LLC
Publishers since 1866
175 Fifth Avenue
New York, New York 10010
www.henryholt.com

Henry Holt® and 𝕳® are registered trademarks of Henry Holt and Company, LLC.

Library of Congress Cataloging-in-Publication Data

Names: Cooper, Andrew Scott, author.
Title: The fall of heaven : the Pahlavis and the final days of imperial Iran / Andrew Scott Cooper.
Description: First edition. | New York, New York : Henry Holt and Co., 2016. |
    Includes bibliographical references and index.
Identifiers: LCCN 2015046095| ISBN 9780805098976 (hardback) |
    ISBN 9780805098983 (electronic book)
Subjects: LCSH: Iran—History—Mohammad Reza Pahlavi, 1941–1979. |
    Mohammad Reza Pahlavi, Shah of Iran, 1919–1980. | Farah, Empress, consort of
    Mohammad Reza Pahlavi, Shah of Iran, 1938– | BISAC: HISTORY / Middle East / General. |
    HISTORY / Revolutionary. | HISTORY / Modern / General.
Classification: LCC DS318 .C655 2016 | DDC 955.05/3092—dc23
LC record available at http://lccn.loc.gov/2015046095

ISBN: 978-0-8050-9897-6

Our books may be purchased in bulk for promotional, educational, or business
use. Please contact your local bookseller or the Macmillan Corporate and
Premium Sales Department at (800) 221-7945, extension 5442, or by e-mail
at MacmillanSpecialMarkets@macmillan.com.

First Edition 2016
Designed by Meryl Sussman Levavi
Printed in the United States of America

3   5   7   9   10   8   6   4   2

To My Friends

CONTENTS

PART TWO
FAREWELL THE SHAH

~

PEOPLE

The Pahlavi Family

Mohammad Reza Shah (1919–1980). King-Emperor of Iran (1941–1979). Son of Reza Shah (1878–1944) and Taj ol-Moluk (1896–1982), whose marriage also produced Princess Shams (1917–1996), Princess Ashraf (1919–2016), and Prince Ali Reza (1922–1954). Mohammad Reza Shah married three times and fathered five children:

1. Princess Fawzia of Egypt (1921–2013). Queen-Empress of Iran (1941–1948). Daughter of King Faud I of Egypt (1868–1936) and sister of King Farouk I of Egypt (1920–1965). Her marriage to the Shah produced one daughter:

   Princess Shahnaz (b. 1940). Married (1) Ardeshir Zahedi (b. 1928), son of General Fazlollah Zahedi (1897–1963), who led the 1953 army coup against Mohammad Mossadeq (1882–1967). (2) Khosrow Djahanbani (1942–2014), scion of a wellborn family whose conversion to fundamentalist Islam scandalized the Imperial Court.

2. Soraya Esfandiary-Bakhtiary (1932–2001). Queen-Empress of Iran (1951–1958). Her childless marriage to the Shah ended in divorce.

3. Farah Diba (b. 1938). Queen-Empress of Iran (1959–1979). Her marriage to the Shah produced two sons and two daughters:

   Crown Prince Reza (b. 1960). Married Yasmine Etemad-Amini (b. 1968). The couple has three children: Princess Noor (b. 1992), Princess Iman (b. 1993), and Princess Farah (b. 2004).

   Princess Farahnaz (b. 1963).

   Prince Ali Reza (1966–2011). His relationship with Raha Didevar produced Princess Iryana Leila (b. 2011).

   Princess Leila (1970–2001).

The Imperial Court and Government

Mahnaz Afkhami (b. 1941). Appointed in 1975 as only the second minister of women's affairs in the world.

Amir Aslan Afshar (b. 1922). Iran's ambassador to Austria, the United States, Mexico, and West Germany. Served as the last grand master of ceremonies at the Imperial Court.

Asadollah Alam (1919–1978). Prime Minister (1962–1964) who crushed Khomeini's June 1963 rebellion and served loyally as minister of the Imperial Court (1967–1977).

Jamshid Amuzegar (b. 1923). Minister of finance (1965–1974) and minister of the interior (1974–1977). Appointed prime minister in 1977 to stabilize Iran's economy.

Gholam Reza Azhari (1917–2001). Chief of staff of the Imperial Iranian Armed Forces (1971–1978). Appointed prime minister in November 1978 to head the military government.

Shahpur Bakhtiar (1914–1991). Opposition politician who served as the Shah's last prime minister. Assassinated in Paris by agents of the Islamic Republic.

Hossein Fardust (1917–1987). The Shah's closest childhood friend. Served as deputy head of Savak (1968–1978) and betrayed him to the revolutionaries.

Reza Ghotbi (b. 1938). The Queen's cousin and close confidant. Served as director of National Iranian Radio and Television for a decade until September 1978.

Amir Abbas Hoveyda (1919–1979). Prime minister of Iran (1965–1977) and minister of the Imperial Court (1977–1978). Executed by the revolutionaries.

Nasser Moghadam (1921–1979). Led Savak's Third Directorate and G2 military intelligence before succeeding Nasiri as new Savak chief in June 1978. Executed by the revolutionaries.

Nematollah Nasiri (1911–1979). Commander of the Imperial Guard, head of National Police, and chief of Savak from 1965 to 1978 who favored tough measures to combat subversion. Appointed Iran's ambassador to Pakistan in June 1978. Recalled and arrested for corruption. Executed by the revolutionaries.

Seyyed Hossein Nasr (b. 1933). Scholar of Islam who served as the last head of Queen Farah's Special Bureau. Favored Islamizing the monarchy to prevent revolution.

Hassan Pakravan (1911–1979). Chief of Savak who reformed the security forces and intervened to prevent Khomeini's execution in 1963. Executed by the revolutionaries.

Parviz Sabeti (b. 1936). Law graduate who rose to lead Savak's Third Directorate in the midseventies. Warned about the dangers of corruption and ill-timed liberalization.

Jafar Sharif-Emami (1910–1996). Prime minister (1960–1961) and president of the Senate (1964–1978). Served as prime minister from August to November 1978.

Ardeshir Zahedi (b. 1928). Son of General Fazlollah Zahedi, who married Princess Shahnaz. Served as foreign minister and ambassador to London and Washington.

The Shia Ulama or Clerical Leadership

Grand Ayatollah Abol Qasem Khoi (1899–1992). Paramount *marja* of the Shia faithful since 1970. Opposed Khomeini's ideas on religious government. Received Queen Farah on her ill-fated trip to Najaf in November 1978.

Grand Ayatollah Ruhollah Khomeini (1902–1989). Leader of hard-line group within the Shia *ulama* opposed to the 1906 Constitution and the Pahlavi state. Formulated the concept of Islamic government called *velayat-e faqih*. Exiled in 1964 for trying to overthrow the Shah. Returned to Iran in February 1979, seized power, and established an Islamic theocracy.

Imam Musa Sadr (1928–?). Iranian-born, charismatic leader of Lebanon's Shia community opposed to Khomeini's doctrine of velayat-e faqih. Disappeared in Libya in August 1978 en route to a secret meeting in West Germany with the Shah's envoy.

Grand Ayatollah Kazem Shariatmadari (1905–1986). Senior marja inside Iran who led the "quietist" ulama. Supported the 1906 Constitution. Opposed Khomeini's velayat-e faqih. Tried and failed to prevent the overthrow of the monarchy.

The Revolutionaries

Mehdi Bazargan (1908–1995). Former National Front official who led the breakaway Islamist group Liberation Movement of Iran. Held secret talks with U.S. embassy staff in an effort to win American support. Briefly held the post of prime minister of Iran after the revolution.

Abolhassan Banisadr (b. 1933). Leftist opposition figure who plotted revolution from exile in Paris. Persuaded Khomeini to lead an umbrella group of anti-Pahlavi opposition forces. Elected and later deposed as the Islamic Republic's first president.

Sadegh Ghotzbadegh (1936–1982). Leftist who cultivated close ties to radical Arab regimes and Yasser Arafat's PLO. Facilitated foreign aid to the anti-Pahlavi opposition. Foreign minister of the Islamic Republic later executed for plotting to overthrow Khomeini.

United States Embassy

George Lambrakis (b. 1931). Led Embassy Tehran's political section under Ambassador Sullivan. Held secret meetings with opposition leaders opposed to the Shah.

John Stempel (b. 1938). Lambrakis's deputy. Liaised with Soviet diplomat Guennady Kazankin. Cultivated Mehdi Bazargan and other prominent opposition figures.

William Sullivan (1922–2013). Ambassador to Iran. Oversaw secret talks with opposition leaders even as he pressed the Shah to restrain his security forces. Favored the Shah's departure from Iran and Khomeini's return from exile.

The White House

Zbigniew Brzezinski (b. 1928). White House national security adviser. Overestimated the Shah's durability and underestimated the threat posed by militant Islam.

Jimmy Carter (b. 1924). President whose ambivalence toward the Shah led to a debilitating split among his advisers about how to manage the collapse of the Pahlavi regime.

Cyrus Vance (1917–2002). Secretary of state who harbored reservations about the Shah. Pressed the Shah to restrain his security forces and opposed U.S. military involvement in Iran.

EVENTS OF THE 1978–1979 REVOLUTION

1978

JANUARY

    1: Carter leaves Iran after one-day state visit.

    7: *Ettelaat* publishes article critical of Khomeini.

    9: Shah flies to Aswan to meet with Egypt's Sadat.
       Khomeini supporters riot in Qom.

14–15: Weekend of religious unrest in several cities.

  27: UFO sighted over Tehran.

FEBRUARY

    1: Shah takes part in "satellite summit."

  11: Shah, Queen Farah open Tehran's new Museum of Persian Carpets.

  18: Riots in northern city of Tabriz.

  27: Shah dismisses religious protesters: "The caravan passes and the dog barks."

MARCH

10–13: Shah, Queen Farah tour Ahwaz and Abadan.

  13: Israeli diplomats leave Kish Island, voice concern about stability in Iran.

  21: Start of Nowruz, Persian New Year festivities.

27–31: Third wave of urban unrest with arson attacks, mob violence.
       Shariatmadari urges Sabeti to assassinate Khomeini.

APRIL

 1–3: Final three days of Nowruz disturbances.

  21: Security forces ambush, arrest students near village of Darakeh.

  28: Shah meets with Ronald Reagan.

MAY

6: Shah returns to Tehran from inspection tour of southern seaports.
9–10: Fourth wave of urban unrest spreads to Tehran's southern suburbs.
11: Shah approves limited crackdown by security forces.
12: Shah opens dialogue with Shariatmadari and moderate ulama.
13: Shah's press conference fails to reassure middle-class opinion.
Security chiefs meet to plot strategy to handle unrest.
16–22: Shah, Queen Farah on state visit to Bulgaria and Hungary.
25: U.S. diplomat Stempel's first meeting with Bazargan.
30: Stempel's second meeting with Bazargan.
28: Shah, Queen Farah fly to Mashad on inspection tour.

JUNE

1: Shah, Queen Farah return from Khorassan Province.
5: Anniversary of 1963 uprising passes without incident.
6: Shah reforms Savak, replaces Nasiri with Moghadam.
Shah meets with Nahavandi's liberals, promises "maximum liberty."
12: Israel's Lubrani predicts overthrow of Iranian monarchy.
19: Forty-day memorial protests contained, no protest deaths reported.

JULY

3: Nasiri tells Lebanon's al-Khalil that Musa Sadr wants to help Shah.
9: U.S. diplomat Nass, Huyser visit Shah at Nowshahr.
18: Soviet diplomat Kazankin tells Stempel Shah has cancer.
Stempel holds third meeting with Bazargan.
21: Death of Haj Sheikh Ahmad Kafi triggers riots in Mashad.
31: Disappearance of Isfahan's Ayatollah Jalal Al-Din Taheri.

AUGUST

1: First day of riots in Isfahan.
5: First day of Ramadan.
In Constitution Day speech, Shah promises democracy and elections.
10–11: Insurrection, martial law in Isfahan.
11: Griffith warns Brzezinski of instability in Iran.
13: Tehran's Khansalar Restaurant bombed in terrorist attack.
17: Shah holds press conference, admits he underestimated unrest.
19: National Uprising Day.
Arson attack on Rex Cinema in Abadan kills more than 420.
27: Shah replaces Amuzegar with Sharif-Emami.
29: Shah hosts China's Hua.
Saddam Hussein offers to assassinate Khomeini.
31: Musa Sadr is missing in Tripoli.

SEPTEMBER

4: Eid-e Fetr march draws large crowds in downtown Tehran.
Shah decides he has lost the *farr* or mantle of kingship.

7: Pro-Khomeini forces stage rally in central Tehran.
Government approves martial law.

8: Violence erupts at Jaleh Square, 88 killed.

10: Carter phones Shah to express support.

11: Lebanon reports Musa Sadr missing.

16: Tabas earthquake.

24: Oil workers strike in the southern fields.

OCTOBER

1: Riots, sabotage attacks hit cities not under martial law.

6: Speaking before Majles, Shah pledges more liberalization.
Khomeini arrives in Paris.

10–31: Iran's economy crippled by strike action.

NOVEMBER

1: Shah tells U.S., UK ambassadors he may leave the country.

2: White House officials hold first crisis meeting.

4: Troops fire on students outside Tehran University.

5: Widespread rioting, arson in central Tehran.

6: Military government installed under Azhari.
Shah tells the nation he has "heard the voice of revolution."
Khomeini pledges to topple the Pahlavi Dynasty.

9: Sullivan's "Thinking the Unthinkable" telegram.

18: Queen Farah flies to Iraq to meet with Khoi.

25–30: Queen Farah meets with Shahpur Bakhtiar.

27: Khomeini's face "appears" in the moon.

DECEMBER

10–11: Millions march during Muharram religious observances.

12–31: Wealthy Iranians, foreign residents flee Iran en masse.

27: Martial law collapses in Tehran amid scenes of anarchy.

29: Shah replaces Azhari with Bakhtiar.

1979

JANUARY

4: Huyser arrives in Tehran with orders to prevent coup.

5: Leaders of four Western powers meet in Guadeloupe.

6: Shah announces he will leave Iran for an extended "vacation."
Western leaders agree the Shah is finished.

15: Youngest Pahlavi children fly out of Iran.
Shah, Queen Farah throw small farewell party at Niavaran.

16: Shah, Queen Farah leave Iran for the last time.

FEBRUARY

    1: Khomeini returns to Iran.

10–11: Islamist, leftist militias assault royalist bastions.
      Imperial Army declares neutrality.
      Rebels triumph, seize power.

APRIL

    1: Islamic Republic declared, monarchy abolished.

Tehran
1978
Alborz Mountains
SHEMIRAN
Saadabad Palace and grounds
Niavaran Palace
Park Niavaran
NIAVARAN
TAJRISH
FARMANIEH
QEYTARIEH
Royal Tehran Hilton Hotel
ELAHIEH
SHAHANSHAH FREEWAY
Saltanatabad army garrison
Imperial Sports Club
ZARGANDEH
SALTANATABAD
Goethe Institute
Imperial Guard
LAVIZAN
Tehran American School (Middle & elementary school campus)
DARROUS
SALTANAT ABAD
OLD SHEMIRAN ROAD
PAHLAVI
JORDAN ROAD
ZAFAR
DAVOUDIEH
Park Lavizan
ARDESHIR-E-BABAKAN
Hosseiniyeh Ershad
SIMETRI-YE-MEMUNE
TARASHT
AYYUBI
Tehran American School (High school campus)
VANAK HIGHWAY
MOHAMMAD REZA SHAH-E-PAHLAVI
DARIUSH-E-KABIR
Supreme Commanders' Staff
ABBASABAD
BISTO PANJ-E-SHAHRIVAR
BASTAN
BAKHTAR
ROOSEVELT
SABALAN
TAKHT-E TAVOUSS
N
W
E
S
Museum of Contemporary Art
Carpet Museum
Park Farah
ELIZABETH II BLVD.
To Mehrebad Airport and Shahyad Monument
U.S. Embassy
OLD SHEMIRAN ROAD
AMIN-OD-DOWLEH
1/2
0
1 mile
0
1 kilometer
DAMAVAND
Tehran University
TAKHT-E JAMSHID
SHAH REZA
Russian Embassy
EISENHOWER BLVD.
AZARBAIJAN
Rudaki Concert Hall
Office of the Prime Minister
British Embassy
Majles (Parliament)
Jaleh Square (Meydan-e Jaleh)
Police Headquarters
FARAH-ABAD
Senate
SEPAH
Ministry of Justice
SHAHBAZ
Ministry of Interior
Ministry of Finance
Golestan Palace (Shamsol-Emareh Palace)
Grand Bazaar
Map by Gene Thorp
U.S.S.R
Caspian Sea
0
400 mi
0
400 km
TUR.
U.S.S.R
Tehran
IRAQ
AFGH.
IRAN
Persian Gulf
PAK.
SAUDI ARABIA
U.A.E.
OMAN
Arabian Sea

PART ONE

LOOKING FOR RAIN

1919–1977

The angel said, "I am Sorush. I came
In answer to your faith, and soon you'll be
The world's king, glorious in your sovereignty:
You'll reign for thirty-eight long years if you
Act righteously in everything you do."
He vanished, and the world has never known
A vision like the one Khosrow was shown.

—*THE PERSIAN BOOK OF KINGS*

I turn to right and left, in all the earth
I see no signs of justice, sense, or worth;
A man does evil deeds, and all his days
Are filled with with luck and universal praise;
Another's good in all he does—he dies
A wretched, broken man whom all despise.

—THE PERSIAN BOOK OF KINGS

Ingratitude is the prerogative of the people.

—THE SHAH

On Sunday, February 15, 2015, under a low gray canvas of threatening skies, two motorcades flanked by police escorts pulled up outside the Unknown Soldier Memorial in Cairo, Egypt. Bodyguards armed with automatic weapons quickly formed a protective cordon, and military officers in attendance smartly saluted, but the smiles on the faces of the two women at the center of the scrum showed they were more interested in each other than in the men fussing around them. Farah Pahlavi, Iran's last queen and empress, and Jehan Sadat, former first lady of Egypt, were old friends and had looked forward to their reunion. They embraced, chatted, and then walked in silence toward the soaring arches of the memorial and beyond to the eternal flame that marked the resting place of Jehan's husband, the late president Anwar Sadat, slain by Islamist gunmen a few hundred yards away during a 1981 military parade. The sight of the two ladies standing with heads bowed stirred powerful emotions among spectators and brought back memories of another time and another place. Forty years ago, Farah Pahlavi and Jehan Sadat were young women at the forefront of progressive change in the Middle East. Passionate advocates for the rights of women and children, they lobbied for passage of laws to empower women in the workplace and in the family. They supported literacy campaigns; women's access to education; health care, arts, and culture; and antipoverty initiatives. They traveled widely in their own countries, delivered speeches and addressed public rallies, received visiting dignitaries, and represented their countries abroad. Their activism was encouraged by two husbands who welcomed the presence of strong, intelligent wives as partners and helpmates. The Pahlavi and Sadat marriages broke the mold in conservative Muslim societies, where the consorts of ruling leaders were expected to maintain a dignified silence in public.

The clouds over Cairo were a reminder of the tempests brewing elsewhere in the region. Four years earlier, the Arab Spring revolutions had raised hopes for a new era of democracy and prosperity in a part of the world sorely lacking both. Euphoria soon gave way to despair. From the shores of the southern Mediterranean to the heartland of the old Babylonian Empire political extremists and religious fanatics rushed to fill the void left by the collapse of the old order, and the region's architecture crumpled beneath the pressure of civil wars, insurgencies, rebellions, assassinations, and terrorist atrocities. Borders dissolved, cities were sacked, and hundreds of thousands were put to the sword in scenes more reminiscent of the thirteenth than the twenty-first century. Women and children were sold as war booty. Barrel bombs and chemical weapons rained down from the sky on once peaceful hamlets and villages. Archaeological ruins that had stood since antiquity were leveled. Journalists and aid workers who rushed to the scene were captured and publicly beheaded. Millions of terrified, traumatized people poured out of Iraq and Syria in search of safe havens and refuge in Turkey, Jordan, and Lebanon. Others decided to abandon the region altogether and make the long, dangerous trek to Europe. Terror followed in their wake: several weeks before Farah Pahlavi arrived in Cairo black-clad gunmen pledging allegiance to the Islamic State and al-Qaeda carried out atrocities near her home in Paris, massacring journalists and shoppers in two separate attacks.

The sight of Farah Pahlavi and Jehan Sadat in Cairo presented a poignant reminder that the removal of their husbands from power a generation earlier opened the floodgates to today's carnage. In the 1970s Mohammad Reza Pahlavi, the King of Iran, and his friend President Anwar Sadat of Egypt dominated political life in the Middle East. The Shah's great hope was that he and Sadat, inheritors of two great empires, could work together to form a bulwark of stability and moderation and keep the forces of extremism at bay. When the ground suddenly shifted beneath their feet, the first pillar fell with surprising ease. After a year of mounting unrest the Shah was forced from power in January 1979 and died in Cairo the following year. Eighteen months later the second pillar fell, this time in a matter of seconds. In October 1981 the Egyptian president was slain when Islamist gunmen attacked the presidential reviewing stand at an army parade. The Shah's eldest son and heir, Reza Pahlavi, had been invited to attend the ceremony as Sadat's personal guest; his last-minute cancellation probably saved his life.

Every summer since then Farah Pahlavi had flown to Cairo to honor her husband's memory and legacy. Her pilgrimages were curtailed in 2011 when Sadat's successor, President Hosni Mubarak, was overthrown in a revolution that brought an Islamist government to power. Farah thought it prudent to stay away until political passions cooled. During her years in exile she had earned a reputation as a tenacious critic of fundamentalist Islam and she continued to champion the rights of women and campaign against religious law. Two years passed and protests by Cairo's middle class led the army under General Abdel Fattah el-Sisi to stage a coup against the Islamists. Eighteen months later, Sisi signaled the Queen that she was welcome to return to Cairo for a visit that he hoped would be brief and low-key. His conditions suited her wishes. "I didn't want to come on the anniversary with the crowds and photographers and flowers," she said. "It is better to be discreet. I want this to be private."

IN THE FIVE years she was away Farah Pahlavi experienced unfathomable personal tragedy and a late life triumph. The suicide of her third child, Ali Reza, in 2011 and the tragic echoes of his sister's death a decade earlier left her in a daze of grief. Both her youngest children had been traumatized during the revolution and suffered from depression and anxiety. Her distress was further compounded when Ben Affleck's movie *Argo* resurrected old allegations that her husband had ruled Iran as a blood-soaked tyrant while she, the Queen, had whiled away her time bathing in milk.

Farah was warned by friends not to watch *Argo* but she attended a screening anyway to see what the fuss was about. She left the cinema devastated and wrote the director a letter defending her husband's record and pointing out *Argo*'s factual inaccuracies and falsehoods. Affleck ignored her and went on to win an Oscar. During that bleak period it seemed as though every time Farah Pahlavi tried to move on with her life events from the past kept pulling her back. Above all, she longed to be near her husband. "She needs to talk to him," said a close friend—she needed to go to Cairo. Yet even in the midst of her sadness and frustration, Farah Pahlavi experienced a remarkable revival of her fortunes.

The Queen's decision to participate in a documentary on the Iranian revolution seemed straightforward enough. *From Tehran to Cairo* was produced by Manuto, a London-based Persian-language television station whose programming is beamed into Iran via satellite. The station's mix of current affairs and pop culture is a favorite among young Iranians. What happened next caught everyone by surprise. When word spread that Iran's last queen was set to talk about the revolution the streets of Tehran emptied out as commuters rushed home to turn on their televisions. Farah's warmth, humor, and intelligence came as a surprise to younger viewers conditioned to see her as one of the "corrupt of the earth." In their tens of thousands, after the broadcast, Iranians wrote to the Queen applauding her courage and thanking her for her years in public life. Many correspondents expressed regret that the 1979 revolution had happened at all. They included ordinary citizens but also government officials, clerics, and even officers serving in the armed forces who sent the Queen their best wishes and apologized for her treatment at the hands of the regime. Remarkably, some regime officials even declared themselves ready to support the overthrow of the Islamic Republic and a restoration of the monarchy.

Their e-mails and letters were filled with regret, longing, and bitter self-reproach. "Dear Lady," wrote one young Iranian, "I did not live during the reign of the Shah nor did I witness the revolution. Each time I look at the photos of you and the Shah, I wonder what our future could have been. My generation was not the cause of the revolution. The people in power are a bunch of Arab worshippers. I was recently beaten up by the Basiji [security forces] who found a photo of the late Shah on my phone. I love you." "As an Iranian," wrote one middle-class woman, "I am ashamed of what my compatriots did to you and your family. We did not appreciate you at the time you were in power. We are now paying the price for our ignorance. How can we ever renew those days? I want you to know that an entire nation is sorry and full of remorse. Your memory is the brightest part of our history. Your good name is eternal." And this, from a young man clinging to a past he never knew: "I take great pride in being born in Iran in 1977 in the last year of the reign of the Shah," he wrote. "I have a big collection of photographs of you and your family and I look at them for solace. It is my wish to visit the grave of the Shahanshah. I thank you for all your interviews and speeches in defense of the Shah. . . . Please call me if you can. And please send me some photographs."

In February 2016 the Islamic Republic celebrated thirty-seven years in power, coincidentally the same length of years as the Shah ruled over Iran. The anniversary provided Iranians with an opportunity to compare and contrast two very different eras and systems of government. Yet if the attitudes expressed by many ordinary people were any indication, the guardians of the Islamic Republic were wary about submitting to the litmus test of public opinion. Many Iranians associated religious rule with failed state policies, corruption, and repression. Even in clerical circles there was a quiet admission that the regime's unpopularity had translated into broad public apathy and cynicism toward religion. Religious and political leaders worried about the secular mood stirring among a new generation of Iranians who were enamored with Iran's pre-Islamic Persian heritage. These rebels sported amulets, necklaces, and rings inscribed with images of Cyrus and Darius, the celebrated kings who centuries before the birth of the Prophet Mohammad transformed Persia into the world's first sole superpower. They made the trek to Pasargade outside Shiraz to stand before Cyrus's tomb, where the Shah celebrated twenty-five hundred years of Persian monarchy in 1971. They immersed themselves in the art and culture of the Safavid and Qajar Eras. Even the tourist store at Niavaran Palace where the Pahlavis once resided now hawked Cyrus memorabilia.

During my visit to the holy city of Qom in 2013 I listened as a group of religious scholars conceded that universities around the country felt compelled to offer special history courses tailored to remind students why there had been a revolution in the first place. As part of its propaganda offensive to discredit the Pahlavi Dynasty, state-run television produced a soap opera that depicted the Shah as an American stooge while his family and courtiers flounced about in ball gowns and elaborate uniforms. In a country where people assume the opposite of what the government tells them to be true, the show's popularity suggested that the public appetite for programming on Iran's former imperial dynasty had only been whetted.

After a long pause the wheel of history was turning again. Nostalgia and reverence for the past were hardly confined to the generation of young Iranians born after the revolution. Their parents and grandparents reminisced about the 1960s and '70s, when their passports were welcomed in every country and when Iran was known for social reforms, a booming economy, and the glamour of royalty, and not for stonings, religious extremism, terrorism, and nuclear bombs. The ceaseless regret for what might have been suggested many Iranians were not at peace with themselves or the past. Their discontent would not have surprised the late Shah, who once predicted that his fickle people would live to regret their decision in 1979 to replace him with Grand Ayatollah Ruhollah Khomeini and the mullahs. Told during the revolution that one of his statues had been pulled down, he offered a brisk rejoinder: "It will be back up soon enough." He liked to cite one of his favorite quotes, "Ingratitude is the prerogative of the people," and on another occasion said, "If the Iranian people were fair and compared their situation with other countries and how Iran was fifty years ago, they would see that they were living in peace. They had it so easy that they decided to have a revolution to supposedly further improve their lives. But this was not a revolution of the Iranian people. In fact it was collective suicide on a national scale that took place at the height of prosperity."

Two days after uttering those words the Shah died in a Cairo hospital.

WHY DOES HE still matter?

The answer to that question is apparent to any visitor to the Iranian capital. Tourists enter Tehran from the south on a carriageway built by order of the Shah. On the city's outskirts they pass through the green belt he envisioned would protect Tehran from the twin scourges of desert wind and dust. In the central city visitors pass by the government ministries, hospitals, universities, schools, concert halls, monuments, bridges, sports complexes, hotels, museums, galleries, and gleaming underground metro that were among his many pet projects. It was the Shah who invested in the technology and purchased the reactors that started Iran's nuclear program. He championed the social welfare state that today provides Iranians with access to state-run health care and education. He raised the scholarship money that allowed hundreds of thousands of Iranian university students, including many luminaries of the Islamic Republic, to study abroad at leading American and European universities. The Shah ordered the fighter jets that made Iran's air force the most powerful in southwestern Asia. He established the first national parks and state forests and ordered strict water, animal, and environmental conservation measures. Perhaps it is no surprise that Iran today has the look and feel of a haunted house. The man who built modern Iran is nowhere to be seen but his presence is felt everywhere. The revolutionaries who replaced the Shah may not like to hear it, but Iran today is as much his country as it is theirs.

The Shah matters as much for his failures as for his successes. Though today he is remembered in the West as a brutal dictator forced from power by a brave people, this one-dimensional narrative is an airbrush of the historical record. The Shah spent the last two and a half years of his reign dismantling personal rule in an attempt to democratize Iranian political life. He ceded power back to the politicians, loosened restrictions on political activity, relaxed censorship, and pulled back the security forces. By the time the Shah left for exile in January 1979 he had reduced his own role to a constitutional figurehead, and made no attempt to save his throne through force. Unlike President Bashar al-Asad of Syria, the Shah surrendered power rather than unleash the army and start a civil war. At a time when a new generation of authoritarian rulers in the Middle East and elsewhere will soon face internal and external pressure to democratize, the Shah's fall raises troubling questions. Did he move too slowly or not fast enough? Would a crackdown have prevented the revolution? If the Shah had not democratized when he did, if he had waited another year, would Iran today be a multiparty democracy with Western-style rule of law?

Today Americans, if they remember the Shah at all, are likely to associate him with massive human rights violations and state-sanctioned repression. In the 1970s the Iranian leader was accused of overseeing a police state responsible for as many as a hundred thousand deaths. According to international human rights groups, an equal number of Iranians were imprisoned and tortured. The Shah became a hate figure for many people. When President Jimmy Carter grudgingly allowed the deposed monarch to enter the United States in 1979 for cancer surgery, his own ambassador to the United Nations, Andrew Young, complained that it was like "protecting Adolf Eichmann." By comparison, Young described Khomeini as "a saint." In addition to the accusations of genocide, the Shah was accused of massive corruption and stashing away at least $25 billion in secret Swiss bank accounts (even higher estimates ran to $59 billion or the equivalent of almost three years' worth of Iranian oil revenues). The Shah rebuffed the charges of mass murder and theft but never denied resorting to authoritarian rule in the latter stages of his reign. "No, I wouldn't deny it," he said. "But look, to carry through reforms, one can't help but be authoritarian. Especially when the reforms take place in a country like Iran, where only 25 percent of the inhabitants know how to read and write."

The controversy and confusion that surrounded the Shah's human rights record overshadowed his many real accomplishments in the fields of women's rights, literacy, health care, education, and modernization. Help in sifting through the accusations and allegations came from a most unexpected quarter, however, when the Islamic Republic announced plans to identify and memorialize each victim of Pahlavi "oppression." But lead researcher Emad al-Din Baghi, a former seminary student, was shocked to discover that he could not match the victims' names to the official numbers: instead of 100,000 deaths Baghi could confirm only 3,164. Even that number was inflated because it included all 2,781 fatalities from the 1978–1979 revolution. The actual death toll was lowered to 383, of whom 197 were guerrilla fighters and terrorists killed in skirmishes with the security forces. That meant 183 political prisoners and dissidents were executed, committed suicide in detention, or died under torture. The number of political prisoners was also sharply reduced, from 100,000 to about 3,200. Baghi's revised numbers were troublesome for another reason: they matched the estimates already provided by the Shah to the International Committee of the Red Cross before the revolution. "The problem here was not only the realization that the Pahlavi state might have been telling the truth but the fact that the Islamic Republic had justified many of its excesses on the popular sacrifices already made," observed historian Ali Ansari. During Khomeini's decade in power, from 1979 to 1989, an estimated 12,000 monarchists, liberals, leftists, homosexuals, and women were executed and thousands more tortured. The single worst atrocity occurred in one week in July 1988, when the Islamic Republic slaughtered an estimated 3,000 young men and women accused of engaging in leftist political activity. Baghi's report exposed Khomeini's hypocrisy and threatened to undermine the very moral basis of the revolution. Similarly, the corruption charges against the Pahlavis collapsed when the Shah's fortune was revealed to be well under $100 million at the time of his departure, hardly insignificant but modest by the standards of other royal families and remarkably low by the estimates that appeared in the Western press.

Baghi's research was suppressed inside Iran but opened up new vistas of study for scholars elsewhere. As a former researcher at Human Rights Watch, the U.S. organization that monitors human rights around the world, I was curious to learn how the higher numbers became common currency in the first place. I interviewed Iranian revolutionaries and foreign correspondents whose reporting had helped cement the popular image of the Shah as a blood-soaked tyrant. I visited the Center for Documentation on the Revolution in Tehran, the state organization that compiles information on human rights during the Pahlavi era, and was assured by current and former staff that Baghi's reduced numbers were indeed credible. If anything, my own research suggested that Baghi's estimates might still be too high. For example, during the revolution the Shah was blamed for a cinema fire that killed 430 people in the southern city of Abadan; we now know that this heinous crime was carried out by a pro-Khomeini terror cell. Dozens of government officials and soldiers had been killed during the revolution, but their deaths were also attributed to the Shah and not to Khomeini. The lower numbers do not excuse or diminish the suffering of political prisoners jailed or tortured in Iran in the 1970s. They do, however, show the extent to which the historical record was manipulated by Khomeini and his partisans to criminalize the Shah and justify their own excesses and abuses.

In the seventies, a decade known for savage ideological struggles, the revised death toll in Iran's 1971–1976 "dirty war" bears consideration. In his lifetime the Shah was often compared to Chile's General Augusto Pinochet, blamed for the deaths of 2,279 people and 30,000 torture victims, and also to the Argentine military junta, held culpable for 30,000 deaths and disappearances. Within the context of Cold War battlefronts in the Middle East and southwestern Asia, the Pahlavi state was not particularly repressive, especially when we consider that Saddam Hussein, in neighboring Iraq, was credited with the deaths of 200,000 political dissidents, while in Syria, President Hafez al-Assad crushed an Islamic uprising with 20,000 casualties. That Iran never experienced violence on such a scale suggests the Shah was a benevolent autocrat who actually enjoyed a greater degree of popular support among the Iranian people than was previously assumed. The television cameras that focused on large, angry

crowds in Tehran in late 1978 told only part of the story, and foreign estimates of millions of anti-Shah protesters calling for the Shah's overthrow
turned out to be vastly inflated. Most scholars now agree that most farmers and workers stayed out of the demonstrations and many in fact supported the Shah to the end. So too did moderate religious leaders and
many of their followers who defied Khomeini and engaged in frantic last-
ditch efforts to find a compromise that would allow the Shah to stay in
Iran and remain on the throne. Though Iran's cities were in turmoil, large
swaths of Iran never experienced the revolution, and for residents living
in many rural districts life continued as before. What, then, are we to
make of the Shah and the Iranian revolution?

Historians often talk about the "uses and abuses" of history, and
researching the Iranian revolution can be compared to entering a dark
tunnel without a flashlight. The tunnel is filled with caverns, dead ends,
and missed turns and lit only by the occasional flare of rumor, conspiracy
theory, and outright lie. The Islamic Republic may be deeply invested in
one version of events, but Iranian exiles remain bitterly divided among
themselves about the Shah, his legacy, and the origins of the revolution.
Many Iranians, even those who left Iran months before the worst unrest,
still blame the Shah for abandoning the country to religious extremists.
Others point the finger at Americans for betraying an ally. According to
their "Green Belt" conspiracy the Shah was pushed out of power by the
United States as part of a secret national security strategy to install a network of anti-Communist Islamist regimes on the southern borders of the
old Soviet Union. No documents have ever surfaced to prove the conspiracy's existence. Nonetheless, I felt duty-bound to raise the topic of betrayal
during my interview with Dr. Zbigniew Brzezinski, who served as Carter's
White House national security adviser. Our subsequent exchange could
have been scripted by a late-night comedy writer. "Green what?" asked
Brzezinski. He listened in silence as I explained his alleged "role" in Iran's
"grassy knoll" version of history. "First I've heard of it," he chuckled and
asked me to repeat the explanation a second time. "I have been accused of
many things in my time but this one might be the best of the lot," he said.
He seemed more flattered than offended to be at the center of an epic
conspiracy theory.

Politicians and government officials with little or no training in history like to cite past events to justify their decisions and policies. This was
certainly true during the Iranian revolution. U.S. officials harked back to

two episodes in 1953 and 1963 when the Shah had approved the use of force to crush protests. When he failed to call out the troops a third time, in 1978, their calculations left them bereft of policy options. Iranian generals and officials used the same events as reference points, but for an entirely different reason. They knew that on both occasions the Shah had actually *opposed* the use of force, relenting only when stronger personalities pressed his hand. Khomeini's totalitarian political views and violent hatred for Americans were matters of public record, yet U.S. ambassador William Sullivan compared him to Gandhi, the pacifist leader of India's independence struggle against the British Raj. Iranians also turned to the past to help explain the catastrophe that befell their country. The Shah's behavior was informed by other dates, most notably 1907, when Russia and Great Britain carved up Iran between them, and also 1941, when the Allies invaded Iran and ousted his father. His family members and aides feared the regicides of earlier revolutions. "I always had in mind the Romanovs," said Queen Farah, who was outraged when a senior courtier compared her to Queen Marie Antoinette and her husband to Czar Nicholas II.

THIRTY-SEVEN YEARS AFTER his exile and on the seventy-fifth anniversary of his accession, Mohammad Reza Shah Pahlavi has been reduced to a bloodless enigma. Puzzled by his decision to leave and not stay on and fight Khomeini, biographers over the years have resorted to dream interpretation and psychosexual analysis to describe his behavior. Others attributed his behavior to personal insecurities stemming from his relationship with a domineering father and the women in his life. "Everyone is a psychologist, you know?" Farah Pahlavi warily observes.

I wondered how the Shah, so often derided as "weak," held on to the Peacock Throne for thirty-seven years, making his the fifth-longest reign in the twenty-five-hundred-year history of the Persian monarchy. If the Shah really was as "stupid" as his detractors said, how did he successfully outmaneuver ruthless and wily American presidents such as Dwight Eisenhower, John Kennedy, Lyndon Johnson, and Richard Nixon? If the Shah was a "coward," how to explain his remarkably cool behavior when he survived a plane crash and assassination attempts? If the Shah was "indecisive," how did he engineer the 1973 "oil shock," the greatest transfer of sovereign wealth in recorded history? Somehow the Shah achieved these feats while steering Iran through the treacherous currents of World War II and the Cold War and implementing one of the twentieth century's great experiments in liberal social and economic reform. The Cold War was a brutal, bloody business during which leaders of frontline states like Iran were regularly overthrown and assassinated. Trapped between that cauldron and the rise of Islam, the Pahlavi Dynasty was swept away in a deluge that few kings or presidents, perhaps not even a de Gaulle, could have held back.

What was true for the Shah was also true for his wife. Throughout history the royal consorts of reigning kings and emperors have usually been portrayed as appendages or spectators, as meddling shrews or naive dilettantes. Farah Pahlavi defied these stereotypes. Early in my research I came across an American diplomatic dispatch from January 1979 that referenced the Queen's role in a final attempt to save the throne. This book provides new details about Farah Pahlavi's life and the remarkable role she played during the critical last days of Imperial Iran. In these pages the Queen finally emerges from her husband's shadow as a truly consequential figure in her own right, not only as one of the great women of Iranian history but also as the most accomplished female sovereign of the twentieth century. It is hardly any wonder that the Islamic Republic regards her as an existential threat or that so many Iranians still address her as *madar*, which translates literally as "mother."

I set out to write a book that would describe the interior life of the Iranian Imperial Family and the Pahlavi Court, while re-creating the fin de siècle atmosphere in Iran in 1978, the momentous year of revolution. Our understanding of Pahlavi-era Iran and the 1978–1979 revolution is moving into a new era of research and discovery. Although many of the principal figures have left the scene, many others were willing to share their experiences. They included Queen Farah; former Iranian president Abolhassan Banisadr; retired White House officials, including former national security adviser Zbigniew Brzezinski; and dozens of former senior Iranian government officials and members of the late Shah's entourage, many of whom agreed to speak out for the first time. Memories change over time and most of my interviewees forgot dates and details of conversations or conflated one event with another. Fortunately, I could fact-check and cross-check their accounts with other interviewees as well as original primary-source documents, including diaries, letters, memoranda, and newspaper clippings. Hundreds of pages of newly declassified documents from the Jimmy Carter Presidential Library provided a unique insight into back-channel communications between the U.S. embassy and the

National Security Council at the height of the revolution. As my research progressed it became clear that I was dealing with two different revolutionary narratives, one American and the other Iranian. As understood by the Americans, Iran's revolution began on September 8, 1978, when army troops opened fire on protesters gathered in Jaleh Square in Tehran. But many Iranian interviewees assured me that the Pahlavi regime was almost certainly finished by the end of August 1978 and that the Shah accepted defeat four days before Jaleh Square.

If the Iranians were indeed correct, if the struggle for Iran really was over before the revolution proper began, I had to make an intensive study of events as they unfolded in the months leading to unrest. To do that I painstakingly constructed a 242-page color-coordinated time line that spanned the crucial twenty-month period from January 1, 1977, through August 31, 1978, that decided the Shah's fate. The time line expanded to include everything from weather reports and traffic conditions to movie and theater listings—anything to help me re-create daily life on the eve of revolution. The time line meant that I could follow the Shah, Queen Farah, President Carter, Ambassador Sullivan, and other personalities on a daily and even hourly basis during a critical two-year stretch. The time line yielded unexpected patterns, trends, and turning points forgotten, neglected, or otherwise overlooked by other scholars.

This book is not intended as the final word on the Shah or the 1979 revolution—far from it. As our knowledge of events from the period expands, so too will our understanding of them change. This book will, I hope, shake up a historical narrative that for too long has felt too settled. No doubt it will upset some and delight others. "Blunt histories do not always meet with warm approval," writes historian Margaret MacMillan. "Historians, of course, do not own the past. We all do. But because historians spend their time studying history, they are in a better position than most amateurs to make reasoned judgments. Historians, after all, are trained to ask questions, make connections, and collect and examine evidence. Ideally, they possess a considerable body of knowledge and an understanding of the context of particular times or events. Yet when they produce work that challenges deeply held beliefs and myths about the past, they are often accused of being elitist, nihilistic, or simply out of touch with that imaginary place 'the real world.' In the case of recent history, they are also told . . . that they cannot have an opinion if they were not there."

This book was researched and written by someone who was not there. Moreover, during the dozens of interviews I conducted for this book I was struck by how many of my Iranian interviewees confided that they felt more comfortable talking to a New Zealand–born historian than an ethnic Iranian scholar, whom they feared would cast judgment on them or misinterpret or even manipulate their words. For my purposes, at least, having an outsider's perspective was a decisive factor in helping me to recover memories, re-create events, and revisit some of the lingering mysteries of the Iranian revolution, perhaps the most important yet misunderstood historical epic of our time.

She flew into Cairo on a Saturday evening.

From the airport, Farah Pahlavi was driven by motorcade to the government guesthouse where she would stay for the next three days. At dinner she joined in the conversation and banter with the same small group of friends and loyalists who have been at her side since she came out in 1979. The table fell silent when she recalled that on her flight from Paris she had sat next to a young man who had been eager to talk about Iran, the Middle East, and politics.

"When did you reveal yourself?" someone asked.

"When he mentioned the Shah," she said, trying to stifle her laughter.

"How did you do that?"

"I said, 'I was his wife.'"

"What was the look on his face?"

Farah mimicked the poor man's look of bug-eyed, openmouthed shock, and the table roared with laughter. She was in good spirits and happy to be back among friends.

The next morning, after paying her respects at President Sadat's bier, Queen Farah drove to the Al-Rifa'i Mosque, which stands on a hill overlooking Cairo. If the view overlooking the city is breathtaking, the mosque itself is one of the jewels of Islamic architecture, with soaring cathedral-like proportions. The Shah's chamber is intimate and elegant. Farah, a trained architect, oversaw the design, and with a team of helpers she managed to purchase a block of Iranian marble, which first had to be shipped through Italy and then conveyed to Egypt without alerting the Iranian authorities. Her husband's strong-willed sisters Ashraf and Shams had insisted that their brother should be buried and entombed with full pomp in the style of Napoleon, and they all but accused their sister-in-law of

skimping on the Shah's burial. She knew her husband preferred simplicity and took the dispute to his five children to ask them what they thought.
"It's beautiful and perfect," they assured her, and the chamber was conse-
crated. Al-Rifa'i is known as the King's Mosque and for a reason: the
room adjacent to where the Shah lies holds the tombs of the last two
kings of Egypt, Farouk and Faud.

The public ceremonies ended and Jehan Sadat and the Egyptians quietly withdrew from the chamber. The doors closed behind Farah Pahlavi
and she stood in silence. After a moment passed she knelt and kissed her
husband's catafalque, then stood with her eyes closed in quiet communion. She was talking to the Shah.

1

THE SHAH

A country's king can never be at peace,
The fears and trials he faces never cease.

—THE PERSIAN BOOK OF KINGS

I want my son to inherit not dreams but
the realization of a dream.

—THE SHAH

His day began at seven o'clock with a soft knock on the bedroom door at Niavaran, the palace compound where he lived and worked in northern Tehran. "Good morning, Your Majesty," said Amir Pourshaja, and by the time he returned from the bathroom the valet had set out a tray with toast, a little butter and honey, five or six pieces of prune, and a glass of orange juice. On occasion, the cook might liven the plate with two or three pieces of grapefruit, but in general he preferred plain, modest fare—he had a sensitive stomach and was allergic to onions, strawberries, and Iran's famous caviar. A military aide brought in official correspondence and the morning papers, both foreign and domestic, to be read while he ate and his wife slept on. He received his first intelligence briefing of the day before he started reading.

The Kingdom of Iran, which Mohammad Reza Shah Pahlavi had ruled over as Shahanshah or King of Kings for the past thirty-six years, occupied a vast southwest Asian desert plateau larger in size than Great Britain, France, Italy, and West Germany combined. An hour earlier, Amir had telephoned officials in each of Iran's twenty-two provinces to collect their individual weather reports. What they told him was important because it usually determined the mood of the Shah—and thus the mood of his thirty-five million subjects—for the remainder of the day. News of rain brought cheer and satisfaction. No rain meant a furrowed brow and gloom. "His Majesty always worried about the weather," said Amir. "He worried all the time. Because he knew weather affected the crops, and crops affected the people." One morning, Amir told the Shah that it had rained during the night: "He was very happy." So happy indeed that he walked over to the window in search of a tree branch moist with precipitation. When he couldn't find one he turned to Amir with disappointment writ on his face: "It's not wet! You told me it rained!" He knew exactly how many millimeters had fallen in each city in each province. He knew the amount of water in each of the dams. He knew because he had built them all, twenty-one to date, and often during the rainy season or after a big snowfall he liked to fly across the country in his executive jet to check the water levels from the air. One day at the Caspian, where he spent a part of each summer, the Shah peered off into the distance, staring up at the cloudless blue sky as if willing something to happen. One perplexed visitor, seeing his head craned for so long in the same position, worried that His Majesty had developed arthritis. "What is he doing?" he implored the household physician. "Looking for rain," sighed his companion.

BEFORE THE CAMERAS and the crowds, His Imperial Majesty Mohammad Reza Pahlavi, King of Kings, Emperor of Iran, Light of the Aryans, Shadow of God, and Custodian of the Shia Faith, exuded the storybook glamour of the bejeweled Peacock Throne and the majesty of twenty-five centuries of Persian monarchy. By December 1977 he had reigned as King-Emperor for so many years that most Iranians could remember no other ruler and most citizens of other nations knew no other Iranian. In the realm of international politics he had outlived or outlasted contemporaries, allies, and adversaries, including Churchill, Roosevelt, Stalin, Kennedy, Nixon, Mao, Franco, and de Gaulle. Three brilliant marriages to three equally remarkable women had sired five children and made Iran's Imperial Family a staple of the picture magazines and gossip columns. The Shah's bemedaled uniforms, aquiline features, and silver hair had graced television news programs and the front pages of newspapers for so long that one visitor to Niavaran, upon meeting him, experienced "a feeling of déjà vu, as you do with some landscapes—as I did when I saw Machu Picchu or the Great Wall for the first time."

The life story of the Shah of Iran was worthy of the *Persian Book of Kings*, the literary epic by Ferdowsi that traced the rise and fall of Iran's royal dynasties through the centuries. After succeeding to the Peacock Throne in 1941, when he was barely out of his teens, Mohammad Reza Shah Pahlavi survived mortal threats that would have broken lesser men: the wartime invasion and occupation of his country, Communist subversion, a plane crash, assassination attempts, coup plots, dynastic intrigue, religious revolts, constitutional crises, and even a brief spell in exile. In an era when other kings and queens were forced from their thrones or reduced to a life spent cutting ribbons and shaking hands, the Shah bucked the tide of royalty in the twentieth century when he decided to rule as well as reign. Not content to merely gather power, in 1963 he embarked on his White Revolution, an ambitious program of social and economic reforms to transform Iran from a semifeudal baron state into a modern industrial powerhouse. Peasant farmers were freed from bondage to landowners. Forests and waterways were nationalized. Women were granted their civil, legal, and political rights. By the time the Shah staged his belated coronation four years later, Iran's rate of economic growth outstripped those of the United States, Great Britain, and France. Critics who had once dismissed Iran's King as a callow playboy now applauded his achievements and acumen. "We are delighted to salute the Shah of Iran on the day of his Coronation," declared Britain's *Daily Mail*. "During his 26-year reign he has never once involved his country in war. He has shown the way to beat hunger, want, squalor and disease by methods from which other countries could learn."

The Shah didn't stop there. In the early seventies he exploited Cold War tensions to achieve regional hegemony over the Persian Gulf, then pulled off the coup of the century by engineering the December 1973 "oil shock." The overnight doubling of the price of oil achieved the single greatest transfer of wealth between sovereign states in recorded history. Flush with his new billions, the leader of the world's second largest oil exporter lavished resources on industry, education, health, welfare, the arts, and the armed forces. At the heart of his program of reform was an ironclad commitment to education. Between 1967 and 1977 the number of universities increased in number from 7 to 22, the number of institutions of advanced learning rose from 47 to 200, and the number of students in higher education soared from 36,742 to 100,000. Iran's literacy programs were among the most innovative and effective anywhere in the world, so that by 1977 the number of Iranians able to read and write had climbed from just 17 percent to more than 50 percent. The Shah embarked on a military buildup, placed orders for nuclear power stations, and announced that the days when foreign powers could get their way in Iran and the region were over. "Nobody can dictate to us," he boasted. "Nobody can wave a finger at us because we will wave back." In 1974 *Time* magazine anointed him "Emperor of Oil" when it declared that the Shah "had brought his country to a threshold of grandeur that is at least analogous to what Cyrus the Great achieved for ancient Persia." American, European, and Japanese corporations rushed to set up headquarters in Iran and enter into joint business ventures. "Boom?" asked an American investment banker. "We haven't seen anything yet. They are now dependent on Western technology, but what happens when they produce and export steel and copper, when they reduce their agricultural problems? They'll eat everybody else in the Middle East alive."

The numbers behind Iran's rise were impressive and few doubted that the Iranian people, reported the *Chicago Tribune*, were "living better than most of their country's neighbors." Since 1941 national income had multiplied 423-fold and since 1963 the country's gross national product had risen 14-fold. Yet Iranian society had paid a price for prosperity. Political institutions and the judiciary were subordinate to the wishes of the Shah, his ministers, and the security forces. "The Shah's power is virtually total," reported one observer. "Only one political party is permitted, and debate is carefully contained." Newspapers, radio, and television were "embarrassingly obsequious" in their coverage of the regime and subject to censorship. The state security police was "one of the most pervasive such organizations in the world" and accused by its critics of imprisoning, torturing, and killing thousands of dissidents. Tens of thousands more Iranians preferred to live outside the country than endure repression at home. The Shah's economic reforms were also scrutinized. Much of Iran's new wealth was concentrated in the hands of a small ruling elite: 10 percent of the population controlled 40 percent of the wealth. Most of Iran's sixty-one thousand villages still lacked "piped water, sanitation, doctors, electricity." One physician claimed that families living in rural Karaj subsisted on four and five grams of protein a week. "People hunt for undigested oats in the droppings of horses," he said. Iranian intellectuals sneered at the Shah's efforts to modernize a poor, semiliterate country. "It's all skin deep" was the common refrain among university students who dismissed the White Revolution as a giant fraud. "It's all fake pretension." The Shah received no credit for his achievements, though even his opponents acknowledged that conditions weren't nearly as bad as they could be: "Given the mentality of the Iranian people, it would be ten times worse here under any other regime."

Despite these controversies, in the last few weeks of 1977 Imperial Iran cut its way through the international scene with the stately grandeur of a Cunard liner on its maiden voyage. While Americans and Europeans grappled with high unemployment, inflation, political scandals, and labor unrest, most Iranians were preoccupied with more mundane affairs. The Shah celebrated his fifty-eighth birthday and was cheered by news of a welcome boost to oil production. He hosted state visits from the presidents of Egypt and Somalia and attended the Aryamehr Cup tennis finals at the Imperial Country Club. He was pleased to hear that America's prestigious Georgetown University now ranked Iran as the world's fifth-strongest nation. His government completed trade deals with France and West Germany to build nuclear power plants, New Zealand to supply lamb, the Soviet Union to increase steel production, and the United States to supply five million telephones. In December 1977 the volume of trades on the Tehran Stock Exchange surpassed 5.9 billion rials for the first time and officials reported a record 380,000 tourists to Iran in the past year. Iran's reputation as a haven to do business was burnished by the presence of more than 100,000 foreign residents inspired by the Shah's vision of transforming his country into the Japan of West Asia, and lured by the prospect of comfortable lives with servants, swimming pools, and tennis courts. The 52,000 Americans living in Iran in 1977 made up the largest concentration of U.S. nationals living abroad. Other expatriate communities in Iran included 8,000 Britons, 8,000 French, 16,000 West Germans, 20,000 Italians, and tens of thousands more Filipinos and Koreans employed as guest workers. "Look at them," crowed an Iranian businessman. "The flies have come to gather at the honeypot."

Foreigners living in Iran considered the country a sure and safe bet for the future. The kingdom was defended by a crack professional fighting force whose 413,000 men and women began each day reciting their pledge to defend "God, Shah, and Fatherland." The Shah's pride and joy were the three branches of the Imperial Armed Forces. The quarter-million-strong army was divided into armored and infantry divisions. Four separate brigades, including special forces and airborne units, "can maintain internal security and halt an invasion by any neighboring state except the Soviet Union." Pride of place in the army went to the Immortals, the twenty-thousand-strong Imperial Guard equipped to fight as infantry and assist regular ground forces at home or overseas. Iran's air force was "capable of defeating any regional air force except that of Israel, and possibly Turkey." The air force dominated the skies over southwestern Asia and boasted the ability to fly hundreds of extra miles outside Iranian airspace. Iran's navy ruled the waves in the Persian Gulf, patrolled deep into the Indian Ocean, and prowled the coast of East Africa. The regular army was complemented by two paramilitary forces. Seventy-five thousand gendarmerie guarded the borders and secured the countryside, trained to provide early warning of foreign aggression or internal subversion, and their 45 regiments and 2,240 gendarmerie posts were equipped with light machine guns, mortars, helicopters, and patrol boats. The National Resistance Force numbered 80,000 personnel and was organized into local-level company- and battalion-size units outfitted with small arms and rifles. The Iranian police was 40,000-strong.

In his fervent nationalism and authoritarian leadership the King of Iran echoed the rulers of centuries past but in particular his idol President Charles de Gaulle of France, the very model of the twentieth-century nationalist strongman. "His is a formidable personality, which he employs skillfully to advance Iran's interests in such matters as increasing oil revenue and acquiring sophisticated military equipment from hesitant sellers," noted an American intelligence assessment. "In short, the Shah has developed into a confident ruler, who knows what he wants and how to get it. He is sure that his way is best for Iran and that monarchical power, wisely used, is essential to the country's well-being. He is, all in all, a popular and respected king. We might ask: Are there no flies in the ointment of Iranian success? Do not some wish him ill and work against him? Can he continue to go onward and upward forever?"

AFTER BREAKFAST, THE Shah returned to his bathroom to shave and brush his teeth. Dressing with the help of his valet, he selected a cravat and slipped a miniature copy of the Muslim holy book, the Quran, inside his front breast jacket pocket. Courtiers recalled the time he walked into his office, patted his jacket, and with a stricken look on his face exclaimed, "My Quran, I forgot it! I have to go back!" Ready for the day and already fully briefed on the domestic and international situation, at nine o'clock he exited his suite accompanied by Colonel Kiomars Djahinbini, his personal bodyguard and the head of palace security. The colonel walked a pace behind and for the remainder of the day never let the Shah out of his sight. Together they crossed a landing, headed down a flight of stairs past smartly saluting military guards, and strolled out onto the sunlit palace grounds. "I remember him coming down the stairs," recalled Crown Prince Reza, who was seventeen years old in December 1977 and in his last year of high school before moving to Texas to train as a pilot at Fort Reese Air Force Base. "He would ask me to walk to his office with him. The first question of the day was always the weather report."

His office was a short walk away from the Niavaran residence along a pathway shaded by plane trees, down a flight of stone steps, and through a small wooded grove that led to a second palace, the Jahan Nama, the low-slung residence of the former ruling Qajar Dynasty. Now refurbished as an office complex, the Jahan Nama boasted exquisite Persian carpets, intricate tile work, and luminous stained-glass windows. Greeted at the entrance by Grand Master of Ceremonies Amir Aslan Afshar, he climbed the stairwell to the second floor along a corridor that passed several ante-rooms, including one for gift wrapping and another for the palace dentist, before entering his office, a vast, cavernous space whose spectacular mir-rored ceiling and inlaid walls resembled a jewel box radiating diamond light. Regardless of the temperature and season, he worked without air-conditioning. Sensitive to chills and drafts, he could not abide modern artificial air to the point where he drove with the windows down and for-bade the installation of cooling devices in his various residences—he hated the expense as much as the air. But by late May, with the heat from the plains climbing up the hillsides, Niavaran became so oppressive that the entire household was forced to decamp farther up the slopes of the Alborz Mountains to Saadabad, a second royal compound of lush, forested acreage whose White Palace served as the Pahlavis' summer residence. When temperatures cooled again in the autumn the family and their servants returned to Niavaran, and the White Palace was converted into a guesthouse for visiting foreign heads of state.

Palace officials were already at their desks when His Imperial Majesty walked in the room. The Shah was a stickler for punctuality who rarely ever ran late for appointments. The bulk of each day was spent behind his desk, though days at a time were spent away on regional inspection tours to open and inspect new factories, dams, schools, hospitals, power plants, and oil refineries, and also abroad, on state visits to capitals in every corner of the globe. After consulting with Afshar, who managed his daily program, the Shah met with Minister of the Imperial Court Amir Abbas Hoveyda, Iran's former long-serving prime minister who four months earlier had assumed the post responsible for the overall running of the Imperial Court and household. "We start getting work from [the Shah's] office at eight in the morning," one aide explained. "We work through meals and until the middle of the night. We go to sleep exhausted, and then we get more work to do." The Shah did not hesitate to bypass the chain of command. "Often I order minor officials to tell their superiors what I want done," he explained. He delighted dropping in to make unannounced inspections. One year earlier, air force commanders at a base near the city of Isfahan learned they had just eight minutes to prepare for his arrival. "I barely had time to get there before he landed," recalled the base's deputy commander. "The plane was a Boeing 727, and he was flying it himself with just a copilot, an engineer, and one other man with him. We were in quite a state here, I can tell you."

Though Iran had a prime minister, cabinet, and parliament, the Shah projected an image of absolute control and made it clear that in the realm of decision making all roads led to Niavaran. "I not only make the decisions, I do the thinking," he famously boasted. He approved and often handled treaty negotiations and defense contracts, negotiated contractual terms and conditions with foreign oil companies, and even agreed to salary increases for oil workers and the timing of oil refinery overhauls. As the son of a general who had seized power in a coup, and in a part of the world where armed revolts were a common occurrence, he kept a close eye on his army, navy, and air force. No military plane took off or landed without his permission. No member of the armed forces was promoted above the rank of lieutenant colonel without his explicit approval. When foreign journalists visited Iran their itineraries were sent to the Shah for inspection. "Copies of every story written about Iran go to his desk, according to aides," recalled a team of American journalists who visited Iran in December 1977. "Once, while visiting a hospital, he ordered a swimming pool dug for the doctors. Plans for building design require his approval. In factories he asks intricate questions on electronics, production rates, and manpower problems. He reads arms catalogues to relax."

The Shah was impatient for results and hated to hear excuses. "He only wanted to get things done," remembered one of his advisers. "He was always asking questions. Questions! Questions! Questions! And he would look at you with those eyes!" Exceptionally well-read and a quick study, the Shah enjoyed policy discussions with his ministers but drew the line at debate. "He would let you explain yourself," said one former cabinet minister. "He was very open in private. I experienced it myself many times and on many issues. And in meetings he would let ministers talk. But he did not appreciate it if they tried to debate him." He prided himself on his breadth of knowledge. "He asks very, very sharp questions," said the manager of an electronics factory in Shiraz who received the Shah. "If you try to b.s. him, he'll know it right away." "He was familiar with everything that was going on in the world," marveled Armin Meyer, President Lyndon Johnson's ambassador to Tehran in the late 1960s. "In military affairs he was smarter than most of our Pentagon people. Very intelligent, very impressive person, and one who had very strong feelings." Ambassadors knew better than to cross him. "Once you lost his goodwill you were finished," recalled Sir Denis Wright, who served as Britain's envoy under Prime Minister Harold Wilson.

Mornings were spent issuing directives, receiving dignitaries, signing legislation into law, and reading the intelligence reports that streamed in from the provinces. The much-feared secret police, Savak, maintained internal security and kept a close watch on events beyond Iran's borders. Once a week the Shah received Savak chief General Nematollah Nasiri to review major intelligence findings, and one morning each week was set aside for separate interviews with the three commanders of the army, air force, and navy. If the foreign minister was traveling, he and the monarch exchanged notes in a case padlocked to the wrist of a close aide. The system was fail-safe—they were the only possessors of the two keys that could open the case—though one time it was fastened so securely in Vladivostok that by the time the go-between reached Tehran his wrist had started to blacken. With these systems in place the Shah felt confident that he enjoyed absolute control and would not be blindsided by events. He dismissed a courtier's advice that he hold regular meetings with ordinary people from different walks of life. "But I already know what the people think," he replied. "I'm fed report after report from goodness knows how many sources." The advent of modern technology meant that he no longer worried about being seen in the flesh: "My voice is heard everywhere, my face is seen everywhere; heard through the radio, seen through the TV. The contact is there." At his desk, while he worked his way through the stacks of paperwork with the help of the head of his Special Bureau, Nosratollah Moinian, he gave instructions on how to respond to individual requests. All this was done verbally and without the use of a stenographer or a Dictaphone.

The Niavaran compound with its two palaces sat perched on a high promontory nestled in the foothills of the Alborz Mountains. Beyond the canopy of plane trees and down the slopes sprawled the capital, Tehran, "the foot of the throne," though on most days its 4.5 million inhabitants were hidden behind a grimy shroud of yellow smog and grit. The Shah had grand plans for Tehran, which one visitor in the midseventies unkindly compared to "some enormous earth slide spilling slowly southward onto Iran's great desert plateau." Six years earlier, at the conclusion of the Persepolis celebrations, the Shah had inaugurated the soaring Shahyad Monument in downtown Tehran in the presence of the Emperor of Ethiopia and the Kings of Greece, Denmark, Norway, and Nepal. The Shahyad's four giant latticed feet thrust skyward as a lyrical if pointed reminder that the spirit of ancient Ctesiphones, capital of Persia's Sasanian Empire, was embodied in the vaulting ambitions of the modern Pahlavi state. Museums, concert halls, and art galleries as fine as any in New York and London already lined the grand central park named after his wife, Queen Farah. Construction on an underground metro had started, building was under way on a new international airport nineteen miles to the south, and approval had been granted for a twelve-mile-long, half-mile-wide forested green belt to improve air quality, preserve agricultural farmland, and protect Tehran from desert sandstorms. The Shah was anxious that his seventeen-year-old heir inherit a capital befitting one of the world's five great powers.

He walked back to the family residence in time for his usual 1:30 p.m. lunch with the Queen, who often ran a few minutes late. The half-hour meal was usually their first meeting of the day. His favorite lunchtime dish was cutlet of roast chicken, which was eaten to the bone. Lunch was followed by the all-important two o'clock national radio news broadcast, which the monarch never missed but which his wife often skipped to attend to business. At the conclusion of the national news report, the Shah retired upstairs to undress and nap. Refreshed, he rose and changed suits, returned to the office, and started the day over again.

AFTERNOONS CONSISTED OF another round of paperwork, meetings, and official engagements, though the Shah almost always found time to exercise. An accomplished equestrian, competitive skier, and tennis player, he also enjoyed swimming, waterskiing, volleyball, and extreme sports such as jumping out of a helicopter into the ocean without wearing a life vest. Several afternoons during the week, usually at about three o'clock if his wife was out of town or on her own engagements, he might drive to a safe house near the palace for an hour or two trysting with a young paramour. These pastimes, outlets to alleviate the pressure of a lifetime spent in the public eye and almost four decades on the throne, merely hinted at the contradiction between his public image and his private personality and character.

Before his people the Shah projected a martial image, "stern, icily correct, almost devoid of humor. He seldom indulges in a smile, never a hearty laugh. He is friendless, suspicious, secretive, and, some say, paranoid." "Some found him a little humorless most of the time," agreed Cynthia Helms, whose husband, Richard, served as America's ambassador to Iran. "The scar on his lip, caused by a 1949 attempt on his life, gave him a slightly cynical appearance. During the day he usually wore a double-breasted suit, and always stood ramrod straight. I could never decide whether this was because of his military training or to give him greater height." The shoes he wore, slightly elevated to add another inch of height to his five foot eight frame, were the only outward sign of insecurity. The Shah's starchy behavior proved too much even for that other model of royal rectitude, Britain's Queen Elizabeth II, when the couple were paired up during celebrations to mark the twenty-fifth wedding anniversary of Queen Juliana and Prince Bernhard of the Netherlands. After the party ended Elizabeth let the British Foreign Office know that she found the Shah "rather a bore" and "very heavy" because all he wanted to do was talk shop. She hosted him a decade later at Windsor Castle and found no improvement; once again she let it be known that she "found the Shah heavy going."

So guarded in his facial expressions that courtiers studied his every gesture to discern the slightest shift in mood, if the Shah was pensive, contemplative, or anxious his fingers would drift up to his forehead to play with a loose strand of hair. If agitated or otherwise stimulated or excited, he would rise from his chair to start pacing back and forth around the office. "The expression in his face never changed," remembered Khalil al-Khalil, Lebanon's ambassador to the Pahlavi Court. "He loved to show that he was as solid as Iran. He always kept a distance from people." "As serious as a mullah, he never said anything stupid, smoked hardly at all, and almost never drank alcohol," recalled Soraya Esfandiary, the second of his three wives. She recalled that even in private he addressed her formally, using the Persian word for "you" normally reserved for acquaintances and strangers. Queen Farah also marveled at her husband's discipline. "He had really great self-control," she recalled. "One time a photographer's flashbulb exploded during a photo shoot. Everybody jumped. He didn't move. It was fantastic." One of the few occasions when he lost his temper with her in front of company came during a drive down the Caspian coast from Ramsar to Nowshahr. Car journeys were fraught affairs because His Majesty was a speed demon who liked nothing better than to floor the accelerator while his wife pleaded with him to slow down before they were killed. "Not so fast! Not so fast!" Farah cried as the car gained speed. Then, just as her husband turned to calm her, a bird flew straight into the windshield, forcing him to suddenly brake and almost lose control of the car. "And then he turned around and shouted at me," she said, laughing at the memory.

His remarkable capacity for self-control revealed itself in an incident at a missile test range in 1976. The Imperial Air Force had taken possession of a new batch of Maverick missiles, and the Shah trooped out to the desert with a group of high-ranking Iranian and American diplomats and generals to watch the first tests. "The missile was fired from six miles away," recalled General Mohammad Hossein Mehrmand. "Then something went wrong. Instead of exploding, the missile executed a ninety-degree turn and flew straight toward the pavilion where the guests were standing. Everyone, including the American generals, threw themselves to the ground." Everyone, that is, except the Shah, who stood ramrod straight, feet firmly planted on the floor, his face immobile, while the missile flew straight over his head and beyond to explode in a fiery ball whose shock waves almost collapsed the pavilion. While the stunned generals collected themselves off the ground, General Mehrmand ran to the Shah's side. "Majesty! Majesty!" he cried. "We should stop!" The Shah was puzzled by the suggestion—why would anyone want to *stop*? "No, no," he replied, "we will continue." The shaken assembly took their seats and the test resumed. The second missile exploded on cue. The Shah took a bet with Mehrmand that the third missile would take just forty-five seconds to strike its target. When the Shah was proven right he momentarily forgot where he was: "He took his hat and threw it on the ground, he was so happy."

On the test ground that day the Shah had shown fatalism and courage under fire but also the boyish side that almost never found public expression.

ONLY FAMILY MEMBERS, close friends, and courtiers were aware that behind the public bravado and gold braid the Shah was a man of surprising modesty and remarkable shyness. For outsiders who met him for the first time, the disconnect between the monarch's public and private sides was jarring. "On a one-to-one, eyeball-to-eyeball basis, he is mild, even a little timid and shy," said a Western ambassador. "He speaks so softly that you sometimes strain to hear him. He likes to hear jokes, but he is utterly humorless himself. Really he is not a colorful personality. But in public he is the forceful striding monarch, stern looking and purposeful, and always slim and fit looking from exercise and careful dieting. Frankly I think the shy quiet man probably is the real Shah. The other one is a personality that he has had to practice in front of a mirror most of his life to master." "He was exactly the opposite of what people thought of him," observed Mahnaz Afkhami, Iran's first minister of women's affairs. Before she entered government she had only ever seen the Shah from a distance. "I accompanied the Shah and Shahbanou to Pakistan. I had the chance to see how he interacted. He was a very mild guy."

Shyness was reinforced by his father's first lesson in leadership: never let the people see you as you are. "My father was shy," confirmed Crown Prince Reza. "He put on a mask in public. Maybe he should have tried more to show his real face. He followed the example set by his father. Part of the reason he put on a mask was that a different face would have been perceived as weak." As a young prince, the Shah had been taught to maintain a certain reserve even in his personal relationships and never to trust anyone completely. "If I take a liking to someone," he once admitted, "I need only the smallest shred of doubt to make me break it off. Friendship involves the exchange of confidence between two people, but a king can take no one into his confidence." On the times when Farah urged her husband to smile more in public, the Shah reminded her that displays of emotion conveyed weakness. On Fridays, when family and friends gathered at Niavaran to eat lunch, watch movies, and play cards, he was careful not to spend too much time in the company of one guest lest the others gain the impression that he held him or her in higher favor.

He dreaded small talk, struggled to make eye contact, and was visibly uncomfortable in informal social settings. These attributes and habits led many observers to conclude that the Shah was arrogant or worse. In November 1977 the Pahlavis visited Washington, DC, and were entertained at the White House by jazz legends Sarah Vaughan and Dizzy Gillespie who performed an after-dinner concert in the East Room. At the end of the show President and Mrs. Carter left their seats and walked up on the dais to personally thank them. Queen Farah rose, too, but everyone noticed that the Shah remained "stiffly seated" in his chair—he had frozen at the prospect of standing up in front of the crowd. His wife, fearing an incident, whispered in her husband's ear to join them onstage. Still he remained glued to his seat, to the point that Farah physically clutched his arm and guided him onto the stage. But the damage was done and the next day the false rumor spread that the Shah of Iran had remained seated because he did not want to shake hands with black musicians. Iran's preeminent dress designer, Parvine Farmanfarmaian, recalled the time she broke her foot skiing in the Alps. The Shah was skiing nearby and when he learned of her misfortune expressed his sympathy. During her infrequent visits to the Imperial Court she sometimes found herself dancing with the Shah. "He was *so* shy," she said. "While we danced, the only thing he could think of to say to me was 'How is your foot?' That was the only subject he talked about. This went on for two or three years— the same question every time—until finally I said, 'Majesty, isn't there *something* else we can talk about? I have told you, my foot healed a long time ago.'"

To shyness was added a capacity for denial and a tendency to avoid conflict, personal confrontations, and bad news. The last thing the Shah wanted to do was cause offense or hurt the feelings of those around him. "There was a gentleman, Mr. Nicknam, who looked after the sports facilities at Niavaran," recalled the Queen, who often ran interference for her husband. "Every morning my husband walked from the residence across the lawn to his office, and every morning this gentleman would walk by his side grumbling about this or that thing. And His Majesty said to me, 'This man is bothering me. I start my day feeling happy and he is always full of complaints.' So I talked to the gentleman. I said, 'Please don't bother His Majesty with these problems. Come to me. You know I am responsible for looking after the household.' My husband was very kind. He didn't want to offend anyone." The Shah's sensitive, retiring nature was also the product of long periods of forced convalescence during childhood. The little prince had almost died of typhoid, was stricken with whooping cough and malaria, and throughout his life suffered from gastrointestinal discomfort. He had a sensitive liver, an enlarged spleen, and a compromised immune system that left him vulnerable to viral infections and frequent bouts of the flu. His preference for sunglasses to shield his eyes, which were sensitive to bright light, only reinforced the image of a remote, untouchable autocrat. For someone already naturally inclined to solitude and with the instincts of a loner, the constant pressure to make decisions and maintain a rigorous public schedule led to stress marked by bouts of debilitating depression, stomach trouble, and anxiety. Insomnia was such a problem that on his worst nights not even Valium could get him to sleep.

Within the Niavaran household the Shah was known as considerate and uncomplaining. When he traveled abroad he made sure thank-you gifts were distributed to attendants and hotel staff. During a state visit to the United States he paid the medical expenses of the mother of his Secret Service agent out of his own pocket. On the same trip he took the serving dish out of the hands of an elderly female server. "I can't allow this," he protested. "She is like my mother." In the palace he never made a fuss. When his valet accidentally gave him the wrong medication for an ailment he insisted the matter be dropped to spare them both the embarrassment of a scene. Grand Master of Ceremonies Amir Aslan Afshar recalled the time they were traveling in Austria and the Shah made his motorcade turn around and go back to their hotel after remembering he had forgotten to say farewell to the porter. "I am sorry I was too busy and I was not able to say good-bye," he said, shaking the astonished man's hand. "Thank you for all the kindness and hard work." Another time, he expressed disappointment with one of his advisers. "Pull this fellow's ears," he told Afshar, and then thought better of it: "Make sure you don't pull too hard. I don't want his ears to fall off!"

His dry, understated sense of humor reflected a fatalistic attitude toward life and its absurdities. An American reporter once asked what it was like to be Iran's king. The Shah pointed to a bullet wound that creased his lip from an earlier assassination attempt and offered a dry one-word retort: "Dangerous." Another time, he reminded a visitor that his people had been ruled by more than a hundred kings from a dozen different dynasties. "And do you know how many died peacefully in their beds?" he asked with a wry smile. Holding up four fingers, he said, "It's not a good job." Asadollah Alam, his closest adviser and one of the few men who could put him at ease, was a former prime minister who went on to serve as Hoveyda's predecessor as minister of the Imperial Court. When the two men were alone they bantered back and forth like two college roommates, though Alam was careful never to overstep the mark. The two men were flying from Tabriz to Tehran when Alam recounted the time he lost his virginity to an older lady who had just downed a plate of garlic. On hearing this, the Shah fell "into such prolonged laughter that Her Majesty the Queen and the others became seriously alarmed."

Though the Shah enjoyed the use of five palaces and was widely assumed to be one of the richest men in the world, he paid no attention to his bank accounts and showed no interest in money except as a means of spreading largesse. For someone who was thoroughly distrustful in affairs of state he was surprisingly, even shockingly, naive about personal matters. When the palace accountant presented him with checks to sign he never stopped to ask what he was paying for; he was unable to conceive that his own servant would ever cook the books. The women in his life despaired at his reluctance to spend money on himself. The suits he wore had long since gone out of style, and his casual clothes hadn't been updated since the early fifties. His wife's efforts to style his wardrobe met with varying degrees of success. Maryam Ansary, the vivacious wife of the minister of finance, tried a different tack. One night at dinner she mentioned in passing that she had found "a fantastic tailor" to make suits for her husband and the prime minister. "Oh, so *now* you're in the fashion industry," the Shah needled her. The lady took the bull by the horns, so to speak, and retorted, "Your Majesty, your suits look *old*!" and the two set off on a good-natured round of sparring about the merits of spending money on clothes. His indulgences were confined to the two or three new wristwatches he purchased each year, the nineteen sports cars he loved to tear about in, and a stable of magnificent Persian, Turkmen, and Arabian horses.

The Shah's portrait hung in every public and many private dwellings in Iran. "You can't throw a stone without hitting one," went the joke. "And if you do, you'll get arrested." Iranians fed up with the cult of personality would have been surprised to learn that the object of adoration shared their frustration. Queen Farah's cousin Reza Ghotbi served as director of Iran's national broadcasting service. He recalled the time he lunched with the Imperial Family and their guests at the Caspian. All chatter and activity ceased when the all-important two o'clock news began with the usual lengthy rundown of the Shah's latest official engagements and speeches. Troubled by the attention, the Shah warily asked, "Isn't there *any* other news at your radio station?" The director returned to his office and raised the subject with one of his staff, a popular radio newscaster. "I'm not feeling very happy with this kind of news," he said, "with this focus on the King and Queen and everything members of the Imperial Family do." His colleague reminded him why they lavished attention on them in the first place. "We're not like the BBC or Radio France," he said. "If we don't lead the news with the Shah, people will think there has been a coup d'état in Iran."

The Shah never denied there were times when he preferred to be somewhere else living a different sort of life. "Let me tell you quite bluntly that this king business has given me personally nothing but headaches," he once told a group of astonished journalists in New York. He was as forthright in private. "It is hardly a pleasant job," he remarked in passing to a visiting scholar. "I can think of many more attractive kinds of work to do, here in Iran or abroad." He was sustained only by his vision to transform his country into a modern state and restore Iran to its former greatness.

IF HE WAS sure of one thing in life it was the love he believed he shared with the Iranian people, whom he affectionately referred to as his "children." Their communion could not possibly be grasped by foreigners or intellectuals. "You Westerners simply don't understand the philosophy behind my power," he said. "The Iranians think of their sovereign as a father. . . . Now, if to you a father is inevitably a dictator, that is your problem, not mine."

Above all the Shah held a fervent attachment to the farr, the Persian mantle of heaven that decreed that so long as a king governed like a benevolent father and kept his people's best interests in mind he was assured their loyalty and devotion. Force could not be used to hold the farr, and monarchs who committed unjust acts such as shedding the blood of innocents could expect to lose their throne and their life. For the Shah, the farr was the ultimate expression of the people's will and democracy because it was a social contract based on mutual respect and trust. The Iranian people, he liked to say, "love me and will never forsake me." "A real king in Iran is not only the political head of the nation," he explained on another occasion. "Rather, more than anything else, he is a teacher and a leader. He is not only a person who builds roads, bridges, dams, and canals for his people, but also one who leads them in spirit, thought, and heart. This explains why, if he has the confidence of his people, the Shah in Iran can on the basis of his enormous prestige and spiritual influence initiate such fundamental and extensive programs—programs which would not be undertaken elsewhere except through revolutions and curtailments of civil and individual liberties, or through slow evolutionary processes."

The Shah's sentimental attachment to the farr helped explain his behavior on two earlier occasions when rivals almost chased him from the throne. In August 1953 he briefly fled Iran during a showdown with Prime Minister Mohammad Mossadeq and left retired army general Fazlollah Zahedi and the army to restore order. In June 1963 religious unrest led by the fiery cleric Ruhollah Khomeini threatened revolution. Once again, the Shah stepped back and allowed a more seasoned and ruthless personality, this time Prime Minister Asadollah Alam, to clear the streets with grapeshot. More than anything, he dreaded the prospect of a confrontation with his people and was temperamentally unable to order his troops to open fire, even on those seeking to destroy him and overthrow the monarchy. His longest-serving advisers understood that the Shah would seek an accommodation or withdraw altogether rather than stand and fight if it meant staining the throne with blood. They fretted that he was too softhearted to rule a country with a long, tortuous history of unrest and rebellion. But the Shah did not see it that way at all. In his eyes, a national leader who used force to stay in power was no better than a dictator, and he never saw himself as one. "I am not Suharto," he repeatedly said in reference to the Indonesian strongman whose brutal crackdown against leftist agitators cost an estimated half a million lives.

So long as he felt certain in his head and heart that he had God on his side and the Iranians at his back, the Shah ruled with confidence and vigor. But if he sensed that he no longer commanded the hearts of his people, and if doubts about his mission should creep in, he tended to

THE FALL OF HEAVEN

waver, lose his way, and prevaricate. The withdrawal of love and support, no matter how temporary, seemed almost to unhinge him by draining him of focus, energy, and determination. A steady guiding hand was then required to steer him back on course. He was, said one government official who enjoyed his confidence, like "a lamb in lion's clothing." Nor was he the decisive administrator he liked to appear. He often left important decisions to the last minute or avoided making them at all. Minor problems left untended became more serious than need be. Too often, this meant that the Shah, who otherwise enjoyed a monopoly on power, risked losing momentum or ceding the initiative to stronger, more forceful personalities.

By December 1977, however, questions of temperament and leadership were abstract concerns, and the unrest of earlier decades was but a distant memory. On a recent trip to the port cities that lined the southern Persian Gulf coastline the Shah had been mightily impressed with the turnout in the streets. "In the afternoon His Imperial Majesty arrived in Kermanshah to the most spectacular display of popular enthusiasm I have ever witnessed," noted Asadollah Alam. The Shah observed that the local Muslim clergy had been in the forefront of the demonstrations of loyalty. "It's incredible, but now that living standards have improved it's the mullahs who are most keen to flatter us on our achievements," he told dinner guests. "You should have heard what their spokesmen said to me whilst I was going in to the residence." "I had indeed heard it and was amazed," Alam confided in his diary.

The Shah firmly believed that "95 percent of the population were in favor of the monarchy." Asked to explain how he knew his people supported him, the Shah had a ready answer: "You can see by the look in their eyes."

POWER MIGHT BE absolute but the Shah, an inveterate planner, had no intention of ruling until his deathbed, and for at least the past decade had talked openly about stepping down once his eldest son was ready to assume the throne.

In October 1971, during the week of the splendid celebrations for the Persian monarchy, he declared before a global television audience that he looked forward to the day when he abdicated his duties. "This is not a new idea," he told reporters from twenty countries in town for the big party. "My father also thought of doing so." At the Caspian Sea in the summer of 1972 he shared his thoughts with a family friend. "The time of Reza will be different than mine," he said. "When Reza is twenty I will retire to the north and they can come and see me if they have any problems." Again, in September 1975 he told the *New York Times* that he would step down once he was confident he had strengthened Iran to the point where "nothing can threaten it." "I want to build a better country for my son to inherit than the one I inherited from my father," he said. "When I was his age I heard voices whispering in my ear about the destiny of Iran. I want my son to inherit not dreams but the realization of a dream." He fully intended to work himself out of a job and stage-manage an orderly transfer of power to his son.

In the spring of 1976 the Shah concluded that Iran had become too big, too complex, and too volatile for one-man rule. With oil revenues stagnant and the economy in the doldrums, the public mood was restless. Though distrustful of parliamentary democracy, which he blamed for the instability that marred his early years on the throne, the Shah concluded that it was time to "let off steam" and open up the political system for the first time since the early sixties. As a first step to reform, he eliminated some of the regime's more unsavory features. To relieve the complaints of liberals and the urban middle class, the Shah supported new laws to protect the rights of political prisoners and outlaw torture. He invited the International Committee of the Red Cross to inspect Iranian prisons. He ordered the relaxation of censorship, encouraged public criticism of the government, and approved investigations into high-level graft. Plans were announced to return power to the provinces, cut waste, and reduce red tape.

Pleased with how this first phase of reform proceeded, one year later, in the summer of 1977, the Shah stepped back from day-to-day management of the ministries and gave his new prime minister the leeway to make decisions. Opposition groups were allowed to gather and organize so long as they did not challenge the basic precepts of the monarchy. At one time the Shah's portrait had adorned the front pages of every Iranian newspaper every day. In the autumn of 1977 shrewd observers noticed that Queen Farah's profile was raised and that she was speaking out on major issues of the day. Crown Prince Reza became more visible, with his first major overseas trip set for Thailand, Australia, and New Zealand in January 1978. These state visits, the first in a series planned over the next year, were to introduce the young heir to an international audience and mark the next phase in his training in kingship.

AT THE CLOSE of each day the Shah strolled back to the big house for an hour of exercise before dinner. Upstairs in the main residence, near his bedroom, he had fashioned a room the size of a large closet into a gym. His valet, Amir Pourshaja, once suggested he might like to enlarge this space and the adjoining bathroom. "No," said the Shah, "this is more than enough space for me." His daily workout consisted of calisthenics followed by a forty-five-minute routine with dumbbells. Pourshaja knew his master's body well. He had trained and been certified in Austria as a masseuse and after each workout he gave the King a rubdown. At fifty-eight years old the Shah still had an enviable physique. Amir noticed that regardless of the year or season, he seemed never to lose or gain extra pounds.

After his massage, the Shah dressed for dinner and joined his wife and family members in the downstairs dining room, or he and Farah might drive to the homes of his mother and sisters for dinner. Almost invariably, they dined on traditional Persian cuisine, though the Shah took care to avoid aggravating his sensitive stomach. One meal he could not resist, even though he knew he would pay dearly for it in the morning, was kalleh pacheh or boiled mutton's head and foot. He rarely drank alcohol and during state dinners would raise the wineglass to his lips but not sip from it—if he indulged at all it was usually with a glass of whiskey after dinner. Tonight, however, New Year's Eve, he might make an exception. Shortly after four in the afternoon the Imperial Family and government dignitaries would drive to Mehrebad Airport to welcome the arrival of President Jimmy Carter, First Lady Rosalynn Carter, and several hundred American dignitaries, news reporters, and White House staff. The president's trip to Iran had already been postponed once, due to domestic politics. Both leaders and their advisers hoped that Carter's visit would help smooth relations after a year of deep strain caused by sharp differences over oil prices, arms sales, nuclear power, and human rights.

The Shahanshah of Iran stood at the wheel of the Pahlavi ship of state, a most formidable structure, which on December 31, 1977, sailed through the night, lights ablaze from end to end, its bulkhead secure, its compartments watertight. There was no reason to worry—he knew the way. Now, as he neared the end of his fourth decade in power, one of the great survivors of the twentieth century seemed destined to go on and on. Only a few embittered enemies, an odd assortment of revolutionaries on the political left and right-wing religious extremists, could imagine a world without him. In recent weeks they had taken advantage of his decision to liberalize by staging protests and launching attacks against symbols of Western modernity such as cinemas, banks, and universities. From neighboring Iraq, where he had lingered in exile for the past thirteen years, Grand Ayatollah Ruhollah Khomeini called for an uprising to demolish the monarchy and establish a religious state whose laws would be based on the Muslim holy book the Quran. But beyond his immediate following Khomeini was still largely unknown inside Iran, and he faced apparently insurmountable odds against the Shah's half-million-strong army, air force, and navy.

Nor were there any signs that the middle class, workers, and farmers, the groups that comprised the bulwarks of the royalist state, would abandon the Shah and his family. And why would they? In an uncertain world the Shah stood strong as their protector but also as the cornerstone of stability for Iran, for the Persian Gulf, and for the whole of southwestern Asia; to overthrow the Shah would be seen as a collective act of national suicide.

ATTACHED TO THE Shah's private suite in Niavaran was a small bathroom, which included a vanity unit. One of its drawers contained several plastic bottles of pills with false labels attached to them. Only the Shah, the Queen, and several Iranian and French physicians sworn to oaths of secrecy knew their real contents. All that the valet Amir Pourshaja knew was that every five days he was required to phone in an order for refills to the local pharmacy, then send a driver down to collect the prescription. The procedure was straightforward enough—at this time in Iran medicines were sold over the counter without proof of identity or residence.

Pourshaja carefully refilled the bottles as he had been shown by the court physician, Lieutenant General Abdolkarim Ayadi. He did not know that the pills contained powerful chemicals to treat incurable lymphoma. He did not know that Iran's King of Kings was slowly, inexorably dying of cancer.

2

CROWN AND KINGDOM

I wish you life and long prosperity,
May God protect you from adversity!
May heaven prosper all you say and do,
May evil glances never injure you.
Whatever purposes you hope to gain
May all your efforts never bring you pain,
May wisdom be your guide, may fortune bless
Iran with prosperous days and happiness.

—THE PERSIAN BOOK OF KINGS

I found myself plunged into a sea of trouble.

—THE SHAH

Fifty-eight years earlier, on the cool autumn afternoon of October 26, 1919, a young woman named Nimtaj went into labor in her family home in Tehran. Her husband, Reza Khan, a ranking brigadier in the Shah of Iran's elite Cossack regiment, stood smoking in an outside courtyard, anxiously awaiting the outcome. Reza's first wife, Tajmah, had died in childbirth delivering a girl. For his second marriage, he wed the sturdy Nimtaj, the daughter of his commanding officer. The couple's first child, a daughter, Shams, was born healthy in 1917, but more than anything, Reza longed for a son. The wait ended when a soldier ran out of the house with the joyous news: "It's a boy!" The father started inside when the midwife met him at the door. "Wait," she told him. "There is another child." Five hours later a twin girl was safely delivered. A clergyman came to the house and intoned a prayer in the ears of each child. Reza Khan held his son up and delivered his own benediction: "O God, I place my son in your care. Keep him in the shelter of your protection."

Destiny had two very different outcomes in store for the twins. "To say that I was unwanted might be harsh, but not altogether from the truth," remembered Princess Ashraf Pahlavi. "To be born on the same day as Mohammad Reza Pahlavi, future Crown Prince and then Shah of Iran, I would always feel I could lay no claim to my parents' special affection." For the boy, crown and kingdom awaited. The tide of history would propel the humble soldier's son from a mud brick house to the palace of the shahs, launching him from obscurity to that rare pantheon of statesmen whose decisions change the destinies of nations and alter the course of history.

PERSIA, HIS FUTURE inheritance, Land of the Lion and the Sun, formed a splendid land bridge between continents, a great salted corridor hemmed in by the Caspian Sea and the Alborz Mountains to the north, stretching almost a thousand miles south to the Zargos Mountains and the warm waters of the Persian Gulf. The Aryan peoples of Central Asia first appeared on the Iranian plateau more than six thousand years ago and lent their name to it. From land as dry as dust and worn as parchment paper, in 550 BC Cyrus II, scion of a dynastic union between two royal houses, the Medes and the Persians, seized power and established the Achaemenid Dynasty. After first securing the high plateau that stretched south from the shores of the Persian Gulf and north to the Caspian Sea, Cyrus ventured forth to conquer Asia Minor, Babylon, Assyria, modern-day Egypt, and Turkey, as well as the seaports of the eastern Mediterranean. Under Cyrus's rule, said the renowned historian Arnold Toynbee, the great Persian Empire stood alone as the world's "first sole superpower." "The establishment of the largest empire in antiquity, one of the most benevolent of any in world history, if any empire is good, is associated with the Persians," wrote historian Touraj Daryaee. "Its founder, Cyrus the Great, changed the map of the world and brought the Afro-Asiatic world together for the first time in history."

The conquest of Babylon in 539 BC inspired Cyrus to inscribe in clay a personal pledge to accord "all men the freedom to worship their own gods and ordered that no one had the right to bother them. I ordered that no house be destroyed, that no inhabitant be dispossessed. . . . I accorded peace and quiet to all men." Cyrus is remembered today as an empire builder but also as the liberator who ruled with social justice and the rights of the individual in mind. His successor Darius the Great pushed the empire west into Libya, south into the Arabian peninsula, and east as far as the Indus River. Outside Shiraz he built a dazzling new capital at Pasargade, "the camp of the Persians." The Achaemenid ascendancy collapsed in 330 BC, when Alexander the Great's legions swept through and the young warrior declared himself King of Persia. His death seven years later, accompanied by the flight of the Macedonians, was followed by the rise of the Parthian Kingdom, which endured for five centuries, and then by the Sasanians, whose mighty empire conquered the Holy Lands of the Levant, including Jerusalem. Though they defended their dominions from frequent Roman incursions, Sasanian defenses were fatally breached in AD 651 by Arab horsemen bearing the green flag of Islam. Ten other dynasties followed until the advent of the "storm from the east," the brutal Mongol invasion and occupation of Persia in the early years of the thirteenth century, which in turn gave way to Safavid, Zand, Afshar, and finally Qajar (1789–1925) dynastic rule.

The Persians had submitted to their Muslim overlords, and exchanged their Zoroastrian faith for Islam, but Persian nationalists were affronted by the thought of rule at the hands of the Arabs, whom they regarded as their racial and cultural inferiors. Persian contempt revealed itself when Reza Khan was elected King of Iran in 1925 and consciously styled himself with the dynastic name "Pahlavi" to honor the written script favored by the Sasanians. His son Mohammad Reza drew similar inspiration from the glories of Persia's pre-Islamic heritage by refusing to even discuss the centuries of Arab invasion and occupation. The mere thought of rule by the Arabs repulsed him, as he made clear during an interview with the Iranian journalist Amir Taheri in the midseventies. The Shah explained that "as a child he had always refused to read those pages in his history textbook that related to Persia's defeat at the hands of Arab armies in the seventh century," and he regarded the invasion of Sasanian Persia as the greatest catastrophe in history. "I simply could not bear the humiliation. I tore those pages out of the book and threw them away. There is no need for us to focus on the negative aspects of our existence."

The Pahlavi Dynasty emerged from the convulsive unrest that gripped Persia at the turn of the twentieth century. Persians frustrated with poverty and feudalism protested the ruling Qajar Dynasty, whose kings had allowed European powers to seize control of the economy and nibble chunks of territory. Corruption, misrule, and a struggling economy provided the bases for insurrection. Matters came to a head in 1905, when a coalition of scholars, clergy, and merchants united and rose in revolt. After months of unrest, on August 5, 1906, Mozaffar al-Din Shah agreed to surrender his autocratic privileges and accept a constitution that restricted royal prerogatives, established an elected parliament on the basis of limited suffrage, and a bill of rights to enshrine basic freedoms. The Constitutional Revolution proved a turning point in Iranian history and also marked a profound change in the status of the country's religious establishment. The majority of the Muslim clergy known as the ulama supported the liberal reformers and were rewarded with the right to inspect parliamentary legislation to make sure it conformed to Sharia, or Islamic law. However, a minority of hard-line religious theocrats rejected the Constitution as a heresy imported from the West. Though their numbers were small, these clerics never reconciled themselves to the notion of separation between church and state.

Far from bringing stability and security, the Constitutional Revolution opened the floodgates to two decades of unrest that brought Persia to the brink of collapse and dismemberment. In 1907 royalists and constitutionalists fought a civil war that drew in Great Britain and Russia, and the two dominant imperial powers in Southwest and Central Asia established cordons of influence in the north and south of the Persian kingdom, with London aggressively asserting its right to monopolize the exploration and production of newly discovered petroleum reserves in its sphere of influence. Over the next half century, successive British governments controlled Persian oil production through their majority shareholding in the Anglo-Persian Oil Company, ensuring that the old kingdom became a playground for great-power intrigue. During the 1914–1918 Great War Persia was invaded, fought over, and occupied by the armies of four foreign powers, who turned vast swaths of the countryside into a wasteland of contagious disease, famine, and tribal insurrection. By the time Brigadier General Reza Khan, the illiterate, courageous, and forceful commander of the elite Cossack Hamadan regiment, marched on the capital in February 1921 and overwhelmed the army garrison, Persians offered no real resistance and even welcomed the promise of a firm hand. Reza Khan saw his first task as reforming the army and pacifying the provinces. The civilian government he installed in Tehran set about with mixed success modernizing Persian government and society with European ideas and technology. Ahmad Shah was allowed to keep his throne, though few doubted that the days of the Qajar Dynasty were numbered.

Change came too slowly for Reza Khan's liking, and in 1923 he made himself prime minister, though he aspired to become the first president of a Persian republic. In neighboring Turkey his idol Kemal Ataturk had seized power, declared a secular republic, and smashed the power of his country's religious establishment. Reza Khan faced stiffer resistance in Persia, a country with more than two thousand years of monarchical heritage. The ulama still regarded the Shah as Custodian of the Shia faith and associated republics with the anticlericalism of Turkey and also France. Where they did find common cause with republicans was on the need to force the Qajars from power. In 1925 the ulama supported a parliamentary vote to replace the Qajar dynasty with a new royal house headed by Reza Khan, and the following spring the newly styled Reza Shah Pahlavi held his coronation and formally ascended the Peacock Throne. The new king surprised and dismayed the ulama when he made it clear that he meant to rule as well as reign and that to modernize Iran he intended to challenge the powers of the religious establishment. For now at least, the democratic spirit of the 1906 Constitutional Revolution remained a dream deferred and a promise unfulfilled.

FROM THE TIME Mohammad Reza Pahlavi was proclaimed Crown Prince of Persia in an elaborate coronation ceremony in April 1926, the boy who would be king was closely scrutinized for his potential as a future monarch. The early signs were not promising. With his jet black hair, sad eyes, and small physique, the new heir struck courtiers as a rather doleful little boy and serious beyond his years. Sickly and prone to stomach upsets and illness, Mohammad Reza "was gentle, reserved, and almost painfully shy, while I was volatile, quick-tempered, and sometimes rebellious," recalled his sister Ashraf. "He was somewhat frail and vulnerable to childhood disease, while I was robust and healthy, in spite of my small frame." Their father joked that Ashraf "must have gotten all the good health." Tough and scrappy, Ashraf saw the world as it really was, as a series of struggles and hardships to be overcome, whereas her shy twin was a dreamer and idealist who saw things as he wished them to be.

Their father, Reza Shah, was a famously taciturn, dominant personality with an explosive temper to match. His son remembered him as "a straightforward kind of man [who] didn't talk much, and sometimes could be very blunt, you know." That was polite understatement. Reza Shah tore the epaulettes off the uniforms of senior army officers and did not hesitate to strike officials in front of their subordinates. In her memoir, Princess Ashraf recalled that her father's "physical presence to us as children was so intimidating, the sound of his voice so terrifying, that even years later as a grown woman I can't remember a time when I wasn't afraid of him." Her twin's second wife, Soraya Esfandiary, described the spell the old man cast over his adult children from the grave. "Despite all the independence which their status as princesses and sisters of the king conferred upon them, [Ashraf and Shams] remained profoundly marked by their childhoods," she wrote. "Over them, as over Mohammad Reza and his brother Ali Reza, brooded the shadow of their father, that colonel of the cossacks who had risen from the ranks, uneducated and brutal, and could with a mere look terrorize his soldiers and those closest to him. Reza Shah, the man who still made them feel afraid."

Later in life, Mohammad Reza Pahlavi protested that his father had in fact showered him with affection. "I was never afraid of my father," he once told a family friend. "There was nothing that I asked him for that he said no to." Those who saw them together attested to the fatherly rapport with his heir. Mohammad Reza was "his father's love—the light of his eye, as the Persian saying goes," confirmed the Shah's biographer. Before bedtime, the boy would climb on his father's back and ride him like a horse, tapping him with a stick to go faster. Only when a servant knocked at the door would they leap to their feet and resume the formalities. "Oh! yes," the Shah agreed. "You may hesitate to believe me, but he was kind and tenderhearted; his sternness and coldness would melt into love and affection as soon as he was with the family, or with me, his crown prince." Father and son even devised a secret code to communicate in front of the other children and courtiers. Reza Shah instructed his other children to address their brother as "Your Highness," making it clear that from now on he was different from them in every way. The other children were jealous of their intimacies.

The Shah once remarked that his mother, Nimtaj, styled Taj ol-Moluk or "Crown of Kings," was "a very dictatorial woman." Taj ol-Moluk lavished attention on her second son, Ali Reza, whom she believed had a more forceful character than his older brother. "In his early days as Shah, Mohammad Reza was not esteemed by his own family," read a U.S. intelligence report from the seventies. "The Queen Mother appeared to hold her eldest son in contempt. She was frequently reported to be intriguing against him and promoting Ali as a more worthy successor, and on one occasion she remarked it was a pity Ashraf was not the Shah." She bullied and schemed against her daughters-in-law, too. Soraya Esfandiary, who bore the brunt of Taj ol-Moluk's machinations, once described her as a "woman of the harem" who "liked to intrigue, to receive political personalities, the wives of officers, courtiers. She questioned them, made them talk, gave her opinion on everything."

The King and Queen intimidated each other. Taj ol-Moluk freely admitted to drinking brandy to get through her wedding night, and her husband was known to flee at the sight of her entering a room. Reza Shah was a brave man indeed when he decided to exercise his marital rights to the full letter of religious law, which allowed Muslim men to take up to four living wives. Shortly after his second son, Ali Reza, was born in 1922, Reza Shah married Turan, who swiftly delivered him a third son, Gholam Reza. After divorcing Turan, in 1924 the King wed the much younger Esmat, who became his favorite wife and went on to provide him with five children of her own. Taj ol-Moluk bitterly fought these arrangements and made life difficult for her rivals. "Although polygamy was commonly practiced, and although women were expected to accept this condition, my mother was very angry," recalled Princess Ashraf Pahlavi, who like her diminutive mother had a very quick temper. "For a long time she refused to see my father. In the face of this unheard challenge to his authority, the Shah would literally hide when he saw my mother coming." Husband and wife eventually agreed to live separate lives, though Taj ol-Moluk retained the title of Queen-Empress and made sure that her two sons remained the sole legitimate heirs to the throne.

Reza Shah worried that his oldest son, doted on by the women in his family, would grow up a weakling. "No, I was not considered strong at all," the Shah later admitted, "but father steeled me by forcing me to become a keen sportsman." When he was six years old the little prince was removed from his mother's care, placed in his own household under strict supervision, and enrolled in a special military school so he could receive a "manly education." He was separately tended by Madame Arfa, a French governess. The Shah's admiration for Madame Arfa suggested that she was the only adult figure in his early life to provide him with anything approaching unconditional affection and emotional warmth. She enthralled her young charge with romantic tales of the lives of the great emperors and empresses and kings and queens of Europe, men and women such as France's Napoleon and Russia's Catherine the Great, who wielded absolute power to improve the lives of their people. Unbeknownst to Reza Shah, Madame Arfa introduced his young son to "the virtues of democracy springing from the ideas of the French Revolution." She taught the Crown Prince that "to become truly civilized, Iranians needed to change themselves culturally; they needed a French Revolution of sorts led by a shah steeped in things modern."

In his memoir, the Shah paid fulsome tribute to Madame Arfa. "To her I owe the advantage of being able to speak and read French as if it were my own language; and beyond this, she opened my mind to the spirit of Western culture." It was Madame Arfa who planted in the impressionable young boy's mind the intoxicating notion that a king could rule as well as reign and be a revolutionary as well as a democrat.

IN THE 1920s the land he was destined to rule nudged the southern border of the newly established Soviet Union for more than a thousand miles, skirting the shoreline of the Caspian Sea, plentiful in sturgeon, whose fine caviar graced tables around the world. The spongy storm clouds that sailed down from southern Russia were squeezed dry trying to clear the mountainous rock face of the Alborz Mountains range, ensuring that Persia's northern coast remained perpetually drenched while the kingdom's interior was almost always parched. "Water is the chief concern of the Persian peasant," an American traveler wrote in the early twentieth century. "Wherever he can find the flow of a mountain stream or build a crude canal from a well or spring, a small portion of the desert becomes a paradise and he prospers. Certain of these regions are said to be among the most fertile in the world, producing in abundance not only the finest of wheat and barley, but grapes, peaches, nectarines, pomegranates, figs and melons which are unsurpassed among the fruits of the Temperate Zone."

The sweeping view from the top of the Alborz ridge was of a "magnificent plateau which seems to stretch to eternity," a visitor to Persia once said. Eighteen thousand feet below, clinging to its mountainous hemline, Tehran basked in the sun like a smug cat whose muddy brick tail extended to the edge of the great salt desert. To the east, beyond Yazd with its lyrical skyline of wind chimneys, travelers entered "the great lifeless desert, shaped like a huge hour-glass, 900 miles in length, from the foothills of the Alborz range, in the north, almost to the Indian Ocean, in the south, and ranging in width from 300 to 100 miles." The sprawling Dasht-e Kavir desert held tight its mysteries and miracles. Mighty dust storms roared through like locomotives. Locals in Sistan Province dreaded the annual Wind of One-Hundred-Twenty Days, when broiling gales lashed the region from June to September, and locals still spoke of the time a shepherd and his flock of sheep were dug out alive after a week buried under a sand drift. "Some sections in their utter bleakness resembled landscapes on the moon," was how one American described Dasht-e Kavir in 1950. "At wide intervals walled adobe villages, with green fields and slender poplar trees, or an upthrust of jagged, rocky hills broke the monotony. . . . A haze wrapped the horizon in mystery. Eastward, seemingly limitless, stretched the great salt desert, shimmering in the heat. To the west, gaunt rock hills, pastel-shaped, made a grotesque skyline. A caravan of camels plodded by carrion birds glided above a burro's carcass."

The main centers of urban life hovered at the desert edge, each a reflection of Persia's dazzling cultural and ethnic diversity. The capital, Tehran, had always been a rough town. Laid waste by the Afghans in 1723, Tehran was a mere cluster of three thousand mud and brick hovels when the Qajar Dynasty appointed it the new Imperial seat. This made strategic sense— the village occupied the gateway to the heights of the Alborz, which overlooked the plateau—but Tehran lacked the elegant artistry and sophistication of the former capital, Isfahan, and most visitors regarded the locals as uncouth and too focused on turning a profit. About seventy-five miles to Tehran's south sat Qom, where the ayatollahs, the country's religious leaders, resided and where important religious schools known as the *hawza* were located. The second major center of clerical power was Mashad, to the northeast, nestled against the border with Afghanistan. Each year pilgrims trekked to Mashad to pay their respects at the stupendous Holy Shrine of Imam Reza, resting place of the Prophet Mohammad's eighth disciple. Isfahan, always elegant, dominated the central provinces, and tourists from around the world admired the Shah Abbas Mosque, one of the finest examples of Islamic architecture in the world, which opened out onto the splendid Naghsh-e Jahan Square, where Persian monarchs watched polo matches from a high pavilion, and also the picturesque "Bridge of Thirty-Three Arches," which spanned the Zayande River. Dominating the southwest was the city of Shiraz, "an oasis situated on a high plateau ringed by barren hills. It is a city of gardens and has never been known as a center of trade and industry. Its fame is due to its poets, its gardens, its wine, and its almost mythical position in the Iranian mind." Persia's greatest poets, Hafez and Saadi, wrote of the Shirazi love of songbirds, sweet wine, and scent of rose.

The southern provinces were Iran's economic lifeline. In the breadbasket province of Khuzestan, which straddled the Iraqi border, the port city of Abadan boasted the world's largest oil refinery. Running along the southern coastline were the Zagros Mountains, rocky sentinels overlooking the Persian Gulf, where mighty tankers crept through the Strait of Hormuz, only twenty-one miles wide at its narrowest tip, on their way to market. In the sixties the Shah poured more than $1 billion into Persian Gulf oil facilities and at a stroke trebled Iran's oil production and established the foundations for the country's spectacular economic takeoff. The Persian Gulf was Iran's "jugular vein," and he brushed aside foreign critics who accused him of harboring territorial ambitions. When an American journalist asked the Shah whether "Iran's entry into the Persian Gulf would affect the country's relations with the Arabs and Israelis," he offered a stiff retort: "We are *in* the Persian Gulf. What we are demanding is what has always belonged to our country throughout history."

The Shah's people embodied the contradictions of life along the highway of history. They retained a distinct identity that set them apart from their neighbors and reflected their unique passage through space and time. Life on the high plateau was a constant game of survival, with everchanging rules. Persians had endured centuries of foreign occupation by absorbing the ways of their overlords to the point where the Greeks, Arabs, and Mongols mirrored *them* back in return. They were Persians first but also Arabs, Baluchis, Armenians, Kurds, and Turks. More than 90 percent were Muslim, but they shared the land with Jewish, Christian, Baha'i, and Zoroastrian minorities. Renowned for their hospitality, artistry, and individualism, the Persians were also inveterate grumblers, too easily slighted and with a capacity to exaggerate and embellish. For a people who prided themselves on their knowledge of science, philosophy, and literature, Persians saw their world as one shaped by elaborate conspiracies that allowed them to shift the blame for their own mistakes and misfortunes onto the shoulders of others. These ultimate survivors were adept at showing different faces to outsiders but also to their own rulers, whom they had a habit of raising up and turning out with bewildering speed—an old saying had it that the people did not often turn, but when they did, it was usually fatal. Persians thrived in adversity only to slacken in good times, so that even when their borders stoved in under relentless pressure from the Russians, Turks, and British in the eighteenth and nineteenth centuries, Persian art, culture, and literature flourished under the Safavid and Qajar Dynasties.

Western visitors regarded the Persians as a brilliant and inscrutable people. The American journalist Frances Fitzgerald traveled to Iran in 1974 and wrote a penetrating account of life under the second Pahlavi king. "Iran is a country of walls and mirrors," she wrote. "Walls surround the villages as they surround every house in Tehran, dividing the public and private lives, creating distances where they do not exist. Behind walls that are mud-brown and anonymous, the rich conceal their fountains and gardens from the desert . . . the great families of Iran have covered the insides of their houses with murals and faceted mirrors so that each room is a visual maze of light and reflections of the real and painted figures. Turn the thought around and the mirrors are a complete defense system, turning away the truth. In Iran, nothing is exactly what it seems. A foreigner finds uncertainty behind arrogance, sadness behind euphoria. But ambiguity may be the only principle of nature in Iran."

As a young boy, and unlike his father, Crown Prince Mohammad Reza never questioned the central tenets of his faith. Palace housemaids kept the young prince and his brothers and sisters entertained by spinning embellished tales about the tragic lives of the Prophet Mohammad's disciples, the imams. These stories of miracles and revelations took on a deeply personal meaning when the little prince almost perished of typhoid at age six. While the boy drifted into and out of consciousness, his mother walked back and forth across the room, holding a Quran over his head and praying for his recovery. When he came around he startled his parents and doctors by informing them that he had been visited in his dreams by Ali, the son-in-law of the Prophet Mohammad. He attributed his survival to Ali's divine intervention. Two more episodes followed, each more intense than the last. After the Crown Prince fell from a horse and struck his head on a rock by the roadside, he told his adult companions that his fall was stopped by a saint who cushioned his head to prevent it from splitting open on the jagged edge.

The third experience was the most revealing, for it went to the very heart of Islam's Shia faith. One day the Crown Prince was walking along a street when he claimed to see "a man with a halo around his head—much as in some of the great paintings, by Western masters, of Jesus. As we passed one another, I knew him at once. He was the imam or descendant of Mohammad who, according to our faith, disappeared but is expected to come again to save the world." This time the young prince kept his vision to himself. Reza Shah had named his sons after the imams and he visited the main holy shrines, but he ruled as an autocrat and did not much care for the divine right of kings. He knew all too well that the sword and not God had brought him to power and placed his family on Persia's Peacock Throne. The Shah regarded his heir's mystical nature as yet another sign of inherent weakness. But the Crown Prince was convinced that his early trials had marked him as a messenger of justice and an instrument of God's will.

Persians were Muslim by conquest if not by choice. In the year AD 610 Mohammad was a forty-year-old trader living in Mecca in the western Arabian peninsula when he experienced the visions and revelations that led him to believe he had been marked as God's messenger on earth. He never claimed to be a divine being and saw in his new religion, Islam, which meant "submission before Allah (God)," fellowship with Judaism and Christianity. His revelations were later transcribed to form the basis of Islam's holy book, the Quran, and the faith he brought to the people was based on the five central pillars of belief, prayer, charity, fasting, and pilgrimage. Within a decade of Mohammad's death in AD 632, Arab armies raided Persia's Sasanian Empire and swept across the length and breadth of the Middle East. By the ninth century, the Islamists ruled over an empire the equal of Rome in terms of size and accomplishment.

Mohammad's death led to a power struggle when his immediate heirs disagreed over who should inherit the mantle of the Prophet and lead the faithful. Two rival camps formed. The majority Muslim party called themselves "Sunni" and followed the rule of the caliphs. But a partisan minority, the "Shia," bitterly contested their claim and argued that Mohammad's rightful heir was Ali, the Prophet's beloved son-in-law. Both groups fought two inconclusive civil wars to settle the matter until Ali's ascendance to the caliphate ended in his assassination. Ali's son and heir, Husayn, fought on, but he, too, was eventually betrayed, hunted down, and beheaded at the Battle of Karbala in AD 680. This outrage made permanent the split between Shia and Sunni and led to two rival lines of succession. Each of the Shia "imams" or claimants fell victim to assassination until the twelfth, a child, disappeared from view completely, apparently having been spirited away to save the Shia line of succession from extinction. The disappearance or "occultation" of the Twelfth or "Hidden Imam" meant that the Shia believed they were condemned to await his return, which would augur the end of days, bringing an end to the injustices visited upon them. Until then, they must accept their bitter lot and not struggle against the vagaries of misfortune and fate. The schism within Islam took on ethnic, political, and nationalist dimensions in AD 1501, when the Safavid Dynasty took power in Persia, seized the Peacock Throne, and declared Shiism the official religion of their new empire. From that moment on the kings of Persia assumed the title of Shia Islam's "Custodian of the Faith."

The Shia clergy occupied a special role in Persian society, one that set them still farther apart from their Sunni brethren. The ulama saw themselves as the people's conscience and "the vehicle for expressing public opinion whenever other means of expression are not existent or insufficient." In practice this meant that the clergy saw their role less as molding public opinion than reflecting it, though the subtlety was sometimes lost during bouts of social and political unrest. On occasions when the people demanded change from a resistant crown the ulama responded by mobilizing the mosques to bring crowds out into the streets. "A fine system of mutual checks and balances has always existed between the clergy and the public at large," wrote one Iranian commentator in 1978. "While no individual would dare do anything glaringly contradictory to religious ethics, no religious leader could adopt a position that was not approved by at least a section of public opinion. The public controls the clergy by financing it and obeying its edicts while it is in turn controlled by the clergy pronouncements and positions. The Shiite mosque is a widespread and loosely organized institution [that] become[s] effective only when and where the community of believers wants to use it. Otherwise, it is kept as a community reserve, a potential capable of effective use whenever the need arises."

Yet Persian attitudes toward Islam, like most everything else, were hardly uniform and at times oddly ambivalent. Public observance and interest in religion waxed and waned according to "the social and political conditions of the society at any given time." The generations worshipped with a different fervor, with parents possibly more observant than their children and vice versa. The Persians were not known for being overly zealous or judgmental in their interpretation of the holy book. There was, too, their cynical use of *taqiya*, an old religious custom that justified lying if believers ever felt threatened for following the Shia line. Though taqiya was supposed to be reserved only for life-threatening situations, mullahs and laymen were quick to exploit this moral loophole for personal use and gain. And though Islam technically forbade alcohol and imposed strict constraints on personal conduct, the Persian appetite for wine, women, and song continued more or less unabated through the centuries. Even while Persians claimed to respect their local mullah or priest, many reserved for him the same cynical contempt for authority they showed their kings. Pious and respectful to his face, behind the mullah's back they gossiped about his women, snickered at his burgeoning waistline, and traded barbed jokes that compared their hapless fate to that of a donkey. "Don't let the mullah ride you," the old Persian saying went, "because once he gets on he'll never get off."

AT AGE TWELVE the young Pahlavi prince boarded a Russian cruiser at the Caspian port of Enzali and set sail for Europe and boarding school in Switzerland. Reza Shah wanted his heir to have a thoroughly modern and Western outlook on life. He allowed his son to take along two companions. The first, Mehrpur Teymurtash, was the son of the minister of court, but it was his second and favored playmate, Hossein Fardust, the son of a noncommissioned officer, who would later play a role in the fall of the dynasty. There was no question that young Fardust should leave his parents for five years to accompany the prince to Europe. The boy already spent five days each week at the palace, where the lonely prince smothered him with affection and treated him almost like a doll to be taken wherever he went. Princess Ashraf later recalled that Reza Shah "did not particularly like Fardust and wondered why his son was so fond of him." Fardust would often run away "and we did not know where he had gone. My brother would then be unhappy and send for him. He liked him very much."

The shy, entitled prince was firmly put in his place by his classmates at Le Rosey, the prestigious boarding school that sat on the shores of Lake Geneva. An American boarder, Frederick Jacobi Jr., later wrote a revealing account in the *New Yorker* of the day the young prince's yellow Hispano-Suiza pulled up. "His entourage consisted of a chauffeur and footman, both in Park Avenue–type uniforms; a valet, who was unmistakable; and a spectacularly handsome, silver-haired gentleman who carried himself straighter than any other man I had ever seen, and who I subsequently learned was a Persian diplomat of high rank." As the new boy walked past the curious crowd that had gathered on the steps he "swept us all with a stare that he must have intended as regal. His efforts were lost on us, however." Later in the day, the prince saw young Frederick Jacobi sitting with his friend Charlie Childs on a small bench. When the boys refused to stand up or otherwise acknowledge the royal presence, the prince "flew at Charlie Childs, seized him by the throat," which prompted Charlie to box him around the ears and pin him to the ground. "It was all over very quickly because Pahlavi soon lay still and grunted for mercy. His black hair dank and falling over his eyes, his face scratched and bleeding, his shirt torn, he slowly got to his feet. His next move surprised me as well. He smiled, shook Charlie's hand a couple of times, and patted him on the back."

The fracas in the school yard showed the prince of Persia as a boy who had thrown the first punch and then sued for peace rather than fight his corner—he wanted to be liked more than respected, a pattern that reasserted itself throughout his life in a series of showdowns with older and more assertive personalities. Gradually, however, the prince won over his classmates, and his election to captain of the soccer team gave him his first real taste of leadership and a sort of popular democracy in action. Still, he was prevented from taking part in many normal student activities by his overzealous Iranian minders. They impressed on the teenager the importance of the farr and the lessons of traditional Persian kingship. Lonely and homesick, the boy found consolation in faith and prayer. "I was determined that when later I came to the throne, my conduct would always be guided by a true religious sense," he recalled. He prayed five times a day and decided that one of his first reforms as king would be to institute a "public complaints" box so that he could stay in touch with his people's wishes. Suffering lay at the heart of Shiism, and his suffering as a child convinced the prince that he had a mission to fulfill in his lifetime. To the dismay of his father, while he was abroad, the Crown Prince became not only more devout in his religious beliefs but also more socially liberal.

WITH HIS SON away at school, Reza Shah set Persia firmly on the road to modernity.

The Shah nursed the ambitions of Peter the Great, Imperial Russia's great modernizer, but he was more personally inspired by France's Napoleon Bonaparte, another junior army officer who rose through the ranks to seize a crown and forge a new civilization. Reza Shah was determined to lay the foundations for a modern state and erase past humiliations. "The hallmark of the era was to be state-building," wrote an Iranian scholar who compared Iran's Pahlavi Dynasty to England's Tudors and Austria's Hapsburgs. "Reza Shah came to power in a country where the government had little presence outside the capital. He left it with an extensive state structure—the first in Iran's two thousand years." He persuaded Britain's Anglo-Persian Oil Company to increase the share of profits it paid the state in taxes and used the money to build dams, railways, ports, libraries, factories, schools, universities, and hospitals. Bank Melli was established as Iran's new national bank, the metric system of measurement was introduced, and the Muslim lunar calendar was swapped for the solar calendar. Vaccination programs eliminated disease. Hundreds of young students were sent abroad on full scholarships to the United States and Europe to train in science, technology, education, and medicine. They returned to take their place as the next generation of reformers. In 1935 the first Pahlavi king renamed Persia "Iran" to make it clear there was no going back to the old ways.

Though the ulama had made Reza Shah's accession to the throne possible, the King was determined to follow the example of Turkey's Kemal Ataturk, who agreed that religion and modernity could not coexist. He closed seminaries, desegregated public places, and changed labor laws to allow women to enter the workforce. He ordered Iranians to don Western garb and forbade women from wearing the flowing black outer garment called the chador. These measures eventually sparked resistance and riots in 1935 in the holy city of Mashad that were put down with force. Faced with severe repression and a loss of status, most Shia clerics chose to withdraw from public life, while others left Iran for permanent exile in neighboring Iraq, another majority Shia society. Reza Shah also reduced Iran's parliament, the Majles, to a rubber stamp, expecting it to bow to his wishes, and hundreds of political dissidents who deplored authoritarian rule were harassed, imprisoned, and exiled.

The schoolboy prince followed events back home with great interest. No single issue gripped his imagination more than the emancipation of women. In a letter dated February 1, 1936, addressed to "my unique and highly esteemed father," the prince replied to Reza Shah's decision to confer on women the same rights as men. "This is a truly massive revelation," the Crown Prince wrote to his father. "The primary care and nurture of every offspring, initiated by its mother's devotion, is pivotal to their upbringing, memories and morals, and my patriotic and progressive noble father, has perpetually been well aware of this fact." Also,

> Hence, women's acquirement of science and arts through education is the key for any nation's progress and advancement. Because achieving such goals would be futile while shrouded by social deprivation, I therefore hope that such fatherly attention and enactments for the benefit of the noble women of our dear Iran will pave the way for the prosperity and well-being of this unfortunate section of our society.

The cruiser that brought the Crown Prince home docked on May 11, 1936, at the renamed port of Pahlavi in the renamed Kingdom of Iran. The Pahlavi family stood assembled on the wharf with Reza Shah "standing alone, watching, calmly it seemed, as the boat approached from a distance." The return of the son after five long years away was an emotional moment that the proud father did not wish to share with anyone, but when the prince walked toward him he appeared briefly not to recognize the once sickly boy, now a handsome young man. Father and son shook hands, exchanged a hug, and walked to where the Queen and the princesses, waiting on the quay, wore stylish European dresses and hats rather than the traditional ill-fitting black chador. Princess Ashraf noticed how "happy and healthy, stronger and more fit" her brother appeared. He was filled with excitement about his future responsibilities. "My brother told me how impressed he had been by the democratic attitudes he had seen at the school, by the fact that all the boys, whether they were sons of businessmen or noblemen or kings, were equals within the school community. He talked about how he had come to realize for the first time how much economic and social disparity there was among the people of Iran."

As the motorcade pulled away from port Pahlavi to rise over the Alborz Mountains headed for Tehran, the Crown Prince felt he had arrived in "a different country. I recognized nothing." Iran's Caspian Sea coastline, previously so wretched, now appeared "as an Iranian version of the south of France." Dodge motorcars hummed along the seaboard and there were "huge new hotels pushing their heads into the air." A decade earlier, travel to Tehran had taken days and involved bribes, opium, brigands, and donkey rides. Now drivers swept over "the superb Chalus road, which ascends in incredible twists and turns up and through the amber Alborz Mountains." Motorists experienced the thrill of driving above the cloud line. Once shabby post houses had been transformed into "elaborate way-side hotels." The bigger surprise lay down in the foothills, where the royal motorcade was greeted by tens of thousands of cheering spectators lining the streets, tossing flowers and bouquets into the prince's open car. "My father had razed Tehran's old walls," he recalled. "Streets were paved and asphalted. The city had begun to take on the look and style of a European capital. I saw it all at first as if in a dream."

The Crown Prince enrolled as a cadet in the Military College of Tehran, a new institution modeled after the elite French academy of St. Cyr, and for the next two years attended maneuvers and studied military strategy and tactics. After graduating as a second lieutenant he was appointed to the post of army inspector. Reza Shah also began tutoring his son in the role and responsibilities of kingship, and together they traveled to Iran's different regions to meet with provincial officials. The Crown Prince noticed how the dignitaries they met along the way were "so much in awe that 'discussion' with [Reza Shah] had none of the give-and-take the word implies." He worried about his father's isolation. He saw that Iranian officials were too intimidated to bring problems to his father's attention and that this left him dangerously isolated from public opinion. Gradually, courtiers who feared Reza Shah learned they could approach his son with their problems, and the prince adopted the role of emissary and mediator. Reza Shah patiently listened to his son's sugges-tions and rarely opposed his recommendations. There was a practical side to this: the old king wanted to test his presumptive successor's judgment. "I advanced my views and made hints and suggestions, but discussion in any usual sense was out of the question," recalled the Shah. "Nevertheless, I, as a young man, of only some nineteen years of age, frequently spoke my mind to the Shah; and the amazing thing was how willing he was to listen to me, and how seldom he rejected my proposals."

As heir to the throne, the Crown Prince exhibited all the zeal of a youthful reformer, even daring to raise with his father the sensitive issue of the Pahlavi family's extensive real estate holdings along the Caspian seaboard. Critics accused Reza Shah of confiscating or purchasing at arti-ficially low prices more than three million acres of prime land. The father, his son remembered, patiently explained that "he concentrated buying along our country's frontier primarily for national security reasons. Although he had in mind a better life for the peasants, he knew it would take time and that national security had to come first." The Crown Prince listened to this explanation and accepted it without comment, though his subsequent behavior suggested he did not believe a word of it. He showed an interest in the cases of prominent political prisoners jailed for dissent and urged his father to release those who claimed unfair conviction. The Shah explained that emptying Iran's prisons would not solve Iran's problems and that showing compassion to one's enemies was a form of weakness. How might it look if men arrested on his orders were later released by his son?

The Shah specifically cautioned his son not to intervene on behalf of Iran's most celebrated political prisoner, an aristocrat related by marriage to the deposed Qajars. Mohammad Mossadeq had opposed the establishment of the Pahlavi Dynasty in 1925, warned Reza Shah against dictatorship, and championed the 1906 Constitution. Mossadeq's children pleaded with the Crown Prince for mercy, explaining that their father's age and infirm health meant he was not expected to survive the harsh prison conditions. In 1940 Reza Shah agreed to release the old man from his confinement but warned in starkly prophetic terms that it was a decision his son would live to regret.

In his sixtieth year, Reza Shah turned his attention to the Imperial succession. He had entertained thoughts of abdication for some time though without spelling out an exact time line for relinquishing power. At first he considered retiring in the late forties but already by the spring of 1941 one of his most trusted advisers was holding preliminary discussions with the Crown Prince to start planning for an orderly transfer. Reza Shah was starting to lose physical strength and may have had a sense of his own impending mortality.

As an upstart dynasty the Pahlavis were faced with a shortage of legitimate candidates to succeed to the throne. Under the Constitution only Crown Prince Mohammad Reza and his full-blood brother, Prince Ali Reza, were eligible to reign. Their half brothers, the children of Reza Shah's other wives, had Qajar blood and were therefore deemed unsuitable. The need for the Crown Prince to produce an heir was pressing. Reza Shah was unsentimental on the subject of marriage. He had already married off his daughters Shams and Ashraf to handpicked suitors, though their joint betrothal turned into a soap opera when Shams decided she preferred her younger sister's beau, Fereydoun Djam, the son of the prime minister and a handsome young army officer, over her own intended. Her father ordered his daughters to exchange fiancés, and Ashraf was married off to Ali Qavam, a man she loathed. "So I was married," she wrote, "in a traditional double ceremony with Shams, complete with white Lanvin wedding dress, though black would have been more suitable for my mood."

With his usual brusque efficiency, Reza Shah took matters into his own hands and betrothed his son and heir to the lovely Princess Fawzia, sister of King Farouk of Egypt. "With his characteristic forthrightness—perhaps better adapted to engineering projects than to affairs of heart—he staged an investigation," Mohammad Reza Shah later recalled with dry understatement. His father was eager to strike a pact with Egypt, the greatest of the Arab states, and legitimize the Pahlavi Dynasty as an established royal house. The engaged couple met for the first time just two weeks before their wedding on March 15, 1939, and discovered they had virtually nothing in common. They were marched down the aisle anyway. Spoiled and adored at home, beautiful Fawzia made no effort to hide her resentment at leaving behind cosmopolitan Cairo for the stuffy provincialism of court life in Tehran. She was bored and lonely and found the intrigues of the Pahlavi women tiresome. The Iranian public regarded her as disinterested in their lot, and they were probably right. Fawzia provided a daughter, Shahnaz, in 1940, but her marriage to the Crown Prince was otherwise not a success. "For reasons still obscure to medical science, there were to be no more children," was his cryptic explanation for the breakdown in marital relations. Rumors flew around town that husband and wife both found solace elsewhere.

Reza Shah's plan for a well-crafted transfer of power to his son was upended during the Second World War when on August 25, 1941, the combined armies of Great Britain and Soviet Russia invaded Iran on the flimsy pretext of preventing the kingdom's road and rail links and oil depots from falling into German hands. The real problem was Reza Shah's policy of neutrality and his refusal to be seen bending to the same foreign powers who earlier in the century had divided the country among them. On the day of the invasion the Imperial Family gathered for lunch. The mood at the table was "so tense and so grim that none of us dared speak," recalled Princess Ashraf. "What I knew was inevitable has happened," her father told them. "The Allies have invaded. I think this will be the end for me—the English will see to it." In a moment of great drama, the Crown Prince handed his sister a gun. "Ashraf, keep this gun with you, and if troops enter Tehran and try to take us, fire a few shots and then take your own life," he told his sister. "I'll do the same." The next day bombers reached the outskirts of Tehran and dropped explosives. The Queen and the princesses sheltered in the palace basement and as soon as the all-clear was sounded packed and fled south to Isfahan.

The Shah and his eldest son stayed behind to rally the generals, but Iran's army disintegrated under the Allied onslaught. On September 16, 1941, Reza Shah signed the formal instrument of abdication, changed into civilian clothes, and drove to Isfahan to join his wife and daughters. He was told by his British captors that he must leave Iran to spend his days in exile—a fitting end for the former Cossack who came to the throne idolizing Napoleon Bonaparte. Princess Ashraf begged to join her father but he said no. "I would love to have you with me, but your brother needs you more," her father explained. "I want you to stay with him. I wish you had been a boy, so you could be a brother to him now." Stripped of his titles, rank, and wealth, Reza Shah boarded a British cruiser bound for his preferred destination of Argentina. Only when the vessel was at sea did the captain inform the deposed monarch that he was actually headed to permanent exile in South Africa. His son later noted the irony—unbeknownst to the British, at the time of their invasion his father had already set his mind on abdication and spending the rest of his life abroad. Mohammad Reza Shah later wrote, "You might say that Reza Shah was exiled by mutual desire and consent."

The British and Russian ambassadors considered turning out the Pahlavis and replacing them with the more pliable Qajars. Fearful of arousing nationalist opinion, they abandoned the scheme but nonetheless snubbed the Shah's investiture. In his maiden speech from the throne the new king assured parliament and the people that he would abide by the Constitution and return his father's estates back to the nation. His speech went down well, but his ministers and the Allied ambassadors were determined to see to it that the second Pahlavi king's wings were firmly clipped and surrounded him with forceful older personalities determined to reestablish constitutional rule and prevent the emergence of a second autocracy. The proud young monarch felt the sting of humiliation every time he drove in and out of the capital, where he was obliged to present his identification papers to the Russian troops manning the gates. Two years later, when Roosevelt, Stalin, and Churchill flew to Tehran to discuss their war aims, only Stalin made an effort to treat the twenty-four-year-old King with the respect he felt he deserved as Iran's head of state. Roosevelt said he would be happy to receive the Shah—at his lodgings in the Russian embassy. The Shah bitterly recalled that "it seemed a curious situation that I had to go to the Russian embassy to see him, while Stalin came to see me." Slights like this left their mark.

The Shah found himself "plunged into a sea of trouble," and perhaps his greatest achievement in those fraught early years was simply to survive. The U.S. embassy in Tehran informed the State Department that the young king had "no solid power base and no political machine" but nonetheless thought they saw promise in his idealism and character.

> Mohammad Shah is a man of much stronger purpose than is generally realized. He stands almost alone, distrusts most advisers, is honest in his efforts to secure a democratic form of government in Iran. He is not easily influenced and cannot be shaken. Installed as a figurehead during the 1941 crisis, he may yet surprise the factions in his country and the outside powers. He thinks along Western lines, and is inalienably attached to his Iranian army. The military budget is half the national expenditure now. Yet, of course, the army is almost his only backing within Iran.

The young monarch could barely hide his frustration with his lot. "I inherited a crown," he protested. "Before I put it on, I want to earn it." He had been on the throne a year when he met with a group of senior politicians to plead his case for far-reaching social and economic reforms. "I told them that we must establish social justice in this country," he said, drawing on his tutelage in Switzerland and bearing in mind Madame Arfa's talk of revolutionary kings. "It is not fair that a number of people should be at a loss what to do with their wealth," he said, "while a number die from hunger." His ministers dismissed his "revolutionary ideas" as empty talk and the naive ramblings of a young man with too much time on his hands.

The Shah's brimming youthful idealism was never more fully expressed than during a reception he hosted for the country's religious leaders in the late forties. In words that would come back to haunt him later in life, he lectured the ulama on their responsibilities as moral guardians of the nation. No ruler of Iran was above the law, he reminded them. "People must not remain silent, or neutral, about the actions of their rulers," he said in reference to the farr, which sanctioned rebellion in case of injustice. "They must rise up if governments trample their rights or break the laws. It is indeed one of the major responsibilities of the clergy to awaken people and make them aware of their legal rights, and thus not allow rulers and governments to engage in reckless and lawless behavior."

3

THE OLD LION

I will never start anything against [him].
—MOHAMMAD MOSSADEQ

Has there ever been a monarch who has
plotted against his own government?
—THE SHAH

On the pale winter afternoon of February 4, 1949, gunshots rang out in front of the University of Tehran, where crowds were gathered to witness the Shah's arrival. He was walking in plain sight of dozens of onlookers when a man pulled a revolver from a camera box, took aim at his head, and opened fire at point-blank range. With no time for the Shah to take cover, the first three bullets "passed through my military cap without touching my head. But the gunman's fourth shot penetrated my right cheekbone and came out beneath my nose. He was now aiming at my heart. . . . So I suddenly started shadow-dancing or feinting. He fired again, wounding me in the shoulder. His last shot stuck in the gun. I had the queer and not unpleasant sensation of knowing that I was alive." The young King's bodyguards returned fire, killing the assassin on the spot, while the Shah was rushed to the hospital "bleeding like a young bull whose throat had been slit." Later in the evening, bandaged and propped up in bed, he delivered a radio address to the nation to assure the people he was not seriously harmed.

The attempted assassination was the Shah's second remarkable escape from death in less than a year. Some months earlier he had been piloting a light aircraft when it inexplicably lost power and dropped from the sky. "We had to make a forced landing in a mountainous region in a ravine full of rocks and boulders," he said, describing the moment when he braced for impact. With no engine to throttle, and unable to maneuver the body of the plane, he managed to pull the nose up just in time to clear a barrier of rocks. The propeller slammed into a boulder, tore off the undercarriage, and the plane landed in a somersault. "There we were, hanging by our seat belts in the open cockpit," he said. "Neither of us suffered so much as a scratch. I remember that the scene amused me so much that I burst out laughing, but my upside-down companion didn't think it was funny." The plane crash and the shooting outside the University of Tehran reaffirmed his fatalistic belief that he enjoyed God's protection.

Faith and luck were in short supply in Iran in the late 1940s and early fifties. The end of the Second World War did not usher in peace or stability but instead hurled Iran into the treacherous currents of the Cold War. Iran's oil wealth and its proximity to the Soviet Union and the Persian Gulf made the country a prize worth fighting for. Though the wartime allies had signed a pact to evacuate their forces from Iranian territory within six months of Germany's defeat, Stalin decided to test British and American resolve by keeping Russian troops on the ground supporting a puppet Communist state in the northern province of Azerbaijan. It was only in the face of tough diplomatic pressure from the Truman administration that Moscow backed down and Azerbaijan was liberated from Communist rule. This first major international crisis of the Cold War convinced the Shah and the army generals that they should cultivate close ties with the United States if Iran was to avoid falling behind the Iron Curtain.

Political disturbances also roiled Iran's southern provinces, where the Anglo-Iranian Oil Company, founded in 1908, still dominated oil production, ruling over a vast swath of territory with all the hubris of a colonial overseer. Iranians angrily protested when the company refused to adopt a more generous compensation agreement in line with favorable taxation deals struck with other oil producers in the Middle East. They clamored for oil nationalization, which would strip Great Britain of its control over Iranian oil assets and end half a century of British interference in their internal affairs. Extremist political and religious groups emerged from the shadows to exploit the unrest and agitate against the royalist establishment. Though police were quick to blame Communists for the attack on the Shah outside the University of Tehran, investigators were well aware that the gunman was in league with the "Warriors of Islam" or "Fedayeen-e Islam," a Shiite group dedicated to the implementation of religious law and ridding Iran of all secular and Western influence. In the same year the Shah escaped assassination, religious fanatics succeeded in murdering his minister of court, and two years later Prime Minister Haj-Ali Razmara was assassinated inside the Sepah Salar Mosque in Tehran.

Poverty and illiteracy were a breeding ground for extremism and violence. "Iran's chief city, like the country as a whole, is still only in the shadow of the machine age," wrote a visitor to Iran. "Though the city boasts broad streets, traffic lights, dial phones, and pretentious buildings, it still lacks sanitary water and sewage systems. . . . Tehran is a city of rags to riches. Expensive American automobiles are legion. Palaces and pretentious walled villas dot the city and its northern suburbs. On the sidewalks well-dressed men brush elbows with barefooted porters, well diggers, and other laborers in rags, while flanking the main road south to the shrine city of Rey families live like animals in caves." The Shah, his ministers, and Western legations worried that Iran's backward economy and weak government made the kingdom susceptible to Communist subversion. The future of the Pahlavi Dynasty hung in the balance at a time when other monarchies were toppled in Europe, the Middle East, and Asia. Queen Fawzia's decision to abandon Tehran for Cairo in 1948 and sue for divorce was yet another reminder that the Pahlavi line was only a bullet away from extinction. Anxious to provide his people and mother with a male heir, the Shah began the search for a new wife.

SORAYA ESFANDIARY WAS descended from the chiefs of the Bakhtiary tribe. Her father, Khalil Esfandiary, had left Reza Shah's Iran for Germany in the late twenties to escape political persecution, and it was while pursuing his university studies in Berlin that he met and fell in love with Eva Karl, the daughter of a wealthy German chemicals industrialist. Following a lengthy courtship, the couple married and moved to Iran, where a daughter, Soraya, was born in 1932. Eva struggled to adjust to Iranian life, and the Esfandiarys soon returned to Berlin. Fearing the outbreak of war, the family moved back to Iran before decamping, this time for good, to Switzerland as soon as peace was declared.

Soraya once explained that her back-and-forth existence meant she felt at home everywhere and nowhere, identifying as Muslim and Christian but feeling neither fully Iranian nor German. "It was a sort of rupture," she explained. "With my eyes which were too light and my skin which was too white for some of them, with my Persian manners which were a little too haughty for the others. I was alone, isolated." After leaving school Soraya decided to take English classes in London in the hope of becoming an actress. She had no idea that she was about to feature in a real-life screenplay, one far more dramatic than any Hollywood starring role. Word of her exquisite beauty had reached Tehran, where Queen Mother Taj ol-Moluk, the indomitable Pahlavi matriarch, investigated her son's prospects for marriage. After a close friend and relative of Khalil Esfandiary handed her a photograph of Soraya, the Queen Mother asked her daughter Shams to summon the girl with the blue-green eyes and luminous complexion to Paris for an inspection. Shams met Soraya and was quickly won over. She informed her mother that their search was over—Iran had its new queen.

The teenager was oblivious to the intrigue. All that Khalil Esfandiary told his daughter was that the Shah had requested her presence back in Tehran and that a marriage proposal was a possibility. Elders in both families, he explained, believed that a union between the Pahlavi and the Bakhtiary clans was desirable. But he made it clear she would have the final say in her fate and that marriage was not a fait accompli. "If he doesn't like me," Soraya pleaded, "promise me that you will send me to drama school in America." Her father agreed to this condition and assured her that a refusal would not cause scandal. Khalil's sentiments may have been well intentioned but they were hardly realistic, and Soraya was passing through Rome when she spotted a newspaper headline that referred to her as the next Queen of Iran. She later admitted that she became swept up in the drama and romance of the moment, behaving like a naive schoolgirl with celluloid dreams of marrying "Prince Charming." Soraya recalled how genuinely impressed she was when she saw the young King stride into a palace reception room wearing the uniform of an army general. He was "imposing, magnificent." He was smitten, too, and before dawn of the next day asked for her hand in marriage. Their passion for each other was obvious, and the Shah made no effort to hide his disappointment when his fiancée fell ill with typhoid on the eve of the wedding ceremony, forcing a six-week postponement of the nuptials.

The bride was still gaunt and feverish when she drove to the Marble Palace on February 12, 1951, dripping in emeralds and wearing a Dior wedding gown so weighty it threatened to topple over like a melted meringue. When Soraya's legs gave out while trying to shake two thousand pairs of hands at the reception, the new Queen was half-carried to an anteroom and revived with smelling salts. Her anxious husband hovered over her and suggested that her lady-in-waiting use a pair of shears to tear off the ten meters of wedding train and petticoats. All the while he tenderly whispered in her ear, telling her how much he loved and desired her. Yet Soraya was struck by her husband's modesty. Even in private, away from the servants, they addressed each other using the formal Persian word for "you." "In spite of a first marriage, in spite of countless mistresses he had before me," she recalled, "he did not like to show his feelings, still less to find expressions of love which his modesty forbade him. His eyes alone were expressive. Dark brown, almost black, shining, at times hard, at times sad and gentle, they exuded charm and reflected his soul." She also remembered the words of Princess Shams, who had warned her in Paris that her brother was insecure and petulant, browbeaten by his mother, humorless and thin-skinned.

Soraya was still a stubborn and highly strung teenager used to getting her way. She had a fiery temper and once banned her husband from the marital bed. He tolerated the outburst and for a while patiently slept outside her door on a camp bed. Several weeks passed before a senior courtier politely suggested that perhaps Her Majesty might allow His Majesty back into his bed. The Queen pointed to a corner and briskly retorted, "He can put *his* bed over there!" Acclaimed abroad as one of the great beauties of the postwar era, Soraya's glacial charm and brusque manner won her few friends at court. She was not afraid to cause a scene. One evening the couple bickered during a dinner with family and friends. Soraya stunned the room into silence by picking up a vase and hurling it against the wall. Courtiers took to calling her "the German woman." She frequently disregarded protocol, refused to wear formal dress when it was required, and absconded from official duties that bored her. Her behavior embarrassed foreign dignitaries and angered her ladies-in-waiting and government officials. During a state visit to India she retired to her suite in the middle of a formal reception, not bothering to offer thanks to her hosts. But her husband adored her and tolerated her petty humiliations. During one dinner party the conversation turned to the sort of qualities that made for the ideal woman. "Well, I'm very lucky, because the Queen is exactly the kind of woman that I like," the Shah told the other guests. Soraya's brisk retort shocked the room into silence: "Well, I cannot say the same for His Majesty."

Palace officials were embarrassed at the hold Soraya had over her husband and dismayed at her treatment of Shahnaz, the Shah's teenage daughter to Fawzia. In her memoir, Soraya claimed she made an effort to get to know the young girl and make her feel welcome. But after their wedding the Shah packed his daughter off to boarding school in Europe, where the girl suffered terribly from homesickness and felt abandoned. One time, when he and Soraya visited Shahnaz at school, the jealous Queen made her feelings clear and "threw an embarrassing temper tantrum." Soraya "wasn't very kind to [the Princess]," said Fatemeh Pakravan, wife of a senior courtier. "For those who knew, it wasn't very pleasant. The Shah liked his daughter very much. I was witness to that. Then he stopped. He completely cut her off, because Soraya didn't like her." He would later pay dearly for the neglect of his firstborn child.

THE NEWLYWEDS' HONEYMOON cruise in the Aegean was canceled when the Fedayeen-e Islam assassinated Prime Minister Razmara, who supported a negotiated settlement with the Anglo-Iranian Oil Company to resolve the dispute over ownership of Iran's oil fields. The speaker of parliament was a clergyman, Ayatollah Abul-Qasem Kashani, a wartime sympathizer of the Nazis, fervent proponent of oil nationalization, and spiritual godfather to a generation of young clerics who wanted religious law to replace secular rule. Kashani's circle of admirers included Ruhollah Khomeini, an ambitious young mullah who was developing new ideas on how the Shia ulama could become more politically involved in public life. Kashani was supported by the Fedayeen-e Islam.

Amid mounting political turmoil the Shah felt obliged to accept the Majles's nominee for prime minister, Mohammad Mossadeq, who commanded a majority of votes in parliament. Mossadeq was the founder of the National Front, a political party composed of left-wing nationalists who demanded an end to Britain's oil concession. Passionate and charismatic, Mossadeq captured the hearts of the people. The Shah granted his assent to Mossadeq's nomination to the post of prime minister, as he was bound to do under the Constitution, and he offered no resistance when the new government voted to nationalize the operations of the Anglo-Iranian Oil Company. With an alliance sealed between Mossadeq's leftist National Front and Kashani's right-wing religious radicals, who also supported oil nationalization, Iranian political life entered a perilous new era. The Shah labeled the two groups "the Red and the Black," and for the rest of his life warned against the unholy alliance of socialists conniving with the clergy to seize power. Mossadeq's ascension to the premiership set the scene for a titanic showdown between two men whose personal relationship dated back to 1940, when the young Crown Prince had intervened to save the older man's life against his own father's advice.

"I WILL NEVER forget what your husband did. I will never start anything against [him]."

Throughout the spring and summer of 1951, Prime Minister Mohammad Mossadeq repeatedly assured Queen Soraya that he understood he owed her husband a debt of gratitude for ordering his release from Reza Shah's prison cell. Now age sixty-nine, Mossadeq, the "Old Lion" of Iranian politics, symbolized Iran's search for democracy and identity in the first half of the twentieth century. Mossadeq had married the granddaughter of Naser al-Din Shah Qajar, whose fifty-year reign over Persia was ended by an assassin's bullet in 1896. Educated in France and Switzerland in politics and law, Mossadeq returned to Persia to enter public life during the Constitutional Revolution. He served in parliament, as governor of the provinces of Fars and Azerbaijan, and later as Iran's minister of finance, and as one of the few parliamentarians to oppose the election of the House of Pahlavi his fierce criticism of Reza Shah's autocracy had earned him a spell in jail. In the late forties Mossadeq founded the National Front, whose central platform called for oil nationalization.

Mossadeq's elevation to the premiership in April 1951, and the swift passage into law of his oil nationalization bill, sent shock waves through capitals in the anti-Communist West. Nowhere was the impact felt more than in Great Britain, whose ailing postwar economy was kept afloat by Persian oil revenues. The Anglo-Iranian Oil Company pumped hundreds of millions of pounds into British coffers and supplied the Royal Navy with 85 percent of its fuel. After losing its base in Iran the British economy faced national bankruptcy. Almost immediately, British officials began planning a coup to depose Mossadeq and take back control of Iran's oil fields. They rushed paratroopers to Cyprus, imposed an oil blockade to choke off oil exports, and sued the Mossadeq government for restitution. In Washington, where the anti-Communist witch hunts of the McCarthy era were under way, U.S. officials braced for a wave of copycat nationalizations targeting Western economic interests in newly independent countries throughout Africa, Asia, and South America. British officials harped on the threat of communism, clearly hoping to rally American support for covert action by implying that Iranian oil would soon fall under Soviet domination. President Harry Truman and his national security team refused to be rushed into action. Secretary of State Dean Acheson hoped for a negotiated solution, and he and Truman hosted the Iranian prime minister at the White House. They dismissed the hysteria over communism as a canard. "The cardinal purpose of British policy is not to prevent Iran from going Commie," Acheson advised Truman. "The cardinal point is to preserve what they believe to be the last remaining bulwark of British solvency."

Iran's young King was intimidated by Mossadeq's street appeal and awed by his reputation as a giant-slayer. It must have appeared to him as though Mossadeq and not he laid claim to the farr. The Shah supported oil nationalization in principle but preferred a negotiated outcome to prevent a full-blown international crisis. Officers in the Imperial Guard watched fascinated as the prime minister's car pulled up outside Saadabad Palace for his weekly audiences with the Shah. Visitors to the palace grounds were required to park outside the gate and walk in. "But Mossadeq was frail and walked slowly with a cane," said the head of the Imperial Guard. "The Shah said several times, 'Open the gate and let him come into the palace grounds with his car.'" But Mossadeq insisted on following protocol and refused to be treated any differently than his predecessors. "He would get out of the car, walk through the gate, pay his respects to the royal flag and then walk on to the palace. The guards were impressed with the loyalty he showed the King. Then he would walk up the stairs." The Shah always made sure his schedule was cleared fifteen minutes before Mossadeq's arrival and patiently stood at the window waiting for his guest to arrive. Then the drama began. Mossadeq had a well-known habit of throwing fainting fits to draw attention to himself, and the sight of the young King at the window was enough to bring on the vapors. "Mossadeq would, when he saw the King, pretend to be about to collapse, and the King would rush down the stairs and help Mossadeq up the stairs. Twice this nearly led the King to fire the head of the Imperial Guard."

The breakdown of their relationship had all the bitterness of an estrangement between father and son. Mossadeq was determined to curb imperial powers and prerogatives and confine the Shah to his palace.

Disdainful of compromise, he resorted to demagoguery and adopted a strategy of bluff and threats to get his way. One of Mossadeq's more sympathetic biographers noted his political genius but also concluded that he probably knew in advance of the plot to assassinate Prime Minister Razmara, yet did nothing to stop it. Nor did Mossadeq express any regret or remorse when the minister of court, a man he knew well, was brutally murdered. The assassinations and the wave of terror carried out by his ally Ayatollah Kashani's Fedayeen-e Islam "saved the National Front in its infancy," wrote Christopher de Bellaigue, and "removed the last obstacle to oil nationalization and a government dominated by the National Front."

The arrival of a new president in Washington in January 1953 led to a sea change in U.S. policy toward Iran and oil nationalization. President Dwight Eisenhower and his national security team led by the two Dulles brothers, Secretary of State John Foster Dulles and Central Intelligence Agency director Allen Dulles, took a more hard-line view of Mossadeq's decision to take back the oil fields. Mindful of Moscow's intrigues in Azerbaijan seven years earlier and haunted by the fall of China, the invasion of South Korea, and Communist coups throughout Eastern Europe, the Americans geared up for intervention. Sixty percent of the world's known oil reserves were in the Persian Gulf region, and the idea that they might fall into Soviet hands was untenable. Eisenhower also worried that his British allies were so desperate they might launch a military operation to seize Iran's southern oil fields and provoke Soviet military retaliation. "Had the British sent in the paratroops and warships as they were wont to do a few years later against the Egyptians at Suez, it was almost certain that the Soviet Union would have occupied the northern portion of Iran by invoking the Soviet-Iranian Treaty of Friendship of 1921," concluded a secret CIA study written in the seventies. "It was also quite possible that the Soviet army would have moved south to drive British forces out on behalf of their Iranian 'allies,' then not only would Iran's oil have been irretrievably lost to the West, but the defense chain around the Soviet Union that was part of US foreign policy would have been breached." At the dawn of the nuclear age, a covert operation provided Eisenhower's men with a menu of options that satisfied Britain's sense of urgency, avoided the risk of a superpower showdown and world war, and allowed for a "hidden hands" regime change operation that ensured the president would not be held publicly accountable if things turned out badly.

While planning for a coup dubbed TPAJAX (Operation Ajax) was under way in Washington, in Tehran the noose tightened around the Imperial Court. Mossadeq cited the economic crisis caused by the shutdown of oil exports as the excuse to dissolve the Supreme Court and the upper house of parliament, impose censorship, reshuffle the senior army command, and propose stripping the Shah of his role as army commander in chief. The prime minister publicly snubbed the monarch when he refused to attend the Pahlavis' traditional New Year celebrations and demanded that the Queen Mother and Princess Ashraf, whose influence he most feared, leave Iran for exile. Since the end of the war, Ashraf had emerged as her brother's lightning rod and the undisputed and greatly feared first lady of Iranian politics. Dubbed the "Black Panther" by her critics, a title she relished, the Princess and her second husband, Ahmad Shafiq, used her inheritance from Reza Shah to build a substantial real estate empire in northern Iran. She plunged into the maelstrom of postwar Iranian public life determined to "make political friends for the regime and to neutralize some of the opposition. Every day I met with individuals and groups representing various points of view." His sister's exile deprived the Shah of his fiercest defender.

Mossadeq was determined to strip the Shah of his remaining powers. Isolated in the palace and ignored by his ministers, the Shah's moods vacillated between elation and despair. The previous year his former brother-in-law King Farouk of Egypt had been deposed and the Shah was keenly aware of the speculation that surrounded his own future. "I have lost my status," he complained to his wife. "Staying in Tehran would mean that I approved the policies of my prime minister. It is absolutely imperative that we go abroad." He sank into such a fitful state of depression that his closest aides "feared complete nervous breakdown and irrational action." Months of continuous stress also triggered severe abdominal pains that required him to have emergency surgery performed by a medical team secretly flown in from the United States. The Queen, already under pressure to conceive a child after two years of marriage, and "wild with anxiety" about the political crisis, suffered her own nervous collapse. She succumbed to anorexia and locked herself in her room for hours at a time, sobbing and barely able to muster the energy to rise from her bed.

Finally, in February 1953 the couple decided to leave the country for what was officially described as an extended overseas vacation, though their final destination of Switzerland raised suspicions that they planned to settle permanently in Europe. The Shah failed to realize that events were turning in his favor. By now many of Mossadeq's allies worried that the prime minister's brinkmanship risked the country's unity and created opportunities for the Communist Tudeh Party and its Soviet backers to seize power. Ayatollah Kashani, who had made Mossadeq's elevation to the premiership possible, dispatched an intermediary to the palace to urge Soraya to change her husband's mind. Kashani also sent crowds to the palace gates to plead with the Shah to stay. For months the Shah had been waiting for some sign that his people still wanted him, and now he had it. "I promise you that I will stay in Tehran!" he cried through a megaphone. The Queen, who presumably knew a ruse when she saw one, looked on and wept. Yet the Shah refused to take the next step, which was to bestow his blessing on a coup against his own prime minister. Though under the Constitution he was well within his legal right to sack the prime minister and appoint a replacement, he knew that doing so would likely provoke street riots and tarnish his own legitimacy. His training as a young prince had taught him that the role of the king was to unify and not divide the people, and he remembered that any monarch who shed the blood of innocents risked forfeiting the farr.

Throughout the spring and summer of 1953 the Shah refused to budge under intense pressure from Washington and London to acquiesce to a coup. U.S. ambassador Loy Henderson, frustrated and perplexed with the Shah's attitude, bluntly informed him that if he did not "take leadership in overthrowing Mossadeq . . . you bear responsibility for [the] collapse of [your] country." His warning reflected the official sentiment in Washington and London that the Shah was expendable: "If the Shah fails to go along [with the coup] his dynasty is bound to come to an end soon. In spite of the Shah's previous misconceptions the United States and the United Kingdom have been and continue to support him but if the Shah fails now, this support will be withdrawn." Ambassador Henderson had no use for the King's sentimental approach to leadership, his reverence for the farr, or his aversion to bloodshed, and in telegrams back to Washington dismissed him as a weakling. Henderson threatened to withhold all U.S. aid to Iran and cabled Washington that the Shah would probably not approve covert action "unless extreme pressure was exerted, possibly including the threat of replacing him." He warned his superiors that "the [Iranian] army would not play a major role in the coup without the Shah's active cooperation, and he urged that an alternate plan be prepared." The

Shah faced the likelihood of ouster at the hands of Mossadeq if he tried to sack him, and removal by American and British agents if he did not. Unsure which way to turn, he dug in his heels and waited, apparently in the hope that events would take care of themselves. He came under pressure from all sides—even from his beloved Soraya. "I could no longer bear the weak man he had become," she recalled in dramatic detail in her memoir, "a king incapable of making a decision, a pawn manipulated by great powers, a puppet ceaselessly torn between the advice of some and the warnings of others."

In a scene worthy of a Wagnerian opera, Soraya confronted her husband with brisk Teutonic firmness and demanded that he pull himself together for the sake of the country. The people, she insisted, wanted action to save them from poverty and communism. She ended her pep talk with a bold appeal to raw power: "Only a coup against Mossadeq can save the country."

"But that's impossible," the Shah replied, the cigarette trembling between his fingers. "Has there ever been a monarch who has plotted against his own government?"

"Well then," she snapped, "you will be the first one to do it!"

The Shah agreed to secretly meet with the leaders of the coup conspiracy but would not say one way or another whether he approved their intentions. "You are pitiful!" Soraya blazed. "You no longer have the right to revel in your depression. You must be the man you once were and whom I respected. If you allow Mossadeq to remain in power, you will be selling Iran off to Moscow."

With tensions mounting, on August 3, 1953, the Shah received Kermit "Kim" Roosevelt, former president Theodore Roosevelt's grandson and the lead CIA operative sent to Iran under cover to organize a coup. Roosevelt was working with army commanders, senior clergy, and wealthy merchants to raise funds, pay bribes, organize street mobs, spread false rumors, and agitate against the government. The conspirators were anxious to strike before Mossadeq uncovered their plot machinations. But they needed the Shah to sign the *firman* or letter of dismissal that would terminate Mossadeq's premiership to provide the coup with the fig leaf of legitimacy. Roosevelt arrived at the palace under the assumption that the Shah had finally changed his mind and consented to sign the firman. He was stunned when the Shah informed him that "he was not an adventurer and could not take chances like one."

General Fazlollah Zahedi, the bravest of the army generals, and the man the conspirators agreed would replace Mossadeq as prime minister, was next ushered into the Shah's office in the second week of August 1953. By now, the monarch had settled on a course of action. If Zahedi was surprised to see the strong-willed young Queen at her husband's side he did not let on.

"When can I act?" he asked, fully expecting to be given the green light to set a date for Operation Ajax to unfold.

"Don't do anything against Mossadeq," the Shah counseled. "It would be dangerous." He had decided that he could not support a coup after all. With these words, the Shah made it clear that he preferred to leave the country and lose his throne than risk the spilling of innocent blood.

These were not the words Zahedi and Soraya had expected to hear, and an awkward silence ensued. The Shah looked first at his wife, and then at the general, who stared back and said nothing. They were not about to provide him with the cover of moral legitimacy he craved. Finally, he conceded defeat. "I will sign a decree," he said with a sigh.

The die was cast, and planning for the overthrow of the Mossadeq government moved into high gear. Fearing assassination, for the next few days the King and Queen changed beds and rooms in the middle of the night, slept with revolvers under their pillows, and worried that their meals might be poisoned.

THE ARMY COUP that deposed Mohammad Mossadeq was a near-run thing.

Originally scheduled for August 15, 1953, logistical delays meant that government agents uncovered the plot in advance and rounded up many of the leading conspirators. Two days later the Shah and Queen were at their summer residence at Kelar Dasht on the Caspian Sea, about thirty minutes' flight from the town of Ramsar, when news came through that Operation Ajax had collapsed. They grabbed a suitcase with clothes and a few valuables, dashed to an airfield, and boarded a small plane and flew across the border to Iraq, where they landed at a quarter past ten in the morning. Iraq's King Faisal II offered the couple and their two attendants safe haven. The Shah assumed he was finished and gloomily informed his wife that he thought they had just enough money to buy a small plot of land in California.

Late on the evening of the first day, the Shah requested a meeting with the American ambassador to Iraq, Burton Berry, whose secret cable back to Washington provided officials with the most detailed account yet of the monarch's fragile state of mind about his agonizing decision to sack Mossadeq. "I found the Shah worn from three sleepless nights, puzzled by turn of events, but with no (repeat no) bitterness toward Americans who had urged and planned action," Berry reported to the State Department. "I suggested for his prestige in Iran he never indicate that any foreigner had had a part in recent events. He agreed." The Shah told Berry that only in the past two weeks had he resolved to sack the prime minister for "flouting the Iranian Constitution." But he explained that after initially approving Roosevelt's idea of a coup he had changed his mind and insisted that any action taken must be within "the framework of his constitutional power." When he heard the plot had collapsed he had decided to leave Iran "to prevent bloodshed and further damage." The Shah added that he hoped to fly on to America, where "he would be looking for work shortly as he has a large family and very small means outside Iran."

Back in Tehran, the coup plotters, who had gone to ground, were beside themselves. "He just took off," exclaimed Kermit Roosevelt when he heard of the Shah's decision to run for the border. "He never communicated with us at all—just took off."

Mossadeq's loyalists crowed over their triumph. "O traitor Shah, you shameless person, you have completed the criminal history of the Pahlavi reign," thundered Foreign Minister Hossein Fatemi. "The people want to drag you from behind your desk to the gallows." In the streets of the capital, CIA agents witnessed Communist mobs "tearing down statues of the Shah and Reza Shah, defiling them, and dragging them through the streets."

The National Front and the Tudeh Party may have won this first round, but overconfidence led them to disaster and defeat. Fatemi's fiery rhetoric alarmed many Iranians who until now had either backed Mossadeq or sat out the escalating strife. The young King, for all his faults, was still revered by the majority of the Iranian people, who dreaded a Bolshevik-style bloodletting. Zahedi, Kashani, and Roosevelt took advantage of the reduced security measures in Tehran to launch a second attempt. On the morning of August 19, Kashani handed out bribes of 200 *tomans* ($26.65) to anyone prepared to march against the government, though bribes likely never touched the hands of the many Tehranis who, fearing Communist mob rule, poured into the streets at the first sight of tanks to cheer Mossadeq's downfall. "Sensing that the army was with them," reported U.S. intelligence, "the demonstrators not only began to move faster but took on a festive holiday atmosphere . . . it had become a mob wholly different from any seen before in Tehran; it was full of well-dressed, white collar people, carrying pictures of the Shah and shouting, 'Zindebah, Shah!' (Long live the Shah!). Then, the troops began to join the demonstrations." The size and enthusiasm of the crowds suggested a groundswell of support for retaining the monarchy. Though opposition groups later claimed hundreds of casualties, only forty-three deaths were reported by nightfall, at which time Mossadeq and his ministers were in detention. General Zahedi imposed martial law and declared himself Iran's new prime minister.

The Pahlavis had just sat down to lunch in the Hotel Excelsior's dining room in Rome when a reporter from the Associated Press ran up to them with a wire service report in his hands: "MOSSADEQ OVERTHROWN— IMPERIAL TROOPS CONTROL TEHRAN—GENERAL ZAHEDI PRIME MINISTER." The stunned Shah was heard to exclaim, "Can it be true? I knew it! I knew it! They love me!" Speaking amid a crush of reporters, he explained his reasons for leaving Iran. "Ninety-nine percent of the population is for me," he said. "I knew it all the time. But if I left my country, it was solely because of my anxiety to avoid bloodshed." Soraya steadied her agitated husband and was overheard to cooly remark, "How exciting." To further bolster the Shah's spirits, Grand Ayatollah Seyyed Hossein Borujerdi, the paramount figure within Shia Islam, sent the monarch a telegram expressing his goodwill and support. "I hope the well-augured return of Your Majesty to Iran will put an end to [temporal] ills therein and will bring glory to Islam and welfare to Muslims," Borujerdi wired the Shah. "Do return, as the Shiism and Islam need you. You are the Shiite sovereign." The Shah interpreted these messages, and the public rallies that greeted him on his return from exile, as proof that he owed his recall to God and the people and not to the generals and foreign mercenaries. Galvanized by this most remarkable reversal of fortune, he concluded that he had finally earned the crown. "Before I was merely a hereditary monarch but today I really have been elected by my people," he told Soraya.

More than two years of political drama, street violence, economic collapse, and international isolation meant that many Iranians, perhaps even a majority of the population, were grateful for a return to peace and stability. But for a hardened minority, and especially the left-wing intellectual class who adored Mossadeq, the Shah's decision to stand back while the army collaborated with foreigners to depose their hero made him a usurper and traitor. Mossadeq's trial on charges of violating the Constitution evoked pity and lingering resentment that turned him into a martyr for democracy. Although CIA complicity in the coup was never publicly admitted in Washington, the U.S. role was widely known inside Iran. American motives were indirectly revealed the next year, when General Zahedi's government was pressured by Eisenhower to accept a new arrangement that allowed American oil companies to dominate an international oil consortium to replace the Anglo-Iranian Oil Company's one-hundred-thousand-square-mile monopoly on oil production. Prime Minister Churchill and his ministers realized only too late that their American partners in the coup had hoodwinked them. From now on the U.S. oil majors determined how much petroleum was pumped in Iran and the price it was sold for on the open market. In return for surrendering control over its own purse strings, the Zahedi government was granted emergency financial assistance and generous economic aid and military hardware.

Many years later, the Shah was asked about the role the CIA played in saving his throne. His interviewer noted that even one of his brothers was on record as saying the "counterrevolution had been scheduled for two weeks later."

"I can't think how he would know it," the Shah answered, "but I can tell you one thing: women in their chadors and children of eight and nine were on the streets. I am certain *they* weren't paid for it."

"To what extent were you apprised of this plot?"

"The plans that I knew were to issue the order for Mossadeq's dismissal," he replied. "Then, if it didn't work, to leave Iran—for various reasons."

He never doubted that his relationship with his people had forever changed. Reminded many years later of how quickly his father had lost power in 1941, the Shah harked back to the events of August 1953 to offer an assurance that history would not repeat itself. "Ah, but the people called for me to return," he chided Court Minister Alam. Alam was no romantic and he gently reminded his master that the people of Iran were fickle souls, capable of turning with stunning speed against the same rulers they once held up to acclaim. Don't forget, he warned, that "it was precisely this nation of ours that fell into line with Mossadeq, so that you were forced to leave the country." The Shah listened but he would not be swayed: he was convinced that he now enjoyed the people's confidence and that the farr was his to lose.

The deposed Mossadeq was placed under lifetime house arrest in his own country residence, a "green-shuttered yellow brick villa" sixty-two miles outside Tehran. The eighty Iranian Army soldiers who surrounded his residence were camped out in the fields in tents stamped "U.S. Army."

MUCH TO THE Shah's displeasure, General Zahedi emerged from the coup as Iran's undisputed new strongman. Government ministers might address the Shah to his face as "Your Imperial Majesty," but behind his back they scoffed at the weakness he had shown during the crisis and referred to him with patronizing disregard as "the boy."

The prime minister's contemptuous treatment of the Shah revealed itself in an incident that occurred shortly after Prince Ali Reza, Reza Shah's widely admired and highly capable second son, was killed in 1954 in a plane crash. Ali Reza's death came at the end of another difficult year for the Pahlavis. Relations between Soraya and the Queen Mother and her sisters-in-law had all but broken down, with Taj ol-Moluk and the princesses spreading poisonous gossip about Soraya's barren state. The Queen Mother confronted her daughter-in-law with matter-of-fact firmness: "So when are you going to give my son a boy?" She encouraged courtiers to spy on Soraya and watch her waist and appetite. "Nobody was entitled to forget that it was from her loins that the kings of Persia were born," Soraya later recalled with great bitterness. She found the pressure unbearable and looked forward to leaving with her husband on a state tour of the United States and Europe. "It is good that we are going on the visit, we can have a break," she admitted to the prime minister one day over lunch at the palace. "No, no, you are not going there to have a break," Zahedi reprimanded her. "You are visiting the United States on national business, and should not regard the time spent there as a holiday." The Shah blanched when he heard his prime minister address his wife in this way. Zahedi's son, Ardeshir, a royal adjutant, kicked his father's leg under the table to silence him. "Why did you kick me?!" General Zahedi shouted. Turning to the Shah, Zahedi tried to restrain his anger: "As you also need a medical checkup, of course you also need some time off [from official duties]."

The damage was done—the Shah had been humiliated at his own table. There were also serious policy differences between the two men. The Shah opposed Zahedi's decision to rehabilitate army officers who had gone over to Mossadeq's side in August 1953. Zahedi disagreed with the Shah's support for Iranian membership in the Baghdad Pact, a security alliance that Washington and London hoped would anchor Muslim states to the cause of anticommunism. Zahedi believed that membership in the Baghdad Pact would only aggravate the Russians. He had no confidence in pledges made by statesmen in far-off capitals—treaties had not prevented invasions of Iran in the past, and he doubted they would do so during the Cold War. The main disagreement between the Shah and his prime minister was over whether the monarch should rule as well as reign, a highly charged question that went to the very heart of Iran's fifty-year struggle to establish constitutional boundaries. Where did the influence of the King end and that of his prime minister begin? Zahedi and the Shah debated this point on several occasions in the presence of the prime minister's son and the Queen. Zahedi argued that government ministers provided an invaluable buffer for the crown should things go wrong. "If you are directly involved in the talks and if you agree with them a few times, they will get into the habit of asking you for what they wish to gain," he explained. "A day will come when the foreigners will make some demands that you will not be able to agree with. At that time, they will take action against you. However, if the government is in charge it will not matter. One government will go and another government will be appointed and the crown will remain immune to any intrigues against it."

Zahedi was fighting a losing battle. Unbeknownst to Zahedi or anyone else in government, for quite some time the Shah had decided that he would do it all without benefit of constitutional restrictions on his role in politics. Indeed, during his visit to the White House in 1949, he had received encouragement from Harry Truman to do so. "Rule, your country needs it!" the president had advised him. Six years later, he was restless and ready to move and take a more active role in the nation's political life. "You know, there is no more lonely and unhappy life for a man than when he decides to rule instead of reign," he confided to a visitor in 1955. "I am going to rule!" Though he realized it was too soon to seize the reins alone, the King fully intended to share power with his prime ministers. In April 1955 the Shah invited Zahedi to lunch and retired him during the main course. Soraya watched the pitiful scene unfold. Her husband, she admitted, "was afraid of General Zahedi's huge popularity. What if one day he tried to topple him from the Iranian throne to have himself proclaimed the Shah of Shah, the sort of thing Nasser had done with Farouk of Egypt? Persecution mania."

TIME WAS ALSO running out for Soraya.

General Zahedi's son Ardeshir had not followed his father into exile in 1955 but chose to stay behind in Iran to continue his service to the crown. His romance the next year with sixteen-year-old Princess Shahnaz brought the Shah's insecurities into painful relief. The Shah had fired General Zahedi because he feared his talents and his ambitions. Now his daughter's wish to marry Ardeshir raised the nightmare possibility that a grandson of the general would one day inherit the throne. The Princess, barely on speaking terms with her stepmother, made no effort to dispel the rumors. "If I have a son before my stepmother [Queen Soraya], he would inherit the Iranian crown," said the Princess. "There is no special law on this issue, but when I was getting married there was an understanding in my family that if I gave birth to a boy, the problem of the inheritance would be solved." Though the Shah finally consented to his daughter's engagement, others in the Imperial Family weren't prepared to let the matter drop. Princess Ashraf was likely behind an effort to smear the Zahedi name in the popular press and portray Ardeshir as unworthy of marriage to the Shah's daughter. More drama followed at the couple's engagement party when Soraya and Taj ol-Moluk exchanged insults and stormed out on each other. Soraya had already hurt her mother-in-law's feelings by refusing to visit her in the hospital after foot surgery, and now she snubbed the old lady's reciprocal engagement party. The intrigue and gossip created such a poisonous atmosphere that Ardeshir Zahedi considered breaking off his engagement to the princess. The Shah felt compelled to invite a senior clergyman to the palace to counsel his embittered relatives.

Still, by July 1957 the truth could no longer be avoided: Soraya could not bear children and provide the dynasty with the long-awaited male heir. Nothing could be done after medical tests revealed she had the womb of a twelve-year-old girl. Ali Reza's premature death meant there was no insurance policy for the dynasty and that in the event of the Shah's sudden demise the Pahlavi line would expire. Legally, his surviving half-blood brothers were ineligible to succeed because of their Qajar lineage, though the idea of a constitutional amendment to legitimize them was briefly mooted. One other possibility remained open to the couple. In Shia Islam temporary contract marriages called *siqeh* allowed men to marry women for periods ranging from a few hours to a few months. These marriages of convenience removed the stigma attached to brothel visits, premarital sex, casual sexual encounters, and affairs. The Shah told Soraya that he was prepared to enter into such a temporary arrangement, promising to divorce the woman as soon as she provided him with a son. The Queen, however, expressed revulsion. "How could you envisage such a thing?" she asked him sadly. He looked away and said nothing. "Then all we can do is separate," she said.

Desperate to keep his wife but also resolve the succession, in February 1958 the Shah threw himself on the mercy of a council of respected elder statesmen, who agreed to study the issue of an amendment to the Constitution. They failed in their task. Though they expressed sympathy for his plight, former prime minister Hossein Ala made it clear that he for one preferred to see Soraya go. He did not regard her as a particularly suitable consort or a positive influence on her husband. The Shah was devastated but understood their decision. Three emissaries were dispatched to Geneva to negotiate the terms of a handsome divorce settlement with the embittered Soraya and her father, who expressed his frank relief that his daughter was now free from the machinations of the Pahlavi Court.

On March 14, 1958, Iranians listened as the Shah announced over national radio his decision to divorce, his voice barely audible over the sobs. Surely his listeners knew that in Persian the name Soraya was taken from the constellation of stars that guided lovers.

4

FARAH DIBA

She was the woman I had been waiting for so long,
as well as the Queen my country needed.

—THE SHAH

But he was my king—how could I possibly have refused?

—QUEEN FARAH

On July 3, 1958, photographers, newspapermen, and hundreds of
spectators crowded Manhattan's West Side docks as the Shah,
accompanied by his sister Princess Fatemeh, boarded the Atlantic liner
Independence at the end of a three-day trip to Washington and New York.
Though billed as informal, few doubted the symbolism behind the Shah's
visit to obtain a $40 million loan with promises of additional investment
and military assistance. His schedule included luncheon followed by a
two-hour talk with President Eisenhower, conferences with the secretaries of state and defense, and a dinner hosted by Vice President Richard
Nixon that featured twenty pounds of Iranian caviar served on gold
plates—the days when world leaders could take the Shah of Iran for
granted were over. The mood aboard the *Independence* was lighthearted
until reporters asked the Shah to comment on his recent divorce from
Soraya. Their breakup, he lamented, was "the hardest decision I have ever
taken. . . . No one can carry a torch more than myself." The crowd fell
silent as the Shah, "his head in his hands and his voice broken by emotion," reminded them that he had taken a coronation oath "to serve my

country. . . . I did that and when you do that you have to forget yourself and dedicate yourself entirely to the country and to the people." Steeling himself, he reiterated that he would not hand over the throne to anyone other than his own male heir: "The next king must be my son."

The *Independence* barely made landfall in Europe when news broke that the Iraqi royal family and government officials had been slaughtered in a coup carried out by leftist army officers. Alarmed at the prospect of a Russian ally on Iran's western border, and fearful that left-wing republicans had him in their sights, the Shah panicked and sent word to General Zahedi in Switzerland that he was welcome to return home to resume the post of prime minister. Zahedi agreed, but only on the condition that Iran invade Iraq with the help of its Western allies to overthrow the new regime in Baghdad. "He said he would accept personal responsibility and that, if anything untoward were to result, His Majesty could dismiss him and put him on trial on charges of acting without official backing," wrote his son. "He went so far as to say that His Majesty could hang him were this to happen." Although Zahedi's offer was not taken up, the Shah's panicked response to the Baghdad coup suggested his continuing need for an older, more seasoned personality to provide a guiding hand. In reaching out to the same man he had so recently dispatched into exile, the Shah revealed a striking weakness of character.

This latest Middle East crisis added urgency to American fears about Iran's stability. In the five years since Operation Ajax had ended Iran's messy postwar experiment with parliamentary democracy, Washington had pumped more than $500 million into the kingdom to develop its economy; the Defense Department had approved hundreds of millions of dollars in arms sales; and the CIA, working in collaboration with Israel's Mossad, had established the Organization of Intelligence and National Security, the secret police known by its Persian acronym as Savak. The 1953 coup and its aftermath had bought time for the Pahlavis but also tainted the Shah's legitimacy amid charges he ruled as an American puppet. Pro-Mossadeq intellectuals driven out of politics retreated to the universities, where they influenced a generation of educated Iranian youth to view the Shah as a traitor and stooge. They accused the Shah of abrogating the 1906 Constitution and concentrating power in his own hands.

The Shah made no excuses for his decision to involve himself in the nation's political affairs. His ambitions were bolstered by his skeptical attitude toward the 1906 Constitution, which he regarded as a European invention imposed on Iran by former colonial powers. He made clear his intention to "Iranize" a document he believed had been foisted on the Iranian people by sly foreigners. "His Imperial Majesty is above everything," observed one Iranian newspaper. "Constitutionally, he can appoint or dismiss the Premier as he sees fit. He can also dissolve parliament if he so chooses. He decides on which projects his country needs, bills that should be presented for passage by the legislature, and on the conduct generally of home and foreign policy." The Shah lavished aid and attention on the armed forces, expanded the role of the state, and involved government in affairs that had once been the realm of the mosques. "The Shah used the military, bureaucracy, and court patronage to pack the cabinet and parliament with his own placemen," wrote one historian. "He amended the constitution, giving himself the authority to appoint prime ministers. . . . To make it doubly clear, the Shah announced that he personally would preside over weekly cabinet meetings."

U.S. officials were ambivalent about the Shah's leadership abilities and believed he had only a tenuous grasp of political realities. Fearing a socialist revolution, they urged him to implement far-reaching social, economic, and political reforms that would bring a measure of hope to the poor and deprived. The Americans saw the Pahlavi elite as wealthy and out of touch with the needs of an impoverished country. "Even yet, the Iranian economy remains primitive enough that a whole family can make a living off a single walnut tree," reported *Time*. "In the rug shops of Tabriz, tiny children work at the looms all day for 20 cents or less." The threat of a Communist takeover was real. Along Iran's northern border the Soviet Union hosted Persian-language radio stations that gleefully denounced the Shah as a "cold war criminal" and called for him to be "dumped in the garbage bin." For Washington, the survival of the Shah was a matter of national interest. "Should the Shah lose his fight, for his dynasty and his nation," observed one American journal, "the Soviets would at last be free to dominate the Middle East." But while the Americans agreed with the Shah that Iran was threatened by communism, they disagreed on the symptoms. Where they argued that the threat came from within and that Iran's economy and society needed restructuring, the Shah countered that the solution was to build up Iran's armed forces as a bulwark against the Soviet Union's predatory intentions. President Eisenhower visited Iran in December 1959 and indirectly chided the Shah when he reminded parliamentarians that weapons alone could not ensure security and that "military strength alone" could not guarantee freedom and security.

Iran's political and economic malaise gave a renewed sense of urgency to the Shah's top priority, which was to settle the question of the Imperial succession once and for all. His initial preference was for a European princess who could provide the House of Pahlavi with the luster of dynastic legitimacy. He soon ran into trouble. The Windsors rebuffed his interest in Queen Elizabeth II's cousin Princess Alexandra of Kent, while his favorite, Princess Maria Gabriella, the Catholic daughter of the deposed King Umberto of Italy, was ruled out owing to opposition from the Vatican and Iran's ulama. Iran's most influential religious figure, Grand Ayatollah Seyyed Hossein Borujerdi, passed on a message to the Imperial Court: "I hope this rumor is baseless, but if true, it must be pointed out to His Majesty that he is the king of a Shia country and must not do such a thing." A second message followed in short order: "If His Majesty were to go ahead, he would be jeopardizing his throne; we cannot remain silent either."

During the Shah's state visit to France in the spring of 1959 he was guest of honor at a reception for Iranian students studying in Paris. At a time when his mother and sisters were selecting and inspecting candidates for marriage, the girls were particularly anxious to make a good impression. Only Farah Diba, a young student of architecture, politely stood back to avoid the crush. When she was introduced in the receiving line His Majesty observed that her choice of profession was unusual—at the time Iran boasted only one other female architect. Farah excitedly wrote her mother back in Tehran to tell of her encounter and provided a vivid description of the Shah's "sad eyes." Few could have predicted that by year's end Farah Diba would take her vows as the Shah of Iran's consort and Queen-Empress over twenty-one million subjects.

THE NAME FARAH means "joy" in Persian, and Sohrab and Farideh Diba were overwhelmed with happiness at the birth of their daughter and only child on October 14, 1938, in the American Mission Hospital in Tehran. Even as a child, Farah exuded a sense of destiny. At the communal baths where she was bathed once a week, the washerwoman would comfort her with a lullaby:

To whom shall we give this girl?
No ordinary man shall she wed!
Should the King come with his army, his Minister in his train,
Perhaps she will not be wed.

Sohrab Diba hailed from a prominent line of courtiers, politicians, and generals who had served the Qajar shahs. He was a direct descendant of the Prophet Mohammad, and as such was allowed to style himself a *seyyed*, a title considered a great mark of respect in the Muslim world. Destined to enter royal service, Sohrab began his training as an army cadet in St. Petersburg and escaped to France during the Russian Revolution to continue his studies at the elite St. Cyr military academy. He returned to Iran with a law degree and married Farideh Ghotbi, "considered one of the prettiest, most delightful girls in Tehran," and the daughter of a well-to-do family from the northern Caspian province of Gilan. Farah retained a lifelong pride in her Diba lineage. "I don't usually talk about this," she once said, "because everybody is his own person and it's not who your family is that's important, but what you are. But my ancestors were ambassadors to Turkey and Russia. My grandfather was an art collector and my father studied at St. Cyr, the French military academy. He also studied law and was a cadet in a Russian school."

Newlyweds Sohrab and Farideh moved into a comfortable walled villa in Tehran with Farideh's brother, Mohammad Ali; his wife, Louise; and their son, Reza, who became Farah's closest childhood friend and confidant in adulthood. Despite the rigors of the war and Allied occupation, the future Queen's earliest years were quite carefree. Each summer, to escape the blazing heat, the Dibas, the Ghotbis, and their friends and servants moved the household north to Shemiran, a popular district in the foothills of the Alborz Mountains. "The days were entirely given up to games and excursions," Farah remembered. "We went climbing, rode donkeys among the hills, wandered through the valleys. Being something of a tomboy, always climbing trees, I preferred to play with my boy cousins." She was only eight years old when her beloved father fell ill with an ailment that at first was diagnosed as hepatitis. "I would not say she loved her father more than myself—we were a deeply united trio—but Farah was completely fascinated by her father; the way he would talk to her in French, and the stories he told her of other lands, all enthralled her," said Madame Diba. Even after the doctors diagnosed pancreatic cancer, Farah was told her father was on the road to recovery. Then one day he disappeared from her life. Her mother explained that Sohrab had been sent to France to continue his medical treatment. As the months passed with no news, the little girl suspected a deception. When she walked into a room she noticed the adults looked away or fell silent. Other times, she caught her mother and aunts stifling sobs. "A pall of melancholy, created by my feelings of emptiness and endless waiting, fell over my existence at that time," she remembered of those sad days. "The unbearable had happened, without my being able to shed a tear." She learned the truth that her father was dead only on the day she left Tehran for Paris on her eighteenth birthday.

Her father's mysterious disappearance matured Farah beyond her years. She grew up to be confident and outgoing but also studious, dutiful, and conscientious, graduating at the top of her class at Tehran's Jeanne d'Arc School for Girls, where she received instruction in French. She led the girls' basketball team to a string of victories and earned two medals at the first national championships for women's athletics. After her picture appeared in the newspapers she became something of a teenage celebrity for middle-class Tehranis. "Look, there's Farah!" the children would tell their parents when they saw her pass by in the streets. The attention did not go to her head. She was active in the Girl Scout movement and spent the summer of 1956 with her friend Elli Antoniades, leading a troupe of teenagers to France to participate in an international scouting jamboree. The trip turned out to be a revelation, and, like her father, Farah developed a lifelong passion for French art, culture, and literature.

Religion played only a peripheral role in her life. Madame Diba observed the rituals of faith, but like so many women in Tehran's upper-middle-class society she refused to wear a chador and would not think of veiling her daughter. Farah did not fast during the holiday month of Ramadan and "learned to read the [Quran] without any explanation of what it meant." As an adult she recalled an unpleasant childhood encounter with a clergyman who angrily berated her for not covering her hair. From that moment on she associated organized religion with anger and intolerance. Nor was there any question of an arranged marriage. Encouraged to pursue a career, Farah Diba had the instincts and temperament of a builder. "Architecture is an act of creation," she once said. "I always wanted to create." For the rest of her life she remained grateful to her mother for breaking with tradition and allowing her daughter and only child to travel to Europe to study.

* * *

IN THE AUTUMN of 1957 Farah left Iran to begin her university studies at the École Speciale d'Architecture in Paris, the preferred training ground for Iran's elite. Her first year away from home was not easy. She experienced homesickness and was troubled by the European students' hazing rituals and casual racism.

Paris in the late fifties was a magnet for refugees, dissidents, and exiles from around the world protesting European colonialism and condemning in particular France's military campaign against Algerian independence. Their activities were monitored by intelligence agencies from several countries, including the Soviet Union. As one of only a few women in the Iranian student contingent, Farah Diba soon drew the attention of a KGB agent, who kept them under surveillance. He noted her attendance at a rally of Communists against the war in Algeria and assumed she shared the marchers' radical sentiments. But Farah had only joined in at the last minute to silence the taunts of friends who accused her of lacking courage, and she found the experience unsettling. The intrigues continued. One time, Farah was introduced to a student from East Germany who later turned out to be a Communist spy. Many years later she attended a play in Gilan Province with her husband when an actor resembling the mystery German from her university days rushed onstage waving an imitation revolver. The mystery man was not arrested and he was never seen again. Scholars who studied the KGB archives at the end of the Cold War judged the spy agency's interest in Farah to be "misplaced." The Russians "failed to realize that [the Queen] remained, as she had been brought up, a convinced royalist." That did not stop rumors circulating in future years that Iran's Queen harbored Marxist sympathies or was even a closet Communist.

Farah was "a hard worker," remembered a classmate, "sitting up late over her studies and never cutting classes, as some of us did." She respectfully stood back during the Shah's embassy reception in the spring of 1959 despite the prodding of Jahingir Tafazoli, the embassy's cultural attaché. Unbeknownst to her, Tafazoli had been groomed by the same KGB agent who decided Farah Diba was a fellow traveler. Now, with the search for a new Queen under way in Tehran, he was anxious that she catch the Shah's attention. Farah was already at the center of a swirl of gossip about her future marriage prospects. "And why shouldn't the Shah marry you?" her friends in Paris joked. "You're pretty." She teased them in return, suggesting they "write to him and try to convince him that there's a very suitable girl for him here." But one of her closest girlfriends mailed her a postcard from Madrid that read simply, "Farah Diba = Farah Pahlavi."

Farah returned home to spend the summer of 1959 in Tehran. With her savings running low, she was anxious to win another round of scholarship funding for the new academic year. As it turned out, the official in charge of approving education grants was Ardeshir Zahedi, the Shah's son-in-law, who also happened to be a friend of another of Farah's uncles, Esfandiar Diba, one of the monarch's former equerries. Diba asked Zahedi to help his niece with her financial problems while dropping the hint that "his niece had all the requisite qualifications for becoming His Majesty's wife." Zahedi agreed to meet the girl and her uncle to discuss the scholarship. Unbeknownst to either of them, they were observed from behind a sliding glass door by Princess Shahnaz. Zahedi was impressed enough to invite Farah back to the house the following day to have tea with his wife.

The Zahedi residence in the hilltop neighborhood of Hesarak enjoyed a panoramic outlook over the capital. The hosts and their awed young guest were chatting away when a car pulled up outside. Noticing a commotion in the hallway, Farah looked up in amazement to see a visitor at the door—it was the Shah. He was curious to meet the girl who so impressed his daughter. "Good Lord!" thought Farah. "I could feel my heart pounding. I was amazed and thrilled all at once." The atmosphere was cordial enough that the Shah canceled his plans for the evening and stayed for dinner. Many years later he was asked what set Farah apart from the other girls. "I think I knew, directly I saw her, saw the way she was, with other people—with myself, too, so natural, so charming . . . speaking excellent French, interested in everything, obviously with a mind of her own . . . and I seem to remember some of us playing a silly game, with counters, or something . . . they kept flipping onto the floor, and she was the one who kept on picking them up for us . . . A little thing, but it told me a lot about her. . . . Yes, I think I knew as soon as we met—certainly within a day or so—that she was the woman I had been waiting for so long, as well as the Queen my country needed."

Farah Diba offered the Shah a fresh start. She was young, modest, cheerful, and a stranger to the petty intrigues of court life. She shared her future husband's athleticism and passion for helping people. There would be potent symbolism in a marriage between the Shah with his dreams of modernizing Iran and the young woman whose life story symbolized the aspirations of Iran's emerging middle class. Marriage to Farah, a descendant of the Prophet, would technically make the Shah a son-in-law of Mohammad and burnish the Pahlavi Dynasty's shaky credentials with the religious establishment. Finally, the Shah told Zahedi that he was determined not to repeat the mistakes of the past. His marriage to Soraya had estranged him from his family and hurt his daughter. "I did not treat my daughter well before," he admitted. "I was not as good a father to her as I should have been. . . . This time I wish to choose a wife who is my daughter's choice. Ardeshir! You know that I am marrying for my country's sake. Had it not been for my country's sake, I would not have wished to divorce and remarry. This will be an opportunity to improve the relationships in our family. Strained family relations make me miserable and unhappy."

When Farah received a second invitation, this time to dinner, she understood the nature of the Shah's interest. "This time I had an inkling that some plan was being devised concerning me," she recalled. Over the next several weeks she joined the Shah for long walks, outings around town in his sports car, and short jaunts in his plane. During their first flight he asked her to adjust one of the controls—it was only after they landed and she saw ambulances at the end of the airstrip that she learned they had had a lucky escape. "The undercarriage wouldn't come down," the Shah casually told her. "You got the wheels out manually." "We could have been killed," she said, "but he remained completely calm through it all."

Farah's inspection before the Pahlavi women was a triumph. Queen Mother Taj ol-Moluk asked after her Aunt Louise, who had known her sisters at school. "It is certain that on that day," Farah recalled, "the King's inner circle saw me as an unaffected girl who knew nothing of their world of courtiers and diplomats." There was still one last hurdle to overcome. Within the Imperial Family there was unhappiness at Zahedi's hand in selecting Iran's next Queen. Gossips tried to undermine her prospects by whispering that the prospective bride was a closet leftist related to the despised Mohammad Mossadeq. Zahedi agreed to investigate the charges but also tried to put the Shah's mind at ease. The Dibas and Mossadeqs might be related through clan ties but it would be "unfair to hold that against her when [Zahedi] himself was also a distant relative [of Mossadeq]." "Everyone in Iran," he reminded the Shah, "is related to each other." This was true enough—Iranians liked to joke that they were one big fractious family. Zahedi offered the further assurance that the young woman and her family were loyal monarchists.

Meanwhile, Madame Diba could not hide her anxiety about sending her daughter to the Imperial Court with its reputation for intrigues. Years later, Madame Diba admitted that had her husband been alive he might well have opposed the engagement. Farah's mentor at the Jeanne d'Arc School, Sister Claire, expressed similar reservations: "I saw, stretching ahead for her, a dazzling but thorny path . . . no Court is without intrigues and jealousies. . . . I looked at her—so young, so vulnerable, and I feared for her." Years later, Farah confirmed that her decision to marry had been motivated more by a sense of duty than by passion or romance—love would come later. "He was the figure-head—the man I and my friends revered," she said. "We were all under his spell. . . . Perhaps it was not a love match, in terms of a romantic novel—not a *coup de foudre* . . . but I think, in my heart, I had always felt a strong emotion about him. And then, when it seemed he needed me, of course I did not hesitate. . . . But he was my king—how could I possibly have refused?"

News of the Shah's engagement broke while Farah was en route to Paris to wrap up her studies. By the time her plane landed, Orly Airport was descended on by a scrum of newspapermen and photographers. She was mobbed at the airport, and the drive to the hotel was a hair-raising affair, with photographers chasing the car through the streets and flashing bulbs in the car windows. A dangerous car chase through the streets of Paris ensued: "I was screaming, thinking that we would kill one of them at any moment." She withdrew from her classes, packed her bags, and bade farewell to her friends and the city she loved so much. At the formal betrothal ceremony, held in Tehran on November 23, 1959, the Shah presented his twenty-one-year-old fiancée with an engagement ring that "shone like the sun" and a blue case that opened to reveal a necklace, earrings, bracelet, brooch, and ring set in diamonds, emeralds, and rubies.

The Shah's fiancée caused a minor stir before the wedding when she acknowledged in an interview that not all Iranians were content with their lot. Farah had been born and raised outside the aristocracy. In Paris she had been exposed to new ideas about social justice and fairness, and the recent creation of Savak, the secret police, and the accompanying crackdown on political dissent and freedom of expression had caused widespread fear and resentment among educated middle-class Iranians who hankered for the 1906 Constitution and Western-style democracy. In Iran the gap between ruler and ruled was as wide as ever. "She said she knew some of the Iranian people were not very happy and she hoped to be able to help them," one interviewer reported. "She said she understood their problems as she had been a simple student." She told the *Times* of London that she would devote her life "to the service of the Iranian people" and encourage women to get an education and enter the workforce. Iranian students marveled that one of their own—someone young, progressive, and idealistic—now lived in the palace of the shahs. Critics scrutinized Farah's comments for signs that she harbored political ambitions of her own. When he proposed to Farah, however, the Shah had made clear that he expected her to take an active role in the life of the nation, one that went beyond the ceremonial duties expected of his consort. He did not want a repeat of the unhappy experiences of Fawzia and Soraya, who had been reluctant queens unwilling to sacrifice and share the burdens of royal life.

The Shah need not have worried: in marrying Farah Diba he gained the partner he never knew he needed.

FARAH SPENT HER wedding eve in the company of her close friend Elli Antoniades, the daughter of Greek refugees. The two young women had known each other since age nine. "We were the only two girls in class without fathers," said Elli. They were up early on the morning of December 21, 1959, in a state of great excitement. It took three hours for the famed Carita sisters, specially flown in from Paris, to style the bride's hair around a diamond hairpiece that weighed four and a half pounds. Designed by Harry Winston, Farah's tiara was delivered after breakfast by a small retinue of security guards and government ministers. Her bridal gown, designed by the House of Dior, was trimmed with pearls and rhinestones and weighed thirty-three pounds. "She wore a matching veil and cape-like bolero," reported the *New York Times*, "a diamond tiara and a necklace of diamonds as large as sugar lumps."

In deference to Farah's wishes, the Shah ended the tradition of ritually slaughtering livestock along the wedding procession route. Like her fiancé, she dreaded bloodshed and could not bear the thought of violence against harmless animals on the happiest day of her life. The couple exchanged their vows before a small audience in the Marble Palace's Hall of Mirrors. The ceremony was about to begin when the bride, overcome with nerves and emotion, remembered she had no ring for her groom. Ardeshir Zahedi stepped in and gave her his ring as a substitute. The newly betrothed couple moved to a grand salon where they hosted a reception for two thousand guests. "By the end of the day, Her Majesty was only thinking of her head," said her friend Elli. "She had a headache [from the weight of the tiara]."

The Shah was determined to avoid the mistakes that had left Soraya isolated and embittered in the palace. He assigned Amir Pourshaja as Farah's valet with instructions to help ease her entry into court life. He also encouraged his young wife to maintain her friendships outside the palace. Two months after the wedding, Elli received the first of the dinner invitations that were to continue over the next two decades. "Her Majesty could fall back on her friends and they could always tell her the truth," she said. "That was a clever thing for the Shah to do." Farah soon learned the limits of her influence and the pressures of life in the palace. She was pregnant with her first child in August 1960, when she visited the port city of Abadan and surprised local officials by asking to inspect the housing conditions of local workers. Feeling nauseous, and almost overcome by stifling heat and the reek of oil fumes, she was so distressed at the poverty that she burst into tears. Her embarrassed host asked her permission to make a financial offering to local families. "Ostentatiously, he collected identity cards, jotted down names—and as Farah Diba drove away, tore up the list and tossed it into the gutter," wrote a witness.

The young Queen was expected to bear children, and the icing on her wedding cake had left no doubt in anyone's mind as to what was expected of Iran's twenty-one-year-old royal consort. "May Allah grant you a male offspring," read the inscription. Farah fulfilled everyone's wishes with the birth of an heir, Crown Prince Reza, on October 31, 1960. But when the delivery proved difficult, the Shah's overly zealous physician administered "rather too much anesthetic." While her husband and the Imperial Family celebrated the arrival of the little prince in the next room, the baby's mother lay passed out in bed. "In the rejoicings, I think I was almost forgotten," she remembered, "and only my mother thought to ask: 'And my daughter, how is she?'" The young Queen was brought around by a nurse tapping her on the cheek and calling out, "Majesty, Majesty." She was immensely relieved when the Shah told her she had given birth to a son and heir. "I burst into tears," she admitted. "My God, I thought to myself, if I had had a daughter, what would have happened? Everyone would have been so terribly disappointed." People danced in the streets when they heard the news, swarming the Shah's car as he left the hospital and picking it up and carrying it on their shoulders. Never before, he told his wife, had he seen "such an outpouring of universal joy and warmth."

THE PAHLAVIS PAID a state visit to the White House in April 1962. Relations between Tehran and Washington were deeply strained by differences stemming from President John F. Kennedy's fear that the Shah was not doing enough to reform his country and that Iran was imperiled by communism. Kennedy's advisers worried that under Eisenhower the United States had aligned itself with an authoritarian leader who lacked popular legitimacy. When they surveyed Iran they thought they saw a country on the verge of a Cuban-style socialist takeover.

Kennedy also held a personal grudge against the Iranian monarch. He was angered by reports that Ardeshir Zahedi, now Iran's ambassador to Washington, had secretly supported Richard Nixon's 1960 presidential campaign with cash donations. The president had also received briefings from liberal officials critical of the Shah's leadership style and his constant intrigues in domestic politics. U.S. Supreme Court justice William Douglas, who knew Kennedy well, concluded that the president favored replacing Iran's monarchy with a liberal republic. "I talked to Jack frequently about conditions in Iran and the corruption that was rampant," wrote Douglas. Kennedy saw the Shah as "not the person we could trust. . . . The idea was to withdraw American support for the Shah causing his abdication." In his first few months in office, Kennedy put pressure on the Shah by ordering a review of U.S. policy and temporarily suspending arms sales. He made it clear that he expected measures to be taken to alleviate poverty, crack down on top-level corruption, and divert funds away from the military and toward education and health. Unlike their Republican counterparts, Democrats on Capitol Hill in Washington believed the Iranian monarchy was doomed at a time when republics were being established throughout the Middle East, Africa, and Asia. Few experts in Washington banked on the Shah's survival. In June 1961 Senator Frank Church told his colleagues on the Senate Committee on Foreign Relations, "I just think it is going to be a miracle if we save the Shah of Iran." At the time rumors were circulating in Tehran of coup plots involving the CIA, army generals, and the head of Iran's intelligence organization.

The Shah suspected that Kennedy and the Democrats wanted him out. The White House, he believed, failed to credit his achievements or appreciate the challenges he faced in reforming a conservative Muslim society. Since childhood he had dreamed of ruling as the people's King and improving their lives with far-reaching reforms. In recent years he had signed decrees breaking up the crown estates and turned over deeds to more than half a million acres, enabling a hundred thousand peasant families to farm their own plots of land. But privately held landholdings were another story. The Majles was still dominated by the so-called Thousand Families, the landed gentry who resisted pressure from the government to sell their estates for partition and redistribution. The ulama, landowners in their own right, were as resistant, and helped the gentry block legislation that the Shah had hoped would enact nationwide land reform. In 1959 he had retreated rather than risk an open breach with the two main pillars of conservative support for the monarchy.

American fears of instability in Iran came to a head in the spring of 1961, when labor strikes erupted in violence. "Four thousand schoolteachers paraded to Parliament to demand a pay increase," reported *Newsweek*. "A policeman opened fire and one teacher was shot dead. Next day, 30,000 teachers and students mobbed the streets, shouting 'butchers' and 'savages.' In the slums of South Tehran, the hungry brickyard workers caught their echo and began to talk of strikes of their own . . . for a precarious few days revolution seemed on the way." Kennedy made it clear that no further aid to Iran would be forthcoming unless the Shah appointed a new, reform-minded prime minister. The White House candidate, Ali Amini, a descendant of the former Qajar Dynasty and former National Front cabinet minister and ambassador to Washington, was despised by the Shah, who noted the irony that eight years earlier Eisenhower had intervened in Iran to depose Mohammad Mossadeq, while his successor, Kennedy, was now prepared to impose one of Mossadeq's loyalists as prime minister. Royalists and the Imperial court thought the U.S. intrigue smacked of a silent coup. The Shah was determined not to return to the bad old days when he had played second fiddle to strong-willed executives such as Generals Razmara and Zahedi. "I must either rule or leave," he told Amini, to which his new prime minister tartly called his bluff: "Whenever you rule, you will leave."

Encouraged by Kennedy's ambivalence toward the Shah, Mossadeq's National Front reemerged on the Iranian political scene for the first time since the early fifties. Demonstrators called for a return to the 1906 Constitution and an end to all restrictions on political activity. Asked what the National Front would do if it took power, one of its leaders admitted he would like to "hang Amini and make the Shah a limited monarch like Queen Elizabeth." Tensions escalated and the National Front's more religious-minded members split off to form the Liberation Movement of Iran, a new political grouping that declared loyalty to former Prime Minister Mossadeq but also emphasized Islam. "We do not consider religion and politics separate, and regard serving the people . . . an act of worship," declared Mehdi Bazargan, a cofounder of the new party and leader of the religious nationalists. His objective was to bridge the gap that until now had prevented the formation of an enduring political alliance between the secular nationalist left and politically minded clergy on the right.

THE FUTURE REVOLUTIONARY Mehdi Bazargan was born in 1907 to a prominent Tehran merchant family with close ties to the ulama. "His father's personal integrity and religiosity is often mentioned by Mehdi Bazargan as one of the chief influences in his life," observed Bazargan's biographer. As a youth he was one of a select group of elite students who won scholarships to study in France. Before the students left for Paris in 1928, Reza Shah received them to congratulate them on their achievement. "You must be wondering why we are sending you to a country whose regime differs from ours," he said. "There, you have freedom and a republic, but they are also patriots. What you will bring back when you return is not only arts and sciences, but also patriotism." Bazargan interpreted the remarks to mean that an Iranian could be a republican and still be considered patriotic. It was a lesson he never forgot.

The seven years Bazargan spent in France left a deep impression. He studied in Nantes and Paris and was rewarded with entry to the country's most prestigious schools. Bazargan was struck by the ease with which the French embraced modernity without sacrificing their religious convictions. This was in marked contrast to Iran, where development and progress were seen as incompatible with organized religion. Bazargan was also inspired by France's lively civil society and the proliferation of voluntary associations with a religious focus. Reza Shah's Iran did not allow citizens to organize groups that operated independently of the state. "The French had voluntary associations for everything," wrote Bazargan. "In Iran, by contrast, one *had* to become a member of whatever state-sponsored associations there were."

Pious and austere, Bazargan returned to Iran in 1935, completed his military service, and taught engineering at the University of Tehran, where he eventually rose to the post of dean of faculty. To supplement his income he founded a successful construction company. Throughout the 1940s he sympathized with the aspirations of Mossadeq's National Front but showed more interest in the activities of the Islamic Society, a group that wanted to include Islam in the national debate about economic and social development. "What the Iranian nation wants is just one word . . . 'Freedom,'" stated the Liberation Movement. "The Iranian people say that one person does not have the right to govern a nation in an arbitrary and tyrannical way. . . . We say that the Shah does not have the right to establish law, to install [or] dismiss a government, and everything, minor or major, be done according to his views and will, and yet he be [considered] sinless, unaccountable, with a sacred, even everlasting, position. This is reactionary, this is despotism, this is dictatorship." Bazargan and other critics of the Pahlavis were inspired by Kennedy's idealism and rhetoric. They expected the White House to pressure the Shah to liberalize his regime and return the country to constitutional rule.

THE KING AND Queen of Iran jetted into New York on April 11, 1962, and the next day flew down to the rainswept American capital. "This is one of our wonderful spring days, for which we are justly celebrated," President Kennedy joked at their official reception in Washington. Nonetheless, the same president who exuded glamour and mastered the stagecraft of the presidency was too slow to appreciate the allure of foreign royalty. Lavish photo spreads and feature articles in the pages of American photo magazines had preceded the arrival of the Iranian couple, whose courtship and glittering wedding ceremony were still fresh in the minds of the American public. For years the Shah's soap opera private life, and especially his heartbreaking divorce from Soraya, had filled pages in women's magazines that cast him in the role of romantic hero. Increasingly, the American public talked about "our Shah," not because they regarded Mohammad Reza Pahlavi as a puppet—the U.S. government's role in Operation Ajax remained a state secret—but because they viewed him as a friend and familiar face, the plucky young King determined to keep his people free from the scourge of communism.

Americans were used to seeing First Lady Jacqueline Kennedy outshine the wives of visiting heads of state. But on the evening of April 12 the gasps were audible when the Shah, wearing an elaborate cape, his uniform festooned in orders and decorations, exited his limousine beneath the White House North Portico in the company of Queen Farah, who dazzled in a jewel-encrusted gown spun of gold thread, a diamond and emerald necklace, and a diamond-encrusted tiara that resembled a bird's nest holding seven giant emeralds the size of robins' eggs. This was the Shah's way of reminding the Kennedys that real titles were inherited and not earned at the ballot box. Wheeled into place, Farah's soft power was illuminated with all the subtlety of a Krupp cannon facing a French cavalry charge. "After that, it was a matter of groping frantically for adjectives superlative enough to describe her gown and her jewels—the most blindingly impressive ever beheld in Washington on any visiting crowned head," noted one society columnist. "Her gold dress was encrusted almost entirely in beading that looked like fair-sized rubies." The only person in disagreement was, ironically, the lady herself. "Actually, I preferred Mrs. Kennedy's gown," recalled Farah. "The simplicity of it. I really liked her style very much." "The Shah and I both have something in common," President Kennedy told ninety guests who dined on cold trout, guinea hen, wild rice with asparagus, and bombe glacée rustique for dessert. "We both went to Paris with our wives and ended up wondering why we bothered. We thought we might as well have stayed home."

The Shah was in New York when he admitted to reporters that "this king business has personally given me nothing but headaches. During the whole of these twenty years of my reign, I have lived under the strain and stress of my duties." He further complained that he had "suffered vilification and attempts on his life" even though he had "presided over the liquidation of the entire royal fortune." The Shah's outburst was maudlin and self-pitying. His was not the behavior of a leader who exuded confidence and inspired respect. His ambivalence left the impression that he might be happier doing something else, like running a corner drugstore.

An intrepid reporter asked him what his wife thought of "the Queen business."

"In addition to giving children to her husband, I think the Queen business is also as serious as the King business," he answered in his usual sober, soft-spoken manner. Alluding to the endless round of public duties, he added, "She must take it to heart."

Farah had eagerly looked forward to seeing America for the first time.

But the memories she took away were not of warm crowds and grand receptions but the hostile abuse from Iranian students studying at American universities who picketed the Imperial couple at every stop along the way. The protesters, a mix of Communists, socialists, and liberals, demanded more democracy and called the Shah a puppet for his role in ousting Mossadeq. Many of the students were Farah's contemporaries, young Iranians who had received scholarships to study abroad. She was embarrassed to be the target of their complaints and harassment, and appalled at the lax security that allowed demonstrators to come within a few feet of them. Five years later, when her husband visited Lyndon Johnson's White House, she chose to stay home. "If I go there to be insulted again, I would be of much more use here in Tehran."

Her husband had his own problems to contend with. During their talks in the Oval Office, the Shah and the president parried over whether political or economic reform should take precedence. Kennedy wanted both to proceed in tandem. The Shah's view was that opening up the political system while trying to restructure the economy could trigger a social explosion. He was supported by experts who argued that it would be suicidal for any Iranian leader to shed power while attempting to tackle the privileges of the ulama and rural gentry, who were bound to resist reforms. The Shah also knew that the president was distracted by more serious crises in Cuba, West Berlin, and South Vietnam. The unrest of recent months had convinced some in Washington that perhaps Iranians weren't ready for democracy after all. The White House had lost the appetite to push for more substantive reform, and with Amini in place Kennedy was prepared to declare victory and move on to other, more pressing concerns. The Shah badgered him to accept that political conditions inside Iran were "obviously improving." He pointed out to his host that "he is not by nature a dictator. But if Iran is to succeed its government would have to act firmly for a time, and he knew that the United States would not insist that Iran do everything in an absolutely legal way." In what must have been for Kennedy a moment of supreme discomfort, the president swallowed whole the Shah's argument that prosperity could be established only in conditions of absolute security and that democracy would have to wait. "There are always special factors that have to be taken into account in different countries," Kennedy glumly conceded. "We are aware that you are the keystone to the arch in Iran."

The Shah left Washington confident that he had inoculated himself from further American pressure and that he could finally embark on a wide-ranging reform program that would burnish the farr. Iranian opposition leaders such as Mehdi Bazargan reacted with suitable outrage when they learned of Kennedy's retreat on political liberty. They vowed to never again be taken in by American pledges of support for democracy and human rights.

5

THE AYATOLLAH

I am going to go faster than the left.
—THE SHAH

I can summon a million martyrs to any cause.
—AYATOLLAH RUHOLLAH KHOMEINI

The chief beneficiary of unrest in the early 1960s was born in the village of Khomein in central Iran on September 24, 1902. Ruhollah Khomeini was raised in a walled compound in comfortable surroundings and attended by servants and guards. His family claimed descent from the seventh of Mohammad's twelve imams or disciples and were entitled to style themselves as seyyeds or direct descendants of the Prophet. Seyyeds wore black turbans and enjoyed considerable prestige in society. The Khomeini family had emigrated from Persia to British-ruled India in the early seventeenth century and lived among Shia Muslims in a small town near Lucknow. Their descendant Ahmad Khomeini returned to Persia in 1834 and established himself as a prosperous landowner. His son Mostafa trained as a religious scholar, and the third of his six children, Ruhollah, was only four months old when his father was slain in an ambush by a local warlord. The boy's childhood coincided with the upheavals of the Constitutional Revolution, civil war, and British-Russian colonial intervention. The Persian countryside was a dangerous, lawless place, and from an early age young Ruhollah showed signs of the remarkable fortitude that defined him as a man. "He was a particularly striking boy of above average build," wrote his biographer Baqer Moin. "Even as a youngster," one of Khomeini's sons later recalled, "my father always wanted to be the Shah in the games he played."

He studied religion in Qom, earned his credentials as a religious scholar or *mutjahid*, and worked as a teacher. His ambition showed in his choice of bride—fifteen-year-old Qodsi was the daughter of a respected Tehran clergyman. "The qualities of autocracy, decisiveness and self-righteousness that were to stand him in such good stead in his later political career were already well ingrained in Khomeini the young teacher," wrote Moin. Khomeini showed no tolerance for classroom debate, still less for compromise in his personal and professional relationships. By age forty he had established a reputation as a critic of Reza Shah's secular state, though he still favored the monarchy over a republic. But Khomeini's impatience revealed itself in publications he authored that called for more religion in public life and the return of the clergy to politics. He became a follower of Ayatollah Kashani, the Shiite firebrand who inspired the Fedayeen-e Islam terror group and later betrayed Prime Minister Moham-mad Mossadeq. Though few knew it at the time, Khomeini also opposed Mossadeq for "pledging allegiance to the Shah and serving as his prime minister when he was strong enough to oust him." He similarly distrusted the National Front for entering into a political alliance with the Tudeh Party, which preached atheist values. Many years later, after Khomeini emerged as the most vociferous of the Shah's critics, Ardeshir Zahedi, who had played a vital role during Operation Ajax as courier between the coup plotters and sympathetic ulama, said he thought the older man's face looked familiar. "I can't be completely sure but I remember seeing that person at Kashani's house."

In the late 1950s Khomeini drew overflowing crowds to a hall where he staked out a position to the right of Shiism's theological divide between constitutionalists and rejectionists. Where other clerics conveyed their thoughts in flowery, arcane seminary language, Khomeini's sermons and speeches had all the subtlety of a sledgehammer striking plate glass; he instinctively understood that in Iran the path to power lay in the gutter. His talents attracted the attention of the security forces, who infiltrated his household with informers, but Khomeini's restlessness also drew the scrutiny of Grand Ayatollah Seyyed Hossein Borujerdi, the paramount figure within Shiism, who resided in Najaf in Iraq. The city of Najaf was home to some of the holiest sites in Islam and competed with Qom as a major center of theological training for young Iranian seminarians. Borujerdi represented the "quietist" majority of clergy who considered themselves monarchists in the spirit of the 1906 Constitution. Despite their reservations about the Pahlavis, who championed pre-Islamic traditions and supported Western-style modernity, the ulama followed Borujerdi's lead and refused to soil themselves in political life. Borujerdi was so adamant on this issue that he once employed club-wielding mobs to forcibly expel the Fedayeen-e from Qom. Khomeini's reputation as a firebrand and his close association with Fedayeen-e Islam were well known, but so long as Borujerdi was alive he felt duty-bound to respect the old man's wishes and stay out of the political fray.

Yet time was on Khomeini's side. The advent of modern communications and transport links meant religious edicts sent from Qom could be wired or telephoned to different parts of the country on the same day. More than his older colleagues, the Ayatollah understood the potential this allowed for closer coordination between like-minded groups and clergy even though they might live hundreds of miles apart.

THE CITY OF Qom was saving itself for the next world. The clocks were set back ninety minutes behind Iran standard time. The preferred spoken language was not Persian but classical Arabic, the language of the Quran. Females over age four wore chadors. "There are, of course, no bars or liquor shops," wrote one British visitor to Qom. "There are no cinemas (one was built but was almost immediately burned by an angry mob). Television is discouraged as are swimming pools, music, and musical instruments. The bookshops have little but religious literature, including numerous anti-Semitic tracts. . . . When the wind whips down the narrow streets and alleys, catching the black cloth of the chadors, the women resemble giant crows." Shops in Qom displayed stylized images of the Twelfth or "Missing Imam" rather than photographs of the Shah. Most Tehranis preferred to drive around rather than through the forbidding little town, where foreigners were shushed away and uncovered women were pelted with stones. Tehranis retaliated by spreading gossip that behind closed doors in Qom "everything goes on. Vodka, poker, opium smoking. . . . There is a secret cinema, there are prostitutes."

The death of Grand Ayatollah Borujerdi in March 1961 created an opportunity for the Shah to ensure that the next generation of clerical leadership in Qom stayed in loyalist hands. Though outwardly hierarchical, Shiism was a remarkably fluid and democratic faith. Mullahs, the

equivalent of parish priests, occupied the lowest rung on the clerical ladder. Above them were the mutjahids, or scholars of religious law. If a mutjahid showed enough talent he might one day graduate to become an
ayatollah, or bishop of the church. Ayatollahs taught and interpreted religious law for the faithful. Very few ayatollahs ever reached the elevated
status of a grand ayatollah or cardinal of the faith, and fewer still reached
the apex of the clerical pyramid to become a marja. It was often said that
marjas were accepted and not elected by the people. Although a marja had
to first become a grand ayatollah, not every grand ayatollah embodied the
qualities to become a marja, and the process by which a grand ayatollah
became a marja was solely determined by the number of people who decided to follow or emulate his personal interpretation of religious law and
apply it in daily life. As a declaration of loyalty the people paid a religious
tax or *khoms*, which entitled their marja to 20 percent of their income or
wealth. Their local mullah took his own cut. "Of the money and goods
donated by the faithful," reported an observer, "the mullah is allowed to
keep a third to support himself, his family, and his own particular projects,
but he must distribute the rest to religious institutions and charities. He
makes extra money through gratuities when he performs such religious
ceremonies as memorial services for the dead. He is also paid for lectures
on religious subjects." Though brilliant scholarship was essential to make
the leap to marja status, other factors such as personality, politics, and
chance played their parts in determining the outcome of Shiism's equivalent of a popularity contest, with prize winnings of millions of fans and
hundreds of millions of dollars.

With his following, money, and moral influence, a marja enjoyed a
stature most kings and prime ministers could only dream of. His position
was strengthened by the fact that there were usually only three to five
marjas alive at any one time. But the marjas had to take care not to grow
complacent. Their followers were free to switch support from one to
another at any time, and so established marjas were wary of any newcomer
who showed himself capable of drawing a decent crowd for fear of losing
their revenue base. Nor were their followers obliged to emulate a grand
ayatollah who resided in Iran—millions of Iranians considered themselves
loyal to marjas who resided in the holy cities of Iraq. The fluid nature of
the marja system posed real challenges for the incumbents but especially
for Iran's kings, who kept a wary eye on these religious barons capable of
mobilizing their admirers and living independent of the state. Marjas

were immune from prosecution and in every respect considered above the law of the land. The greatest fear of any shah was that a marja would send the signal to his followers to come out onto the streets and enter the political arena. The last time this had happened was in 1906, when the country was swept by revolution; at that time the ulama had successfully forced the Qajar Shah to relinquish his monopoly on power. The greatest fear of the ulama, on the other hand, was the Pahlavi state's emphasis on secularism and state power. Every time public interest in religion waned, the decline in mosque attendance meant fewer followers and a sharp drop in their income.

Though each marja was technically equal to the others, it also happened that one among them enjoyed more moral authority than his colleagues. By a quirk of tradition, exactly who that was depended on the wishes of the monarch. When Grand Ayatollah Borujerdi died the Shah, as Custodian of the Faith, wrote his letter of condolence to the ulama. Whomever among the surviving marjas received the letter was allowed to claim the exalted status of paramount marja. In 1961 the Shah was anxious not to strengthen the hand of any of the marjas living inside Iran. So he sent his letter of condolence to Grand Ayatollah Mohsen Hakim, who, like his predecessor, lived in Najaf and was firmly opposed to clerical involvement in politics. By now the Shah was determined to proceed with radical social reforms that he knew would anger the clergy.

Since childhood the Shah had dreamed of ushering in an era of social justice in the tradition of the Shia imams. Madame Arfa's nursery lessons had not been lost on him—kings could be revolutionaries, too. "If there is to be a revolution in this country," he said, "I will be the one to lead it." He believed he had survived illness, the plane crash, and an assassination attempt for a reason. "I concluded that my destiny had already been designed and ordered by God," he said. "And I must carry it out." Self-preservation was also a factor in his decision. Five years earlier, King Faisal II of Iraq had been butchered in his palace by renegade colonels. The Shah was determined to avoid his fate by placing Iran's monarchy not only on the side of social progress but also at the forefront. "I am going to show that revolutions to advance the poor and underprivileged can come from kings and are not the exclusive field of Marxists or socialist-minded young colonels," he explained. "I am going to go faster than the left." His Swiss education had convinced him that feudal societies could be reshaped by theories and policies that redistributed income and strengthened the reach of government. But the Shah's fascination with state activism went very much against the grain of the Iranian experience. Historically, though most Iranians revered the monarchy, and held the king above politics, they viewed government as predatory, corrupt, and oppressive. The idea that government would have a more forceful presence in their lives caused ripples of discontent that spread beyond clerical circles.

With Hakim now the titular head of the clergy, the Shah decided the time was right to unveil the reforms he dubbed the "White Revolution" and that he hoped would transform Iran from a semifeudal to a modern industrial state in a generation. The White Revolution included land reform; granting women the vote; nationalizing forests; selling shares in government-owned factories to the public; profit sharing for factory workers; and establishing a literacy corps composed of army conscripts whose job would be to bring education to the provinces. Though landowners were promised compensation to surrender their estates they also lost their political clout. The ulama would also have to surrender their landholdings. There was no doubt that both groups would resist this landmark attempt to sweep away their privileges and prerogatives.

To manage the reform process, in July 1962 the Shah turned to an old friend and confederate, Asadollah Alam, a prominent landowner and aristocrat from eastern Iran whose climb to the pinnacle of power began in 1945, when he was appointed governor of Sistan and Baluchistan. Five years later, Alam received his first cabinet appointment. During the showdown against Mossadeq he had rallied to the Shah's side, and though a hardheaded realist when it came to politics he held a romantic, almost feudal attachment to the Crown. In marked contrast to the rest of the political establishment, Alam flattered the Shah's pretensions to rule as well as reign. In appointing Alam as his new prime minister, the Shah chose wisely and with foresight. Alam and the Shah understood that the White Revolution faced defeat if left in the hands of the conservative-dominated Majles. They decided to bypass the legislature altogether and take their plans to the country in the form of a nationwide referendum. The government's announcement of the referendum in January 1963 caused disquiet in Qom but no immediate unrest—Grand Ayatollah Hakim was hundreds of miles away in Najaf, and the other marjas followed their usual policy of neutrality. Their silence appalled Ruhollah Khomeini, who felt obliged to vent his outrage at the Pahlavi assault on tradition and heritage. The radicals were angered by land reform but above all by women's rights. "The son of Reza Khan has embarked on the destruction of Islam in Iran," he thundered. "I will oppose this as long as the blood circulates in my veins."

Everyone understood that with Ayatollah Khomeini's entry into the political arena an important taboo had been broken. Wealthy merchants angered by the government's economic policies donated generously to Khomeini's cause. Left-wing students and intellectuals rallied to the side of the first public figure since Mossadeq to challenge royal prerogatives. In other circumstances they would have welcomed the Shah's efforts to improve the lives of the rural and urban poor. But the opportunity to use an ayatollah as a battering ram against the king who had deposed their hero a decade earlier was too tempting an opportunity to pass up. The political class was mesmerized by Khomeini's ability to fill the streets with supporters who displayed a fanatical level of devotion. "If you give the order we are prepared to attach bombs to ourselves and throw ourselves at the Shah's car to blow him up," one local merchant told the Ayatollah. "It won't come to that," Khomeini answered him. "[When] you come here, if there is something to be done, you will be asked to do it." Out of this feverish atmosphere emerged the Coalition of Islamic Societies, an underground organization that formed the nucleus of a religious revolutionary movement. Established and led by a secret cell made up of Khomeini's most devoted seminary students, the coalition raised money, spread propaganda, and organized other underground groups within the hawza, the network of seminaries in Qom. They endorsed assassination as a political tactic and collected money from the *bazaaris* (merchants).

One of the coalition's most aggressive strategies was to smear the Shah as an apostate or nonbeliever. The allegation appeared absurd on its face— the Custodian of the Faith's piety was well known to his family and friends. He carried a miniature copy of the Quran in his suit jacket pocket and made frequent references to his faith in speeches and interviews. His childhood visions of the imams were a matter of public record. Each time he left the country to travel overseas, the senior Muslim cleric in Tehran joined him at the airport, put his hand on his shoulder, and recited a special verse of the Quran to wish him a safe journey. Yet as a prince educated in Switzerland and trained to think logically, the Shah followed the Enlightenment rule that called for strict separation between church and state. He refused to accept the supremacy of religious over secular law and dismissed out of hand the 1906 Constitution's guarantee of a clerical veto over parliamentary legislation. Shyness and emotional reserve played their parts, too. The Shah was uncomfortable with public displays of piety, which he viewed as another sort of demagoguery. His reticence set him apart from his own people, who reveled in passionate and very public displays of faith. Shia mosques were at the very center of neighborhood life in most Iranian villages and towns. He did not attend Friday prayers, nor did he observe fasting during the month that marked observance of Ramadan. In his thirty-seven years on the throne, the only time the faithful saw their king make his devotions was during his highly publicized annual trip to the holy city of Mashad and his attendance at ceremonies in a Tehran mosque to mark the Ashura holiday. Niavaran was the first palace since Achaemenid times not to include its own house of worship.

The Shah's visible discomfort with public displays of piety and his disregard for Islamic symbolism stood in marked contrast to the behavior of the Arab world's Sunni kings. The reigning monarchs of Jordan, Morocco, and Saudi Arabia were not necessarily more religious than their Iranian brother, but they made a great show of attending the Friday prayers read out in their name. In so doing they retained a feel for the street and a connection to the mosque that their brother king in Iran did not have.

"EVEN IN THE womb I was a revolutionary," Abolhassan Banisadr once said, beaming with pride. Thirty years earlier, in March 1933, Banisadr's father, the prominent cleric Ayatollah Nasrollah Banisadr, had left the city of Hamadan with his pregnant wife to deliver a statement of political protest against Reza Shah. The Shah had recently renegotiated the terms of Britain's monopoly of Iranian oil production and appealed to the ulama for support. But rather than send the obligatory telegram of congratulations, Banisadr chose to snub the King by making an excuse to leave his home in the city of Hamadan. Husband and wife reached a village on the outskirts in time for the Persian New Year, and it was there that their son Abolhassan, the future first president of the Islamic Republic of Iran, was born.

The Banisadrs were well acquainted with two other prominent religious families, the Khomeinis and the Sadrs. In the 1930s Ruhollah Khomeini liked to visit Hamadan in the summer to take the cool. "I met Khomeini as a child," Abolhassan recalled of his playdates with the cleric's young sons Mostafa and Ahmad. As a teenager he might have been expected to follow his father into the seminary. Abolhassan's great teenage passion was not religion but politics. "My last days of high school coincided with the Mossadeq era," he remembered. "That led to activism at an early age. I was a nationalist. I was in favor of independence and liberty. I was a Mossadeqi." It was a thrilling time for a young boy fired with dreams of nationalism, secularism, and Cold War neutrality. "As a student I saw many of my classmates sympathized [with the Communists]," he said. "But I was convinced the Tudeh were Russian stooges." He sharpened his debating skills during hours of discussions and by eleventh grade was out in the streets circulating petitions in favor of oil nationalization. Whereas loyalists of Tudeh looked to Stalin for leadership, Banisadr favored the more nationalist and moderate left-wing National Front, and he idolized Mohammad Mossadeq.

The events of August 1953—Operation Ajax and the Shah's brief exile followed by his triumphal return to power—proved turning points. Bitterly disillusioned with U.S. policy toward Iran, a generation of left-wing students such as Banisadr saw the Americans as the latest in a long line of imperialist occupiers dating back to antiquity. "The monarchy was against independence. We were convinced it was used as a staging ground for the foreign powers. I personally became a republican the day after the 1953 coup d'état." In the late fifties he joined the underground National Resistance Movement and spent two short spells in jail for political offenses. "We would write tracts, do anything to show our resistance to the coup d'état."

Though he identified as a socialist, Banisadr never renounced religion and admired Shiism's sympathy for the downtrodden and oppressed. In 1963 he watched in fascination as his father's old friend Khomeini began openly criticizing the Shah's social and economic reforms. Many students and intellectuals supported Khomeini not because they opposed women's rights or land reform but because they envied his ability to bring many common people out into the streets to demonstrate against the Shah, whom they blamed for the ouster of their hero Mossadeq. "It was not known then that Khomeini played a role in 1953 against Mossadeq," Banisadr later grimly conceded. "We [only] understood afterward that he stood with those who supported the coup. . . . At the time [in 1963] we had no real knowledge of his views."

THE WHITE REVOLUTION referendum passed with 99 percent support, providing the Shah with a clear-cut victory and earning him a laudatory telegram of congratulations from the White House. But the results were clouded by reports of voting irregularities and the decision by the marjas to call for a boycott. Nor were Khomeini's hard-liners about to concede defeat. They smarted from the Shah's ill-tempered denunciation of them as a "stupid and reactionary bunch whose brains have not moved. . . . They think life is about getting something for nothing, eating and sleeping . . . sponging on others and a parasitic existence." In a second venomous speech, he denounced rebel ulama as "sordid and vile elements . . . a numb and dispiriting snake and lice who float in their own dirt . . . the fist of justice, like thunder, will be struck at their head in whatever cloth they are, perhaps to terminate their filthy and shameful life."

Throughout the spring and early summer of 1963 sporadic clashes occurred in Qom between pro-Khomeini seminarians and the security forces. The Shah's public attacks against his religious opponents made it all but impossible for the moderate clerical majority to stand up to Khomeini, and momentum quickly shifted to his extremists, who spoiled for a showdown. Tensions ratcheted up still further when paratroopers stormed through the Feiziyah, the seminary attached to the Holy Shrine of Fatima, one of the most sacred sites in all of Islam. They assaulted the young seminarians and wrecked their rooms. At least one student fell to his death from a high rooftop. Then the troops lit a bonfire in the courtyard and fed the flames with turbans, books, and furniture. All of Qom was traumatized by the raid. "With this crime the regime has revealed itself as the successor to Genghiz Khan and has made its defeat and destruction inevitable," declared Khomeini. "The son of Reza Khan has dug his own grave and disgraced himself." He issued a defiant call to arms: "I can summon a million martyrs to any cause."

The Shah and his government had good reason to believe they could maintain order and forestall a religious revolt. Khomeini was not a marja but a lowly ayatollah. His supporters were fervent but still few in number. Middle-class Iranians, the workers, and the farmers were excited by the White Revolution and the promise of prosperity, education, and medical care. They showed no sign of turning against the one man who stood for progress and reform. "We did consider the possibility of violence," recalled Parviz Sabeti, who in 1963 was a young Savak analyst responsible for monitoring religious dissent. "But we didn't anticipate it spreading among the people." The problem, he said, was that although the Shah "spoke in a very tough way [against the ulama] he didn't follow through with actions. He should have crushed them."

Ayatollah Khomeini made his move on June 3, 1963, which in the lunar calendar fell on Ashura, the tenth day of the month of Muharram and the fateful anniversary of the death of Imam Husayn at the Battle of Karbala in 680. The security forces had discovered that Khomeini planned to deliver a speech critical of the Shah on the grounds of the martyred Feiziyah school. They surrounded Qom with six thousand paratroopers and dispatched an emissary, Colonel Nasser Moghadam, who tried and failed to persuade the Ayatollah not to proceed. By the time Khomeini arrived at the Feiziyah in the afternoon to address the crowd, the streets surrounding the shrine were thronged with thousands of admirers. "Let me give you some advice, Mr. Shah!" Khomeini declared, addressing the King much as a headmaster might scold an errant schoolboy. "Dear Mr. Shah, I advise you to desist this policy and acts like this. I don't want the people to offer thanks if your masters should decide one day that you must leave. I don't want you to become like your father." Khomeini warned that the Americans were fickle allies, "friends of the dollar; they have no religion, no loyalty. They are hanging responsibility for everything around your miserable neck! . . . I feel anxiety and sorrow at the state of Iran, at the state of our ruined country, at the state of this cabinet, at the state of those running our government."

Khomeini's fiery words electrified his devotees, who acclaimed the speech as the "Second Ashura." They swept into the streets calling for the overthrow of the Shah and smashing and burning symbols of the regime and modernity. Police and soldiers rushed to downtown Tehran to secure the parliament building and protect the palace from mobs who chanted, "Death to the dictator!" The speed with which the violence spread caught everyone by surprise. Members of the Imperial Family not already at Saadabad for the summer were evacuated to safety in the north. Queen Farah and her two young children, Crown Prince Reza and Princess Farahnaz, were driven in a convoy to Saadabad. The young mother had only recently given birth to her daughter. "The tension was evident even in our immediate environment: this year the king had us go earlier than usual to Saadabad Palace in Shemiran, far from the center of town," the Queen recalled of those dark days. "I remember that as I tightened my arms around our little Farahnaz, then only three months old, I noticed that the guards had put on combat uniforms."

ON THE EVENING of June 4, 1963, Prime Minister Alam summoned to his office the heads of the different branches of the security forces. With the country on the brink of a religious revolt he warned them he was about to order the seizure of Ayatollah Khomeini, an act that he assumed would lead to open clashes in the streets. "Tomorrow is going to be very crucial," he advised the officers. "The fate of the country depends on us and how the generals behave." Everyone in the room understood the implication— they should be prepared if necessary to use live rounds to prevent the overthrow of the monarchy.

"Mr. Prime Minister, are *you* asking us to shoot people?" inquired Lieutenant General Mozaffer Malek, the head of the National Gendarmerie.

Alam took this remark to mean that the general would refuse an order to open fire on the demonstrators. He angrily ordered Malek to leave the room and telephone his deputy to come and replace him. General Hassan Pakravan, the head of Savak, intervened on his colleague's behalf. "Mr. Prime Minister, General Malek didn't mean that," he offered. The generals, he explained, were confused because only their commander in chief, the Shah, could give the order to shoot. When Alam said nothing it dawned on the men in the room that the Shah had removed himself from the line of command: everyone now understood that their own commander in chief was unwilling to issue an order that might lead to civilian casualties.

Alam was understandably on edge. What the generals did not know was that he had just helped steer the Shah through a crisis with striking similarities to the showdown ten years earlier with Mossadeq. Fearful of issuing the order that might result in deaths and injuries, once again the Shah had procrastinated. But where the earlier crisis had been allowed to drag out for months, this time Alam took matters firmly in hand. His intervention steadied the Shah's nerves even as rumors spread that he was on the verge of packing his suitcase and repeating his earlier flight into exile. "He was panicking," confirmed Parviz Sabeti, who spent the crisis at the side of General Pakravan. "But he wasn't ready to leave. He didn't know what to do because he didn't want to kill people. There was no talk of the Shah leaving. But he dreaded the prospect of bloodshed." Ten years earlier, General Zahedi had stepped in to save the day; now Alam took charge and issued the order for the army to use force if necessary to prevent revolution. "I had to," Alam confided years later to the British ambassador. "His Majesty is very soft-hearted and does not like bloodshed." "I was determined to make a stand since the very survival of our country was at stake," Alam told a courtier. In public the prime minister told a different story. "His Majesty was as a rock," he later told the English writer Margaret Laing. "I could really feel that I could rely on that rock. . . . Therefore when I proposed to His Majesty 'Do you allow me to shoot? To order shooting?' he said 'Yes, not only I allow, I back you.' "

The great revolutionary drama unfolded in the early morning hours of June 5, 1963. As Alam predicted, news of the arrest of Ayatollah Khomeini unleashed a storm of protest. In Tehran, mobs surged through the center of town and besieged the national radio station, parliament, ministries, and the Marble Palace. "They had no plan [as such] to take over," recalled Sabeti. "They targeted the radio station so they could make a broadcast to the nation and provoke a popular uprising." Similar tactics had been tried in 1953. Rumors flew that as many as a hundred thousand people were in the streets, but the security forces estimated only one-fifth that number were in open revolt. Still, the authorities were shocked by the scale and ferocity of the unrest. Though Alam radiated outward confidence, he was painfully aware that the fate of the dynasty and the country rested in his hands. His usual routine was to take an afternoon nap after lunch. "My stomach was upset," he later reminisced. "I thought I would throw up. I was scared. I thought, 'If I don't take my nap that bastard attendant will go out and tell people, "The Prime Minister is too upset to take his nap today." ' " So Alam stuck to his usual routine, pretending to nap though "too nervous to sleep." When he dressed to return to his office he found his attendant in a state of near hysteria: "Mr. Prime Minister, how can you take a nap when the city is burning?!"

By midday, Khomeini's followers were on the rampage in the cities of Mashad, Isfahan, Shiraz, and Kashan. Plumes of smoke rose high over the Tehran skyline. Arsonists and rioters approached the center of town from four directions in a well-coordinated assault that suggested careful advance planning. "In the Ministry of Justice, files were burned, the Ministry of Interior was wrecked, [and the] office of News and Broadcasting was destroyed," reported American diplomats from the stricken city. The building that housed the newspaper *Ettelaat*, which had criticized Khomeini, was saved from destruction only by troop reinforcements. "Police stations were destroyed, petrol stations fired, telephone lines ripped up, phone booths destroyed, buses and bus stations were destroyed . . . this had obviously been well planned and the targets were both strategic and places hated by many of the people . . . there was relatively little looting, although deliberate destruction of government property." The

municipal library, built with American money, was burned. Repeated
attempts were made to storm the perimeter around the Marble Palace,
but the palace guard stood their ground and prevented a massacre.

With Iran's cities put to the torch, Prime Minister Alam drove to
National Police headquarters to issue the order to clear the streets. He
erupted when he saw that his driver had concealed his license plate to prevent their car from being identified and possibly targeted by rioters. "Eat
shit!" snapped the prime minister. "If there is one day I need to be seen
driving into town it is today!" The convoy encountered no problems, and
Alam was met at police headquarters by Police Chief Nematollah Nasiri
and General Gholam Ali Oveissi. Alam made a few light quips but then
turned deadly serious. "Who has the guns?" he asked his commanders. "I
don't know why you're not using them. I want to save Tehran." Martial law
was declared, troops began moving through the streets, and the crackle
of rifle fire was heard through that night and into the next day. When
one squad of troops phoned General Nasiri asking for reinforcements,
he responded that the only assistance they could expect from him were
trucks to collect bodies. Wild rumors spread of thousands killed, but the
actual death toll turned out to be much lower. Whereas the Shah and his
advisers were told that about 120 people died, after the revolution the
Islamic Republic's Martyr's Foundation surprised everyone by scaling
down the final death toll to 32. Some of the casualties had been policemen
and gendarmerie fired on by rioters.

Prime Minister Alam's decisive action had saved the day. But even he
was left uneasy by the sight of troops firing on religious students. "It was
not an easy decision for me," he admitted. "I too was raised by a devout
mother."

WITH LAW AND order restored, the Shah faced the dilemma of what to
do with his nemesis. The call for leniency came from a surprising direction. Two years earlier Hassan Pakravan had succeeded General Teymour
Bakhtiar as head of Savak after Bakhtiar fled the country amid charges of
coup plotting. Pakravan had banned the use of torture and opened a dialogue with the regime's critics, who included many leading clerics. Queen
Farah admired Pakravan as "a man of great culture, intelligence, and
humanity, who pleaded clemency to the king." Though Pakravan was not
personally religious he was wary of doing or saying anything that might
provoke more unrest in the mosques. "He said he knew that, after all,

the population of the country is not its elite," recalled his wife, Fatemeh. "It's the real people. They are not very literate. They are simple. They are full of superstition. And even though most of the Iranians have no respect for the mullahs, they still have [respect] for what they represent."

The Ayatollah's courage in standing up to the regime marked him as a potent threat for the future. He was detained on an army base while the Shah and his advisers debated what to do with him. The list of available options ranged from execution, imprisonment, and exile to freeing him without conditions. Pakravan's aide Parviz Sabeti, who closely followed the deliberations, dismissed speculation that execution was ever seriously considered. "If it was discussed I didn't hear about it," he said. The regime was not prepared for, nor could it afford to risk, a second explosion of religious violence and more martyrs. These concerns were shared by the marjas. Regardless of their feelings about the Shah's reforms, the marjas loathed Khomeini for provoking bloodshed and stirring unrest. They regarded his interest in politics as heresy and his demagoguery as a threat to the entire religious establishment. Grand Ayatollah Kazem Shariatmadari, the most influential marja living inside Iran, took the lead in brokering a settlement with the regime. Shariatmadari, who bore a striking resemblance to the British actor Alec Guinness, had taught Khomeini when they were in seminary school together in Qom and was well versed in his ambition and fanaticism. He came up with an ingenious plan that he hoped would placate the ulama, satisfy the palace, and tame the radicals.

Shariatmadari led a procession of senior religious figures to Tehran to publicly petition the Shah to spare Khomeini's life. Behind the scenes, the Marja worked with Alam to come up with a compromise formula that would allow both sides to back down without losing face. Shariatmadari's subsequent decision to elevate Khomeini from the rank of ayatollah to the exalted status of grand ayatollah was made with the full knowledge that no king of Iran would dare execute a senior member of the ulama. "Khomeini is a grand ayatollah like us," he declared. Alam and the Shah accepted the formula as the price of peace. Nor was Khomeini given a say in the matter: Shariatmadari wanted him to feel indebted to his colleagues and hoped the promotion would satisfy his drive for power. Now the whole of Qom would know that the moderates had "saved" Khomeini's life. Better yet, his new title was tainted because he had not earned it on his own merits. This and his reputation for extremism made it highly unlikely he would ever be acclaimed as a marja. Prime Minister Alam noted that even while the marjas negotiated they discreetly signaled that "their appeals [on behalf of Khomeini's life] should be disregarded."

General Pakravan went to great lengths to make sure the newly styled Grand Ayatollah Khomeini was treated with respect and held in comfortable surroundings. After a few weeks he was transferred to a spacious guesthouse and spared the indignity of a formal interrogation. Pakravan even made a point of lunching with his "guest" once a week. Khomeini was polite to his jailer, and the atmosphere between the two men was outwardly cordial. Together they discussed religion, history, and philosophy. "He is very handsome," Pakravan told Fatemeh when his wife peppered him with questions about the man from Qom. Like others in the ruling class, she was fascinated by the clergyman who had come so close to toppling the King. "He has extraordinary presence, a power of seduction. He has great charisma." He described Khomeini's most striking trait as "ambition. You know, it made my hair stand on end. It was frightening." Pakravan described Khomeini as immune to reason and logic. "I felt like a helpless wave, smashing my head against solid rock."

The Shah accepted the arrangement that spared Khomeini either execution or a lengthy prison sentence for treason. In response, Grand Ayatollah Shariatmadari released a conciliatory statement declaring that the ulama were not "reactionaries opposed to liberty and progress" and that they would support "genuine reforms." He did, however, call for "social justice and the implementation of the Constitution."

Grand Ayatollah Khomeini was released from detention in April 1964. He received a hero's welcome back in Qom, where tens of thousands of people cheered and danced in the streets. He had the crowds with him. "Khomeini is now an important national figure that the regime must handle with extreme care," the U.S. embassy cabled Washington. The Americans had anticipated an uprising from the Communist left but never considered the possibility of a threat from the religious right. Iran's highly complex interplay of religion, politics, and intrigue was beyond their understanding. Hossein Mahdavy, a leading figure in the National Front, which had been sidelined by Khomeini's revolt, warned diplomat William Green that the Shah and his government "greatly underestimated" the strength of religious feeling among the common people and the loyalty they felt to the marjas.

One admirer who did not travel to Qom to welcome Khomeini home was Abolhassan Banisadr. "I had a phone call from [Khomeini's eldest son] Mostafa to tell me that his father had been released," he said. But Abolhassan's father, Ayatollah Banisadr, said he would make the trip instead—he did not want his son to get picked up by Savak—and it would be another nine years before Banisadr and Khomeini met to plan the overthrow of the monarchy.

THE SHAH TOOK advantage of the 1963–1964 crackdown to make a crucial decision. After years of lurching from one political crisis to the next, impatient to put his reforms in place, he decided to seize the reins of executive power in his own hands and establish personal authoritarian rule. Since 1955 he had involved himself in politics but essentially shared power with his prime ministers while meddling in cabinet affairs. From now on, however, Iran's prime minister, cabinet, and parliament could question and debate his decisions but otherwise not oppose them. The events of June 5, 1963, which became known as Fifteen Khordad, had proven the last straw. Never again would he allow a strong personality or demagogue to emerge as a threat from within the ranks of the clergy, the military, or the political class. There would never be another Mossadeq, Zahedi, or Khomeini to threaten the ruling dynasty or distract him from his mission to develop and modernize Iran on his own terms and at his own pace.

The Shah was unapologetic: "Finally I became so exasperated that I decided we would have to dispense with democracy and operate by decree." His decision to rule without cultivating the support of the political establishment carried risks and made him dependent on the army to stay in power. "Having successfully stripped his traditional supporters of power, the Shah has come as near to a monopoly of power as at any time in his reign," the U.S. embassy informed Washington. The Americans concluded there would be no repeat event: "Whatever the ups and downs of the Shah's future relations with the mullahs, it seems clear that the standard bearers of Shia Islam as it exists today in Iran are fighting a losing battle." The Shah's own advisers were less confident. They warned of the risks involved in shutting down legitimate political activity and involving the Crown in government. Five years earlier, former prime minister and court minister Hossein Ala had been instrumental in ending the Shah's marriage to Queen Soraya. Now he convened a meeting of grandees to plead the case for restraint. They worried that Alam's crackdown had gone far enough. The regime could not afford to alienate the clergy, students, intellectuals, and the urban middle class who recoiled at the prospect of dictatorship. The Shah was furious when he learned of their meeting. He suspected they were plotting and saw to it that all but one of the participants was sacked from office. Ardeshir Zahedi, now Iran's ambassador to the Court of St. James's in London, wrote his father-in-law a long letter urging him to reconsider and slow down. "I urged His Majesty to reign and not rule," he explained, "because the risk was that he would be blamed when things went bad, like the economy. The White Revolution was not well thought through. I told him, 'When you paint a new house, you have to clean it first, and then you paint it in layers. You have to get rid of the old paint first. I have to tell you, something is wrong. Khomeini is like a cancer.'"

RUHOLLAH KHOMEINI COULD not stay quiet—it was not in his nature.

The next crisis arose in 1964, when under intense pressure from Washington the Iranian government quietly announced plans to approve legislation that would provide legal immunity to U.S. military personnel, their family members, and household staff stationed in Iran. President Lyndon Johnson's administration placed a high priority on a Status of Forces Agreement between the two countries. Privately, the Shah and his advisers expressed deep concern. With their history of colonialism, Iranians were deeply sensitive to any suggestion that foreigners should receive special privileges or be exempted from the laws of the land. Washington's insistence that the flow of military and economic aid to Iran was contingent on passage of the law showed staggering insensitivity toward their ally, who had just put the lid on revolt. As an incentive, Johnson offered a $200 million loan to purchase additional military hardware. Iranians predictably reacted with widespread outrage to what they regarded as a "capitulation bill" with bribes attached. The parliamentary debate over the proposed legislation reopened old wounds still unhealed from Operation Ajax and completely undermined the Shah's efforts to calm passions and reassert his authority in the wake of Khomeini's rebellion.

On October 27, 1964, Khomeini stood outside his home in Qom and delivered a thunderous second attack on the Shah and the Pahlavi state. This time he ventured beyond religion to appeal to the people's sense of nationalism and pride, savaging the King and his ministers as a nest of traitors. "They have reduced the Iranian people to a level lower than that of an American dog," he protested. "If someone runs over a dog belonging to an American, he will be prosecuted. Even if the Shah himself were to run over a dog belonging to an American, he will be prosecuted. But if an American cook runs over the Shah, the head of state, no one will have the right to interfere with him." Khomeini called on all sections of Iranian society to revolt. He also issued a dramatic pan-Islamist call to arms. "Ulama of Qom, come to the aid of Islam! Muslim peoples! Leaders of the Muslim peoples! Presidents and kings of the Muslim peoples! Come to our aid! Shah of Iran, save yourself! . . . O God, destroy those individuals who are traitors to this land, who are traitors to Islam, who are traitors to the Quran."

This time the government did not wait for the popular reaction. Within a week Khomeini found himself bundled onto a Royal Iranian Air Force Hercules bound for Turkey and a life in permanent exile. For the first eleven months he lived with the family of Colonel Ali Cetiner, a Turkish intelligence officer, until the Iranian government agreed that he could move to Najaf in Iraq, where they could keep a closer eye on him. Colonel Cetiner was sorry to lose his houseguest. He thought how strange it was that the man who left his house was the same in every respect but one. "When he arrived from Iran he did not have a penny on him," recalled the colonel. "But when he left Turkey in November 1965 he was a million-aire, even by the standards of those days. He was given money by visitors from Iran. Khomeini left Turkey with his fortune and went to Iraq."

6

"JAVID SHAH!"

Shah is a kind of magic word with the Persian people.
—THE SHAH

Now I could do more than sympathize;
I had the means to act.
—QUEEN FARAH

Each morning the Shah and four-year-old Reza strolled hand in hand from their residence in the Ekhtessassi Palace in central Tehran across the road to the Marble Palace, the Shah's office, from where the toddler was picked up by a governess and taken to kindergarten. But on the morning of April 10, 1965, the little prince left home earlier than usual to welcome a new playmate to class. The change in routine prompted his father to drive instead of walk to work, and the decision saved his life. As the Shah exited his car and walked toward the palace's main entrance, a young soldier opened fire on him with a small M3 machine gun. At the first sound of shots two sentries on duty abandoned their posts and ran for cover. An attempt by a valet to close the door failed when a bullet struck his hand. With the gunman in hot pursuit the Shah dashed inside, up the stairs, and into his office, where two lightly armed bodyguards mounted a courageous last stand. Colonel Kiomars Djahinbini, the head of the Shah's security detail, ran to the scene after hearing the attack over his walkie-talkie. "As soon as [the gunman] started shooting, my two agents shot back. They hit him but didn't kill him. My people were armed only with revolvers." During the final shoot-out a bullet crashed through the Shah's office door, whistled over the desk, where he took cover, and thudded into the chair he usually sat in to do paperwork. The final spray of automatic gunfire was followed by an ominous silence. The Shah opened the door and stepped outside to find three blood-soaked corpses strewn on the floor. Incredibly, one of his mortally wounded bodyguards had managed to take down the assassin with a single shot before succumbing to his own wounds.

The telephone rang while the Queen was putting on her makeup in preparation for an early-morning meeting. "Oh, my God, Farah, darling!" Queen Mother Taj ol-Moluk sobbed on the line. "Do you know what has happened?"

"No."

"Someone has fired on the King!" On hearing this news the young mother "gasped and my heart stopped beating." Finally, after repeating the words over and over as though in a daze, her mother-in-law had the presence of mind to tell Farah that her husband had survived the attack. "Do not worry, all is well," she said and abruptly hung up.

Farah went into shock. "I continued putting on my makeup, like an automaton, chanting, 'Thank you, God! Thank you, God!'" Then it dawned on her that only Reza's change of routine had saved the lives of both her husband and her son. She ran to her husband's blood-soaked office suite, where courtiers, family, and friends stood gathered around the bodies. They watched with astonishment as the Shah went back to work, display-ing his usual sangfroid in times of crisis. "Four times in my reign I have been threatened seriously, and four times my life has been spared," he had recently told a visitor. "I must confess that I am beginning to have a mys-tical sense about my job. I am reaching the conviction, anyway, that I must be here for something!"

His bodyguards could not afford the luxury of believing in a higher power or expecting a sixth miracle—they knew that luck and not divine intervention had prevented a palace massacre. "After that the system was changed," explained Colonel Djahinbini, whose Special Protection Unit was responsible for the security of the Imperial Family. The Special Pro-tection Unit was comprised of three hundred volunteers from the elite Eternals division of the Imperial Guard. New rules were laid down. From now on no regular army soldiers were allowed onto the palace grounds. Colonel Djahinbini's men had their revolvers replaced with automatic weapons and were sent to the United States to receive training from the

Secret Service. They also started wearing earpieces for easier communications. The security cordon around the King, Queen, and their children was tightened to the point where casual interactions with the public became rare. The most obvious result of the tragedy was the decision to move the Pahlavis away from the crowds and bustling streets of downtown Tehran. The Ekhtessassi Palace was too small anyway for the young family, and construction of a new guesthouse for foreign visitors was already under way in the fashionable neighborhood of Niavaran, to the north. Now the decision was made to transform it into a temporary residence for the Pahlavis until a new, more secure palace could be built elsewhere in the capital.

The Shah accepted these strictures without complaint, though he insisted he still drive himself everywhere. But there were to be no more incidents of the sort that used to give Colonel Djahinbini and his agents heartburn. "Once we were driving back to Saadabad from downtown," he recalled. "We entered a narrow street and had to slow down. We saw a big man running after a little girl. I saw His Majesty push the brake." He braked so suddenly indeed that they were almost rear-ended by the tail car following behind. The Shah leaped out of the driver's seat and started after the man. Colonel Djahinbini and his agents, who did not understand what was going on, also sprang into action. "I jumped out and said, 'Is there something wrong?'"

"Stop that man!" cried the Shah.

His bodyguards ran off, grabbed the culprit, and brought him back to where the Shah was standing. The young girl he had been chasing was in floods of tears.

"Why are you running after this girl?" the Shah demanded.

"She is very naughty!" replied the man, who claimed to be her father.

"But you are *big*!" protested the Shah, who had personal experience of childhood bullying. He began to lecture the man on the need to show kindness to his daughter.

Suddenly the father recognized who was talking to him. He became very emotional, begged the Shah's forgiveness, and promised not to punish his daughter once they returned home. The Shah accepted his assurance and left the scene. But once they reached Saadabad he asked Colonel Djahinbini to send one of his agents back to the girl's house to make sure the father kept his word. This sort of behavior unnerved the Shah's bodyguards and courtiers: the same King who had stopped to help a single child was now responsible for making life-and-death decisions that affected a kingdom.

HE WAS READY to show what he could do with his untrammeled powers. "I want to build a government that is based on democratic practice at the bottom," said the Shah, "although perhaps a better term is 'cooperatively based.' I know that my people are very individualistic and find it difficult to work with each other, but I am certain this can be overcome. It can be conquered, particularly now that the whole nation is behind it." In the spirit of making a fresh start, he installed in government a team of young technocrats and businessmen who he believed reflected his modern interests and outlooks. Because they were his appointees and owed him their careers, he felt more confident in the saddle. They shared his builder's instincts, his impatience with party politics, and his admiration for the great cultures of Western Europe. Like him, they wanted to get on with the job and see how far they could go with the resources of the state at their disposal. Ever alert to the rise of a new demagogue and potential rival, the Shah made sure none was able to develop an independent following among the people.

The new era got off to a bloody start, however, when in January 1965 Hassan Ali Mansur, the Shah's pick to succeed Asadollah Alam as prime minister, and the brightest of the young liberal reformers, was shot to death by Mohammad Bokharai, a teenager found carrying "a copy of the Quran and a picture of Ruhollah Khomeini." The police investigation revealed that Bokharai had been sent on a mission to kill the prime minister by the Coalition of Islamic Societies, the militant group that represented Khomeini's interests inside Iran. In his absence the coalition had absorbed the terrorist group Fedayeen-e Islam. The story behind Mansur's murder was typically Persian in its level of intrigue. His death had been ordered by a secret religious "court" composed of Khomeini loyalists. One of the judges was Seyyed Mohammad Hussein Beheshti, a special adviser on religious affairs to Prime Minister Mansur's very own Ministry of Education. When he learned that a death sentence had been passed, Khomeini approved the fatwa or religious edict that rendered it legal under Sharia law. With permission in hand, Akbar Hashemi Rafsanjani, a young clergyman loyal to the Ayatollah, and a future president of the Islamic Republic, handed the gunman his weapon.

The shooting of Hassan Ali Mansur was an act of revenge for the humiliation of Khomeini's exile, the prime minister's association with the White Revolution, and his role in pushing through the controversial legislation that granted legal immunity to U.S. military advisers. At the top of the coalition's list of thirteen targets for assassination was the Shah himself, followed by other senior regime officials. The objective of Khomeini's men was to decapitate the entire national leadership and provoke another religious uprising. The soldier who shot up the Marble Palace three months after Mansur's death was publicly accused of Communist affiliations, but he, too, was later revealed to be part of Beheshti's underground terror network.

Khomeini did not yet have a million martyrs willing to die for him, but exile imbued him with the irresistible aura of outlaw and man of God, two attributes highly prized by the Shia faithful, who saw themselves as victims of historic injustices dating back to the Battle of Karbala. The narrative of the "tyrant king" and "pious man of God" resonated with religious radicals. Ironically, in the months before he was shot Mansur had tried to persuade the Shah to end Khomeini's exile and bring him home in the spirit of national reconciliation. The Grand Ayatollah was not looking for favors, let alone a charitable compromise from a man he despised as a traitor: Mansur's liberal moderation suggested weakness that in Khomeini's view invited only contempt and a bullet.

SEVERAL DAYS AFTER the assault on the Marble Palace, Farah collapsed from nervous exhaustion. One night, hearing voices outside her bedroom, she crept onto the landing and stood in the shadows as a young man was brought into the downstairs lobby and forced to stand against the wall with his hands tied behind his back. He was a confederate of the gunman who had tried to shoot her husband. "I was filled with sadness and felt deeply sorry for him," she said. She watched as her husband came down, talked to him, and then escorted him into his office, where they conversed for an hour. The culprit was pardoned and let go.

Since the birth of her two children Farah had steadily increased her workload. "When I was first married, well, marriage is a big change in anyone's life so I was content with that for a year or so." But she was soon dissatisfied. "I had nothing to do. At times I just drove my car around Shemiran to kill time." Wearing a pair of jeans, she rummaged through palace basements "sticking my nose" into dusty hideaways that few had

ventured into over the years. She rescued valuable artifacts, started restoration work, and figuratively and literally let in the light after years of
darkness and neglect. The palaces were in a terrible state. "I remember in
the Golestan Palace, the Court had to borrow candelabras from the outside. The officer on duty at Saadabad was sleeping on the job."

After successfully tackling the family's living quarters, Farah decided
to carve out a public role for herself. She became patron of the national
organization that helped orphans and children abandoned by their parents
and supported national groups representing underprivileged youngsters,
the handicapped, the deaf, and the blind. Farah became a strong and early
proponent of mainstreaming the disabled into society by helping them
gain an education, skills training, and enter the workforce. At her behest,
sports facilities for deaf students were built in every major town. One of
her earliest causes had a transformative impact on how she saw her role
and how she in turn was seen by the people. She accepted the presidency
of the Lepers' Aid Association at a time when the Muslim clergy refused
to administer to lepers or even set foot in Iran's two isolated leper colo-
nies, a fact that did not escape Farah's attention. But even she admitted to
feelings of apprehension on the eve of her first visit to the leper center
near Tabriz. "For the first time I saw those ashen, disfigured, ragged faces,
and the deep distress in their eyes," she remembered. She brought cakes
and candy for them and was appalled when her guide, instead of presenting them to the lepers as gifts, tossed them on the ground so that they
were trampled in the dust. She broke away from her entourage and walked
into the crowd, touching the lepers, talking to them, listening to their
stories, and allowing herself to be touched in return.

In dispensing with protocol Farah broke the biggest taboo associated
with the disease. She convened doctors and specialists from around the
world and embraced the role of advocate for medical advancements in
the treatment and early detection of leprosy. Her husband consented to
her request to donate a large parcel of crown land on which was built the
world's first economically viable and self-sufficient leper community. With
the help of a board of trustees, and support from wealthy donors, the new
village acquired "all the facilities, schools, shops, even a theater, to the
point that the village was more advanced than some of the villages around
it. And the people from the other villages started coming to work with the
lepers. It was a *fantastic* place." Doctors traveled to Iran from around the

world to do facial reconstructive surgery and repair hands that had never opened. The Queen made periodic inspection visits and insisted on regular progress reports on improvements undertaken since her last trip.

Farah's encounter with the lepers taught her an invaluable lesson: "Now I could do more than sympathize; I had the means to act." She threw herself into her public duties with the gusto and optimism that epitomized the go-go atmosphere of Iran in the late sixties. Where her husband identified with the military, foreign affairs, and business interests, the Queen challenged old taboos through symbolic gestures. To erase the stigma associated with blood transfusions in a Muslim society, she allowed herself to be photographed donating blood. Deeply affected by the plight of burn victims in hospitals, Farah lent her name and prestige to Queen's University Hospital's special burns unit and signed on as the organization's patron and chair of the board. Together with her friend Lili Amir-Arjomand, she launched the Organization for the Intellectual Development of Children and Young Adults, which raised funds to build a network of children's libraries across the country. "We built libraries in public places like parks," Farah recalled. "I wanted libraries built that reflected the style of each city, and also to have writers write storybooks for children and designers illustrate them. To start production, I symbolically translated *The Little Mermaid* into Persian and drew some pictures like Disney cartoons." The libraries and books were free. By 1977 Tehran boasted 28 children's libraries, many located in the poorest neighborhoods in the city. A second initiative included sending 118 mobile libraries out into the provinces to educate children living in 2,400 villages. The children's libraries led to other free initiatives, such as children's concerts, poetry recitals, movies, and eventually the world-renowned Children's Film Festival. By the late seventies, Iran's success in reducing illiteracy attracted the attention of educators from around the world.

Farah had one major advantage over her husband in that she could move more freely around the country with a small entourage and minimal security. On occasion her old friend from childhood Elli Antoniades filled in as lady-in-waiting. She remembered these excursions as exhausting but exhilarating. One day Elli, by now the principal of Tehran's French school, received a phone call from the Queen asking if she could replace her regular lady-in-waiting, who had fallen ill. "When?" she asked. "Now," came the reply. "But I have to pack. I have no clothes." "Elli, there is no time. The car will pick you up in a few minutes. We will get you clothes when we arrive." But when the women arrived in the south their days were so jammed with engagements they had no time to shop for Elli's new wardrobe. "So at the start of each day I wore the clothes Her Majesty had worn the day before. But she is taller than me and . . . nothing fitted!" The two women tried to suppress their mirth during official engagements but at the end of each day once the door was closed they roared with laughter.

Farah returned home to be peppered with questions from her husband, who was curious to hear firsthand what was happening in the countryside. "His Majesty was always asking me about my day," she said. "Where had I been? Who had I seen? You know, at some point it was difficult because even in bed before sleeping we were talking about road building projects. His life was Iran. And progress for Iran. It was part of us."

IN OCTOBER 1967 an American visitor contrasted Tehran to the city he had first visited at the end of the Second World War. The Iranian capital was no longer "a sprawling city of one- and two-story buildings, where horse-drawn carts and donkeys clattered through ill-paved streets, and the municipal water supply ran through open gutters," he wrote in *National Geographic*. "Now I had spent a week walking the neat streets of a modern city, looking into shop windows full of electric refrigerators, gas stoves and television sets, and staring up at 16-story office buildings. And on the broad avenues where automobiles had been few, I had fretted through some of the most stupendous traffic jams the world has ever produced. Not that Tehran had lost all its old flavor. Vendors still crowded the sidewalks. Fruit stands offering grapes, melons, figs, and pomegranates took advantage of the shade cast by a modern skyscraper. The odor of roasting kebab floated from a hundred small food shops, and corner vendors offered glasses of tart pomegranate juice—fresh from an electric blender." Other foreign visitors were as impressed with the benefits of the Shah's economic and social revolution. "The beaches bounce with bikinis," said *Time*, "and teen-agers in Tehran have joined the transistor generation. The ancient, withered men of Yazd are being taught to read. In Qom and Bam, in Dezful and Gowater and 50,000 villages throughout Iran, 15 million peasants have been transformed, almost overnight in history's terms, from feudal serfs into freeholders whose land is now their own."

With internal security ensured and demand increasing for Middle East oil, Iran's economy in the late sixties took off with a 10 percent annual growth spurt that convinced American diplomats that the threat of social- ist revolution had receded. Per capita income doubled from $130 to $250 and at last a start was made to fight the twin scourges of poverty and igno- rance. Annual oil revenues surpassed $700 million, and 75 percent of the new wealth was channeled into big development and infrastructure proj- ects. For the first time, the Shah's 26 million subjects experienced a taste of real prosperity, with 98 percent of Iranian villagers now released from landlord control. The Shah and his admirers were convinced that the key to the boom was his style of authoritarian leadership. In the late sixties and early seventies, leaders throughout the developing world but particu- larly in Asia suspended constitutions, imposed censorship, and exiled or imprisoned their adversaries in the belief that Western-style democracy contributed to social instability during periods of economic reform. "Iran must first become an economically democratic society and then a politi- cally democratic society," the Shah insisted. "Shah is a kind of magic word with the Persian people," he told the *New York Times* in 1967. "If I were not the King of this country, I could never have implemented one- hundredth of what we've been able to do with the White Revolution. A dictator could not do it. The leader of a political party could not do it. But the King could do it."

The Shah believed that at least a decade of personal rule was required to strengthen the economy and broaden the base of the middle class. Once a conservative, moderate center was established, he could begin disman- tling the trappings of personal rule and quietly disengage from the politi- cal process. His confidence in his abilities and judgment soared along with the economy. He rebuked Iranian intellectuals, university students, and Mossadeq supporters who questioned his belief that the Iranian people were not ready for democracy. "When everybody in Iran is like everybody in Sweden, then I will rule like the King of Sweden," he declared. Nor did the Shah have patience for those who wondered whether the pace of reform was more than an ancient society could handle. He said he had no choice but to drive the kingdom as he drove his sports cars. "If you don't say to the Iranians run one hundred kilometers an hour, they wouldn't go five kilometers," he explained. There were "always ridiculous reasons" to explain delays. "And we have enough bad economics in this country! These are the reasons why I am pushing on and on, and every day I am going to push harder."

Many Iranians and most foreign observers agreed with the Shah that Iran had a long way to go before it became a stable parliamentary democracy. "The ignorance of rural Iran is incredible," said one American visitor in 1967. "One village elder, watching his first movie, ordered a feast prepared for all the actors, convinced that they could somehow step out of the screen and join him for a chelo kebab. In another village the audience wrecked the screen by giving chase to the villain of a Hollywood western."

The Shah understood that present conditions could not last forever. In the midsixties he was influenced by American ideas on modernization after reading a study positing that "by the year 2000 the world would be divided into industrial and agricultural countries, and by then it would be too late for the laggards to industrialize." This document became the blueprint and justification for the pell-mell industrialization of Iran within a single generation. "In the life of a nation you have only a few periods where everything gathers to make [swift progress] possible," said the Shah. "This is one of those periods. We have got to take the fullest advantage of that." He would not allow Iran to lose precious time by indulging in yet another ill-fated experiment with Western-style democracy. "We have *got* to catch up, and in a certain limited time."

Kennedy's successor in the White House, President Lyndon Johnson, encouraged and supported reform of Iran's economy and society, though the State Department's Bureau of Intelligence and Research warned that "the realities of the future will not include the indefinite prolongation of one-man rule; in some fashion that cannot yet be discerned, it appears likely that the Shah will confront a choice between allowing greater participation in government or seriously risking a fall from power." The bureau noted that "while there is no evidence that a conflagration is imminent, there is no room for complacency. . . . Though it enjoyed stability imposed from above and its short-term viability appears reasonably good so long as nothing happens to the Shah, Iran's future is clouded by hazards which could profoundly affect its political climate." Other observers noted the extent to which the security forces had strengthened their grip over Iranian society to the dismay of intellectuals, students, and the clergy who bitterly complained that independent thought and basic freedoms had been extinguished. The Shah "uses [parliament] mostly for window-dressing. All candidates must be approved by Savak, his powerful security police, and elections are arranged so as to give the Shah's Iran Novin (New Iran) Party an overwhelming majority of the seats. . . . The press is controlled, and all public criticism of the Shah is forbidden by law."

These concerns barely registered when in August 1967 the Shah paid a triumphant state visit to Washington. Five years earlier, Kennedy had interfered in Iran's internal affairs, foisted his candidate for prime minister on the Shah, and predicted the imminent demise of the Pahlavi Dynasty. Half a decade later, the president was dead from an assassin's bullet, American cities were torn by urban riots and civil rights protests, and Americans were deeply split over the war in Vietnam. The Shah made it clear that with security and prosperity established Iran had strengthened itself to the point where it could pursue "positive nationalism" and adopt a less deferential posture toward the United States. Speaking to the *New York Times* in September, the Shah confirmed "that our independent policy is now firmly established." He basked in the praise of Johnson, who lauded him as a visionary statesman. His effort to modernize his ancient country "beckons all the Middle East," said the president. "You are winning progress without violence and bloodshed—a lesson others have still to learn." Johnson approved the Shah's request to purchase two squadrons of advanced fighter jets. Diplomatic observers interpreted this as the first step in an ambitious plan that called for Iran to eventually replace Great Britain as the guardian of Western security interests in the Persian Gulf.

The Shah's decision to finally stage his long-delayed coronation in the autumn of 1967 was the surest sign yet of his confidence that he and his country had put to rest the bad old days of riots, assassinations, and revolutions. "It is not a source of pride or satisfaction to become King of a poor people," he explained. "So in the past I had felt that a coronation ceremony was not justified. Now I am proud of the progress we have made." He was the same age his father had been when he was crowned in 1926. He had turned seven that year, the same age Reza was now. He took delight in his young family. The birth of Farahnaz on March 12, 1963, coming so soon after the birth of the heir, had been a cause for great celebration. Father and daughter, both shy, developed a close bond. One evening, the Shah was presiding over a meeting of his ministers at Saadabad Palace when the door was pushed open and Farahnaz, three and a half years of age, cried out, "Daddy, it's time to come!"

The Shah pretended not to notice the interruption and continued with his presentation. Heads turned at the sound of a scuffle as the little girl broke free from her nurse and "ran the length of the chamber and tugged on the monarch's trousers, looking up at him brightly."

"Daddy, come now!" she insisted.

The Shah smiled, rose to his feet, and escorted his daughter out of the room "murmuring something about 'disgraceful behavior.'" While he was away the ministers chatted among themselves. They straightened up when the monarch returned but noticed that he was visibly relaxed. He was determined not to repeat the mistakes of his own childhood. Much to his wife's dismay, he indulged the children and seemed quite unable to discipline them.

CORONATION FEVER HAD been building for the past year. "This month, Iran will hold a blowout the likes of which few countries have ever seen," reported *Time* magazine. "The country is being shaken by a two-pronged revolution—social and industrial—that is bringing to the mass of its people the first real taste of prosperity in 6,000 years. . . . For seven roaring days and seven joyous nights, it will celebrate the coronation of the man responsible for it all." Earlier in the year, astrologers had encouraged husbands to make love to their wives so their newborns would receive a Coronation Day blessing and "hospitals all over Iran are expecting a population explosion on Coronation Day." Iranians were confident and optimistic about the future. "God bless His Majesty," said the chief of a village awarded a new water well, radios, and a refrigerator. "He has made our lives better."

To celebrate the milestone, the government opened thousands of new schools, hospitals, and big development projects that included Tehran's stock exchange, the Rudaki concert hall, and docking facilities in the Persian Gulf. The barbaric practice of hanging criminals in public squares was ended. Among the 4,811 convicted criminals pardoned by the Shah were the men who had planned the attack three years earlier on the Marble Palace. In Shiraz, the Queen inaugurated the first in a series of annual arts festivals that placed Iran in the forefront of the avant-garde arts scene and became a draw for foreign tourism. A performance by renowned violinist Yehudi Menuhin was broadcast to the nation from the ancient ruins of the palace of the Achaemenid kings. Museums around the world held exhibitions of Persian art. Europe's Telstar announced that its satellite would transmit the coronation live to a global audience of 270 million television viewers. Millions of lights decorated city streets so that from the air Tehran resembled a "box of jewels."

In recognition of his wife's hard work, and to emphasize that there was no going back to the days when the women of Iran hid from society, in September 1967 the Shah announced his intention to ask the Constituent Assembly to name Farah regent-designate in the event he died before their son reached his maturity. The symbolism of the gesture was unmistakable. The regency initiative was hailed at home and abroad as an important step in the advancement of women's rights in the Muslim world. Behind the scenes, however, it set off a fight led by court conservatives already uncomfortable with the Queen's high public profile and social activism. They opposed the idea of granting power to a young woman with liberal views and fought a rearguard action to defeat the measure. Within the cabinet, Ardeshir Zahedi spearheaded the opposition. Zahedi, now serving as Iran's foreign minister, had at one time championed Farah Diba's credentials as a suitable consort and assuaged concerns about the Diba family's ties to the Mossadeq clan. Now he worried that Farah's influence threatened to eclipse his own. During a meeting of the cabinet he declared his outright opposition to the regency bill. "I told the Shah it was foolish," he recalled. "The other ministers signed it knowing that without my signature it would never become law. No one liked the idea."

The Shah did not confront Zahedi over his objections but neither did he aggressively defend his plan to overhaul the Constitution. As was often the case in domestic matters where decisive action was needed, the Shah thought about it, hesitated, and gave conflicting signals in an attempt to placate both sides. Inevitably, this caused confusion and hurt feelings. The Constituent Assembly ultimately approved the change to the succession but noted conservative objections when it inserted an opt-out clause that allowed the Shah to name a new regent should he ever change his mind. If she did ever ascend the throne, the Queen would also be required to share power with an eight-person advisory council. But Foreign Minister Zahedi, who never recognized Farah's new legal status, regarded the regency as one of the Shah's most ill-advised and sentimental follies. Court Minister Asadollah Alam, who ran the Imperial court and kept a shrewd eye on events, was more understanding of Farah's liberalism, which he interpreted as the natural outgrowth of a sensitive nature and social conscience. "Long may her influence be felt; a valuable safeguard against the abuse of power," he wrote in his diary. "She alone has the ability to open His

Imperial Majesty's eyes to the truth. In this respect I run her a very poor second, but I do try my best to be truthful, which is more than can be said for anyone else at court."

IN THE SOFT autumn light of October 26, 1967, gilt carriages cantered past hundreds of thousands of cheering spectators on their way to Tehran's Golestan Palace, the fabled palace of the garden of roses. Hundreds of guests wearing black ties, gaily colored floor-length gowns, and diadems were already in place when shortly after eleven o'clock the Pahlavi princes and princesses entered the Golestan's great Salaam Hall, with its Naderi Throne encrusted with more than twenty-five thousand rubies, sapphires, and emeralds and embellished with images of lions, peacocks, and dragons. The Pahlavis were followed by the Shah's senior generals and aides-de-camp, bearing raised swords, flags, and the Imperial standard. Then, against a swelling backdrop of choral music, Crown Prince Reza entered to smiles and nods. The little Prince's parents had made him watch old newsreels of Queen Elizabeth II's coronation so that he could take a lesson from Prince Charles, whose behavior that day had been impeccable. Next to enter the grand hall was Queen Farah, who dazzled the assembly in a white silk gown, her hair worn up in her signature chignon, her swan neck adorned with her favorite emerald earrings and necklace. A fanfare of trumpets announced the Shah's arrival in the hall.

The coronation ceremony began with a prayer offered by Seyyed Hassan Emami, the Imam Juma of Tehran, who hailed the monarch's commitment to social justice and offered the King a copy of the Quran, which he kissed. "This could have been a ceremony at the court of Imperial Russia," wrote one observer. "[The Shah] buckled on a rich sword belt and a sword knobbly with gems. The soldiers put a gold and blue cloak round his shoulders and then they offered him the crown." "The Shah and Queen remained generally impassive throughout the ceremony," reported the *New York Times* correspondent, "but the Crown Prince fidgeted in his chair during his father's brief address. The Queen's eyes surveyed the audience of dignitaries, who were in full evening dress and long gowns, even though the temperature was in the seventies. Two hidden fans cooled the Shah and Queen during the ceremony, but the Shah perspired slightly under the hot lights of the cameramen. Princess Shahnaz, the Shah's 27-year-old daughter by the first of his three marriages, wept copiously during the ceremony."

The Shah meant to crown himself and his consort in the style of Napoleon and Josephine. He had already conferred on his wife the new title of "Shahbanou," or "King's Lady," to distinguish Farah from her predecessors. The Pahlavi crown had been fashioned for his father's coronation, and with more than three thousand diamonds and pearls it was "shaped rather like a wastepaper basket with a tail plume at its front." At the designated moment the Shah seized the Peacock Crown and set it on his head amid cries of *"Javid Shah!"* ("Long Live the King!"), and the roar of cannons from a 101-gun salute could be heard from one end of town to the other. Now the Queen approached the throne while her attendants fastened around her shoulders a twenty-six-foot-long green velvet train edged in white mink and studded with emeralds, diamonds, and pearls. She knelt before her husband on a pillow spun of gold thread while he pressed down on her chignon a crown of diamonds, rubies, and emeralds shaped like a sunburst and "as spectacular as a city in flames." Struggling to hold back tears, the first crowned empress in Iranian history had never looked more radiant. "It was the Queen and her son, indeed, who stole the show in the icing-sugar extravaganza of the mirrored coronation hall," observed the correspondent for the *Times* of London. "Queen Farah, cool, smiling and composed, wore her crown gracefully and unbent to the extreme of acknowledging her young daughter, Princess Farahnaz, who sat bouncing on her peacock blue chair throughout the half-hour ceremony. The Shah, by contrast, seemed to feel the weight of his ostrich-plumed scarlet and gold crown and the constraint of the tight-waisted uniform of Commander-in-Chief of the Armed Forces. He spoke in soft, almost breathless tones after his coronation, referring to his hopes that he and his wife and son would fulfill their responsibilities for the future."

At the conclusion of the speech "guns fired, bells rang, trumpets sounded, people shouted acclamations and a nationwide celebration began." The King, Queen, and Crown Prince Reza left the Salaam Hall, reported one guest, "ignoring the bows and curtsies that bent the audience like the wind does the wheat," to the accompaniment of a choir who sang the special coronation ode: "The King of Kings is wearing the crown. May you reign forever in the kingdom of [our] hearts." They processed through the grounds of the Golestan along a 150-yard red carpet, past sun-dappled rose gardens and dancing fountains to receive the acclamation of several thousand guests clustered in viewing stands.

From Golestan the newly crowned King and Queen rode back to the

Marble Palace in a gold coach specially built for the occasion by Viennese craftsmen and drawn by eight magnificent white Hungarian stallions. Lancers on horseback wearing silver Prussian helmets led the way as planes overhead bombed the procession route with 17,532 roses, one for every day of the Shah's life. "The crowds were enormous," reported the *Washington Post* correspondent, "mostly male and young and mostly shabbily dressed. The spectators cheered and clapped and in places were nearly out of control, trampling down trees as they surged. A few women set up the high ululation of the Muslim world. Bands played and whole battalions, drawn up in close order, saluted." The Pahlavis smiled and fluttered their hands in appreciation. "The procession moved at a walking pace through a city that had been decorated in the manner of a country fair but on an infinite scale. There were vast gaudy crowns, millions of electric bulbs, new fountains, triumphal arches made of hardboard and everywhere the green, white and red flag of Iran." The festivities continued until well after midnight, the mood on the streets joyous and exuberant. "The sleepless population either arranged parties, attended carnivals or simply took delight in roaming the streets, with or without vehicles, causing endless traffic jams," reported Tehran's English-language *Kayhan International* newspaper. "In the streets, and in the smaller hotels, all forms of dialects, from the south to the north of the country, could be heard. Farmers, who normally go to bed at dusk, were still on the streets by 1:30 a.m. this morning."

In the afternoon, the Pahlavis attended a three-hour military parade, and in the evening there was a banquet at the foreign ministry followed by a royal command performance of Iran's first scored opera at the Rudaki Hall, Tehran's gleaming new concert pavilion. At midnight the capital was the scene of a spectacular fireworks display. Even the Shah's severest critics, the intellectuals, were prepared to concede him a day in the sun. "He launched a revolution without killing the kulaks [wealthy peasants], and he rode out the cold war without becoming a satellite," conceded a Tehran university professor who admitted that he still opposed the Shah. "On balance, the price we're paying for so much progress—and you can toss in the price tag of the coronation—has so far been quite acceptable."

Foreign guests left Tehran deeply impressed by the pageantry and popular show of support for the monarchy. "It had been a dignified, rich and popular coronation," noted a British observer. "It was a morning of dazzling jewels that really were as big as pigeons' eggs, of innumerable diamonds, of heavy robes encrusted with gold pearls, of curved swords held high in the air at the salute," said an American present. "It was Byzantine in its remote magnificence. It was heavily military. It was the sort of occasion which when it happens causes people to say that it can never happen again."

7

ROYALS AND REBELS

Wake up! Pay some attention to reality and the
questions of the day.

—GRAND AYATOLLAH RUHOLLAH KHOMEINI

I always had in mind the Romanovs.

—QUEEN FARAH

In his place of exile a world away from the Ruritanian scenes of splendor unfolding in the Shah's capital, the old man was up before dawn and for the rest of the day kept a routine so exact that locals in Najaf liked to say they could set their watches by his daily walk to the holy shrine. After rising at five to pray, and breakfasting two hours later on cheese, bread, and nuts, Grand Ayatollah Ruhollah Khomeini spent the morning catching up on the latest news, reading books, writing lectures, and meeting with admirers and aides. The midday prayer was followed by lunch; a long nap; and more reading, writing, and meetings. The workday ended at five, when family members joined him for a half-hour stroll. After a modest dinner and evening prayers, then more reading and writing, the lights were dimmed at ten. "Even we were affected by his discipline," said one young admirer who later served as Khomeini's bodyguard. The Grand Ayatollah's rigid focus, work ethic, and modest diet were if anything reminiscent of the man he sought to destroy, and like the Shah he went to great lengths to conceal his true nature from the Iranian people, whom he also believed instinctively preferred strongman rule. "In private meetings," recalled his bodyguard, "he was very happy and joking. But at the same time, when he had public meetings he was stern and unsmiling."

Khomeini brooded and contemplated his future. "I do not know what sin I have committed to be confined to Najaf in the few remaining days of my life," he complained during his first bitter years in the dusty town. Living in a foreign country surrounded by Sunni Arabs, isolated from his admirers, shut off from everything he knew in Qom, the Grand Ayatollah referred to himself as "this old man who is spending the last moments of his life." The Pahlavi regime hoped that the longer Khomeini remained out of the public spotlight, the greater the chance he would fade from memory. Savak's Parviz Sabeti infiltrated his household with informers. General Nasiri informed the Shah that "the old shark has had his fangs pulled out." Now in his midsixties, the Grand Ayatollah faced the very real prospect that he would never set foot in Iran again, let alone live to see the destruction of the Pahlavi Dynasty.

Najaf's clerical establishment regarded Khomeini as an interloper and viewed him as an unwelcome troublemaker. Grand Ayatollah Mohsen Hakim, Shiism's paramount marja, made his feelings clear when he publicly snubbed the newcomer upon his arrival in Iraq. "Najaf, like Qom and Mashad, was a center of intrigue and gossip at the best of times," wrote Khomeini's biographer. "Religio-political rivalry is as intense among the Shia clergy as in any political party and sometimes borders on the childish, with grand ayatollahs refusing to speak to each other. With their lives of loyalty that resemble those directed by tribal chieftains rather than spiritual elders, the great Shia religious centers have always looked like a confederacy of fiefdoms."

During one of their rare encounters, Grand Ayatollahs Hakim and Khomeini debated the merits of launching a second rebellion against the Pahlavis and their White Revolution. In the Shia tradition there was no more epic religious narrative or morality play than the martyrdom of Imam Husayn and his family at the hands of the wicked Caliph Yazid at Karbala in AD 680. Hakim disputed Khomeini's claim that the Shah had become the new Yazid and that the ulama had a duty to lead a second revolt against the Iranian monarchy.

"If we staged an uprising and people suffered there would be chaos and people would curse us," Hakim warned. Though Khomeini had gained infamy for his leadership role in challenging the Shah, his fellow marjas still commanded greater support among the people.

"When we staged the uprising it only raised the esteem in which we were held," Khomeini challenged Hakim.

"What should be done?" replied Hakim. "We must balance our actions against the result. There is no point in sending people to their deaths."

Khomeini argued that deaths were *exactly* what the revolutionary movement needed. Martyrdom was to be celebrated and welcomed, not feared or discouraged. "We must sacrifice our lives," he retorted. "Let history note that when religion was in danger a number of Shia ulama stood up to defend it and a group of them were killed."

REBELLION OF A different kind was brewing in the palace.

Less than eighteen months after Princess Shahnaz was seen weeping at her father's coronation, the Shah decided his daughter was "full of crazy ideas," so crazy indeed that he questioned her sanity and threatened her with disinheritance. With her finely sculptured cheekbones as though carved from marble, her father's expressive brown eyes, and a striking physical resemblance to the ill-fated Hollywood actress Sharon Tate, Princess Shahnaz was as beautiful as she was restless. Her marriage to Ardeshir Zahedi had crumbled following the couple's return to Tehran after years abroad representing Iran in London and Washington. Ardeshir's rapid ascent through the ranks continued with his appointment as foreign minister. His former wife chose a very different course. Like so many young educated Iranians from well-to-do families, in the late 1960s Princess Shahnaz embarked on a quest for personal and spiritual self-enlightenment that led her to the great love of her life and the man many royalists would later blame for helping seal the fate of the dynasty.

Khosrow Djahanbani was the son of a respected former general who had served Reza Shah as the heir to one of Iran's great families. The Djahanbanis were related to the Qajar princes and princesses and circulated in the highest echelons of Pahlavi society. Khosrow's brother Nader was a dedicated air force pilot, beloved by his men, and so good-looking that he earned the moniker "the blue-eyed general." Khosrow, with his wild mane of coal-black hair, angular good looks, and penetrating eyes, cut an equally dashing if decidedly more mercurial figure. He returned home from several years spent studying in New York and affected the mannerisms, dress, and louche drug habits of a Greenwich Village hippie. His admirers and critics attested to his handsome, brooding charm but also his danger and arrogance. Djahanbani moved around town with northern Tehran's beautiful young things, the sons and daughters of prominent businessmen, public officials, and generals who dabbled in pseudo-Marxism, indulged in cocaine, hash, and heroin, and entertained utopian fantasies about throwing in their lot with the working class and joining the barricades for a republic that would presumably abolish their titles and privileges and take away their trust funds. In choosing Khosrow Djahanbani, Princess Shahnaz could not have taken a more unsuitable lover, though that was undoubtedly part of his allure. To her father's consternation, Shahnaz adopted Khosrow's lifestyle and financed the couple's habits with the stipend she received as his daughter.

Every effort the Shah made to separate the couple only strengthened the girl's willful determination to be with her lover. Djahanbani's conscription into the army backfired when he was court-martialed and imprisoned for a minor offense, so that by the early summer of 1969 the Shah's firstborn child could be found standing in line each morning outside Tehran's main prison awaiting the start of visiting hours. The Princess, who made no effort to cover her head or otherwise disguise her appearance, emulated her lover as she would a marja so that she no longer cared what people thought. When Djahanbani was transferred to a second prison, outside Tehran, Shahnaz exiled herself to Switzerland and wrote her father a letter declaring her intention to marry the convicted criminal. Matters came to a head in the first week of August 1969 when Djahanbani was released from prison to avoid public scandal. His lover returned from Geneva for one final attempt at winning her father's approval for marriage. On the evening of August 5, Alam instructed the Imperial Guard to prevent Djahanbani from entering the princess's residence until he had arrived to escort her to Niavaran to see her father. To his fury, he learned the released felon had already made his way inside the house. Alam ordered the commander of the guard to enter the property and expel Shahnaz's lover, by force if need be. But Shahnaz told him over the phone that if Djahanbani was taken away she would join him. Alam begged her to avoid confrontation and scandal. She finally backed down but only on the condition they spend another hour in each other's company. Alam agreed and in the event was kept waiting until three in the morning for the lovers to finish.

The next morning the exhausted Alam received Djahanbani at Saadabad. To his surprise, the young man promised "to abandon his hippyfied ways and face up to reality." Father and daughter held a separate meeting elsewhere in the palace and their reunion also went better than expected. The Shah assured the Princess that he loved her and promised not to stand in the way of her happiness even if her heart was set on marriage. All he asked was that she show respect for her family, whose public reputation was threatened by her scandalous behavior. Like Khosrow, Shahnaz agreed to change her lifestyle. The two older men were relieved at the outcome, sure that the two youngsters had sobered up to their familial responsibilities. But six weeks later, following a lovers' quarrel, Shahnaz took an overdose of sleeping pills. She was revived just in time, and the couple was reunited.

Court Minister Asadollah Alam asked the question on the everyone's mind: "Where on earth is this love affair going to lead us?"

IN JANUARY AND February 1970, while the Shah, Queen Farah, and their children left Iran for an extended forty-day ski vacation in Switzerland—far longer than usual—Grand Ayatollah Ruhollah Khomeini delivered a series of thirteen lectures to seminary students in Najaf that laid out his blueprint for the overthrow of the monarchy and the establishment of an Islamic state.

In his lectures, known colloquially as the *velayat-e faqih* ("guardianship of the jurists"), Khomeini challenged the conventional belief within Shiism that Islamic religious scholars should remain above the social and political fray and that the laws of Islam "remain in abeyance or are restricted to a particular time or place" until the return of the Hidden Imam, twelfth successor to the Prophet Mohammad. Khomeini bolstered his case by pointing out that the Prophet had not only founded a religion but also led a government and commanded an army. By this logic, the only individuals qualified to make, interpret, and implement laws were the mutjahids (religious scholars). They, and not any king, or president, or constitution, were the only acceptable guardians of the state until the Hidden Imam returned to usher in the end of days. Any form of government that was not Islamic in character was therefore illegitimate and must be annihilated: "We have in reality, then, no choice but to destroy those systems of government that are corrupt in themselves and also entail the corruption of others, and to overthrow all treacherous, corrupt, oppressive, and criminal regimes."

Khomeini ferociously rejected the 1906 constitutional settlement and declared his intention to bury it once and for all. In that vein he expressed disgust with the mainstream moderate religious establishments head-quartered in Qom, Najaf, and Mashad. By discouraging their followers from entering politics the marjas and grand ayatollahs were little more than "pseudo saints" and "negligent, lazy, idle and apathetic people." "Wake up!" he sneered. "Pay some attention to reality and the questions of the day. Do not let yourselves be negligent. Are you waiting for the angels to come and carry you on their wings? Is it the function of the angels to pamper the idle?" True Islam, in Khomeini's rendering, was not moderate or mainstream or quiet—anything but. True Islam "is the religion of militant individuals who are committed to truth and justice. It is the religion of those who desire freedom and independence. It is the school of those who struggle against imperialism." He all but challenged his eager young followers to return to their seminaries, overthrow their teachers, and launch a cultural revolution.

> [The ulama] must be exposed and disgraced so that they may lose whatever standing they have among the people. . . . Our youths must strip them of their turbans. . . . I do not know if our young people in Iran have died; where are they? Why do they not strip these people of their turbans? I am not saying they should be killed; they do not deserve to be killed. But take off their turbans! Our people in Iran, particularly the zealous youths, have a duty. . . . They do not need to be beaten much; just take off their turbans, and do not permit them to appear in public wearing turbans. The turban is a model garment; not everyone is fit to wear it.

Khomeini's plainspoken delivery, rough street language, and call for violence resonated with young militants in the late sixties and early seventies, a time when university campuses and high schools around the world were in open revolt against authority. Among Iran's educated youth population—prime beneficiaries of the Shah's reforms—the air was thick with talk of revolution against his authoritarian, pro-American regime. Iran was an old country with a youthful population. In 1970 an estimated 54 percent or 14.5 million Iranians were aged under twenty-four years and thanks to the White Revolution were on average the most literate generation in the country's history. As their families moved through the ranks of the middle class, and as they gained an education, many young Iranians who a generation earlier might have toiled in the fields had the luxury of focusing on broader philosophical issues and indulging in politics. They were inspired by events in the region. Though they were not Arab they could hardly be unmoved by the staggering setbacks their fellow Muslim brethren had suffered in recent years. For many Muslims, Israel's victory in the 1967 Six-Day War shattered the belief that Western ideas held the key to a prosperous and just future. With the old panaceas—nationalism, socialism, and secularism—identified with failure and humiliation, their search for solutions led many young Muslims, Sunni and Shia alike, back to the mosque and the old ways.

Disillusioned with the West, young students and intellectuals rediscovered Islam with all the fervor of first-time love. A new generation of leftist scholars, most notably Iran's Ali Shariati, helped bridge the gap between Marxism and Islam by explaining that the Prophet Mohammad had also emphasized social justice, brotherhood, and opposition to tyranny. Shariati's interpretation of Islam as a revolutionary belief system proved a drawing card for throngs of young liberals and leftists who associated the Pahlavi monarchy with dictatorship, state repression, censorship, and foreign interference. Iranian students blamed the United States for propping up corrupt regimes throughout the Middle East to ensure a plentiful supply of cheap oil, support for Israel, and containment of the Soviet Union and Arab regimes. Their teachers encouraged their cynicism by reminding them of the American role in the overthrow of the martyred Mossadeq, which had ended Iran's messy postwar experiment with democracy and paved the way for the Shah's royal authoritarianism.

The real radicalization of Iranian youth took place outside Iran's borders. Each year the Shah spent $50 million to send his country's best and brightest to the United States and Western Europe to learn the skills needed to modernize Iranian society. The students' time in America coincided with the explosive events of the late sixties, when the United States was rocked by urban riots, social movements, street protests, and political assassinations. Caught up in the spirit of people power, the students returned home to a still deeply conservative Muslim society where strict censorship was enforced, drug traffickers went to the firing squad, and secret police informants sat in their classrooms. In 1970 the U.S. embassy was concerned enough about the emergence of a leftist fifth column to conduct a study of Iranian youth opinion. "The liberal states of Western Europe and North America are measures by which young Iranians judge themselves and their society," it concluded. "Thus, as elsewhere in the world, most of the educated youth in Iran dislike living in what they see as a totalitarian society. They deeply desire the civil liberties which are standard in the United States and other Western nations; they are annoyed that their newspapers are censored and controlled, their activities subject to secret police scrutiny, their movements (particularly in and out of the country) under heavy control, and the free public expression of their personal freedoms forbidden. They regard these aspects of Iranian society and government as a direct creation of the Shah."

Young, politically astute Iranians admired Ruhollah Khomeini as the only public figure who had stood up to the Shah and paid the price for his principles. Though they knew very little about him, the young idolized Khomeini as an Iranian Che Guevara, imbuing him with a leftist revolutionary aura based on their own naive hopes for a better tomorrow. The Iraqi authorities who kept the Grand Ayatollah under observation were more apprised of his true nature. Iraqi intelligence chief Sadoun Shakir informed his French counterpart, Count Alexandre de Marenche, that Khomeini was "a terrible character" with the personality traits of a "medieval tyrant." Shakir passed along a report of a disturbing incident that had recently involved the Grand Ayatollah and a neighbor's child.

> One day, a child of his family had a fight with a neighborhood youngster. [Khomeini] wanted the boy who had dared raise a hand to his offspring to be put to death.

BEFORE HE BECAME the public face of Savak, Parviz Sabeti earned his law degree at the University of Tehran. Bright and exceptionally well-read, with ambitions to enter political life, at twenty-two he went to work for the security organization as an intelligence analyst in the hope it would serve as a springboard to enter government. His intelligence and acumen so impressed his employers that within five years he was appointed to head the agency's political reporting unit. "Our task was not only to fight the opposition but to fight injustices and corruption within the system," he said. "The cycle of popular grievance led to actions [by the security forces] and then counter-actions [by the opposition]. We had to break the cycle."

In the aftermath of June 1963 Iran's senior security officials reorganized Savak with the goal of anticipating and preventing another bout of revolutionary unrest. The Iranians accepted an Israeli recommendation that they merge the separate offices responsible for collecting and processing intelligence. The next year Sabeti was put in charge of the new Office of Anti-Subversion, which fell within the jurisdiction of Savak's powerful Third Directorate, headed by General Nasser Moghadam. Moghadam was the same officer who had tried and failed to persuade Khomeini not to deliver his Ashura speech. He reported directly to General Nasiri, who had replaced General Pakravan as Savak's new chief, and both men enjoyed reputations as hard-liners within the security forces. Moghadam's Third Directorate was responsible for domestic security and for monitoring the activities of subversive groups as well as farmers and workers. Separate directorates were devoted to the National Front and its Islamic offshoot, Mehdi Bazargan's Liberation Movement of Iran; the Kurdish minority; other minority separatist groups, including Arabs, Baluchis, and Turks; Iranian students abroad; domestic religious radicals; and the Fedayeen and Mujahedin terrorist groups. Khomeini lived in exile, but Sabeti regarded him as a domestic threat and kept tabs on him, too, infiltrating his household with informers who garnered information on who he saw and what he said and wrote.

Savak agents gathered intelligence on subversives but also on officials whose behavior and activities they believed posed a threat to public confidence. Sabeti and Moghadam were particularly concerned about the corrosive effects of corruption. Years earlier, Prime Minister Fazlollah Zahedi had warned the Shah that in the absence of a strong parliamentary executive the monarch would be held personally responsible for scandals and failures. To prevent that from happening Savak monitored the business activities, financial dealings, friendships, and sex lives of members of the Imperial Family in addition to government ministers, senior military officers, business executives, the ayatollahs, and poets, writers, playwrights, and entertainers. Government ministries were infiltrated with informants and subjected to investigations. The head of state was not immune from Savak's prying eyes. When Sabeti discovered that the Shah was seeing women in a safe house near the palace, he took action. "I often used to see the Shah driving to this house [near Niavaran] at three in the afternoon," he said. "I started asking around and soon found out what was going on. My concern was security. I thought the house was too exposed, so I made sure security in the area was tightened."

The Shah made certain that the intelligence service remained in loyal hands. Nematollah Nasiri, born in 1910, had first made the acquaintance of Crown Prince Mohammad Reza at the prestigious Officers' Academy.

Later, he served as a lieutenant with Hossein Fardust, the Shah's confidant since childhood, and it was Fardust who selected him to help guard the royal palaces when political unrest boiled over in the early fifties. Nasiri played a key role during Operation Ajax, when he was arrested on August 15, 1953, while trying to serve Prime Minister Mohammad Mossadeq with his letter of dismissal. The Shah rewarded Nasiri's loyalty by promoting him to the rank of three-star general and appointing him to lead the national police. In June 1963 it was Nasiri who enforced Alam's shoot-to-kill order that earned him the title "Butcher of Tehran." Two years later, when the Shah swept aside his father's advisers, Nasiri received the Imperial warrant to replace General Hassan Pakravan as head of Savak. Nasiri was loyal to a fault, though not regarded as especially creative or original in his thinking. That suited the purposes of the Shah, who had no intention of hiring a Mark Antony to run his secret service.

Nasiri had a taste for the finer things in life. "He parlayed his power into wealth and illicit gains not only for himself and his allies, but for his family," wrote one critic. He earned a fortune in real estate and invested in industrial farms with Hossein Fardust, once his patron and now his deputy at Savak. While Sabeti and Moghadam rooted out corruption, their superiors enriched themselves at the public trough. It was hardly a surprise that Nasiri went to great lengths to protect the names of his business associates and others cashing in on Iran's economic boom. "Any time I wrote reports on the Shah's family and friends," complained Parviz Sabeti, "Nasiri wouldn't take them to him." The general transformed Savak into a personal empire whose grip extended deep into every sector of society as well as into government ministries, embassies, and universities. In the early seventies he personified the agency's Orwellian reputation as all-knowing, all-seeing. But no spy agency could see or know everything, particularly when the men at the top were censoring themselves.

As a boy, Hossein Fardust had been selected by Reza Shah as a companion for his son, and he had accompanied the young Crown Prince of Iran to boarding school in Switzerland.

When the Shah reshuffled Savak's top leadership in 1965, he appointed his oldest friend, Fardust, to the highly sensitive post of deputy director to make sure he had his own "eyes and ears" in the agency. Fardust's job was to report to the monarch each day with summaries from the different directorates. One biographer described him as "the ultimate 'clearinghouse' for all reports [and he] had his hands on the pulse of the country." Fardust struck most observers, including Queen Farah, as a rather strange and mysterious fellow, the sort of courtier who lurked in the shadows and prowled the palace corridors, scuttling into and out of anterooms, and entering and leaving meetings without feeling the need to say a word to anyone. His influence was such that everyone at court, from the Queen and the commanders of the armed forces on down to the lowliest palace courtier, believed that Fardust's opinions and instructions carried the full weight of the Shah and were to be carried out accordingly. Like his friend General Nasiri, Hossein Fardust was not especially smart, bright, or cultured. He shambled when he walked and was "notorious for wearing the same shirt and shoes for long stretches of time." Despite his attempts at modesty, however, Fardust's business dealings with Nasiri made him a very wealthy man.

The Shah refused to hear a word said against his old school chum. He dismissed as slander the rumors and reports that Fardust was in the pay of either the Russian or the British intelligence services. "They can't even let me have one friend," he grumbled. He trusted Fardust to the point that he told his wife to consult him if she ever needed to corroborate information or could not obtain satisfaction elsewhere in government. The Queen was aware of the stories that Reza Shah had selected Fardust to accompany her husband to Le Rosey and then decided he didn't like him. Reza Shah had discouraged his son from making friendships, with the predictable result that he grew up to be a generally terrible judge of character. The Shah had a tendency to push away smart, capable people who genuinely had his best interests in mind and surrounded himself instead with men such as Fardust and Nasiri, feckless mediocrities who exploited and manipulated their proximity to the throne for self-interest. In the case of Fardust, the viper at the breast nursed a bitter, vengeful grievance. He had never forgotten his origins as the son of a poor soldier taken away from his parents at a tender age to serve the most powerful family in the land. One interpretation is that he associated his royal service with a form of psychological imprisonment. "He grew to despise all those whose birthrights granted them advantages in life," wrote Abbas Milani. "Envy became a permanent part of his emotional vocabulary. Yet he spent nearly all his life serving someone whose very right to rule—and to lord it over him—was an accident of birth." From an early age he had learned to tell the Pahlavis what he thought they wanted to hear. The first lies he told were as a boy

on the tennis court—he fibbed when he assured Reza Shah that his son
the Crown Prince was his superior in tennis. His habit of covering up, dis-
sembling, and deceiving escalated from the tennis court to the palace.
This, then, was the twisted personality of the dark soul who presented the
Shah with his daily portrait of conditions inside the country. In his personality and motives, Hossein Fardust had all the makings of a traitor.

Perhaps it was not surprising that when the Shah read the Third Directorate's periodic reports on corruption and policy failures he was often
too quick to blame the messenger. Since childhood he had avoided dealing with unpleasantness and bad news to the point where he tore references to the Arab invasion of Persia in the seventh century out of a school
textbook. In the palace he dismissed as spoilers the few brave officials who
tried to bring evidence of mismanagement and corruption to his attention.
"Why is Savak pushing so much negativity?" he complained to Fardust.
"Go and see what is wrong with Sabeti and Moghadam. What are their
family backgrounds like? Why are they the only ones complaining?" He
was so used to receiving optimistic assessments of Iran's progress from
Nasiri and Fardust that he wondered if their two underlings suffered from
psychological problems. "I didn't blame His Majesty but Fardust [for not
telling him the truth]," said Sabeti. "I told Fardust that he needed to
explain to His Majesty that it was not our job to tell him good news." Fardust's solution was typical: he advised Sabeti that in the future he should
edit his intelligence reports so that any bad news was balanced alongside
the good. But even then the Shah complained that his reports were too
negative, sniping to Court Minister Alam that Savak's most senior and
talented intelligence analyst was most likely a CIA plant. Alam did nothing
to allay his paranoia. He, too, feared and resented Sabeti—agents from the
Third Directorate compiled damaging material on his own extralegal
commercial investments and properties.

Yet by age thirty-five Parviz Sabeti had become Iran's untouchable
man. No one could match his breadth and depth of knowledge on conditions inside Iran, the regime's strengths, and its vulnerabilities. His intelligence on opposition groups, terrorist networks, and dissidents was
unmatched. His files contained the most intimate secrets of anyone of any
consequence at court, in government, the mosques, and in the bazaars.
The Shah knew this and warily kept Sabeti, the regime's "Mr. Security," at
arm's length—the two men met each other on only one occasion—but he
knew how much Nasiri depended on Sabeti's skills as an analyst to suc-

ceed. Sabeti emerged from the shadows on three separate occasions in 1969 and 1970, when he appeared on national television to explain the activities of the Third Directorate to the Iranian public. Television viewers were struck by Sabeti's telegenic looks, sharp intellect, and soft-spoken demeanor—he was no one's idea of a ruthless secret police operative. The decision to raise Sabeti's public profile had another quite remarkable and unintended consequence.

"Farah knew me from television," said Sabeti. "The people around her asked her to call me. I told her, 'I want to see you. But not without His Majesty's permission.' She asked, he approved, and we met for the first time in 1970 at Nowshahr on the Caspian. Our meeting lasted five hours."

THE DIARY OF Court Minister Alam revealed that on May 9, 1970, he accompanied Queen Farah on a day trip to Mashad. She had a complex relationship with Alam, her husband's oldest, devoted, and most indispensable adviser. Farah was painfully aware that it was Alam who arranged the Shah's afternoon trysts with young women in a safe house near the palace. She bridled at his sycophantic behavior and worried that her husband, shy, isolated, and surrounded with flatterers, risked losing touch with the realities of daily life in what was still a poor country with serious social and economic challenges to overcome. Alam was loyal to the point of servility. "He is very, very independent," he once said of the Shah. "You know, a man who is missioned by the gods, how can he choose a model for himself?"

On the flight back to Tehran the Queen asked Alam if she could talk to him alone. Though she blamed him for pandering to her husband she still appreciated his loyalty, discretion, and political acumen. She also knew he shared her concerns about the behavior of the Shah's relatives. "In general I get the impression that Her Majesty fears for the future, and not without cause." Farah was sensitive to the widespread perception that her husband's brothers and sisters used their titles and connections to advance their own interests. "In general," the U.S. embassy observed in a devastating 1970 assessment, "young people in Iran, like other Iranians, find the numerous members of the Royal Family, other than the immediate family of the Shah, a shadowy and vaguely distasteful group. Innumerable rumors and occasional substantiated accounts, which are in circulation in Iran, produce, particularly among Iranian youth, a general image of parasitism, constant corruption, and personal laxness."

The wives of Reza Shah had between them produced seven sons and four surviving daughters. "The Shah had too many brothers and sisters," said Fatemeh Pakravan. "That's not good for a king. Not good at all." He kept them firmly in their place, restricting their ability to play any role in public life. "We never spoke politics in family gatherings," confirmed Prince Gholam Reza, the Shah's half brother, who was respected for his involvement in the army and sporting life. "I was His Majesty's Special Inspector for the Army. This position was important at the beginning as I could report directly to His Majesty, but in the last few years this was changed. I kept the title but had no real impact." His wife, Princess Manigeh, a Qajar princess, was not allowed to hold official patronages, which were reserved solely for Queen Farah and the Shah's sisters. The prince recalled that as children the Pahlavi siblings were raised in separate households so that relations between them "were never shown in a warm way. We had no casual gatherings together. It was always a bit official between us. We avoided talking Iranian politics as it could be considered interfering in government decisions or influencing this or that. I'm not exaggerating by saying *not a word*." The prince recalled that Princess Shams maintained her own social circle and kept to herself, while Princess Ashraf "had the best parties and was a very interesting lady. There was always very good conversation and she had very bright mind. We always had a very good time in her place." He was personally closest to Prince Ali Reza who was "as a twin to me. We loved each other and made lots of things together. His loss [in a plane crash in 1954] for me remains very painful. Prince Abdul Reza was very sportive and a very good hunter, very elegant and refined. Princess Fatemeh was very sociable, down to earth and sportive. She was also a helicopter pilot. Prince Hamid Reza was fun and smart. When he was younger he would hide under the car from his own guards. He liked to go out and have fun—he had a good sense of humor."

Denied any official role, the Shah's brothers and sisters entered into commerce; jockeyed for proximity to the throne; and lobbied for favors, appointments, and increases in their stipends. The Shah's view was that largesse was a small price to pay for keeping them out of trouble. If his siblings enjoyed the perks of status, then all the better. Dispensing favors and money was the Shah's way of keeping his fractious siblings onside but also led to jealousies and resentments. No member of the Pahlavi family aroused more public animosity than Princess Ashraf. The CIA described Ashraf as one of her brother's "most ambitious supporters and one of his major liabilities during most of his career." After her brother consolidated power in the midsixties the Princess's interests moved from politics to business and she entered into a series of highly lucrative business partnerships to build residential and commercial developments. The Princess "has not hesitated to use her influence to obtain government contracts for her friends or acquaintances willing to pay her a fee. In recent years . . . she no longer demands a pay-off from contractors but only comments that she would be happy to be able to rely on them should it ever be necessary." Though reports of her involvement in the drug trade were based on "scanty evidence," they too had become "a fixture in the catalogue of charges against the Pahlavis."

The CIA report was based on the usual Tehran tittle-tattle and contained few if any proven facts and even less original analysis. Talk of the Princess's influence was vastly exaggerated, not only in government but also in her charity work. Much of the enmity directed at female members of the Pahlavi family in particular originated with men troubled by their influence in a conservative Muslim male-dominated society. Everyone who knew Ashraf attested to her humor, passion for life, and above all her devotion to her brother. Her extensive patronage of charities and philanthropies mainly reflected her staunch support for women's rights, a cause that stirred resentment from the ulama. The Princess built a powerful network of loyalists within the regime who kept her informed at all times. Yet there was no doubting her tenacious, opinionated personality or her business acumen. Her intrigues against the Queen, whose liberal tendencies she distrusted, caused so much havoc that in the late sixties her brother, who usually retreated from personal confrontations, sent her into exile to cool off. She returned to find her influence at court greatly diminished and Farah in the ascendant.

Princess Ashraf's first, brief marriage, to Ali Qavam, had produced a son, Shahram, described by U.S. intelligence as "a wheeler-dealer" invested in twenty holding companies that ranged from transportation, nightclubs, and construction to advertising and distributorships. The holding companies were set up, the CIA reported, to provide cover for "quasi-legal business ventures." Prince Shahram's "most flagrant act of irresponsibility," according to the agency, was a smuggling operation that involved "the sale of national art treasures and antiques, notably the gold artifacts from Marlik, a prehistoric archeological site of great significance." According to U.S. intelligence, the loot was ferried out of Iran in his mother's name to evade inspections by customs officials. Ashraf was stunned and humiliated when she learned of the ruse and gave orders to put an immediate end to it. The companies were wound up and her affairs were put in order, but the Princess's reputation with the Iranian public never recovered from the scandal, and her standing with her brother and sister-in-law was further undermined.

The Shah was so angered by his nephew's behavior that he briefly considered jailing him and then sending him into exile. He relented only in the face of emotional pleas from his sister. The Queen was not nearly so understanding or forgiving. She understood the concerns of middle-class Tehranis who worked hard, played by the rules, and were appalled by official greed and corruption, and she worried that her sister-in-law's family threatened the Crown Prince's chances of ever taking the throne. By now Farah was under no illusions about the life she had married into. When she accompanied her husband to the Soviet Union the Pahlavis exchanged knowing glances when their Russian escorts made them linger in the private apartments of the ill-fated Czar Nicholas II and Empress Alexandra Feodorovna, shot, bayoneted, and clubbed to death with their children by the Bolsheviks in 1918. The Shah understood that the Russians were playing a psychological game and pretended not to notice. His wife followed his cue but couldn't help identify with the star-crossed couple. Looking around the room, she noted that they had left their possessions behind when the revolutionaries came for them. The trip made an indelible impression. "I always had in mind the Romanovs. I remember thinking, 'If this happens in Iran, I never want them to say that we took everything away.'"

Queen Farah's decision to sound out Court Minister Alam during her trip to Mashad in May 1970 marked an important step in her political maturity. Her dissatisfaction with Alam's response to her concerns about corruption meant that when she returned to Tehran she decided to follow the advice of trusted friends and place a telephone call to Parviz Sabeti, whose appearances on television explaining the role of Savak had also drawn her husband's close attention. Sabeti agreed to meet with her but only on the condition that she first obtain the Shah's approval—he wanted the monarch to know exactly what was going on.

* * *

PARVIZ SABETI FLEW to Nowshahr on the Caspian Sea, where the Pahlavis spent the later part of each summer on vacation. He found the Queen in a state of great anxiety. "She was obsessed with corruption," he recalled. They met alone. The Nowshahr residence was small but somehow Sabeti never caught a glimpse of her husband.

For five hours Sabeti briefed Farah on his findings, providing her with damning evidence of corruption within the Imperial Family and at the highest levels of Pahlavi society. "I spoke against corrupt courtiers and family members," said Sabeti. He rattled off the list of names in his usual cool, perfunctory manner and spared no one. By the end of their exhausting session Farah grasped the magnitude of the problem and the powerful forces arrayed against her. The scales had finally fallen from her eyes. The Queen was stunned. "She cried hard," remembered Sabeti. "She asked, 'How can my son become king if this is going on?'"

After their first encounter the Queen kept in close touch with Sabeti, phoning him to arrange for the delivery of reports and seeking his advice. She also used their back channel to intercede on behalf of citizens who contacted her office claiming they had been falsely accused of dissident political activities. Sabeti was generally amenable to her requests, though they bickered over specific cases. More meetings followed. Over the next several years they held at least two lengthy sessions specifically devoted to corruption, and on both occasions the Queen again wept in despair. But Farah was also galvanized into action. She started asking questions and pursued her own lines of inquiry. She showed a closer interest in the workings of the Imperial Court and government. Another time, Farah asked Sabeti to prepare a report on the corrupt business practices of a prominent leader of the Tehran trade guild who happened to be a protégé of both Hoveyda and General Nasiri. She said she intended to raise the matter with her husband in the hope that he would take action. "It took three days to write," said Sabeti. "I gave it to her. It was a very long report." The Queen handed the report to her husband, who, unbeknownst to her, gave it first to Hossein Fardust, who then presented it to General Nasiri. The next thing Sabeti knew, Nasiri summoned him to his office and in the presence of one of Fardust's aides informed him point-blank that the contents of the report he had compiled were categorically false. "It's all wrong," said Nasiri, and sent him smarting back to his office.

Two days later, Farah telephoned Sabeti. She said her husband had embarrassed her by discounting the corruption allegations in their entirety. "Mr. Sabeti, the report you gave me was all wrong," she said. He could tell by the tone of her voice that she was distressed. They met the next day, and Sabeti explained to her what had happened. The confidential report he had prepared for her eyes only had been handed over to his superiors—the same men he had accused of malfeasance. "Now, I have to say it is all wrong," he patiently explained. Realizing what had happened, the Queen wept with frustration and offered to help Sabeti secure a meeting with her husband so he could present the evidence in person. She telephoned him from a small resort area beside a lake outside the capital. "His Majesty has offered to see you," she said, sounding optimistic. "We will be together." Sabeti insisted that he see the Shah alone because "He won't let me talk frankly about his sisters and brothers with you in the same room as me."

The Queen helped Sabeti prepare for the meeting, which they both hoped would focus the Shah on the need to confront his brothers and sisters and purge his inner circle of corrupt elements. But in the end the Shah backed out of the meeting. Shy, averse to bad news, and surrounded by loyalists who had their own reasons for encouraging his distrust, the monarch declined his wife's request to meet alone with Sabeti. In so doing he missed a golden opportunity to learn more about the corruption that was already starting to gnaw away at public confidence in the regime.

PRINCESS SHAHNAZ MARRIED Khosrow Djahanbani in the winter of 1971 at Iran's embassy in Geneva, an out-of-the-way location dictated by the bride's embarrassed father. The Shah instructed Alam to prevent the transfer of his daughter's financial assets out of the country and to bar the groom from ever showing his face at court. Iranian law stipulated that drug offenders face the firing squad, and the couple's hedonistic lifestyle made him appear a hypocrite. "As her father I may be able to forgive my daughter her mistakes, but as Shahanshah of Iran I can never accept a good-for-nothing as my son-in-law," he said. "It would imply that I am willing to condone his morals." Princess Fatemeh represented the Pahlavi family at the wedding ceremony. The couple, wearing elegantly tailored caftans, their long hair falling loose over their shoulders, wept, smiled, and held each other during their vows. Shahnaz had never looked more lovely or more happy.

In the months leading up to his marriage, Khosrow Djahanbani had moved into the house of his fiancée's cousin Prince Patrick Ali, the Shah's nephew by his late brother Prince Ali Reza, who had died in a plane crash in 1954. The young prince dabbled in religion and was under the influence of a fundamentalist Islamic preacher who saw an opportunity to make a spectacular conversion. Patrick Ali was not alone in turning to religion. In 1971 U.S. diplomats reported "an unexpected growth of interest in religion among a small segment of youth in Iran, especially those studying and teaching in the universities." The Islamist Union was strong on all campuses "and attendance at the Tehran University Mosque is continually increasing." The embassy concluded that youth interest in religion was "basically conservative in nature" and a backlash against the White Revolution, which emphasized the use of American and European ideas, technology, and personnel. "A small number of students have also embraced religious orthodoxy as a means of criticizing the Shah and his method of rule in Iran," read the report. "Criticism of the Shah which might be unacceptable in a secular context, can often be voiced under cover of an interest in strengthening the role of religion in Iranian life."

Savak generally left the mosques alone. With Khomeini in exile and his lieutenants underground or in prison, and Iran's mainstream ulama solidly anti-Communist and in receipt of generous state subsidies to reward their quiescence, there seemed little reason for the secret police to harass the clergy. That made the mosques even more attractive to leftists, who saw them as sanctuaries for political activity. Through their contacts with the mullahs some students did rediscover and embrace religion. Mostly they were allies of convenience who could offer shelter and support while they fomented plans to overthrow the Shah and replace the monarchy with a republic. Both sides set aside religious and philosophical differences for the greater good of the struggle against what they saw as injustice and repression. "The banning of political parties, the turning of the Parliament into a club for sycophants, the muzzling of the press, and the continued underdevelopment of trade unions and other associations, deprived society of its natural means of self-expression and political activity," wrote an Iranian political commentator. "This led to a gradual return to the mosque as a multipurpose institution that could counter the inordinate expansion of the state as a super institution."

The U.S. embassy decided that Islam did not pose a threat to the Shah or to Iran's essentially pro-Western orientation. If anything, the "conservative, inward looking, and antiforeign basis for the revival of interest in religion among the young educated classes" actually precluded it from becoming a "force for change in the country" because the country was moving inexorably toward a future that was modern, liberal, and secular. "It is necessary to re-emphasize that this growth in interest is on a small scale and affects an extremely limited percentage of the student body. It is interesting, however, as an indication of one of the possible paths reaction against Westernization and modernization can take in Iranian society."

8

THE CAMP OF GOLD CLOTH

We stand on our own feet.
—THE SHAH

Ah yes, Khomeini. One does what one can.
—IMAM MUSA SADR

Let's go and visit the halls. We're going to pay a visit to the students."
The Shah's casual suggestion to his startled entourage was
made on the grounds of Pahlavi University in Shiraz. Having decreed 1971
the "Year of Iran" to mark the 2,500-year anniversary of the Iranian monarchy, he traveled to Shiraz to open a sparkling new sports facility on the
grounds of the university. The White Revolution was under way, income
from oil revenues was surging, and dozens of world leaders were expected
to arrive in October to attend the anniversary festivities outside Shiraz
at Persepolis. More than two thousand schools, three dams, highways,
mosques, a vast irrigation system, and one of the world's largest pumping
stations were on target for completion. Resources including a municipal
library were lavished on Tehran. The Shah opened a new housing complex to serve hundreds of poor families in the southern suburbs and whose
amenities included arts and sports facilities. During a stroll through the
University of Tehran's new central library, which housed more than six
hundred thousand volumes, and a collection of priceless Persian manu-
scripts, he asked a university official, "What status does this library, as one
of the world's institutions of this kind, give us?" His escort replied that the
university was now one of the best equipped of its kind. "We've given them

a good hiding, haven't we?" the Shah said, beaming. As ever, he was determined to show *them*—the Europeans and the Americans who had once dominated Iran—that his people were catching up.

In the countryside, where land reform was in full swing, millions of farming families now lived on their own plots. "Of course my life is better," said a peasant living in a village near Shiraz. "Ten years ago, I could neither read nor write, nor could my wife. Our children were not in school and they worked here on the land with us—another man's land. I got one-fifth of the fruit of it each year, if I was lucky. Sometimes there wasn't much fruit. Now our farm belongs to us. We have machines for work. All my children have gone to school. My eldest daughter has married an engineer in the city. My wife and I vote for our village council. We can read and write because a young man from the Education Corps [the national service group of young men drafted for military duty who are assigned to adult education] taught us to." Women were eligible to vote and stand for election. They could divorce their husbands and veto them taking a second wife. Idealistic young volunteers from the universities joined the literacy and medical corps and ventured into the countryside to teach reading, writing, and health care.

The Shah was at the peak of his powers and popularity. Despite the bitter criticism leveled at him by left-wing intellectuals and religious radicals, in 1971 he enjoyed broader public support than at any time in the previous three decades. Sixty thousand had recently turned out to cheer his visit to the Holy Shrine of Imam Reza at Mashad, the same spot where his father's troops had once fired on crowds to enforce the ban on hijab, or Islamic dress. In 1971 the CIA described him as "a worthy successor to earlier monarchs, of whom some have been notable—Cyrus, Darius, Xerxes, Abbas to name a few. His is a formidable personality, which he employs skillfully to advance Iran's interests in such matters as increasing oil revenue and acquiring sophisticated military equipment from hesitant sellers." The Shah was "a confident ruler, who knows what he wants and how to get it" and "all in all, a popular and respected king." The agency did express concern about "soft spots, actual and potential" in the overall picture. He was isolated from the realities of daily life in Iran and from different viewpoints: "Few of his ministers or officials are ready to express to him an opinion differing from his own; virtually none are able to tell him he is wrong about something. Even foreign ambassadors cringe before the Shah's responses in official presentations which displease him." Most

Iranians were too preoccupied with making money "to fuss much about politics," though that was likely to change and "there are a few signs of ferment—after a decade of political torpor." The Shah's isolation would not lessen as he grew older: "The chances he will fail to comprehend the intensity of, say, a political protest movement, are likely to grow. Hence, so will the miscalculation for dealing with it."

Despite the general image of peace and prosperity, among middle-class Iranians there was rising impatience with authoritarian rule and criticism of the secret police "and the monarchy itself, particularly since extensive corruption is associated with the royal family." The Shah's suppression of legitimate political activity had pushed the opposition underground and caused younger activists to abandon hope of peaceful reform and take up arms. On February 8, 1971, a group of poorly trained, lightly armed insurgents attacked a gendarmerie post at Siakal on the Caspian. The arrest and execution of the thirteen culprits was followed by the revenge killing of the army's special prosecutor and a series of tit-for-tat assassinations and shoot-outs in southern Tehran neighborhoods between the security forces and armed militants. The CIA's view was that the Shah was likely to remain in power for "the foreseeable future" though it cautioned that "Iran's fundamental vulnerability lies in the unique concentration of power in the hands of the Shah. He has over the years deliberately cut down any leaders who have shown signs of acquiring an independent political base. He talks of giving the responsibility to elected representatives but shows no sign of actual movement along these lines. He hopes to hand the throne to his son; he may be able to do so." But he couldn't rule forever and his departure from the scene "will usher in change, perhaps involving tumult and chaos."

Tumult and chaos were the last things on anyone's mind on the bright morning of April 28, 1971, when the Shah made his impromptu stroll over to Pahlavi University's student halls. Usually unsmiling and taciturn, today the monarch was "obviously happy, almost radiant," remembered his escort Chancellor Hushang Nahavandi. He was all the more cheerful knowing that his officials dreaded exactly this sort of spontaneous gesture. They usually preceded his arrival to ensure that the facilities he inspected were orderly and the people he met were loyal. He waved aside his officials' security fears and walked on. His face lit up as he ventured onto the grounds. The architecture, he told Chancellor Nahavandi, was ideal because it was "modern, but so suited to the climate and the surroundings—so Iranian!" He expressed his hope that one day the university would be "the Persepolis of our times."

The Shah and the chancellor entered a dormitory and started up the stairs. In the Iranian tradition the Shah was "in his own home, wherever he may be," observed Nahavandi, and the two men knocked on the first door they encountered. Two students were in the room, surrounded by books and cups of tea, one sitting on the floor while his friend leaned against a wall. The Shah's appearance stunned them into silence. "We've come to ask for your news and how you are," he politely inquired. "It's about time for your exams. You're getting ready for them, aren't you?"

The student who had been seated on the floor stood up, started weeping, and in the tribal custom knelt at the Shah's feet and gripped his legs. His friend took the monarch's hand and touched his shoulder. Everyone was overcome with emotion.

The Shah asked them about their studies. He applauded them for studying science, a profession he saw as essential to Iran's development, and asked them about their families, where they were from.

By now news had spread throughout the dormitory of the Shah's arrival. Excited students thronged the hallway and soon the chant went up, *"Javid Shah! Javid Shah!"*

After a few more words the Shah bade the students farewell and ventured into the corridor, where he shook hands and exchanged greetings. Students converged on the dormitory from around the campus, some still in their pajamas. They cheered and called out their support. The Shah smiled, waved, and urged them to go back to class.

"We want to come with you!" they cried. "Thank you for coming to see us."

Downstairs, the Shah greeted the dignitaries with a sardonic aside. "You see," he said, "we're still alive."

Cynics might dismiss the Shah's public receptions as staged, but no cameras were present to record his encounter with the students at Pahlavi University: at the first sight of their king they had melted in his presence—won over by his modesty, self-effacement, and politesse, they had dropped to their knees. The royal magic still worked.

THE PERSEPOLIS CELEBRATIONS were the inspiration of Shojaeddin Shafa, an Iranian scholar who eleven years earlier had first proposed the idea of celebrating two and a half thousand years of Persian monarchy. The Shah approved the concept and established a planning committee with a budget. But the unrest and financial constraints of the early sixties, followed by the great national crusade to implement the reforms of the White Revolution, led to a nearly ten-year delay, and it wasn't until the summer of 1970 that the Shah announced his intention to host "the most wonderful thing the world has ever seen." It was from Persepolis that Darius had ruled the ancient world, and a pageant there would "rewaken the people of Iran to their past and reawaken the world to Iran."

The Shah liked the idea of building a tent city in the desert to house his foreign guests. He blanched at the cost but eventually assented in the face of Court Minister Alam's persistence and flattery. Envisioned as a contemporary take on the royal encampment built by Francis I, who hosted England's Henry VIII in 1520 at the Field of the Cloth of Gold, Persepolis appealed to the Shah's sense of history, romance, and grandeur. But it was only after Queen Farah accepted patronage of the Celebrations Council that she learned that the design and construction of the Tent City had already been outsourced to French companies. To speed up the planning process, on his own initiative Alam had contracted Jansen of Paris to design and build the tents, Maxim's to provide catering, and Lanvin to dress officials and guests. Sensitive as ever to public relations concerns, Farah reminded the council that the whole point of the celebration was "to prove that the times we are living in now, the Pahlavi era, is a period of renaissance for Iranian civilization." The idea that Iranians would pay foreigners to plan their own national event "went against my Iranian sensibility," and she anticipated a backlash from foreign media. Though she made an impassioned plea to scrap the contracts, the majority of the council stayed loyal to Alam and accepted his argument that it was too late to change course. Farah doubted Alam's excuse that Iran lacked the expertise to stage the event in one year. His older generation of Iranians, she believed, had an inferiority complex when it came to their own culture, having been raised to assume that "whatever was European was good, noble, beautiful and praiseworthy. They thought that Iranian things were ugly, mean and open to condemnation." Privately, she seethed. "Of all the tasks that fell to me in preparation for the festivities," she wrote, "coping with that mishap was the most difficult and the most depressing, for just as I had predicted, a wave of acerbic criticism about expenditure on luxuries slowly arose from the West."

The Court Ministry stumbled again when it announced that the price tag for Persepolis came to a staggering $100 million. Alam failed to point out that the sum included the cost of new construction projects such as rural schools, tourist facilities, roads, and other infrastructure projects. The actual cost of the weeklong festivities came to $22 million, of which one-third was covered by generous donations from the Iranian business community, one-third was paid for by the Court Ministry, and one-third was rolled over from the budget of the Celebrations Council, which had a ten-year reserve to draw on. The Court Ministry's inept handling of public relations presented opposition groups with a priceless opportunity to tarnish the Shah as a cruel dictator who preferred to dine on foie gras while his poorest subjects went hungry. In a society that thrived on conspiracy theories and was prepared to believe the very worst about its rulers, wild rumors soon spread that the true cost of the event had soared as high as $300 million. The Shah bridled at the criticism. "Why are we reproached for serving dinner to fifty heads of state?" he snapped. "What am I supposed to do—serve them bread and radishes?" He had a point— Jacqueline Kennedy had hired Jansen to redecorate the White House, and she had not faced this sort of personal criticism. But his defensive attitude showed how out of step he was with the toned-down modesty of the early seventies. Four years earlier, on the eve of his lavish coronation, he had been lauded abroad as a benevolent and progressive king. Now he was criticized for indulging in a Bourbon-style extravaganza while international aid agencies still supplied eighty thousand Iranian mothers and children with powdered milk. Tehran lacked a proper sewer system, one-third of children admitted to hospitals in the capital suffered from malnutrition, and cholera remained a persistent threat.

The celebrations drew the attention of young socialists who had fled over the border and made their way to Palestinian terrorist camps in Iraq, Lebanon, Libya, and South Yemen to receive weapons training and learn how to plant explosives and stage bank robberies and hijackings. An attempt had already been made to kidnap U.S. ambassador Douglas MacArthur II outside the grounds of the American embassy in November 1970. The incident at Siakal three months later raised the dreaded prospect of a terrorist attack on the Shah's golden city in the desert. Hamid Ashraf, the sole survivor of the original guerrilla cell, evaded capture to mastermind a series of bank robberies that raised funds to buy weapons and earned him the cult status of a modern-day Robin Hood. The regime responded in kind by harassing, arresting, and detaining hundreds of suspected radicals, extremists, and dissidents but also many moderate critics of autocratic rule. In late September, on the eve of the celebrations, four armed men staged a clumsy bid to kidnap Princess Ashraf's errant son Shahram Pahlavi on the streets of downtown Tehran. Though the prince escaped with minor abrasions, a parking attendant who ran to his aid was shot and killed. "Theoretically the guerrillas must have hoped to impose top-level negotiations—humiliating for even a less autocratic regime—in which the prince's release would have been contingent on that of the rumored 600 to 1,000 political prisoners detained in recent months," reported the *Washington Post*.

Determined to prevent more attacks, the Shah's security advisers established the Anti-Terrorist Joint Committee, a special extralegal body specifically set up to combat terrorism and antistate subversion. The joint committee's leadership included the heads of Savak, the gendarmerie, military intelligence or G-2, and the national police. Working in complete secrecy, these officials made the momentous decision to determine the fate of individual detainees and captured terrorists outside the court system. In some cases that meant approving the use of force during interrogations. The joint committee was structured to ensure a measure of collective responsibility among the regime's top security officials. Detainees were not taken to Evin Prison, where political prisoners were normally held, but instead to a special holding facility at the national police headquarters for their initial interrogation, from where they were transferred to Evin. Members of the joint committee took care to shield the head of state from the methods used to extract information. The Shah was informed of their deliberations on a need-to-know basis and apparently believed Nasiri's explanation that only psychological pressure was applied to inmates. His fear of bloodshed and his record of pardoning assassins and plotters were well known to Nasiri and the others, who regarded him as far too soft-hearted to understand the sort of unpleasant measures required to crush an insurgency.

Torture was not new to the Iranian experience. Dark tales had always swirled about the rumored bloodlust of Iran's kings. According to legend, Shah Abbas reportedly "kept a retinue of cannibals . . . and when someone angered him he would turn to the cannibals and say, 'Eat him,' which they would promptly do." In 1794 Shah Agha Mohammad Khan's troops pillaged the city of Kerman and reputedly had the male population blinded and their wives and daughters raped and enslaved. Torture was a violation of the teachings of the Prophet and the holy book. "God shall torture in the next world those who have tortured in this world," decreed Mohammad. Yet his admonition had not stopped Persian religious courts at the turn of the twentieth century from approving the use of "an array of corporal punishments. . . . They gouged out eyes. They amputated fingers, feet, and ears. They hanged, decapitated, strangled, impaled, disemboweled, crucified, hurled from cliffs, buried alive, and drew-and-quartered. Most common of all, they flogged the soles of the feet in a process known as *falak*." Yet systematic torture had not been employed in the prisons of Reza Shah in the 1930s, and his regime had still enjoyed internal stability. At that time the police administered beatings to common criminals, though political prisoners and disgraced government officials were generally treated with leniency. It took the feverish, paranoid onset of the Cold War in the late forties for political extremists on the far left and right to resort to torture. Abuses were reported in Iranian Azerbaijan during the Communist rebellion at the end of World War II, and also during the unrest of the early fifties political detainees had been routinely abused. Pro-Mossadeq loyalists had thrown young Ardeshir Zahedi in prison, strapped him down, and beaten him so savagely that he suffered crippling spinal injuries and a lifetime of chronic pain.

Still, the creation of the Anti-Terrorist Joint Committee signaled the start of something new and disturbing in Iran—the introduction of state-sanctioned torture. Though the Shah was not aware of the most extreme forms of interrogation, and though the regime considered itself at war with fanatics, bomb throwers, and revolutionaries, as head of state he bore ultimate responsibility for any suffering caused and any deaths that resulted.

AT ELEVEN O'CLOCK on the morning of Tuesday, October 12, 1971, the boom of a 101-gun salute echoed across the vast windswept plain at Pasargade, outside Shiraz. The Shah had brought his family, government officials, generals, and tribal leaders to this remote desert place to honor the founder of empire, Cyrus the Great, before traveling to the Camp of Gold Cloth, some twenty-five miles away at Persepolis, where Cyrus's grandson Darius had ruled. For the Shah, who as a boy had savored tales of Cyrus's epic rise to the pantheon of greatness and resolved to revive the splendors of the Persian Empire, this moment marked the symbolic high point of his thirty years on the throne. He believed that he had succeeded where his father and dozens of other kings had failed by erasing past humiliations and consigning several hundred years of reversals and defeats to the dustbin of history. Television viewers thought his voice shook with emotion when he stood before the tomb of Cyrus wearing the uniform of commander in chief, his gold braid and ribbons of medals and decorations ablaze under the desert sun, to deliver a heartfelt eulogy to the architect of the world's first great empire.

"O Cyrus," the Shah intoned, "great King, King of Kings, Achaemenian King, King of the land of Iran. I, the Shahanshah of Iran, offer thee salutations from myself and from my nation . . . the Iranian flag is flying today as triumphantly as it flew in thy glorious age; the name of Iran today evokes as much respect throughout the world as it did in thy days; today, as in thy age, Iran bears the message of liberty and the love of mankind in a troubled world and is the guardian of the most sublime human aspirations. The torch thou lit has never died in stormy times." His concluding words burst forth like an agitated thunderclap: "Cyrus! Great King, King of Kings, Noblest of the Noble, Hero of the history of Iran, and the world! Rest in Peace, for we are awake, and we will always stay awake!" "With that," wrote the *Washington Post*'s Sally Quinn, "a huge sand storm, a good omen in Persia, arose in an abrupt funnel and hovered for a few minutes, then blew away."

Standing behind him, with Crown Prince Reza at her side, the Queen looked on with pride and trepidation. Wearing a traditional white and green silk gown handsewn by seamstresses in Baluchistan, elbow length white gloves, and her diamond and emerald tiara, Farah had turned to cigarettes and tranquilizers to conceal the strain of months of planning and relentless criticism. Her rail-thin figure attested to severe weight loss. Several days earlier she had spoken to the *Washington Post*'s Quinn, who described the Queen as looking "quite thin, drawn and tired. Her fresh makeup did not hide the circles under her eyes." Farah was alternately defensive and defiant. "People are quite right in their criticism," she conceded. "The problem was that the plans for the festival were starting to be made 10 years ago. And I was not involved in the beginning. I came in only because they said they needed me and then it was too late. . . . We would have done the interior decorations of the tents in Persia and the design could have been done in Persia but it was all so rushed. Everything happened at the last moment and I just didn't have a chance to see to it. There were so many more important things. And also it was a committee point of view. I tried to get them to see it my way." She lit up one of her favorite Winston cigarettes and looked down at her hands. "You have to accept your destiny. It's no good to dream of a life you might have had. You have to be happy the way you are. The strain and the mental and moral fatigue are overcome by the satisfaction of knowing you have achieved something. I guess you just have to develop inside you a kind of philosophy."

Her husband, by contrast, was in an ebullient mood. On the flight back from Pasargade, the Shah saw crowds gathered outside the gates of the Bagh-e Eram Palace in Shiraz and ordered his pilot to set the helicopter down. After alighting he stalked off into the streets of Shiraz, to be greeted by thousands of cheering locals. The Pahlavis and their aides strolled as far as the grounds of Pahlavi University, where the Shah had enjoyed himself so much back in the spring. After a half-hour inspection of the press center, where a thousand journalists from around the world were already filing their first stories, the couple returned to Bagh-e Eram in time for a cocktail reception at sunset to honor the world's leading scholars in Persian history and culture. But the Shah found the crush of admirers an ordeal and was disconcerted at the absence of security. "This is a fine place for a murder," he grimly confided to one guest. "Little by little, the guests backed the rulers against the palace wall and they slipped inside where they had a tea while their guests peered in at them," reported the *New York Times*. "Then they were off again in their helicopters—back to their tent in Persepolis and then on to the sound-and-light spectacle in the mountains above the ruins."

HE WAS NOT physically present, but as dawn broke over Persepolis on the morning of October 13, 1971, the chilling echoes of a familiar voice made itself heard.

Grand Ayatollah Ruhollah Khomeini could not resist the opportunity to shade the Pahlavis' big day. From his place of exile in Najaf, Khomeini issued a statement that for the first time called for the abolition of the Iranian monarchy, an institution that he deemed incompatible with Islam. Even as dozens of world leaders jetted into Shiraz, Khomeini furiously denounced "a regime founded on oppression and thievery whose only aim is to satisfy its own lustful desires—only when it is overthrown can the people celebrate and rejoice." Khomeini referred back to the events of June 1963, when he sensationally claimed that fifteen thousand innocents had been mowed down in the two days of unrest. His Iran was a country where the flower of Iranian youth were tortured and murdered and where virgin girls had "boiling water poured on their heads. . . . Nobody's life is safe." The story of the Persian monarchy was a black tale of oppression. "The crimes of the kings of Iran have blackened the pages of history. It is the kings of Iran that have constantly ordered massacres of their own people and had pyramids built with their skulls. . . . Monarchy is one of the most shameful and disgraceful reactionary manifestations." The Persepolis celebrations were "abominable" and he advised Muslims "to refrain from participation in this illegitimate festival, to engage in passive struggle against it, to remain indoors during the days of the festival, and to express by any means possible their disgust and aversion for anyone who contributes to the organization or celebration of the festival."

The Grand Ayatollah said he would rather die than live through the shame of Iran's rape at the hands of the Pahlavis. He called on 150,000 Iranian religious students and scholars to launch a revolt against injustice. "The crimes committed by this tyrannical regime and the acts of treachery against Islam and the Muslims have robbed me of all peace," he lamented. The reigning monarch was like a "beast . . . who pays no attention to the condition of the people or to the ordinances of the law— such a man lives like an animal. A ruler who fits this description and wishes to rule over the people and the nation in accordance with his carnal and bestial desires will produce nothing but disaster."

BACK AT THE Persepolis campsite, Princess Grace of Monaco was explaining the daily whirl to William McWhirter of *Life* magazine: "And then, of course, everyone meets informally at the club for lunch." "Calling cards and small gifts were sent around the neighborhood on small silver trays," said McWhirter, "and who called upon whom didn't seem to present a problem of protocol. King Constantine of Greece, for example, 'just popped in' to see Princess Grace and her husband, Prince Rainier." The Grimaldis had flown into Shiraz and were enjoying the royal roundabout in the Tent City with their friends. The Monegasque royals were among more than sixty heads of state in attendance at the "party of parties," the biggest gathering of world leaders in recent history. Others who made the trip included the Emperor of Ethiopia, the kings and queens of Denmark, Greece, Norway, Jordan, and Nepal, the Grand Duke and Duchess of Luxembourg, and the presidents of Romania, Russia, Yugoslavia, Turkey, and Pakistan.

The Shah was delighted with the turnout but miffed that the heads of state of the major Western powers decided to stay away. President Richard Nixon accepted the advice of his ambassador, who warned that logistics and security were problematic. France had reaped millions in business from the affair, but President Georges Pompidou turned down his invitation when he learned that mere presidents would be seated well below the salt. "If I did go, they would probably make me the headwaiter," he huffed. Emperor Hirohito of Japan sent his regrets. "The Queen does not go on international jamborees," sniffed Britain's ambassador, though his predecessor, Denis Wright, later admitted that Downing Street had been furious with the Shah for drumming up anti-British sentiment in Iranian newspapers during protracted negotiations over the Royal Navy's impending withdrawal from the Persian Gulf. "Why should we, having all this abuse hurled at us in the press, bring our queen out just to please the Shah?" To add insult to injury, heir to the British throne Prince Charles had refused to interrupt his naval training to fly in. The Shah had to settle for Prince Philip and Princess Anne, who arrived in predictably foul temper. "What's the panic?" they barked at photographers who mobbed them at the airport.

The Camp of Gold Cloth consisted of three large tents and fifty-nine lesser tents surrounded by fifteen hundred imported Cyprus trees, fifty thousand carnations, and "acres of other floodlit flora including great carpets of petunias and marigolds." The tents were laid out in a star formation, not unlike a pleasant retirement community in the Florida panhandle, with five avenues branching off and each named after a different continent. This snowbirds' nest, however, was surrounded by barbed wire and an electronic monitoring system and patrolled by hundreds of soldiers bearing submachine guns. "The entire area looks like the Berlin Wall," noted one visitor. The planning committee had considered every worst-case scenario. The tent windows were bulletproof and the canvas had been treated to withstand fire and desert gales up to seventy miles per hour. For the past several months workers had carefully swept the encampment site clear of thousands of poisonous snakes, scorpions, and lizards. The foreign press gawped over the details. "The entire tented city was brought from France on 120 planes, including four planes just for Maxim's Restaurant alone," reported the *Washington Post*'s Jonathan Randal in a feature article that he later conceded was his way of "pissing on the Shah's party." "All the butter, cream, eggs, pheasants, veal, etc., will be flown in each day," said *Time*. "The planes used for all this shuttling are Iranian Air Force planes (originally American C-130s). Peasants in nearby villages may have been impressed—but not exactly pleased—that the government spent $50,000 on fifty Lanvin-designed uniforms for the royal court, each requiring one mile of gold thread." The fifty tents constructed to house the Imperial Family and their guests "were completely air-conditioned and furnished with Baccarat crystal, Ceralene Limoges china and Porthault linens. Providing the trappings kept Paris merchants—who supplied everything—busy for a whole year. Bimonthly flights of aircraft and convoys of trucks that made the overland trips from Paris with relays of drivers transported the wares to the desert."

After settling into their desert quarters, the Shah's illustrious guests went door knocking to greet their neighbors or headed over to the club tent for lunch and a martini. In one instance they literally bumped heads when King Constantine II of Greece collided with his father-in-law, King Frederik IX of Denmark, as they both knelt down to pick up a dropped bouquet. Frederik's run of bad luck continued when he was mistaken for an impostor and assaulted by an overzealous Savak agent. The guard's suspicions had been aroused when he saw "a rather dowdy man" try to enter the club tent; when challenged to produce identification "the man went through his pockets, shrugged and started to walk into the club tent." The guard grabbed the intruder and yanked him away from the door, "only to be told by a horrified bystander than the man was the king of Denmark." Out in the ruins of Darius's old palace, eighty-year-old Emperor Haile Selassie shuffled around in his suspenders calling out for his pet chihuahua, Cheecheebee, who had escaped her leash and run off in a diamond-studded collar. One guest who kept a low profile was Nixon's representative: U.S. vice president Spiro Agnew stayed indoors battling a nasty case of what his Iranian hosts politely termed "the Shah's revenge."

On the evening of October 14, the Shah hosted a grand banquet in the dining tent, entry to which was gained through a scarlet reception room hung with twenty plastic chandeliers. First in the receiving line was King Frederik who after greeting the Shah and Shahbanou turned around and bellowed, "Does anyone know where the hell I have to go?!" "The reception room for the arrivals was totally silent except for the loud howling of the sand storm which suddenly blew up in the desert and was rocking the tent back and forth and rattling the plastic chandeliers," remarked one guest. "There was no music at all and the effect was deadly." Then as the wind picked up outside the tent "the monarchs and heads of state [started] pushing and shoving each other to get inside," so quickly indeed that the official greeter lost his head and announced Spiro Agnew as the representative for Afghanistan. The uncomfortable silence was broken by a familiar warble heard floating over the receiving line. "At last, a woman in a decent dress," cried television personality Barbara Walters when Christina Ford, the statuesque wife of Detroit auto mogul Henry Ford II, entered wearing a suntan and diamonds and little else, her barely there modesty covered by a "kind of swimsuit halter top and low dipping back."

The blue damask dining hall was arranged with a two-hundred-foot-long serpentine-shaped head table designed to create the illusion that each monarch and president was on equal footing when Court protocol dictated that they most certainly were not. Branching off from the head table were another thirty-six tables that seated thirteen apiece. The Shah entered to the strains of Mozart with Queen Ingrid of Denmark, consort of King Frederik, on his arm while Farah towered over her companion, the diminutive Emperor Haile Selassie. "Most [guests] had remarkably little to say to one another, at least before the wines were served," reported the *Los Angeles Times*. "Most remained wooden faced." As the high desert winds picked up outside, more than a few anxious eyes peered up at the chandeliers swaying overhead. "When Marie Antoinette said, 'Let them eat cake', she could never have dreamed of this performance," sniffed one of Maxim's catering staff. "The conspicuous consumption of this thing," rapped a Western diplomat, "is simply shocking in a country such as this."

The banquet of the century lasted five and a half hours and was followed by a spectacular *son et lumière* light and fireworks show that lasted into the early morning hours. At its conclusion the grounds were unexpectedly pitched into darkness when the light operator forgot to turn on a switch. For a minute or two everyone sat in embarrassed silence. The Queen, her nerves frayed by fear of a terrorist attack, turned over her shoulder and rounded on Court Minister Alam, who was relishing his role as grand master of ceremonies. "Whose foolish idea was it to have these fireworks?" she remarked. "There is *nothing* wrong," he briskly retorted in a voice loud enough for everyone around them to hear. "Everything has gone *exactly* according to plan." If the Shah was offended by his servant's tone of lèse-majesté he did not let on, nor did he bother to defend his wife's honor. As usual, he sat in silence.

The following day, after a restful afternoon, the Pahlavis and their guests trooped over to view a grand pageant representing eras in Iran's history since 500 BC. They sat on a dais in a single row that extended along the perimeter of the Persepolis archaeological ruins and for ninety minutes under a blazing sun watched as twenty water buffalo, seven hundred horses, and two thousand costumed men marched past the Shah, who took the salute accompanied by martial music. "The setting was spectacular," reported the *New York Times*. "Men in Achaemenian gold and scarlet uniforms stood high on the ruins. Trumpets sounded in the hills. Cavalry troops on matching black horses were followed by foot soldiers in link armor. Oxen pulled copies of mobile battlements. The men on 26 camels wore plumes. At least two sailing vessels motored by." The Russian president in particular could have hardly missed the parade's militarist theme. "After 25 centuries Iranian soldiers once again march past the upright pillars on this vast plain, this monument to the age-old grandeur and glory of Persia," the Shah declared. He wanted all the leaders assembled to understand that the honor of Iran had been restored and that after centuries of slumber the Iranian people were back on the world stage and ready to assume a leadership role.

From Persepolis and Shiraz the party moved on to Tehran, where on Saturday the Shah inaugurated the Shahyad Monument, whose intricate latticed archways were intended to firmly anchor the Pahlavi Dynasty to the Sasanian Empire, whose achievements he admired so much. The next day the Imperial Family opened Tehran's new one-hundred-thousand-seat Olympic stadium, which had already been selected to host the 1974 Asian Games.

THE PERSEPOLIS FESTIVAL scandalized the ulama, who interpreted it as a deliberate attempt to whitewash Iran's Islamic heritage. Iranian student leaders chimed in from exile, sardonically congratulating the Shah for making their job much easier by bringing to light his "crimes, Iran's poverty, the wide chasm separating the economic classes, and the regime's militarism." The Shah paid them no mind. On Monday, October 18, he hosted a press conference at Saadabad Palace attended by 136 reporters from more than 20 countries, with many of the journalists sitting at his feet like four-year-olds at reading time in kindergarten. He defended the cost of the event by pointing out that "the many buildings, hotels, roads, communication systems, schools and other infrastructure projects [were all] included in the current development plan," and that the economy had already surpassed its growth targets for the year. The cost of the Shahyad Monument had been met through public donations. "The only expense which perhaps did not have investment value" were the entertainments provided in the Tent City but they were budgeted for anyway. He conceded that the security crackdown had been excessive but "we had to take precautions after all that you wrote about dangers. So we did it."

The most important thing was that the Iranian people felt pride in their nation and history. "We stand on our own feet," he declared. By turns proud and combative, he lectured a West German reporter that "we are not affected in the slightest way by what is said about us by biased people. . . . We shall regain our prestige. I say this without vanity. I am, in fact, full of humility. But I have full faith in my people." For the first time he publicly announced his intention to eventually abdicate the throne. "This is not a new idea," he said. "My father thought of doing so. That is to say, in 1941, a few months before those events happened in our country [the Allied invasion of Iran], he wanted to give me the crown and see how I would run the country, how I would take my first steps. . . . It is natural that I, too, should have the same idea because succession will take place smoothly in this way. I think it is a good idea that we should do that." The Queen was thinking about the succession, too, when Court Minister Alam inquired whether she and Crown Prince Reza would like to attend the screening of a documentary film about the party of the century. "For goodness sake, leave me alone," she retorted. "I want our names to be utterly disassociated from those ghastly celebrations."

THE ORANGE AND lemon groves that graced the far eastern shores of the Mediterranean were a world away from Niavaran, but the Shah had every reason to keep a close eye on developments in Lebanon, where Imam Musa Sadr, a young Iranian-born cleric, had emerged as the conscience of the Shia peoples of the Levant, an important regional power broker, and a future candidate for the post of Shiism's paramount marja. The Persepolis celebrations had barely concluded when Musa Sadr arrived in Tehran in November 1971 to pay his respects and seek an important favor from the Custodian of the Shia Faith.

Seyyed Musa Sadr, born on June 4, 1928, was the scion of two of Shiism's most revered clerical dynasties. His father, Grand Ayatollah Sadreddin Sadr, was a marja whose own father had helped lead the revolt against the Qajars. From an early age Musa Sadr's boundless energy, charisma, and intellect left an indelible impression on everyone who met him. Blessed with a sunny disposition, gentle demeanor, and breathtaking good looks, the young man was as comfortable in the secular world of the Pahlavis as he was in the hawza, where his teachers took note of his erudite scholarship and marked him out as a major future talent. On the day in 1943 when he was formally welcomed into the ranks of the ulama, Musa Sadr was feted by family and friends, and also by his teachers, who included the firebrand cleric Ruhollah Khomeini. After entering the ranks of the clergy, the young mutjahid broke a major barrier by becoming the first "black turban" to graduate with a law degree from the secular University of Tehran. From there he set out for Najaf to study under Grand Ayatollah Abol Qasem Khoi, the marja who became his spiritual and theological mentor. Restless, ambitious, and impatient to make his mark, in 1959 Khoi and his fellow marjas agreed that Musa Sadr should be dispatched to the southern Lebanese port city of Tyre and take up the post of spiritual guide to that country's poverty-stricken Shia community, which at the time numbered more than three hundred thousand.

Lebanon held a special place in Iranian hearts and minds. For the past four centuries the former French colony had played an outsize role in Iranian affairs because of the steady flow of young seminarians who traveled from Tyre to Qom to study and replenish the town's seminaries and mosques. In the late fifties and through the sixties Lebanon was threatened by Egypt's General Gamal Abdel Nasser, who made no secret of his ambition to replace moderate, pro-Western Middle East regimes with his own brand of radical Arab socialism. Nasser was a sworn enemy of the Pahlavis—the Shah suspected that Nasser had played a role in stoking unrest in Iran in June 1963—and Lebanon's large Shia population created opportunities and challenges for both leaders. The Iranians feared the spread of radicalism from Lebanon into Qom's seminaries. Young Musa Sadr opposed clerical involvement in politics and adhered to Grand Ayatollah Khoi's acceptance of the monarchy. Accordingly, he went to Lebanon with the blessing of the Shah, whose title as Custodian of the

Faith meant he took a close interest in the promotions of senior clergy, and also of General Nasiri, whose agents conducted the requisite background check to assess Musa Sadr's loyalty to the throne.

Once installed in Tyre, Musa Sadr established himself as a passionate advocate for the poor in a country with a long history of discrimination against Shia Muslims. He built an orphanage, founded a trade school, and established social programs that eradicated beggary. The first of his groundbreaking efforts to forge coalitions and partnerships with the leaders of Lebanon's non-Muslim faiths got under way. His followers acclaimed him as "Imam" Musa Sadr, an accolade that struck his elders back home as premature but that cemented his reputation among the poor of Lebanon as a champion for social justice in the tradition of the martyred Imam Husayn. He dazzled his contemporaries. "[He was] tall, very tall to the point of seeming to soar above the often frenzied crowds that his presence drew together," recalled a prominent member of the Greek Orthodox community. "His black turban tilted back with a slight negligence. His enemies seemed charmed by his enigmatic and benevolent smile, whereas to his friends, his bearded face always reflected a profound melancholy. . . . His personal contacts were a ritual of seduction." Musa Sadr, wrote another Lebanese, had "an exquisite slightly self-disparaging sense of humor, head bowed as if in some private act of reverence, a shy, boyish smile, but luminous and perceptive eyes. His speech was slow, deliberate, well-stressed, the accent derived from purest Farsi interspersed with Shia slang and lilt." Musa Sadr had his detractors. They feared his popularity, accusing the cleric of wanting to have it both ways and engaging in demagoguery while cutting deals with the establishment. Even they found him irresistible. "He was different, he was open," said Khalil al-Khalil, the scion of one of the established families of Lebanese Shiism whose influence was eclipsed by Musa Sadr's arrival in Tyre. "If a woman was not veiled, he would not make a scene of it. He used to come and visit us at home. He would smoke the hookah pipe."

The Shah admired Musa Sadr's commitment to social justice, open mind, and his willingness to challenge the Beirut establishment, and saw in him a fellow reformer and kindred spirit who embraced modernity. Court Minister Alam had a soft spot for Musa Sadr, too—Grand Ayatollah Sadreddin Sadr had been his own father's marja. The Imam's November 1971 meeting with both men was clandestine and for good reason: he had traveled to Tehran to congratulate the monarch on his anniversary but also to lobby the palace for help in building a $30 million hospital and university complex to serve his poor constituents in Tyre. The trip placed Musa Sadr in a precarious position vis-à-vis the Khomeini family. The marriage between Khomeini's son Ahmad and Musa Sadr's niece had formally allied two powerful Shia dynasties. Musa Sadr needed the Shah's largesse and goodwill but naturally feared antagonizing Khomeini and the Ayatollah's sons, Mostafa, his father's closest counselor, but especially Ahmad, a ruthless operator who trained in guerrilla warfare in Lebanon's Bekaa Valley. Musa Sadr respected Grand Ayatollah Khomeini but was under no illusions about his driving ambition. "Ah yes, Khomeini," he once murmured. "One does what one can."

The meeting logistics were handled by Savak's Parviz Sabeti. "We had a mutual friend," Sabeti explained. "A classmate from his town. He brokered the dinner meeting at Saadabad." The nighttime rendezvous at Saadabad Palace was so secret indeed that it was kept from Colonel Djahinbini, the Shah's bodyguard, who insisted he never saw Musa Sadr in the Shah's company. "This undoubtedly happened," recalled Kambiz Atabai, Court Minister Alam's deputy. "When the Shah wanted to meet someone in total secrecy, either at his or their instigation, the name of the visitor would not be disclosed to Djahinbini or palace security. Instead, Mr. Alam or myself would personally inform security that Mr. X was entering the palace grounds in Alam's car or mine. The car lights would flash at the entrance and the guards would let it pass. Security would withdraw from the Shah's office, and even the office staff and secretaries would be sent away. Even the tea server would be sent away. Mr. Alam and myself might serve the tea ourselves. The anonymity might be at the Shah's instruction, but it could have been at the visitor's request and this made sense in the case of Musa Sadr."

Parviz Sabeti, who met separately with Musa Sadr the following day, found the Imam to be in high spirits. "He was very happy with the way the Shah treated him," said Sabeti. He listened as the Imam cheerfully recounted that the Shah had offered him a seat—guests usually stood during their audiences with the monarch—and that two servants had served tea instead of the usual one, which he interpreted as a royal gesture of equality. The Shah, he said, had agreed to pay the building costs for the hospital and the university. The Imam again repeated how "very impressed [he was] with the Shah. At that time he was very happy with the Shah." Sabeti took a less sanguine view of the visitor from Lebanon. The Imam, he decided, was "charismatic, a smart man, but not principled."

9

THE PAHLAVI PROGRESS

Our lives pass from us like the wind, and why
Should wise men grieve to know that they must die?
—*THE PERSIAN BOOK OF KINGS*

They told me it was treatable.
—THE SHAH

Niavaran Palace was a curious blend of traditional Persian design and the boxy, brutalist strain of urban architecture in vogue in European and American cities in the late fifties and early sixties. Visitors approaching the building from the main gate were startled to encounter a "four-square, lofty white cube, strangely window-less on the same side approached from the gates." If first impressions counted, the immediate effect was of the harsh military bearing and stern public countenance of its chief occupant. But around the side, floor-to-ceiling windows and a portico with columns offered a more inviting view, and when entering the softly lit grand hall that doubled as a reception area Queen Farah's influence was felt for the first time. Despite the height of the grand hall, which extended to the ceiling and engulfed most of the structure's interior, the residence exuded warmth, intimacy, and taste. Small lounges discreetly occupied each corner of the cube so that guests waiting to be received could pass the time viewing Iranian artwork, paintings, tapestries, carpets, and pottery in display cases. Overlooking the reception area was a wraparound gallery with a landing that led to the family quarters.

Niavaran's private suites were hardly spacious and so close to the balcony, which afforded a bird's-eye view of the activity below, that the raised voices of the Pahlavi children were overheard in the public area. During state receptions the two mischievous younger children, Prince Ali Reza and Princess Leila, delighted in creeping out of their rooms in their pajamas to drop peanuts and hurl bread pellets on the heads of guests in the hall below, much to their parents' amusement. Fitted with all the latest conveniences, the residence's most impressive feature was the high ceiling that retracted at the flick of a switch to open up the grand hall to sunlight and fresh air. Niavaran had been designed as a government guesthouse and was never intended as a permanent residence. The Shah preferred several minor additions rather than approve the cost of building a new palace southwest of the capital. These included an adjoining wing with a private cinema that was attached to the Queen's library. Farah put her training as an architect to good use by overseeing the design of a split-level library that served as a personal retreat where she could read, reflect, and entertain away from the bustle of the residence. "In this vast, bright room I had gathered together the works that meant the most to me," she said. There were sculptures, paintings, and objets d'art collected during her travels. She admired the pop art of Andy Warhol, and his lithograph of her was on display. The library looked out over a broad manicured lawn, and beyond were the tennis courts where husband and wife often dueled blistering backhands.

The emergence of a terrorist threat in Iran meant the safety of the Imperial Family became ever more a focus of concern for Colonel Kiomars Djahinbini and his security detail. The hilltop neighborhood of Shemiran, which included Niavaran, had been a backwater when the Pahlavis moved to the Alborz foothills in the late sixties. But by the early seventies a building boom was under way, with residential complexes and mansions sprouting along the northern hills. Neighbors could stand on their balconies and rooftops and look down over the palace grounds. "We put restrictions on the height of apartment buildings," said the colonel, "but the real problem with security were the helicopters." The Shah and Shahbanou were constantly on the move in blue and white choppers, which functioned as highly efficient mobile offices. Djahinbini's fear was that a terrorist cell would rent a nearby apartment and use one of the high rooftops to launch a rocket at the Shah's helicopter as it approached to land or take off. Motorcades posed their own challenge in a city famous for its traffic-choked streets. "We were already thinking about suicide vests worn by the Mujahedin. We provided security on the roads but that meant stopping traffic, which took too long. We were also worried that traffic delays antagonized the people." The streets of the capital were clogged and the palace did not want to be seen adding to the problem. But the Shah's munificent gesture backfired in spectacular fashion when gridlocked Tehranis, seeing his helicopter flit back and forth overhead while their cars idled below, bitterly complained that he was more removed than ever from the daily travails of life on the streets.

Security inside the palace complex was as elaborate. Before every meal, food tasters made sure the dishes were free from poisons. For Farah, even a stroll around the grounds at Niavaran or Saadabad meant hearing the crunch of gravel behind her, a constant reminder of the men with guns who lurked in the bushes and observed her every move. Her bedroom was guarded, too. "Three or four of my men were stationed inside the family residence through the night," said Djahinbini, "and there were also officers of the Imperial Guard." The Shah suspected that foreign intelligence services intercepted his telephone conversations and had placed bugs and listening devices inside his residence and office. "We had electronic devices that swept the rooms. They were Swiss-made, handheld devices that came in a little suitcase. My people were specially trained in communications." France's President de Gaulle had visited Iran in the early sixties and invited Djahinbini to France for additional training. The colonel and one of his colleagues spent a month in the Élysée Palace discussing the strengths and weaknesses of palace security with French intelligence officials. By the time they returned home they were fully trained in electronic countersurveillance. The Iranians also trained with the U.S. Secret Service, who exchanged their walkie-talkies for earpieces. A thorough sweep of all rooms at Niavaran, including the lavatories, was conducted before the family returned to the residence at the end of summer from their time away at Saadabad.

Niavaran was the Pahlavis' primary residence and one of five palaces dedicated to their exclusive use. The family spent a considerable part of each year on the road. "It was very important when the Shah moved around," said Kambiz Atabai, deputy to Court Minister Alam. "Mr. Alam argued that the Shah should have a residence in every corner of the kingdom." Iran had tribal traditions, and Alam understood the importance of the personal touch and being seen in the flesh. The Pahlavi progress was planned months in advance and involved transporting the immediate members of the family but also dozens of courtiers, servants, and security officials many hundreds of miles. Always sensitive to local concerns, the Court Ministry encouraged the cooks and servants to order supplies of fresh produce to give a boost to the local economy. "There was always great excitement and the area he visited was cleaned up in advance."

The Pahlavis were officially in residence at Niavaran from midautumn in late October until late May, which marked the onset of summer. During that time they broke away only for vacations, state visits, or to make regional inspection tours. In late December they flew to Zurich in Switzerland, and from there choppered to their ski chalet in St. Moritz to spend two or three weeks on the slopes. Armed guards patrolled the perimeter of the chalet grounds. One time, feeling lucky, Queen Farah placed a bet with her skiing companion, a Savak general, that she could escape from the chalet without alerting security. He cheerfully accepted her dare, which was sealed in Swiss francs. Later, while the household rested, the Queen stole out of her room, took the general's boots from under his nose, clambered out a window, jumped to the snowpack below, then scampered down the hill to the village hotel, where she placed a telephone call to the chalet. The same general's wife answered the phone and was stunned to hear the familiar throaty voice on the other end of the line: "I'm not there. Come and join me at the hotel." From where the two ladies sat drinking tea, they enjoyed a clear view up the hill of the chalet, delighting at the sight of "the security, Iranian and Swiss, running around the chalet, up on the roof and around the building, trying to find me." For one brief moment, Farah enjoyed the thrill of life outside the royal cocoon.

The Pahlavis returned to Tehran in mid-January to stay in residence until the Persian New Year, Nowruz, which always fell on the equinox in the third week of March. Nowruz was spent on Kish Island, sixteen miles off Iran's Persian Gulf coast. The Shah also used Kish as a base from which to jet over to the mainland to inspect regional oil facilities and military installations. The Pahlavis returned to Niavaran at the end of March and stayed until the last week of April, when the Shah made his annual excursion to the city of Shiraz. He was in residence in the Bagh-e Eram Palace for two weeks, during which time he received regional governors, mayors, tribal leaders, industrialists, and other leading men and women of influence in the southwest. These audiences allowed him to press the flesh, listen to gripes, and gain a better understanding of the people's needs.

The Shah spent the next six weeks in Tehran, where he tended to affairs of state. Then he was off again, this time accompanied by the Queen for their annual ten-day trip to the holy city of Mashad, on Iran's northeast border with Afghanistan. Mashad was the most sensitive of the annual inspection tours because of the city's significance as the site of the Holy Shrine of Imam Reza, one of Islam's most revered mosques. Imam Reza held a special place in the affections of the Pahlavi family—the Shah and his brothers all bore the name Reza—and the King used the trip as an opportunity to reestablish his credentials as Shia Islam's Custodian of the Faith. He received proclamations of fealty from ulama throughout the northeast. Despite her low opinion of the clergy, Farah enjoyed her time in Mashad. "Mashad is like nowhere else in all Iran," she said. "It is so lovely, so quiet, tree-lined streets, and then the great mosques with their golden domes rising above the pilgrim crowds. Its atmosphere of devotion is so intense . . . it is profoundly moving . . . and then—those trumpets and drums and saluting the sunrise and sunset. . . . Mashad has an extraordinary ambience." Her husband much preferred Mashad to Qom, the dour and dusty town seventy-five miles south of the capital; Qom's seminaries were in a near-constant state of agitation. He wanted to strengthen Mashad at Qom's expense. The project he envisioned was a new Islamic university that would be administered by progressive scholars such as his wife's adviser Seyyed Hossein Nasr, who would teach modern sciences and languages alongside the world's major religions.

The next big move came on the first day of June, when the entire household fled the first heat of summer and decamped to Saadabad, a short ten-minute drive higher up the Alborz slopes, where they stayed at Saadabad's White Palace until the end of October. Though Saadabad was cooler than Niavaran, and boasted thick woods and forested trails, the White Palace was not Farah's favorite residence. She thought it "dark and gloomy with a rather overgrown garden," though Saadabad's compensations included the splendid view of the Alborz Mountains "and to the east you can see the Damavand volcano with its mantle of snow."

The hottest weeks of the summer, from the middle of July to the third week of August, were spent at the Caspian Sea resort town of Nowshahr. "That was the time we had the most fun," said the Queen. The family lived in an old wooden barrack precariously perched on stilts over the water. The Shah loved its simplicity. When Farah's friend Fereydoun Djavadi was invited to stay at Nowshahr he expected luxurious quarters. "We arrived at 9 a.m. and were introduced," he said. "I kept thinking to myself some-one would come and take us to the palace. I thought this was the place for their staff." "In the first year our bed was on a tilt," the Queen said, laugh-ing. "And in the evenings they would remove the chairs [on the deck] and put up a screen and we would watch movies." One warm summer afternoon the couple were entertaining guests at lunch on the veranda when Farah, known for her high spirits, disdain for protocol, and mischievous sense of humor, started a food fight. "It was very casual," she confessed. "And I don't know, but I started throwing bread with someone else." Others soon joined in and the rolls began flying. But the commotion interrupted the sacrosanct two o'clock national radio broadcast and led to a swift royal dressing-down from the other end of the table. While they relaxed, Soviet ships assumed to have sophisticated electronics surveillance gear were moored nearby. "We would see the Russian ships were just on the other side of the harbor," said Farah. Sometimes the Iranians poked fun at them by waving. The water was polluted, she added, but they went swimming and water skiing anyway. "We became immune to it." Her brother-in-law General Mohammad Khatami, Princess Fatemeh's hus-band, taught her how to monoski, ski-jump, and eventually fly-ski by "hanging from parachutes that take you up twenty or thirty meters above the water."

The Shah always made his entrance on the beach at exactly ten o'clock in the morning and plunged into the surf. After lunch the Imperial couple, his brothers and sisters, and the older Pahlavi children piled into a heli-copter that flew them away from the coast and far out to sea. While the chopper hovered in place everyone took turns jumping into the water from a great height. But when it came to the Shah's turn the pilots made a point of lowering the machine almost to water level to prevent injury or accident. Unbeknownst to the Shah, they had received strict orders from General Khatami not to ever place the monarch in physical danger. This happened every time and it always drove him to distraction. He loved heights, he loved speed, and he loved the thrill of the jump. If the children could jump, why couldn't he?

"Why are you taking it down?" he would exclaim. "Higher! Take it back up!"

"Your Majesty, it is not safe! We cannot allow you to hurt yourself!"

"Take the bloody thing *higher*! I order you!"

"No Majesty, please it is not safe!"

"Higher, damn it!"

The others in the party, treading water down below, would watch this scene unfold in a state of great mirth, laughing at the string of expletives that accompanied the Shah's final leap into the blue. The pilots stayed on the scene until a flotilla of small boats trailing inflatable rafts arrived from the mainland. Everyone in the water then climbed aboard the inflatables and a race ensued back to the shore, with speedboats whipping the children through the water amid gales of laughter. If ever a child lost their footing and was flung off, one of the boats would stop, circle back around, and scoop them from the sea. One afternoon, however, fun almost turned to tragedy when Princess Mahnaz, the daughter of Princess Shahnaz and Ardeshir Zahedi, was lost at sea.

Each summer, Mahnaz returned to Iran from boarding school in Switzerland. Her time in Nowshahr was when she had the chance to catch up with her grandparents, uncles, aunts, and the cousins. One day she slipped into the Shah's helicopter unobserved just before it took off with its cargo of royal vacationers. She was the last to make the jump into the water and in the confusion somehow missed grabbing onto a line or climbing into the last inflatable before the convoy of boats roared back to shore. Suddenly, she was alone in the water. With no land in sight and dusk setting in, she calmed herself by lying on her back to save energy. The minutes passed slowly. Back on land, the adults and children were cleaning up in preparation for supper when someone noticed that Mahnaz was missing. After one of the children recalled seeing her in the water, the adults realized that the Shah's only grandchild had been left behind. They raised the alarm and boats and aircraft sped to the area. The search party faced a daunting challenge. The currents were shifting and the pilots could only hazard a guess as to where they had set her down. The girl, meanwhile, lay still in the water with sea creatures nibbling at her limbs. Mahnaz was spotted from a helicopter with only a few minutes of light left and winched to safety.

From Nowshahr, the Pahlavis returned to Saadabad to round out the summer and early autumn before heading back down the hill to Niavaran in late October. This final move completed the annual progress. Though the Court Ministry was responsible for maintaining the five palaces and twelve hundred staff scattered around the country, many problems still ended up on the Queen's desk. She was the first to admit that the logistics involved in moving so often between different residences taxed everyone's patience. "Often I have instructed the staff to use a certain set of tableware for an official occasion at Saadabad Palace," she said. "They have immediately informed me that the set is at Niavaran Palace. In Nowshahr, I used to ask for something and receive the answer that it was in Kish Island. In Kish, I would be told that the thing I wanted was in Saadabad."

NIAVARAN WAS A working palace and a family home. The residence and the grounds were filled with the sights and sounds of children laughing and tearing through the halls and animals scampering about. With the birth of Ali Reza on April 28, 1966, followed four years later by a sister, Leila, on March 27, 1970, the family was complete. The King and Queen had always wanted four children, and with two male heirs the line of succession was finally settled.

Even before he was born, Crown Prince Reza was the subject of endless gossip and conjecture. "The rumors were that my mother was never pregnant, I was mute, and I was not my father's son," he recalled. One popular rumor had it that the young prince was born with webbed hands that resembled duck feet. The rumors of muteness were laid to rest only in 1973 when the thirteen-year-old opened a youth soccer tournament in Shiraz and officials made sure his speech was broadcast to the nation. Street gossip about the Imperial Family was part of the fabric of Iranian daily life. "They said absolutely anything, anything—the most fantastic rumors," remembered Fatemeh Pakravan, wife of General Pakravan. One persistent rumor was that each day the Shah entered a secret underground tunnel that took him from Niavaran to Savak headquarters, where he presided over torture interrogations and watched as students were fed to the lions. The tunnel in question was actually a short passageway only a few hundred yards long that connected Niavaran's basement to a small outhouse that stored machinery and a power generator. "Do you know how many *miles* my father would have had to walk each day to get to Savak headquarters?" said Reza with a laugh. "Savak was located *downtown*." Still, the underground passageway came in handy when Reza filmed a high school remake of the hit television show *The Six Million Dollar Man*, starring Lee Majors. "In another life I would have been a director of films," he admitted. He corralled his younger siblings and friends to act out a script that called for a jewel thief to sneak into Niavaran, snatch one of his mother's diadems, and then escape through the tunnel.

Great expectations were attached to the young prince. "I was far more scrutinized. I never saw the stroke of midnight until I was sixteen. I recall from my childhood, eighty percent was going to school and twenty percent was in my capacity as crown prince." There were snatches of normality. "One night my father was chasing me down the hall while waiting for my mother to get dressed for dinner. I got hyper and ran into the bathroom, slipped on the shower rug and fell nose first into the back of my mother's chair." His parents canceled their plans, bundled the bleeding child into the car, and drove at high speed to the nearest hospital. Needless to say, their sudden appearance made it a night to remember for the medical staff and other patients in the emergency room. In his teenage years the prince showed an assertive streak that his father did nothing to discourage. He approved the thirteen-year-old's request to make a solo flight without his flying instructor. Despite his mother's reservations, both the King and Queen accompanied their son to an air force base and looked on with pride as his Beechcraft F33C Bonanza danced around the sky before executing a perfect landing. Farah bit her lip so as not to cry with pride—and relief. The young prince's father looked on with barely concealed satisfaction. Reza was friendly with his bodyguards but that didn't stop him from trying to break out of his security cordon. One day he sped off in his Mini Cooper, leaving the drivers of the tail car shaking their fists in traffic. Another time, he and his sister Farahnaz armed themselves with tape and paper and covered over the dozen security cameras installed in the palace compound. For this impertinence they earned a rare scolding from their father. By the time of his sixteenth birthday, the prince's dark good looks drew stares and swoons from Tehran schoolgirls, who reported sightings of him shopping in the music stores that lined Pahlavi Avenue. At the Tehran American School, the American girls and a few boys decorated their lockers with photographs and posters of the prince decked out in football gear or wearing his flying togs.

Princess Farahnaz was her brother's confidante and close confederate in their escapades around the grounds of Saadabad and Niavaran. "She was a real tomboy," said her mother. "She drove a three-wheel motorbike up the palace stairs." Personally shy and sensitive, Farahnaz most closely resembled her father in temperament. From an early age she showed a keen interest in the lives and well-being of the servants and lavished affection on the family's growing menagerie of pets. For a while the children were entertained with a lion cub given to Reza by President de Gaulle until it grew too big and was sent to Tehran's zoo. Farahnaz's pet fox often joined the family at mealtimes, though Madame Diba refused to enter her granddaughter's bedroom for fear of encountering the mice. The teenager inherited her mother's social conscience. "If she came across people in the street who were poor or unhappy, it always affected her," said Farah. In the Niavaran neighborhood where she lived, locals often saw the little girl standing at the palace gates staring at them in the vain hope another child would come over to invite her to play or chat. But more than anything, Farahnaz loved spending time with her father. She would listen with big eyes as he described to her his latest travels and the important people he had met during his day.

The couple's third child, Ali Reza, had a personality and spirit that called to mind his grandfather Reza Shah. The boy was as charming as he was tough. He was five when one night he crept out of his bedroom in his pajamas, stole along the gallery, and flung bread pellets over the balcony and onto the heads of his parents, who were receiving guests in the grand hall. He was the same age, his mother remembered, when he jumped into a barrel of tar being used to coat the terraces. "He was so *naughty*," she said with a smile. "At the entrance to Niavaran there was a guard who sat at a table. He kept a loaded gun under it. One day Ali Reza crept beneath it and stole the man's pistol." Her son enjoyed his first day at nursery school so much that he ordered his driver to turn around and go home without him. One morning, impatient to play outside, he admonished his mother to hurry up and get dressed. "People will say, what kind of majesty is this still in her bathrobe?" he lectured her in fluent French. The Queen recalled that though Ali Reza was slow to speak, when he did it was in full sentences and with a directness that often brought conversation to a halt. One night at dinner he told his family that he liked "free love." When the children raced across the gallery to keep their father company while he exercised before dinner, it was Ali Reza who would jump on his back, issue riding instructions, and start the pillow fights.

Leila was the baby of the family and Ali Reza's closest friend. At bedtime the Shah would ask her, "Pray for rain, Leila *joune*." Rain was always on his mind, and Leila was often heard to say, "I like it when the sky is gray." The Queen thought, "Her father has passed on his love of rain to her. Forever." But he was a hopeless disciplinarian and a soft touch. "The children were conscious of the power they had over their father, and for his part my husband knew how to delight them and with just a few words restore the closeness interrupted by official trips or long working days at home."

Both parents were often away or at official events, and their absence was keenly felt. "I physically didn't see my parents much," Reza remembered. Farah admitted that she struggled and often failed to balance home life with her public duties. "Basically, we were never able to live as a normal family and give the children as much time as we would have liked," she said after the revolution. "While they have a certain understanding of what our responsibilities were, the children remark on it to me today, and if I had my life to live over again, I would give more time to them and to my husband."

IN THE EARLY seventies the rumor took hold that Queen Farah bathed in milk. She became aware of it herself when one of her maids mentioned the latest gossip at school. "Behind me, in class, there were two girls speaking about you," said the young woman. "They said that the Queen bathes twice a day in milk." The tale was so absurd that Farah dismissed it as nonsense. But she noticed that journalists soon began raising the subject of her bathing habits in interviews. "Is it true that you bathe in milk like Cleopatra?" they inquired. The exasperated Queen put the rumors down to the usual backstreet tittle-tattle but also to the demands of her role. "I am never photographed at work. The only photographs published always show me wearing the crown jewels. Unfortunately, ninety-nine out of a hundred people judge by appearances. No one wonders, 'What is she, herself, like?' They do not want to know that we, too, are human and, like others, have problems and feelings."

Other rumors could not be brushed off or set aside so easily. In a society where so many were prepared to believe that the Shah fed young people to lions, that his wife bathed in milk, and that his sister ruled behind the scenes as Persia's Lady Macbeth, it was inevitable that the Pahlavi marriage would become fodder for the gossips. The Shah and Shahbanou were twenty years apart in age and the product of different generations, his more conservative and authoritative, hers more liberal and idealistic. He had been raised in an atmosphere of total obeisance and was not used to being questioned or challenged, least of all by a woman. Farah had suffered the loss of her father at a young age, been encouraged to stand on her own two feet, and understood the impatience of the younger generation for more freedom. Her family pedigree meant she need never feel insecure in the company of the Pahlavi clan. She refused to indulge her husband and did what she could to challenge the enablers who surrounded him at court. One evening she watched in rising anger as Bruno, the Shah's pampered Great Dane, sidled up to the dinner table and started licking food off people's plates. "Flatterers everywhere!" she snapped. "I refuse to follow their example. Even this dog is fawned upon just because he is yours. I alone refuse to stoop to such nonsense."

The Shah, exasperated, returned the sentiment. After the state opening of parliament in October 1972, while the couple waited in an anteroom for the return trip to the palace, the Queen observed that her husband's speech from the throne "had done nothing but praise our achievements without mentioning a single shortcoming." His testy reply betrayed his insecurities and also the suspicion that perhaps she had a point. "You're becoming quite the revolutionary yourself," he rounded on her in front of their aides. "I'd like to see you try and run this country at the same time as making revolutionary pronouncements and heaping your own administration with abuse. But do tell me, now that you've joined the revolutionaries, how is it you continue to dress yourself in jewels and finery?"

Farah felt no need to apologize or back down. She worked hard and had earned the right to make her voice heard. She took the view that more candor and not less was needed in the palace. "His Majesty and I see eye to eye on nothing; almost invariably I disagree with him," she once told a startled Court Minister Alam. Farah's outburst was a rare indiscretion probably meant to shock the man she regarded as her husband's chief enabler. She did what she could to keep him grounded. She refused to suppress her competitive streak, beating him in straight sets at tennis, keeping up with him on the ski slopes, and once sensationally outwitting him during his favorite after-dinner word game. The Shah loved games and was a keen bridge player. There was one word game he favored over all others and that allowed his intellect to shine. According to the rules of Botticelli, each player was allowed to ask questions of the protagonist. "For example," said the Queen, "you are thinking of a famous person starting with 'B,' and the other people ask another question, 'Are you, for instance, from a country in South America?,' and you have to answer, 'I'm not Bolivian.' If you cannot answer, you may ask an indirect question: 'Are you alive? Are you a man? A woman?'" One evening Farah shocked her husband into silence by correctly naming the head of a German tank division. He was so flummoxed that he brought the game to a halt and incredulously asked, "*How* do you know this? Tell me, *how*?" She collapsed in laughter.

The Shah ceded the domestic realm to his wife's better judgment. He indulged her passion for modern art and held his tongue when the sculptures and paintings she favored but that he found incomprehensible appeared in their homes. Only occasionally did he put his foot down. One day he noticed the bronze relief of a giant thumb mounted on a pedestal in her library. He decided this was going too far—in Iran the thumb symbolized the middle finger. Recalling the incident, the Queen blushed and said with a chuckle, "His Majesty banished it from the residence." She moved the thumb to a pavilion outside her library, where it stands to this day, and Ali Reza later bought her a smaller-scale replica made out of glass. In its place in the library she installed a second bronze relief, this one intended to symbolize "nothing."

Among the things the couple shared in common was a love of the outdoors and athletics, French literature and culture, Dean Martin movies, and wildlife conservation. It was in response to his wife's appeals that the Shah finally gave up hunting. Work often intruded in their personal life. The Queen advocated on behalf of groups and issues that her husband's more conservative circle regarded as liberal and therefore suspect. "It's very difficult for me," Farah conceded. "I try to talk to him, not as a queen talking to a king but as a wife talks to her husband. Sometimes, though, I care so much about something, I get so excited I can't breathe. But I have to be careful because if I'm not, and I start raising my voice he will think I am blaming him for what's wrong and he'll get angry." Pressed for time, and fighting for his attention, Farah wrote her husband notes. "I don't want to take up his time; I don't want to trouble him with my problems during the day so the only time I can talk to him is at lunch or in bed and that's the worst time to talk about your problems. Once in a while I have him alone for five or ten minutes in the car. But generally I write to him. If I talk to him he forgets. So I write little notes to him and send them to the office so he will read it with the rest of his papers."

Weeks passed when they saw each other only briefly and mainly at joint official engagements. One visitor to Niavaran in the midseventies recorded the following scene.

> I have watched her dash out (already changed from the clothes she was wearing when we were talking ten minutes earlier), at the same moment

as a throbbing machine drops to earth on one of the terraces which
serves as landing pad. It has come down to whisk her off, maybe to a
distant province, or just the other end of the city.... At the same
time there is another insistent buzzing overhead, and a second helicopter plumbs down at nudging distance from the first. This one is
returning the Shah to his Palace for the series of audiences and conferences that make up his day. He is in uniform—perhaps he has been
attending army maneuvers.... At this moment, while the helicopters
throb and quiver, one coming to a standstill, the other raring to lift off
into the skies, there is a frantic surge of children and dogs. Hugs,
farewells, greetings, shrieks, laughter and barking sound below the
whirring machines. Then the Pahlavi parents are off, each to their
respective obligations.

Now well into their second decade of marriage, their relationship held
few surprises. "Farah and the Shah loved each other, but the love was more
companionate than passionate," wrote the Shah's biographer Gholam
Reza Afkhami. "The Shah, being in an oriental patriarchy had more leeway; the Queen was bound by custom and tradition to make sure her
actions did not violate the honor of the family and in her case the nation."
The greatest strain placed on the marriage was the Shah's philandering.
The Shah, like John Kennedy, the American president he professed to
loathe, was a client of the legendary Madame Claude of Paris, who ran the
world's most exclusive gentleman's club and whose clientele reportedly
included General de Gaulle, Italian industrialist Gianni Agnelli, Greek
shipping magnate Aristotle Onassis, and the actor Marlon Brando. Claude
handpicked the young women who flew out on Air France's regular
Friday night flight to Tehran. Their encounters with the Shah were hardly
romantic. "Often a conversation, a dance, or a drink sufficed," wrote
Afkhami. "But these occasions were soothing, and the Shah enjoyed them.
He called them *gardesh*, outings." He also felt he needed them. "If I don't
have this recreation a couple of times a week," he told Court Minister
Alam, "there is no way I could bear the burden of my office."

The Queen had no choice but to look the other way, though her husband's adventures wounded her. "At times she would grumble or cry, and
on rare occasions even threaten to harm herself," wrote Afkhami. "The
worst crisis of this sort occurred in the summer of 1973." The Shah had only
himself to blame when one of his lovers, a mouthy blond teenager named

Gilda, flaunted their affair by spreading the lie that the Shah had promised to take her as his second wife. When the gossip reached the ears of the Diba family, the Queen's formidable mother, Madame Farideh Diba, confronted Alam and briskly demanded that he stop the public humiliation—or else. The threat from the Diba matriarch was unmistakable—her daughter had reached the limits of endurance and would leave her husband if he did not end her humiliation. The Shah sputtered that he, too, would welcome divorce, though his idle talk fooled no one and he scrambled to make amends. Once again, Alam saved the day by seeing to it that Gilda was discreetly handed off, this time to the Shah's brother-in-law General Khatami, the husband of his sister Princess Fatemeh.

Though passions eventually cooled and the crisis passed, there was a subtle shift in the marriage. Farah carved out a greater public role and declared herself a feminist. In 1975 she made a point of speaking out in support of a proposal to establish a radical government-administered alimony fund that would issue married women with "divorce insurance." It was important for wives "to have some security," she told *Women's Wear Daily*. She said she had sold the only piece of personal property she owned for about $1 million "and, like other women, I put aside some of the money."

The Shah might grouch about his wife's ambitions and politics, but he ceded her more influence in public life than any Iranian female sovereign since the Islamic conquest of Persia in the seventh century. He dispatched Farah to China on a highly sensitive landmark state visit that paved the way for the normalization of diplomatic relations. The trip was a success, and Farah soon became a familiar presence on the world stage as a diplomat and envoy. Her status at home was further boosted with the establishment of the Empress Farah Foundation, a multimillion-dollar charitable endeavor that supported and promoted artistic and cultural activities. Rather than settle for her usual role as honorary patron, Farah took the title of CEO and Head of the Board of Directors and ran the foundation like a business. She donated the endowment and the plot of land where the headquarters was built and made sure it became a self-financing entity with a stable revenue stream provided by the state oil company, private donations, and public fees charged by museums, exhibitions, and festivals.

Organizations affiliated with the Empress Farah Foundation included the Negarastan Museum, headed by Farah's cousin by marriage Layla

Diba; the Carpet Museum; the stunning Museum of Contemporary Arts, whose design was inspired by New York's Guggenheim; and a network of nationwide landmark museums and galleries that celebrated Iranian ceramics, clay, bronze, and miniatures. In addition there were four cultural centers; three national arts festivals; three research, exploration, and science institutes; and the City Theater of Tehran. The Queen's leadership ensured that the 1970s would forever be remembered as a golden age for Iranian avant-garde and traditional artistic expression.

IN JANUARY 1974, the Shah followed his usual custom of breaking away from the family winter ski vacation in Switzerland to fly by helicopter to neighboring Austria for his annual medical checkup. Several weeks earlier he had noticed swelling in his abdomen, and made the self-diagnosis of an enlarged spleen. Secretive as ever, he decided to keep the news to himself until he reached the consulting rooms of Viennese physician Dr. Karl Fellinger, the renowned "Doctor to the Kings" whose roster of patients included the Shah of Iran but also the Kings of Jordan, Saudi Arabia, and Morocco.

In Vienna, Dr. Fellinger examined the Shah's abdominal swelling and ran routine blood tests that revealed some devastating news. His Majesty, he informed General Ayadi, the monarch's personal physician, had developed incurable lymphatic cancer. The diagnosis did not come as a complete surprise to the patient. The Shah's family history showed a genetic predisposition to cancer. Reza Shah had died of stomach cancer and Queen Mother Taj ol-Moluk was under treatment for the same exact strain of lymphoma that now afflicted her son. "They told me it was treatable," the Shah later explained. Fellinger warned him that the disease would flare up if he did not keep stress to a minimum. For the ruler of a country with a history of rebellion and revolution, invasion and occupation, assassination and unrest, the physician's parting admonition may have been the cruelest cut of all. From the moment of diagnosis, every decision and every plan he made would be determined by the knowledge that he had only a short window of opportunity, perhaps as few as seven and as many as fifteen years, to complete his life's work.

10

EMPEROR OF OIL

My problem is that I haven't enough time.
—THE SHAH

This is the juice of a sick mind.
—IMAM MUSA SADR

In 1972 Abolhassan Banisadr traveled to Najaf in Iraq to mourn the death of his father, Ayatollah Nasrollah Banisadr, a prominent clerical opponent of the Pahlavi Dynasty. By now he was living in Paris in exile, teaching economics, and thinking about Iran's future. He was not intimidated by the Shah's popularity or the apparent strength of the Pahlavi regime. "Ten years before the revolution, a group of us concluded the Shah's regime was headed for serious difficulties and will end up completely lost," he recalled. "We started from that period to create an alternative in terms of programs for action in different fields and put together a group of people ready to take over." The exiled intellectuals studied the army and concluded that its emphasis on combating foreign threats presented a major weakness in dealing with domestic discontent. Iranian soldiers were well equipped but were not trained to fight an internal insurgency or put down an uprising. In surveying the White Revolution, Banisadr and his friends noted that many peasant families had walked off the land and moved to the cities in search of a better life. Now congregated in urban slums, they comprised a lumpen proletariat, which would eventually demand a greater share of power and resources. His conclusion was that the Shah was headed for a crisis down the road because his regime's "social basis was shrinking. . . . So you see on one side a phenomenon of crumbling, and on the other side the opposition pulling itself together, developing a platform, and presenting an alternative."

Banisadr and the other exiles recognized that the path to power lay in the streets. Equally, they understood that they lacked the leadership, charisma, and resources to mobilize vast crowds. Only a marja was capable of mounting an insurrection. Khomeini enjoyed a record of defying the Shah, but he was not considered a marja and languished in exile in Najaf. "The way we looked at Khomeini was, 'What role could he play in a revolution?'" said Banisadr. Though Khomeini was not a marja, Banisadr and his confederates had the idea of imbuing him with the authority of one in the same way they might sell a new brand of laundry detergent. "In Khomeini we saw a voice who could reach all of Iran. And as a marja, everything he would say would have a religious message and would be accepted. If the movement's objectives would be articulated by Khomeini, this would be a big gain. We had some thoughts but not the means to make a public discourse. That would be Khomeini's role. Without Khomeini, it was not clear a revolution could take place."

When he traveled to Najaf in Iraq in 1972 to mourn his father, Banisadr met with Khomeini to discuss how they might work together. The experience left Banisadr distinctly underwhelmed—he found Khomeini to be neither friendly nor collegial. "Khomeini was not one of those who believed a revolution would happen," he recalled. "My first impression was that [he] was isolated. He was not in contact with the rest of the community. The other grand ayatollahs did not consider him part of the community. So I asked him, 'Why is it this way?'"

"You do not know these people," Khomeini glumly replied. "If you go along with these people you will have to go along with these people." Khomeini liked to talk in circles. What he meant was that he would not be accepted by the other marjas unless he moderated his views, something he was clearly not prepared to do.

Banisadr returned to Najaf one year later to mark the anniversary of his father's death. Since his last visit he had read Khomeini's thirteen-part lecture series calling for a religious dictatorship. Many of Banisadr's leftist comrades had decided the thesis was so extreme it must be part of an elaborate forgery by Savak to discredit Khomeini as a religious fanatic. But Banisadr, with his background in religion, knew better. "You are doing a great favor to the Pahlavi government," he warned Khomeini. "You are advocating the creation of a government by people who are so incompetent they cannot even manage the affairs of a town like Najaf, which is filled with dirt and garbage."

If Khomeini was offended by Banisadr's criticism, he didn't let on. "I have written this book as an attempt to open a discussion," he replied. "This is not the final word. It is for people like you to start thinking about forming a government."

"Very well," replied Banisadr, who accepted Khomeini's flattery and his explanation that the book merely served a tactical purpose. "Very good. Please publish this."

Then they got down to business. Banisadr and the nationalist left were good organizers but lacked a popular following among the people. They needed to forge alliances with Khomeini's religious supporters in exile but especially with groups back in Iran who could open up the religious networks and mosques to their political activity. Khomeini's pride and ambition, not to mention his hatred for the secular left, which he regarded as insufficiently Islamist, meant that he was much more comfortable dealing with Mehdi Bazargan's rival offshoot the Liberation Movement of Iran. "There were some talks about the ambiguity of Khomeini's relationship with the nationalist movement," Banisadr recalled. To test Khomeini's goodwill and to reassure his supporters on the left, Banisadr asked if Khomeini would be prepared to donate a percentage of his tithings to finance a propaganda effort to tarnish the Pahlavi name in Western capitals. The Grand Ayatollah swiftly gave his consent, and hundreds of thousands of dollars soon began flowing into bank accounts in Houston, Texas, where a supporter named Ibrahim Yazdi represented the American chapter of the revolutionary movement, and also in Paris, where Banisadr and his clique were based. Banisadr used the money to found a publishing house that churned out crudely effective propaganda that accused the Shah of committing monstrous human rights abuses.

Banisadr was most anxious to influence foreign press coverage of Iran. Banisadr and his colleague Sadegh Ghotzbadegh made a point of cultivating American and European reporters who covered events in Iran from their regional offices in the Lebanese capital, Beirut. They studied their reporting methods, fed them story ideas, steered them toward sympathetic interviewees, and supplied them with the revolutionary movement's facts and figures. Banisadr became particularly close to Eric Rouleaux, a reporter from *Le Monde* who had covered the 1963 insurrection. He was especially pleased when his French friend, a supporter of Third World nationalism and various radical causes, wrote the first article predicting the overthrow of the Shah. Another sympathetic ear was Jonathan Randal, the former foreign correspondent for the *New York Times* who now reported for the *Washington Post* from Beirut. Randal's critical coverage of the 1971 Persepolis celebrations had presented a devastating portrait of conditions inside Iran and helped define the Shah as a corrupt, cruel dictator. Randal became friendly with Sadegh Ghotzbadegh, a raconteur and womanizer whose romances with female Western foreign correspondents were widely known. The Iranian would drop by his bureau and charm him into writing stories about human rights in Iran. On one of his trips to Tehran, Randal even agreed to Ghotzbadegh's request that he drive to the bazaar to collect a suitcase that turned out to be full of cash and bring it out of the country.

Back in Najaf, Khomeini made sure his thesis was republished with an innocuously worded introduction that merely explained the author's intention "to discuss certain related matters and questions." Copies of the book and Khomeini's periodic statements on politics and religion were mass produced with the help of a Gestetner photostat machine set up in his compound. From there they were smuggled back into Iran, to be stashed in a warehouse in Tehran's overcrowded and poor southern suburbs. Khomeini's advisers also had him start recording his sermons on cassette tapes, then the latest audio technology. The tapes were flown to Beirut, West Berlin, and Paris, where they were duplicated in safe houses by sympathizers. From there the tapes were smuggled back into Iran by courier to be reproduced and distributed around the mosques and bazaars.

Khomeini's classes in Najaf began to steadily increase in size and number. By the latter stages of his exile, the Grand Ayatollah had trained as many as five hundred mutjahid and lectured to twelve thousand religious students who made the trek over the border from Iran. Each wave of acolytes returned home filled with Khomeini's message of hatred toward the Shah.

WHILE KHOMEINI LINGERED in exile, the Shah exploited the international scene to emerge on the world stage as a confident, seasoned statesman. In 1971 President Richard Nixon welcomed his Iranian ally's offer to shoulder the burden of defense in the Persian Gulf at a time when the White House was focused on ending the Vietnam War and avoiding new foreign entanglements. "The Persian Gulf delivers about 70 percent of Europe's energy needs and about 90 percent of Japan's," explained the Shah. "If these lines of communication are not secure, then Japan and Europe will crack. So while we are doing this for ourselves, at the same time I think we are rendering a great service to the whole of Europe and Japan." At a time when anti-American sentiment was running high throughout Asia and the Middle East, the Shah's staunch pro-Western credentials made him stand out as a loyal ally. In return, Nixon agreed to end restrictions on U.S. arms sales to Iran and tacitly approved the Shah's demand that he charge higher oil prices to Western consumers to finance his country's military buildup, nuclear program, and industrialization. "But I like him, I like him, and I like the country," Nixon enthused. "And some of those other bastards out there I don't like, right? I just wish there were a few more leaders around the world with his foresight. . . . And his ability, his ability to run, let's face it, a virtual dictatorship in a benign way."

The Shah's foreign policy triumphs masked a growing malaise at home. Ten years had passed since he decided to rule and reign, and the White Revolution had achieved many of its immediate objectives. Wealthier peasant farmers tilled their own land and sent their produce to market. Women enjoyed the right to vote, divorce, work, receive an education, and secure abortions. The rising tide of prosperity enriched and enlarged the urban middle class. Even many of the Shah's most severe critics on the left, including opposition leaders such as the Liberation Movement's Mehdi Bazargan, worked in the private sector and put their connections and skills to good use to enjoy a high standard of living. Yet materialism brought with it a host of new problems and challenges. Many Iranians were disoriented by the pace of change and increasingly questioned the logic behind rapid modernization. They worried that it diminished and threatened family life, culture, and traditional values. The old ways still exerted a strong pull. "Our economic progress is a wonderful thing, but we are being swamped by you," former Savak chief Hassan Pakravan told the American journalist Frances Fitzgerald. "No one cares for anything but money nowadays. We are overwhelmed by material goods, and we are losing our own values. Children don't respect their parents. Of course, there's nothing we can do about it. The modern world must come, and we are powerless. But what you have, is that really a way of life?"

The Shah was beginning to understand that total political power and full coffers could not solve every problem. He could impose laws but not enforce them. Despite the money he lavished on his country's best and brightest, the elite universities remained in a constant state of upheaval and rebellion. After spending a fortune to build up the Iranian Imperial Navy, he had recently attended maneuvers during which every cannon fired had missed its target. "These are the people that I rely on in planning my foreign policy, in risking confrontation with foreign powers; and yet you can see for yourself what a bunch of cretins they've turned out to be," he told Alam. He pumped billions in oil revenues into the domestic economy only to learn of food shortages and inflation. Despite thousands of new schools, rapid population growth meant the government was falling behind in its campaign to improve literacy. Many poorer peasants had been freed at great cost only to walk off the land in search of better lives in the big cities. Women emancipated a decade earlier were now covering their heads and in some cases even returning to full hijab. Recently a popular preacher had delivered a radio address without bestowing the usual blessing on the head of state. "What a farce," he groused. "Anyone courting popularity does his damnedest to steer clear of the court."

The proud monarch who only two years earlier had led a parade of kings, queens, and presidents at Persepolis struggled to contain the worries that kept him up at night. Even the 5- and 10-milligram capsules of Valium he took each night to combat anxiety failed to keep the insomnia at bay. Iranian students reserved a special loathing for the man who thought of himself as their father. Nothing he did for them was ever good enough. They cynically dismissed land reform, women's emancipation, free education, free health care, and economic growth as a giant fraud perpetrated to please his American and Zionist "puppet masters." "I believe that the peasantry are with me," the Shah lamented, "but it is not so true of the younger intelligentsia. The younger people—they are in the National Front—have no ties to the ordinary people. They are a problem for me. Everything they have advocated I have done. We have made more reforms than they have asked for. I do not understand why they are not with me."

The Shah was too slow to understand that his people's spiritual malaise could not be solved with more charts, studies, projections, and forecasts. Their ailment was one of the heart and not the head. Court Minister Alam gingerly suggested that His Majesty might wish to change the way he spoke to his people. Ten years had passed since he had imposed reforms from the top down. Security was too tight. The people needed to breathe. Perhaps, recommended Alam, the time had come to "reform popular attitudes. But by subtlety; it cannot be achieved merely by issuing commands." The real culprit, in Alam's view, was not the Shah, whom he regarded as the visionary Iran needed, but Prime Minister Amir Abbas Hoveyda, whom he caustically referred to as "old Quasimodo" and regarded as a corrosive and cynical influence in public life. Since taking office in 1965 after the assassination of his friend Ali Mansur, Hoveyda had defied the odds and retained the monarch's confidence through several terms in office. The scion of an aristocratic family, like so many of Iran's ruling elite, Hoveyda was also related to senior religious figures, in his case the marja Grand Ayatollah Khoi, who resided in Najaf. Hoveyda was intelligent, charming, and erudite, but also servile, obsequious, and well versed in the Persian art of court flattery.

The Shah enjoyed Hoveyda's company and relaxed visibly in his presence. A palace aide recalled that he was once taken aback when His Majesty broke protocol and requested a whiskey for his prime minister. "They shared a love of French culture and the French language," wrote Hoveyda's biographer. "In Hoveyda, the Shah also found an intellectual of sound credentials, with a voracious appetite for books and ideas, who could banter about the history, culture, and politics of the West with the best of his Western counterparts. More important, Hoveyda was also accommodating toward the King's growing appetite to concentrate more and more of the government's daily functions in his own hands." Smart enough not to debate the Shah in his presence, the prime minister fed the perception that he existed only to carry his master's water. "The Shah is the Chairman of the Board and I am the Managing Director," was how he described his role to Britain's ambassador Antony Parsons. "Well Tony," he said on another occasion, "you know His Majesty's definition of a dialogue. It is—I speak, you listen. He will not change." "Hoveyda was a very good friend," said Mahnaz Afkhami, who served as Iran's minister of women's affairs. "He was charming, cultured and good with people. But he established the situation where he got technocrats to run the country. We had complete freedom to do what we loved. We had resources. We didn't have to deal with constituencies. Just as long as we didn't meddle in politics. The security was taken care of. But no one was taking care of the political system. Hoveyda kept saying, 'The Shah is making all the decisions,' which wasn't true. He made it appear as though it was the Shah doing everything. But in three years I only had three meetings with the Shah and no direction from him."

No one doubted Hoveyda's competence as a manager. He had a knack for spotting talent and his cabinet was staffed with highly capable administrators and technocrats. The prime minister was smart, charming, and cultivated friendships with members of the Imperial Family, ambassadors, intellectuals, and the clergy. They tolerated his alcoholism and rumored homosexuality, though not everyone was patient or forgiving. "Amir, are you drunk already?" Ardeshir Zahedi once barked at him during a daytime reception. His door was open to all comers—even the young student revolutionary Abolhassan Banisadr had enjoyed access to Hoveyda. As early as 1959, when Banisadr was already in open revolt against the regime, he had found a sympathetic ear in Hoveyda who at the time was serving on the board of directors of the National Iranian Oil Company. "I was usually frank and ruthless in my criticism of him and the regime he served," Banisadr later said of his encounters with Hoveyda. "He bore it all with a grin. On more than one occasion, I asked him to help free friends who had fallen into the hands of the secret police, and he usually did what he could. I grew to like him; his problem was that he had no religious faith at all." Hoveyda was the only government official Banisadr bothered to call on before he left for exile in Paris. Hoveyda's willingness to entertain the very agent who sought the Shah's overthrow hinted at not only his bald cynicism—he liked to keep all his options open—but also his need to be liked even by his enemies. Perhaps the most persistent criticism of Hoveyda, the technocrat par excellence, was that no one really knew what he stood for except the maintenance of his high office with its perks and privileges.

Hoveyda encouraged the popular perception that the Shah refused to heed advice or listen to reason, and that he exhibited the tendencies of a megalomaniac. The Shah was stubborn and proud, it was true, and already far too isolated. He could be petulant and thin-skinned in the face of criticism. Far from having a closed mind, however, he enjoyed discussing and debating ideas and policies with his ministers as long as they did not oppose his wishes in public, and he showed himself open to consider any and all new concepts and proposals as long as they could strengthen Iran and improve the lives of as many Iranians as possible in the shortest possible time. His mind was like a sponge. The Shah's main problem was that with an education no higher than that of a high school student, like so many self-taught experts he had a dangerous habit of embracing fashionable theories and accepting them as fundamental truths rather than broad-stroke policy guidelines. What he needed was a prime minister with a confident personality matched by an understated demeanor. By finessing the royal ego, lauding each of His Majesty's new initiatives, dismissing legitimate criticisms, and offering assurances that all was well despite his own reservations to the contrary, Hoveyda did the Shah and the monarchy a grave disservice. He withheld disagreeable information that he feared might cause disfavor, agreed to carry out imperial edicts even as he consigned them to the graveyard of committees of experts, and quietly manipulated the monarch's paperwork and instructions to his benefit. Right to the end, when not even his young friend Banisadr could save him from the executioner's bullets, Hoveyda insisted he had just been following orders.

Alam was puzzled as to why the Shah still retained confidence in a politician whose government "should be so negligent . . . its indifference and, on occasion, its brute aggression toward the people remind me of the way an army of occupation might treat a nation defeated in war." Criticizing Hoveyda, of course, allowed Alam to avoid the real elephant in the room, namely his master's obsession with control, his chronic distrust of subordinates, and the personal insecurities that meant he preferred to surround himself with yes-men who told him what he wanted to hear. He observed on more than one occasion to the Shah that the security forces went overboard in roughing up the regime's opponents. He worried that too many young Iranians were alienated to the point they favored the overthrow of the monarchy. Nor did the Shah object in December 1973 when Alam admitted that he feared "a growing sense of alienation between the regime and people." "I'm afraid you're right," he finally conceded. "I've sensed the same thing myself." They discussed the matter, and Alam felt that a turning point had been reached, that the Shah understood that materialism on its own was not a panacea. Hoveyda's government should be replaced and a caretaker cabinet appointed to lead the country into free elections.

The U.S. intelligence community watched with interest the Shah's repeated efforts and persistent failure to broaden his regime's base of support among the people. "There is considerable anxiety," reported the CIA, "that the Shah, in his impatience to move [Iran] ahead now, is failing to prepare institutions and leaders that could make [the] transition to post-Shah Iran without serious political turmoil and without serious damage to social and economic progress." The intelligence agency took note of the "essentially negative role" played by the "educated professional class—some even from establishment families—who refuse to cooperate with the ruling elite, and the clergy, whose strength lies in the emotions of the Iranian masses and whose opposition to the Shah's government is nearly total." But the CIA was hampered in its ability to conduct more in-depth assessments of the domestic mood. As part of the hosting rights for two CIA listening posts that monitored Soviet missile tests in Central Asia, the Shah had extracted a concession from Washington to forgo intelligence gathering inside Iran. "Iran was in the category of states that we agreed not to conduct intense political intelligence activities," recalled Dr. Zbigniew Brzezinski, who served as President Carter's national security adviser in the late seventies. "That left us at a disadvantage because we relied on independent observers and we had no backup of our own [to assess conditions inside Iran]."

Iran's domestic discontents were overshadowed by the earth-shaking events of late 1973 and early 1974 in the Middle East. Simmering tensions between Israel and Egypt erupted into open warfare in October 1973. Furious that the United States airlifted military supplies to Israel, Arab states in the Middle East imposed an oil embargo that triggered panic buying in the West and sent crude prices soaring. The Shah's decision to remain neutral in the conflict earned him Nixon's gratitude. But he also saw an opportunity to exploit the crisis to Iran's benefit. On December 23, 1973, he hosted a meeting of Persian Gulf oil producers who followed his suggestion that they double the price of oil for the second time in a year. The Shah's oil coup stunned his admirers back in Washington. The "oil shock" devastated the economies of Western oil consumers even as Iran's income from oil doubled to $4.6 billion in 1973–1974, then rocketed to $17.8 billion a year later to a total of $98.2 billion for the next five years. In just a few months the Shah had seized control of the oil markets and established himself as the dominant figure within OPEC, the oil producers' cartel that set prices and determined levels of oil production. Rather than invest Iran's new billions offshore in bonds, treasury notes, and real estate, the Shah decided to pump it straight back into the domestic economy to give it the push he felt was needed to break the cycle of poverty and underdevelopment. Finally, after decades of struggle and turmoil, the Shah felt himself to be untouchable and indispensable. He had broken free from the Russians, the British, and now the Americans. "Iran is not a volcano now," he assured a visitor to Niavaran. "I want the standard of living in Iran in ten years' time to be exactly on a level with that in Europe today. In twenty years' time we shall be ahead of the United States."

The Shah stood at the apex of a new world economic order. "Once dismissed by Western diplomats as an insecure, ineffective playboy-King, this emperor of oil commands new respect these days, as much for his ambitions as for his wealth," declared *Time* magazine. "In the 33rd year of an often uncertain reign, Mohammad Reza Shah Pahlavi has brought Iran to a threshold of grandeur that is at least analogous to what Cyrus the Great achieved for ancient Persia." Bankers joked that when the Shah sneezed, Wall Street caught cold. Iran's astonishing 33 percent economic growth rate for 1973 was outpaced by 40 percent the following year, and gross national product was set to expand at the rate of 50 percent in twelve months. The economy took off like an Apollo rocket to the moon. "We have no real limit on money," boasted the government's senior economist. "None." The Shah interpreted this remark in the most literal sense. He ordered billions in new military equipment and made all elementary school education free and compulsory. Iran was not a major dairy producer, but he decreed that every schoolchild was entitled to a free glass of milk each day. He purchased a 25 percent stake in the West German steel company Krupp and spent $16 billion in the fiscal year 1974–1975 "on projects ranging from schools to hospitals." Eager to buy international prestige and influence, the Shah contributed $700 million to the International Monetary Fund and another $1 million to the University of Southern California to endow a professorial chair in engineering. U.S. intelligence analysts were confounded by the Shah's oil coup against his former patrons. "He *was* our baby, but now he has grown up," complained a CIA official whose admission signaled that the United States had finally lost the ability to influence Iranian foreign and economic policy.

ALI KANI, A prominent member of the Iranian political establishment, stopped off in Beirut in 1973 to see his old friend Imam Musa Sadr. The two men met at the St. George Hotel, and from there drove to Musa Sadr's residence in the capital. Although this was a social visit between two friends who had known each other since childhood, Musa Sadr also had serious business to discuss. He had a secret message he wanted Kani to pass on to the Shah that concerned the behavior of his old teacher Grand Ayatollah Khomeini.

Reza Shah, seen here with his young son and heir, Crown Prince Mohammad Reza, founded the Pahlavi Dynasty. Through sheer force of will he revived the fortunes of the Persian monarchy. (Getty)

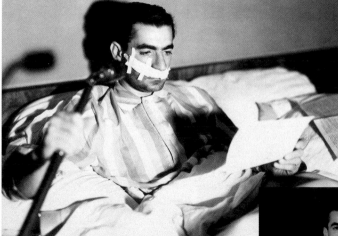

Following the 1949 attempt on his life, Iran's young King broadcast a reassuring message to the nation from his hospital bed. (Corbis)

The Shah's wedding to Soraya Esfandiary in 1951 was a sumptuous affair. (Getty)

In 1959 the Shah married Farah Diba, an architecture student. (Getty)

The birth of an heir, Crown Prince Reza, here with his parents in 1964, secured the Imperial succession. (Magnum)

In 1967 Iran's glamorous Imperial couple attended a parade. (Magnum)

The Imperial coronation in 1967, an occasion for old-world pomp and pageantry. (Magnum)

The Shah of Iran was first among equals at the 1969 funeral of former U.S. president Dwight Eisenhower. (Corbis)

In 1971 the Pahlavis welcomed to Persepolis Prince Rainier III and Princess Grace of Monaco. (Getty)

The Imperial family visited
Shiraz in 1971. While the
Queen tended to Princess
Leila, her husband posed with
Prince Ali Reza, Crown Prince
Reza, and Princess Farahnaz.
(Getty)

In 1972 the Pahlavis enjoyed their winter ski vacation
in St. Moritz. From left: Queen Farah, Prince Ali Reza,
the Shah, Princess Farahnaz, Crown Prince Reza,
Princess Leila. (Corbis)

The King and Queen of Iran, partners in marriage
and in power. (Pahlavi family photograph)

Asadollah Alam, minister of the Imperial Court, was a shrewd political operator who kept a watchful eye over his master and the Iranian scene. In 1974 he supported the Shah at a formal court reception. (Getty)

Prime Minister Amir Abbas Hoveyda, who ran the government his way. (Getty)

The Shah was happiest in the company of his generals. In the midseventies he attended maneuvers with General Mohammad Khatami, Princess Fatemeh's husband, and with General Nader Djahanbani, the "blue-eyed general" whose brother Khosrow married Princess Shahnaz. (Pahlavi family photograph)

Queen Farah, whose influence was felt throughout the old Persian kingdom.
(Getty)

During a trip to the provinces, the Queen was surrounded by adoring schoolchildren.
(Pahlavi family photograph)

In 1974 the Imperial family gathered for a family portrait: the Shah and Queen Farah, seated front row center; Princess Shahnaz, seated to her father's right; to the Queen's left, with Prince Ali Reza between them, Princess Ashraf; Princess Farahnaz and Crown Prince Reza behind their parents; Prince Gholam Reza and his wife, Princess Manigeh, fifth and sixth in from the left, second row from the rear; Khosrow Djahanbani, partially obscured in the back row, second from the right. Seated in the front row, far left, Princess Hamdamsaltaneh, the Shah's rarely seen half-sister. (Pahlavi family photograph)

Throughout most of his reign the Shah enjoyed correct if strained relations with senior Muslim clerics. In this telling image he conversed with Seyyed Hassan Emami, a prominent Tehran clergyman. (Pahlavi family photograph)

Grand Ayatollah Ruhollah Khomeini, whose vendetta against the Pahlavi family led to rebellion and revolution. (Corbis)

Imam Musa Sadr, whose disappearance in 1978 sealed the Shah's fate. (Sadr family photograph)

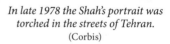

*In late 1978 the Shah's portrait was
torched in the streets of Tehran.*
(Corbis)

*The tearful scene at Mehrebad Airport
on January 16, 1979, the day the King
and Queen left Iran to avoid civil war
and bloodshed.* (Corbis)

As the sons of two of Iran's most revered grand ayatollahs, Ali Kani and Musa Sadr had more than friendship in common. Theirs was the insular, tightly knit world of the highborn families who dominated the Iranian religious and political elites. In the early 1960s, while Musa Sadr was busy establishing himself in Lebanon, Ali Kani had served in the cabinet of his friend Asadollah Alam, whose premiership coincided with the uprising of June 1963. Kani was at Alam's side during the showdown with Khomeini. He always believed that had Alam remained in power as prime minister he would never have allowed Khomeini to leave Iran for the relative safety and comfort of exile. "They crushed the uprising. But Alam wanted Khomeini to stay in Iran under watch. But [Alam's successor as prime minister] Mansur asked the King to send him to Turkey." Kani regarded the Status of Forces Agreement, which provided immunity for U.S. military personnel based in Iran, as nothing short of "a disaster" for the regime.

Through the years, Ali Kani and Musa Sadr stayed in touch. They exchanged letters and whenever Kani traveled back and forth to Paris he made sure to stop off in Beirut to see his old friend so they could compare notes on politics and religion. "Musa Sadr was a very intelligent man," remembered Kani. "Very charismatic and attractive. He was too intelligent to be influenced by others."

At the end of his short stay in Beirut, Musa Sadr took his friend aside and handed him a twenty-page booklet written in Arabic that contained "the concise thoughts of Khomeini." This was the bound version of the Grand Ayatollah's lectures calling for the overthrow of the monarchy and the establishment of an Islamic government.

"This is the juice of a sick mind," warned the Imam. "However you wish, by any means, let the King know about this," he urged Kani. "Give it to your friend [the King]. Tell him to publish 200,000 copies and distribute them to the universities so the intellectuals can read Khomeini and learn who he really is."

Ali Kani read Khomeini's treatise on the plane trip back to Tehran. What he read shocked him to the core and he instinctively understood why the Imam wanted the Shah to read the tract. It was imperative that he understand the nature of the threat he faced in Najaf. Once back home, Kani wrote an executive summary of the text in Persian and took it to the palace.

"The Shah read it and he loved it," Kani recalled. The Shah understood that if handled the right way, Khomeini's thesis calling for a clerical dictatorship could expose the idol of Iranian youth as a religious fanatic and dangerous heretic. He instructed Prime Minister Hoveyda to publish *half a million* copies of the booklet and spread them around the universities, bazaars, and mosques—anywhere the people could learn for themselves the truth about the elderly cleric who presented himself as a benign champion of social justice and liberty.

"The next thing I learned, it was with the prime minister," said Kani, who fell into a state of despair when he learned the news. The two men had a long-standing rivalry that had recently ended with a final bitter falling-out and Kani's decision to leave political life. "And Hoveyda sent the plan to a committee to 'study.'" Hoveyda had a standing habit of agreeing with the Shah to his face and then taking the opposite action in private. He regularly sabotaged proposals and plans that he felt undermined his authority, advanced the ambitions of his rivals, or threatened his own agenda. The prime minister's three-man committee was composed of reformed Communists who had been turned by Savak and now worked for the regime. But they were still atheists who cared little for Iran's religious traditions. Months passed while they dithered over what to do. Eventually they chose what they thought was the safest option and decided to recommend suppressing the report altogether. "They maintained that the text would only promote Khomeini, give him a platform, and they opposed publication," said Kani, who personally blamed Hoveyda for what happened next.

In the hands of the regime, the text could have been a powerful weapon to force a public discussion about Khomeini's true intentions. Instead, its suppression only increased its currency as a forbidden tract in the seminaries. University students, who never read the thesis, remained in the dark about its central message.

"Musa Sadr understood the influence of this sick mind and the potential for his ideas to spread," said Ali Kani. So, too, it might be said, did the Shah.

THE PAHLAVIS GATHERED on Kish Island in the Persian Gulf in spring 1974 to celebrate the Nowruz holiday, which fell on March 21. In the eight weeks since his initial diagnosis for lymphoma, the Shah had not felt the need to start the anticancer treatments required to manage his condition.

Events on Kish soon forced his hand.

On the morning of Tuesday, April 9, the Pahlavis were about to leave their beach retreat on Kish Island and fly back to Tehran when General Ayadi startled Alam with the request that he urgently send for Professor Jean Bernard, a renowned hematologist who worked in a hospital in Paris. The swelling in the Shah's abdomen had apparently reappeared. By strange coincidence Asadollah Alam, his closest aide and oldest confidant, was also being treated for a similar form of rare and incurable blood cancer, though without either his or the Shah's knowledge. Alam's Iranian physician, Dr. Abbas Safavian, had successfully persuaded Bernard and his young protégé Dr. Georges Flandrin not to tell their patient the truth about his condition; Alam knew he was ill but did not know his condition was incurable. Now General Ayadi asked Alam to send for Bernard and Flandrin at once, though he withheld the real reason for his request. Alam observed that the Shah remained his usual calm self. All that he said as they flew out was that he wanted the island's construction projects hurried up: "I want them finished in my lifetime."

The French physicians left Paris amid great secrecy on May 1, 1974. When their Air France flight landed at Mehrebad Airport they were greeted on the tarmac by Dr. Safavian, Alam's doctor, who explained that they had been summoned to examine the court minister. Out of his earshot, Bernard confided to his younger colleague that this seemed improbable because Alam's health problems were well known to them. Only when they reached Alam's house did the minister himself reveal the real purpose of their visit, and that they had been called to see "the boss." From there the doctors were ferried to Niavaran, entering the compound's modest right-side entrance, whose lower driveway led to the old Qajar palace, where the Shah maintained his office. Through this entrance it was possible to smuggle visitors into and out of the palace compound without alerting anyone in the main family residence, which sat a few hundred yards up the slope behind a bank of plane trees. From there they walked up the hill to the big house. Georges Flandrin recalled the sensation of seeing the legendary Shah in the flesh for the first time. He and Bernard were surprised and impressed when the Shah casually related his symptoms to them. The two doctors surmised they were dealing with a remarkably well-informed and well-read patient.

Neither the Shah nor Ayadi mentioned their previous visit to Fellinger. This was in keeping with the monarch's preferred way of doing business. He liked to consult different experts about the same problem and get a variety of opinions that would help him reach his own determination. In this case, he wanted Bernard and Flandrin to tell him what *they* thought was wrong. They drew blood, performed their tests, and returned to inform General Ayadi that the Shah had lymphoma. Ayadi did not register surprise but insisted they not mention the word "cancer" to the patient. The formal diagnosis they eventually settled on was "Waldenstrom's disease," a technical term used to describe cancer of the blood. Still, it defied belief that the Shah, when presented with their conclusions, did not grasp their meaning. Unfortunately for the doctors, at this exact same time Waldenstrom's disease had been attributed as the cause of death of France's president Georges Pompidou, and the Shah had followed the Pompidou case with great interest. He and Alam had both expressed admiration for the president's decision to conceal his disease from the French people: his honorable decision to die in the saddle in the spring of 1974 showed that it was possible for a head of state to work with dignity right up to the end.

In May 1974 the burden of knowledge was still limited to the Shah, General Ayadi, Jean Bernard, Georges Flandrin, and most likely Alam, though nowhere in his diaries did he reveal his knowledge. Alam arranged for the doctors to treat the Shah either in the same house he rented in northern Tehran; in a small room at Saadabad Palace; in the main residence at Niavaran, which was usually quiet when the Queen and her children were away on duty or at school; or in a safe house in northern Tehran. Bernard and Flandrin started treatment by prescribing a daily dosage of three chlorambucil tablets and monitoring the patient's progress from Paris. There was little else they could do but manage the disease until it reached the next critical stage. They returned to Tehran in September. By now three others were privy to the secret: Dr. Abbas Safavian; his French mentor Dr. Paul Milliez; and most likely the unknown Iranian official whose residence in northern Tehran was used as the doctors' safe house when in Tehran.

Bernard and Flandrin saw the Shah again in January 1975 at St. Moritz during his annual ski holiday. They arrived at a particularly sensitive time for the world economy: financial markets were on edge because of the Iranian monarch's refusal to countenance lower oil prices. Statesmen including President Valéry Giscard d'Estaing, Pompidou's successor, and U.S. secretary of state Henry Kissinger flew to Switzerland to see the Shah and lobby their national interests. The doctors' visit to St. Moritz, an area saturated with television camera crews and journalists, entailed an extraordinary level of risk, but the Shah displayed his usual sangfroid and carried on as usual. Flandrin watched in horror as he barreled past him down the slopes when both men knew a serious fall could fatally rupture his spleen.

Giscard d'Estaing later recalled that during their discussion he had asked the Shah why he was in such a hurry to get things done back home. The Shah told the French president that he preferred to step down sooner but knew that his son was too young and inexperienced to take over. He said he was determined to stay on and put in place the building blocks for Iran's transformation to a modern industrialized state. More than anything, he made clear, what was needed was time.

FROM HUMBLE BEGINNINGS in a small office staffed by a single private secretary, Queen Farah's Special Bureau by 1974 boasted a $5 million annual operating budget and employed forty office workers to manage her caseload, travel schedule, twenty-six patronages, and respond to the staggering fifty thousand letters a year that poured in addressed to her. Writing a letter to the King or Queen was a Persian tradition, and many of those Farah's office received were appeals for help. "We will have to continue to do this until our welfare system is more spread out," she explained. "Many problems touch me and I can be a good advocate," she said. "My husband is interested in Iran's GNP. I am interested in its GNH—Gross National Happiness." Not since Catherine the Great of Russia had the world known a female sovereign entrusted with as much influence and as many resources. By now Farah had emerged as a political force in her own right. Each week she received Prime Minister Hoveyda in audience to discuss policy initiatives. She lobbied government ministers to support her causes and worked the phones to cut through red tape. She enjoyed influence at every level of the national bureaucracy. She learned the hard way that the more active she was the more people depended on her, which in turn meant more problems arrived at her door.

The Queen was sensitive to charges that the White Revolution had disrupted traditional life. Tehran's building boom blighted the capital with smog, construction, and traffic congestion. "The only beautiful thing we had in Tehran was the view of the mountains," she said. "And I didn't want people to build higher, to ruin the view." Flying back and forth between engagements in her helicopter, she scouted the horizon for land that could be turned into parks. "I didn't want to repeat the mistakes of other countries." One of her triumphs was the transformation of a horse race track in Tehran's western quarter into a grand park. The Shah was traveling in Europe when his wife heard the land was about to be turned into another concrete monolith. She wrote him a letter urging him to dedicate the grounds as the centerpiece of a campus dedicated to the arts, culture, and education. But when it came to real estate even the Queen's influence was limited. She opposed construction of Tehran's Inter-Continental Hotel, condemning it as an eyesore, but the project went ahead anyway. In Mashad her efforts to preserve the ancient bazaar were foiled when the local governor proceeded with demolition. She was horrified when she learned only after the fact that hundreds of houses and shops had been bulldozed in an egregious act of vandalism that helped turn local sentiment against the regime.

Day-to-day operations within the Queen's Special Bureau were managed by a secretary appointed at her husband's discretion. In the early seventies the job was filled by Karim Pasha Bahadori. He was later replaced by Hushang Nahavandi, the scholar and chancellor who had welcomed the Shah onto the grounds of Pahlau University in April 1971. "He was very hardworking and the head of my office," Farah remembered, though she was also aware of Nahavandi's abrasive personal style. "People said that he was using my office as a stepping-stone to becoming prime minister. He had friends but he was not popular." Farah's cousin Reza Ghotbi, her closest confidant, was appointed Managing Director of National Iranian Radio and Television (NIRT) in 1969. From his sinecure he influenced the media and cultural affairs with his liberal views. Seyyed Hossein Nasr, one of Shia Islam's preeminent scholars, was another prominent adviser. Nasr made Farah's acquaintance when he returned to Iran in the early sixties after studying at Harvard and the Massachusetts Institute of Technology. "I met her and she became very interested in my devotion to Persian culture," Nasr remembered. "For many years in the 1960s and seventies I used to cooperate with her very closely on projects such as saving old crafts and urban planning."

The Queen's party, though never formally declared, stood for more political freedom, restraints placed on Savak, and an end to censorship. Liberals argued that these reforms were essential if the monarchy was to stay relevant in the affections of a population becoming steadily younger, more educated, and more worldly. Many intellectuals and even some leftists who could not abide the Shah were prepared to set aside their qualms

to work for his wife. Consciously or not, Farah replicated the role of intermediary and mediator her husband had carved out during Reza Shah's
reign forty years earlier. "The Queen," said Reza Ghotbi, "was always the
person to whom intellectuals would go for support, to get her protection
against the government, Savak, the police, so she was involved and concerned and in contact with these people."

Farah used her influence at court and her back channel to Parviz
Sabeti to quietly help artists, writers, playwrights, and poets arrested or
harassed by the security forces. "They once arrested a man and gave him
three years in jail for reading Chekhov!" she said, her voice rising in incre-
dulity. "Can you *believe* it? I intervened on his behalf and he was released."
The acclaimed artist Zenderoudi turned to her when he was arrested on
the streets of Tehran for having shoulder-length hair, taken to a police
station, and forcibly shorn. "Furious, I spoke to my husband about it,"
said Farah. The Shah agreed to sack the national chief of police. But not
even his wife was immune from Savak's heavy-handed tactics. Before the
Queen attended public events, her staff forwarded the names of attendees
so they could be prescreened. But her attendance at the opening of a new
art gallery was marred when security agents prevented some guests from
entering the building and subjected others to humiliating interrogations.
One of her oldest friends, Fereydoun Djavadi, now lecturing at the University of Tehran, was approached by a Savak agent who pressed him to
become an informant. Djavadi refused and demanded the man leave his
office. This sort of intimidation, directed at someone who regularly social-
ized with the King and Queen, sent the chilling message that no one was
beyond reach or surveillance.

The Queen drew the lightning for her husband whom establishment
conservatives were loath to criticize. The ulama were disturbed that a
woman should occupy such a prominent role in national affairs and speak
out on family issues, which they regarded as their prerogative. Within the
regime, conservatives such as Ardeshir Zahedi blamed Farah for giving
false hope to the same subversives they had helped crush twenty years
earlier. "Why do you hire so many leftists?" he once challenged her. But
Zahedi's criticism could also have been directed at Court Minister Alam,
another rival, whose deputy, the former minister of justice, had previously
been a high-ranking member of the Communist Tudeh Party. The Shah's
preference was to co-opt as many leftists as possible. He viewed their
placement at all levels of government not as evidence of a conspiracy but

as a sign of progress—finally, the intellectuals were coming around. If the Queen hired former Marxists and Maoists it was with her husband's express permission. Foreign diplomats to the Pahlavi Court welcomed her moderating influence. "I saw the Empress as the perfect complement to the Shah," wrote Britain's ambassador Tony Parsons. "Where he inspired awe and fear, she inspired love and affection. Beautiful, intelligent, artistic, compassionate, she seemed to have a remarkably free and open relationship with her husband. The general view was that she was one of the very few people who could speak their minds to him and that her influence was beneficial."

11

THE TURNING

Right across Islam, the mullahs are doomed.
—THE SHAH

People are turning to Islam.
—GRAND AYATOLLAH KAZEM SHARIATMADARI

In centuries past the Persian Gulf island of Kish had prospered as a trading port and pirate anchorage. When the Shah first saw Kish in the late sixties the island had fallen on hard times, reduced to a few settlements that survived on fishing and smuggling. He was entranced, however, and decided that Kish's long beaches, temperate winter climate, and strategic location sixteen miles off Iran's southern coast made it the ideal venue for a holiday home and a convenient base from which to visit nearby ports and military and oil installations. He also hoped to revitalize the island by establishing it as a mecca for European and regional tourism. The Pahlavis flew down to Kish in March 1976 to spend the Persian New Year Nowruz holidays in their seaside palace on the western shore, a large whitewashed bungalow nestled amid sand dunes. The palace's strikingly modern design was "simple, sharply angled, steeply gabled, and with a retreating, pyramidal formation of balconies, those at the top being set back far from those at the base." Kish Palace had the ambience of a big beach house with children and animals running around and toys littering the public rooms. The Queen rode her bicycle through the corridors. "Kish was fantastic," she said. "Architecturally it was very nice. We swam but we were very careful because there were sharks." Her husband was not deterred and swam out as far as he could, his head spotted at a center of a bobbing circle of Colonel Djahinbini's bodyguards.

While his guests enjoyed themselves on the beach, the Shah reached a fateful decision about his future. Thirteen years after the army crackdown that paved the way for personal rule, and more than two years since Court Minister Alam first advised him to start sharing power, the Shah decided to embark on the immensely difficult task of reforming the political system to allow for a greater measure of democracy. His health problems and the succession were his foremost concerns, but he was also disturbed by the economic convulsions set in motion by the oil boom, realizing that "an informed and urbanized society could not be run in the old way." The Shah followed his usual pattern of establishing a committee of experts to consider the problem and make a series of recommendations. Their report made for sober reading. They pointed out that the Shah faced a daunting series of challenges: economic problems, institutional corruption, political stagnation, youth rebellion, popular resentment of foreign and especially American influence, and the emergence of an urban proletariat with all the makings of a revolutionary underclass. Pressure for reform was coming from different directions. Since the Shah had so far failed to build independent political institutions that could outlast him, the survival of the Pahlavi state still relied to a large extent on the quiescence of three traditional groups: the ulama; the merchants, or *bazaaris;* and intellectuals. The Shah believed that the 1963 crackdown, the White Revolution, and the oil boom had eliminated the potential for a repeat of the coalition that led the 1905–1906 revolution. By 1976, however, each of these three groups was disillusioned enough with the Shah's rule to set aside their differences and start a mobilization against the state. The complaints of the clergy and intellectuals were well known. Less understood were the fears and insecurities of the guardians of the old economy, the merchants whose way of life was threatened by the emergence of Pahlavi state power, big corporations, and foreign investment.

If the mosque was Iran's beating heart, the bazaar was the lung that drew in commerce and exhaled prosperity to everyone's benefit. "The bazaar is not just a collection of shops, as it might appear at first sight," wrote an Iranian journalist. "In it there are merchants worth hundreds of millions of dollars as well as small businessmen, artisans, craftsmen and a whole army of middlemen. The bazaar also invests in agriculture, the building sector and, in recent years, the nation's expanding industries."

The bazaars were built beside the mosques and for good reason: the ulama ᵗᵃ ?
relied on the merchant class to handle their business transactions and provide them with banking and investment advice. As late as 1976 fully
80 percent of clergy income was reinvested in charities, religious schools,
publishers, and theological colleges. Merchant-clergy relations extended
beyond commerce. The bazaaris played an important role in helping the
ulama mobilize large crowds for religious processions. In Tehran, for
example, the mullahs could expect to call on five thousand agents from
the bazaar to help them organize annual big religious processions that
typically drew tens of thousands of participants during the holy months
of Muharram and Ramadan. The Tehran bazaar's network of operatives
extended deep into the southern and eastern suburbs, where Khomeini
supporters predominated. In the absence of democracy, the bazaaris found
it convenient to use "the religious processions and leaders for political
purposes" and formed tactical political alliances with the mullahs. The
mosques were run by their relatives, clients, and customers and served as
a convenient means to an end, not least because religious devotees were a
captive audience that could be readily mobilized in support of a good
cause. "Politically, it is the bazaar that influences the Shiite clergy and not
vice versa," noted an Iranian observer. "This is because the bazaar, in addition to holding the purse-strings, has all the networks . . . and is also
capable of doing something concrete and valuable by closing down. Without the active backing of the bazaar virtually no section of the clergy
could wield political influence for any length of time."

The Shah and his ministers, determined to build a strong, centralized
state on the French model, saw the bazaaris as an impediment to modernity and reform. "The Iranian government, on the other hand, has developed an increasing fascination for economic 'etatisme', complete with
'planning' laws to protect the consumer and institutions needed to consolidate its domination of the nation economy," observed *Kayhan*. "This
trend was accelerated as the flow of oil money, together with an equally
profuse flow of Western-oriented technocrats, enabled the government to
assume the role of Providence itself." The bazaaris protested when the government asked small businesses to report their total number of employees so that even temporary workers could be paid social security. Iranians
were by nature suspicious of central authority and resented clumsy official efforts to impose and collect taxes or interfere in price-fixing. The
Ministry of Commerce further angered the business community by

accusing shopkeepers and merchants of greed and graft, then hiring zealous students to harass anyone they suspected of overcharging and con-
tributing to inflation. The government's shock tactics hurt profits and
drove many bazaaris into politics for the first time since the early sixties.

The old merchant class worried that the Shah's economic reforms
threatened their power and wealth. The injection of billions of dollars in
oil revenues into manufacturing, textiles, petrochemicals, and the auto
industry, but especially the introduction of new rules and regulations to
introduce modern taxation and banking systems, directly threatened the
living standards and profits of the bazaaris, who adhered to the slogan
that "government is best that governs least." As long as the general economy prospered, the merchants held their fire. But the Shah and his ministers miscalculated when they decided to inject most of the country's oil
stimulus back into the domestic economy. They rejected the alternative
course of action, which was to temporarily invest oil revenues abroad until
a domestic infrastructure was in place to safely absorb and distribute the
money. The consequences of the decision to spend everything at once soon
became apparent. "The cost of living in Iran—where more than 60 percent
of the families have a subsistence level income of $15 a week—is jumping
almost daily and is expected to rise soon to 20 percent above what it was
last year," the New York Times reported in October 1974. "Prices for staple
foods, textile goods and home appliances have been soaring, in some cases
to 100 percent above last year's levels. A black market has developed to
circumvent the Government's price controls." Other problems caused by
the oil boom included shortages of affordable housing, basic foodstuffs,
and skilled labor. While poor Iranians suffered, Tehran's northern hills
became a flashy showcase for the nouveaux riches, whose boorish behavior
shocked traditional tastes. "There's something a little desperate in the
air," observed Newsweek magazine. "The spiraling price of oil has made
Tehran a boom town reminiscent of San Francisco in the days of the great
Oil Rush. Hordes of bankers, brokers, super-salesmen and carpetbaggers
of every description fill the three major hotels to overflowing. . . . By day a
haze of smog drifts skyward against the magnificent backdrop of the
Alborz Mountains. By night the city's restaurants and nightclubs are
jammed with expense-account tycoons wolfing down caviar and stuffing
wads of money into the bosoms of belly dancers."

Boom was followed in short order by bust. Iran's economy was left peri-
lously exposed when Western oil consumers, their economies battered by

high oil prices, entered recession and sharply reduced spending on fuel imports. For the Shah, who had personally approved billions in new expenditures, the unexpected dip in oil revenues had immediate political consequences. His main objective until now, observed *Newsweek*, "was to raise Iran's standard of living fast enough to prevent his subjects from falling into the temptation of organizing a revolution of their own against him." Court Minister Alam was beside himself with worry. He understood that the social contract between the Shah and his people was at risk of dissolving: "I genuinely fear that this may be the first vague rumbling of impending revolution."

The Shah suspected a plot. Three years earlier, he had issued Western oil companies with an ultimatum: surrender production rights or leave the country. The companies had settled for a new deal by which they ceded the right to produce oil in Iran in return for the right to sell Persian crude on the world market. The problem was that the oil companies were not obliged to take to market quantities of oil they couldn't sell. With global markets glutted, they preferred not to place new orders with the National Iranian Oil Company until consumer demand in the West picked up. The result was that Iran's national oil company was left with many millions of barrels of unsold oil. The Shah suspected the oil companies were punishing him for his decision to nationalize production and end their lucrative pumping rights.

The Shah's next two missteps were entirely self-inflicted. In an attempt to distance the crown from his government and stay relevant in a rapidly changing society, in March 1975 he abolished Iran's two nominal political parties and replaced them with a single party, the Rastakhiz (Resurgence) Party. In theory, the "King's Party" was supposed to inoculate the throne from the threat of future social unrest, bring the crown closer to the people, and prepare the Iranian nation for a more open, democratic political system. But the Shah utterly failed to communicate that vision to his people, who interpreted the formation of Rastakhiz as a final, brazen attempt to bury their cherished 1906 Constitution. The Shah's next folly was to approve a proposal to scrap the Islamic Hegira calendar and replace it with the Persian Imperial calendar, which dated back to the coronation of Cyrus the Great in 599 BC. This gesture to mark the Pahlavi Dynasty's half-century celebrations in 1976 caused needless offense to religious conservatives and confused the public—Iranians went to bed in the year 1355 and woke the next morning in the year 2535. By now it was clear that the Shah and his chief minister had ruled in isolation for too long. The Shah's public pronouncements hinted as much. "My motto is: ask the advice of the technocrats and . . . well, just do the opposite and you'll succeed," he boasted. Another time he said, "I not only make the decisions, I do the thinking."

These debacles suggested the Shah was losing touch. Years earlier, Britain's ambassador Sir Denis Wright had fretted that he "was taking on too much, he wouldn't delegate. . . . He had got into a position where he was taking all the small decisions, all sorts of decisions, and no man could cope with that. What one was frightened of was that he would do something silly because he just hadn't got the knowledge, and might resort to brinkmanship in a way which would get him into serious trouble."

WHILE IRAN'S ECONOMY weakened, popular interest in religion gathered strength as Muslim clerics rejected modernization, which they associated with corruption, income inequality, and political repression. The phenomenon was hardly limited to Iran: in the 1970s tens of millions of Sunni and Shia Muslims shared a horror of Western-style corporate capitalism. They instead found solace in tradition and the old ways. "People are turning to Islam because they recognize that modernization and development have not brought peace of mind," observed Grand Ayatollah Kazem Shariatmadari. "It takes religion to do that." In November 1974 the authorities in Saudi Arabia reported a surge in attendance at the annual hajj, the pilgrimage by observant Muslims to Mecca's Grand Mosque, the holiest site in Islam, whose Kaaba, a fifty-foot-high cloth-covered stone structure, was revered as the "House of God." Each successive hajj broke the record of the previous year until November 1977, when an estimated 1.6 million pilgrims gathered on the plain of Arafat, a barren field twelve miles east of Mecca, to recite verses from the holy book the Quran and to pray for forgiveness of their sins. Their devotions symbolically represented both an end and a beginning: the end of centuries of decline and the beginning of a new, more militant phase in the history of a faith that had emerged from the deserts of western Arabia in the seventh century.

Nowhere was the pace of Western-style development as rapid, or the side effects of the oil boom more keenly felt, than in Iran, where religious sentiment quickened in response to a slowdown in the economy. The first sign of unrest came in June 1975, when supporters of Grand Ayatollah Khomeini staged demonstrations at the Feiziyah seminary in Qom to commemorate the twelfth anniversary of the Fifteen Khordad uprising. Iran, cried the students, was "like a harlot running after the evil ways of the West." The Shah initially interpreted the unrest as a last gasp by "the unholy alliance of black reactionist[s] and stateless Reds." Khomeini's name had recently been raised in his presence. "Khomeini?" he asked. "No one mentions his name any more in Iran, except, perhaps, the terrorists. The so-called Islamic Marxists pronounce his name every now and then. That's all." But Court Minister Alam's diaries traced the gradual realization on the part of both men that old forces were starting to stir and that the ground beneath their feet had shifted. On April 12, 1976, the Shah told his minister that he had interceded on behalf of Grand Ayatollah Khoi with Saddam Hussein, the young Iraqi strongman who had recently launched a crackdown against his country's Shia population. But he said he doubted the Iraqis would pay attention: "Right across Islam, the mullahs are doomed." Then, on the twenty-sixth, Alam delivered a speech at Pahlavi University in Shiraz, where he was "rather alarmed to see so many of the girls wearing the veil."

The revival of popular interest in Islam was not confined to the poor and uneducated. Members of the government and top-ranking generals made pilgrimages to the holy sites and joined Quran study groups. Attendance at Friday prayers marked atonement and was a way for the wealthy and privileged to show solidarity with the less well-to-do. "There seems to be a need for religion, as if we have moved too fast in a direction that is not native to us," said Mahnaz Afkhami, Iran's minister for women's affairs and a self-proclaimed feminist. She spoke from personal experience, having visited holy shrines in Iraq and completed the hajj. "I found it in myself," she told the *New York Times*. The Shah saw attitudes like this as evidence of backsliding. In October 1976 he erupted when Alam broke the news that a party of society ladies led by his sister Princess Fatemeh and his mother-in-law, Madame Diba, requested use of a 707 army plane to fly them to the holy city of Mashad, where they planned a pilgrimage. "Do they suppose the military have nothing better to do than to act as courier to a bunch of redundant old bags in search of God's mercy!" the Shah snapped. Still, nothing prepared him for the most bitter blow, the decision by his daughter Shahnaz to reject secular life and become a religious convert. The beautiful young woman who at one time had resembled a San Francisco flower child now covered herself head to toe in black, her long tresses hidden by a flowing chador.

* * *

PRINCESS SHAHNAZ'S CONVERSION from royal rebel to religious revolutionary mirrored the experiences of her generation of young, well-heeled northern Tehranis. Raised in the gilded ghettos of Tajrish and Niavaran, cut off from their cultural roots, educated in the world's finest universities, they returned home surprised to learn that they lived in a developing country with serious social problems. They cast the Shah in the role of villain and held him responsible for more than two thousand years of poverty and illiteracy. Anxious to identify with the masses and their deprivations, these sons and daughters of privilege exchanged one set of drag for another, donning austere Muslim garb as a way of distancing themselves from everything their parents held dear. Few had ever opened a Quran, and fewer still had any in-depth knowledge of Shia theology, but in their rebellious naïveté they rushed to embrace the latest opiate. "Young professional people want to escape the establishment," said Karim Pakravan, the son of General Hassan Pakravan, the former Savak chief. He had been raised in comfort and privilege but he too felt no compunction in rejecting the security offered by the Pahlavi state. "The establishment is everybody who has real power. In one way or another, either morally or financially, it is corrupt. We are not brave enough to join the opposition, but by being at the university we maintain a passive opposition. Our case against the government is lack of freedom."

In the months that preceded his marriage to Princess Shahnaz, Khosrow Djahanbani had moved into the home of his fiancée's cousin. Prince Patrick Ali was the son of the Shah's late brother Prince Ali Reza, killed twenty years earlier in a plane crash. During the brief interregnum between his father's death and the birth of Crown Prince Reza, Patrick Ali had been recognized as the legitimate heir to the Peacock Throne. Raised a Catholic—his mother, Christiane Choleski, was Polish—the prince lived in San Francisco in the late sixties, where he studied Taoism and became interested in all religions. After returning to Iran he immersed himself in Islam as a student of Ayatollah Malayeri, a radical cleric, and began publicly criticizing his uncle's regime as unjust and corrupt. At the time he was in a relationship with Catherine Adl, the daughter of Professor Yahya Adl, the Shah's surgeon and one of the monarch's closest male friends. Their relationship ended soon after a rock climbing accident that left Cathy paralyzed. The spirited young woman had been an accomplished equestrienne. Now confined to a wheelchair, she fell into despair and drug addiction.

Cathy Adl eventually married Bahman Hojat, a fellow drug addict and the son of a major general in the Shah's army. Against the odds, she became pregnant and gave birth to a baby girl. The couple weaned themselves off drugs and followed Patrick Ali's example by embracing political Islam. But they went one step farther in 1975, when they fled to the hills with a cache of guns and explosives and declared their intention to overthrow the state. They didn't get very far—Cathy was crippled and the couple had brought along their baby girl and his son from an earlier marriage—but they still managed to ambush and kill several rural police officers. The security forces eventually tracked them down, cornering them in a cave, where they were shot to death in a final blaze of gunfire. The children were found alive, hidden beneath their parents' corpses.

The tragedy in the cave stunned Pahlavi high society. The King and Queen had known Cathy since childhood and considered her a part of their extended family. The depths of her sudden, ferocious turn were almost impossible to fathom. The tragedy led to a bitter generational family rift. Prince Patrick Ali issued a public denunciation of his uncle's regime, an act of defiance that led to his arrest and imprisonment in Evin Prison. The onetime heir to the Peacock Throne claimed he was interrogated for seventeen days and "psychologically tortured, notably with a fake execution." As soon as he was released he was placed under house arrest to prevent further scandal. U.S. intelligence sources reported back to the State Department that Princess Sarvanaz, the daughter of Prince Abdul Reza, the Shah's half brother, declared she hated her uncle and "would like to lead a revolution to overthrow the government." Most affected by the deaths were Princess Shahnaz and Khosrow Djahanbani, who had counted Cathy Adl and her husband as among their closest friends. Their response to the carnage was to emulate their friends' example by converting to Grand Ayatollah Khomeini's brand of fundamentalist Islam.

The Shah was deeply hurt and bewildered by his daughter's rejection. In June 1975 Alam witnessed a heated exchange between the pair at the dinner table, where they bickered over "the recent outrages by Muslim fanatics (outright lunatics I would call them)." Shahnaz vigorously defended her friends even though they had shot to death several farmers and gendarmes during a short-lived rebellion. Alam was so incensed that he cut in to deliver a lecture on what he regarded as the true meaning of Islam. Looking directly at her, he told the princess that religious fanatics should be sent to psychiatric wards or given the lash in a military prison. "This put the Princess in her place," he observed, "and much to His Imperial Majesty's relief she preferred to change the subject."

Though Khosrow Djahanbani proved himself a reliable and loving stepfather to his stepdaughter Mahnaz, his influence over her mother caused great alarm at court. Despite rejecting the Pahlavi inheritance, the couple insisted on maintaining their right as members of the Imperial Family to reside at Saadabad for free. They even sought permission to raise a wall around the couple's villa, though their request was rejected by Alam on the grounds that no walls were permitted within the park. Djahanbani sent his wife to request more pocket money from her father and lobbied for state support in a harebrained scheme to import luxury motorbikes into Iran. More serious were his ties to the Mujahedin terrorists, who assassinated government and security officials, ambushed police officers, murdered American military personnel, and were dedicated to overthrowing the monarchy. If the Shah was looking for evidence of treason he need only lock eyes with the brooding young man who stared across from him at his own dinner table.

The Shah tried to be philosophical. "It is human nature to be in opposition to society and its values for a certain time," he admitted in an interview. "That certain time often coincides with the years of youth—exactly at the time some of our children are about to go abroad to pursue their studies, thus virtually suspending their time with their families and their country." Privately, he struggled to understand why so many educated students from Iran's best families not only rejected him but also wanted to burn down their inheritance. Their willingness to die for their cause appalled but also impressed him.

HE HAD NEVER enjoyed a strong constitution, and the barrage of daily stress now began to aggravate his lymphoma.

During their first few visits to Iran, French physicians Jean Bernard, Georges Flandrin, and Paul Milliez had agreed with Dr. Abbas Safavian, the specialist treating Court Minister Alam for his own terminal blood disease, that the monarch's personal doctor, General Ayadi, was incapable of providing the right palliative care. Ayadi's valise was crammed with so many potions, pills, and creams that they lent him the air of the village quack rather than physician to a king. The French team expressed concern that the Shah was not receiving the correct dosage of medication. They observed that Ayadi appeared anxious not to be assigned blame if anything went wrong. The Shah agreed with Bernard's recommendation that his junior colleague Flandrin should take over supervision of his treatment and progress. Flandrin flew out to Tehran on February 19, 1975, and in total made forty-seven secret trips to Tehran until his final visit at the height of the revolution in December 1978.

Flandrin's schedule rarely varied. He left Paris on the third Saturday of each month and was back at his office each Monday morning to make sure no one noticed his absence. He usually traveled alone but from time to time was accompanied by Jean Bernard or Paul Milliez. On occasion, he might make two trips to the palace over a two- or three-day period. When he departed Paris, Flandrin drove away from Saint-Louis Hospital at midday for Charles de Gaulle Airport, boarded the afternoon Air France flight to Manila via Tehran, and disembarked at Mehrebad Airport after dark. Flandrin traveled as discreetly as possible, always sitting in the front row of first class so he was the first passenger to exit the aircraft. At the bottom of the gangway he was met by a car with flashing lights sent by Colonel Djahinbini. Their nighttime drives from the airport to the safe house sometimes involved a change of vehicles to shake off tailgaters. After a short and difficult night's sleep, Flandrin was up at dawn for his early morning appointment. Depending on the Shah's routine he was taken either to Niavaran; to Saadabad, where a small bedroom was set aside for his use; or to another safe house.

Flandrin's movements into and out of the palace grounds were carefully choreographed. Shortly after dawn two cars would approach Niavaran's lower right-side entrance. Either Colonel Djahinbini or one of his deputies watched from the shadows as General Ayadi, in the first car, stopped at the gate to present his papers for inspection. But the second car, with Flandrin, never stopped and was briskly waved through by the guards. The Shah's chief bodyguard preferred not to know what was going on. "I knew they were doctors," recalled Djahinbini. "I saw them at least once a month. Sometimes they came in with lots of equipment like microscopes to check blood but I never asked why they were there. I could have given their names to my friends in the Imperial Guard who were studying in Paris, and they could have found out immediately who they were. But I didn't. I didn't know they specialized in cancer. I didn't want to ask."

The Shah's blood samples were sent to Paris from a medical laboratory in Tehran under the name of his valet, Amir Pourshaja. Every five days Pourshaja sent a driver to a local pharmacy to pick up the phoned-in refills of chlorambucil. General Ayadi was supposed to oversee the tests and refills. "Each bottle lasted five days," said Pourshaja. "I called the pharmacy and sent the driver to get the pills. Dr. Ayadi chose the medicine." But when Flandrin visited the Shah at the Dizin ski field he noticed that his spleen had once again become swollen. Worse, new blood tests revealed elevated levels of abnormal cells. The Shah's medication was not working—but why? Flandrin deduced that the Shah's second valet had accidentally refilled the bottles with the wrong pills. This was an easy enough thing to do. To avoid discovery, the doctors had agreed to substitute chlorambucil for Quinercyl, another medication whose white pills resembled the original anticancer drug. In their medical reports they substituted the word "Quinercyl" for "chlorambucil" and also placed the real medication in bottles labeled Quinercyl. One day, as a precautionary measure, and in advance of a state visit abroad, the valet decided to stock up on an extra supply of Quinercyl, and these were the pills that he used to refill the Shah's medicine bottles for the next two months.

The prescription mix-up had still not been discovered by the time the Pahlavis flew to Kish Island for the 1976 Nowruz holidays. Farah noticed that her husband's lip was swollen but was reassured by General Ayadi that nothing was amiss. By June, however, the Shah complained to Alam of stomach pains, skin rashes, and a headache, and it wasn't until the end of summer when proper medication was restored that his condition stabilized.

Try as he might, the Shah could not escape the reality of his terminal illness. More than ever, he thought about the succession. Two weeks before flying down to Kish he granted an extensive interview to *Newsweek* magazine and explained his plans for Crown Prince Reza's education and his own desire to eventually step down. "Secondary school, then certainly a military training," the Shah explained. "Even in the European royal families, where the monarchs are doing what they do, the Prince still has military training. But in this country, if the King is not the real commander in chief of the armed forces, anything can happen. . . . Also he must understand that the people of our country expect the King to be the father, the teacher, the leader, the confidante. These are the characteristics of our people and monarchy. That's why it has lasted so long." He was "not pressing at all" for his son to learn the ropes. "But every day I can feel that he's more and more interested . . . maybe knowing a little less, but always terribly interested—in the dams, in atomic energy, in everything."

The Shah answered in the affirmative when his interviewer asked if the Crown Prince "would play an active role earlier than he would normally."

"Yes," the Shah replied. "I intend to retire, really, in about twelve and a half years' time—if I live until that time—and let him take over. Before then, he will be gradually introduced to all the problems. This is my normal position and if everything goes in a normal way, there is nothing to change that decision."

Though his publicly expressed intention was to hand over the reins in 1988, the qualifier to the statement was significant: *if I live until that time.*

ON KISH ISLAND, Queen Farah struggled to contain her own anxieties about the future.

Several days earlier, on March 21, 1976, she had noticed the cool way the public had responded to the lavish fiftieth-anniversary celebrations to mark Reza Shah's coronation. She compared the indifference of the crowds to "a sudden icy wind." Farah startled the Shah and Alam when she said she wondered if the Iranian people had lost interest in the monarchy. The two men waved away her fears, blaming them on an overactive imagination. They decided it was *she* who was out of touch with public attitudes. "The internal situation is sound," Alam assured her. The regime's generous social programs kept the middle class, workers, and farmers onside, and the complaints of a few intellectuals were of no concern. "I saw the problems while His Majesty saw the achievements," said Queen Farah. "In bed we would compare notes. I would report about what was going wrong in the regions I had just toured. His Majesty would try to dismiss my report as exaggerated or one-sided. At times he would tell me that such minor problems were *des accidents de parcours* or the heritage of the past, and that all would be well in a few years' time. Sometimes, however, he would get impatient and edgy. 'No more bad news!' His Majesty would command. And I would, naturally, change the subject."

In June 1976 Farah returned from a trip to the countryside to sound the alarm. This time, rather than write a letter to her husband or have a private chat over lunch, she decided to take her concerns public. Speaking to journalists, she warned that "the rate of migration from villages to towns is dangerous." Tehran could no longer absorb the newcomers, and she feared a social explosion if they did not receive adequate housing and jobs. "What had happened was when land reform was done, of course the agriculturalists were very happy, but there were people on the lands who were just the workers," she later explained. "They suddenly didn't have anywhere else to go and that created some social problems. We tried to see what we could do to help them. I remember that the government gave money for instance to those whose villages had been destroyed when a dam was built. But you know, they did not know how to properly use the money, they spent it, and then they were left with nothing. In the villages, except for agriculture they made handicrafts but they wouldn't make enough money [to survive]. They would come to town, to Tehran, hoping to find work and a better salary." Farah supported initiatives to tackle the problem of rural migration by promoting village handicrafts and small businesses. At her urging, wealthy businessmen agreed to open showrooms to display village wares. Still, the scale of the problems dwarfed the solutions.

During the oil boom the Shah approved the creation of an American-style think tank, the Group for the Study of Iranian Problems, which he hoped would provide the government with fresh ideas on how to manage policy challenges arising from the oil boom. Scores of scholars, industrialists, and lawyers joined the new association under the aegis of Hushang Nahavandi, head of his wife's Special Bureau, who took charge as its chief executive. The group served to reassure Tehran's liberal community that the Shah understood their concerns and took them seriously. Nahavandi's leadership and the Queen's patronage, however informal, gave the assembly the imprimatur of legitimacy. The Shah was also aware that Nahavandi had ambitions for the premiership, though he never regarded him as suitable for the task. In classic divide-and-rule fashion, Nahavandi's appointment as head of the think tank became a device to keep Hoveyda from becoming too comfortable in his job. The prime minister retaliated by encouraging the secret police to harass Nahavandi and obstruct his work.

The group's report on public attitudes came as a rude shock at court. Although living standards had improved considerably, the interviewees spoke more about their frustration and disillusion with modernization.

The authors of the report were especially critical of the security forces, which they blamed for alienating young Iranians and the middle class from the monarchy. Rounding up and detaining students for weeks at a time created a lawless atmosphere that angered their families and friends, who pointed the finger of blame up the hill, at Niavaran. They warned that Savak's harsh tactics were driving even moderates into the arms of the opposition. Unless steps were taken to reform the political system and address underlying grievances, there would be trouble. The middle class had to be engaged and a measure of democracy injected into Iranian political life. The Shah was deeply upset with the report's conclusions. He rejected the implication that the regime was off-track or that he was out of touch with public sentiment. But his decision to hand the report off to Hoveyda for action suggested it had made an impression. Hoveyda, however, had no intention of lending credence to anything Nahavandi did, nor was he about to boost his rival's credibility. The report was quietly shelved, its recommendations never debated. Had the prime minister bothered to read it, the Queen lamented, its findings "would have alerted the government to the dissatisfaction."

More than ever, the Queen worried about the corrosive effects of corruption. Her sharp eye led to the exposure of one of the last great scandals of the Pahlavi era, an episode that some saw as an Iranian version of the doomed French Bourbon Dynasty's celebrated "affair of the diamonds." At the center of the scandal was an exquisite set of jewels that included a necklace, earrings, and a bracelet valued at $1 million. Farah had admired the collection and made discreet inquiries to the jeweler. "I am very sorry," the jeweler told her representative, "the set was brought yesterday by the wife of Admiral Atai." Admiral Atai, commander of the Imperial Navy, lived on a modest salary and could not possibly afford such extravagance. Farah told her husband, who ordered an immediate investigation. By the time the probe was finished the admiral was under arrest, and graft had been uncovered at the highest levels of the armed forces.

Corruption in the senior ranks of the armed forces was a dangerous development for a royal dynasty whose survival rested on the competence and integrity of the military. An official investigation revealed a culture of corruption with vast fortunes that had been acquired by Iranian officials who demanded kickbacks from foreign defense companies anxious to secure lucrative contracts to furnish Iran with their weapons systems. The Shah was also dealing with a scandal closer to home, this one involving the family of his sister. Princess Fatemeh, only daughter of Reza Shah and Esmat ol-Moluk Dowlatshahi, had first married an American, Vincent Hillyer, a union her brother had opposed to the point of stripping his sister of her royal prerogatives. Following their divorce in 1959 the Princess had returned to Iran, resumed her titles and responsibilities, and married General Mohammad Khatami, chief of the air force, and one of only two attendants who had accompanied the Shah and Queen Soraya on their desperate flight out of the country in August 1953. Khatami was a strong personality and talented leader, who enjoyed the Shah's complete confidence, and who was also widely rumored to be the U.S. embassy's preferred successor in the event the Shah was assassinated or removed in a coup. But in the last few years of his life Khatami had piled up a fortune estimated at more than $100 million, and at the time of his death in a hang-gliding accident in 1975 investigators in Washington were exposing his complicity in a brazen kickback scheme involving the sale of American Grumman fighter jets to the Imperial Iranian Air Force.

This, then, was the unhappy state of affairs that confronted the Shah in early 1976 and that convinced him of the need to take action. He set up a committee of experts "to recommend changes that would improve Iran's image and loosen controls without affecting anything basic." Committee members included senior ministers, security chiefs, and newspaper editors. The report they produced became the basis for the Shah's subsequent policy shift, which was dubbed "liberalization." They urged him to open a dialogue with Amnesty International and other international groups critical of Iran's record on human rights. They recommended lifting the ban on twelve hundred books and easing censorship of newspapers and magazines. "There was a realization," said one participant, "that Iran cannot develop technologically without a more open political environment." A case in point was Aryamehr University, supposed to be the MIT of Iran, where classes were seriously disrupted by student protests. At the same time, "an effort was being made to pump some life into the flaccid body of Rastakhiz" when the Shah allowed Nahavandi's Group for the Study of Iranian Problems to become a quasi third wing of Rastakhiz. He hoped this would stimulate the political establishment and encourage the exchange of ideas and a degree of informed debate. Yet he remained adamantly opposed to working with the National Front and the Liberation Movement of Iran, the two leftist groups that had tormented him in the 1950s and early '60s. He hoped that Nahavandi's liberal think tank would supplant them as a moderate centrist force that could reinvigorate Iran's moribund political system.

SENSING A SUBTLE shift in atmosphere, Tehran-based diplomats began quietly comparing notes. Though the Shah projected an air of confidence and power, Iran's economic and political malaise coincided with almost daily confrontations between the security forces and Mujahedin guerrilla fighters, who melted away into the warrens and slums of the southern suburbs. In 1976 almost one hundred people, including police, terrorists, and innocent civilians, were killed in shoot-outs that sometimes spilled over into the downtown commercial district. Iranian society was coming to a boil. In 1976 U.S. senator Charles Percy visited Tehran and asked Israel's ambassador, Uri Lubrani, for his assessment. "Everything is okay with the Shah, except he has a big problem with the clerics," said Lubrani. "He can't control them in the way he can control the politicians and the others."

Every few weeks American diplomat John Stempel, deputy political counselor at the U.S. embassy, held regular meetings with Guennady Kazankin, the second secretary at the Soviet embassy, at restaurants and coffee bars around Tehran. On April 14, 1976, the pair met in a booth at the Pizza Roma restaurant. The Russian asked Stempel "whether we had any recent difficulties with terrorists." Stempel answered that "things had been mercifully quiet for the past couple of months, but that we remain concerned." He asked Kazankin if he agreed with the Shah's assertion that Yasser Arafat, chairman of the Palestine Liberation Organization, was arming, training, and sheltering the Mujahedin in camps in Lebanon: "[Kazankin] said he thought this was not true, although perhaps a few Iranians were being trained in 'centers abroad.'"

Two weeks later, on April 28, Stempel and Kazankin met again, this time for lunch at the Tehran Steak House, a popular watering hole for the sixty Russian families stationed in Tehran, and then on to Tiffany's Restaurant for coffee. Kazankin wanted to hear Stempel's view "about the future of U.S.-Iran relations and gradually pushed the discussion toward what happens in Iran when the Shah goes."

The American admitted "there was a great deal of uncertainty as to what would happen when the Shah eventually left the scene."

"No, no," Kazankin pressed him. "I mean if he were to be taken away by accident, what do you think?"

If there were no suspicions of foul play, said Stempel, "the Regency

Council and the Empress would take over. The US would support the legitimate succession to the Throne."

At this point Kazankin broke in: "But aren't you already preparing yourselves for the next step after that?"

"Of course not," replied Stempel. In response to Kazankin's next question on whether the State Department thought Farah "was strong enough to take control," the American admitted that Farah appeared "quite capable and was obviously appearing more in public but that of course her eventual role would depend upon circumstances. In fact, the whole problem of political succession in Iran was much more uncertain than most countries."

Stempel then asked Kazankin what Moscow thought of Iran's future. The Soviet Union, answered Kazankin, "favors the people's determining their own form of government."

"With a little Cuban help?"

"No," he added, "we have confidence that the will of the people will determine what happens."

12

THIRSTY FOR MARTYRDOM

Something is in the air.
—THE SHAH

I wonder when we're going to have a revolution in Iran.
—AMBASSADOR WILLIAM SULLIVAN

In the spring of 1977 Iran's economy was destabilized by a sudden short-fall in government revenues caused by Saudi Arabia's decision to flood crude markets with cheap oil. The Saudi move, undertaken with U.S. encouragement, prevented the Shah from raising prices yet again to finance Iran's development projects and military buildup. The Americans had finally lost patience with their Iranian ally, whose aggressive oil policies threatened not only Iran's economy but also the economies of Western allies in Europe and Asia. The U.S.-Saudi gambit worked and oil prices stayed in line. For the Iranian economy, however, the loss of billions of dollars in anticipated income from oil revenues precipitated a grave financial crisis. In the first nine days of the new year, Iran's oil production fell 38 percent over the previous month, or two million barrels a day. "We're broke," the Shah glumly conceded. "Everything seems doomed to grind to a standstill, and meanwhile many of the programs we had planned must be postponed."

Prime Minister Hoveyda abandoned his government's budget fore-casts, imposed a spending freeze, and sought a bridge loan from a consortium of American and European banks. Credit dried up and many large industrial and defense construction projects were postponed or canceled.

The shortfall in oil revenues, combined with a drought in the south, led to a 50 percent drop in industrial production, and in the summer the national electricity grid failed, causing widespread power outages. "Government officials must walk up seven and eight stories to their offices," reported the *New York Times*. "Tourists get caught in elevators. Office workers swelter in 100-degree-plus temperatures without air conditioning. Housewives complain that electrical appliances are damaged by the abrupt cuts and restorations of power." The southern suburbs, which lacked even a basic sewage system, bore the brunt of power cuts lasting up to ten hours. Court Minister Asadollah Alam begged the Shah to replace his prime minister, warning that "we are now in dire financial peril and must tighten our belts if we are to survive."

Government efforts to bring spending under control only made matters worse when the construction sector ground to a halt and tens of thousands of young male laborers lost their jobs and ended up on the streets. "People were flocking to town from the countryside, from the small villages all over the country, hoping to get in on the gravy train and crammed into impossible living quarters in south Tehran, by and large," recalled William Lehfeldt who headed up the local branch of the U.S. Chamber of Commerce and represented General Electric's business interests in Iran. "And all looking for jobs. You could go down there with your truck and fill it with with people to go out working on day labor, and you didn't have to pay them very much, because they were really paid starvation wages. . . . There was more disguised under- and unemployment than you could shake a stick at." The government's official unemployment statistics were "ludicrous. I realize they had to manufacture things, but if you went down into south Tehran in 1977 on a warm summer's day, you wondered why the place didn't blow up sooner."

The economic contraction coincided with the Shah's plan to liberalize Iranian society and "let off steam" by tolerating more dissent and relaxing censorship. But with the economy in free fall, Parviz Sabeti presented the Shah with an analysis that recommended a temporary halt to liberalization. He pointed out that similar measures in the early sixties had quickly spiraled out of control and culminated in Khomeini's attempt to overthrow the monarchy. Since then, Iran's population had grown to 35 million and "we have more students and workers than ever before, and many farmers migrating to the cities who are vulnerable. Today we also have what we did not have then—terrorist groups. It will be more difficult than in 1963 to maintain order." If street demonstrations erupted while the Shah was trying to introduce liberal reforms he would be faced with the painful choice of ordering another crackdown and risking bloodshed, or offering more concessions to avoid a bloodbath. Sabeti considered it vital that the authorities demonstrate strength from day one "to show we are not intimidated, and we will not cave in to pressure." The Shah read Sabeti's report but rejected its conclusions. He had half a million men under arms, and the army was rock solid in its support. Iran's economy and society had been thoroughly restructured in the past fourteen years. Despite bad news on the economy, he retained full confidence that the great silent majority of the Iranian people were with him. "Sabeti sees everything as black," the Shah told General Nasiri, who handed him the report. "Negative. He doesn't see anything positive. We have been careful. We have grown the military. He has not mentioned any of the positives. We are going to be okay." The Shah was apt to remind pessimists such as Sabeti that the farr had always seen him through. He never forgot the dark days of 1953, when the people came into the streets to save the country from communism. Whatever hardships they faced, he never believed his children would turn against him.

If anything, the Shah believed that more reforms and concessions were needed to satisfy the mood of unrest. Though he took a dim view of Western-style democracy, which he associated with the turmoil of the war years and early fifties and sixties, he grudgingly accepted that a return to the 1906 Constitution was inevitable and that the window of opportunity that had allowed him to reshape Iranian society on his terms was closing: his health was failing, the economy was stalled, and the ambitious experiment with one-party rule had failed to broaden support for his regime. If the monarchy was to survive, it would have to identify with the aspirations of the emerging middle class, which demanded an end to authoritarianism and a return to constitutional rule. The Shah had made abrupt course corrections before. The problem this time was that no one, not his most devoted supporters, and certainly not his foes, could imagine that the king who relished power as much as he did would ever voluntarily relinquish it.

The Shah first intimated his game plan to his sister. In March 1977 Princess Ashraf visited Niavaran to pass on the concerns of her network of admirers and contacts. They were warning her that political and religious extremists were using liberalization as a cover to organize, agitate, and mobilize. She pointed out that the recent election of Jimmy Carter to the American presidency was another complicating factor. During his election campaign Carter had criticized Iran's human rights record and called for restrictions to be placed on U.S. arms sales. Carter's rhetoric, said the Princess, "feeds and encourages the opposition . . . it tells them that you do not have the support of an ally."

The Shah did not disagree with her assessment, though she was taken aback with his proposed remedy. "All the more reason to speed up our reforms," he explained. "We have established the basis for economic democracy. Now, if I have the time, I want to see political democracy. I'm thinking of a first for Iran . . . free elections in the summer of 1979, with the participation of all parties, except perhaps the [Communist] Tudeh. I've discussed this with my aides." The Princess was astonished to hear her brother talk this way. Free elections two years from now? And what did he mean when he said "if I have the time"?

In Washington, Ambassador Ardeshir Zahedi, who knew nothing of the Shah's plan to democratize Iran, was also hearing from his constituents and friends. Like Ashraf, he passed on their concerns to the monarch. "People were telling me things were bad," he remembered. "They were giving me a very gloomy situation. I wrote a letter to the Shah."

BY HIS OWN estimate, fifty-five-year-old William Sullivan was a reluctant American envoy to the Pahlavi Court. Tall, brusque, and imposing, with a shock of white hair that suited his proconsul pretensions, after serving in the early seventies as an aide to Secretary of State Henry Kissinger during peace talks to end the war in Vietnam, Sullivan was sent to Laos to oversee the Nixon administration's secret air war against Communist insurgents. From Vientiane he was ordered to Manila to manage Washington's fraught relations with the mercurial president Ferdinand Marcos of the Philippines. Famously acerbic, Sullivan once had a memorable run-in with First Lady Imelda Marcos. When she mentioned that she did not know what more she could do to help the poor, Sullivan tartly advised her to "try feeding them cake." He had no time for fools and invariably regarded himself as the smartest man in any room he entered. Sullivan expected his sunset diplomatic post to be in Mexico City, near where he planned to retire to the resort town of Cuernavaca. The incoming president and his national security team had other plans. Sullivan was dismayed to learn that the State Department was sending him to Tehran instead. "The nearest I had been to Tehran was in Calcutta nearly thirty years before," he recalled. "I had never lived in the Islamic world and knew little about its culture or ethos. While I recognized the importance of Iran, the proposal did not make me jump for joy." He knew he was out of his depth. "I make no pretense of understanding these people," he once said of the Iranians. "I find the Iranians a lot more inscrutable than Asians." He appeared not to know that Iran was *in* Asia.

Following Jimmy Carter's election victory in November 1976, Secretary of State Cyrus Vance had contacted William Sullivan to inform him that the incoming Democratic administration wanted to reset relations with Tehran. The White House believed that Carter's two Republican predecessors, Nixon and Ford, had surrendered America's strategic leverage over Tehran. Arms sales to Iran had spiraled out of control, with Iran's armed forces struggling to absorb billions of dollars' worth of systems they lacked the expertise to operate and maintain. U.S. military personnel were caught taking bribes and fixing defense contracts. Oil prices were a major point of contention in U.S.-Iran relations and so, too, was the Shah's insistence on enriching uranium on Iranian soil. U.S. officials suspected their ally of harboring ambitions to acquire nuclear weapons using American and European technology.

Carter's emphasis on human rights as a core principle of U.S. foreign policy was another sticking point in relations. The downfall of President Nixon in the Watergate scandal had revealed widespread abuses by the CIA at home and abroad. American public opinion was shocked at revelations that their government plotted coups and assassinations and supported unelected leaders in the developing world. In 1976 Amnesty International published a report that claimed the Shah ran one of the world's most repressive regimes. The group repeated claims made by Iranian opposition groups that between twenty-five thousand and a hundred thousand people were in jail on trumped-up political charges. The International Commission of Jurists piled on when it described human rights violations in the kingdom as "unprecedented," a statement that implied conditions inside Iran were worse than in Pol Pot's Kampuchea and Idi Amin's Uganda. Simultaneously, Iranian poet Reza Baraheni's best-selling prison memoir *Crowned Cannibals* described his country as a charnel house of misery and murder. "Thousands of men and women have been summarily executed during the last twenty-three years," he wrote in gripping prose. "More than 300,000 people are estimated to have been in and out of prison during the last nineteen years of the existence of Savak; an average of 1,500 people are arrested every month. . . . There have been occasions when 5,000 people have been kidnapped in one day. This puts the number of kidnappers in the thousands. Sometimes even tanks are used in order to get a suspect out of his lodgings." Amid a wave of moral indignation, *Time* magazine lamented Washington's inability to influence domestic policy in "largely self-sufficient and comparatively wealthy" states like Iran: "One widespread hope is that torturing dictatorships will be overthrown."

For years the Shah, Prime Minister Hoveyda, and government officials had looked the other way, dismissing antigovernment protesters as "a bunch of Clockwork Orangers," and allowing the security forces to get on with the job of defeating the urban guerrillas who carried out bombings and assassinations. "There has been enough of this preaching, moralizing, and telling others that they are trash or that they are third or fourth rate," the Shah erupted in an audience with a U.S. diplomat. "It won't work, you will see. Don't be encouraged even if 200 dissidents write letters to you. It doesn't mean anything." The U.S. embassy cabled Washington that the Shah "has been stung by rash of unfavorable publicity appearing in US and western media about human rights conditions in Iran. Basically, he considers it unfair, unwarranted, and lacking in recognition of major socioeconomic advances his country has achieved during his reign." Was it a coincidence, he demanded to know, that Saudi Arabia, America's chief ally within OPEC, received a free pass on human rights? Iranians enjoyed far greater freedoms and a higher standard of living than the Saudis. "If you Americans are going to be so moral, you must apply a single standard to the whole world," he lectured *Newsweek* in an interview in early 1977. "If I have a few thousand Communist people in prison so that others can live in a free society, it is magnified and talked about endlessly. But do you ever talk about the hundreds of thousands who were murdered in Cambodia? . . . I cannot believe that the US would be so shortsighted as to cut off arms sales to my country."

The Shah was genuinely mystified by the lurid reports that appeared in the American and European press of mass arrests, cases of torture, and executions. His weekly meetings with General Nasiri had always focused on broader questions of intelligence, not what he described as "petty" matters such as prison conditions or interrogations. He might have followed the example of most every other Middle East leader and either ignored the critics and rebuffed the Americans or introduced superficial reforms that could later be withdrawn. But he knew that the Iranian middle class, whom he regarded as his most important supporters, wanted to see an improvement in the political atmosphere. The Shah was paying the price of the "don't ask, don't tell" policy on prisoner detention adopted five years earlier by the regime's Anti-Terrorist Joint Committee. Worried that General Nasiri had not been straight with him, he took the unprecedented step of inviting the International Committee of the Red Cross to investigate Iranian political prisons. He ordered his own parallel internal inquiry to make sure the Red Cross inspectors received full cooperation. In addition to meeting Red Cross envoys, the Shah met with Martin Ennals, head of Amnesty International, and also with William Butler, president of the International Commission of Jurists, and listened to their complaints. Parviz Sabeti gave a rare interview to the *Washington Post* correspondent in Tehran and dismissed Amnesty International's report as "pure fabrication and not at all true. In all Iran there are only 3,200 political prisoners. We don't have enough jails to house 100,000 prisoners." The Shah had already banned the use of torture during interrogations and anybody caught "will get six years in prison." The number of "active terrorists at large in Iran may not exceed 100." Before 1970, he admitted, "Iran had not felt it necessary to execute people for anti-state activities." However, following the outbreak of guerrilla warfare in 1971 the "new wave of terrorism had 'caused us to get a bit rougher.'" Sabeti's counterclaims raised the question: Who was telling the truth?

The Red Cross inspectors reported their findings in June 1977. They counted 3,087 political prisoners, down from a peak of 3,700 inmates two years earlier. Approximately one third of the inmates, or 900, reported having been subjected to some form of torture or abuse while in detention. The inspectors found no evidence of torture "over the past few months." The striking discrepancy between the Red Cross and Amnesty International investigations was explained by the fact that Amnesty relied solely on statistics provided by opposition groups and foreign press reports. Western journalists like Jonathan Randal of the *Washington Post* had also been manipulated by Abolhassan Banisadr and anti-Shah propagandists in Paris and Beirut. The truth was that from 1971-1978 at most 386 and as few as 312 Iranian dissidents were killed by the security forces or died in detention.

The findings of the International Committee of the Red Cross confirmed that hundreds of Iranians had been tortured by the security forces but exonerated the regime of the worst charges leveled by Reza Baraheni and others. Yet his Iranian critics and their Western sympathizers simply ignored the report or accused the Shah of a cover-up. The same American and European newspapers that had fulminated against the Shah lost interest in the story and never made the necessary corrections. This was a shame. In an internal intelligence memorandum published in November 1977, Jimmy Carter's State Department reported that the Shah's intervention had been decisive and that there had been not a single case of torture in Iran in the past twelve months. "During the past year the Shah has moved further and more rapidly on human rights than most leaders with a similar image. Because he does not wish to be labeled as a US puppet, he particularly resents inferences that his efforts are in response to US pressure, but the fact remains that they only began after Iran received considerable bad publicity in the US and candidate Carter looked like a winner in the US elections." The Shah had followed through with reforms to the judicial system and released almost half of all political prisoners. He had even gone so far as to instruct his security forces to "assist needy families of 'anti-security' prisoners." Indeed, the Red Cross inspection team had "praised the 'indispensable' interest and backing of the Shah" for its work. In a separate report, the CIA concurred with State's assessment.

> The human rights situation in Iran has been improving. Only government opponents advocating violent overthrow of the regime or who are suspected of terrorist activity are now being arrested, greatly reducing the number of persons being detained on security grounds.

Savak's influence and importance had always been overstated. At its peak, the security agency employed no more than five thousand office workers and agents in the field—a far cry from the twenty thousand claimed by critics. Ten thousand additional names—not the millions alleged by Baraheni—were listed on the books as either full-time or part-time informants, though even the latter figure was inflated because it included individuals who had been approached by the secret police and refused requests to cooperate. The Shah's "eyes and ears" had the technical ability to monitor just fifty conversations at a time. "People worried about Savak," recalled British journalist Martin Woollacott, the *Guardian* correspondent who was married to an Iranian. The reporter later admitted that he had investigated and largely dismissed claims made by opposition groups of mass torture and brutality. "We were dubious. Savak worked very well in instilling passivity, some fear, and a large degree of acquiescence with a minimum of violence. But the picture of Savak as bloodthirsty did not stand up to scrutiny."

By now Parviz Sabeti, who had succeeded General Moghadam as head of Savak's Third Directorate, worried that the Shah's decision to "hand over the prisons to the Red Cross" had led to a loss of control. His men were confused and demoralized—why were terrorists trying to overthrow the regime and credited with killing high officials now getting a free pass? "He got advice to allow prison inspections and put them under [Red Cross] control," said Sabeti. "And this sent the signal [to opposition groups] that the Shah was not in charge. That he was finished."

Queen Farah favored placing restraints on Savak and was an enthusiastic proponent of liberalization. Like her husband, she thought Sabeti was too much of a pessimist. "You warned us and nothing happened," she said after the Red Cross inspectors left Iran.

"It will," Sabeti answered back. "You wait. Evin Prison has become like a hotel."

Sabeti's view found support from an unexpected quarter. Mohammad Ali Gerami, a close associate of Grand Ayatollah Khomeini, had been locked up in Evin for the past several years. He recalled the dark days before prison inspections. "No one dared talk among the prisoners," he said. "Even if we went to prison we did not look each other in the eyes for fear of violent reprisals." Everything changed when the Red Cross arrived. "In Evin, the facilities improved. We were allowed the Quran."

Gerami and other revolutionaries sensed that change was coming to Iran, that there had been a subtle shift in mood. They decided that the Shah was acting on the defensive, most likely under pressure from his American allies. They watched and waited, ready to make their move.

AFTER A LENGTHY interregnum, William Sullivan finally presented his credentials to the Shah on June 18, 1977. His instructions from Washington were to restore order to arms sales, resolve the nuclear standoff, press for relief on oil prices, and encourage liberalization. Sullivan was intrigued to discover that Iran's King was anything but the ruthless dictator he had read about. He recalled the time they both attended a joint Iranian-American air force exercise in the desert south of the capital. The Shah arrived separately, piloting his own transport plane. After landing, he ignored his officials, walked straight over to Sullivan, and asked the ambassador to accompany him for the van ride across the desert. While the crowds assembled in the reviewing stand the two men kept cool in an air-conditioned trailer. "Once inside, he unhitched his tunic, relaxed, and talked in his usual easy, gracious way about a number of things," said Sullivan. When the time came to leave, however, the Shah let out a sigh, straightened his military tunic, and prepared to make his public entrance.

> From the gracious, easy, smiling host with whom I had been talking, he transformed himself suddenly into a steely, ramrod-straight auto-crat. This involved not only adjusting his uniform and donning dark glasses but also throwing out his chest, raising his chin, and fixing his lips in a grim line. When he had achieved this change to his satisfac-tion, he thrust open the door of the trailer and stalked out across the few remaining steps to the reviewing stand.

Sullivan might have shown the Shah more respect if he really had been a Suharto, Pinochet, or Marcos. But his host's shyness, soft-spoken demeanor, and European sensibilities seemed only to invite contempt. Sullivan deci-ded the Shah was a slightly ridiculous marionette who liked to play dress-up. He gave his host virtually no credit for lasting thirty-six years on the Peacock Throne—the fifth-longest reign in the history of the Iranian monarchy—let alone his life-and-death struggle to reform a conservative Muslim society averse to change. He showed little if any sensitivity to the unique pressures the Shah faced at home by supporting U.S. foreign policy in the Middle East, selling oil to Israel, and guarding the approaches to the Persian Gulf from an array of adversaries. Sullivan received a polite wel-come at the palace. The Shah's entourage were less receptive, viewing the new ambassador as they would a spider climbing up the drainpipe. His rep-utation for asserting himself and involving himself in his host countries' internal affairs was already well known. "Everyone buckled up when Sullivan arrived," remembered Maryam Ansary, wife of the Shah's finance and economy minister. "He came in with his reputation and the devil on his back." When she heard that Bill Sullivan was on his way to Tehran, Imelda Marcos placed a phone call to Queen Farah and passed on a stark warning: "Be careful. Sullivan is trouble. Wherever he goes he makes trouble."

The ambassador's jaunty irreverence dismayed and offended his hosts. It was customary for new envoys to visit the offices of the major daily newspapers. Farhad Massoudi, publisher of the evening paper *Ettelaat*, arranged for Sullivan to be shown around his newsroom and meet with his editors. "I was quite surprised on a number of occasions in the way he spoke about the Shah," said Massoudi. "He did not give the necessary respect that I had been expecting from a new American ambassador." Sullivan's tone and attitude only encouraged the rampant speculation that he had been sent to Tehran to sow mischief. Sullivan was still settling in when he attended a dinner party hosted by Britain's ambassador Tony Parsons. "I wonder when we're going to have a revolution in Iran," Sullivan cheerfully mused to his female dinner companion. "Every country I go to, after a while there is a revolution." Unfortunately for the ambassador, the lady in question was the wife of Seyyed Hossein Nasr, Queen Farah's adviser on cultural and religious matters and a regular visitor to the palace.

IN THE SUMMER of 1977 a tall, austere, twenty-six-year-old seminarian named Ali Hossein divided his time between Qom, where he studied religion, and Tehran, where he was enrolled in Western philosophy classes at the University of Tehran. He spent Sundays through Wednesdays in the capital and on Thursday mornings drove down to Qom, ostensibly to receive instruction in religion for two days in the hawza. But his studies were a ruse—the young clergyman was a courier for the revolutionary underground whose job was to convey secret messages and materials back and forth between safe houses in both cities. After leaving the bus depot in Qom he made straight for the home of Ayatollah Rasti Kashani, Grand Ayatollah Khomeini's personal representative in the holy city. Two days later, Hossein was on his way back to Tehran, holding a satchel that contained tape cassettes of his hero's latest revolutionary pronouncements. The tapes, which had been flown in from Paris, West Berlin, and Beirut, were distributed to Hossein's family members and friends, who in turn took them to the bazaars, where they were sold. Others passed them hand to hand. Hossein was not afraid of being caught by the security forces. "There was no fear in the followers of Imam Khomeini," he recalled. "If they arrested me and killed me I became a martyr and martyrdom was a very great blessing. We welcomed martyrdom. We were thirsty for martyrdom. We knew that in this situation we could not fight the power. We could show by martyrdom that Western slogans about human rights and democracy were big lies."

Hossein's personal journey from pious student to revolutionary zealot mirrored the experiences of a generation of young, educated Iranians who rejected the Shah's vision of a secular state and dedicated their lives to establishing an Islamic republic. "Before the revolution I liked to study Western culture," he said. At the age of twenty-three he had sold a parcel of land to pay for a trip to Europe. But instead of returning home feeling inspired and uplifted, Hossein found that his encounter with modernity left him deeply disillusioned. "When I traveled in Western countries I used to ask people the same question: 'What is the acceptable philosophy for the creation of the human being?' Each time the answer was the same: 'comfort and pleasure.' They claimed to believe in individualism. They believed in multiculturalism. In nationalism. In rationalism." Western societies, he decided, were "animalistic and not human." Appalled by their loose morals, their individualism, and their obsession with material goods, Hossein returned to Iran with a sharper awareness of what the White Revolution meant for Islam. "After that trip I became ready to tolerate every type of torture in prison and made a firm determination to fight with [the Pahlavi] regime. I found that Iranian governments wanted to make Iran in [the Western] image."

An opportunity came up to work for the government, and Ali Hossein accepted an offer to accompany an official from the Ministry of Education to Shiraz. On the trip from Tehran his bus pulled over at the side of the road to pick up an American traveler. None of the Iranians on board wanted to sit beside the foreigner but the seminarian, who spoke English, told them, "I am ready to sit with this American." Over the next twelve hours he and the traveler talked about many things. The American admitted he was overcompensated for the work he did and that Iran offered him a much higher standard of living than he could ever have back home. He was so pleased with his new status that he had decided to bring his daughter over from America to study at Pahlavi University in Shiraz. "The Americans could do whatever they wanted in Iran without observing the customs of the people," concluded the Iranian. When he reached Shiraz his hosts at the Ministry of Education "showed me some Westernized youth and said, 'We are going to establish an organization to change the culture of youth to make them look like this.'" This was the last straw: at the age of twenty-six he joined "the movement" and went underground.

Ali Hossein was the quintessential true believer. "Since we were active and new to the circle of Ayatollah Khomeini, we used to follow everything exactly." He repeated verbatim Khomeini's solemn pronouncements that the Shah's plan to liberalize Iranian public life was "a plot by America to deceive the people and nothing more," and that President Carter's support for human rights was little more than a trick to prolong the enslavement of the Iranian people. The Shah "gave" women the right to vote, but who was he to "give" anyone anything? Who was he to decide such matters? If Iranian men were not free to vote as they wished, then "how does he claim he is giving women *their* freedom?" The real enemy was not the Shah ("the Shah was nothing") but America. "[The Imam] was fighting the international power of the United States. The Shah was the first step. He had attacked the United States and Israel in 1963. *They* were the *real* targets. He felt a prophetic responsibility on his shoulders to save humanity." The revolutionaries understood that the Shah's decision to liberalize provided them with an opportunity to organize and mobilize. "We saw [liberalization] as weakness!" said Hossein. "Yes, of course!"

For more than a decade the Coalition of Islamic Societies had represented Khomeini's interests inside Iran while he remained in exile. In the midseventies their revolutionary cells began to sense a shift in momentum. Opposition to the White Revolution was growing, and interest in Islam among younger Iranians led to a surge in seminary enrollments. In 1977 some 60,000 "undergraduates" studied at 300 religious schools around the country, while 180,000 mullahs were active in 80,000 mosques, holy shrines, schools, and other Islamic sites. In the aftermath of the June 1975 uprising in Qom, more seminarians and younger clergy concluded that the Pahlavi regime could not be peacefully reformed and that their entire way of life was at stake. They agreed with Khomeini on the need to reject the 1906 constitutional settlement, revolt against the regime, and replace the monarchy with an Islamic state. These converts studied and employed tactics used by other successful revolutionary movements throughout Africa, South America, and Asia. To escape Savak's prying eyes, sympathetic teachers in the hawza devised "hidden classes" that never appeared in the official academic curriculum. "In my hidden classes we learned revolutionary activism, which we could not learn in an official course," said Ali Hossein. "We participated in classes on the characteristics of Islamic government. First, they used to teach us the necessity of revolution, Islamic government, corruption and the oppression of the Shah and his superpower supporters. We studied how to make the people ready to participate in demonstrations and make them aware."

The young revolutionaries scrutinized the Pahlavi regime's strengths and weaknesses but also those of his more mainstream opponents. Just as leftists such as Abolhassan Banisadr accepted that they could not overthrow the monarchy without the help of the ulama, Khomeini's supporters accepted that they would have to adopt a moderate posture and work closely alongside liberal and leftist opposition groups that enjoyed the support of the middle class. Both sides agreed that if the middle class deserted the Shah, his regime would collapse. The two main opposition groups favored by middle-class liberals and leftists were the National Front, the party of former prime minister Mohammad Mossadeq, and the Liberation Movement of Iran, the spin-off from the National Front led by moderate Islamist Mehdi Bazargan. Khomeini's agents studied these men and their beliefs like insects under a microscope. "We knew that these groups did not believe in Khomeini," said Ali Hossein. "But the requirements of revolution sometimes make use of people who are not in complete agreement with the leaders. We were aware of Bazargan's objections to Khomeini even before the revolution began. He did not believe in revolutionary activities and we knew what he and his people said in private." The Khomeini movement had already infiltrated Bazargan's circle and spied on him: "There were people who were with Khomeini who pretended to be close to Bazargan." In their "hidden classes," the religious students read and critiqued works by Bazargan and Banisadr. "We did not believe in them even then. The Imam recognized that [these] Westernized people could not run Iran for Muslims. Their preoccupation was with the West and not Islam."

The dangerous game began. Banisadr and Bazargan believed *they* were the ones who would inherit power by manipulating Khomeini. Khomeini had the same idea, but in reverse. His plan was always to outmaneuver liberals and the left, and the "democracy" he envisioned was purely Islamic in form and content. "Khomeini did not believe in parties or in parliamentary struggles, even though he recognized a parliament was essential," said Ali Hossein. The challenge was to cultivate the support of Iran's urbane middle class, which in turn would earn him sympathy from the Western powers and international public opinion. Then once the Shah was deposed Khomeini's men planned to follow the example the Bolsheviks had set in Russia when in 1917 they seized total power for themselves.

Perhaps more than even he knew, Khomeini had already won the hearts and minds of the children of the Pahlavi elite and many in the middle and upper-middle classes. They decided that poor religious students like Ali Hossein represented the true voice of a nation corrupted by sterile Western materialism. Karim Pakravan, the son of General Pakravan, told an American visitor to Iran that in his youth he too had once supported Mossadeq. "The young had absolutely no interest in religion," he said. "Khomeini became important only after he was driven into exile by the Shah. The Shah's father, Reza Shah, had been very successful in fighting the mullahs. He made a direct assault on the clergy—forcing women to take off veils, riding into the shrines and beating the mullahs. He had public sympathy, because then the clergy were corrupt and wealthy. They were hated by everybody. Now they have lost their lands and the religious foundations. The mullahs have been purified. They have the power of poverty." Intellectuals like Pakravan believed that Khomeini and his followers were to be pitied and helped. "Khomeini is merely a symbol of opposition. He is a respected Muslim, but he has no power. Ten years ago, no prayers were said in universities. Religious students were mocked. Now there is a genuine student problem. Many of the students come from poor families in the provinces. They have to rent homes, and the financial burdens are unbearable."

Young Iranians educated at the Sorbonne returned to Iran as committed Marxists willing to subjugate themselves to Khomeini's leadership of the anti-Shah opposition. "[Marx] exposes the imperialists and their rape of all the countries of the Third World, including Iran," parroted one student, a leftist who donned a chador not because she understood or believed in Islam but because she wanted to make a political statement against the Shah's regime. Though Marx had condemned religion as the "opiate of the masses . . . in developing countries it is different. At times, religious feelings and social movements go hand in hand. That is the way it is now in Iran. We are all of us united against the Shah. We are in an Islamic country, and all social movements inevitably have a religious coloring. We do not believe there will ever be Communism here as there is Communism in Russia or China. We will have our own brand of socialism." Remarks like hers pointed to a curious phenomenon last seen in Imperial Russia sixty years before: Iran's best-educated minds helping their future executioners erect scaffolds in their name.

By the summer of 1977 the combination of a genuine Islamic revival and leftist and intellectual support for Khomeini had led to disorienting, alarming scenes on the streets of Iran's cities. "More and more women are seen on the streets of this Middle Eastern capital wearing the chador, a long enveloping veil, in what looks like a women's backlash," reported the *New York Times*. Popular culture reflected the new mood of sobriety. After the Quran, the second-best-selling book in Iran that year was a fundamentalist tract called *The Keys to Heaven*. The Shah saw with his own eyes what was happening when on May 29, 1977, during a rare public outing to southern Tehran, he was disturbed to see "thousands of women wearing the veil." Events in the region that spring and summer suggested that the revival of Islam was not limited to Iran or the Shia. In Egypt, President Sadat called out the army to crush street protests. The country's former minister for religious affairs was murdered in July by zealots who carried out a wave of terror attacks against cinemas, nightclubs, and other symbols of Western culture. "We don't want your civilization!" cried one of the Egyptian defendants on trial for the minister's murder. "We want to live in the desert under the clear blue sky, where we can pray to God!" Extremists in Syria staged attacks against government officials and assassinated Russian military advisers. In Turkey, dozens were killed and injured when gunmen opened fire on workers celebrating May Day in Taksim Square in Istanbul. But nothing prepared the Shah for the overthrow of his ally Prime Minister Zulfikar Ali Bhutto of Pakistan in that same month. The new Pakistani leader, General Zia ul-Haq, was a devout Muslim who announced his intention to adopt a new constitution based on Sharia. Through the Muslim world, leaders who had previously shown disdain or outright contempt for religion suddenly found the need to prove their credentials as men of faith. President Hafez al-Asad of Syria was photographed at Friday prayer services, and Libya's Colonel Muammar Gadhafi, ostensibly a socialist, closed nightclubs, imposed Sharia law, and declared his support for an Islamic state.

Religious fervor was on display even at Niavaran, where a small cadre of the Shah's own household staff emulated Grand Ayatollah Khomeini as their marja. "Afterwards, we found out that one of the young men who was working at Niavaran was in the [Khomeini] movement," recalled Queen Farah. Her own entourage had been infiltrated. "And the funny thing was, my, one of my ladies, she traveled with me, and suddenly I realized she was wearing a scarf. I didn't ask her why. And then with me she would put the scarf down, and when a man came she would put it up. We were hearing that in the universities some women were wearing veils and scarves, and the universities wanted to regulate them because they could catch fire in the science laboratories, or they could hide something during the exams." It apparently never occurred to the King and Queen to purge their household of malcontents or screen employees for their beliefs, though the security implications were obvious: some of the same men and women who cooked and served the Imperial Family their meals, cleaned the floors, and stood guard duty already questioned their allegiance to the dynasty, struggling to reconcile service to the Pahlavis with their fervent devotion to the man they upheld as their marja.

By now the Shah's relationship with his daughter had completely broken down. Princess Shahnaz and Khosrow Djahanbani were barred from the palace grounds, much to the relief of the Shah's bodyguards, who, unbeknownst to him, were secretly operating under orders not to leave him alone in the same room with his son-in-law. If Djahanbani made any sudden movements toward the King they were instructed to shoot him dead on the spot. The Queen's efforts to mediate came to naught, and the last time father and daughter met before the revolution was at a house party in Tehran. Informed that Shahnaz was on the property he at first refused to acknowledge her. Farah nudged him to make the first move but their last exchange was brief and awkward. The Shah's anxieties were revealed in an interview to mark his fifty-eighth birthday. He reminded the women of Iran how far they had come—and how much they had to lose if they returned to "medieval" ways. "How could we write off half the population—that is to say all Iranian women?" he said. "If our women continue to hide behind veils we shall not achieve our national aims. How could such women score victory at the Olympics or, when and if the need arose, fight patriotic wars? If we want a progressive Iran we ought to accept its terms also. A person's appearance has nothing to do with his or her moral standards, and refusing to work while hiding oneself away from society does not indicate purity or chastity either." The Shah had lost one daughter to the siren call of Islam, and now he began to worry that if he did not take action the rest of his children might soon slip from his grasp.

Determined to inoculate the throne from charges of apostasy, the Shah decided to highlight his role as Custodian of the Faith and offer the clergy small, tactical concessions until the religious fever broke. As a fifty-eighth-birthday gift to the nation he announced his intention to build a new Islamic university in the city of Mashad. The Shah hoped that Mashad, a more moderate seat of Islamic learning, would displace Qom as Shiism's most important center for religious scholarship. He assigned management of the project to Hossein Nasr, the Islamic scholar who advised his wife on cultural issues. The Shah also invited Nasr to enter politics when he offered him the post of secretary-general of the Rastakhiz Party. If he agreed to serve in that position for one year, the Shah said he hoped Nasr would consider taking the job of prime minister to lead Iran into free elections in the summer of 1979. Though Nasr preferred to stay out of politics and turned down the appointment, the Shah had revealed his thinking. As he surveyed the horizon in the summer of 1977 he recognized that storm clouds of a different, unwelcome sort were forming, and that interim measures were needed to batten down the hatches and clear the decks. If that meant Islamizing the Pahlavi monarchy in the short term, then so be it.

At the end of the summer Princess Ashraf returned to Niavaran to warn her brother for a second time that her contacts had told her that opposition groups were exploiting liberalization to organize and agitate. The annual ritual of Ramadan, one of the central pillars of the Muslim faith, was under way. During the monthlong observance—the date each year varied slightly according to the lunar calendar—the devout sought to purify their hearts, minds, and bodies through fasting. During Ramadan no food or beverages were consumed in daylight hours, though the rules were not as strict as they appeared: travelers, diabetics, and women pregnant, breastfeeding, or menstruating were exempted from fasting. Nonetheless, Ramadan was a time when individuals, families, and communities renewed their commitment to the Prophet and their faith in Islam. Long hours were spent in the mosques listening to prayer leaders deliver sermons and speeches. After dusk, at the end of fasting, families and their friends gathered for celebratory meals to socialize and exchange news. The combination of fasting, prayer, and celebration produced feelings of elevated spiritual unity. In the late summer of 1977, at the height of Ramadan, Tehran's mosques took advantage of liberalization to host large political gatherings at which the Shah and his reforms were denounced as un-Islamic. "We have not been allowed to form political parties," said a dissident lawyer. "We have no newspapers of our own. But the religious leaders have a built-in communications system. They easily reach the masses through their weekly sermons in the mosques and their network of mullahs throughout the nation. That is why so many nonreligious elements cloak their opposition in the mantle of religion." Mosque orators spoke in code to avoid provoking a reaction from Savak but their meaning was understood by all. At the same time, everyone was talking about the marked drop-off in terrorist activity by the Mujahedin.

The Shah told Ashraf that he couldn't quite put his finger on it but he too sensed an undercurrent of unrest. "Something is in the air," he agreed. "What concerns me most is this renewal of the alliance between the Red and the Black." He explained that Savak had recently uncovered evidence that the Mujahedin and Fedayeen had agreed to form a united front and share resources. His next remark suggested that he understood the implication: "It is clear they will settle for nothing less than the overthrow of our regime." He resolved to stay on track. Nothing, he assured his sister, would deter him from democratizing Iran—there could be no going back.

QUEEN FARAH SPENT the first half of July 1977 on a speaking tour of the United States. She was puzzled to see young Iranian student protesters holding aloft portraits of an elderly clergyman whose face she did not recognize. "And so I asked the name of this mullah who was idolized by our young demonstrators and whose defiant look meant nothing to me," she recalled. Mention of Grand Ayatollah Khomeini's name brought back unpleasant memories of the summer of 1963, when his mobs had threatened to storm the palace. To see the old man hailed now as an icon, like some Iranian Che Guevara, made no sense to her.

Farah's party was scheduled to fly on the Concorde to France on July 14 with a brief stopover before returning to Tehran the next day. After landing in Paris the Queen was handed a cryptic note from Dr. Abbas Safavian, someone she knew well from her work in academia. "I have to stay on an extra day," she told her party and they left without her. The next morning Farah was in her suite when Safavian entered with her husband's medical team. For the past few months Bernard, Flandrin, and Milliez had debated the ethics of staging a medical intervention. They worried that the Shah was not receiving the correct dosage of medication and that his health was already starting to deteriorate. Yet whenever they raised the topic of informing the Queen he would change the subject. By the summer of 1977 the physicians agreed that regardless of the patient's wishes they were obliged to break confidence. It was Jean Bernard who broke the devastating news of her husband's cancer. He explained that the Shah's condition was "chronic but serious . . . he knew it and had not wanted to say anything about it. All this had to be understood, if not accepted in such a short time, and then kept to herself. More difficult still: how was [the Queen] going to tell her husband that she knew about it?"

For Farah, the shock of diagnosis was compounded by the knowledge of her husband's years of deception. She couldn't help but feel betrayed. There was a harrowing parallel too with her father's cancer diagnosis thirty years earlier. As a child she had been lied to by her mother about her beloved father's illness. Now, as mother, wife, and Queen, she had to cope with the bitter reality of history repeating itself. "I thought that was the end," she remembered. "I cried all night long. I could not bear the thought of returning to Tehran and facing him. What would I tell him?" She flew back to Tehran on July 16, anguished but composed. She smiled through the arrival ceremony and concealed her distress from the battery of photographers and government officials on hand to greet her at the airport. The Shah, meanwhile, knew nothing about the medical intervention. All that he had agreed to do was allow Bernard and Flandrin to meet his wife when they were next in Tehran.

THE SUMMER OF 1977 was a heady time for Ali Hossein and his band of young revolutionaries. Their handlers made the crucial decision to start testing the reflexes of the security forces. They wanted to gauge the extent to which the Shah's pledge to loosen controls and tolerate more dissent was purely symbolic or a genuine concession. Younger men in the movement were ready to put their training to good use and stage provocations. They hoped a bloody crackdown would discredit liberalization by exposing the Shah as a hypocrite in the eyes of the Iranian middle class and isolating him still farther from his allies. "We would move in groups, through alleyways," said Hossein, "and we would meet in different homes."

For the past year terrorist operations against the Pahlavi regime had halted in response to appeals from the leaders of the two best-known mainstream opposition groups. The secular National Front and the Islamist Liberation Movement of Iran urged the Mujahedin and Fedayeen to give President Carter time to show he was serious in pressuring the Shah to improve human rights and return to constitutional rule. U.S. intelligence experts described the Mujahedin as "fanatic religious conservatives" who opposed the Shah because his reforms threatened to weaken the power of religious leaders. They described themselves as "Islamic Marxists" because of their commitment to the Prophet but also to social justice and equality. Khomeini had forged a tactical alliance with the Mujahedin in 1972, boosting their fortunes when he declared it "the duty of all good Muslims to support [the group] and overthrow the Shah."

Khomeini's blessing legitimized the Mujahedin in the eyes of Shia fundamentalists. Mujahedin recruits trained in terrorist camps run by Yasser Arafat's Palestine Liberation Organization and George Habash's even more radical Popular Front for the Liberation of Palestine. After completing training in Lebanon, Libya, and Syria they slipped back into Iran, some posing "as clergymen . . . [they] took code names, formed cells and provoked incidents of terrorism." "The quantity and sophistication of weapons available to the terrorists is impressive," concluded a secret U.S. intelligence assessment produced in September 1977. "Their arsenal includes assault rifles, armor-piercing rifle grenades and possibly mortars, which allows them considerable flexibility in their tactics." Mujahedin guerrillas also enjoyed ready access to radios, handheld walkie-talkies, and "electronic devices such as oscilloscopes, transformers, condensers, relays and grated circuits." Some of the Mujahedin's funding came from followers of Khomeini who traveled to Najaf to make their financial donations in person. The Marja "siphoned off a portion and gave the rest to the [Mujahedin]." The group's other lucrative source of income came from Colonel Muammar Gadhafi of Libya, who "provided financial assistance to both Khomeini and [the Mujahedin]. The Libyan embassy in Beirut allegedly forwarded $100,000 to the Mujahedin every 3 months." The financing and training paid off; by 1977 Mujahedin operatives had infiltrated Ambassador Sullivan's embassy and secured jobs working in the motor pool used by U.S. army advisers.

The second major terrorist group, the Fedayeen, were secular Communists, dedicated Maoists bitterly opposed to any form of organized religion. They did not target Americans in Iran and focused their attacks exclusively on Iranian buildings and military and government personnel. The Fedayeen underwent training in guerrilla warfare operations in terrorist camps in Oman, South Yemen, and at bases in Libya run by George Habash's Popular Front for the Liberation of Palestine. The Fedayeen were well stocked with explosives, machine pistols, revolvers, submachine guns, high-powered hunting rifles, and Tungsten armor-piercing ammunition supplied by Communist regimes in Poland, Czechoslovakia, and East Germany. Financing for group operations came predominantly from Libya's Colonel Gadhafi, who kept the group on a retainer to the tune of

$400,000 each year. Fedayeen leaders also enjoyed close ties to an assortment of international terrorist groups, including Swiss anarchists, West Germany's Baader-Meinhof Gang, the Irish Republican Army, and the Popular Movement for the Liberation of Angola. Fedayeen agents earned notoriety by disguising themselves as Iranian student protesters and storming Iranian consulates in European capitals. Though they claimed the attacks were staged to draw attention to human rights abuses in Iran, their real motive in assaulting diplomatic missions was to seize as many Iranian passports as possible, which were then used to create fake identities for sleeper agents sent back into Iran.

Libya's Gadhafi boosted Khomeini's fortunes at a crucial moment. In 1977 Grand Ayatollah Kazem Shariatmadari and the other moderate marjas and grand ayatollahs noticed a marked drop-off in the religious taxes they garnered from their supporters. They watched with dismay as many of their youngest and brightest emulants drifted to Khomeini's side. Hassan Shariatmadari served as his father's closest adviser and aide during this time and recalled his father's shock when Khomeini attracted enough adherents to emerge as a marja in his own right. "Most people had still not heard his name," he said. At this time, Iranian newspapers and television were still expressly forbidden from mentioning Khomeini's name or even publishing his portrait. Later, Shariatmadari and the others found out what had happened. "Two years before the revolution, Khomeini got $16 million from Libya through the son of Ayatollah Montazeri. He used this money to pay the *talebs* [religious students], and this allowed Khomeini to become a marja." Seminarians were reliant on the stipends they received from their marja, and in Khomeini's case he simply purchased their allegiance by outbidding his peers. "We knew a mullah in a far village who was getting 20,000 tomans from Khomeini, whereas my father had been giving him 5,000 tomans," said Shariatmadari. "We were astonished. We did not know the sources of the money."

Libyan cash supplemented even vaster sums raised inside Iran to support revolutionary activities. In 1977 Khomeini's field commander at home was Seyyed Mohammad Hussein Beheshti, now Ayatollah Beheshti, who twelve years earlier had condemned to death Prime Minister Hassan Ali Mansur. In the late sixties Beheshti, described by CIA analysts as "rabidly anti-Shah and an unwavering and unquestioning supporter of Khomeini," moved to Hamburg in West Germany to found the city's Islamic Center. Beheshti was a brilliant organizer and tactician who played the lead in forging alliances between religious hard-liners and secular left-wing Iranian student groups based in Europe, two groups united solely by their hatred for the Shah and the monarchy. From Hamburg, Beheshti returned to Iran to serve as Khomeini's liaison to the National Front and Liberation Movement. His biggest contribution, however, was as the revolutionary movement's fund-raiser in chief. "The funds Beheshti has been able to raise in the bazaar are considerable," reported CIA agents who estimated that "on a normal day" friendly merchants donated $285,000 or 2 million tomans to Khomeini's underground cells. The U.S. intelligence agency made one other notable observation: "Beheshti also functions as Khomeini's conduit for distributing funds to the terrorist group Mujahedin which targeted Americans for assassination in the early 1970s."

These immense sums ensured that student revolutionaries like Ali Hossein were never short of money and resources. Some of his friends volunteered to be sent to terrorist training camps in Lebanon's Bekaa Valley to learn how to handle guns and explosives. They returned home to form paramilitary groups, which were quietly dispersed around Tehran mosques whose basements became storage places for military hardware. "The level of organization was very developed and quite complex," said the young revolutionary. "It was not difficult to get guns. Guns were available. We produced our own hand grenades in Tehran." There were even training grounds inside Iran, up in the mountains, where hardened fighters trained recruits to handle weapons, plant bombs, and use large crowds as cover from which to attack the security forces.

The Shah was repeatedly assured by General Nasiri that terrorist groups posed no threat to Iran's stability or his survival. In September 1977, he boasted to *Kayhan* that "there are still between 100 and 200 terrorists left in Iran." He made it clear he wasn't worried. The captures and killings of the Mujahedin's top leadership in the summer and autumn of 1976 had been followed by the lull in terrorist activity that led the Shah and Nasiri to believe—erroneously, as it turned out—that the security forces had finally gained the upper hand in their "dirty war" against subversion. "We totally destroyed them," confirmed Parviz Sabeti. "Two thousand were in prison or killed. We had the best security conditions in six or seven years." With this assurance in mind, the Shah believed he could achieve his objective of loosening controls while reining in the security forces. Back in Washington, the CIA expressed skepticism. "On the basis of fragmentary information, we estimate Iranian terrorists to number more than 1,000," concluded a U.S. intelligence estimate compiled in late 1977. "Terrorist organizations appear to have no trouble in recruiting members from Iran's large student population." The terrorists "have the expertise to assemble powerful explosive devices, probably efficient enough, if properly placed on a major petroleum facility, to do substantial damage." The Americans found evidence that "terrorists are indeed interested in disrupting the economy. Terrorists in 1975 bombed electrical power lines outside Tehran that resulted in power outages." Iranian counterterrorist measures had so far focused on crushing the threat from inside the country. But these measures "will probably not be effective until the security services devise means to cut off the internal terrorist network from its external base of support." Remarkably, the Americans were unaware that Mujahedin agents had infiltrated their own embassy even as they concluded the terrorist group had developed the capacity to monitor Savak's internal communications.

Ambassador Sullivan's embassy rejected the CIA analysis and shared Nasiri's confidence that the insurgency was broken. "We knew firepower was coming in," said diplomat John Stempel, deputy head of the political section. "We didn't know how much of it there was. There was enough border fluidity in northern Iran to make it possible. But the light weapons and machine guns were not significant. A lot of the revolutionaries were trained in Lebanon, so you would expect there would be a cadre trained there. We were aware of it."

In July 1977 Court Minister Asadollah Alam flew to his rented villa in the south of France. Racked with cancer, Alam was anxious about the mess he had left behind in Tehran. He saw only one bright spot on the horizon: the Shah had finally summoned the nerve to replace Hoveyda as prime minister. For months, Alam had been patiently urging the Shah to clean house and appoint a strong, independent executive who could withstand American diplomatic pressure. Before he left Tehran, Alam thought he secured from the Shah a pledge to appoint Iran's tough-minded finance and economy minister Hushang Ansary, an official who enjoyed good relations with the commanders of the armed forces and senior clerics. Alam felt confident that Ansary, a consummate negotiator, would not hesitate to maintain order during liberalization. The mood at Niavaran was expectant and the Ansary family began receiving congratulatory telephone calls and floral bouquets. Ansary's wife, Maryam, was visiting Alam in Antibes, and the French government prepared to send bodyguards down in anticipation of her husband's appointment. In the event, they weren't needed.

On Friday, August 5, the Shah telephoned Alam and asked for his ailing minister's resignation. Alam may have been grateful to be relieved of the burden. His mood darkened the following day, however, when the Shah called again, this time with the news that he had decided to replace Hoveyda not with Ansary but with Jamshid Amuzegar, Iran's minister of the interior and chief oil negotiator. Known as a talented economist, and reputed to be on warm terms with senior U.S. officials, Amuzegar lacked the common touch that Iranians expected from their politicians. In public he came across as officious, haughty, and disdainful. This suited the Shah, who was still distrustful of professional politicians. Hoveyda, despite his faults, was a raconteur who could charm people in small groups or large gatherings. Alam was doubly outraged that instead of consigning Hoveyda to oblivion or exile the Shah appointed him as the new head of the Court Ministry. The Shah had apparently buckled when Hoveyda burst into tears at the news he would lose his post as prime minister and placated him by assigning him to the Court Ministry. "His Majesty is not thinking clearly," Alam mused out loud. "This has nothing to do with his sickness. The country is lost."

13

LAST DAYS OF POMPEII

Stop it when it gets into the streets.
—THE SHAH

This time either Islam triumphs or we disappear.
—GRAND AYATOLLAH KHOMEINI

On September 23, 1977, the King and Queen attended the University of Tehran's forty-fourth annual graduation ceremony, a routine event on an otherwise quiet day in the Iranian capital. Liberalization was moving ahead. Hundreds of political prisoners had already been released, censorship laws relaxed, and newspapers were permitted to publish articles on corruption, government incompetence, and the economy. Senior civil servants were ordered to make their assets and salaries public, and reforms were announced to make the judiciary more accountable and independent. The Iranian people were encouraged to attend assemblies organized by the Rastakhiz Party, where they could debate politics and air grievances. Most striking was the Shah's announcement of an "open space," allowing respectable regime opponents to meet and organize on condition that they refrained from criticizing the Shah or calling for a republic. Longtime activists such as Mehdi Bazargan suspected a ruse. They recalled the open atmosphere of the early 1960s, when reforms had been followed by repression. Younger activists, however, looked forward to testing the limits of the open space.

For Queen Farah, the ceremony at Tehran University came at the end of a difficult few weeks. For the past several years conservatives at court had argued that the Shiraz-Persepolis Festival of Arts, one of her signature patronages, was too avant-garde for Iranian tastes and caused needless offense to the clergy. Scorn turned to anger in August 1977 when the eleventh Shiraz-Persepolis Festival almost descended into street riots. The Squat Theater, an experimental Hungarian troupe based in New York, staged a production of its show *Pig, Child, Fire!* in an empty storefront window in the main Shiraz bazaar. In the play's climactic scene a young mother was raped by a soldier in front of her child. The atmosphere in the bazaar was already a combustible scene, with American tourists buying trinkets from stall owners, who broadcast cassette tapes of Grand Ayatollah Khomeini calling for revolution and railing against American influence. By way of coincidence, the Shah's granddaughter Princess Mahnaz was in the bazaar that day and overheard Khomeini's voice. She stumbled across *Pig, Child, Fire!* as the show was already under way and noticed the crowd start to boil as a rumor spread that the actors had actually performed a live public sex act. Police officers rushed to the bazaar to prevent an outbreak of rioting, but public revulsion could not be contained. From Najaf, Khomeini issued a statement condemning what he described as the "indecent acts" perpetrated on the people of Shiraz and demanded local religious leaders "speak out and protest."

The scandal provided ammunition for Farah's conservative critics in government and at court. At a time when religious passions were running high they argued that the Queen needed to lower her public profile. Shiraz, they argued, had been an accident waiting to happen. These critics reserved special enmity for her cousin Reza Ghotbi, whose state radio and television monopoly sanctioned programming that took sly digs at the Shah's authoritarian regime. But Farah's public works were more nuanced than they appeared to conservatives. She used the proceeds from her foundation to preserve and restore old mosques that had fallen into disrepair. Iran's most ardent feminist defended the right of women to stay home and raise children in the conventional manner. One of her new initiatives was the Festival of Popular Traditions, which championed traditional village culture. In the rush to find a scapegoat for Shiraz, however, these achievements were overlooked.

One month later, Farah sat mute beside her husband while university graduates filed past to collect their diplomas. She had attended hundreds of similar events over the years, each one following the same unerring script. This time, however, something unusual happened when several students stood up before the assembly to warn that extremists had infiltrated the university with the intention of instigating "plots to create campus unrest." One student referenced the involvement of religious radicals in the 1949 assassination attempt on the Shah's life and the 1963 uprising against the White Revolution. A second student rejected international criticism of Iran's record on human rights, while a third appealed to Iranians living abroad to return home "to become acquainted with the new realities of modern Iran, and to enjoy the fruits of our success and prosperity." This clumsy piece of staged theater caused outrage among faculty, administrators, and students who regarded it as an effort by Savak to hijack and politicize the signature event of the academic calendar. Tensions were already running high on campus, and the demonstration of loyalty before the Imperial couple was all that was needed to strike the match of conflagration.

AT THE START of the new school year, student revolutionary Ali Hossein was on the run.

The young man's identity as a courier for the Khomeini movement was discovered by Parviz Sabeti's agents, who ordered his arrest. He fled his dormitory room at the University of Tehran for a safe house where "we could become more and more active." Hossein's underground cell received orders to start testing the boundaries of the "open space" and bait the security forces with staged provocations that they hoped would draw blood, create martyrs, and generate public sympathy. Violent disorders would embarrass the Shah before the eyes of the world and expose liberalization as a sham. In the absence of a crackdown, however, revolutionary cells would take advantage of the resulting security vacuum to cause further instability. Either way, the revolutionaries would win. "Our goal was to confront the regime in some way, show our opposition in some way," said Hossein. The debacle at the university graduation ceremony created new opportunities to stoke unrest. "We made demonstrations and created problems for the regime under the banner of some excuse, pretending that our activities were not political." The provocateurs decided to stage their biggest attack yet inside the university's student cafeteria, acting under the guise of protesting the mingling between male and female students at mealtimes. Hossein was already personally offended by the behavior of young women on campus. "In the mosques the genders were segregated. The girls [on campus] wore makeup and Western clothes.

In the cafeteria at that time when we were taking tea there was no separate facility for the girls."

On Sunday, October 9, 1977, twenty religious extremists wearing balaclavas rushed into Tehran University's parking lot and set fire to student buses. The attack on the buses proved a diversionary tactic. While security guards doused the flames, the young men stormed into the student cafeteria, smashing and kicking in windows and forcibly pulling apart the boys from the girls. The scene inside was one of panic and pandemonium. Screaming students ran for cover, and those who offered resistance were set upon and beaten to the ground. Before the assailants ran off they dropped a pamphlet titled, "Warning to the Elements of Corruption." In it they threatened the life of any female student caught socializing with male friends.

> Don't ever come to the self-service restaurant in the boys' section [of the dormitory]. Don't ever, under any pretext, even for getting food, come to the boys' area. In no way may you ride the boys' bus. Put pressure on the officials of the dormitory and demand a separate self-service restaurant, as well as a bus. If you violate the guideline, your lives will have no guarantee of safety.

The assault on Iran's oldest and most prestigious university made front-page news across the country. One professor described the episode as a "revolting attempt to revive medieval horrors," an allusion to Sharia law, which forbade casual mixing of the sexes. The chancellor said it was the worst display of violence he could remember in his eleven years on the job. The head of the student union appealed to the anonymous assailants to come forward to talk about their concerns rather than resort to violence. University coeds staged a four-hour sit-in, promising they would "not allow shameful ideas to be propagated on the campus, which is a center of progress and the home of the nation's enlightened youth." They were supported by the Women's Organization of Iran, a women's rights organization headed by Princess Ashraf, which held a press conference on campus to denounce religious extremism.

Ultimately, however, the efforts of student leaders to rouse their peers was met with a sullen wall of silence. Leftist students suspected the secret police had staged the attack to smear their hero Khomeini as a fanatic. Religious students fully supported segregation anyway. Most students, not wanting trouble, warily submitted to intimidation. The result was that Tehran University's self-service cafeteria was segregated, and bus drivers refused to drive onto campus grounds. Ali Hossein's revolutionary cell had succeeded in its mission to paralyze the administration of the nation's top university and terrorize the student body into submission.

Students and intellectuals weren't alone in assuming that Savak was behind the cafeteria invasion. In the shadowy world of counterintelligence and subversion, the secret police had a long history of staging provocations to discredit opponents of the regime. Even government officials such as Minister of Women's Affairs Mahnaz Afkhami suspected Parviz Sabeti's Third Directorate was to blame. His agents targeted her for harassment because they believed her ministry employed too many leftists and dissidents. "The only negative article written about me was planted by Savak," she claimed. "They said I wore a see-through blouse with boots and drank whiskey." Galvanized by the attack on Tehran University, a pro-Khomeini mob took to the streets of Rey three days later demanding the release of Seyyed Mehdi Hashemi, a hard-line mullah sentenced to death for his role in a series of assassinations in Isfahan.

Both incidents drew the Shah's condemnation. On Saturday, October 14, he received a delegation of parliamentary leaders at the palace. While they stood in respectful silence he read out a tough statement deploring those who would try to take advantage of liberalization. "All these developments smell highly of counterrevolution, black reaction, and outright treason," he lectured his audience. "They want to set the country back, not only to pre-Shah-people revolution times, but also to circumstances prevalent fifteen hundred or two thousand years ago." Without naming Khomeini, the Shah made it clear who he believed was behind the violence. "How coordinated these internal and external developments are! One should not be surprised because they originate from the same center. Their orders come from the same source." He insisted that he would not be deterred from opening up the political system. Liberalization was irreversible: "And those who think otherwise or act in response to orders from foreigners or their agents should realize that their actions will not delay our progress as much as one ten thousandth of a second." As though to prove his point, the Shah allowed a series of open poetry readings hosted by West Germany's Goethe Institute to proceed. European and American diplomats were shocked when as many as fifteen thousand Iranians showed up to attend the receptions, using the venues to debate the country's political future without fear of censorship or arrest. The security forces watched warily outside the institute but otherwise made no effort to break up the gathering. "It was absolutely unbelievable," said one lawyer. "I thought I wasn't in Iran. I kept expecting the goons to come in and take us all away, but nothing happened."

Opposition leader Mehdi Bazargan also decided to test the new open space by announcing his first public speech in almost fifteen years. His choice of venue, a large mosque in the heart of downtown Tehran, was highly provocative, and his remarks warning against false idolatry were clearly aimed at the Shah, whose portrait was displayed in every public and many private buildings. But Bazargan's event passed off peacefully, too. "His people were well organized with loudspeakers so they could reach a crowd which at times numbered twenty thousand," reported one observer. "Going among them [were the] young and fairly well to do."

QUEEN FARAH'S THIRTY-NINTH birthday fell on October 14. Around the country, hundreds of local development initiatives were inaugurated in her name. She spent the day handing out awards to a group of eight hundred science and medical researchers at Tehran University. Prime Minister Amuzegar and Minister of Education and Science Manuchehr Ganji arrived to help her blow out the candles on a huge birthday cake.

To celebrate Farah's birthday the Pahlavis invited their good friends former U.S. vice president Nelson Rockefeller and his wife, Happy, to attend the gala opening of Tehran's new Museum of Contemporary Art. "A huge filmy sky sculpture floated above Farah Park Thursday evening, a symbol of the heady new status of Tehran in the artistic world," wrote one observer. Farah had conceived the project ten years earlier and kept a close eye on all aspects of design and construction, to the point of inviting her cousin Kamran Diba to assume the job of principal architect. They both shared a vision of making art accessible to the people. "A lot of Iranians still think of museums and art galleries as religious places, only for scholars and artists," Diba told reporters. "But we have the ideal setting in the park, and we hope people will just wander in." Rather than cater to a specialized clientele, the museum's board approved an admission fee of only twenty rials and made opening hours six days a week until eight in the evening. There were live musical and theatrical performances, workshops and film theaters for children, and specially funded programs to encourage young artists. Children's books and audiovisual presentations were commissioned and taken to local schools so schoolchildren could be exposed to art from an early age.

Farah's hectic work schedule never let up. On a single day in October 1977 she flew to Isfahan to open the first Festival of Popular Traditions, a weeklong affair intended to highlight tribal arts and culture; inaugurated an exhibition of Iranian handicrafts; awarded prizes to the winners of the Third and Fourth Festival of Theater; visited the historic Naqsh-e Jahan building; received the board of directors of the Reza Pahlavi Cultural Foundation's local branch; and watched a play put on by students of the Isfahan International School. Two days later she flew to Kerman to open one of her personal projects, a new museum dedicated to Iranian folk art. Back in Tehran, the leading advocate for Iran's disabled communities called on the government to devote more resources to helping the blind and the deaf. In the autumn of 1977 the Queen seemed to be everywhere. Her husband, by contrast, appeared to be quietly receding from the spotlight.

QUESTIONS OF MORTALITY were on the mind of Grand Ayatollah Khomeini following the sudden death of his eldest son on the twenty-third of October. Mostafa Khomeini had been his father's most trusted aide and the last voice of moderation in his inner circle. Though Mostafa suffered from health problems related to obesity, his father made no attempt to correct conspiracy theories that claimed he had been poisoned by Parviz Sabeti's agents. Eleven of the twelve imams of Shiism had been assassinated by poison, and Mostafa Khomeini's death conveniently played into the Shia narrative of martyrdom at the hands of an unjust ruler. Later, Khomeini ascribed the death of his son to "God's hidden providence."

The Shia tradition called for forty days of mourning followed by a memorial service. The release of pent-up grief after more than a month usually accounted for very public displays of emotion. Though Khomeini was forbidden from returning home, his representatives in Iran petitioned the government to permit mourning vigils in the mosques. Parviz Sabeti suspected they wanted to use the services as an excuse to organize, and he warned General Nasiri of his misgivings. The Shah was hesitant to deny the Marja's relatives the right to grieve and assented to their request, never doubting that the security forces would maintain order if trouble started. "Stop it when it gets into the streets," he instructed Nasiri.

With permission in hand, Khomeini's relatives and admirers published a notice of mourning in the newspaper *Kayhan* referring to Mostafa as "the offspring of the Exalted Leader of All Shiites of the World." This public letter provided an excuse for several hundred sympathetic clergymen to sign their own notice of condolence. At Mostafa Khomeini's memorial service at the Jam'e Mosque in Tehran, presiding cleric Ayatollah Taheri Esfahani prayed for "our one and only leader, the defender of the faith and the great combatant of Islam, Grand Ayatollah Khomeini." In an instant the fourteen-year taboo against mentioning Khomeini's name inside Iran was broken and "thunderous cries of 'Allah Akbar' " or "God is Great" echoed through the mosque. "And it spread," recalled Parviz Sabeti. "The forty-day mourning period was the time when the Khomeini people really got organized." Groups on the left took their cue and also published open letters praising Mostafa Khomeini. Heartened by the expressions of support, Khomeini decided that Iran was on the brink of upheaval. He had been closely following the bad news on the economy, the corruption scandals, and the Shah's attempts to reform his regime. He spoiled for a final showdown with the man he ridiculed as "that unfit element."

The Coalition of Islamic Societies ordered its revolutionary cells to step up provocations. In the first incident of its kind, on November 5 an anonymous caller telephoned the Paramount Cinema on Takht-e Jamshid Avenue in Tehran, just down the road from the U.S. embassy, and accused the owners of screening Western "pornography." A bomb was discovered hidden in a lavatory, and the complex was hastily evacuated while it was defused. The extremists were also galvanized by the behavior and attitudes of President Carter and his representatives in Iran. Convinced that the Shah's liberalization program was the result of U.S. pressure, Khomeini's men rejoiced on November 15 when the Pahlavi state visit to Washington, DC, was disrupted by violent protests outside the White House. Televised images of the Iranian and American First Couples teargassed and harried by demonstrators gripped the imagination of the Iranian public, whose culture and historical awareness did not allow for accident or incompetence. They concluded that the American president had staged the unrest to embarrass his guests, whom he now apparently regarded as liabilities. This leap of logic, so alien to American sensibilities, made complete sense from an Iranian perspective.

The Islamic Coalition's revolutionary cells were fully activated, and saboteurs like Ali Hossein fanned out around the country to stoke unrest and cause mayhem. Isolated acts of violence were reported in several towns where banks, travel agencies, cinemas, and facilities identified with modernization and the White Revolution were attacked. On November 24 in Shiraz pro-Khomeini militants rioted outside a mosque smashing windows, setting fire to two cinemas, and storming the main synagogue, whose carpets were doused with gasoline and set ablaze. Bomb threats were phoned in to more than a hundred family welfare centers established to cater to mothers living in poor neighborhoods such as the Tehran slum districts of Darvazeh Gar and Naziabaz. Women came to the centers, run by the Ministry of Women's Affairs, to learn to read and write and receive instruction in postnatal care, hygiene, health, and nutrition. Trained staff provided them with family planning information and employment and legal counseling services. Ninety of the centers also offered child-care facilities for mothers with infants and toddlers. Starting in November, male callers threatened to blow up welfare centers in Tehran, Isfahan, Shiraz, and Kerman. "There was a lot of panic and disruption," recalled Minister of Women's Affairs Mahnaz Afkhami. "We would have to evacuate the children to safety. Then we would bring them back and another threat would be phoned in and it would start all over again." Unrest erupted on major university campuses, where leftists broke windows and assaulted administrators. The first targeting of American citizens was reported on December 7, the anniversary of Pearl Harbor, when a touring American college wrestling team was attacked in the cafeteria at Aryamehr University by Iranian students chanting anti-U.S. slogans. The Iranians desecrated the Stars and Stripes and declared their support for the opposing Russian team.

One of the Shah's proudest achievements was the infusion of Western technology to develop Iran's economy. But just as the security forces could not possibly stop every tape cassette of Khomeini's speeches from entering the country, so too were they powerless to prevent the Xerox machines then coming into fashion in offices in the capital from being used as weapons to fight the regime. "Tens of thousands of copies of protest petitions have found their way into circulation because nearly every office in Tehran has a copying machine," reported one American who visited the capital in the autumn of 1977. "Thank God for the Xerox machine," chortled an opposition activist. "I don't think the man who invented the copying machine was aware of what he was doing for freedom of expression."

Even the Shah's efforts to tackle corruption and waste in government had a boomerang effect. When Jamshid Amuzegar became prime minister he had sought the advice of Parviz Sabeti. "I never had any political experience before now," he admitted. "What can I do to succeed?" Sabeti told him that opposition parties such as the National Front, Liberation Movement of Iran, and Tudeh already had well-crafted political programs that told the people what they stood for. "You have to set your agenda," he advised. "I told him [Rastakhiz] should be moderate, pragmatic, and nationalist. He needed a short-term program." He also recommended the new government start airing grievances in a public forum such as a stadium. Amuzegar liked the idea and took it to the Shah, who rejected it as "ridiculous. If you do it, bring it to the royal court." This was the origin of the notorious Imperial Commission, tasked with rooting out evidence of corruption and waste in government agencies and in the business community. The Shah appointed Hossein Fardust, his oldest friend and Nasiri's deputy at Savak, to head the commission, whose proceedings were televised live rather like the Nixon-era Watergate investigation in the United States. He expected to be applauded for making government more transparent and accountable—isn't that what the liberals had been clamoring for all these years? But Sabeti was aghast that his original idea had evolved into a public witch hunt of the civil service: "I thought party members would talk about lifestyle problems but when it was on TV it reached a mass audience."

Month after month, Iranians watched in dismay as public officials were hauled in front of a panel and grilled under klieg lights about project overruns, missing millions, and kickbacks. In the second week of November 1977 the commission released reports on delays in road, rail, and port construction; problems affecting the electrical grid; and shortages of skilled labor to keep power generators running. Nosratollah Moinian, head of the Shah's Special Bureau, took the lead in denouncing "incompetence and negligence among certain government executives," and the Shah personally ordered the arrest of a former energy minister and two associates for their role in the summer power outages that had left the capital blacked out during a heat wave. But the Shah's decision to involve himself in matters best left to prosecutors and the court system sent the signal that he was putting his own regime on trial. The depressing catalog of failures and lost public funds only served to reinforce the widespread popular belief that the White Revolution had run aground. The commission reinforced the idea that the government was corrupt and inept, and it helped collapse the confidence of the civil service, which was staffed by the white-collar middle class. These professionals regarded the Shah's personal involvement in the investigations as a singular act of disloyalty. Business-men also began to lose confidence in the regime, regarding the commission as an attempt to find scapegoats for the government's own failures. Far from helping to restore public confidence in the system, the Imperial Commission played an instrumental role in discrediting state institutions and undermining public morale.

AMBASSADOR WILLIAM SULLIVAN closely followed the sudden surge in unrest around the country, though from the start he misunderstood its origins. Sullivan and his political counselors, section head George Lam-brakis and his deputy John Stempel, appeared more concerned with the behavior of the Shah's security forces than the shadowy men behind the unrest. In recent weeks, anxious to build relations with the anti-Shah opposition, they had made contact with moderate leftists and republicans who assured them Parviz Sabeti's Third Directorate was staging provoca-tions to prove to the Shah that the "open space" had gone too far and that tough measures were required to restore law and order. The Americans accepted this explanation. They were certainly aware of who Khomeini was but made no real attempt to learn about his philosophy of Islamic governance; translate his writings; or track the flow of money, men, and arms from radical Arab leaders such as Arafat and Gadhafi.

On December 7, the same day the American wrestlers were set upon at Aryamehr University, and while the Shah was outside the country on a state visit to Oman, Sullivan met privately with Prime Minister Amuzegar to receive his assurance that the Iranian government would not use force to put down peaceful protests, nor would it resort to the sort of crack-downs that had led to human rights abuses in the past. He told Amuze-gar that he was particularly upset over a recent incident where Savak agents had stormed a Tehran home where opposition leaders were holding a political meeting. Sullivan sent a cable to Secretary of State Cyrus Vance explaining that Amuzegar had agreed to a "hands off" strategy and that he was determined to avoid at all costs repressive measures that would invite condemnation from foreign governments and human rights groups. "Amuzegar said GOI [Government of Iran] had decided to eschew police measures in handling dissent," explained Sullivan. "Prime Minister went on to say that government particularly sought to avoid making arrests, because 'these people want to be arrested.' He said their tactic was to have some of their members arrested, convey the information directly to [the foreign news media], and have exaggerated reports of the arrests circulated in the United States. Then, he said, I would get a letter from a Congressman and in effect become an advocate for the person arrested." Amuzegar told Sullivan that his government "would permit dissenting groups to continue having public meetings, signing letters, and otherwise remaining active."

Amuzegar's remarks reflected the Shah's view that the Rastakhiz Party should take the lead in channeling popular unrest and directing political passions toward constructive measures rather than into the streets. That, after all, had been the basis for its establishment three years earlier. Amuzegar told Sullivan that Rastakhiz had recently organized an impressive turnout of parents to protest the violence at the University of Tehran. But Sullivan wasn't satisfied. He wanted a promise from Amuzegar that there would be no more "head bashing" by Savak or pro-regime vigilante groups: it was important that peaceful protesters felt there were legitimate venues in which they could "vent their views. Otherwise they would become convinced there was no way within the system to advocate opposition. This in turn could convince them that violence and terrorism were the only alternatives to the current system." Amuzegar said he "emphatically agreed" with Sullivan and that there could be no retreat from liberalization—the "open space" must remain open.

To reinforce the Shah's message of tolerance and moderation in the face of extremism, violence, and threats, one of Iran's most respected politicians delivered a speech that summed up government strategy. "Patience is the imperative of the current situation," declared Abdol Majid Majidi, the leader of the more liberal of the Rastakhiz Party's two ideological wings. The agitators, he insisted, *wanted* the authorities to crack down hard, to discredit liberalization. But the government would not take the bait. He repeated a recent statement by the Shah to the effect that young people often did things to "prove and test their presence before entering society." What was going on was not so unusual. Young people were "letting off steam," and there was no reason to be alarmed: incidents of unrest occurring around the country were harmless and to be expected.

MANY WEALTHIER Iranians did not see it that way. The Shah had launched liberalization in the hope it would strengthen middle-class support for the monarchy and show that he too was on the side of political reform. But many of the same liberals who had spent the past few years calling for democracy became alarmed at the sudden spike in unrest: Iran's propertied class was already holding an election of sorts, and the ballots they cast were with their feet.

The 1973–1974 oil boom had been accompanied by the lifting of restrictions on the amount of capital Iranians could take out of the country. With real estate prices and inflation soaring at home, many middle- and upper-middle-class Iranians purchased properties in Europe and North America as a nest egg. The pace of capital flight began to accelerate over the summer of 1977. "I was aware of it," recalled Hassan Ali Mehran, governor of Iran's Central Bank. "What was a good investment policy in 1975 was a good insurance policy in 1977." Mehran's analysts watched as private capital worth an estimated $100 million began leaving Iran each month, bound for foreign safe havens. At the same time, consular officials at the U.S. embassy on Takht-e Jamshid Avenue noticed a sharp increase in the number of Iranians seeking visas to enter the United States. Thousands of miles away, real-estate agents in California's San Francisco Bay Area were startled by an influx of Iranians "buying up the place," with properties going for between $250,000 and $400,000. Farther south, Iranians were "pouring" into Los Angeles to the extent that they had "rejuvenated the place."

Foreign residents who knew Iran well or had close ties to the government and military also began to take the Shah's measure. They were aware of the rumors that he was ill, and they, too, doubted that liberalization could work. Businessman James Saghi "saw the writing on the wall," remembered a colleague, "and sold his house at the top of the market for something approaching two and a half million dollars cash, which he took out of the country immediately." American Lloyd Bertman, who ran the Jupiter Trading Company and who had lived in Iran for twenty-eight years, told associates "there are things that are happening that make me uncomfortable, so I'm going to leave." Others were struck by the sour public mood. Chris Westberg, the twenty-one-year-old daughter of an American lawyer, had lived with her family in Iran since the midsixties. On returning after several years away at college, she was disturbed by the sour public mood and tension on the streets of Tehran. "The men seemed even more hostile than I remembered them," she recalled. "Instead of the comments about my blue-eyes-like-the-sky or more brazen appraisals of my anatomy, there were vicious murmurs of 'foreign whore!'" She spotted anti-American graffiti daubed on walls around town proclaiming, "Death to

Jimmy Carter" and "Yonkee Go to Home." Then there were the austere uniforms worn by young women of university age. They were decked out in "grey or khaki-colored tunics over long pants or ankle-length skirts, with matching scarves tied tightly under their chins, absolutely no make-up." One day the young American chanced to talk to one of these stern young creatures when they shared a cab ride together. Her fellow passenger explained that she was a devout Muslim "who hoped to serve Allah and her country by obtaining a science degree from Tehran University." Westberg suggested that the student's education might conflict with the teachings of the Quran. Her fellow traveler retorted, "It is necessary for the changes to come."

IN DECEMBER 1977, in the same week that Prime Minister Amuzegar assured Ambassador Sullivan that his government would not use force to suppress dissent, Grand Ayatollah Khomeini issued a public fatwa, or religious edict, from Najaf in which he declared the Shah an illegitimate ruler and condemned his rule as illegal. The editor of the *Kayhan* newspaper, Amir Taheri, recalled receiving "a strange handwritten [two-page] letter . . . peppered with a number of amusing spelling errors." The letter had been dictated by Khomeini to his younger son Ahmad, a guerrilla fighter trained in Lebanon who since his brother Mostafa's death had taken on the role of his father's principal secretary. In his fatwa, Khomeini boldly announced that he had "deposed the Shah and abrogated the Constitution." He referred to the King as the *Taghut*, or Satan, and signed the letter "Imam," claiming for himself the title of one of the Prophet's original disciples—an audacious and highly provocative gesture that had no precedent under Quranic law. Furthermore, Khomeini called on the people to withhold their taxes, refuse to obey the laws of the land, and stay away from school. Iranian intellectuals ignored the fatwa, regarding it as so outrageous and so fantastic that it could only have been produced by Savak to smear Khomeini as a lunatic.

The Shah learned of the fatwa after it had been in circulation for a week and only then from the Iraqi ambassador. According to Taheri, who saw the Shah in early December, the monarch was "still angry enough to mention [the fatwa] himself and turn it into a major topic of conversation. He would soon, he warned, call on all Iranians to choose sides." Like Khomeini, he wanted the Iranian people to make a choice. "They must decide," the Shah told him. "Do they want our great civilization, or would they rather live under the great terror our foreign enemies are plotting with that crazy fanatic as their instrument?" His remarks echoed his earlier comments to Princess Ashraf at the end of the summer: he wanted his son to inherit a throne without thorns. As December drew on, the Shah established a special committee and instructed it to come up with a list of strategies and measures to isolate and discredit the Islamists. At the same time, Khomeini wrote a letter to the leaders of the Coalition of Islamic Societies informing them to start their long-awaited insurrection. "The Shah must go," he insisted. "This time either Islam triumphs or we disappear." He left it to them to formulate a plan for revolt. This would be no easy task—the revolutionaries faced the unenviable feat of stirring unrest without bringing down upon their followers the full weight of the fifth-strongest army in the world.

Week by week, day by day, the provocations escalated. In the last two weeks of December 1977 the Iranian embassy in Denmark was invaded and ransacked, and in Tehran and other major cities banks and businesses associated with Americans, Jews, and the Baha'i, a minority Islamic sect, were assaulted.

There was a respite only on Christmas Day when Queen Farah and her children welcomed to Niavaran a group of American students traveling around the world to promote their message of peace.

THE SABOTAGE OPERATIONS and violent protests staged by the Khomeini movement were choreographed to coincide with the arrival in Tehran on New Year's Eve of President Carter. The American was on the second stop of a seven-nation, nine-day presidential tour of European, Asian, and Middle East capitals. Originally scheduled for late November, Carter's trip had been pushed back to the New Year when the centerpiece of his domestic agenda, legislation to promote energy independence, faced defeat on Capitol Hill. The significance of the trip did not become apparent until much later when it became a symbol for political collapse and the opening act in a grand historical drama, the prelude to disaster and a terrifying metaphor for future shock.

Despite his personal disdain for the Shah, Carter was anxious to mend fences with the only leader in the Middle East who enjoyed close relations with the president of Egypt and prime minister of Israel, both of whom were involved in intensive U.S.-sponsored peace negotiations. The Shah was President Sadat's friend and as Israel's main supplier of oil the Shah was well placed to exert leverage on Prime Minister Menachim Begin to accept painful territorial concessions. Still, Carter did not want to appear too closely associated with the Shah, whose human rights record had earned international opprobrium. The seventeen hours he planned to spend in Tehran seemed about right, just enough time to make a courtesy call and to refuel on the way to New Delhi. Carter was about to depart the Polish capital Warsaw when a time bomb exploded in the washroom of the Iran-America Society's language school in Tehran, wrecking the ground-floor administration offices and injuring a security guard.

Air Force One's slow descent over the mountains of eastern Turkey and northern Iran on the afternoon of December 31, 1977, afforded Jimmy Carter his first look at the country that over the next year would dictate his political future, decide the fate of Islam as a force for change in the world, and define the contours of the new century whose blurred lines were already taking shape. In the hour before he landed, Carter conferred one last time with his senior aides Secretary of State Cyrus Vance, Assistant for National Security Affairs Zbigniew Brzezinski, and officials who handled Iranian affairs. Also aboard was Gary Sick, the desk officer for Iranian affairs serving on the National Security Council. The presidential caravan included dozens of White House advisers, support staff, bodyguards, newspaper and television reporters, celebrity interviewer Barbara Walters, and *Doonesbury* cartoonist Garry Trudeau. But as Air Force One approached the Iranian frontier over Turkey, starting its final approach over the great desert plateau that Cyrus and Alexander had once conquered, the fifty-three-year-old president had thoughts other than politics and diplomacy on his mind.

Jimmy and Rosalynn Carter had prepared for the trip by showing their daughter, Amy, an illustrated picture book of life in Iran. The Carters were both born-again Christians and had looked forward to seeing the lands of the Old Testament for the first time. The couple peered out the windows of their compartment over the arid moonscape, hoping to catch a glimpse of the mountain where Noah's Ark settled during the Great Flood. Excitement quickly turned to disappointment. "Although it was a clear day," Carter wrote in his diary, "we never were sure whether or not we saw Mount Ararat to the north." Despite the unobstructed view, the president of the United States could not see what he was looking for in the open skies over southwest Asia.

* * *

ON THE EVE of President Carter's arrival in Tehran, a cold front rolled down from Soviet Central Asia, coating the Alborz Mountains with a foot of silver frosting that chilled the air in the Iranian capital. The ski fields at Dizin, a short drive from the northern suburbs, were open for the season, and the northern cities of Mashad, Tabriz, and Kermanshah were already well blanketed. To the south, the Kharkeh River in Khuzestan Province burst its banks and flooded farmland, and mud seeped into the municipal water supply of Ahwaz. Iranians cheered their football team's victory over Australia to advance to the play-offs of the soccer World Cup, due to be held the following summer in Argentina. A team of Iranian mountaineers declared their intention to become the first non-Chinese climbers to scale Mount Everest from Tibet. The death toll from the recent temblor in Kerman rose to six hundred. Iran's broadcast authority announced that next summer state television would make the switch from black-and-white to color.

Artists and audiences flew in from around the world to enjoy what promised to be Tehran's most brilliant winter season yet for the performing arts. Acclaimed mime artist Marcel Marceau, French pop singer Joe Dassin, and renowned Swedish soprano Birgit Nilsson were all booked to perform in the New Year, with Nilsson at the Rudaki Hall reprising her signature role in *Tristan und Isolde*, accompanied by the Tehran Symphony Orchestra. Large crowds turned out for exhibitions celebrating the art of Andy Warhol and Jasper Johns in Tehran's dazzling new Museum of Contemporary Art. The King and Queen opened an exhibition of African art and inaugurated the Tenth Festival of Arts and Culture by attending the opening night performance of *Romeo and Juliet*. Iranian film director Shahpur Gharib scooped top honors and the prized golden statue at the Twelfth International Festival for Children and Young Adults for his movie *Summer Vacation*. Hollywood had recently discovered Iran's potential as a movie location. Filming was under way on *Caravans*, starring Anthony Quinn, Christopher Lee, Joseph Cotten, and Jennifer O'Neill. O'Neill delighted the social pages when she announced her engagement to a local businessman from Isfahan. Novelist Alex Haley, the author of *Roots*, was received at Niavaran by the Queen. Movie buffs flocked to the Tehran International Film Festival to see Sylvester Stallone's *Rocky*, Woody Allen's *Annie Hall*, and Barbra Streisand's *A Star Is Born*. At the Italian Theater on Avenue France, the Crown Players, an amateur expatriate theatrical group, held final dress rehearsals for their Persian-themed pantomime version of *Dick Whittington*. In a nod to their surroundings, the streets of London were given Iranian names, and references to Christmas were struck in favor of Nowruz, the Persian New Year.

At the central fish market, housewives waited in line to buy white fish from the Caspian, though over the winter dealers charged such exorbitant prices for a single fish—as much as 2,500 to 3,000 rials—that dark brown halva from the Persian Gulf was once again back in fashion. Shoppers in the main bazaar grumbled about high prices and shortages of basic food items such as table salt, eggs, and chickens. Eager to cash in, merchants were caught cheating customers by selling nylon bags half filled with sand instead of salt. Demand for dairy products far outstripped supply. "Get your milk and yogurt before 8 a.m. or you will go without," Tehranis were warned. Consumption of milk had shot up 36 percent in just twelve months, far in excess of the capital's 560-ton daily milk supply. Power outages didn't help. The influx of new migrants from the provinces and construction of new factories and office buildings placed enormous strain on the city's power grid. Electrical failures temporarily knocked out milk and yogurt production at the pasteurized milk plant. A nationwide shortage of eggs prompted the government to import two thousand tons of eggs to meet demand in Tehran and other cities. Even beer, a staple in a city that proudly boasted its own breweries, rose 10 percent in price so that a small bottle of beer now cost 25 rials and a big bottle went for 30 rials.

In the thirty-sixth year of the Shah's reign his capital resembled a glass, steel, and concrete behemoth that flooded an eighty-five-mile-square radius stretching from the foothills of the Alborz Mountains to the edge of the great salt desert. Tehran's population now exceeded 4.5 million, with 200,000 new arrivals expected each year and the number of city residents doubling on average every eleven years. The runaway growth of recent decades had outpaced the ability of local government to maintain services, and the combination of weather and traffic served only to aggravate popular discontent. In the autumn of 1977 unseasonably heavy rains caused the water table beneath southern Tehran to suddenly rise, backing up sewers, overflowing drains, and flooding poorer neighborhoods in the southern suburbs as well as the central business district. Surface water brought traffic to a halt in a metropolis where every morning another five hundred vehicles were added to rush-hour traffic, which peaked as early as seven in the morning. "Private cars, taxis, minibuses, single- and double-decker city buses, heavy trucks, and trailers can be seen as early as four in the morning to late at night," remembered one resident.

With only 1,200 traffic police to monitor 12,000 roads, and 109 filling stations to service almost 1.5 million cars, daily travel around the capital was a real challenge. The traditional Persian disdain for regulations and laws of any sort didn't help. In Tehran there was a sort of freewheeling anarchy on the streets, with motorists slicing across divider lanes, driving up on sidewalks, barreling through traffic intersections and red lights, and heading in the opposite direction down one-way streets. Collisions led to raised tempers, fistfights, and broken bones. Iran had one of the world's highest rates of fatalities involving children because ambulances were often stuck in traffic. Traffic was so bad that Crown Prince Reza made front-page news when he placed an anonymous phone call to Mayor Javad Shahrestani's live radio and television program *Direct Contact*, pointing out that too many traffic lights did not work and that uneven hatches covering sewage ducts made the roads even more hazardous.

The capital's poor southern suburbs were plagued by overcrowding, poor sanitation, and shortages of clean drinking water. An estimated 700,000 residents who lived there were either unemployed or underemployed. The heavy autumn rains that flooded "sewage wells and filth-choked jubes" caused a cholera outbreak made worse by "the piles of garbage left on street corners and the presence of packs of wild dogs, both threats to health." City councillors representing southern wards complained that the municipal budget was weighted in favor of the wealthier north. Whereas northerners were allotted one street cleaner per sixty residents, said Councillor Hossein Sharbiani, in Mesgarabad in the south there was only one cleaner for 720 residents. In the southern districts of Naziabad and Javadieh there was one worker for every 540 residents, but in Takhte Tavous in the north there was one municipal worker for every 190 people. Disparities like this fed the grievances of poorer Tehranis who every day took buses to Shemiran to clean, sweep, and cook for the wealthy.

The authorities were finally responding to mounting public anger. In December, Mayor Shahrestani unveiled a five-year roadworks plan to tackle congestion and get the city moving again. Construction started on the first section of Tehran's new French-designed subway, whose 2.8-mile tunnel connecting Mirdamad to Abassabad Avenue was set to open in January 1981. The proposed new metro stations were specially designed to double as bomb shelters in the event of aerial bombardment during a war.

Work also began on a new international airport nineteen miles south of the capital. Final approval was granted for what would be remembered as one of the Shah's finest urban legacies, a twelve-mile-long, half-mile-wide forested green belt designed to improve air quality, preserve agricultural farmland, and protect the city from desert sandstorms. The National Iranian Oil Company announced the installation of new equipment at its Tehran refinery to reduce the content of lead in gasoline. The Ministry of Energy announced plans to build a 20-billion-rial sewage treatment plant to service southern Tehran. The city's fourth water filter plant was on the brink of completion.

One group of young entrepreneurs decided not to wait for official action and imported forty-two battery-run cars capable of driving distances of up to sixty kilometers. Demand was not exactly overwhelming in Tehran for automobiles that sat only two passengers, had limited mileage, and cost 225,000 rials. Nevertheless, by the end of the year four battery-powered CitiCars had appeared on Tehran city streets. They were taken as yet another sign that Iranians had embraced science and technology and were ready for the challenges of the eighties. Help was on the way. The question was whether they had the patience to wait that long.

PART TWO

FAREWELL THE SHAH

1978–1979

And Seyavash said, "As the heavens roll
They cast my spirit down and sear my soul.
The wealth with which my treasury is filled,
The goods I've sought, the palaces I build,
Will pass into my enemy's fell hand.
Before long, death will take me from this land."

—THE PERSIAN BOOK OF KINGS

14

LIGHTS OVER NIAVARAN

Caesar, I never stood on ceremonies,
Yet now they fright me. There is one within,
Besides the thing that we have heard and seen,
Recounts most horrid things seen by the watch.
A lioness hath whelped in the streets,
And graves have yawned, and yielded up their dead.
—JULIUS CAESAR, ACT 2, SCENE 2

All the elements of trouble are on the loose
and unleashed.
—THE SHAH

From the heights, the winter city unfolded like a crush of black velvet and white light, spilling down the slopes of the Alborz Mountains as though every diamond in the Queen's jewel box had been flung onto the desert floor. Tonight, the lights of northern Tehran shimmered and glowed with a special brilliance. With the New Year only a few hours away, a round of house parties was about to get under way. Hostesses and servants put the final touches to dinner tables; checked place settings; and strung lights, streamers, and decorations. One of the biggest house parties was a fancy dress bash at the home of John Hoyer, general manager of Scandinavian Airlines, and his wife, Hanne. Their guests included Canadian ambassador Ken Taylor and his wife, Pat, and diplomats and business executives from a dozen countries. The hilltop home of Iran's ambassador to Washington, Ardeshir Zahedi, back in town for one of his infrequent visits, was a "busy hive of activity," with baskets of flowers arriving "almost every other minute" from admirers.

Tehran's hotels anticipated a busy night. The InterContinental boasted Polynesian and French-themed restaurants, a "snazzy disco" on the ground floor, and assured guests a celebratory midnight glass of champagne "on the house." The Sheraton promised "an exciting and unforgettable New Year's Eve special" with a fixed-price menu in the Supper Club, accompanied by live entertainment featuring Persian singers and belly dancers. The Hilton's French restaurant, Chez Maurice, offered romantic dinners by candlelight. In the hotel discotheque, DJ John Coulson was on hand to spin the latest pop hits flown in on audiocassette tapes from New York and London. Abba's "Name of the Game," "How Deep Is Your Love?" by the Bee Gees, and "We Are the Champions" by Queen were the hot tracks of the winter, and "Mull of Kintyre" by Wings finally toppled Debby Boone's "You Light Up My Life" after eight straight weeks at the top of the charts. Iranian playlists included disco tracks by popular local stars Darioush, Manouchehr, Giti, Ramesh, and Googoosh. The fun would continue well into the night. After-dinner entertainment ran the gamut in Tehran, where every taste, fancy, and quirk was catered to. In a city where an exotic dancer had recently been paid a staggering $50,000 to disrobe at a private party, nightclub patrons at Club Vanak looked forward to a smorgasbord of "belly dancers, strip teasers, sexy dancers, go-go girls, jugglers and musicians."

Moviegoers in Tehran had fewer choices over the new year. New foreign movie releases were a rarity in a country that for the past several years had been blacklisted by Hollywood studios because of the Shah's stubborn refusal to approve an increase in cinema ticket prices. The boycott ended when the government reached a deal to raise prices, but the big studios still insisted that Iranian cinemas first screen a backlog of movies that dated back to the midseventies. The result was a slew of disaster pictures that opened in late 1977 and kept audiences on the edges of their seats, each film emphasizing failure of leadership, loss of control, and public panic. In *Towering Inferno* (1974), which opened just before Christmas 1977, a group of hapless celebrants were stranded when fire broke out in what was supposed to be the world's newest and most luxurious skyscraper. In *Earthquake* (1974), the glamorous, sun-drenched metropolis of Los Angeles was flattened by a powerful temblor and dam collapse. The protagonists in *Jaws* (1975), which opened in Tehran cinemas in the New Year, kept trying to swim to safety but never quite made it.

Tehranis would have to wait before they could see *Saturday Night Fever*, *Star Wars*, and *Close Encounters of the Third Kind*, the three blockbuster releases that swept American and European box offices that winter. John Travolta was the biggest movie star in the world and every teenage girl's crush. The slim pickings on New Year's Eve in Tehran were the usual fare of obscure horrors, spaghetti Westerns, and dated romances. Over on Old Shemiran Road the Bowling screened *The Graduate* (1967). Showing at the Ice Palace on Pahlavi Avenue were two movies whose titles eerily portended how most Americans living in Tehran spent their next New Year's Eve, *The Getaway* (1972), starring Steve McQueen and Ali MacGraw, followed by Peter Cushing's *Now the Screaming Starts* (1973). For those planning a quiet night in, National Iranian Radio and Television's English-language television station cut away from its regular nighttime lineup of *Charlie's Angels*, *Space 1999*, and *Shaft* to broadcast the evening movie, *The Pendulum*, a 1969 murder thriller with George Peppard and Jean Seberg with sly political undertones. At the time of its release the American movie critic Roger Ebert had denounced it as "a fascist movie, defending strong authority figures against citizens' rights."

Tonight's big show, of course, was the televised state banquet in honor of the Carters.

JIMMY CARTER ROSE to deliver his toast shortly after ten o'clock. A hush fell over the dining hall in Niavaran and in private homes and in bars, hotels, and restaurants across Tehran, and indeed around the country, the meal chatter subsided, drinks were set aside, and celebrants gathered around television sets to listen to what the American president had to say. Every word the president said would be parsed and analyzed for some hidden or deeper meaning. Television audiences noticed the anxiety on the Queen's face. From her seat at the top table, Princess Ashraf also thought she knew what was going on. "I looked at his pale face," she remembered. "I thought his smile was artificial, his eyes icy—I hoped I could trust him." "The situation in Iran was already bad," recalled Elli Antoniades, Queen Farah's friend since childhood. Farah's circle regarded Carter with a wariness bordering on distrust. "We were in such a bad mood. We were so suspicious of Carter."

This president had a habit of laying it on thick with foreign heads of state. Previously, Carter had praised Yugoslavia's Communist dictator Marshal Josip Broz Tito as "one of the world's greatest fighters of freedom," and he had lauded President Hafez Assad of Syria, no one's idea of a pacifist or diplomat, as a great "peacemaker." Both leaders ran tough dictatorial regimes. In his banquet speech in Warsaw, the first stop on his trip, Carter had startled his Communist hosts by telling them that their two countries shared similar values. "I wish you'd quit saying how great a friendship you've struck with some leader after meeting only briefly," grumbled the *Washington Post*'s Haynes Johnson. The press pool cringed when Carter began his remarks describing the Shah's riot-torn visit to Washington the previous month as "delightful." There were more raised eyebrows when he offered that he had traveled to Tehran in deference to his wife's wishes. Carter said he had asked Rosalynn: "'With whom then would you like to spend New Year's Eve?' And she said, 'Above all others, I think, with the Shah and Empress of Iran.' So we arranged the trip accordingly to be with you." Then Carter turned serious. To everyone's surprise, he lauded the great strides made in Iran during the Shah's reign. "Iran, because of the great leadership of the Shah, is an island of stability in one of the more troubled areas of the world," he declared. "This is a great tribute to you, Your Majesty, and to your leadership and to the respect and the admiration and love which your people give to you."

Ambassador Sullivan's staff, seated at the rear of the banquet hall, looked at each other in astonishment. What on earth was the president *doing*? For the past year they had been quietly monitoring the rising level of unrest around the country. Jack Shellenberger, the embassy's head of public affairs, watched the scene unfold, with Carter "throwing away all the material that had been prepared. So like most of these visits by presidents, the mix of words that goes into the final speeches comes from many players," he recalled. "But I think Carter was in such rapture at being in this palace among the friendly family, the Pahlavis, he felt, well, this guy has got it together and he won't fall, he'll survive." White House speechwriter James Fallows, who crafted the final version of the toast on the drive in from the airport, knew nothing about the loaded history of "island of stability." But if his goal was to offer the Shah assurance, his penmanship did the trick.

After dinner the two heads of state retired for a private conference with King Hussein of Jordan, who had flown in to discuss the prospects for a

Middle East peace deal. The Carters originally intended to withdraw to their suite to see in the New Year but changed their minds after the Queen prevailed on them to stay for a celebratory glass of champagne. The party moved into her library. "I have a happy memory of that evening, which was peaceful, friendly, and warm," she recalled. On the library balcony, overlooking the floor where the heads of state and their guests danced and chatted, Crown Prince Reza and Princess Farahnaz played the latest disco hits on a record player and practiced their dance moves to applause from the adults. Their father grimaced at the racket. He waved his hands, trying to signal them to turn down the volume, but eventually gave up and let them have their fun. The New Year was greeted with a round of cheers, hugs, and handshakes.

WHILE JACK SHELLENBERGER sat shaking his head in the Shah's palace, his daughter Katie Shellenberger and her friends were dancing in the Hilton's disco before moving on to other venues around town. The American celebrants didn't notice the stern-faced young man who watched them with disdain from the shadows. "I went to the InterContinental," said the student revolutionary Ali Hossein. "The discotheque. Alcohol was prevalent. They were against the values of the nation. The Pahlavis did not see any limit for them. They felt they were free to do whatever they liked."

THE NEXT MORNING the Pahlavis accompanied the Carters to Mehrebad Airport. As the president climbed the stairs to Air Force One he stopped, turned to the Shah, and dramatically declared, "I wish you were coming with me." The irony of his farewell remarks did not become apparent for quite some time. After Air Force One took off, the Shah did something that for him was quite out of character. Usually reticent before large crowds, he was buoyed by Carter's visit and agreed to Ambassador Sullivan's suggestion that he greet several hundred members of the American community who waited patiently behind a rope line. To the surprise and delight of the crowd, the King and Queen strolled over and began shaking hands. It was a spontaneous gesture and one greatly appreciated by the Americans, who clapped and called out expressions of support. "We admired the Shah for what he was doing for the Iranian people," said Bruce Vernor, an oil company executive who took photographs while his wife, Pat, greeted the royal couple. "And we liked to say that with the Shahbanou we had the most beautiful head of state in the world!" The Pahlavis left to a round of cheers and applause. The Shah was delighted with the reception. "You Americans are really very nice people," he complimented the ambassador, who thought the remark unintentionally revealing.

Sharp-eyed readers who picked up their copy of that morning's *Kayhan* newspaper might have noticed the teasing headline on page nine: "Period of Trepidation Ahead Says Zodiac Calendar." According to the Asian zodiac, 1978 was the Year of the Horse. "It may be an occasion for trepidation," the paper reported. People born in horse years were distinguished by their "energy but are prone to be impatient and emotional, often going too far and creating friction with people around them." In a horse year, people tended to do whatever they wanted "without being nervous over small details." It was a time to let loose and not think of the consequences. It so happened that previous horse years in Iran had coincided with great upheavals. They included 1906, which *Kayhan* omitted to mention was the year of the Constitutional Revolution, when the Qajar Dynasty surrendered to a popular uprising, and also 1930, when "a worldwide economic depression brought widespread bankruptcy in many countries, encouraging the rise of extremist movements." One "startling prediction" even had it that in 1978 the holy book the Quran would become well known in the United States. *Kayhan* advised its readers to hold on—this year might be a wild ride.

Internationally syndicated newspaper columnist Gwynne Dyer indulged in the sort of idle but provocative speculation that often fills newspaper copy over the holiday season. He had history on his mind. Dyer reminded his readers that "the past we are condemned to relive (with only the names changed) is a past that included vast surprises. The Black Death, the French Revolution, the rise of Islam, the creation of the Soviet Union: nobody knew those things were coming, and yet they changed practically everyone's lives." Revolutions and religious unrest were historical "wild cards" that no one could predict with any certainty. As an example, he cited the Shah of Iran.

A modest example of a present-day wild card is the 'one bullet regime' of Iran. The Shah is clever, but he is not bullet-proof. If an assassin should get him (and several have tried) there is no guessing what would happen in Iran. Since the country supplies a large slice of Western Europe's and Japan's oil (and, according to foreign sources, almost all of Israel's oil imports), radical change in Iran would mean crisis not only in the Gulf but much farther afield.

Yet history had a way of pulling surprises. Before she flew out of Iran, celebrity journalist Barbara Walters sat down with the Shah to gauge his views on developments in the Middle East. The previous day, Yasser Arafat had presided over a four-hour military parade in Beirut to mark the Palestine Liberation Organization's thirteenth anniversary. Before a crowd of eight thousand supporters in the war-torn city's municipal sports stadium, Arafat denounced National Security Adviser Zbigniew Brzezinski's recent comment that the Palestine Liberation Organization had "written itself off" for refusing to participate in regional peace talks. "It's not bye-bye PLO, Mr. Brzezinski," thundered Arafat. "It's bye-bye America again and again in the Middle East. Let it sink into Mr Brzezinski's and even Carter's brain that America's entire interests shall be written off rather than the PLO." Arafat was flanked by top Palestinian commanders and faction leaders including George Habash, leader of the more radical left-wing Popular Front for the Liberation of Palestine. "There will never be an alternative except the gun, the gun, the gun!" Arafat told the cheering crowd.

Arafat's threat to attack U.S. interests in the Middle East held special resonance for Washington's chief ally in the region. The Shah was Israel's main oil supplier, President Sadat's friend, and the most vocal regional supporter of the Egypt-Israel peace talks. No other Muslim leader dared express support for a treaty resolving the conflict between the two states. If the Shah was removed from the scene the U.S. strategic position would be severely weakened and Israel left dangerously exposed. The Shah's remarks to Barbara Walters suggested that he understood he had been threatened by Arafat and Habash, who ran the terror camps where young Iranian revolutionaries trained. He made it clear that he expected a rough time of it over the next twelve months. "But the destructive, negative elements everywhere are in turmoil," he told Walters. "Everywhere they are up to some mischief. And somewhere, all the elements of trouble are on the loose and unleashed. So every country should expect those elements to try to foment some trouble." Iran's rain catcher saw storm clouds on the horizon.

Hours later, the great primal, subterranean forces the Shah had dedicated his life, his reign, and billions of dollars trying to contain and suppress came unloosed. The tectonic plates that underpinned a millennium of Iranian history began to strain and buckle. For 35 million Iranians, and for the hundreds of thousands of foreigners who made Iran their home, a way of life and an entire world was about to end. Over the next year the choices they made and the decisions made for them would seal their fate. The cleaners at the Hilton Hotel on Pahlavi Avenue had barely mopped the floors and swept up the streamers when the first stirrings of unrest that led to revolution erupted in Iran.

THE NEXT FEW days were quiet enough.

Across town, the Crown Players' production of *Dick Whittington* opened at the Italian Theater on France Avenue, and an open casting call was held for a production of Eugene O'Neill's *Long Day's Journey into Night*. On the resort island of Kish the House of Christian Dior staged a fashion show featuring the latest swimwear. In local news, the head of Tehran's Criminal Investigation Division, General Farzaneh, reported that the capital remained one of the safest big cities in the world, with crime rates well below those in European and American capitals. But he cautioned that crime was steadily rising in Iran's metropolitan areas: "The new, mechanized way of life, the migration of the population from rural areas to the congested cities, the sudden picture of wealth and affluence which greets the young and often uneducated people who come to Tehran for the first time, all contribute to the increasing number of thefts and murders in the city."

The economy rallied. After months of depressing news, Iran registered its biggest gains in oil production in a year, with daily output back at 6.4 million barrels. Crown Prince Reza arrived in Bangkok on the first leg of his three-nation Asia-Pacific tour. From Niavaran, the Shah spoke out in support of wildlife conservation—he condemned "hunting for pleasure" motived by "bloodlust"—and met with a team of international experts advising the government on a long-term plan to transform Iran into a global hub for science and medical research. Iran had already entered the computer age. There were three hundred computers in service in Iran in 1977, demand was growing by 300 percent a year, and the market for business equipment and systems was projected to hit a record figure of $500 million within the next eighteen months. This at a time when only thirteen countries had more than a hundred computers per million of population.

Iran Air's new computerized ticketing center was scheduled to come online in January 1978, at which time the Concorde would start flying American and European jet-setters to Kish.

The Shah announced plans to fly to Aswan to confer with the leaders of Egypt, Jordan, and Morocco on peace talks with Israel, followed by a stop in Riyadh on the way home to brief King Khalid of Saudi Arabia on their progress. He chose not to attend the Rastakhiz Party's one-day special session held on Wednesday, January 4, at the Aryamehr indoor sports stadium in Tehran. But a statement read out in his behalf called on the ten thousand delegates to combat "subversive intrigues" through "political education" of the masses. Other speakers took up the theme that "red and black reactionaries" were trying to destabilize the country. Prime Minister Amuzegar warned that "a few innocent deceived youths shouting here and there, and breaking windows," had been manipulated by more experienced foreign instigators. His government, he vowed, would "crush any attempt at anarchy, slavery, disorder and colonization ruthlessly."

The prime minister's game of bluff was starting to wear thin. Though in public he liked to talk tough, Amuzegar had already made it clear to Ambassador Sullivan that there would be no crackdown on dissent.

THE ROOMFUL OF women at Damavand College erupted in laughter.

On Saturday, January 7, 1978, Tehran's celebrated liberal arts university for women marked its tenth birthday and the forty-second anniversary of the abolition of the veil by royal decree. Damavand College was named after Iran's highest mountain to symbolize the spirit of endurance and excellence in women's education. Designed by Frank Lloyd Wright Associated Architects in the 1960s, the campus grounds were built on a parcel of land donated by the Shah in the hills above northeastern Tehran. Iranian and foreign-born women studied a mixed curriculum that focused on Persian and Western civilization. This morning students were gathered for a special panel discussion to commemorate Reza Shah's bold decision in 1936 to ban the veil. Mrs. Effat Samiian reminisced about her participation in the first unveiling ceremony. She reminded the audience that American missionaries had done "a great deal to prepare fertile ground for the subsequent emancipation of women." One former missionary, Miss Jane Doolittle, talked about the conditions that prevailed when she arrived in Persia in 1921: "Iranian women were hidden from society, and prevented from an active life." She stood beside a student modeling a chador, pointing at it like a museum exhibit, and eliciting laughter from her audience.

The students of Damavand College believed the future belonged to them. In the 1960s and 1970s the legal and civil protections accorded Iranian women were the most progressive in the Muslim world. The Shah granted women the right to vote, enter politics, and own property. The age of marriage was raised and abortion was legalized. Divorces were now handled by the courts and not decided by husbands and the clergy. Laws were passed guaranteeing equal pay and opportunity in the workforce. The civil service allowed women with children under age three to work half days with full benefits. The Shah's emphasis on promoting higher education paid off: in 1978 women made up a third of all university students and half of all medical school applicants. Women were moving into politics. Mahnaz Afkhami, a thirty-six-year-old graduate of the University of San Francisco, was Iran's first minister of state for women's affairs, and there were twenty female members of parliament and four hundred female city councillors. Women were entering corporate boardrooms and the performing arts. Iran Air appointed Minu Ahmadsartip as its deputy managing director, popular singer Aki Banai returned home in the New Year following a triumphant tour of American cities, and Anahid Moradian opened the country's first hair salon to cater to a male and female clientele. Young women of the middle class dressed in skirts, jeans, and blouses and styled their hair after American celebrities Farrah Fawcett, star of the hit TV show *Charlie's Angels*, and ice skater Dorothy Hamill. They studied abroad, drove around town unaccompanied by male relatives, and dated and danced the night away in discotheques in northern Tehran.

Iran was changing. But even as the students at Damavand College celebrated four decades of progress, across town one hundred women marched for the return of the veil, strict segregation of men and women in public places, and the repeal of the 1963 emancipation proclamation. They protested in Isfahan and also in Mashad, where police moved in to arrest several women blocking traffic on Naderi Avenue. But police stood back in Qom when religious students poured from the seminaries to chant antiregime slogans. The voice of the political establishment, the newspaper *Kayhan*, chastised the protesters as deviants. "Their demonstration was in effect a call to return to the Stone Age, to negate achievements of modern Iranian society, and to deprive half the population of their basic human rights," declared an editorial. "Had they looked around themselves while shouting their reactionary slogans they would have seen scorn and utter disgust in the eyes of the passersby."

The following day, when photographs of the event at Damavand appeared in the press, college administrators began receiving anonymous threatening phone calls. "There is nothing to be afraid of," a school spokesman assured the students. "We cannot turn back to where we were a generation ago."

BY THE TIME the students left for home on that chilly Saturday afternoon the fuse of revolt had been lit. Most Tehranis missed the January 7 evening edition of the newspaper *Ettelaat*, and fewer still bothered to read the mundane headline printed on page seven in small type: "IRAN AND RED-AND-BLACK COLONIALISM." On closer inspection, however, the article, ostensibly a letter to the editor, consisted of a virulent attack against Grand Ayatollah Ruhollah Khomeini. The anonymous author accused the Marja of treachery and fraud. "By his own admission, Ruhollah Khomeini had lived in India and there had relations with the centers of English imperialism. What is clear is that his fame as the chief instigator of the events of 1963 has persisted to this day. Opposed to the [White] Revolution in Iran, he was determined to install a red-and-black imperialism, and unleashed his agents against the land reform, women's rights and nationalization of the forests, shed the blood of innocent people and showed that even today there are people ready loyally to put themselves at the disposal of conspirators and [foreign] national interests. . . . Millions of Iranian Muslims will ponder how Iran's enemies choose their accomplices as need arises, even accomplices dressed in the sacred and honorable cloth of the clergyman."

The article in *Ettelaat*, the official response to Khomeini's fatwa, was the brainchild of the special committee set up a month earlier to devise strategies to discredit the Marja. Asadollah Alam would never have allowed a newspaper to publicly attack a marja, let alone one with Khomeini's track record of extremism. His replacement, Court Minister Hoveyda, however, saw an opportunity to cause trouble for his successor, Jamshid Amuzegar, whom he blamed for usurping the premiership. Amuzegar lacked experience in crisis management and had no background in dealing with the ulama. Hoveyda's decision to hand the article to Savak's General Nasiri with orders to publish was an act of spite more than anything else. "Hoveyda wrote the letter to prove his loyalty and then blamed it on Amuzegar," said Ardeshir Zahedi. Parviz Sabeti felt sure the article would incite disturbances in Qom. "I told Nasiri," he recalled, "do not do this unless we are ready to arrest them."

The two officials were still debating what to do when Minister of Information Dariush Homayoun, in attendance at the Rastakhiz Party's January 4 plenary, handed a copy of the letter to a reporter from the newspaper *Ettelaat*. "Homayoun was leaving the conference hall when he gave our reporter the envelope," said Farhad Massoudi, *Ettelaat*'s young publisher. "When he saw that the flip of the envelope contained the Court's seal he took it back, tore off the seal, then handed it back to the reporter." Massoudi read the letter and decided not to publish. "It was personal and vitriolic, in very poor taste. It accused Khomeini of not being Iranian and implied he was homosexual." Massoudi had a poor relationship with Homayoun, whom he regarded as arrogant and conceited, and asked his senior editor, Ahmad Shahidy, to make the call to the Ministry of Information. Shahidy told Homayoun the letter was ill-advised and put them all at risk: "If we print this letter they might burn us down." "If *Ettelaat* has to burn down, it's better it be so," Homayoun retorted and hung up. Massoudi telephoned the prime minister's office out of desperation. "He was most kind but he knew nothing of the letter. He said: 'Let me look into it. I'll get back to you.'" Homayoun called later in the day to inform Shahidy that "though Mr. Massoudi is concerned, the letter must be published." Fearing trouble from religious fanatics, the staff at *Ettelaat* tried to minimize the impact by printing the letter in small type beside a large advertisement for machinery.

By the dinner hour on January 7, 1978, copies of the newspaper had been rushed to Qom. No one could remember such a slanderous attack against a marja. "Writing such an article about a brave, pious marja was a strategic mistake," said religious revolutionary Ali Hossein, who read the paper in Tehran. "No one can degrade a marja. Even the Shah couldn't do so." Within two hours, Khomeini's agents were on the streets of Qom, setting fire to *Ettelaat*'s newsstands. The next day they marched to the homes of the town's three most prominent grand ayatollahs—the men responsible for Khomeini's elevation fifteen years earlier—to demand that they issue public statements condemning the regime and declaring their support for their fellow marja.

* * *

ON THE AFTERNOON of Monday, January 9, while the Shah was in Aswan for talks with President Sadat of Egypt, Queen Farah was en route to Paris for a two-day trip, and the Crown Prince was in Australia, police officers in Qom were set upon by several thousand rioters. The mob tore through the downtown district and attacked and set alight "banks, government offices, girls' schools, bookshops selling non-religious publications, the homes of officials and the city's only two restaurants where men and women could dine under the same roof." By nightfall a crowd of twenty thousand had taken over the streets and for the first time the cry of "Death to the Shah!" was heard in what was to become a familiar chilling refrain over the next year. Khomeini supporters besieged Police Station Number One, set cars alight, and tried to force their way inside. The officers retreated to the rooftop and opened fire on the crowd, killing six people and wounding a dozen others. A thirteen-year-old boy was crushed underfoot in the stampede to escape the gunfire. Order was restored only with the help of army units rushed to the stricken town. Though none knew it at the time, the first shots of revolution had been fired.

The Shah returned to Tehran on Tuesday, January 10. He betrayed no outward signs of anxiety and appeared relaxed at an evening reception for six visiting American senators. He had spent the morning with President Sadat in Aswan, where the two old friends had driven through the streets in an open car basking in the adoration of cheering crowds. His remarks to his guests focused exclusively on the Egypt-Israel peace negotiations. While the senators circulated, Court Minister Hoveyda took aside U.S. embassy Deputy Chief of Mission Jack Miklos for a private chat. Rumors were circulating in Tehran that the army had massacred seventy religious students and dumped their bodies in a salt lake on the edge of Qom. Hoveyda assured Miklos there were only six confirmed casualties and that they had been rioters armed with "stones, iron bars, and wooden staves" who had rampaged through the streets of Qom "smashing windows of shops and destroying premises of [the] Rastakhiz Party headquarters."

Over the next two weeks scattered outbreaks of violence at universities and strikes in the bazaars were reported in several cities. In Tehran, religious zealots attacked the Arya Cinema on Zahedi Avenue, while further south in Shiraz congregants poured out of a mosque and hurled rocks at police. Undergraduates rioted at Aryamehr University, Aryamehr Technical

College, and Tehran University. At Narmak College, six hundred students overwhelmed security guards, broke into the chancellor's office, and "virtually destroyed the administration building"; over seventy percent of windows on campus were smashed. At Isfahan University, a "volley of rocks broke 60 percent of windows in the faculty of foreign languages. There were no casualties and no class disruption, but university authorities were disconcerted by the level of organization shown and by [the] fact that this is the first time that this faculty has been hit this school year." The cycle of unrest accelerated sharply over the weekend of January 14–15 with protest marches reported in Mashad, Abadan, Ahwaz, Dezful, and Khorramshahr. Prime Minister Amuzegar's clumsy response was to stage a large progovernment demonstration of loyalty to the throne on the outskirts of Qom, a highly provocative gesture at a time when city residents were in deep mourning for those killed earlier in the month.

Princess Ashraf Pahlavi watched events unfold with a gnawing sense of anxiety. On the eve of the pro-government rally in Qom she received a call from Mahnaz Afkhami to say that the Ministry of Women's Affairs was having trouble rounding up volunteers to make the trip—Qom was regarded by liberated Iranian women as a no-go area. The Princess phoned Parviz Sabeti to seek reinforcements. "I can provide more," he assured her. While she was on the phone, Ashraf asked Sabeti his thoughts on the security situation.

"What is going on?" she asked. "[General] Nasiri is stupid. But you are intelligent. What is happening?"

"You had better ask your brother," answered Sabeti. "He was the one who tied the dog to the stone and set it free." Sabeti's point was that the Shah's policy was doomed to fail: he could not on the one hand expect the security forces to maintain order while insisting they avoid violence. "The way His Majesty is going, Fifteen Khordad will be a picnic. We will have to bring machine guns and tanks into the streets."

"You *dare* talk like this!" snapped the Princess, her brother's most fervent defender. "You people only think of force. To you, killing people is as easy as drinking water."

"Who wants to kill people?" replied Sabeti. "I don't want to see us get to a point where we are faced with exactly that situation."

IN THE EMBASSY on Roosevelt Avenue, Ambassador Sullivan and his political advisers huddled. They understood that the events of the past week signaled a major escalation of unrest. "I counted the crisis as starting from January 1978," recalled George Lambrakis. "In the embassy we always counted that as the beginning. We were pretty sure the Shah had ordered the publication of the article in *Ettelaat* attacking Khomeini. Our best guess was that he was preparing to turn over to his son. Then the question was why. He was getting older, his son was growing up, and maybe at that point someone mentioned an illness. We didn't know he had cancer. But the French head of intelligence in *their* embassy believed the Shah was finished." On January 11, Sullivan cabled Washington that "in most serious incident of this sort for years" five demonstrators had been killed and nine wounded when a crowd attempted to storm a police station "in the religious city of Qom." There was still confusion as to which clerical faction had been involved in the protests. According to Sullivan, police sources blamed "conservative religious opposition elements (though not specifically to followers of Khomeini or to Islamic Marxists as such)." Ten days later, Sullivan warned there was a very real danger that the regime would lose control and find itself in a confrontation with "fundamentalist religious leaders," as had happened in 1963.

On February 1, Sullivan sent a follow-up airgram to Washington with the first detailed description of the men orchestrating the unrest. Crucially, he already understood that moderate and extremist groups in Iran were in contact and coordinating a joint strategy. The lull in guerrilla activity over the past year had little to do with Savak's counterinsurgency techniques and everything to do with a secret deal reached between the National Front and Liberation Movement and the Mujahedin and Fedayeen. The moderates had persuaded the men with guns to pause their operations to give the Americans time to pressure the Shah to cede his powers. Attacks would resume if Carter showed that he was either unable or unwilling to force the Shah to make political concessions. Sullivan also explained that senior religious leaders enjoyed separate ties to the Mujahedin terror group. "At the present time, we do not know how these connections take place, but they have been hinted at second and third hand by a number of individuals who have dealt with the oppositionist movement." Religious hard-liners favored launching a frontal assault against the Shah's regime, which they felt sure could be toppled. Their strategy was to provoke a crackdown by the security forces and publicize civilian casualties as a way of stoking public anger. "The loose and fluid religious structure of Iran offers perhaps the only country-wide network for an oppositionist group," Sullivan advised. "Embassy sources suggest religious groups are talking about joining together for certain demonstrations similar to those which eventually led to confrontation in 1963. Circumstances would appear to be important—if additional incidents involving the religious community, such as firing upon marchers, either occurs or can be generated, religious fervor could be activated to provide the mob manpower for demonstrations."

But Sullivan's assessment contained a single devastating flaw when he described Khomeini as "the true leader of the Shia faithful," a statement that was not only factually incorrect but also theologically impossible. Shiism's paramount marja was Grand Ayatollah Khoi, who enjoyed the biggest popular following and who resolutely opposed clerical involvement in politics. Grand Ayatollah Shariatmadari shared Khoi's dim view of Khomeini's activism. American ignorance of Shia Islam and Iran's Shiite hierarchy led Sullivan and his political officers to prematurely confer political legitimacy on the most radical of the marjas and overlook the two men who represented the great moderate center of Shiism.

In Qom, Grand Ayatollah Kazem Shariatmadari faced a dilemma.

The Marja's silence in response to the *Ettelaat* article had provoked charges of cowardice from Khomeini sympathizers who paraded outside his home in drag, waving female undergarments and demanding that he condemn the regime's use of force to put down the riots. Shariatmadari understood that by staying silent he risked creating a leadership vacuum that Khomeini would be all too ready to fill. The Marja also wanted to send the Shah a message. He believed the Shah had not done enough to curb his relatives' financial dealings, clamp down on corruption, and restrict foreign cultural influence. He wanted the Shah to declare that he would abide within the strictures of the 1906 constitutional settlement that guaranteed the ulama a role in approving government laws. Clerical frustration extended to more temporal matters and in particular Amuzegar's austerity budget, which had ended his predecessor Hoveyda's practice of paying "subsidies" to thousands of mullahs around the country. If the money did not ensure their loyalty to the regime it at least kept them off the streets and in the mosques. The amount involved, an estimated $35 million annually, was hardly worth the political price. "Austerity during liberalization was a disaster," said Parviz Sabeti. "Cutting the deficit was a disaster. Amuzegar cut the subsidies but the amount [for each mullah] was never much, around 300 tomens. He also cut credit and loans to the bazaaris." These policies meant that the mullahs and their friends in the bazaars had a shared grievance. "The sudden cut meant that a large number of mullahs no longer had any reason to support the regime," said journalist Amir Taheri.

With these concerns in mind, Shariatmadari issued a rare public letter condemning the bloodshed in Qom as "un-Islamic and inhumane." Though he did not mention the Shah by name—the Marja preferred to spare the monarch embarrassment and cast blame instead on his government— his anger was palpable. He invited three foreign correspondents to his home in Qom and explained his position. "The government says we are reactionaries and backward," he said. "Well, if being backward means we want the constitutional laws to be respected, then we accept that definition." Shariatmadari warned that if he wanted "he could have ordered all the bazaars and mosques in Iran closed, sending thousands of people into the streets, but that this would only risk more shootings." His decision to speak out electrified the ulama and shocked public opinion. Many Iranians who until now had ignored the unrest in Qom were suddenly made aware of a looming confrontation between crown and clergy.

Over the winter Reza Ghotbi, Queen Farah's cousin and the head of Iranian television and radio, drove down to Qom to see Shariatmadari. Ghotbi often fielded complaints from the ayatollahs about television programs such as *The Mary Tyler Moore Show* and *Rhoda*, which depicted women in the workplace and ran story lines on abortion, homosexuality, and premarital sex. But National Iranian Radio and Television devoted far more resources to religious programming, and Ghotbi's staff were always careful to consult with clerical experts while filming special projects such as the annual televised reenactments of Shia passion plays. During his trip to Qom, Ghotbi asked his religious hosts to explain what they thought Grand Ayatollah Khomeini meant with his call for an Islamic government. One ayatollah explained to Ghotbi that it would be like a return to the sixteenth century, when the Safavid Dynasty had shared power with the ulama. "The Shah is the son-in-law of the Ayatollah," he said. "And the Ayatollah is the son-in-law of the Shah." Shariatmadari added that he had talked to Khomeini about that very issue. He wanted to know if Khomeini meant to establish a dictatorship. He said he had asked Khomeini flat out, "Do you mean that you want to run the state?" Khomeini's reply made clear that he saw himself as occupying a far more elevated position, that of "supreme leader" or intermediary between God and government.

Besides, he told Shariatmadari, he already had someone in mind to run a future Islamic government. He was not interested in a political post. "No," he said, he had no such ambition for himself. "I have Musa Sadr in mind as prime minister."

Reza Ghotbi was familiar with Musa Sadr. "I had heard about his work in Lebanon. One of his cousins was a colleague of mine. I was aware that Musa Sadr was in conflict with our ambassador in Beirut and that he had traveled to Cairo to talk about his problem with our ambassador there. He wanted to assure His Majesty that he was not against him."

FIVE YEARS EARLIER, Musa Sadr had enjoyed a warm rapport with the Shah and Court Minister Alam. Since then, however, relations had cooled to the point where the Shah refused to receive the Imam or listen to his requests for financial assistance.

Lebanon's descent into anarchy in the early 1970s had made the country a magnet for extremist groups. The Shah was especially concerned because of the number of Iranian revolutionaries who traveled to the Bekaa Valley to be trained as bomb throwers, while in the capital, Beirut, zealots copied and distributed Khomeini's speeches and propaganda tracts in a safe house. These materials were then smuggled into Iran and stored in a warehouse in the capital's southern suburbs. In the south of Lebanon, as conditions deteriorated, Musa Sadr felt compelled to form a loyalist militia, the Amal, led by Mustafa Chamran, an anti-Shah exile who had trained in electrical engineering at the University of Berkeley California, completed a PhD, and went to work in NASA's Jet Propulsion Laboratory. Chamran built the Amal militia into a formidable fighting force that drew recruits from disaffected Lebanese Shia youth but also from the hundreds of Iranian dissidents who came to Lebanon to learn how to overthrow the Pahlavi monarchy. Outraged by what he perceived to be disloyalty, the Shah ordered that Musa Sadr be stripped of his Iranian passport. As far as the Shah was concerned, the Imam could swim with the sharks. Musa Sadr appealed to the Shah to understand the delicacy of his position and explained to Iranian officials who contacted him that his primary responsibility was to the Shia of Lebanon and not to the Pahlavi state. He bitterly complained that Iran's ambassador to Lebanon, Mansur Qadar, a Savak general and confidant of General Nasiri, was trying to frame him as an anti-Shah revolutionary.

Musa Sadr's estrangement from his patron in Tehran left him dangerously isolated and vulnerable to men such as Abolhassan Banisadr and Ahmad Khomeini, who suspected he did not share their extremist agenda. They were deeply angered when he blamed their ally Yasser Arafat for provoking Israeli military action in and around his stronghold of Tyre. His next heresy was to ally himself with Syria and support President Hafez Assad's decision to send troops into Lebanon to try to dampen the civil war and prevent the Palestinian leader from setting up his own puppet state inside Lebanon. Musa Sadr received death threats and after evacuating his wife and children to Paris spent his days on the run, shuttling between safe houses in the Lebanese capital. Despite Musa Sadr's open breach with Arafat, Khomeini retained a soft spot for him. He entertained the notion of appointing his former pupil to serve as the first prime minister of an Islamic republic. Talk like this disturbed his son Ahmad, a fanatic who nurtured his own political ambitions. "Ahmad was someone thinking in terms of power," recalled Abolhassan Banisadr. "He had no scruples in terms of religion, clerics or whatever. His wife was Musa Sadr's niece but he was not someone who necessarily liked Musa Sadr."

OUTWARDLY AT LEAST, the streets of Tehran appeared calm in late January, though the mood of complacency tended to rise with the elevation. "Many Iranians appear to have ceased to believe newspaper reports of religious incidents and regard counter-demonstrations as government inspired," observed the U.S. embassy. But others, acting on tip-offs from friends and family members in high places, suspected there was something wrong in the palace. Since the summer they had purchased residences in Europe and North America. Now they began quietly moving family members out of the country to safety.

Then, at six thirty on the morning of Thursday, January 19, an explosion tore through Tehran's Bowling Recreation Club, a popular hangout spot for American teenagers that housed a cinema, indoor pool, skating rink, and bowling alley. The fire on Old Shemiran Road "raged for hours," reported *Kayhan*, "and brought frightened householders in the neighborhood to the scene." Eight days later a second explosion and fire tore through the three-story Sabouri furniture store on Pahlavi Avenue. The inferno on Friday, January 27, broke out at six forty-one in the morning, raged for four hours, and almost detonated a nearby gasoline station. Both fires were reported in the local press without comment. The authorities worried that if the public learned the truth—Islamic sabotage squads were at work targeting businesses owned by Jews and members of the Baha'i faith, regarded by the Shia as apostates—there would be panic. Knowledgeable Tehranis read between the lines anyway. There had already been a run on Iran's largest private commercial bank, Bank Saderat, whose three thousand branches also made it the most accessible for depositors. They didn't need the government to tell them that Bank Saderat was owned by a Baha'i, or that Khomeini had ordered his followers to suddenly withdraw their savings in an attempt to collapse the banking system.

On that same Friday evening, at the end of another long week of suspicion and rumor, strollers leaving Tehran mosques after evening prayers claimed they saw an unidentified flying object approach northeast Tehran and the hills around Niavaran from the direction of "the southern end of the city." In the words of one eyewitness, the object was "shining brightly, regularly changed its colors and flew for about fifteen minutes over the area in a revolving manner before it suddenly gained speed and disappeared."

For the past two years, UFO sightings and paranormal disturbances had escalated in direct proportion to the intensity of Iran's Islamic revival. Two weeks earlier, on the same day that *Ettelaat* published the article attacking Khomeini, police officers were called to a house on Vanak Square in Tehran to investigate alarming reports of a mysterious intruder. Twelve-year-old housemaid Zari, who spoke as if in a trance, described her friendship with an "extraterrestrial being" named "Honar" who stood over two meters tall and whose arms and legs were "longer than an ordinary human being [with a] body [that] was covered with something like a black fur coat. . . . Some strange light reflects off the eyes of this creature and this light causes the attention of the onlooker to be drawn on it rather than to any other part of its body." Her employers said they too had experienced "strange and unexpected things connected to an 'outer space creature'" and felt the intruder's presence. Furniture was moved around rooms, the radio turned itself on and off, the refrigerator was unplugged, and trays of food were missing. Police officers confirmed that fingerprints found in the house were "not those of any human being."

The most notorious incident involving UFOs had occurred fifteen months earlier, and had drawn the Shah's close attention. At 11 o'clock on the evening of September 18, 1976, the control tower at Mehrebad Airport received four telephone calls from residents of Tehran's Shemiran district who reported seeing bright lights and a fast moving object in the sky overhead. The unidentified aircraft was picked up on radar and two F-4 fighter jets were scrambled from Hamadan air base to investigate. Air force generals suspected a Russian intruder, possibly to test the readiness of Iran's aerial defenses. The pilots radioed ground control with detailed descriptions of a large cylindrical object with flashing lights that released a smaller orb, which flew toward and around them—no mean feat considering the pilots were flying at almost the speed of sound—and started circling them. One of the pilots turned back to base. Fearing an attack, his colleague, Lieutenant Parviz Jafari, made an attempt to fire a sidewinder missile at the intruder when he reported the electronics in his cockpit suddenly failed, shutting down all radar and navigation equipment. After regaining power he returned to Hamadan for a debriefing that drew the attention of CIA investigators. He told them he had seen a second small orbit plummet into the earth north of Shemiran. The American briefing on the incident was sent to President Gerald Ford, Secretary of Defense Donald Rumsfeld, and Secretary of State Henry Kissinger.

The Shah's reaction to the mystery intruder in the night sky over Tehran was telling. He knew the intruder hadn't been a Russian aircraft testing Iran's aerial defenses. "The Russians weren't coming over Iran anymore," said Lieutenant General Mohammad Hossein Mehrmand, the Hamadan base commander. "Our new F-14 jets flew with Phoenix missiles that could reach Russian aircraft even if they were flying at a higher altitude. The Shah knew this. And Jafari was a good pilot." Five days later, the Shah flew down to Hamadan to learn more. "He listened carefully to the pilots for thirty to thirty-five minutes," said General Mehrmand. "He didn't ask any questions." At the end of the presentation the Shah made one of his typically oblique observations. "Yes," he said, "for sure there was something out there. But it did not come from the human hand." He paused before adding, "Maybe it came from the other side." Though the events of September 18, 1976, were never fully explained, astronomers did observe that on the same evening a meteor shower rained debris over a broad arc of territory that stretched from Iran as far west as Morocco.

There was no easy explanation for the monster of Vanak Square and the sightings of bright lights circling over Tehran. Throughout human history, however, such events have often been interpreted as precursors to the fall of kings and the collapse of empires. The faithful saw the flying lights over Niavaran as an omen that Allah was on their side and that Islam would triumph.

15

THE CARAVAN PASSES

Death to the Shah!

—GRAND AYATOLLAH KHOMEINI

Khomeini has to be assassinated.

—GRAND AYATOLLAH SHARIATMADARI

On February 1, 1978, the Shah took part in the first "satellite summit" or televised video conference between heads of state from different countries. He joined France's president Giscard d'Estaing and West Germany's president Walter Scheel on the three-way call to inaugurate two satellite relay stations built in Tehran and Shiraz by the Franco-German telecommunications company Symphonie. Nineteen seventy-eight was the "Year of the Microchip," which ushered in the era of personal computing, and the Shah was eager for Iranians to be seen as at the forefront of technological innovation. In his remarks to d'Estaing and Scheel, the King quoted Hugo and Goethe on the importance of brotherhood and expressed his hope that their satellite linkup "was solid proof of the fact that geographical distance had lost its meaning. The time was now ripe for technology to be used to remove non-geographical gaps—remnants of the past—and replace them with understanding and cooperation."

Here was proof, if proof was still needed, that a modern, secular Iran was within reach. New satellite and computer technology proved that the Persian fable "about a prince who had a glass ball in which he could see all he wanted" would come to pass. The next day, the Shah and Queen Farah flew to India to begin a four-day state visit. On arrival in New

Delhi, he again spoke out forcefully in support of his friend Anwar Sadat's peace plan with Israel and lobbied for two of his most visionary foreign policy initiatives: a "common market" binding Asian economies and a "zone of peace" in the Indian Ocean. As usual, the Imperial couple were dogged by boisterous protests organized by Iranian student groups. Responding to Western criticism of Iran's record on human rights, the Shah told reporters that the first world leader to address the issue had been Cyrus the Great, more than six hundred years before the birth of Christ. At that time, he tartly reminded his audience, "we [Iranians] were civilized . . . and those people [Westerners] were climbing trees. I don't think that we can really take lessons from anybody. They should first put their own house in order."

Ten days later, the Pahlavis opened Tehran's new Museum of Persian Carpets on Aryamehr Avenue. They were joined for the gala celebrations by Prince Gholam Reza, Princess Pari Sima, Prime Minister Amuzegar, Court Minister Hoveyda, and a phalanx of high-ranking court and government dignitaries. The carpet museum and its neighbor the Museum of Contemporary Art firmly anchored the Farah Park fine arts district in the downtown commercial district. Built to resemble "a giant-size nomadic tent, stretched and pinned to the ground at all sides," the new museum's inaugural exhibit boasted two hundred of the finest Persian rugs in the world. The facility's upper story was painted turquoise blue, a color "used a great deal in mosques, from which many of the carpet designs . . . are copied." Inside, the dignitaries strolled through a large, well-lit hall with "a pond and bubbling fountain in the center and singing canaries all around." The outside garden included an Islamic prayer room.

In his opening remarks, the Shah said he hoped this latest dazzling addition to the capital's skyline would "turn Tehran into an international cultural center within a few years." He noted the importance of carpet weaving to Iranian society and reminded the guests that he had outlawed child labor in the carpet-weaving industry and introduced salaries to end exploitation of young and poor workers. He pledged state aid to support local weavers in the face of "tough foreign competition." But there could be no doubt in anyone's mind as to whose day it really was. In the late sixties the Queen had envisioned a network of museums that would revive and preserve art but also make the country's cultural treasures more accessible to the people. By the spring of 1978 the fruits of her years of labor could finally be seen not only around Farah Park but also in northern

Tehran, where the Negarastan and Reza Abbasi museums were located, and out in the provinces—in Lorestan, which boasted a new museum to house bronze, and in Kerman, where there was now a modern art museum.

The Queen's pride was tempered by the private agony of her husband's cancer diagnosis. Six months earlier, the Shah's doctors had staged their dramatic intervention in Paris and informed his wife that he was stricken with terminal lymphoma. She felt constrained from raising the subject with him because he had not been informed that she knew. To further complicate matters, his shyness prevented him from sharing personal matters. She tried to draw him out, but to no avail. Farah and the medical team were also still unaware of the Shah's initial diagnosis at the hands of Dr. Fellinger in Vienna four years earlier. All she could do was monitor his weight and make sure he took his medicine. The Shah hinted that he was aware that she knew the extent of his illness, though the word "cancer" never passed his lips. If he felt discomfort he would lift up his shirt and ask Farah to touch his abdomen and check his spleen. "What do you think?" he would plaintively ask. "Does it look swollen to you?" "We talked a great deal about His Majesty's illness," she recalled. "I was sure that he knew that I knew the truth. He might have even known that I knew that he knew. But he played the game as if I didn't know while I pretended not to know what was wrong. It was a strange game: sweet and sour, tender and painful at the same time. I loved him desperately. I wanted to rush into his arms, put my head on his chest and cry. But I kept my cool: *raison d'état oblige*." The knowledge that they shared the secret "brought me closer to His Majesty than ever before."

Finally, Farah summoned the French doctors and told them that enough was enough. It was no longer tolerable for them to simply refer to her husband's lymphoma as "Waldenstrom's disease." She asked them to be straight—it was time for the word games to end. The doctors met with the Shah in the first few weeks of 1978, intending to break the news. To their great surprise, he preempted them and made a poignant request that left no doubt in their minds that he already knew he was marking time. "I am only asking you to help me maintain my health for two years," he said, "enough time for the Crown Prince to finish the year in the US [where he planned to train as an air force pilot] and spend another in Tehran."

* * *

IN FEBRUARY 1978 Tabriz was a "somewhat dingy" city of eight hundred thousand, located in Iran's northwestern frontier near the Turkish and Russian borders. Tabriz occupied a special place in Iranian history, having served several stints as the national capital, most recently in the 1500s, when the Safavid dynasty established Shiism as the state religion, and locals enjoyed a reputation as observant and proud defenders of the 1906 Constitution. The Islamic revival sweeping the region was evident in the market, where butchers had recently announced they would refuse to sell imported meat because the animals had not been slaughtered the halal way, according to Muslim tradition. The American consulate's new visitors' guide warned that "it is not comfortable for women to shop in the bazaar during certain seasons of religious activity. At all times they must expect and be prepared to deal with a certain amount of molestation. Conservative clothing should be worn at all times." The economy was also behind the recent sharp rise in popular discontent. Shortages, inflation, corruption, red tape, and harsh government austerity measures hurt credit and consumer spending, which in turn angered the bazaaris.

Tabrizis enjoyed close ties to Qom, where their favorite son, Grand Ayatollah Kazem Shariatmadari, reigned over the Shia hierarchy. His public criticism of the Shah's handling of recent unrest had made an impact; for weeks the Tabriz bazaar had been "plastered with signs" announcing a citywide strike set for February 18. The security forces were already expecting trouble in the third week of February because it marked the end of the forty-day mourning period for those killed in the assault on the police station in Qom. Parviz Sabeti's Third Directorate learned that Khomeini's agents planned to exploit the funeral ceremonies to provoke further unrest. "People in charge of the movement made the decision to make use of [the mourning period] to try to request the marjas to issue announcements about it and try to request the people to demonstrate in different cities," said Ali Hossein, the young revolutionary who had also grown up in Tabriz. The country had to be brought to a boil, which meant producing a fresh batch of martyrs every forty days. This remarkably cynical but effective strategy became known as "doing the forty-forty."

On the morning of February 18, extra police were stationed outside the university and around police stations, and officers with walkie-talkies were placed at most traffic intersections. The day began quietly enough with government offices, schools, stores, and banks open for business.

Trouble broke out when enraged mourners discovered that the gates of the Masjed-e-Jomeh Mosque had been locked as a precautionary measure. Large crowds formed and started chanting anti-Shah slogans. They attacked stores that sold liquor and television sets and then set off for the center of town, setting fire to a traffic kiosk and police motorcycles. The windows of the Tabriz Justice Department were smashed. The crowd surged into Kourosh Square, chanting "Death to the Shah!" They attacked branches of the Saderat, Melli, Irano-British, and Shahyar Banks with crowbars, clubs, axes, and stones, and tossed Molotov cocktails into four other bank branches as well as cinemas, hotels, and electronic appliance stores. With the central city in the hands of rioters, police regrouped and mounted a charge, pushing the swelling crowds back to Shahrdari Square, where they splintered into four smaller groups and then rampaged along Pahlavi Avenue, the main shopping district, collecting support as they went and overwhelming the security forces. Tabrizis were stunned when local police abandoned their posts and fled the scene rather than obey orders to open fire.

At midday the Tabriz fire department battled as many as 134 blazes in different parts of the city. Supermarkets, child-care and welfare centers, and even hospitals were attacked and set ablaze. A truck carrying Coca-Cola bottles was lit up. The local Youth Palace, the Rastakhiz Party headquarters, and commemorative panels celebrating the White Revolution were wrecked. The Iran-America Society building was put to the torch, and billboards advertising movies were pulled down. Women seen wearing jeans and skirts, or whose heads were uncovered, were chased down and assaulted. Outside the Aria Hotel, a woman "was dragged from her car and has disappeared, rumored to have been burned." "Women in Western clothes were dragged out of taxies and beaten up," confirmed an American eyewitness. Another witness to the mayhem, Henry Marchal, director of the French Cultural Center, stated that "more than twenty girls at the Parvin School, a somewhat progressive girls' school, were severely beaten when they attempted to leave the school and that authorities called parents to come with automobiles and chadors to pick up the remainder." Order was briefly restored in the early afternoon, when the police opened fire with live rounds. But at four o'clock, while police helicopters clattered overhead, mobs tried to force their way into the Shah-Ismail Guesthouse, where foreign workers lived, and set the twelve-floor structure on fire. Eyewitnesses reported seeing "people in the mob throw 'ball-like things' into places they intended to set on fire. Upon contact with the target, the device would explode into huge flames." The long and bloody day ended only when army tanks rolled into the center of town to enforce martial law.

The government made no effort to cover up the extent of the disaster, with the official death toll standing at 12 dead and 125 seriously injured. A total of 73 bank branches had been gutted in addition to 22 shops; 4 hotels; the Institute of Technology; all major government buildings; 9 cinemas; and countless telephone booths, parking meters, and liquor stores. Tabriz's banking system was devastated. The Central Bank of Iran evacuated all deposits from local banks as a safety precaution, and many branches reported the destruction of files and account books. "Banks and trading companies now face irreparable damage to their books," a Tabrizi businessman told *Kayhan*. "This means the city's economy is going to suffer, even though shops have reopened." The extent of the unrest pointed to a social explosion fed by genuine social and political grievances. But the events of February 18 also suggested an unusual degree of planning and preparation. The crowds had been well armed and carefully selective in which businesses they attacked and which they spared. Government officials gathered evidence that proved the rioters had been equipped with "imported incendiary bombs." Police also reported the arrests of several Lebanese and Libyans "who had passed through Palestinian training camps." Even the dispersal of the main crowd into smaller groups suggested a degree of tactical coordination by men trained in the basics of crowd control. "The attacks seemed extraordinarily well planned," recalled a foreigner in Tabriz at the time. "At one time a huge mob controlled all 7.5 miles from the university to the railroad station."

The Islamic underground had thrown down the gauntlet to the Shah. An attempt had been made to challenge political authority and collapse the economy of one of Iran's most important municipalities, purge the city of Western influence, and intimidate secular Tabrizis into accepting Khomeini's new religious order. They succeeded with stunning swiftness. "It is rare now to see a woman in Western dress," reported a *New York Times* reporter who ventured into the city in the aftermath of the riots.

Grand Ayatollah Khomeini issued a public statement applauding the "courageous and God-fearing" people of Tabriz "who with their great uprising have given a painful punch in the mouth to those babblers!" Referring to the Shah as "this wretch," Khomeini pledged to "expunge every trace of this anti-Islamic regime that wishes to revive Zoroastrianism. . . ."

The slogan heard in every street and alley of every city and village is: 'Death to the Shah!'"

NINE DAYS LATER, on Monday, February 27, the Shah addressed thousands of women gathered to attend the Grand Congress of Iranian Women at the giant Aryamehr indoor stadium. Flanked on either side by Queen Farah and Princess Ashraf, both passionate advocates for women's rights, the Shah reassured the cheering delegates that he would not bow to pressure from religious extremists. The savagery of the attacks on young girls and women in Tabriz had caused widespread shock and alarm. "We shall continue with our liberalization policy because the fundamentals of the state rest on it," he declared. "But the unholy alliance of red and black forces continues to work toward dividing our population once again."

The Shah reminded his audience that until the advent of the Pahlavi Dynasty "little remained of Iran except in name; there was no one to stand up to foreign tyranny. In such an environment women were considered insane by the society." He made specific reference to the assault four months earlier on the student cafeteria at the University of Tehran. "Does freedom mean that some people in the universities should say women are not allowed to use the self-service facilities?" he asked. "Apartheid is against Iranian policy, especially this apartheid, which is directed against a person of one's own race." He insisted that the recent wave of unrest, far from exposing weaknesses in the regime, represented "the death pangs" of fanatics on the left and right who acted out of a sense of frustration born of failure. The Shah wrapped up his remarks with an old Persian saying that brought the crowd to its feet. "The caravan passes and the dog barks!" he cried. He wanted there to be no doubt in anyone's mind that he intended to move forward with his reforms and pay no heed to his critics.

The Shah's confidence was informed by decades of past experience. Fifteen years earlier his most trusted advisers had urged him not to proceed with the White Revolution, arguing that Iranian society was not ready for land reform and women's emancipation. He had overruled them anyway and in so doing built the foundations for middle-class prosperity and created the moderate center in Iranian politics. He was not about to start listening to the naysayers now. He believed that the unrest in Qom and Tabriz served at least two useful purposes. First, the riots were a classic case of "letting off steam." Social unrest was to be expected as restrictions were loosened after so many years of rule from the top down. Second, the carnage showed Iranians the choice they faced between chaos and order. Eight weeks earlier, the Shah had explained to Amir Taheri, the editor of *Kayhan*, that the Iranian people would soon have to choose between two competing visions of the future, between their King with his jet-age vision and a bearded fanatic with a seventh-century mind-set. He never doubted their final decision. He, not Khomeini, held the farr. He, not Khomeini, had dedicated his life to modernizing the country and restoring it to the level of an international power. No sane person would ever choose *that* to *this*. As if to show his people that he would not be provoked into a crackdown, the day after his speech at the Aryamehr stadium the Shah recalled the governor of Eastern Azerbaijan Province and appointed the most moderate of three candidates. He sacked senior police commanders in Tabriz and ordered an inquiry into the origins of the unrest. Newspapers and members of parliament were encouraged to criticize the decision to close the doors of the Masjed-e-Jomeh Mosque and to use live rounds against demonstrators. Several hundred rioters were tried in civilian courts, charged with minor offenses, and then released back onto the streets.

The Shah's handling of dissent was applauded in foreign capitals as convincing proof that the maestro of Persian politics knew exactly which corrective measures were required to defuse tensions. "I am not going to change my policy of liberalizing to the maximum," the Shah told the *Washington Post* in early March. "Yes, you can say that this [violence] is related completely to this liberalization program, but this is the price we have got to pay." At the same time, he described opposition groups as "obviously illegal" and warned, "obviously, we will not let [violence] get out of hand." But he downplayed the possibility of more serious unrest. "If I have to defend my country, I could be the toughest guy, but when it is not necessary why should I be? I think we are strong enough, the basis of our society and state are strong enough to allow at least this limit and even more." He expressed disappointment that Savak had failed "to uncover plans for the demonstrations which degenerated into a violent rampage in Tabriz." But he was confident that he knew what his opponents were up to. "We are not babies, we know what contacts they have with all the foreign correspondents here. We know when they go to Qom. We know they try to excite the clergy." The *Post*'s conclusions reflected the assessment of most foreign observers that the Shah had matters firmly in hand.

The autocratic 58-year-old Shah's new tactics not only have reduced tensions caused by the Tabriz events but also are thought by analysts to stand a good chance of limiting damage to the government's prestige, which he has worked so tirelessly to promote. . . . The Shah is credited with understanding the traditional Muslim leadership's latest disruptive power in this fundamentally religious country and its potential ability to channel discontent arising from an exodus from rural areas, scarce and expensive urban housing, inflation and other ills.

The Shah was satisfied that liberalization and the open space met middle-class demands for reform. But he underestimated the extent to which televised images of burned-out cars, smashed windows, and torched banks shook public confidence in his ability to protect their interests. They questioned his belief that the violence signaled the "death pangs" of extremism. What if liberalization actually *fed* the unrest? Tabriz had also shown that the security forces were capable of losing control of a major urban center. For the past six months middle-class Iranians had comforted themselves with tall tales and conspiracy theories that the Shah was orchestrating unrest as part of a diabolical plan to justify an army crackdown; Tabriz raised the even more chilling prospect that power was slipping from his hands. Now the same liberals who only a few weeks earlier had complained about the lack of democracy clamored for law and order.

The unsettled mood on the streets of Tehran was heightened by the kidnapping and murder of a young boy, Mehdi Pournik, the nine-year-old son of a wealthy Tehran businessman, snatched on his way home from school. Violent crimes involving children were a rarity in Iran and the brutality of this one struck terror in the hearts of parents, who began walking their children to and from school each day. "Those with younger children are especially worried," reported *Kayhan*. "Almost every child in Tehran has by now heard the warning: do not talk to strangers and do not under any circumstances accept offers of rides from anyone." The crime, motivated by greed and avarice, was seen as yet another curse of modernization and a sign of innocence lost. The sour public mood was aptly summed up by Googoosh, the country's most celebrated female singer, actress, and femme fatale, whose rags-to-riches success story made her a middle-class heroine. In March 1978 Googoosh's new movie *During the Night* opened to packed houses and told the story of "a young couple who fall in love but are finally forced to succumb to the conventions of traditional society." The film suggested that the personal freedoms of the Pahlavi era were illusions and that no one, not even the most beautiful star-crossed lovers, could outrun their fate and that in the end, rather than struggle and make their own way in the world, young Iranians would submit to tradition, history, and religion. In her promotional appearances Googoosh sounded exhausted, brittle, and disillusioned with the phenomenal success that had brought her fame and fortune. "If only I could have a simple, normal life," she said with a sigh. "I'd be quite happy to do without a big house, travel and the money. But somehow, the 'devil you know' keeps its grip on my life and I stay." She freely admitted singing commercial songs that meant nothing to her but everything to the "leeches" who surrounded her.

The malaise did not stop middle-class Tehranis from planning their annual spring vacations in Europe and North America. London had recently fallen out of favor with northern Tehran's bright young things. "But I am pretty certain I shall not be visiting London this year, but seek new places in Europe," remarked a young government employee on a quest to find the perfect pair of panties. "At any rate, I only buy most of my underwear from London since the city lacks highly fashionable clothing and shoes. Most of the underwear I usually buy in London is now sold at various stores in Iran and at prices pretty much the same as those sold in London." Another young Iranian, an engineer, complained how terribly difficult it was to obtain decent theater tickets in London "since foreign tourists, particularly from the oil producing countries, crowded the theaters and lengthy queues formed." He said he visited the West End now only "on condition that my friends can reserve seats in cinemas and theaters well in advance." He added that he felt sorry for "the ordinary Britons who had to suffer and compromise for the sake of more income for the government."

The young Iranian's striking lack of self-awareness—he seemed not to realize that he *was* a foreign tourist from an oil-producing country— would have been laughable but for the fact that the Shah expected the new middle class to defend the gains of the White Revolution from the likes of religious extremists trying to overthrow the state.

AROUND THE COUNTRY, hundreds of thousands of cars, buses, and trucks set out on the eve of the Nowruz spring holidays with traffic jams starting at four in the afternoon in southern Tehran and lasting well into the evening. In the back streets of the southern suburbs, soothsayers pulled out their astrological almanacs. For Iranians, too, the Year of the Snake had changed to the Year of the Horse. "Hang in there," advised one astrologer, "it will not all be smooth sailing. It will be a year of variable weather and sometimes cloudy skies. All the people who bought studded snow tires and chains for the slopes of upper Tehran and the mountain passes, and had no opportunity to use them last year, will have their full share of hazards and landslides."

Merchants relied on the Nowruz holiday to boost their retail earnings for the year. But March 1978 was one of the worst seasons on record with the popular shopping districts of Kouche Berlin, Valihad Circle, Lalezar, and Naderi Avenue reporting "no increase in sales." The Tehran bazaar was full of new products but few shoppers. Travel, however, was a different story, with the national passport office reporting "its busiest period so far, dealing with a greater number of requests for exit every day." An estimated twenty thousand Iranians planned to travel abroad. At home, families appeared to be making an extra effort to get together. The authorities in Shiraz reported that all two hundred thousand hotel rooms were booked up, while Isfahan expected a full holiday season and warned visitors they risked fines if they pitched tents in public spaces. Otherwise, life in the capital continued as normal. Audiences at the Rudaki Hall thrilled to performances by the Tehran Symphony Orchestra, the Leningrad Ballet, and Swedish opera diva Birgit Nilsson. The trial was under way of Maryam, a love-struck fan who threw acid in the face of pop singer Darioush in the middle of a concert. Broadway star Pearl Bailey arrived to perform two concerts in aid of Queen Farah's National Leprosy Fund. Now on her third visit to Iran, Bailey was warmly received at Niavaran by the Queen and Crown Prince Reza. "I am always moved by the warm response and hospitality of Iranians," the singer and actress told reporters. Downtown, Sullivan's embassy announced plans to build a large new facility to handle the escalating volume of visa applications to enter the United States.

On Tuesday, March 21, the first day of the New Year, clocks moved forward an hour and the Shah and Queen Farah hosted their traditional salaam reception for political, military, and religious figures. In his remarks to the assembly, the Shah made no reference to domestic problems but instead called for a "new international economic order" to correct imbalances between rich and poor nations. If the gap in wealth was allowed to grow "it will lead to an international conflagration." In his traditional Nowruz address to the nation, however, he referred to the challenges of the past year. "But we all know that in rapid growth such difficulties are predictable," he explained, and added that "the possibility that such freedom might be misused by elements whose identity is known to us was predictable." Farah held her own reception for the wives of the ministers and ambassadors. Usually, the wife of the prime minister would respond on behalf of the group. But Mrs. Amuzegar was German-born and the Queen's Special Bureau quietly let it be known that this year she would prefer the respondent to be of Iranian origin. Maryam Ansary stepped in at the last minute to deliver the annual felicitations.

Their final engagements of the year complete, the Imperial couple and their children, friends, and courtiers boarded a plane at Mehrebad Airport and set out for the Persian Gulf island of Kish. The children were in high spirits with Princess Farahnaz, who had just turned sweet sixteen, set on learning to play the guitar, though against the wishes of her father, who thought the piano a more suitable instrument for his beloved daughter. But the adults in the party reported a more subdued atmosphere than usual. Everyone was braced for the end of the Tabriz mourning period and the likelihood of another round of unrest. Reza Ghotbi used his audience with the Shah to warn that his network of journalists around the country had received information that violent protests and acts of sabotage were being planned. "In Kish I presented an assessment of what had happened in Qom and Tabriz," he said. "Our reporters and analysts thought these incidents would start happening every forty days. They predicted Yazd would be next—Yazd was preparing. Apparently my presentation was too gloomy and pessimistic. When His Majesty was not satisfied or unhappy with me, our meetings would be spaced longer and longer until the next time." The Shah was so displeased with Ghotbi that he refused to receive him in private for several weeks. Though he personally liked his wife's cousin, he considered National Iranian Radio and Television a bastion of liberal and leftist views.

Minister for Women's Affairs Mahnaz Afkhami tried to pass on her own warning. Five months earlier, she had suspected the secret police had staged the raid on the University of Tehran canteen. Now she realized the hidden hand was coming from another, more sinister direction. Around the country, her network of women's rights activists reported they were coming under attack and that religious zealots were trying to force women to cover themselves. In several shocking cases, young toughs roaming the streets of Tehran threw vials of acid in the faces of young girls and women wearing Western dress. "Several foreign companies told employees to stay home," reported Britain's *Guardian* newspaper, "and there were at least four reports of girls being attacked with acid." Fearing for their safety, more women—even those who did not consider themselves religious—began wearing chadors when they ventured outside. But the sight of even more black crows on city streets served only to strengthen the perception that the women of Iran were electing to submit to Islamic law.

Defenders of women's rights, stunned at what was happening, had almost no time to react. "People around us were shocked that things were moving so fast," said Mahnaz Afkhami. "The government didn't take it seriously. I remember talking to [Prime Minister] Amuzegar. I said we should set up a committee to do something, and he said, 'I don't know why you are so worried.'" She called Princess Ashraf and begged her to intervene with her brother. "We are hearing it is getting serious," she said. "He needs to do something dramatic like the White Revolution and appoint a new prime minister like Amini. Someone from the outside." But the Princess had elected to spend her Nowruz vacation on pilgrimage to Mecca and Medina and wasn't there to pass on the message. "I spoke to His Majesty," Ashraf told Mahnaz Afkhami after she returned from Saudi Arabia. "And he said, 'Afkhami is a good minister but she seems hysterical. Ask her why she is so worked up.'"

ISRAELI DIPLOMATS CLOSELY monitored events in Iran, a country whose Jewish population of sixty thousand to seventy thousand dated back to the time of Esther. Jews were sensitive to the Islamic revival sweeping their homeland and anti-Semitic incidents had become more noticeable in the past several years. "Anti-Jewish books can be bought in Tehran and anti-Jewish slogans sometimes appear on the walls of buildings," the *Jerusalem Post* reported in March 1978. "Anti-Semitism in Iranian Kurdistan has spurred many of the Jews in that area to move to Tehran." Though Muslims assumed Iran's Jews had prospered from the Shah's reforms, half of the fifty thousand Jews living in Tehran were described as poor by Jewish relief organizations, and four thousand of those were indigent. About 20 percent of Iranian Jews were affluent, while the remaining 30 percent enjoyed middle-class status. Jewish resettlement organizations encouraged families to move to Israel to better their lives and end their isolation.

Under the Shah, Iran and Israel enjoyed unusually close ties. The Shah saw Iranians and Jews as natural allies and strategic partners as the only two non-Arab peoples in the region. He admired Israel's stubborn resilience, its remarkable string of military victories over the more populous Arab states, and the young country's impressive record of economic and social development. Fifteen hundred Israeli citizens worked in Iran under the terms of a bilateral trade relationship worth $210 million, training the military; helping the security forces; and running horticulture, electronics, and construction companies. They shuttled back and forth on six weekly flights operated by Israel's national airline, El Al. Bilateral ties provided Iranian Jews with an insurance policy of sorts. "The Jews have every confidence in the Shah," reported the *Jerusalem Post*, "though there is always the lurking fear of a change in regime."

Israel's unofficial ambassador Uri Lubrani enjoyed a close working relationship with the Shah and top government officials. Unlike his American counterpart, Lubrani was trusted in the palace, and the ambassador's staff spoke Persian and were well acquainted with Iranian history, culture, and religious traditions. The Israelis had closely followed the outbreak of unrest in the autumn of 1977 and been shocked at the speed with which the security forces in Tabriz surrendered to the mob. Days after the riots, Brigadier General Yitzhak Segev, Lubrani's military attaché, confided to an Israeli journalist that "the Shah was finished and his days were numbered."

Three weeks later, on March 13, Lubrani and Reuven Merhav, the Mossad station chief, secretly visited the Shah on Kish Island armed with a proposal that Iran strengthen Musa Sadr in southern Lebanon as a counterweight to Iranian opposition groups. The Israelis were curious to see Kish, which "is rapidly taking on the symbolism of Sodom and Gomorrah to the Muslim faithful." Far from being impressed with the louche ambience, the visitors decided conditions in Iran were comparable to Ethiopia just before the fall of Haile Selassie. On the flight back to Tehran the Israelis "concluded that the combination of a disconnected leadership that enjoyed an extremely lavish life and a growing popular frustration and civil unrest made a radical regime change highly likely." Lubrani sent a secret communication to Foreign Minister Moshe Dayan to alert him that "the main challenge to the [Pahlavi] regime came now not from the liberal and communist opposition, but from the Islamists who had gathered strength and were expressing a strong anti-Israeli sentiment."

On his own initiative, the ambassador quietly stepped up purchases of Iranian crude oil to ensure that Israel would be protected if the oil supply was suddenly cut off. He also placed phone calls to Israeli businessmen living in Iran and advised them to start putting in place emergency contingency plans.

AS PREDICTED, THE tempo of unrest flared again in late March. Groups of men set fire to banks and smashed windows in Tehran, Qazvin, Babol, and Kashan. Ambassador Sullivan reported that a bomb threat had been called in to Tehran's Community Church, where many Americans worshipped. Elsewhere, flames destroyed thirty-five shops along Shohoda Street in Babol, and disturbances were reported in the towns of Abadan and Abadeh. Police in Qazvin were involved in a shoot-out that left one gunman dead and his accomplice fleeing on foot: inside the getaway car police found a handgun, thirty-one rounds of ammunition, two hand grenades, forged identity papers, and stacks of antiregime literature. Bands of rioters attacked businesses in Tehran, Isfahan, Yazd, Mashad, Qom, and Kashan in violence that lasted into the early-morning hours. The governor of Lorestan's car was torched, gunmen opened fire on a police station in Qom, and evening strollers were set upon and assaulted on the streets of Yazd.

The violence ramped up over the long holiday weekend of Friday, March 31, to Saturday, April 1, with daylight attacks reported for the first time against banks, cinemas, and other public buildings in more than a dozen cities and towns, including Tabriz, Bandar Shah, Arak, and Chalus. Machete-wielding assailants smashed in the windows of a restaurant at Saqi-Kalayeh on the Caspian, terrorizing patrons but causing no casualties. In Khomein, birthplace of the Marja, the governor's residence and many private dwellings and vehicles were set upon by organized mobs. In Zarand, saboteurs "sprinkled petrol on the roof of the Kuroush Cinema Hall and set it ablaze. Firefighters got there in time and put the blaze out before it could spread to the structure and neighboring buildings." Each wave of provocations, unrest, and violence was more intense than the last. But nothing prepared the police in Isfahan for the gruesome crime scene that awaited them in a field on the outskirts of town. Iranians prided themselves on the hospitality they showed foreigners. That made the discovery of a bloodied foreign worker whose tongue had been cut out, presumably to prevent him from identifying his attackers, all the more shocking. The battered victim died of his injuries in the hospital.

TWICE A YEAR, and always at Nowruz, Parviz Sabeti made the drive down to Qom to pay his respects to Grand Ayatollah Shariatmadari. Sabeti always took great care to travel incognito and arrived in town after dark to protect the Grand Ayatollah's reputation. "I drove down at night with a security car in the rear," he recalled. "I always drove myself—I never trusted my guard. That way I could keep an eye on the rearview mirror."

Sabeti had a vivid memory of his final meeting with Shariatmadari. The Marja handed him a gold coin, as was custom, and the two men began a lengthy discussion about the unrest sweeping the country. The Marja was alarmed by the latest unrest, fearful of where the kingdom was headed, and puzzled by the Shah's inaction. More than anything, Shariatmadari was "scared of Khomeini" and "furious" that Savak was not doing more to remove the source of the problem. The Shah, he said, did not seem to understand what and who he was up against. The most respected and popular of the Shia marjas living in Iran got straight to the point. "Khomeini has to be assassinated," he declared. "I, as a marja, can give you a fatwa to send someone to kill him."

Sabeti was impressed and astonished with this most unusual request. He explained to the Grand Ayatollah that his hands were tied. "Your Holiness," he answered, "we are not in the business of killing people. If you want this taken care of you can give the fatwa to one of your followers."

16

FIVE DAYS IN MAY

My headstrong lord, consider now and say
Whether you want to fight or run away!

—*THE PERSIAN BOOK OF KINGS*

The Americans want to eliminate me.

—THE SHAH

The thirteenth day of Nowruz, the final day of the spring break, was traditionally an occasion for family outings to public parks, gardens, and picnic spots. This year, Sizdeh-Bedar fell on Sunday, April 2, and many Tehranis took day trips to the countryside, while others stayed closer to home, motoring the short distance to Karaj to the west, to the Abbasabad hills in the east, or to the Latian Dam, a beauty spot popular with the Imperial Family. Downtown, tens of thousands of picnickers filled the broad lawns that marched outward from the grand archway of the Shahyad Monument. "There were only a few cases of quarrels among picnickers," reported *Kayhan*, "and police and Gendarmes said most people, in a jovial mood, enjoyed their Sizdeh, which was made even more enjoyable by the beautiful sunshine." The arrival of warm spring weather saw fresh snowfall in northeastern Iran, Gilan on the Caspian was drenched by heavy rains, and there followed several days of high winds in Tehran, which "raised the dust and scattered garbage, causing inconvenience to many pedestrians. In the mornings after the winds, the city has suffered a typical heat wave that is apt to suffocate many."

From overseas, dignitaries and celebrities lined up to see the Shah like so many airliners circling over Mehrebad Airport. "Foreign trade delegations poured into Iran," recalled Britain's ambassador Tony Parsons, "and it was hard to imagine that we were living on the edge of a volcano." Formal state visits were paid by the presidents of West Germany and Senegal. The Shah received the commander of the Indian Navy, and the Queen welcomed to Niavaran a delegation of prominent American feminist leaders. Two American politicians, Ronald Reagan and George H. W. Bush, both presidential aspirants, flew to Tehran to burnish their foreign policy credentials. Ambassador Ardeshir Zahedi had taken special care to arrange the Shah's audience with Reagan. The Iranian was friendly with the glamorous Ron and Nancy Reagan, who fondly regarded him as an honorary member of their "kitchen cabinet" of advisers. Convinced that Reagan had a good chance of defeating Jimmy Carter in 1980, Zahedi wanted the Shah to be his preferred partner on the world stage and hoped that a Reagan victory would get U.S.-Iran relations back on track. "Ron and Nancy stayed in my house," he said. "I sent them by plane from the south of Iran to the north and from the east to the west. I wanted to show the geopolitics of Iran's position in the region. Reagan and the Shah spoke about geopolitics. The Shah was terribly impressed." The Shah's interview with Reagan took place the same day another prominent conservative politician, Margaret Thatcher, the leader of Britain's opposition Conservative Party, flew in to Mehrebad. Princess Ashraf and Prime Minister Amuzegar feted the Iron Lady at separate luncheons, and Ambassador Parsons took her to Isfahan and Shiraz for a spot of sightseeing. "Isfahan was full of European and American tourists, as was customary in the spring," Parsons wrote in his memoir. "The only evidence that everything was not entirely satisfactory was that Mrs. Thatcher's visit to the Isfahan bazaar was quietly dropped, her escort explaining to me that there was 'the possibility of a little trouble there.'" The Shah's session with Thatcher had no sooner ended than George Bush, the former CIA director and future forty-first president, was escorted into his office.

In downtown Tehran, and despite the return to piety, grind houses, strip bars, and nudie cinemas that lined Avenue Lalezar, formerly known as the "Street of Ambassadors," attracted a steady trade. Elsewhere, office workers looking for a shady lunch spot strolled over to Avenue Kakh, the old royal quarter built by Reza Shah with its rambling lawns, trees, and fountains, while to the north Shemiran and the surrounding hills were as charming as ever. "The parks are immaculate, studded with sculpture and fountains," wrote one visitor. "Along tree-lined Pahlavi Avenue, apartment buildings, 30 stories high, shade splendid mansions only partly hidden by brick walls and iron-latticed gates. There are restaurants and nightclubs with names like Miami and Chattanooga. Department stores and supermarkets offer almost anything that can be found in an American suburban shopping mall. The Yves St. Laurent and Charles Jourdan boutiques cater to stylish customers." But the languid spring atmosphere was deceptive. Iranians counted the cost of the Nowruz holiday disturbances that left at least five dead and ninety-eight injured. Violence had been reported in fifty-five towns and cities, with hundreds of commercial properties put to the torch.

FOR THE FIRST time since the outbreak of unrest in January, longtime observers of the Iranian scene studied the Shah's prospects. "Mohammad Reza Pahlavi is beset by grave economic, social and political problems he set in motion when he spearheaded the successful oil producers' fight to quadruple oil prices in 1973," reported the *Washington Post*. "Rarely would contemporary history appear to provide such an example of a people's ingratitude towards a leader who has brought about an economic miracle of similar proportions." The Shah faced a tough economic climate at a time of rising popular expectations. "A year ago you wouldn't have found all these people to go rioting," stated an Iranian economist. "They would have been working in the construction sector." But with the economy slowed down and the construction sector in the doldrums, unskilled laborers saw their daily wage packet fall from $10 to $7. An Iranian-based ambassador said, "The only way out for him now is to deliver the goods— and fast. But can he?"

The final spasms of unrest were felt on Monday, April 3, the day the King, Queen, and their children returned to Tehran from Kish Island. Police officers responding to an anonymous tip rushed to the Takht-e Jamshid movie theater to discover explosives planted and timed to detonate under seats. The packed hall was quickly evacuated and the devices defused just in time. In Zarand, firefighters managed to put out a fire caused by gasoline sprinkled on the roof of a local cinema. But police were too late to reach a cinema in Veramin, whose eastern wall "was suddenly engulfed in flames." Fire consumed a large manufacturing plant on Karaj Road, a bus depot in the town of Shushtar in Khuzestan Province, and the Physical Culture Organization building in Sirjan in Kerman. The Youth

Hostel in Kermanshah was firebombed. A policeman was blinded in a grenade attack in Mashad. The use of accelerants and explosives suggested the revolutionary underground was determined to cause maximum panic and casualties. "These groups have obviously taken to arson now," reported the Pars News Agency. "Attacks with pickaxes and crowbars on bank buildings have continued as in the past. But they are increasingly using fire-bombs." According to the authorities, the saboteurs traveled in small commando units of between two and five people. Paid for hire, and "mostly drawn from the marginal strata of the society," they fanned out from Tehran to strike public facilities "in order to promote commotion throughout the country."

The Islamist underground was determined to draw the security forces into a series of confrontations that they hoped would lead to more deaths and another round of forty-day memorial services. They also hoped that bloodshed would discredit liberalization in the eyes of Iran's middle class and the Shah's American and European allies. The Shah refused to play their game. He believed that a sweeping security crackdown would destroy the progress he had made to clean up Iran's human rights image and would only taint the throne. He could not afford to freeze liberalization and disrupt political activity for at least one and perhaps two years, during which time he expected his health to decline: intellectuals and moderate dissidents whose participation he needed in the elections would denounce the open space as a fraud. He also understood that his son could not inherit a blood-stained throne. It was essential that Iranians accepted Reza's legitimacy but recognition by the foreign powers who guaranteed Iran's security and engaged in commerce was also crucial. For these reasons he vetoed any measures that increased the likelihood of bloodshed.

The Shah, who had always held the mullahs in low esteem, suspected they could not stage unrest without a great deal of help from foreigners. To those who dismissed talk of a conspiracy as evidence of paranoia, he reminded them of Iran's experiences during the Second World War, when British, Soviet, and American armies had occupied his country and divided it into three sectors. The Shah remembered this bitter history and wondered whether he was starting to see old patterns of behavior reemerge. Carter reminded him of Kennedy, another liberal Democrat who held republican sympathies and interfered in Iran's internal affairs. Then there were the big oil companies. Their contracts to take Iranian oil to market were due to expire, and they held out for better terms. The Shah saw this as a blackmail threat. Above all, he suspected that the U.S. and British intelligence services were taking revenge for the 1973 oil price hike and were determined to install in Tehran a more compliant, less nationalistic regime.

When Reza Ghotbi's latest request to see the Shah went unanswered, he asked Akbar Etemad, the president of Iran's Atomic Energy Organization, to gauge the King's view of events. "The Americans want to eliminate me," the Shah told Etemad. "Take me out of my place. But they are wrong. Because if they succeed Iran will become a satellite of the Soviet Union and it will be the beginning of chaos in the region. The domino effect they worried about in Vietnam will happen if Iran goes Communist." Ghotbi reeled when Etemad relayed the contents of his conversation. "This was shocking for me," he remembered. "It was normal to hear [the Shah] saying that 'the Americans are plotting against me.' He often talked about the oil companies and their influence over the religious people. That part was not new. What *was* shocking was that he did not say he would fight it. Instead he said, 'If they succeed . . .'" The Queen's cousin wondered what was going on. "My reaction was, 'There are forces against him, trying to use his people, and that may help to open the political space in Iran,' but it also means he has a very pessimistic assessment, and if so we are in trouble."

Other prominent officials and personalities suspected the Shah did not understand the true dimensions of the crisis. They saw inaction as the very worst choice at a time when bold gestures were required to regain the political initiative. On the evening of April 19, 1978, former Savak chief General Hassan Pakravan hosted a small dinner party at his home and took aside the American diplomat Claude Taylor for a discreet chat. Pakravan explained that unlike some of his younger friends "he no longer exercised access to the Shah," Taylor reported back to Ambassador Sullivan. Nonetheless, said Pakravan, he was confident he knew the Shah "like a book." The Shah, he explained, was "greatly concerned about economic and political conditions in Iran" as well as "the increasing dissidence of a political, social and religious nature." But he was too isolated and dependent on advice from a small group of loyalists who told him what they thought he wanted to hear. Pakravan said he hoped the White House might send over a trusted emissary, someone like David Rockefeller, who could "actively pursue an advisory role with the Shah." The Shah "might get angry and shout," as was his nature, "but he needs to be told before the present trends are even less reversible." Pakravan emphasized to Taylor that the Shah was committed to reform and that he had known since the early sixties "that he must set in train the democratization of Iran." Pakravan's unusual intercession with Taylor had undoubtedly been prompted by the death five days earlier in New York of former minister of court Asadollah Alam. The general was one of the last of the generation of older courtiers who understood that it had been Alam who had issued the decisive order to call out the army in June 1963—his cool head and firm hand had saved the kingdom. But with Alam gone, who would the Shah turn to if the unrest spiraled out of control?

General Nasser Moghadam, now the head of G-2 military intelligence, avoided talking to the Shah and instead tried another tack by taking his concerns directly to Queen Farah. He telephoned Hushang Nahavandi, the head of the Shahbanou's Special Bureau, to request a private meeting. During his long tenure at Savak, Moghadam had enjoyed a reputation as a hard-liner but also as someone who was incorruptible. Over the Nowruz holiday he had stopped off at the home of Parviz Sabeti, his old deputy, to let him know that he had accepted an invitation to fly to Washington, DC, to meet with top CIA officials. Moghadam told Sabeti that the Queen had asked him to provide her with a report on the problems facing the regime and the causes of unrest. Sabeti agreed to write the report, which Moghadam then presented to Nahavandi at their assignation at the Reza Abbasi Museum. The general wore a civilian suit so as to avoid stares from the crowds.

Nahavandi read the "brutally frank" document at the table, apparently unaware it had actually been written by Sabeti. The report named corrupt individuals within the Imperial Family, at the Imperial Court, and in private business. It revealed that former prime minister Hoveyda had not only tolerated but also encouraged corrupt business dealings with government officials and that General Nasiri had carried out extortion. It described in detail the breakdown in crown-clergy relations and how problems with the economy were exacerbating unrest in the streets. The report urged that "dramatic measures must be taken 'at once if not sooner.'" Nahavandi later claimed that the Queen was furious that he had read the report without her permission. She dismissed his version of events as "nonsense." "There was nothing so secret," she said. "I knew about the problems, everybody was coming and telling me their problems."

* * *

THE LOWER SLOPES of the Alborz Mountains were near enough to Tehran for day trips but far enough from the capital that dissidents could meet
away from the prying eyes of the security forces. Young student admirers
of Grand Ayatollah Khomeini often spent their Fridays hiking around the
small hamlets debating politics and Iran's future.

On Friday, April 21, even as the King and Queen extended a warm
welcome to West Germany's President and Mrs. Scheel at Mehrebad Airport, several hundred students assembled near the village of Darakeh to
distribute subversive literature and listen to new cassette tape recordings
of Khomeini's latest diatribe against the Pahlavis. They had no sooner
gathered when they were surprised by gendarmes dressed in full riot gear
who began corralling them to higher ground, while from the air ten Chi-
nook helicopters swooped down and landed on a nearby field. Those
who resisted arrest were beaten and clubbed. "Eyewitness said he saw
more than 50 individuals with serious injuries such as severe head cuts,
cheeks cut open, and bones broken," Ambassador William Sullivan reported
back to Washington. "Several other dissident sources point to roughness
of events and police preparation as evidence that [the government of Iran]
is determined to crack down on dissenters, in violent manner if necessary."

U.S. officials were furious. They believed that the Shah and Prime Minister Amuzegar had reneged on the promises they had made to restrain
the security forces and allow peaceful demonstrations. They were aware
that in recent weeks the homes of several prominent Iranian dissidents
had been firebombed, reportedly by vigilante groups acting at the behest
of Savak. Sullivan condemned "brownshirt tactics" that he feared would
cause opposition leaders to break off their contacts with the embassy and
blame Washington for repression. The ambassador received support from
Secretary of State Vance and his deputy Warren Christopher. Their concerns continued to be focused on the Shah's handling of the unrest rather
than the unrest itself. Senior administration officials scoffed at reports
that opposition groups were part of a conspiracy by the Soviet Union and
its proxies in the Middle East to overthrow the Shah. Parviz Sabeti recalled
a contentious meeting he had with CIA officials in Washington in 1977.
They got into a "big fight" on the subject of foreign subversion in Iran.
"I told them the Mujahedin was getting help from the Czechs, the PLO and
others," he said. "And they said, 'You're telling us that everyone who is
against the Shah is Communist?' And I said, 'No, you are missing the

point.'" The meeting ended in acrimony, with the Americans convinced the Shah was hyping the threat from radicals and extremists to justify the use of force to suppress legitimate dissent.

The Americans came down hard on the Shah because they assumed he could end the unrest when he thought the time was right. They not only misinterpreted his intentions but also overestimated the durability of his regime to withstand pressure from within and without. U.S. policy rested on the latest CIA review of the Shah's prospects. Based on four key assumptions, the agency provided officials in Washington with a glowing picture of Iran as it prepared to enter the 1980s. The report's first assumption was that the Shah enjoyed "good health" and was likely to be "an active participant in Iranian life well into the 1980s." Reports circulating in Tehran that the Shah was "suffering from a dread but usually unspecified disease" were "unfounded and are probably the result more of wishful thinking than of medical fact." Second, there would be "no radical change in Iranian political behavior in the near future." Now in his final decade in power, the Shah was "not likely to change voluntarily the style of rule which he has found so successful." He would continue to rely on a "small inner circle of confidantes, whom he uses as hatchet men, enforcers, advisers, and go-betweens with other elements of the Iranian power structure." Third, "Iran will not become involved in a war that would absorb all of its energies and resources." Iran was the bulwark of stability in southwestern Asia and at peace with its neighbors—the Shah kept a close eye on developments in the region. Fourth, oil production and exports "will continue to dominate the Iranian economy."

Central Intelligence admitted that any one of its four assumptions might be proven wrong. "The Shah *could* die suddenly or be assassinated; a combination of political personalities and forces *might* reduce the Shah to a figurehead; Iran *could* become involved in a war with one of its neighbors or in a more general outbreak of hostilities." Though none of the scenarios could be predicted, there was no doubt that the Shah's "forced-draft approach" to modernization had placed enormous strains on Iranian society. His programs were so interrelated that the failure of one could affect the others, and all were dependent on "a continuing flow of income from oil revenues: declining oil sales have recently forced a cutback in some programs, and a sharp decline could affect everything else." The CIA failed to point out that the decline in oil sales and program cutbacks was the direct result of the U.S.-Saudi oil coup that had shaken the foundations of the Iranian economy and weakened the regime's pillars of support.

EVEN AS THE White House was assured by the CIA and Sullivan's embassy that all was well in Iran and with the Shah, on Saturday, May 6, U.S. consul David McGaffey reported from Isfahan that thousands of American defense contractors and their families were "on the verge of panic" and that the city itself was a tinderbox of tightly coiled anger and resentment. McGaffey expressed alarm at the "strength and growing violence" of religious groups whose mullahs "have begun inserting inflammatory anti-foreign and anti-American rhetoric into already anti-Shah sermons, and that they and their students are forming 'self-defense squads.'" The city was filled with wild rumors: "I was called from several sources about the kidnapping of an American child, an acid attack on two American women, student bodies on the street near American residences, attacks on American school buses, and numerous break-ins, assaults, and rapes. The Elementary School saw a sharp drop in attendance after rumors of an attack and serious vandalism at the school." Though none of the rumors was true, American parents had decided to keep their children at home, others had fled the city for safety, and contract workers were requesting transfers out of the area.

McGaffey believed the rumors were part of a concerted effort to stampede the American civilian community into leaving Isfahan. "The general population," he reported, "while unhappy with the situation, is largely sympathetic to the conservative [religious] reaction. As it grows in strength, there is an increased danger that additional targets will be added to the anti-government actions: Isfahan's Jewish, Armenian and Baha'i communities are increasingly fearful, and Americans are on the verge of panic. . . . Security officials are now beginning to issue warnings to Americans, after weeks of assurances that there was nothing to fear."

ON SATURDAY, WHILE McGaffey warned of a brewing insurrection in Isfahan, the Shah returned to Tehran from a highly successful visit to the southern seaports. He had toured naval installations, attended maneuvers in the Persian Gulf, and been feted by large and enthusiastic crowds. The trip reinforced his own view that Tehran was a bubble and that the Imperial Court in particular was filled with elitists, nervous Nellies, and naysayers who failed to understand his rapport with the great, silent majority of the Iranian people.

Usually reticent before the cameras, today the Shah was practically bursting with good cheer. Everything was going so well, he told reporters assembled at Mehrebad Airport. "I talked with people from all walks of life and could see how happy and hopeful they were," he said. "You hear about the naval maneuvers but beyond that visible aspect there is the sense of national pride, that intangible achievement which some nations may never succeed in attaining while Iran has fortunately attained it." He said he had met with local leaders, including senior clergy, who praised him for "generating a new sense of awareness among Iranians in their cultural and religious values." Iran's southern provinces would be "turned into an industrial powerhouse competitive with any in this part of the world. . . . The income of the people, according to the local elders, is high and signs of progress are everywhere." Before returning to Niavaran, the Shah ended his remarks on a positive note: "This preparedness, vigilance, sense of pride and faith in the future could be seen everywhere in our visit to Tabriz and Kermanshah last year and in our numerous visits to Mashad."

Not for the last time, the Shah appeared curiously detached from the pall of anxiety that hung over the country. Courtiers worried about his capacity for denial, his aversion to unpleasant news, and his decision to cut out anyone who suggested the situation in the country was anything but agreeable. Even *Kayhan*, a pillar of the establishment, expressed concern at the official policy of leniency toward rioters and provocateurs. "Over the last three months, the country has witnessed various instances of individuals or small groups of people taking the law into their own hands and choosing to express their 'views' by acts of violence and hooliganism," the editors warned toward the end of the latest forty-day mourning period. The universities were in turmoil, banks had been attacked, shop windows smashed, and private and public property destroyed. "Iranians should stand together in the firm determination that, during this time of liberalization, the rule of law shall prevail." As if to prove their point, over the next several days students stabbed the head of the faculty of literature of the University of Tehran and threatened another senior administrator; University of Melli students torched two cars, attacked a cinema and a bank, and assaulted another student in his bed; University of Kerman students clashed with police; and Pahlavi University's central administration building was bombed.

In this strange season of contrasts, with the Shah feeling supremely confident, Sullivan convinced the Shah was strong in the saddle, and

Sullivan's consul a few hundred miles to the south predicting an urban insurrection, perhaps it was oddly fitting that 120 American tourist operators flew into Tehran for a nine-day junket meant to sell them on Iran's advantages as a major tourist destination. On the evening of Sunday, May 7, the Americans were treated to "a lavish cocktail and dinner" hosted by the Hyatt International Corporation. Managers from Hyatt Regency Hotels in Tehran, Mashad, and the Caspian were on hand to extend a warm welcome for what everyone hoped would be an unforgettable trip. The events of the next few days proved them right.

THE FIRST SHOTS in the latest round of unrest were fired in Tabriz on Monday, May 8, when police clashed with demonstrators outside a mosque, killing two men. From there, the end-of-mourning protest cycle spread like a brushfire. The next day Qom erupted when mourners destroyed three hundred vehicles and pushed past police lines to rampage through the central railway station, attacking commuters and trashing shops. Mobs attacked buses and beat passengers, then set fires in banks, shops, hotels, and factories. By midday barricades blocked major thoroughfares and prevented emergency crews from dousing the flames. Amid mounting chaos, police officers chased several rioters through alleyways and into a private residence, where they shot to death one person and wounded a second. Only too late they realized they had invaded the home of Grand Ayatollah Shariatmadari and that the two victims had been in search of sanctuary. The riots continued even after the authorities cut off the power supply. But even with the town plunged into pitch-black darkness, it took "squads of anti-riot police backed by army units and helicopters more than ten hours to restore law and order in the city."

On the morning of Wednesday, May 10, demonstrations and riots erupted in nineteen cities, including Mashad, Kashan, Ahwaz, Shiraz, Kerman, Hamadan, Yazd, and Qazvin. The size of the demonstrations—a mob estimated at more than a thousand rioted in Kerman—and the speed with which protesters seized control of streets in major urban centers stunned the palace and unnerved the security forces. Their worst-case scenario—that the Tehran slums would detonate beneath their feet—was on the verge of becoming reality. This time, Sabeti convinced the Shah and Amuzegar to issue a tough public statement warning rioters of severe consequences. For the past few weeks he had drawn up a contingency plan that proposed that the Shah move to a naval base and allow his security forces to smash revolutionary cells, uproot terror networks, and break the cycle of unrest. Liberalization would be halted and the "open political space" closed until religious and political passions had cooled. The reform process would restart only when calm returned to the streets and the threat of rebellion had receded. Sabeti anticipated that the crackdown would be in the main bloodless—he already had at his fingertips the names and addresses of those he wanted to detain. "We had the names of five thousand people divided into five categories," he said. "I drew up plans to immediately arrest the first and second categories which came to fifteen hundred names." Sabeti received support from other officials who by now were convinced that the Shah's liberal policies were leading Iran to disaster.

Sabeti presented the prime minister with his plan. "Now we have to do our job," he told Amuzegar.

"And what is our job?" asked Amuzegar.

"For the past year," said Sabeti, "we've been told not to arrest anyone. We relied on the regular courts. On the Red Cross. We are not doing our jobs. We have to arrest fifteen hundred people."

Amuzegar was aghast: "How are we going to respond to international public opinion?"

The prime minister and the head of internal security then argued over how the White House and Ambassador Sullivan would respond to tougher security measures. Sabeti told Amuzegar to ignore Sullivan and do what was right for the Iranian nation—the survival of the regime was at stake. His own confidence in the Americans had long since collapsed. He was furious that his CIA counterparts protested the arrests of Iranian dissidents: "I told [my CIA counterparts that] if an American is arrested here you have the right to ask questions. But we don't ask you about a black man arrested in Texas."

Amuzegar refused to approve Sabeti's plan, which prompted Sabeti to make an appeal to Court Minister Hoveyda. "Now you have to help us," he pleaded. "You can't let Amuzegar persuade the Shah not to proceed."

Hoveyda asked: "Who are they?"

Sabeti showed him the list of fifteen hundred names, divided among five separate groups. Their numbers included:

Pro-Khomeini clergy: three hundred
National Front, Liberation Movement: fifty to sixty

Seminary students in Qom: four hundred
Fedayeen, Mujahedin: six hundred
Intellectuals, writers: fifty to sixty

Hoveyda took the list to the Shah. Later in the day, he called Sabeti and told him that His Majesty wanted General Nasiri to provide him with a report the next morning to justify such drastic action as making "collective arrests."

WHILE THE SHAH's advisers debated their options, Queen Farah took matters into her own hands when she canceled her appointments, called for her car, and ordered her driver to head straight for the slums of southern Tehran. More than her husband or his advisers, she understood the power of a symbolic gesture during a national emergency. Iranians, frightened, confused, and anxious by this outbreak of violence and mayhem, were looking for some sign that the palace understood the gravity of the emergency.

Wearing a plain business suit, her hair pulled back in its signature chignon, and accompanied only by Minister of Education and Science Manuchehr Ganji, the Queen left her car on a downtown block trailed by her wary security detail and "simply went from door to door and street to street, talking to people about their needs, expectations and problems." It was a bravura performance—the Queen had ventured into a Khomeini stronghold on a day when his men ruled the streets to listen to the concerns of the local people. At one point she took the hand of a small boy and allowed him to guide her through his neighborhood. They chatted together about his life, problems at school, and what he and his friends hoped to be when they grew up. "I went to try to find out what was going on," she said. "I couldn't understand that there were so many problems that people had to come out into the streets. I believed the basis of a just foundation had been built." Like most everyone else in government, the King and Queen had assumed the worst problems associated with modernization would sort themselves out over time. The latest bout of unrest, however, suggested that time was not on their side. Late on Tuesday afternoon, shortly after Farah's inspection tour ended, a mob attacked a branch of Bank Saderat in tony Shemiran, and a large printing press affiliated with Princess Ashraf's social welfare agency was put to the torch.

* * *

THE SHAH READ the Sabeti plan on the morning of Thursday, May 11. Cautious as ever, he rejected it as unnecessary and fraught with risk. His trip to the southern ports the week before had convinced him that he was on the right path. The people had responded to him magnificently—the bond they shared, the farr, was indissoluble. The problem he faced was that his advisers and supporters in government and in the security forces lacked confidence in the people and were too easily cowed by bomb throwers. At the same time, though he was not worried about the National Front and Liberation Movement—their supporters numbered in the low thousands—he was anxious not to do or say anything that might provoke the mosques, which could turn millions into the streets.

For the first time the Shah understood that inaction was no longer an option—the sewers had been flushed to the point where they were now at risk of overflowing. Even as he considered what to do next he learned that rioting had erupted in southern Tehran, outside the mosque attached to the downtown bazaar near Golestan Palace. Riot police fired warning shots into the air and hurled tear gas canisters to disperse the crowds. "Such large demonstrations attacking the Shah personally are virtually unprecedented in Iran, particularly in Tehran," reported the *Los Angeles Times*. British and American schools sent their pupils home, and American companies announced restrictions on employee travel. The Shah was sufficiently alarmed to rearrange his schedule, cancel his appointments for the rest of the day, and postpone his planned departure for Hungary and Bulgaria— the official reason given was a lingering head cold. When he emerged from his office he handed Sabeti's report to Court Minister Hoveyda. The Shah now accepted that arrests had to be made. But he still resisted the idea of a forceful crackdown, opting instead for what he hoped would be seen as a velvet hammer rather than an iron first. Beside the names of the five groups identified for arrest he made the following notations:

Pro-Khomeini clergy:+
National Front, Liberation Movement: −
Seminary students in Qom: −
Fedayeen, Mujahedin: −
Intellectuals, writers: −

Hoveyda informed Sabeti that the Shah would not give the order to make "collective arrests." The father of the nation could not behave as a dictator. Sabeti was dismayed: "In the end he only approved three hundred arrests."

"We are going the wrong way," he told Nasiri.

"Don't worry," Nasiri assured him. "His Majesty knows how to handle it."

The mood in Niavaran was for conciliation, consensus, and compromise—anything to buy time until things settled down. The Shah was particularly anxious to make amends with Grand Ayatollah Shariatmadari, whose house had been invaded by troops several days earlier. On the evening of Friday, May 12, he dispatched to Qom Deputy Court Minister Jafar Behbahanian, who managed his personal finances and property, for a secret nighttime rendezvous with the country's most popular marja. Behbahanian was accompanied on the trip by Hedayat Eslaminia, a former member of the Iranian parliament whose impeccable religious credentials masked dubious morals. Eslaminia was not an easy man to read. "He was a Savak agent," Sabeti explained. "He was a friend of General Pakravan, who introduced him to Nasiri. But Nasiri became his enemy for personal reasons. He took information on Nasiri and his corruption to the American embassy." Eslaminia was also a CIA informant. Like other Iranian officials he was careful to always hedge his bets and kept an insurance policy in his back pocket in case the situation soured— loyalty was only as good as the last paycheck.

Eslaminia's presence in Qom ensured that Ambassador Sullivan and his political counselors were kept apprised of the negotiations that the Shah and Shariatmadari assumed were highly confidential. At one point during the discussions, Eslaminia asked Shariatmadari if he agreed with a recent remark by Khomeini that the current unrest "foreshadowed a gigantic explosion with incalculable consequences." Shariatmadari said he did not. Shariatmadari lectured his visitors that he wanted the government to "stop constantly interfering" in religious matters and presented them with the names of four religious leaders he wanted released from detention. Princess Ashraf, he added, should lower her visibility. The Marja said he understood that the Shah could not possibly "accept 100 percent of his requests, but he would be happy with sufficient indications to show the Shah was cooperating." If he saw good faith from the Shah he would issue a statement of support to the people. Eslaminia then expressed the hope out loud "that some people around the Shah, such as General Nasiri, might be removed."

*   *   *

On Saturday, May 13, 1978, at the end of a tumultuous week, the Shah's top security chiefs met in private conference to discuss the raft of challenges facing the regime. By now there could be no doubt that their opponents sought the overthrow of the monarchy. A unified approach to the unrest would be essential if the regime was to survive what looked like a protracted siege. So far, at least, the Shah's support among the middle class, workers, and farmers held firm, and they had not joined in the demonstrations.

General Nasiri told the others that arresting a few hundred dissidents and troublemakers was only a temporary solution: they should move forward with the tougher approach outlined by Parviz Sabeti. The Savak chief "put forth the view that the way to handle the disturbances was to close the bazaars in cities such as Qom and use all necessary force, including killing people." But General Hossein Fardust laid out the case for moderation, dialogue, and more concessions. "He pointed to [the] difficulty of Nasiri's approach if prominent leaders such as Shariatmadari were to appear at the head of their followers carrying a Koran." If the soldiers opened fire, said Fardust, "It would be a disaster if someone shot a leader in that situation, while failure to put down the demonstrations might even result in some of the soldiers going over to the other side." He strongly argued against putting conscripts on the front lines. Many were young religious men who "should not be sent into the city of Qom, for example; only police should. Beyond that, he recommended the government open a dialogue with the people and talk to them rather than simply repressing them."

The split between Savak's two senior officials was a worrying sign for a regime that relied so heavily on unity at the top. Nasiri's authority was undermined when his colleagues voted to reject his hard-line prescription and instead support Fardust's compromise measures. Fardust's special role at court helped shift the outcome, as he later admitted to Hedayat Eslaminia. The others had followed his lead because they assumed he spoke on the Shah's behalf. But did he? "Fardust never saw the Shah in his last few years," said Parviz Sabeti. "He stopped having audiences with the Shah. He was not in meetings with senior officials." Queen Farah had also noticed a change in their relationship. "In the last years he wouldn't come anymore to the palace," she said. Instead of delivering his weekly briefing in person, Fardust communicated with the Shah through a briefcase that contained sensitive intelligence dispatches. Though no one knew what if anything had happened between them, Fardust never corrected the impression that he still retained the monarch's favor. The Shah was presumably cheered by the news that his security chiefs favored dialogue and moderation over harsh repression. Army troops were pulled out of Qom, and the tanks that lumbered at traffic intersections in southern Tehran returned to base.

While his security chiefs debated strategy, the Shah delivered his first public remarks on the troubles. Millions of Iranians tuned in to watch the live television broadcast from Jahan Nama Palace, and expected the Shah to condemn lawlessness, issue new security measures, and provide them with a clear time line for reforms to regain the political initiative. What they saw instead was a king on the defensive, unsure of himself and in denial about the challenges facing the country. Instead of taking responsibility for the turmoil, the Shah warned of a conspiracy to destroy the country's unity. "These people are politically bankrupt cases whose only hope is the dismemberment of Iran in the 1907 style," he said. Rather than engage the left and moderates, he ridiculed the National Front and insisted he would not curtail liberalization "just because these persons may abuse it." The Shah, snorted one prominent dissident, looked and sounded "like a man in retreat, unable to concentrate or grasp hold of anything. A dictator should be more confident in his own judgment. That, after all, is the only benefit of dictatorship."

Queen Farah, touched by her earlier walking tour of south Tehran, drove back to the area on Sunday, May 14. Determined to rally public support for her husband, she strolled into a supermarket where she was cheered and applauded by friendly crowds. From there she set out in an unmarked minibus for the southern suburbs, where hundreds of people surrounded her vehicle crying, "Javid Shah!" Women hugged her and poured out their troubles. Hushang Nahavandi, who witnessed the scene, observed that although a section of the middle class "was already beginning to challenge the regime at this time . . . the lower classes remained loyal to the Sovereign and had no inhibitions showing it. That's how it was, right to the end."

ON SATURDAY, MAY 20, while the Shah and Queen Farah were on a state visit to Hungary, the American consul in Tabriz, Michael Metrinko, attended a four-hour dinner as a guest of the Armenian archbishop. During the meal, Metrinko listened as Archbishop Diyair Panossian "expounded at great length on his fears for Iranian political stability."

The archbishop told Metrinko that it was no longer a question of "if there is trouble" but exactly "when the trouble will really begin." Since the Tabriz riots in February, Panossian said he had traveled widely throughout Iran but also to Syria and Lebanon to consult with other Armenian church leaders. "The reports he has received and meetings and discussions he has had all point to serious trouble, he said, and he no longer believes the Pahlavi regime will survive it." Fearful of Islamic pogroms and an orgy of religious bloodshed, the archbishop informed his American guest that the only option left open to him was to evacuate his entire flock of seven thousand out of Iran to safety. He said he was already helping anyone who wanted to leave to do so. "He cannot see any real future here for Armenians or Christians as a whole, and is caught between maintaining a very ancient and valuable presence in Azerbaijan, or thinking about the real safety of his people."

CUSTOM REQUIRED THE Shah and Shahbanou to spend the last week in May in Mashad, capital of Khorassan Province. Before the couple flew out they had an important family matter to attend to. For the past year Prince Ali Reza had been taking flying lessons with an instructor. Now the twelve-year-old begged his parents to allow him to make his first solo flight. The Queen could barely stand the tension as the family gathered at Mehrebad Airport to watch the littlest Pahlavi prince take off. The nose of the aircraft dipped slightly just as he was coming in to land and she exclaimed, "O my God!" His instructor radioed a warning and Ali Reza took evasive action and landed without a hitch. Custom demanded that a new pilot be doused with cold water—the Queen had done the honors when her husband piloted his first F-5—and Crown Prince Reza raised cheers and applause by tipping the bucket over his brother's head.

If the Shah was looking for proof that he still enjoyed the people's affection he found it in Mashad, which had remained peaceful throughout the winter and spring. The Pahlavis drove through the city's crowded streets standing in the back of an open car, receiving the acclaim of tens of thousands of admirers who lined the route tossing bouquets and singing, "Greetings to the king of kings." The scene was an extraordinary reminder of the Shah's enduring personal appeal in the provinces. Mashad was far from the intellectual hubbub of Tehran, with its cynicism and snobbery. The city was not a Khomeini stronghold, and its clerical establishment seemed determined to send the Shah a message of support after months of bad news. Like Shariatmadari in Qom, Mashad's moderates feared Khomeini and looked to the Shah and the army to prevent an extremist takeover. At the Holy Shrine of Imam Reza he reaffirmed his complementary functions as Keeper of the Realm and Custodian of the Faith. "You know about my faith in Islam and my methods of statesmanship," he told the city's religious leadership. "My faith is reflected in my words and actions. The Islamic world, especially the Shia community, is of course aware of my other responsibility, which is the protection of the country's borders and independence." Then he uttered a warning that in hindsight could only be regarded as prophetic.

> If we protect this country we can also protect our religion, our sacred beliefs and our convictions. But if, God forbidding, the country should be rendered shaky, then I fear our religion will be harmed too. There are examples of such an eventuality. But I do not want to mention them.

The senior cleric who replied on behalf of the ulama made the pointed observation that too many young Iranians lacked "sufficient understanding of the true principles of Islam" and were too easily influenced by "distorted views"—a none-too-subtle dig at Khomeini's call for an Islamic government—and he urged the media and school system to "be more responsive to the need to steer the public away from corrupt views and unethical practices."

The next day, while the Queen made several spontaneous walkabouts in the center of town, where she was cheered and hugged by the crowds, the Shah took his message to perhaps his most loyal supporters, the factory workers who owed him their livelihoods. He reminded his audience at the Iran National Automobile spare parts complex of how far Iran had come in recent decades, returning to his theme of foreign interference in Iran's internal affairs and mentioning the country's division in 1907 between the Russians and British and the 1941 Russo-British invasion and occupation. "If the principles of the [White] Revolution are harmed, not only your children will have to play in dirt, but also you yourselves will be deprived of living," he reminded the workers. His enemies wanted to "restore the old regime in which workers were ruthlessly exploited, farmers were little different from slaves, women were classed with criminals and the insane, and the country was condemned to eternal backwardness." The workers rewarded him with rousing cheers and pledges of support for the monarchy. He enjoyed a similar reception at Ferdowsi University, where he mixed with a crowd of a thousand academics amid only light security. As the Shah left the three-hour event he turned to the governor, who had tried to prevent the attendance of twenty leftist professors, and with a mocking smile said, "If only all agitators were like that!"

The Shah returned from his inspection tour of Khorassan Province with a much-needed confidence boost. But he was rattled when a newspaper reporter asked him "why some Iranians felt scared and were leaving the country after liquidating their assets." This was apparently the first time the Shah had heard that middle-class Iranians were fleeing the country. "What point is there in living abroad as a refugee, even if one is leading a good life?" he asked and reminded them that the "protection of the state required active cooperation on the part of patriotic Iranians as well." Yet he failed to appreciate the panic gripping Iran's middle class. The absence of a moderate alternative to the Shah's rule was driving young people toward extremism. Terrified that religious fanatics were making their bid for power, worried that the Shah was either ill or out of touch, and fearful that the earth was breaking open beneath their feet, the middle class felt pushed and pulled between two extremes. "My God, we would like a decent opposition, a decent alternative, but the idea of the mullahs bringing the mob out to burn the place down is absolutely terrifying," one middle-class Tehrani told Colin Smith of Britain's *Observer* newspaper. In a dispatch he filed in late May 1978, Smith observed that "much of the [religious] protest movement seems to be aimed against the growing secularism of a society where, because oil has made possible what the Shah's father only dreamed of doing, changes that took centuries in Europe have been telescoped into a couple of decades. Rioters have broken up shops selling televisions, liquor stores, boutiques, cinemas and in accordance with Islamic strictures against usury banks."

Iran's secular urban middle class felt the noose drawing around its neck. More cases were reported of young men on motorcycles throwing acid in the faces of women seen wearing Western clothing. The pace of middle-class flight picked up after the Shah's dismal performance at his press conference. "Bankers suggest that wealthy and middle-class Iranians are prudently transferring funds abroad," warned the *Washington Post*. "We're angry about the Tehran traffic when the shah is spending billions on military gadgets," said one frustrated Tehran resident. "We're angry about the pollution in the capital. Face it, everyone has got a complaint." Prime Minister Amuzegar offered the assurance that the trouble "will play itself out" and "poses no threat" to the stability of the regime. "Many Iranians are not so sure, however," reported Nicholas Gage of the *New York Times*, "and some are hurrying to sell property in a declining market in order to send cash abroad. They know that when reformist elements put their liberal, revolutionary and even heretical ideas aside and ally themselves with the mullahs, it means trouble, because the mullahs have the power and influence to threaten the Government."

17

INTO THE STORM

Nobody can overthrow me. I have the power.

—THE SHAH

The Shah will be gone before I leave.

—U.S. CONSUL MICHAEL METRINKO

To everyone's relief, except for a strike that closed shops in southern Tehran, the fifteenth anniversary of Khomeini's June 1963 uprising passed uneventfully. The Shah had rejected Sabeti's raft of tougher measures, but even the limited arrests of several hundred religious opponents was enough to calm the streets. "Rumors and alarmist reports notwithstanding, Tehran and the rest of the country had a quiet day yesterday," reported one observer. "Workers went to their factories and employees to their offices. The shops were open; the streets were as usual jammed with traffic." The government had succeeded in puncturing the rumors and gossip flying about town and the vast majority of Tehranis "gave clear indication that they opt for moderation and that the extremists of any color have little following."

Hopeful that the "forty-forty" protest cycle had ended, the Shah wasted no time in moving forward with the next phase of liberalization. On Tuesday, June 6, he fired General Nasiri as Savak's chief and appointed him to the post of Iran's ambassador to Pakistan. "Political sources said the surprise dismissal indicated the Shah's displeasure with Savak, and claimed it will probably lead to stricter control on its future activities," reported the *Washington Post*. The next day the Imperial Court announced that

Lieutenant General Nasser Moghadam, chief of military intelligence, would run the secret police. Moghadam had led the effort to reform the trials of civilian suspects hauled before military courts, and the previous month he had presented Hushang Nahavandi with the report documenting corruption at the highest levels of court and government. The Shah presided over his two-minute swearing-in ceremony but kept his remarks to the bare minimum: "I'm sure you know your job." No newspaper reporters or cameras were present to record the moment.

From there, the Shah walked out onto Niavaran's front lawn to deliver his second major announcement of the day. Waiting for him on the sun-dappled grass under the plane trees were several hundred members of Hushang Nahavandi's think tank of intellectuals, lawyers, industrialists, and civic leaders. In years past the Shah had dismissed the group as a talk shop. Now he wanted the liberals to know that he was with them. It was at this moment that he removed the mask of authoritarianism with which he had never been comfortable and revealed his true colors as a progressive and social activist. With Savak reformed, the king who had emancipated women, liberated the peasants, enacted profit sharing for workers, and nationalized the forests and waterways was finally free to be himself. He believed that his decision to replace Nasiri with Moghadam had removed the shadow of police state repression. Fresh from his triumph in Mashad, and with the streets quiet, commerce resumed, and classes over for the summer, Niavaran's warm summer day felt like a fresh start. A burden had been lifted—finally he could be the sort of father to the nation he had always aspired to be. Just before they walked out before the television cameras, the Shah turned to Nahavandi and with a broad smile said, "Well, I hope you're satisfied."

"I think Your Majesty made the right choice," answered Nahavandi.

They strolled into the center of the gathering and the Shah smiled again and shyly remarked, "Who says the intellectuals don't like us?" He soaked up the cheers and applause.

Nahavandi spoke first. He began by reminding everyone that "the stability and unity of Iran depend upon cooperation between the religious authorities and the monarchy." He spoke of popular unhappiness with corruption, gently reminding the Shah that "those who surround Your Majesty and are closest to you ought to be exemplars of moral rectitude, virtue and integrity." Then he pointed out that the Rastakhiz Party had failed in its mission to bring the crown closer to the people and that more than ever the regime had to initiate a dialogue with opposition groups. He ended his remarks by urging the nation "to renew its confidence in the King, to direct us at this decisive turning point, deal with the problems of the present and prepare for the future."

The Shah said he was "gratified to see you here again in such strength." He proceeded to deliver his most detailed explanation yet of what he hoped to achieve with liberalization and why he was not worried about street protests. "Eighteen months ago we began to give the people greater freedom and more opportunities in every field," he told the crowd. "Some say by giving these freedoms we have caused all the commotion and events that we witnessed, that they have led to attacks on banks and window smashing. But this is the price we must pay to achieve maximum freedom. Obviously, this freedom must be within the framework of the country's laws and sovereignty. . . . You have surely seen the results of the advancement of freedom. This process will continue and lead to maximum liberty—liberty minus treason." A decade ago Iran had needed strong leadership from the center to push through reform programs and industrialization schemes in the most efficient and time-saving manner possible. Now, with the first phase of reforms completed, it was time to return power to the people. He was confident that the White Revolution "has led to enough social, political, economic, and cultural progress to sustain such liberalization policies. If such confidence did not exist, the government would not so heatedly pursue decentralization and the promotion of individual liberties." The Shah complained that more attention was being paid to "troublemakers" than to the reformers in his audience. Once again, he recapitulated Iran's recent history by reminding his audience of how far the country had come in recent years. He ended by pledging his support for measures that would respect constitutional conventions and ensure the separation of the executive, judiciary, and legislative branches of government.

The Shah's speech was a tour de force. "This was the first time that the Monarch has directly replied to those who are known to have reservations about the overture towards greater freedom of debate and dissent that began nearly two years ago," wrote journalist Amir Taheri in the pages of *Kayhan*. "It is now clear that the critics of liberalization will either have to find stronger arguments than broken windows or step aside, allowing those who understand and support the process to continue with the current reforms and changes of attitude." Liberalization had never been intended as "a tactical move" but was the result of the Shah's carefully considered assessment that Iran was not the country it had been fifteen years ago and that the political system had to be reformed. The Shah's view was that some unrest was to be expected as controls on speech and assembly were loosened. "Disturbances began to spread, first on university campuses and later in the streets and bazaars," wrote Taheri. "Part of this was, no doubt, the work of traditional opposition groups that had remained dormant for many years. But a good part was also due to an accumulation of discontent with tight control, over-centralization, lack of sufficient open debate and a general feeling that corruption and inefficiency together with arrogance have struck the bureaucracy. All this had to come out in the open." Part of it came out in "aimless riots" that received widespread coverage in the international news media. But most dissent has been "aired in a responsible and constructive manner." Millions of Iranians were debating the country's shortcomings and ways of overcoming them. Part of this process was taking place within the Rastakhiz Party. In the media, articles critical of the system could now be published. Even state-owned television has "encouraged and organized a series of pertinent debates on various aspects of the nation's life." Tension with the clergy was also natural. "Periods of disaffection between the government and the Shi'ite clergy have punctuated Iran's history during the past 400 years. But both sides have always succeeded in sorting out their differences in the end. Seen from every angle it appears impossible to counsel against liberalization. If anything, the counsel of wisdom would be aimed at speeding up the process, giving it more tangible form on the way."

In laying out his vision for Iran's future, the Shah hoped to rally the disaffected middle class, consolidate the support of workers and farmers, and reassure his foreign allies that he was committed to liberalization. His view that riots were the price of progress found support from prominent foreign scholars and academics, most notably Iranologist George Lenczowski, who taught political science at the University of California–Berkeley. In May 1978 Lenczowski visited Tehran in his capacity as chairman of the Hoover Institute's Committee for the Middle East and assured his Iranian audiences that the recent violence was actually proof that the Shah's policies were working. Such dissent was "unthinkable in a totalitarian system," which was why it was not seen in the Soviet Union. Nor was he especially worried about the resurgence of Islam throughout the region or "any basic conflict between the Iranian clergy and leadership . . . judging by the notions of progress nursed by the regime, very close cooperation between Church and State in Iran seemed the most natural option." The Shah felt encouraged by Lenczowski and others to believe that the best antidote to unrest was more and not less liberalization. He had always been impressed by academics boasting Ivy League credentials, and now they confirmed his own instincts to stay on course. He seemed not to grasp that having set down his sword and shield he was walking naked into the storm.

Six days after the Shah's June 6 speech, Israel's ambassador Uri Lubrani sent Foreign Minister Moshe Dayan a memorandum that warned the Pahlavi Dynasty was doomed. "Many feel that an accelerated process of challenging the Shah has started; this process is irreversible and will ultimately lead to his fall and to a drastic change in the structure of the regime in Iran," he warned. "It is very difficult to estimate time scopes and my personal estimate, which is not based on any objective factors, is that we speak, more or less, about five years." Lubrani's pessimistic report recommended that Israel start looking for oil elsewhere and prepare to walk away from its extensive military and commercial investments in Iran.

Ambassador Sullivan took the opposite view. On the eve of his departure for a summer-long vacation in Mexico he wrote a long memorandum to the State Department in which he assured his colleagues that while the Shah was not yet "out of the woods," the end of unrest was in sight. Tougher security measures and the Shah's effort to find common ground with Grand Ayatollah Shariatmadari and moderate ulama had eased tensions and yielded results.

Sullivan and his political counselors Lambrakis and Stempel were anxious to start their own dialogue with Shariatmadari. Sullivan played tennis on Tuesdays with Hossein Nasr, Queen Farah's cultural affairs adviser, and knew him to be well connected in clerical circles. Sullivan, Nasr recalled, "began to pester me for a meeting with Shariatmadari independent of the government. It really began after Tabriz. He picked my brains. He wanted to meet these people." Nasr was coolly indifferent to the ambassador's overtures. Sullivan had more luck with Mehdi Bazargan, leader of the Liberation Movement of Iran and the only mainstream opposition leader inside Iran who everyone assumed had Khomeini's ear and shared the Marja's confidence. On May 25 diplomat John Stempel was introduced to Bazargan at the home of an associate, and they talked about the Shah's liberalization and the Carter administration's human rights policy. Bazargan admitted that opposition groups had taken advantage of the "open space" to test the limits of censorship and the regime's tolerance of dissent. They had felt encouraged when Parviz Sabeti's Savak agents stood on the sidelines and did nothing. Bazargan insisted that Savak and not the religious underground was behind the riots around the country.

Both sides were pleased with how the meeting went. Stempel went back to the embassy to tell his colleagues that Bazargan was someone they could do business with. Bazargan in turn said he "looked forward to a dialogue with the American embassy and was quite pleased with the initial talk." Following the discussion, Bazargan's associate Mohammad Tavakoli confided to Stempel that moderates like Bazargan were in a race against time against young hotheads and supporters of Khomeini were were pushing for an open confrontation with the regime. Six months ago, he explained, the Mujahedin and Fedayeen had almost given up on the prospect of peaceful change in Iran. When Stempel asked how he knew this to be true—was Bazargan in contact with these same terrorist groups?—Tavakoli became vague, "indicating the LMI had learned this from 'friends.' I did not press the point." Tavakoli assured Stempel that the Islamic movement opposed to the Shah was basically pro-Western and "it would be a pity if the Shah drove it into the hands of other hostile forces."

Sullivan flew back to Washington to start his summer vacation and told his colleagues not to worry: the cycle of unrest was broken and the Shah had matters well in hand. "The fix is in," he told Henry Precht, the Iran desk officer at the State Department. "He told us he had been assured that the mullahs had been bought off," said Precht. "Then he went off to Mexico."

In Sullivan's absence the day-to-day running of the embassy was left in the hands of Deputy Chief of Mission Charlie Naas, a new arrival from Washington. Naas was settling in when he chaired a meeting of senior political officers and consular officers to get an update on where things stood. Senior political counselor George Lambrakis began by pointing out that the Shah's policy of all-out liberalization "raised the question whether [he] is in full control or not. Has the process come so far as to be irreversible?" He reminded everyone that moderate, leftist, and nationalist groups like the National Front and Liberation Movement were once again speaking out, and students felt free to stage protests without fear of retribution.

Senior military and civil service officials were puzzled by the Shah's inaction, and there was an upsurge in anti-American sentiment on the streets of Tehran. U.S. support for the Shah meant that it was by default the "fall guy for Iran's problems." The presence of tens of thousands of American citizens in Iran was also causing problems because they "pushed up rents and food costs. . . . At the moment, US power is not respected and we are seen as a weak, indecisive nation. . . . There are situations in which the US could turn very swiftly into a scapegoat for Persian problems."

Isfahan consul David McGaffey told the group that his local contacts were convinced that "the Shah does not know the breadth and depth of popular discontent," and that in an attempt to buy social peace he was giving away too many concessions to the clergy. "While the Shah shows moderation, his opponents never will. . . . Hence there is pressure from the bureaucrats favoring strong action against discontent." The same was true of younger officers in the air force who were "very uneasy about a liberalization which would give substantial concessions to those [they] opposed." McGaffey observed that Isfahan's senior religious leaders had their own concerns. Worried that they were losing their younger followers to Khomeini's extremism, they feared the Marja but were powerless to challenge his appeal.

Mike Metrinko painted a depressing picture of life in Tabriz. The once-vibrant city, he told the room, was now in the grip of Islamic hard-liners. "Virtually the only entertainment that exists is through the mosque," he explained. "The normal social structure has been reduced. Social clubs and movies have been closed. In Tabriz, Empress Farah (who is widely respected elsewhere) is despised even by members of her family, who claim the Tehran Dibas have ceased being Turkish. There is some belief that the Shah is not fully informed about what has been unleashed in Tabriz."

Religious minorities were in a state of panic and looking for ways out of the country, chimed in Metrinko's colleague Thomas Dowling: "The Armenian archbishop is reportedly encouraging his supporters to leave Iran."

Those around the table agreed that if anything happened to the Shah "the military will be the final arbiter in a succession crisis. Although there is some religious influence in the military, it is expected to remain loyal to the Empress or the Crown Prince. If the entire royal family is killed, Iran will be up for grabs."

"What do you think, Mike?" Naas asked Metrinko.

"The Shah will be gone before I leave," he confidently answered.

Naas laughed and said, "Well, I hope your next tour is a long ways away."

"No, it's next summer."

THE FIRST HEAT of summer rolled in the second week of June 1978.

In Khuzestan, 124-degree Fahrenheit temperatures and forty-mile-per-hour wind gusts sandblasted thousands of acres of farmland, scorching crops and burning freshwater melons in the fields. Television antennae, tree branches, and shop signs were blown down. In Aghajari trees were torn up by the roots and "the city was left in total silence with all residents keeping indoors." In stricken Ahwaz, "hot winds hurling hot dust into the faces of pedestrians have caused many to pass out, while others have been hospitalized with heat stroke. The city has taken on the air of a ghost town with many shop owners not opening in the afternoons, and taxi drivers parking their vehicles, leaving the streets empty."

Rolling power cuts that lasted up to eight hours a day pitched the port cities along the southern coast into darkness and left millions at the mercy of the cruel heat. Earlier in the year the Water Board had provided the public with an assurance that Iran's dams were full. There was no need to measure water levels "to see if there is enough water to meet the needs of everyone" over the summer. Electricity Minister Taqi Tavakoli had been careful not to rule out future power cuts. "The national power network is linked by only one line, which can create problems in the entire networks," he pointed out. But he explained that the grid would double its capacity in time for the hot season and said he saw no need to take the precautionary step of purchasing electricity in advance from neighboring Turkey and the Soviet Union. But four months later, with pumping stations in the south "forced to shut down due to the lack of electricity, leaving residents with no running water for most of the day," hospitals in Abadan reported ten heat-related deaths and numerous cases of food poisoning involving children eating spoiled food. With all sea travel in the region halted, thousands of residents thronged the airport and rail and bus terminals each morning, desperate to find a way out of town.

The Shah had devoted the greater part of his reign to taming Iran's unforgiving terrain and climate, investing billions to construct dams, reservoirs, and canals and put in place ambitious reforestation and conservation projects. But the collapse of the power grid in June 1978 exposed the limitations of rapid industrialization and the White Revolution. Even the north experienced dry conditions. When Queen Farah visited Mazandaran in the same month she was told by local officials that the biggest problem they faced was "a shortage of drinking water." In a year when nothing seemed to go right, a second disaster, of biblical proportions, threatened when the United Nations warned Iran to prepare for a plague of East African locusts. Observation posts were erected along the southern coast, forty aircraft and two thousand ground-spraying units were rushed to the region, and in the fertile southwest locust detection centers were built near fruit, cotton, and wheat fields. By unhappy coincidence, the last locust invasion had occurred in 1963 at the time of Grand Ayatollah Khomeini's rebellion.

The regime made three other major missteps. Thanks to austerity, over the past year, the budget for the Customs Department had been slashed, with seventeen hundred staff laid off and another eight hundred employees retired. To reduce bottlenecks at the borders and speed the flow of merchandise to market, customs protocols were changed so that "trucks importing materials for a firm would not be stopped at the border, but rather would be inspected and charged customs levies only upon arrival at the site of the industrial unit." What this meant in practical terms was that a truck driver could pick up his cargo in a European city and pass through Iran's frontier without having his load inspected until he arrived at the depot in Tehran. This devastating gap in border security played into the hands of the Palestine Liberation Organization and black market smuggling networks, which were stockpiling guns and explosives inside the country. "There were no controls and everything flooded into Iran in 1978," lamented one former senior Savak agent. "Most people in Savak did not know about this. It wasn't seen as such a big deal at the time. But on one occasion a customs officer ordered an Austrian driver to open a single crate in the back of his truck. The driver had been paid to drive the cargo to Tehran no questions asked. When the crate was forced open the inspector and the driver discovered a cache of automatic weapons. We tried to trace the contents back to Vienna but it was too late—the trail had gone cold."

While one government policy left Iran's borders unguarded, a second, this time involving taxes, hastened the flight of capital, property, and people to safe havens abroad. In a country where tax avoidance was regarded almost as a birthright, wealthy Iranians were stunned in June by the news that their tax burden would increase. Worse, the criminal statute of limitations would no longer apply in cases of tax evasion, and specially trained agents would be hired to "hunt down" tax cheats. Wealthy individuals and businesses immediately began off-loading their property and assets. Reform of the travelers' exit tax also backfired. Under the new rules a traveler who paid $30 to fly from Abadan to Kuwait was soaked with $300 in exit taxes. Iran's new exit tax, the most punitive in the world, was intended to boost government coffers but had the perverse effect of punishing short-distance travelers and rewarding those who flew the farthest and stayed away the longest. "The further abroad you go," explained one travel writer, "the smaller the exit tax becomes as a percentage of the total fare. The Iranian tourist is thus looking at more distance destinations. Similarly, the exit tax applies to a trip of one day or one lasting months. In this context, on a one-day trip the exit tax costs $300 per day. On a 30 day trip it costs $10 per day." The new tax regime encouraged middle-class and wealthy Iranians to spend the entire summer of 1978 abroad rather than the usual month of August. This was to the benefit of the religious revolutionaries, who chose that month to make their bid for power.

The third miscalculation involved the security forces. The Shah sent several intermediaries, including his trusted financial adviser Mohammad Behbahanian and General Nasser Moghadam, the new Savak chief, down to Qom to try to broker an accord with Grand Ayatollah Shariatmadari and moderate ulama who had not sided with Khomeini. Flattered that Moghadam was interested in hearing their views, the clerics issued a series of tough preconditions for talks. First, they demanded the release of the several hundred religious activists arrested in the wake of the May riots. Second, they insisted that the clergy and not the government should decide who attended pilgrimages to holy cities in Saudi Arabia and Iraq. Third, the government should suppress publication of "antireligious articles" in the popular press. Fourth, justice should be meted out to Savak officials implicated in human rights abuses. Fifth, the government should pay handouts "to people who are ill or whose families are in bad shape." Sixth, the regime should "pay more attention to the religious people." Finally, they opposed an agreement that would allow Austria to send its nuclear waste to be buried in Iran's deserts.

General Moghadam's decision to meet their demands and approve the release of religious extremists from prison shocked his own rank and file. To those who protested, Moghadam explained that the plan to buy off the clergy with concessions was the brainchild of the unscrupulous double agent Hedayat Eslaminia and had won the support of Court Minister Hoveyda and General Fardust. Parviz Sabeti's suspicions were aroused by Moghadam's change of tone. Two and a half months earlier, Moghadam had asked him to prepare the report for Queen Farah detailing the main causes of unrest before flying to Washington, DC, for a series of briefings with U.S. intelligence officials. "When he came back he was no longer a hard-liner," Sabeti recalled. The head of Savak's Third Directorate was convinced that Moghadam had been "turned" by the CIA, persuaded that he would be rewarded if he stood down the security forces and entered into negotiations with regime opponents. In early June, Sabeti and Moghadam attended the wedding of a mutual friend. The younger man challenged the general to justify his decision to release the prisoners. "His Majesty said this is wrong," protested Moghadam. "We got into a fight," said Sabeti. "I said, 'We should not release these men until the forty-day cycle is over.' Moghadam believed I was sabotaging him. Our fight lasted for almost five months." The split within Savak weakened the security forces at a critical time. On two earlier occasions, in 1953 and 1963, the Shah's dread of bloodshed and his natural instinct to avoid conflict had been countered by the intervention of strong-willed personalities such as General Zahedi and Prime Minister Alam. Fifteen years later, Zahedi, Alam, and General Khatami, the strong-willed air force chief, were dead, and the Shah was surrounded by advisers who reinforced his own personal conviction that further concessions would defuse political and religious tensions.

Sabeti managed to keep the agitators off the streets until the June 19 memorials and the state visit of the Spanish King Juan Carlos and Queen Sofia passed uneventfully. The army's show of force included Qom, where troops with bayonets standing guard at key intersections worked wonders. "I control this city," declared Shariatmadari, who fully endorsed the regime's decision to flood the streets with armor. "I didn't want bloodshed and insisted there be peace." He personally banned street protests and limited strike calls to prevent an escalation of unrest. Even so, demonstrations were reported in Isfahan, Tabriz, Ahwaz, Yazd, Zanjin, and Khorramshahr. In Mashad, saboteurs attacked Ferdowsi University, setting fire to the university generator and lobbing Molotov cocktails into the security office, causing a fire that incinerated one guard and mortally injured his colleague. Khomeini's agents were determined to claim a new batch of martyrs to reinvigorate their dwindling protests. In Tehran on Monday, June 19, fire quickly spread from the basement of the Kasra Cinema on Shah Reza Avenue, sending plumes of smoke billowing over Bahar Street. Two moviegoers perished from smoke inhalation during a hasty but otherwise successful evacuation.

Still, palace and government officials were relieved that the security forces had avoided deadly clashes with religious demonstrators. Once again, the Shah's determination to avoid bloodshed and confrontations looked like it had paid off. The avoidance of casualties meant "no new 'martyrs,'" observed the *Washington Post*, which meant "there seems no ceremonial basis for new demonstrations 40 days from now." Days later Khomeini's men, who had been in detention since the May riots, were released and walked to freedom.

The Shah, as inscrutable as ever, gave little away in his meetings with ministers and courtiers. But his shrewdest advisers suspected the pressure was getting to him. In late June Lieutenant General Amir Hossein Rabii, commander of the Imperial Iranian Air Force, saw his friend and palace courtier Kambiz Atabai at the Imperial Country Club, where the two men often played tennis. "This morning I had an audience with His Majesty to discuss the F-16s," Rabii said in reference to an order the Shah had placed for new American jet fighters. "For the first time he didn't seem very interested. What has happened to him?"

"I don't think you should read too much into it," Atabai assured him.

"Kambiz, he's lost his balls."

"He trusts you."

"This is not the same Shah we knew," said Rabii. "He is no longer commanding me."

SHORTLY BEFORE HIS departure for Nowshahr on the Caspian Sea, where he planned to spend the remainder of the summer, the Shah sat down for a lengthy interview with the American newsmagazine *U.S. News & World Report*. He made it clear he fully understood that his decision to loosen the reins was fueling unrest—but that he felt he had no option than to accelerate the pace of reform. If unrest flared again he said he would try to maintain order without resorting to repression. "The liberalization will

THE FALL OF HEAVEN   349

continue, and I view law and order as a separate issue," he said defiantly. "Nobody can overthrow me. I have the power. I have the support of 700,000 troops, all the workers, and most of the people. Wherever I go there are fantastic demonstrations of support. I have the power, and the opposition cannot be compared to the strength of the government in any way."

The Queen completed her last engagements of the season, flying to Mashad to attend the Fourth Tus Festival, dedicated to the poet Ferdowsi's literary masterpiece *Shahnameh*. Entering the festival grounds and "escorted to the Imperial Stand by Zaboli dancers and musicians and Quchani men carrying trays of crystalline sugar cones and burning frankincense," the Queen received a "rapturous traditional welcome" from thousands of spectators and participants. Farah sat on a dais from where she was entertained with wrestling displays followed by a garden concert performed by Azerbaijani musicians, whose "mellow music against the backdrop of Ferdowsi's majestic marble mausoleum, and the tall silvery poplars rising into the evening sky created an enchanting atmosphere."

ON MONDAY, JULY 3, on the eve of General Nasiri's departure for Islamabad to take up his new post as ambassador, Pakistan's envoy threw a farewell luncheon in his honor at his residence in Tehran. While the guests mingled, Nasiri took aside Lebanon's Khalil al-Khalil for a quiet word. He explained that a Savak agent in Beirut had arrived bearing a secret communication from Musa Sadr that included a gift for the Shah. Fully aware that Ambassador Qadar despised the Imam, the agent had agreed to Musa Sadr's request to bypass the envoy and deliver the letter in person to General Moghadam. Nasiri and Sabeti were both briefed on the contents. "In the letter, Musa Sadr offered to help the Shah," said Sabeti. "He offered to talk to Khomeini on his behalf. He also offered to help change the Shah's policies to make them more reflective of Islam—he was offering his services."

Lebanon was in the third year of the brutal civil war that devastated Musa Sadr's kingdom in the south. In March 1978 Israel's invasion to uproot Palestinian bases forced 250,000 Shia villagers from their homes and collapsed the local economy. The Shah condemned the Israeli action and rushed food, clothing, and medical supplies to the region in C-130 transport planes, earning praise from local Shia and presenting Musa Sadr with an opportunity for rapprochement. "By responding quickly to the material needs of the Shia refugees," said the *Christian Science Monitor*, "the Shah's intervention had exposed Musa Sadr as powerless: the Shah, many observers believe, has struck a decisive blow at Imam Sadr's already declining prestige since the Imam's self-styled 'Movement of the Impoverished,' aimed at self-help for the impoverished Shia farmers in south Lebanon, lacks funds or other means to help." The Shah's intervention in Lebanon served a dual purpose: the UN peacekeepers he sent to Lebanon included Savak agents who operated under cover to hunt down PLO-trained Iranian dissidents. By now the regime fully understood that the Khomeini movement was using Lebanon as the springboard to launch insurrection inside Iran. The Shah's action made it clear that he "plans to end if he can the role of south Lebanon as a sanctuary for what he has termed 'outlaws, terrorists, and Islamic Marxists' trying to escape pursuit by Savak."

Musa Sadr was also under intense pressure from Iran's revolutionary movement and its Palestinian and Libyan allies to overcome his resistance to clerical involvement in politics and finally throw the full force of his moral weight against the Shah and behind Khomeini. They were already furious with the Imam's support for Syria's invasion of Lebanon. "Musa Sadr was not considered as someone who was particularly anti-Shah," confirmed Abolhassan Banisadr. Banisadr harbored a visceral dislike for his old childhood playmate and suspected him of playing a double game. Over the summer of 1978 he and other senior figures in the anti-Shah revolutionary movement "were in disagreement with Musa Sadr's position in regards to the Syrian involvement in Lebanon."

Colonel Muammar Gadhafi of Libya had his own set of grievances with Musa Sadr, this time to do with millions of dollars in donations he had given to the Imam's Amal militia to buy weapons to use against the Israelis. "[Musa Sadr] promised Gadhafi to take action in the south of Lebanon against Israel and he never did," said Ambassador al-Khalil. "Gadhafi wanted him to motivate the Shia to work against the Israelis and work with the Palestinians. He gave him a lot of money and he did nothing. He did not live up to his promise." Gadhafi offered to broker a meeting at his residence in Tripoli between Musa Sadr and Ayatollah Mohammad Beheshti, Khomeini's most trusted aide and a key architect of the Islamic underground's assault against the Pahlavi state. Gadhafi believed it was time the clergy patched up their differences and joined forces for a final push to topple the Shah's regime. Beheshti was no stranger to Musa Sadr. During the Ayatollah's years living in exile in Hamburg he had also cultivated a reputation among Western diplomats and foreign correspondents as a cosmopolitan and a moderate. But Beheshti's erudite personality and admiration for German culture masked a fanatical side—he had after all played the key role in the assassination of Prime Minister Mansur of Iran thirteen years before.

Imam Musa Sadr still harbored the dream of returning to Iran to play a role in public life. There were those who believed he wanted to enter politics. "He actually had a great ambition to become something great in Iran," said Ambassador al-Khalil. "He used Lebanon as a stepping-stone to move politically into Iran. He involved himself in Lebanese and Iranian political life." But Musa Sadr's ambitions were confined to the religious sphere. By temperament and training he was staunchly opposed to Khomeini's idea that the ulama should rule Iran. Among moderates in Qom he was seen as the hope of the "quietists," the natural successor to the great marjas Khoi and Shariatmadari, and the only senior cleric with the skill and charisma to reconcile Shiism with the modernist thrust of the Pahlavi state. They also saw him as their best means of blocking Khomeini's power grab. By the summer of 1978 he and the Shah were two men in search of a lifeline. From the Shah's vantage point, the humbling of Musa Sadr in Lebanon made him a more acceptable candidate for negotiation.

At his farewell luncheon, General Nasiri explained to Ambassador al-Khalil that Musa Sadr had extended an extraordinary offer of assistance to help the Shah reach an accommodation with moderate ulama. "He wants to improve relations," said Nasiri. "What do you think? What do you think is behind this letter? What is he thinking?" The ambassador asked if he could see the letter for himself. The next day, Nasiri sent one of his aides to al-Khalil's residence with the letter. Its contents were explosive. "I am ready to help you if you bring Mehdi Bazargan and the people from the Liberation Movement into government, and if you dissolve parliament and allow free elections," read the missive. "If you do these things I am going to help you as much as possible." Musa Sadr's offer of help came with unpalatable conditions—the Shah associated Bazargan with his old nemesis Mossadeq—but it also provided the palace with an opportunity to break the impasse with Qom.

Ambassador Khalil listened as the letter was translated from Persian to Arabic, and then telephoned Nasiri to say that he was impressed with what he had heard. "And why not?" he said. "What do you have to lose by meeting with him? You have every reason to hear him out and no reason to close the door to him."

The next day Nasiri's aide told al-Khalil that the Shah, who was apparently informed of Musa Sadr's message but not the detailed conditions, had agreed to send a personal representative to confer secretly with Musa Sadr in West Germany from September 5 to 7.

VISITORS TO NOWSHAHR found the Shah engaged in his work and active in his leisure pursuits. "The holidays of the summer of 1978 began relatively peacefully for the Shah, who believed he had defused the crisis, and for the Imperial family," wrote Hushang Nahavandi. "There was almost no change to the usual routine. The Shah had more visitors than previously, and the Shahbanou, who had taken a complete break in preceding years, also began to give audiences in order to keep pace with events." "He would work until one o'clock," recalled Elli Antoniades, who spent part of the summer at Nowshahr with the Pahlavis. "He received guests, ambassadors, ministers, then had lunch and then recreation." After dinner, "the elder folk would play cards, without stakes, while the younger ones danced on the terrace."

Back in the capital, however, and as far away as Isfahan, the streets were "awash with rumors of the Shah's health." "At every social occasion embassy officers and I have received anxious inquiries from Americans, Iranians and other diplomats," Charlie Naas cabled the State Department. "By now most of the home offices of US firms have probably received the story of ill health. The rumors range from terminal malignancy, leukemia, simple anemia to having been wounded in the arm or shoulder by General Khatami's son or Princess Ashraf's son. The latter rumor has the assassination attempt taking palace at Kish Island earlier this year or recently at the Caspian and has on occasion included the death or wounding of security guards." In his telegram, Naas noted that the rumors had been spurred by the cancellation of official events in late June and early July and the Shah's absence from the front pages of the newspapers. He also recounted his most recent visits to see the monarch, the first on July 1, when he had escorted Lady Bird Johnson, the widow of Lyndon Johnson, to Niavaran for tea with the Imperial couple.

Gossip about the Shah's health reached Nowshahr. Prime Minister Amuzegar sent officials to the Caspian "to see if the rumor was true," remembered the Shah's valet. "There was a rumor that the son of Princess Fatemeh killed him," said Amir Pourshaja. "His Majesty was water-skiing and the officials cried, 'Look, look! Thank God, Thank God!'" Another rumor had it that the Shah couldn't walk by himself and so he and the Queen staged a photo opportunity for the press where they walked "hand in hand" up and down the beach together. Cynics back in Tehran decided the photos had been doctored to fool the public.

Charlie Naas and Under Secretary of State David Newsom flew to the Caspian on July 9 to break the news that the Carter administration had decided not to sell Iran a ground-to-air missile system. The official reason given was that the United States had decided to cancel development of its own project. But even Naas "wondered whether there was growing concern [back in Washington] about selling such a sensitive program at that stage to Iran. The Shah's disappointment was seen in his face." Not surprisingly, he interpreted the decision as a loss of confidence in his leadership. Naas's trip to the Caspian masked an ulterior motive. Embassy staff were worried enough about the rumors of ill health that they asked Naas to make a studied inspection of his appearance. "We sent Charlie up to see the Shah," admitted John Stempel. During his conference with the Shah, Naas looked for any sign of obvious distress or illness. "He looked a little tired but was otherwise fine," Naas reported back. At one point the American watched as the Shah took a small medicinal bottle out of his pocket and swallowed some pills—he was so close he could see their different colors. "He did take some medication with his tea," Naas wrote. But an Iranian palace source had assured him that "that the Shah is fine and enjoying his rest. . . . [He] blames the Russians for starting the rumors. Our own sources indicate that there is no doubt the Russians in fact are spreading the stories, but at this point everybody is in on the act. At this time I tend to discount well over 90 percent of the nonsense but we shall continue to try to keep ourselves informed. We are taking the line, when comment is unavoidable, that 'to the best of our knowledge the Shah is fine.'"

Back at the embassy, meanwhile, Naas's consular officers were issuing on average six hundred to seven hundred nonimmigrant visas every day to Iranians impatient to gain entry into the United States.

* * *

THE START OF the summer vacation season, coinciding with the closure of high schools and university campuses, reinforced the illusion of normalcy. The government's tough austerity measures were finally starting to pay off. Inflation had fallen to 12 percent, and in the past fiscal year the gross national product had registered a modest 2.4 percent increase. Each weekend in July more than a million people flocked to beaches along the Caspian Sea. The European Community expressed optimism that Iran would be granted favorable trade status by the end of the year to sell its manufactured goods within the Common Market. West Germany signed an accord to work with Iran on joint projects related to science, engineering, and "advanced technologies." Hungary agreed to build a $12 million date processing plant at Banpur. Work resumed on local infrastructure projects, including Tehran's underground metro and international airport. Construction began on the Trans-Iranian Gas Pipeline, one of the Shah's more visionary projects to increase European reliance on Iran as an energy provider. By 1981 the pipeline would bisect Europe's east–west divide transiting Czechoslovakia, Austria, West Germany, and France; the Czechs alone were expected to earn transit rights of $100 million each year. In the same week, Paris agreed to sell to Iran four nuclear power plants at a cost of $4 billion. The nuclear deal bailed out France's nuclear industry, which "has been running into increasing financial difficulties of late because of the slowdown of nuclear power plant construction programs in France and abroad."

The old anxieties lurked just beneath the surface. In a year when everything fell apart, and when Iranians looked skyward for answers to their terrestrial troubles, it made sense that so many people found inspiration in Steven Spielberg's science fiction epic *Close Encounters of the Third Kind*, which opened at the Goldis Cinema over the summer, with its hopeful depiction of what might happen if the heavens did actually open. On July 16, at two o'clock in the afternoon, two young men in southern Tehran were taking pictures with their new 150-rial camera when they saw overhead what they claimed was a spaceship. "Suddenly, we spotted something flashing an orangish color over our heads," said Ali Farboudi, who with his best friend, Amir Barjan, enjoyed national celebrity status in the days that followed. The boys contacted Mehrebad Airport to report the sighting, and their infamous photograph was splashed across the newspapers. The skeptics had a field day. "We think Ali and Amir are having us on," chided the editors at *Kayhan International*. "Everyone we have shown the picture to says the same thing—clever, but it's not a UFO."

Twenty-four hours later, however, duty officers in the control tower at Mehrebad Airport watched in disbelief as an unidentified aircraft with flashing lights moved at high speed through the night sky. The strange vessel was also spotted by the flight crew and passengers aboard a Lufthansa airliner as it prepared to make its final descent into Tehran. On the ground below, eyewitnesses contacted a radio station to report a UFO sighting. No one was joking this time.

JOHN STEMPEL AND his Russian counterpart Guennady Kazankin sat down for lunch, this time at a Chinese restaurant on Pahlavi Avenue. The talk around town was of the UFO sighting the night before, but their discussion focused on more mundane events, specifically what they thought was happening in the palace. The Russian pressed Stempel for his views on the Shah's decision to democratize Iranian life. The American, "pleading a return from vacation, merely said he had heard the political system was opening up," and noted that elections were planned for next year.

Kazankin snorted in derision. "If the Shah is still around next year," he acidly remarked, "everything will be rigged by the government."

Stempel "picked up on the 'if'" and asked whether Kazankin "has any news that would suggest differently. Were the Soviets planning something in Iran?"

The Russian "cleared his throat and treated Stempel to the rumor that the Shah was reportedly sick with cancer or some other blood disease."

Stempel rolled his eyes. As he explained in his account of their conversation, rumors of a possible illness affecting the Shah "abounded in many quarters and may be of Soviet inspiration." Later, he defended his decision to ignore Kazankin's tip. "The Russians always believe conspiracy rumors," he protested. "And when it came right down to the revolution, Kazankin knew nothing."

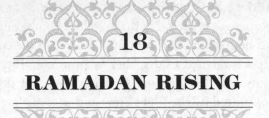

18

RAMADAN RISING

What do you think is going on in my country?
—THE SHAH

*Iran is not in a revolutionary or even a
"pre-revolutionary" situation.*
—CIA

In a year when the fortunes of the old Persian kingdom hinged on a cancer diagnosis, funeral processions, and visions of spaceships hurtling through the night skies, perhaps it was fitting that a fatal car crash on a lonely stretch of highway outside Mashad proved enough to tip Iran back into a state of siege. It was the Shah's bad luck that Haj Sheikh Ahmad Kafi was no ordinary traffic fatality but one of Tehran's most popular preachers. At age eleven the former child prodigy had dazzled crowds in his hometown of Mashad by leading prayers at the Holy Shrine of Imam Reza, and in his early forties Sheikh Kafi presided over a network of religious institutes and enjoyed a sizable following among the people. The traffic pileup that claimed his life on Friday, July 21, and injured his wife and five children was an accident, but Khomeini's agents were quick to spread the legend that Parviz Sabeti's men had rammed their car off the road. The death in London of a second respected cleric, Ayatollah Molla Ali Hamadani, only added to the Shah's woes. The passing of these two mullahs ensured that Shia mosques would be packed with memorial services through the holy month of Ramadan, set to begin on Saturday, August 5. Two other calendar events loomed as major tests for the security forces. This year the first day of Ramadan also happened to fall on Constitution Day, the national holiday that served as a reminder of how far Iran had strayed from the democratic ideals of the 1906 revolution. The twenty-fifth anniversary of Mossadeq's ouster, National Uprising Day, fell on August 19 and promised to be another flash point for royalists and republicans.

Among the thousands of mourners who thronged the streets around Mashad's main shrine for Sheikh Kafi's funeral procession on Saturday, July 22, were young knife-brandishing provocateurs loyal to Khomeini who began chanting antiregime slogans. They leaped from the crowd and slashed police officers, butchering one on the spot and wounding seven others, and triggered street brawls with the security forces that lasted through the day. One week after the Sheikh's death, mourners in southern Tehran blocked traffic, smashed bank windows with bricks and rocks, and attacked the headquarters of the Boy Scouts. Buses ferrying American workers in Isfahan were stoned. Even as King Hussein of Jordan presented his new bride, Lisa Halaby, to the King and Queen, who were in residence at Nowshahr, riot police in the capital teargassed demonstrators who converged along Amireh Avenue. In Qom, a police officer was blown up when he caught a device thrown from a passing car that turned out to be a live grenade. Rioters in Shiraz assaulted banks, cinemas, and the Iran-America Society building. Mobs ran wild in Kashan, Hamadan, Rafsanjan, Behbehan, and Jahrom, setting fires and attacking public buildings and businesses owned by religious minorities. By the end of the weekend the authorities counted at least six deaths and had made three hundred arrests.

Khomeini's agents staged the latest provocations to reinvigorate a protest movement that had petered out eight weeks earlier. "The relative calm evidently did not sit too well with the monarch's more extreme opponents," reported the U.S. Department of Defense. "Followers of the exiled Khomeini appeared to have been behind much of the violence, or at least exploited the genuine commemorations of the religious majority. Other cities also reported some incidents, which apparently were perpetrated by religious extremists."

The tempo of religious dissent sharply accelerated on the eve of Ramadan. From sunrise to sunset during the month of Ramadan observant Muslims deprived themselves of food, liquids, and sexual relations to cleanse their minds and bodies. The mosques were more packed than usual, and evening meals were a time for families and neighbors to come together. In their elevated spiritual state the devout were more likely to listen to and act on the urgings of Khomeini's agents. "The preachers took advantage of Ramadan," explained the young revolutionary Ali Hossein. Since staging the attack on the cafeteria at the University of Tehran he had risen to become a close aide to Ayatollah Rasti Kashani, Khomeini's representative in Qom. "The people were high. There was fasting. The companions of Khomeini and the preachers held gatherings throughout the country, and intellectuals and young people propagated in favor of an Islamic government." From the pulpit, the Shah was indirectly compared to Yazid, the treacherous villain who had assassinated Imam Husayn at Karbala. "Khomeini made use of this point to the maximum extent," said Ali Hossein. "He used the mourning ceremonies to ask preachers to talk about this interpretation of the uprising and provoke people. The preachers told their congregations but in a way that did not mention the Shah by name but made it obvious he was Yazid in their eyes."

IRAN WAS AT war on two fronts. The first, between the Shah and Khomeini, was over which leader would wield ultimate political power in Iran. The second, between Khomeini and Shariatmadari, would decide the future of the Shia faith. Since 1906, tension had always existed between the ulama's majority "constitutionalists" and minority "rejectionists." Over the past several years the "rejectionists" had won the hearts and minds of younger clerics, whose energy and enthusiasm began to overwhelm the "constitutionalists." If Grand Ayatollah Shariatmadari was to prevail in this contest he would have to show his supporters that moderation could yield results, which in turn meant the Shah would have to pledge to respect and enforce the Constitution.

If the Shah was slow to act it was because just eight weeks earlier he had been feted in Mashad by senior clergy and acclaimed by vast crowds. Meanwhile, the dwindling of religious unrest in late May had restored the illusion of normalcy. Convinced that the worst had passed and that enough steam had been let out of the system, he saw no need to hurry along the dialogue with Shariatmadari or announce new reforms. He groaned when Hushang Nahavandi flew up to Nowshahr to deliver the Marja's latest list of complaints and demands. "Oh, that old man!" the Shah said with a sigh. "Of course, you'll have to keep on going to see him." He was too insensitive to the pressures weighing on Shariatmadari. In early August Khomeini used Ramadan as a cover to step up his campaign to isolate, discredit, and smash Qom's moderates. As a pretext he cited a recent interview Shariatmadari gave to a French publication in which he criticized the use of violence to achieve political goals and expressed support for the 1906 Constitution. "Within [the] past few days Ayatollah Khomeini sent Shariatmadari a message to stop talking about a constitution and parliament since Khomeini opposed them all," reported the U.S. embassy. The contempt was mutual. "Source who has been involved in government/religious discussions tells us Shariatmadari sent Khomeini a 'put up or shut up' message to effect that if Khomeini was so strong, he should come to Tehran and speak face to face with the ayatollahs who live in Iran. Shariatmadari noted Khomeini lived far away in Iraq and had refused to criticize Iraqi government when it took severe action against demonstrators in Najaf about two years ago."

The Shah was not entirely to blame for inaction. For months he had held out for some form of acknowledgment from Shariatmadari that he was making a sincere effort to open up the political system and reform the government and the Imperial Court. The Marja's defenders argued that to do so would violate Iran's church-state divide, which the Shah had enforced with such enthusiasm. The role of the clergy, they reminded the palace, was to reflect and not shape public opinion, and so the marjas were duty-bound to keep their silence. "My father was not pro-monarchy or anti-monarchy," explained Hassan Shariatmadari, who served as his father's private secretary. "He saw the ulama as the voice of the people— we do not involve ourselves in politics." Still, by late July the Marja's preferred list of demands extended to sacking not only the prime minister but the entire cabinet, silencing Princess Ashraf, and firing the Shah's personal physician—General Ayadi was a Baha'i whose faith singled him out in the eyes of the clergy as an apostate. Speaking to Nahavandi, Shariatmadari rapped the monarch's casual attitude toward religion: "I can't just ring him up and give him a moral lecture, although God knows he needs it; do you dare take this message?"

Royalists cried foul. They recalled Shariatmadari's decisive intervention in 1963 when he had orchestrated Khomeini's elevation to grand ayatollah, and they pointed out that even now the Marja insisted that the Shah give away his powers without offering so much as a public blessing. "Shariatmadari was very weak," said Ali Kani, one of many establishment figures who begged him to lend public support to the Shah. "One day I went to him and said, 'Do something.' The Marja protested to Kani that he was under intense pressure from the militants. "His own students wanted him to do something," said Kani. "He was nothing."

The impasse weakened both leaders and the moderate cause. "The failure of the Shah was that he never agreed to make real reforms," said Hassan Shariatmadari. "The moderates were losing ground in late 1977 and early '78. My father urged the Shah to reform. The various middle men sent from the Court to Qom misinterpreted his words. The Shah was too distrustful and showed more interest in international politics than in domestic reform." The senior marja was especially worried that with the onset of Ramadan the situation in Iran would deteriorate. When Hushang Nahavandi visited Qom at the Shah's behest he received an earful from his host. "We have a constitution which ought to be honored and applied both in the spirit and the letter, and a Sovereign who ought to act as an impartial judge, completely detached from factional interests," said Shariatmadari. "Indeed, he's throwing himself away at the moment; he is terribly exposed. . . . I am convinced that the time has come for him to take a radical decision, in order to change the course of events. He is still in a position of strength, and the situation can be managed without any appearance of retreat; but, if the King fails to take this decision within the next few weeks, he will lose everything."

U.S. diplomats watched as the Shah's attempt to strike a deal with Shariatmadari faltered. Charlie Naas concluded that the King's efforts "to come to some sort of arrangement with religious forces have not been successful . . . the competition between Iranian mullahs for politically religious prominence can have the effect of forcing all mullahs to support their more extreme brethren, however lukewarmly, in any civilian confrontation with security forces." Privately, Naas and his colleagues suspected sabotage from within the Shah's inner circle. "The paradigm we were working under in the summer of '78 was to reach an accommodation with the moderates," explained John Stempel. "There was some suspicion that someone wasn't getting the message out. We decided Hossein Fardust wrecked the chances of an accommodation. He felt he had been treated badly by the Shah, treated like a peasant—he wanted to do the Shah in."

Regardless of who was to blame, or whether sabotage and high treason were involved, there remained a striking gulf in perceptions between Niavaran and Qom. "Still one finds [Prime Minister Amuzegar] to be relaxed and conciliatory in his spacious office, not ready yet to call for the display of force that might have been expected in this monarchy not so long ago," *Wall Street Journal* correspondent Ray Vicker informed his readers on August 2. "He is convinced that dissenters represent only a small minority of this country's 35 million people." Ever the loyal techno-crat, Amuzegar took his cues from the Shah. "Our problems stem from the fact that we have been making rapid progress toward liberalization without having the institutions necessary for a democratic society," he said. Amuzegar admitted that the government had been caught flat-footed by events. Remarkably, the Majles had still not passed legislation allowing for peaceful protests, and his prescription for future action was hardly reassuring: "We have convinced ourselves we are moving in the right direction. We must convince the people, and I think we are doing that."

EARLIER IN THE summer, Isfahan consul David McGaffey had warned his colleagues that Isfahan was a tinderbox. The incident that pushed the city over the edge was the disappearance of Ayatollah Jalal Al-Din Taheri, a prominent Isfahan cleric and Khomeini supporter, from his home on the evening of Monday, July 31. His followers accused Savak of detaining their leader, but there was enough confusion initially that McGaffey wondered if the entire incident had been staged by Khomeini's agents as another pretext to stage a riot. The next day, Ayatollah Taheri's acolytes seized control of the streets around the main shrine, erected and set ablaze bar-ricades, hurled explosives into banks, and attacked public buildings. The security forces lost control and fired live rounds into the crowd. One American caught up in the violence told diplomats that "one child was hit in the head and died. Others may have been injured and possibly killed as well. Same source saw small groups of police chase some rioters into small alleys and return after single shot had been fired." Isfahan's Ameri-can Club was firebombed, an American was shot at on his way to work, and a pipe bomb was thrown over the wall of the U.S. consulate. Mob attacks were carried out against a cinema, restaurant, and businesses either popular with Americans or owned by Jews or Baha'i.

The return of unrest cast a pall over the holiday atmosphere at Now-shahr, where guests and courtiers quietly passed on the latest grim reports of the unrest to the south. "Every day His Majesty heard on the phone the bad news," recalled his valet Amir Pourshaja. Too late, the Shah accepted Shariatmadari's advice that he needed to make a bold gesture if he was to convince Iranian public opinion that his commitment to constitutional rule was genuine.

On Saturday, August 5, Reza Ghotbi flew to Nowshahr with a film crew from state television to film the Shah's annual Constitution Day speech, which was broadcast to the nation. Ghotbi read the speech before the taping and was struck by the contrite, defensive tone. "He talked about when he and his father took leadership of the country, how we had more students and universities," said Ghotbi. "It was a list of accomplishments, mostly material, but also how other countries now respected Iran and treated it as a partner. I said it was somehow apologetic." Reporters invited to a pre-broadcast briefing were assured by Minister of Information Dariush Homayoun that the Shah "is serious about opening up the system, but plans to do it carefully. Local newsmen were told [the] Shah remains in full control, and plans to loosen up as [the] system shows it can take it. Press was told criticism was all right except of [the] Shah himself and [the] prime minister by name, pending new press law."

Millions of Iranians turned on their television sets and radios to hear the Shah promise the most sweeping political reforms in decades. He pledged to hold free and fair parliamentary elections in 1979 and challenged his opponents to test their strength at the ballot box instead of in the streets. He provided the assurance that "in terms of political liberties we will have as much liberty as democratic European nations, and, as in democratic countries, the limits of freedom will be specified." Peaceful public gatherings would be allowed and freedom of the press and speech regulated by a press code that guaranteed criticism of every institution except the monarchy and the Shia faith. Yet if the Shah expected gratitude for this latest round of reforms he was very much mistaken. Conservatives despised them as concessions to mob rule that made the palace and government appear weak. Leftists, meanwhile, denounced the Shah's "Father knows best" attitude and dismissed the promise of elections as a cynical gimmick. "They are glad the Shah has given them a weapon to beat him with—the promise of political freedom—but distrust his commitment to specific measures and remain deeply suspicious of his ultimate intentions," Charlie Naas reported back to Washington. "His public commitment to free elections will keep [the] political pot boiling." For Khomeini's followers, the promise of democratic elections was like waving a red flag to a bull. In their eyes the national parliament, the Majles, a holdover from 1906, was the ultimate symbol of Western liberal decadence: only an

Islamic legislature was truly capable of representing the people. Sensing that the Shah was on the defensive, Khomeini's forces launched a wave of arson and sabotage attacks in Tehran and instigated a full-scale insurrection in Isfahan.

On Thursday, August 10, hundreds of young men fanned out from Pahlavi Square in Isfahan chanting antiregime slogans. They invaded banks, forced out staff and customers, and "proceeded to pour benzine and set the banks on fire." Police responded with tear gas, firing rounds into the air to disperse demonstrators, but the rioters regrouped, took back the avenues, and tossed bags full of benzine at passing army trucks. In the evening and through the next eighteen hours this most elegant and sophisticated of Iranian cities passed into the hands of the mob. Amid scenes of complete anarchy the barricades went up and cinemas, banks, department stores, and hundreds of private cars and rescue vehicles were set alight. For the first time, small bands of heavily armed men trained in Palestinian terror camps in Lebanon and Yemen engaged the security forces in running gun battles. Five police officers died of bullet wounds, and the streets were turned into deadly crossfire zones. Hospital emergency rooms were jammed with the dead and the dying. With Isfahan on the verge of becoming a second Beirut, the Shah had no choice but to send in the troops. Martial law was declared and a thirty-day curfew imposed. At 8:00 p.m. on Friday evening, with plumes of smoke billowing into the night sky, helicopter gunships clattered overhead and Chieftain tanks rumbled along Isfahan's broad avenues trailed by hundreds of heavily armed soldiers. But even as calm returned to Isfahan, protesters in Shiraz demonstrated outside the New Mosque, scaling its high towers and hurling projectiles onto police lines below. Other rioters set fire to motorcycles, mopeds, bicycles, and cars, turning them into explosives and ramming them through police lines. The security forces opened fire, causing "a number of deaths" and many injuries.

Foreign tourists were caught up in the drama when several hundred rioters launched an assault on Isfahan's luxurious Shah Abbas Hotel, running for cover as the mob threw bricks through windows and tossed an incendiary device into the hotel's fabled Golden Hall, which quickly caught fire. Bruce and Pat Vernor, who eight months earlier had greeted the Pahlavis at Mehrebad Airport, were on a driving tour of the south when they stopped for the night in Shiraz. From the streets outside they heard the pop of firecrackers. The next morning the couple and their daughter

Eileen were at the checkout desk and about to set off for Isfahan when they learned that the firecrackers had actually been shots. Bruce was handed a newspaper "that said someone had thrown a firebomb through the window of the Shah Abbas Hotel where we had reservations." He called ahead and was told it was still safe to travel to Isfahan but to avoid the area around the bazaar, which was surrounded by tanks. A run-in with Iranian soldiers left the family sufficiently shaken up to end the trip early and head back to Tehran. "For us, August was when the trouble began," said Bruce.

ISFAHAN WAS LIKE a distress flare that lit up the night sky. Over the next several days a wave of riots struck major urban centers, including Tehran, Abadan, Ardebil, Kermanshah, Khoramabad, Qazvin, Tabriz, Arsanjan, Arak, Ahwaz, and Qom. "In Babol on the Caspian Sea," reported *Time*, "a mob tied to prevent the opening of a touring Italian circus, retreating only after its owner threatened to let loose his lions on the crowd."

As the pace of unrest escalated, so too did the level of violence directed at foreigners. On Sunday evening, August 13, a man carrying a black bag walked into the Khansalar Restaurant, a favorite Tehran nightspot for American and European diners. He surveyed the room and strode out back, where the kitchen and bathroom were located. Seconds later, a blast and fireball tore through the building, collapsing walls, hurling debris, and burying patrons beneath rubble. With the lights knocked out, survivors clawed their way to safety amid horrific scenes. "While I was going to help the injured I felt myself walking on something soft," said one survivor. "I touched it to find that it was an injured woman's body. You could see men, women, and children panicking and running here and there, trying to find the door out. The bodies of many whose limbs were nearly torn off could be seen lying on the ground with blood and destruction all around." Another bloodied victim who staggered over twenty bodies to make his escape noticed that "the heads of two of them were split and blood could be seen oozing out."

With Ramadan under way, the anniversary of Operation Ajax fast approaching, and mosques gearing up for the birthday celebrations of Imam Ali on August 24–26, August was the month when Shariatmadari's religious moderates were overwhelmed by Khomeini's extremists. August was also the hottest month of the year, a time when the streets of northern Tehran's wealthy enclaves emptied. That meant the men and women who ran the kingdom—the Shah and Shahbanou, the prime minister and his cabinet, senior generals and leading industrialists—were absent during the critical few weeks when Khomeini's men made their power play. Only too late, the few who remained behind became aware of the southern suburbs rising from the desert floor to start the inevitable advance toward the northern foothills. "August was the crucial time," recalled an Iranian physician who ventured into southern Tehran during the hot season. "There was a very feverish atmosphere. Preachers were in the mosques giving fiery speeches. Thousands of people attended, some hanging from trees outside mosques and halls. People were excited at the prospect of 'change.' That was the cry, 'We want change.'" "Rhetoric and crowd activity in Tehran" was on the increase as religious leaders prepared to commemorate the death of Imam Ali, the U.S. embassy reported on August 17. "Eyewitness Iranian source tells us there has been almost continual minor upheaval in south Tehran for past seven to ten days. Ayatollahs at major mosques have become more anti-government and in some cases anti-foreign and directly anti-American." In one incident, demonstrators were chased to the corner of Takht-e Jamshid and Old Shemiran Road, just six blocks from the embassy grounds. The embassy obtained documents linking a prominent Khomeini follower, Ayatollah Yahya Nouri, to a virulent campaign of anti-Semitism. "Even before the inception of Zionism, Jews have never lived in peace and harmony with their neighbors," Nouri preached. "Due to their transgression and hostility to others they were always rejected by society." Without naming the Shah, Nouri condemned governments in the region that dealt with Israel, "the aggressive enemy," and insisted Muslims boycott Coca-Cola, which was "a big Jewish company." He urged the devout "to avenge Jewish bloodletting in Lebanon by an 'eye for an eye.'"

The simmering unrest was brought to the attention of Reza Ghotbi, who had stayed at his post at National Iranian Radio and Television. He dispatched correspondents to southern Tehran to keep an eye on the mosques and then report straight back to him. Their accounts made for chilling reading. "People would break their fast before going to the mosques," he recalled. "When they came out they were shouting for Islam and against the Shah. My reporters were shocked. They made some interviews and smelled alcohol—these were very secular people, leftists, communists, so they had the protection of the holy place." For the mullahs to find common cause with socialists, atheists, and anarchists who drank alcohol and ate during the day in Ramadan could mean only one thing: something big was about to happen.

Minister of Women's Affairs Mahnaz Afkhami was so worried she went to see Court Minister Hoveyda. "Things are terrible," she told him. "I feel really scared."

"Why don't you go to the prime minister?" said Hoveyda.

"I've tried. I tried the Princess. Now I'm trying you. You have access to the Shah."

Hoveyda picked up the phone and dialed Nowshahr. Afkhami listened as he relayed her concerns over the phone to the Shah, though without mentioning her name. "He is going to have a press conference when he gets back," Hoveyda assured her.

"Does he want us to prepare anything for him?"

"No. He will do it himself."

ON AUGUST 11, the same day tanks rolled into Isfahan, White House national security adviser Zbigniew Brzezinski received a written report from Professor William E. Griffith, an old friend who had recently returned from a visit to Iran and the region. Griffith was an expert on communism and a scholar whose opinions Brzezinski greatly respected.

Since late May Brzezinski had been following news of the troubles in Iran prepared for him by his Iran desk officer, Gary Sick. Griffith's deeply pessimistic analysis went one step further, reflecting the outcome of his meetings in Tehran with officials including the Shah, Prime Minister Amuzegar, Iranian government officials, and foreign diplomats. Griffith was that rare Cold War warrior who understood that something new was taking shape not only in Iran but also throughout the region. Crucially, he perceived that the real danger to the Shah was coming not from communism and the far left but from Islam and the far right. The Shah's liberal social and economic policies, he warned, were stoking an inferno:

> On balance, I should think the domestic situation [in Iran] is serious and the future of the dynasty is in question (this is *not* the view of the Embassy, and I saw no opposition leaders, but I am still of this view). The Shah began liberalization and is continuing it; the demonstrations are primarily fundamentalist Moslem; the new Prime Minister, Amuzegar, whom I saw, is impressive and committed to continue the liberalization; but the Shah (whom I also saw) seemed to be less so, and

I fear that the intelligentsia is largely alienated. . . . The Shah is, even more than usual, concerned about US steadiness of will; and the Soviets seem to him regionally successful and on the offensive.

Griffith urged Brzezinski to order up a fresh intelligence analysis of the situation in Iran and indeed throughout the Middle East. Second, he recommended that the White House publicly throw its weight behind the Shah's attempts at political reform. "The Middle East and indeed most of the Moslem world, is in the grip of a rising fundamentalist Islam," he advised. The main causes for religious fervor, he argued, were "strains of modernization and the perceived failure of both Western models, parliamentary democracy and Marxism. Thus the return to Islam is the current solution for the problem of identity." An Islamic resurgence posed a real threat to the president's foreign policy goals in the Middle East and especially his efforts to build peace between Israel and its neighbors: "A gloomy picture, in short, but there is no point in not realizing it—and in not continuing to try to prevent it coming true!"

Bill Griffith had never lived in Iran, did not speak or read the language, and had never been regarded as an expert on Islam or indeed the Middle East. As a result, Brzezinski read the memo with interest but ultimately decided not to act on it. "On the one hand, his warning was probably one of the first," said Brzezinski. "On the other, I knew he didn't speak Farsi and he was not an area specialist. So I decided his view was not decisive." Griffith's insights were also private, which meant no official follow-up was required or requested. To date, President Carter had not been briefed on the unrest in Iran. From the West Wing to Roosevelt Avenue, the consensus among U.S. officials was that the Shah had matters firmly in hand. "Iran is not in a revolutionary or even a pre-revolutionary situation," the CIA concluded in early August 1978. "There is dissatisfaction with the Shah's tight control of the political process, but this does not at present threaten the government. Perhaps most important, the military, far from being a hotbed of conspiracies, supports the monarchy."

In mid-August President Carter left town for a two-week white-water rafting vacation in the Rockies. Secretary of State Cyrus Vance was fully absorbed with preparations for the Egypt-Israel peace talks, set to start at Camp David in the first week of September. NSC Iran desk officer Gary Sick was away on leave for the rest of the month, and Ambassador Sullivan was enjoying his second month of vacation in Mexico. For the American public, the big story of the late summer was not Iran but the death of Pope Paul VI and the election of Albino Cardinal Luciani as John Paul I. Only in hindsight did it become clear that the last two weeks of August were the critical time when the fate of the Shah and the Iranian nation was decided.

KHOMEINI TOOK ADVANTAGE of Ramadan to mobilize his followers. The fatwa he issued was the moral equivalent of a declaration of war against the state. "The people will not rest until the decadent Pahlavi Dynasty has been swept away and all traces of tyranny have disappeared," he thundered. Free elections were pointless because "as long as the Shah's satanic power prevails not a single true representative of the people can possibly be elected." Khomeini ordered his followers in the army, security forces, and government to lay down their arms and abandon their posts. "Do your duty by Islam," he instructed. "Put yourselves where you belong, and you will be rewarded in this world and the next." The Marja went still further when he called for the murder of the head of state: "Death to the Shah is an Islamic slogan which all men of religion should take up."

In the Shia tradition a marja's followers were expected to emulate his teachings. Khomeini did not boast as many adherents as Grand Ayatollahs Shariatmadari or Khoi, but those he did have were more likely to share his fundamentalist interpretation of the Quran and emulate his conservative social views. They were, in fact, prepared to give their lives for him. Though most were poor and illiterate laborers, others were army conscripts or had risen from the ranks of the petty bourgeoisie to work in government as low-level civil servants. Still others were powerful in the bazaar, wealthy industrialists, society ladies, and even senior ranking army officers. Khomeini's fatwa tore at their consciences, as he surely knew it would. He was making it clear that now was the time of choosing—they were either with him or against him. Was their loyalty first to God or man, to the mosque or to the state? Soldiers who disobeyed Khomeini's fatwa were deemed legitimate targets for reprisal and attack.

Rattled by this latest escalation, the Shah finally awoke to the danger and sent General Moghadam to Qom for an urgent nighttime rendezvous with Shariatmadari's son-in-law Ahmad Abbasi, who restated the demands the Marja had presented earlier in the summer. The Shah was mulling whether to accept them when he received two American officials at Nowshahr. Charlie Naas escorted General Robert E. Huyser, deputy commander of U.S. ground forces in Europe, to brief the monarch on Huyser's proposed blueprint to reform the command and control system operated by the Imperial Armed Forces. The Shah broke the ice by raising the sensitive subject of unrest. He restated his commitment to liberalization but declared that the "recent vandalism" had to end. Turning to Huyser, he reminded the general that "he had predicted this development" in a conversation the two men had earlier in the year. The Shah admitted that the crisis "had come more quickly than he expected" and that although the situation "was very serious . . . he did not want me to become overly alarmed." He added that "he was not going to lose control." The Americans interpreted this to mean that the Shah was prepared to call out the army to prevent the collapse of law and order.

As the meeting broke up the Shah asked Naas if he could have a quiet word.

"Mr. Naas," he asked, "what do you think is going on in my country?"

"Your Majesty, we in the embassy have come to no particular conclusion about what is happening. We are following it very closely."

"But what do *you* think?"

"Your Majesty," Naas replied, "I agree with your assessment. You are opposed by the Red and the Black." Later, Naas admitted that his answer had been calculated not to offend: "As chargé, I was very conscious of not being ahead of government policy."

The Shah sensed as much. He looked at him doubtfully and signaled it was time to leave.

THE SHAH'S QUESTION to Charlie Naas was a tacit admission of his bewilderment at the rapid turn of events. Two years earlier, when he first decided to open up the political system, he had expected a certain amount of unrest. But this? Cities in flames? Mobs with knives? Suicide bombers blowing up restaurants packed with women and children? The King who prided himself on always having a plan was at a loss as to what to do. For the first time doubts crept in, and with the doubts came hesitancy, second-guessing, and bitterness. At Nowshahr, family and friends were startled to hear their host, always so quiet and confident, repeat the same question over and over. "The Shah was asking, 'What do you think is going on?'" said Elli Antoniades.

His unease was on display at the press conference held to mark his return to Tehran in late August after forty-two days away and on the eve of National Uprising Day. Drawing parallels with that earlier time, the Shah directed his fire at "Islamic Marxists," whom he accused of fomenting riots and for wanting to turn Iran into "Iranistan." "We offer the people the Great Civilization with all the benefits we have detailed," he said. "They offer the Great Terror." "But the situation is different now," he told his audience of newspaper editors. "As I said earlier . . . the patriots, the Armed Forces and I will not let them execute their plot." Reminiscing about the Mossadeq era, he conceded that he had taken a long time to act in 1953 because "perhaps the conditions of the time did not permit an alternative response. But the situation is drastically different now." For the first time he admitted to doubts about his decision to dismantle authoritarian rule. He had "considered riots to be the price of democratization" but "did not think this price would be so high." Many people in government "were already afraid of the consequences of political liberalization and asking the question 'Where are we going?'"

The Shah asked himself the same question. Still determined to win over the skeptics, he provided more explicit details of his road map to democracy. Liberalization would continue, and the first bills to be submitted to the Majles after the summer break would provide guarantees for freedom of speech, press, and assembly. The Rastakhiz Party would no longer hold a monopoly, and other political groups were free to form. Parliamentary elections would take place as scheduled next year, and opposition candidates could participate as long as they were prepared to swear the parliamentary oath of allegiance to the Throne and the Quran. Addressing the issue of corruption, the Shah announced that members of the Imperial Family were henceforth banned from government affairs and private business. Denying rumors of illness, he insisted he was in good health: "I have never felt better." He took a swipe at upper-middle-class Iranians fleeing the country, calling them "chicken-hearted." Their departure would only "cause house prices to fall even further." Asked what he might do if the riots continued, he left the door open to a temporary suspension of elections and civil liberties until order was restored. "If, despite all the civil, individual and political liberties they are to enjoy . . . they still refuse to quiet down, then what are we supposed to do? I do not need to spell it out. You can readily come up with the answer." Few reporters took him at his word—by now they sensed he was in full retreat. "Press noted this could mean change in liberalization plans but Shah saw it as reaffirmation of [his government's] decision to move forward despite heavy sledding," reported the U.S. embassy. "The press conference went badly," said Mahnaz Afkhami. "He lost an opportunity."

In light of the Ramadan riots, the Shah's decision earlier in the summer to send an envoy to meet with Imam Musa Sadr now assumed real significance. Behind the scenes, Shariatmadari and the moderates struggled to come up with a formula that would satisfy most ulama without humiliating the palace. They found inspiration from the Safavid period, when Persia's kings had shared power with the marjas. Modern-day Morocco offered another model in King Hassan, who had shown a canny ability to keep his country's clergy on his side. One idea was to ask the Shah to replace his prime minister with a statesman with impeccable religious credentials, "somebody with [the] confidence of both Shah and people." As early as mid-August the U.S. embassy reported to Washington that the moderates favored Senate president Jaafar Sharif-Emami for the post of prime minister "because he is a religious man himself and has solid political backing."

The religious moderates' most intriguing and creative proposal was that an invitation should be extended to Musa Sadr to return to the land of his birth to lead them against Khomeini. The Imam's attributes were obvious. He was a highly respected Shia theologian and had the personal skills to draw large crowds. He had once enjoyed the Shah's admiration and was known to favor Grand Ayatollah Khoi's opposition to a religious state. Worldly, tolerant, and a brilliant communicator, some in the clergy even dared hope that the Shah would appoint Musa Sadr to the post of new prime minister. "When the revolution began, many people said Musa Sadr knew more about the affairs of the world than Khomeini," said Hossein Nasr, Queen Farah's adviser on cultural affairs. "Musa Sadr was not known inside Iran either, but he was known in Iraq, the Arab world, and he knew the present day situation. He knew the ulama in Qom. To be frank, I thought it was an interesting idea. Musa Sadr had the experience and the exposure." The plan, he said, was for Musa Sadr to return to Iran "and keep the Shah on as a figurehead. I had heard it from younger ulama in Qom and in ulama circles in Tehran, from people involved in religious circles." The Imam would "establish a formal religious government and restore order. Khomeini would come back to Iran, go to Qom to live, and stick to scholarship. This was discussed with the generals. The Shah and Empress knew about the plan to put in Musa Sadr as head of government."

The moderates believed Musa Sadr was the only cleric capable of standing up to Khomeini and preventing what they feared was an inevitable slide toward civil war and massive bloodshed. "I have heard [the ulama] believed Musa Sadr could be an alternative as a leader," confirmed Hassan Shariatmadari. "Relations between Musa Sadr and my father were very good. He had the ambition to become the leader of Lebanon—he also wanted to become the leader of Iran. The Khomeini people feared him." "Musa Sadr was a threat to Ayatollah Khomeini," agreed Ali Kani. "Khomeini was scared of him."

Musa Sadr's admirers in Iran had every reason to believe he would accept an offer of leadership if it was extended. In early August in Beirut the Imam hosted an old friend, Ali Reza Nourizadeh, the political editor of Iran's *Ettelaat* newspaper. The two men reminisced about Iran, and Musa Sadr was brought to tears listening to tape cassettes of Marzieh, the Iranian chanteuse who sang traditional Persian music. He confessed that he had been so excited by Googoosh's recent tour of Lebanon that he had asked a friend to film the concert so he could watch it at home. The two men spent long hours talking about the troubles in Iran. "You don't know Khomeini," Musa Sadr told Nourizadeh. "He is a dangerous man." The Imam said he had recently asked Ahmad Khomeini to talk to his father and try to calm him. "You don't want Iran to become Lebanon," he had warned Ahmad. "He didn't want the Shah to fall," said Nourizadeh. "He was very worried about Khomeini's intentions."

With Iran and the region coming to a boil, Musa Sadr's friends worried about his safety. When he told them he had decided to accept Colonel Gadhafi's invitation to stop over in Tripoli before flying on to Rome in early September, they begged him to reconsider. King Hussein of Jordan and the president of Algeria suspected the Libyan leader had laid a trap. Gadhafi was "crazy," they told him, and prone to violence. Iranian diplomats sympathetic to Musa Sadr also advised him to cancel his travel plans. "Our ambassador in Syria told him not to go because Gadhafi might kill him," recalled Parviz Sabeti. But Musa Sadr was undeterred. Supremely confident in his powers of persuasion, he could not imagine that a Muslim head of state—not even Gadhafi—would dare harm one of Islam's most beloved and respected figures.

ON THE MORNING of August 19, National Uprising Day and the anniversary of Mossadeq's downfall, the editors of *Kayhan* published a special editorial that warned the country was "in a virtual state of war. What is taking place now is nothing less than an open, concerted and tenacious aggression [from the religious right]." "The Shah is on a tight rope—trying to minimize violence while channeling political conflict into [the] electoral realm," agreed Charlie Naas. The air was thick with tension. "Goose-stepping Iranian soldiers paraded in Tehran, and the government organized pro-Shah rallies in most major cities," reported the *Washington Post*. "The parades in Tehran drew crowds of mildly curious onlookers, but public enthusiasm for the display was visibly lacking. There was virtually no applause and the generally listless spectators did not join in the troops' shouts of 'Javid Shah' (Long live the Shah)."

To the south, residents of Abadan endured another miserable day of appalling heat, water shortages, and power blackouts. "More than half the doctors in Abadan have left, because of the intense heat," reported the press, "but a medical spokesman in the city said it had not caused any inconvenience because 150,000 other residents had left with them." Air-conditioned cinemas remained the preferred place of refuge from the heat and on Saturday evening the six-hundred-seat Rex Cinema was filled almost to capacity for a screening of the Iranian movie *The Deer*. Two months earlier, religious extremists had made an abortive attempt to bomb the Rex, and it was to prevent a second incident that the proprietor had taken the precaution of bolting the exit doors from the inside to prevent saboteurs from sneaking in unobserved. Halfway through the screening, ticket holders near the rear noticed a commotion behind them and smelled smoke. Out of the darkness a cry went up, "The cinema is on fire!"

19

THE GREAT TERROR

What did I do to them?

—THE SHAH

He will lead us straight into the abyss.

—GENERAL MOGHADAM

The cries from the back of the Rex Cinema auditorium set off pandemonium. "In total darkness," said a survivor, "I with the rest of the spectators was watching the beginning of the movie when we suddenly heard noise from the back seats and felt smoke and then saw flames . . . all in minutes. Soon all the spectators had found out the cinema was on fire. But darkness and panic caused some to die under the feet of spectators trying to escape. People cried, jumped over each other." Groping in the dark, the panicked crowd rushed to the emergency exits only to find them locked. Those who were not crushed to death or asphyxiated by toxic fumes were engulfed by a raging inferno. "It began at the corner near the top and soon spread everywhere," said another survivor. "Everybody was screaming and running around. But all the doors were locked and kept in place despite our frantic efforts to force them."

News of the tragedy quickly spread, and the streets around the Rex filled with anguished family members, friends, and neighbors who tried to force entry but were beaten back by the smoke, heat, and flames. "The cries for help were so pathetic that I could die hearing them," said one bystander. "There were hundreds watching a disaster take place, but there was very little they could do." The first fire crew arrived after twenty-five minutes to discover the closest fire hydrant had a broken knob, the second nearest was underground and covered by tiles, and the third lacked enough water pressure to be of any use. "The cinema was engulfed in the conflagration," said one firefighter injured by a falling brick. "I saw tongues of flames emerging from the air-conditioning ducts. We managed to reach the upper floor and extinguish the fire near the lavatories. All the entrance doors remained shut." Rescuers successfully pried open one door, pulled several survivors to safety, and then ran in. "We raced to the rear of the cinema and while my colleagues directed water hoses on the fire, I used a pickaxe to unhinge the door. I gave a loud call above the din of the raging fire but no one, not a single soul moved forward. There was no movement among the doomed audience, only whining and whimpering, terribly muffled, as if from the bottom of a sepulcher." The firemen were confronted with a hellish scene. "Several rescuers collapsed in nervous hysteria when they gained entrance to the charred building," said a witness. "For many the greatest fear was that those unrecognizable heaps of flesh lying on the floor may have been their friends, their relatives, people they knew."

One of the few survivors was Hossein Takbalizadeh, an unemployed welder, heroin addict, and recent convert to fundamentalist Islam. The day before the fire he had left a drug treatment facility and met up with three friends affiliated with the local chapter of the Khomeini underground. They were under orders to carry out a sabotage operation to mar the formal ceremonies marking August 19, 1953, and National Uprising Day. Though Takbalizadeh had been out on the streets for only a few hours, he agreed to help the others set fire to the nearby Soheila Cinema. Fortunately for the patrons inside, the solvents used in the attack failed to explode. The next day, the four men went to a field on the outskirts of town to test and strengthen the fuel. They drove back into town in the evening only to find the Soheila's box office closed, and it was by chance they noticed that the Rex Cinema was still selling tickets to the eight o'clock screening of *The Deer*. The young men paid the entry fee, took their seats at the rear of the hall, and shortly after intermission slipped out into the lobby, where they sprinkled four small bottles of solvent around the concession stand and along the corridor leading to the main stairwell and only exit. Takbalizadeh proudly lit the first match and fled the scene. Passersby told police they saw a man running from the cinema as the fire took hold.

Iranians awoke to the appalling news that a single act of arson had caused the deaths of 377 men, women, and children; the final death toll reached at least 430. The inferno, the worst anywhere since the Second World War, was at the time modern history's deadliest recorded act of terrorism. "The holocaust stunned Iranians from all walks of life," reported one newspaper. "Radio Iran stopped its music programs and declared, 'The slaughter of innocents in Abadan has plunged all Iran into mourning.'" Around the country, cinemas closed their doors in sympathy. The streets of Abadan, said one visitor, "echo with scores of muezzins reciting the Quran, and many people on the streets are wearing black, weeping for relatives or friends lost in the holocaust. Thousands of people have attended memorial services and mosques are booked for the next 15 days for ceremonies for the dead." Businesses and homes were draped in black. Physicians treated hundreds of people for shock, and local pharmacies ran out of tranquilizers. Throughout Khuzestan Province, crowds gathered in town squares to demand that the authorities investigate the shoddy rescue effort and find and punish the culprits.

FEW DOUBTED THAT the arson was connected to the Ramadan riots. The date of the fire, National Uprising Day, was significant, and so too was the location—the Rex had been targeted once before by religious fanatics. Over the past nine months, Khomeini's revolutionary cadres had burned twenty-nine cinemas and hundreds of private businesses. The Marja's incendiary rhetoric criminalizing the Pahlavis, and the Islamic underground's use of solvents and explosives in crowded spaces, made the Rex Cinema a massacre waiting to happen. "The Khomeini people selected August 19 to show their power even though it was the day the regime had to show its strength," said Minister of the Interior Assdollah Nasr. The Rex Cinema was not the isolated act of a bunch of misfits but the centerpiece of a concerted terrorist campaign to destabilize and panic Iranian society and shake the foundations of the Pahlavi state. During Ramadan the authorities reported 123 bombs planted in public places and 184 acts of arson. There were 158 assaults and 3 armed attacks against police officers. At least 336 public and commercial buildings were attacked. In the same twenty-four-hour period that coincided with the Rex Cinema tragedy, religious fanatics set fire to a cinema in Mashad, killing three people, while in Shiraz another two were hurt in a cinema fire. Tehran's famous Hatam Restaurant, on Pahlavi Avenue, was badly damaged by arson, and the Baccara, the capital's biggest nightclub, was gutted.

Khomeini's agents were not deterred and may even have been encouraged by the slaughter in Abadan and subsequent chaos. Five days after the outrage an attempt by two men to plant explosives on the roofs of two cinemas in Shiraz was foiled by alert pedestrians who spotted them on the street below. Properties owned by Jews and Baha'i were assaulted. Southern Tehran's vegetable market was destroyed by arson, and three children were injured when their family's furniture workshop was firebombed. Elsewhere in the capital, arsonists destroyed a brewery, a mob threw rocks at a school for intellectually handicapped children, and the Darvish nightclub was firebombed. In Khorramshahr, a large blaze gutted the harbor authority's warehouse, a restaurant was bombed in Yazd, in Qouchan a private construction company was burned down, and near Elam a restaurant was set alight in forested parkland. "There is no question now that a stupendously savage and sinister hand is behind this spreading bloodbath," declared one newspaper in a front-page editorial. "There has been no dearth of violence since the political liberalization program started. Thousands of people have been hurt and hundreds killed. Now, the situation seems to be getting out of hand. Extremists on the Left and the Right seem to have gone berserk. The madness must be stopped in the most urgent manner possible."

Thousands of angry Abadan residents besieged police headquarters to demand expulsion from the city of preachers "who have urged people to go to mosques instead of to movies. The demonstrators put the brunt of the blame on the preachers." Observers noted that Khomeini was the only marja who did not immediately condemn the arson, and Grand Ayatollah Shariatmadari all but accused his rival Khomeini of culpability when he condemned "hot-headed people with whom we have no link whatsoever." He added, "Such a crime must be the work of Nazi-type people. We are still not sure who is responsible, but you can be certain that no true Muslim was in any way involved."

The Shah issued a ritual statement of condolence and urged the authorities to find and punish those responsible, but he blundered badly when he allowed his mother's annual garden party to mark National Uprising Day to proceed. Each year Queen Mother Taj ol-Moluk marked the anniversary of her son's return from exile with a lavish soiree in the gardens of Saadabad Palace. Court Minister Asadollah Alam would never have allowed the festivities to take place, but his successor, Hoveyda, feared crossing the eighty-two-year-old grande dame even in the midst of national mourning. Iranian public opinion was scandalized that the Pahlavi elite drank champagne while Abadan mourned its dead. "As always, the reception was sumptuous, the buffets beautifully laid out and the quality of food and drink was exceptional," recalled Hushang Nahavandi. "Two orchestras, one Iranian and one Western, played alternately. Gentlemen wore evening dress and ladies wore gowns and jewels which would have been the envy of the finest receptions in Paris and Rome." Inside the palace, however, the smiles were as tight as the gowns. The Shah "mingled with the guests, as was his wont. He seemed relaxed; but he was wearing his habitual mask, through which no hint of his real, inner misgivings could penetrate." The Queen struggled with her own emotions. Earlier in the day the government had rejected her offer to fly to Abadan to console families of the victims. Farah was told that her safety could not be guaranteed and that her presence in the stricken town might actually trigger riots. "Usually when there was a tragedy I would go down," she recalled. "I asked if I could go to Abadan and was told, 'No.'"

For three days Khomeini, with his usual flair for the dramatic, maintained a stony silence. When he did finally speak out it was to sensationally turn the tables and accuse the Shah of orchestrating a massacre. "This heart-rending tragedy is intended by the Shah to be his masterpiece, to provide material to be exploited to the utmost by his extensive domestic and foreign propaganda apparatus," Khomeini declared. "Who benefits from these crimes other than the Shah and his accomplices? Who is there—other than the Shah—that has ever enacted savage slaughter of the people every now and then, and presented us with barbaric scenes such as this?" Khomeini warned that "the regime may commit similar savage acts in other cities of Iran in the hope of defiling the pure demonstrations of our courageous people, who have watered the roots of Islam with their blood." The crime was the Shah's devilish attempt "to show the world— and in particular the Americans—that the Iranian people are not ready for his program of 'liberalizing' the political atmosphere." Khomeini's protégé Ayatollah Yahya Nouri, architect of a campaign of virulent anti-Semitism, was also quick to claim the moral high ground when he denounced "the burning of human life" that "could only be regarded as inhuman in Islam." In mosques in the capital, sympathetic preachers read out an open letter repeating the smear of Pahlavi complicity, while to the east, in Mashad, a crowd of thirty thousand gathered at the Holy Shrine of Imam Reza to listen as the Shah's "crimes" were broadcast in lurid detail over loudspeakers.

With public emotions running high, Khomeini and Nouri succeeded in convincing many devout Iranians that the Shah had ordered the fire lit and then tried to shift blame onto the ulama. Public grief boiled over in Abadan, where ten thousand mourners packed the town cemetery. "Men, women and children poured earth on their heads and writhed around in the dust in scenes that even shocked and sickened hardened detectives and veteran crime reporters," reported one eyewitness. "Scores of ambulances, on standby to rush those overcome by grief to hospital, were very busy throughout the sorrowful ceremony." Fearing riots, the City Council barred police and firemen from the site and turned over crowd control to young Boy Scouts, who sobbed as relatives of the dead tore their hair, clothing, and leaped into grave pits, begging to be buried with friends and family. Newspaper reporters and photographers ran for their lives when the mob turned on them, leaving several beaten and bloodied. Mourners rioted in the streets of downtown Abadan, smashing up banks and store-fronts and lighting fires. Faced with a second major urban insurrection in as many weeks, the Shah made it clear to his security chiefs that he wanted no civilian casualties, and the police were instructed to fire live rounds over the heads of the crowd. When he was informed that order had been restored without loss of life, the Shah telephoned Khuzestan governor Baquer Nemazie to express his gratitude.

Iranians braced for more attacks to coincide with the birthday of Imam Ali, and the security forces instituted bag checks in government ministries, hotels, restaurants and public venues. Worried officials noticed that with each passing day the crowds of unruly demonstrators and rioters were swelling in size. Protests that one month earlier might have drawn dozens or even hundreds of people now attracted thousands. With Savak emasculated, the army confined to barracks, and the police holding fire, the crowds lost their fear and took over the streets. On the evening of Friday, August 25, demonstrators in Qom waving black flags clashed with police and lit fires around the town, prompting firemen to turn their hoses on the crowds. The next day, when several thousand demonstrators chanted slogans and hurled bricks, stones, and explosives, police were ambushed by men tossing Molotov cocktails out of house windows. The unrest quickly spread to the streets of the capital, where a crowd rioted outside a mosque in southern Tehran, while in Shemiran a group of thirty men set fire to a branch of Bank Saderat. In nearby Karaj, rioters assaulted a cinema and broke bank windows. To the south, zealots in Abadan burned the grand bazaar to the ground and destroyed several hundred stores. Police in Hamadan fired live rounds into the air to clear the streets, and a terrorist was killed when his bomb prematurely exploded. Violent unrest was reported in another half dozen cities and towns.

REZA GHOTBI WAS in Vienna when Cinema Rex burned down. "I cut my stay short and went back because of the government's reaction," he remembered. He was alarmed when Information Minister Dariush Homayoun all but dared the public to challenge the government's version of events.

Back in Tehran, the Queen's cousin attended meetings where government officials and courtiers discussed the worsening security situation. Everyone was waiting for a signal from the Shah to do *something*. "At many different meetings people would say, 'We hope he knows what he's doing,'" said Ghotbi. "If he is not reacting it is because either (1) Carter and the Americans have told him to democratize or (2) people thought he was intriguing and would come back even harder. People wouldn't even believe there wouldn't be a reaction." Ghotbi agreed with the others that "something has to be done." Still, he recalled that "no one at that time except some in the military said we need a military solution." He joined Hushang Nahavandi and Savak's General Hossein Fardust at a meeting in Court Minister Hoveyda's office. They wanted to know what was going on. "Things are going awry," said Fardust, "and I hope His Majesty knows what he is doing because it is not possible he has no plan. I hope you, Mr. Hoveyda, will ask him and tell us so that we have nothing to fear. Otherwise things are going to end badly."

AMERICAN DIPLOMATS IN Tehran remained curiously detached from the crisis. "We were not panicking in August," explained Deputy Chief of Mission Charlie Naas. "With Rex, all we could do was report it and the different explanations for it. We thought the Savak story [of culpability] was weak. It was a terrible tragedy—it boggled my mind that anyone could say the Shah did it. We did not recognize it as such a severe blow." Still, Ambassador Sullivan's first day back at the embassy after his summer on the Mexican riviera coincided with the mass burial in the Abadan cemetery. Sitting on his desk at the top of a stack of papers was a memorandum written by John Stempel describing the dreadful events of recent weeks. The headline he wrote reflected the somber mood: "While You Were Away . . . the place really didn't turn to crap, but it might have looked like it."

ISRAELI DIPLOMATS, BY contrast, saw the Rex Cinema as the decisive turning point in the Shah's fortunes. After deciding that the Shah's reluctance to use force meant he was finished, Ambassador Uri Lubrani, who was about to return home to accept a new diplomatic assignment, requested the Foreign Ministry to start drawing up emergency plans for a wholesale evacuation of Israeli nationals. The Israelis were also acutely sensitive to the panic sweeping Iran's Jewish community. Ayatollah Nouri's campaign of anti-Semitism had awakened the beast. "Some of the slogans say 'Jews out of Iran,' while others blame the Shah for being a 'Zionist stooge' and not supporting the Arab Muslim cause," reported the *Jerusalem Post*. Propaganda leaflets were distributed in the oil fields "calling on Iranian oil workers to stop working on oil production to Israel." Iranian Jews followed the example of the Armenian Christian population by drawing up evacuation plans, selling property, and sending wives and children to safety abroad. "Many of those who have already left are well-to-do families who have settled in either North America or Western Europe," reported the *Post* on August 25. "Some of them have been operating various businesses abroad for some time in preparation for such an eventuality."

Confounded by the pace of events, Sullivan visited Lubrani, who "expressed concern that Jews will be the next target of Muslim fanatics." When the American asked him to describe what he thought was happening, Lubrani's deputy interjected. "It's a revolution," he said, a remark that prompted his boss to look at him as if to say, "Shut up."

THE TUMULTUOUS EVENTS of August 1978—the Ramadan rising, the Isfahan insurrection, and the fire at the Rex Cinema—ended any hope the Shah had for a peaceful transition to Western-style democracy. For the first time in twenty-five years he began to have doubts about his mission. Visitors to the palace noticed he was more subdued and reflective than usual. The old confidence and buoyancy were gone. "When the King came back from Nowshahr he wouldn't talk much," said Reza Ghotbi. "He was not active in conversations. He would listen much more than he talked. I went to the residence and you could feel some sort of isolation."

He could no longer dismiss the unrest on the streets as the work of a few terrorists and malcontents—the sight of crowds massing in late August suggested broader opposition to the regime and a more personal rejection. The question he asked friends and family members changed from, "What do you think is going on?" to "What did I do to them?" He succumbed to feelings of guilt, self-pity, and bitterness, and on his worst days he lashed out at family members, advisers, and ministers, wondering who among them he could trust. At other times he blamed the Iranian people for behaving like spoiled children—if they no longer wanted him then they could run the country on their own and see what happened. In late August, Prime Minister Amuzegar offered a disturbing insight into his agitated state of mind. "If the people are so ungrateful, His Majesty may leave," Amuzegar warned General Moghadam. He repeated the remark to shocked cabinet ministers. No one needed to be reminded that the Shah had left Iran under similar circumstances once before.

Disoriented by events, the Shah miscalculated when he lurched from one extreme to another. He abandoned his plan for a gradual transition to democracy, deciding instead to give the people what they wanted now by simply lifting the lid off. "In the past few days that I have been back in Tehran," Ambassador Sullivan informed Washington, "it has become clear to me that the Shah has made a fundamental political decision, as announced in his Constitution Day speech, to transform his authoritarian regime into a genuine democracy. He has reached this decision as a result of his own intellectual convictions, because he feels Iran has become too complex and too volatile to govern through the current processes of benevolent authoritarianism. He therefore feels that the only way to preserve the integrity of the country is to change the political system, even if that change puts the monarchy at risk. Indeed, he realizes that, unless the system changes, the monarchy is predictably doomed."

Sullivan explained that the Shah believed that events were forcing his hand and that he was moving faster than he ever intended or indeed wished to open up the political system. "The Shah had not made his dramatic decision in a burst of exhilaration," wrote the ambassador. "He is remorseful, morose, nervous and suspicious. His game plan, which he nurtured in such confidence for two decades, has had to be scrapped. He has little confidence in the wisdom or the responsibility of the Iranian people even though he has decided to put his faith and that of his country in their hands. He fears that everyone will perceive him as slipping and then in the best Middle East tradition join in kicking him as he goes down. He especially fears the United States will do this." Sullivan warned that the Shah's enemies "will try to frustrate political liberalization and prove that the Shah's 'democracy' is a farce by taking to the streets and forcing the Shah to institute a martial law regime. . . . The fabric of this society, under the stress of a genuine democratic opportunity, may disintegrate and the Shah may feel he has to reimpose strict political controls. That sort of thing has happened before and the US assisted in the reestablishment of internal security." Senior Iranian officials were themselves unsure what to do or how to react. Even those who have encouraged the Shah in that direction "are nervous, because they have never played the democratic game before and they are not sure how things will turn out. . . . They are nervous and afraid of 'that great beast,' the people of Iran."

The Shah announced a new raft of concessions that signaled weakness to supporters and opponents. He canceled the controversial deal to allow the burial of nuclear waste in the Kavir Desert, sent his brothers and sisters and their families out of the country, and agreed to sack Jamshid Amuzegar as prime minister and replace him with Jafar Sharif-Emami, the Senate president who he was told enjoyed good relations with Shariatmadari and other senior ulama. He had chosen poorly. Sharif-Emami was a lackluster politician widely suspected of skimming profits from the assets of the Pahlavi Foundation, which managed the Imperial Family's wealth. The foundation's portfolio of investments, which he oversaw, included many of the same casinos and hotels that were now under attack from Muslim fundamentalists. Even the Shah's most devoted followers reacted with shock and amazement when they heard that he was on the verge of demanding Amuzegar's resignation in favor of Sharif-Emami's appointment.

On the morning of Thursday, August 24, Hushang Nahavandi, who aspired to the prime ministership himself, drove to Saadabad Palace to find out if the rumors were true. He arrived just as a clearly distressed General Moghadam left the Shah's suite. When the two men saw each other, Moghadam approached and asked Nahavandi if he could secure an immediate audience with the Queen. Farah listened as the general begged her to help him stop Sharif-Emami's appointment. "I permit myself to intercede with you about this appointment, because it is the worst which could possibly have been made, at this critical juncture in the nation's affairs," begged Moghadam. "Sharif-Emami is not the man for this situation.

Not only does he have no following, popular or otherwise, but he has an abominable reputation. His appointment as prime minister—it is my duty to tell you—is nothing less than catastrophic. He will lead us straight into the abyss; but there is still time to stop it. Please, Your Majesty, persuade the Shahanshah to reconsider."

Farah picked up the phone and dialed her husband's office. "Sire, your chief of Savak is here, begging me to throw myself at your feet and implore you by no means to make Mr. Sharif-Emami your head of government," she explained. "His reputation is execrable and he's the most dangerous choice you could have made at this time." Listening in silence to what the Shah had to say, she put down the phone after a few minutes and looked at her two visitors. "Unfortunately," she said, "there's nothing to be done about it as far as I can see."

Outside the Queen's office, Moghadam vented his frustration. "I just can't believe it. How can the Shah be so ill informed? Sharif-Emami! There will be a general insurrection within two months! I've done all I can to stop the worst from happening—you are my witness to that—and even now I beg you to keep trying."

The Queen tried again, too. She favored Nahavandi for the job of prime minister. Though his arrogance alienated many of his colleagues, Farah recognized his credentials as a liberal reformer loyal to the throne. "I thought Nahavandi should be prime minister but His Majesty wouldn't have him," she recalled. "He said, 'Is Nahavandi *again* trying to become prime minister?' He didn't like him."

Reza Ghotbi made a similar appeal. "I proposed Nahavandi as prime minister," he recalled. The Shah rebuffed him. "Nahavandi?" he queried. "He has no weight." To emphasize his point the Shah held out his hands, palms facing upward, and raised and lowered them in quick succession: "The Shah took [Nahavandi] as a loyal, good intellectual who could be of interest as a contact between the palace and scholars and intellectuals."

ON SUNDAY, AUGUST 27, the palace confirmed that Jafar Sharif-Emami would replace Jamshid Amuzegar as Iran's new prime minister. "I thought it was a joke," recalled Iran's ambassador to Washington Ardeshir Zahedi. "I didn't take it seriously. It wasn't possible. His name was 'Mr. Five Percent'—he was totally corrupt." Princess Ashraf also was "astonished at the choice. I felt the situation called for a stronger leader." She told Parviz Radji, Iran's ambassador to the Court of St. James's, that "for us—and by us I mean the Pahlavis—it is virtually over, it being only a matter of time before a republic based on Islamic principles is proclaimed. His Majesty will never agree to be King in a country where Khomeini or Shariat-madari exercise the ultimate power. He will never have anything to do with the mullahs." The Princess criticized "the Iranian people who are incapable of gratitude after all that my father and brother did for them."

On Sunday, the day of Sharif-Emami's appointment, the new prime minister's televised speech to the nation included the admission that the reforms of the White Revolution "had been too rapid and uncoordinated, resulting in an unprecedented spread of corruption and unsuitable bureaucracy." His remarks signaled that the Pahlavi state was in full retreat before the Islamist onslaught. The new government replaced the Imperial calendar with the Muslim lunar year—Iranians found them-selves plunged back into the year 1357—and Mahnaz Afkhami's Ministry of Women's Affairs, the first in the Muslim world and one of the only ministries of its kind anywhere, was abolished. Bars, clubs, and liquor stores were shut down, copies of *Playboy* and *Penthouse* were hurriedly pulled from store shelves, and for the first time since 1963 Iranian news-papers were permitted to display Khomeini's portrait and mention his name on their front pages. "The Club Discotheque, normally a place of frenzied activity for Iran's newly rich upper middle class, was shuttered," reported *Time*. "Television stations broadcast readings from the Quran and Islamic sermons in place of *Cannon* and *Police Story*. It seemed that Iran's uncertain advance into the 20th century had stumbled again, and that the nation had been thrust back into the dark Islamic puritanism of the 18th century." Khomeini's campaign of intimidation combined with Sharif-Emami's concessions brought a sudden, ignominious end to the Pahlavi Dynasty's half-century effort to balance Iranian religious tradi-tions with secular government and Western-style modernization.

Two days earlier, Imam Musa Sadr had arrived in Tripoli on the first stop of a three-week trip scheduled to take him to Rome and then on to West Germany, where he planned a secret meeting with the Shah's envoy. Musa Sadr was accompanied by two close associates, his aide Sheikh Mohammad Yaqub and Abbas Badreddin, a Lebanese journalist assigned to cover the trip for the Beirut press. Shortly before his departure he had written an essay in France's *Le Monde* that described his view of events back in Iran. In "The Call of the Prophets" the Imam drew an idealistic portrait of different classes and social groups joining together to fight injustice. The language and spirit of the article reflected mainstream Shia thinking and were in keeping with French Enlightenment traditions. They provided a real contrast to Khomeini's message of fundamentalism and violence. Where he used the word "revolution" to describe the troubles, Musa Sadr was referring to a revolution of ideas and not politics. Though careful to acknowledge the guiding role of "the great Imam Khomeini" in leading the opposition to the Pahlavi state, nowhere did Musa Sadr personally condemn the Shah or advocate the replacement of the monarchy with religious rule. Senior clerics often cloaked their opinions in carefully phrased sentences, and Musa Sadr's essay, written to assuage the doubts and suspicions of men such as Ahmad Khomeini and Abolhassan Banisadr, actually left open the door to rapprochement with Niavaran.

Musa Sadr and his companions were picked up at the airport in Tripoli and whisked to the al Shate' Hotel. Ayatollah Beheshti was expected to arrive shortly. Curiously, the Libyan press failed to mention the presence in their country of one of Islam's most revered leaders. Musa Sadr usually phoned his office and family when he was away, but on this trip they never heard from him. Journalist Badreddin's employers noted that he did not file a single news dispatch during his stay in the hotel. Gadhafi finally consented to receive Musa Sadr on the evening of August 29–30, then begged off, pleading a busy schedule. Beheshti's party never arrived. Musa Sadr became impatient to leave—perhaps he realized he had walked into a trap after all—and at one o'clock on the afternoon of August 31, 1978, the trio was spotted by a group of Lebanese visitors in the lobby of their hotel. An aide to Yasser Arafat later confided to his contact in American intelligence, CIA Beirut station chief Robert Ames, what he was told happened next:

> Arriving at the Tripoli airport, Musa Sadr was escorted to the VIP departure lounge. In the meantime, Beheshti told Qaddafi over the phone to detain Musa Sadr by all means necessary. Beheshti assured Qaddafi that Imam Sadr was a Western agent. Qaddafi ordered his security force to delay Musa Sadr's departure. Qaddafi instructed that the imam should just be persuaded to go back to his hotel. But Qaddafi's security officers accosted Imam Sadr in the VIP lounge and addressed him disrespectfully. An argument ensued, and the imam was roughed up and thrown into a car. Things had gotten so out of hand that the imam was taken to a prison.

In Beirut, one of the Imam's friends passed in the street Mohammad Saleh Hosseini, the founder of the Farsi Brigade, which trained Iranian guerrilla fighters in Lebanon. Hosseini knew Musa Sadr and enjoyed good relations with Colonel Gadhafi. When Hosseini mentioned his intention to fly to Tripoli to attend Gadhafi's festivities, the Imam's friend asked him to pass on his greetings to Musa Sadr. Hosseini fixed him with a hard stare and without explanation said, "Musa Sadr is gone."

ON AUGUST 29, while Musa Sadr cooled his heels in a hotel room in Tripoli, the Shah and Queen Farah received Chinese Communist Party leader Hua Guofeng at Saadabad. The first ever trip by a Chinese Communist leader to Iran couldn't have come at a worse time. Security was so tight that the usual ride from the airport in a gold coach was scrapped and the two leaders drove to the Shahyad Monument by car, and from there flew by helicopter the short distance to Golestan Palace. "Security around Hua's Golestan Palace guest residence in teeming South Tehran, a short distance from the teeming Bazaar area, was drumtight to prevent the approach of any demonstrators," reported the *Washington Post*. They came anyway. An evening rally drew thousands of protesters to downtown Tehran. They attacked a bank and a cinema, lit fires in backstreets, evaded police lines to block traffic, and hurled burning garbage cans.

At Niavaran the Shah, Queen Farah, and their Chinese guests were halfway through their banquet dinner when the King was approached by an aide who whispered in his ear. The Shah thought for a few moments and then rose from the table and excused himself, unheard of behavior for someone so concerned with protocol. The Iranians in the room exchanged furtive glances—what could be so important that His Majesty would leave his own table during a state dinner? Several minutes later the Shah returned but instead of entering the dining room signaled to Prime Minister Sharif-Emami and General Moghadam to join him outside. Moghadam went to pick up his hat but the Shah made it clear it was not necessary. The two men listened in stunned silence as the Shah told them he had just taken a phone call from Saddam Hussein, the leader of Iraq, where Khomeini lived in exile: "Saddam Hussein was telling me, 'This mullah, Khomeini, is causing problems for you, and for me, and for all of us. It would be wise to get rid of him. But I need your agreement to take care of it.'" The Shah said that he responded, "I personally cannot make this decision. I have to speak to my responsible officials." He looked at

Sharif-Emami and Moghadam and added, "Saddam Hussein is waiting on the phone for my answer. I wanted to know your thoughts about this."

Sharif-Emami and Moghadam then conferred between themselves for several more minutes. Moghadam had nothing to say and preferred to hear the prime minister's opinion. Neither man wanted to take responsibility for the assassination of a marja. "Your Majesty," said Sharif-Emami, "you know better than anyone else what should be done."

The Shah looked at them and gravely said, "In my opinion, this is not the right action." He turned and walked back up the stairs to give his reply to Saddam. For the second time in fifteen years, the Shah saved the life of the man he knew wanted to destroy him. Then the Shah walked back down the stairs, returned to the dining hall, and resumed his seat as if nothing untoward had happened.

THE NEXT DAY, Wednesday, August 30, the Israeli ambassador Uri Lubrani recommended that his government establish an emergency committee to monitor the worsening unrest in Iran. Prime Minister Menachem Begin was at Camp David in the United States, negotiating a peace treaty with Egypt's president, Anwar Sadat, and President Carter, when his deputy back home authorized the Israeli security forces to start planning for the evacuation of Israeli citizens from Iran.

RESIDENTS OF THE northern Tehran enclave of Shemiran, "flooding back into town from Europe," spent the last evening of August at the newly refurbished Farahabad racetrack, mingling at the new Café de Paris restaurant, and taking in dinner and a fashion show. They looked forward to the splashy opening of the Tehran skyline's latest addition, the luxurious new twenty-six-story Hyatt Crown Tehran, which boasted a rooftop restaurant and nightclub, health club with sauna, and indoor swimming pool. Despite the closure of many watering holes and clubs around town, the autumn still promised another rich season in arts and culture entertainment. *The Merry Widow* was set to open at Rudaki Hall, and symphonic recitals of works by Corelli and Tchaikovsky were scheduled. The Museum of Contemporary Art featured exhibitions of modern Iranian works and Finnish and Italian architecture, and the poetry of Hafez was set to music by Shahin Farhat at the City Theater. The yacht club at Karaj Dam Lake hosted the final weekend of water skiing, and children's rides were still open at the Mini-City amusement park on Lashkarak Road.

If outward appearances counted, Shemiran residents were more focused on their social plans and preparing to resume work and school than the troubles several miles to the south. But the glamorous scene at Farahabad was deceptive, and an undercurrent of tension ran through the salons. Returning vacationers were shocked at the changes they encountered at home. Parts of the capital were deemed no-go zones, too unsafe to venture into even during the daytime. Their maids wore head scarves, interrupted their chores to pray, and recited quotes from the strange man they called "Imam Khomeini." Friends who had stayed in town through the summer sported Islamic garb and stopped returning their calls. One wealthy couple noticed something was amiss when their chauffeur failed to pick them up at Mehrebad Airport. They arrived home in a taxi to find that their palatial residence had been requisitioned by the servants, who hurled abuse and refused to follow instructions. Royalists found "the windows of their homes broken and dead cats thrown into their gardens." Queen Farah's friend Elli Antoniades returned from Nowshahr to discover the graffitied message "Death to the Shah!" scrawled across her front door, something that would have been unthinkable six months ago.

ON FRIDAY, SEPTEMBER 1, at the end of another long, grueling week of riots and civil unrest, Queen Farah decided her husband was in need of a change of scene. Fridays were the one day of the week set aside to entertain family and friends at the palace. "There was usually dinner for forty people," said Elli Antoniades. "It was the only time the King and Queen were free to be human beings. There was horseback riding and playing bridge with his friends." Today, however, Farah arranged an excursion by helicopter to Lake Latian, a popular boating and nature destination north of the capital. The Queen pleaded with the small party not to mention the troubles in conversation with her husband. "We felt the situation was serious," said Elli Antoniades, "but we were afraid to talk about it. I remember the Queen said, 'Whatever is happening, please don't discuss it. It stays here.'"

20

BLACK FRIDAY

By saying this he lost God's farr, and through
The world men's murmurings of sedition grew.
—*THE PERSIAN BOOK OF KINGS*

If my people don't want me, I will not stay by force.
—THE SHAH

On Monday morning, September 4, fifteen thousand people gathered in a dusty lot in the northern hills neighborhood of Qeitariyeh in Shemiran to mark Eid-e Fetr, the joyous last day of the monthlong Ramadan fast. After morning prayers and a speech by a clergyman who condemned the Shah and Prime Minister Sharif-Emami's government as un-Islamic, the large crowd began an eight-mile "long march" down into the center of town. Along the way they were joined by tens of thousands more demonstrators waiting at designated meeting spots, their way cleared by an escort of "Motorcyclists for Allah." Though the marchers refrained from calling for the overthrow of the Shah, they held aloft banners displaying Grand Ayatollah Khomeini's face and chanted slogans calling for their hero's return from exile. "Iran is our country!" "Khomeini is our leader!" "Why do government troops kill our people?"

Army units posted at key intersections along the route warily eyed the marchers. "At one point shortly after the march began, nervous troops surrounded by the teeming thousands seemed to get riled by some of the strong slogans they chanted," reported an Iranian journalist. "But the marchers quickly gathered around their army trucks, shouting 'Soldiers, brothers don't shoot brothers,' and 'We've got nothing against you if you've nothing against us.'" An army officer rose from the back of his truck and declared, "You are indeed our brothers but we have our duty to fulfill." The tension broke and the crowd threw flowers into the truck, a sight repeated again and again along the route. Many onlookers came out of their homes with melons and pitchers of water to quench the marchers' thirst. Not everyone was happy with the display of religious power, and many Tehranis, "clearly frightened by the size of the demonstration, stayed indoors, fearing the worst." As the procession moved through the busy commercial district, marchers appealed to curious bystanders to join them in celebrating the end of Ramadan, and by early afternoon a carnival atmosphere prevailed with an estimated two hundred thousand religious protesters, students, office workers, middle-class housewives, and pensioners exchanging flowers, kisses, and handshakes. The urge to participate proved irresistible. "I was in the middle of the crowd," said one middle-class Tehrani. "In front of me, behind me, to my side, wherever I looked I saw people in this great wave as drops in the sea, and I too was in the sea of this immeasurable gathering of the people of Iran. There was no 'I' there, we were nothing but 'We.'"

Visions of a "Persian Spring" with asphalt streets turned into a field of flowers heartened liberals and leftists, whose lingering fear of the mullahs was replaced by respect and admiration for the ones who had come out into the streets to defy the Shah and his army. Some even joined in the scattered chants of "Down with the Shah!" "The never before sighted demonstration of 'flower power' followed pleas for restraint from religious leaders and the police," wrote one newspaper. "They said it with flowers not the sticks and stones that have marked demonstrations after religious meetings throughout Ramadan. The sight of women and children putting garlands around the necks of troops and throwing flowers into their trucks could not help conjuring up the Vietnam peace demonstrations of the late 1960s in the United States." The news from the provinces was more ominous. Radio and television news bulletins reported violent clashes, with five demonstrators killed in Elam; two in Karaj; two in Khomein; and one death in Qom, where police struggled to contain a crowd of thirty thousand protesters.

In advance of Eid, moderate clerics and opposition leaders had counseled moderation. The Qeitariyeh rally had been approved only after the authorities received assurances from National Front spokesmen that "the meeting would be similar to such gatherings in past years and would not develop into street marches or demonstrations." Khomeini's men agreed to the plan and then simply hijacked it by flooding the venue with their followers and marching them down the hill into town to invade the bastion of middle-class commerce. The Shah paid the price for his steadfast refusal over the past two years to legalize political activity by the National Front and Liberation Movement, his more moderate opponents. At one time both groups might have channeled popular discontent into the political process. "These groups and 'parties' provide the basis of what could develop into a constitutional opposition, capable of helping Iran achieve a true system of democratic debate and accountability," noted one political commentator. "Ultimately they could serve the nation by helping create the moderate center that a truly balanced democracy needs in order to function effectively and smoothly." Instead, their absence from the political scene allowed the opposition movement to "fall into the hands of the extremist and radical groups." Prime Minister Sharif-Emami's decision two weeks earlier to end restrictions on political activity had caught them unprepared. With no time to raise funds or campaign, the moderate left was swamped by the rising groundswell of support for Khomeini and a more radical approach to forcing political change.

ON NIAVARAN HILL, palace courtiers reacted with shock and disbelief to news reports that as many as a million people were protesting in the streets of downtown Tehran. The Shah, who had spent the morning in a salaam ceremony with high government dignitaries, generals, and ambassadors, asked his bodyguard Colonel Djahinbini, commander of the Imperial Guard General Abdul Ali Badrei, and commander of Air Corps Forces General Manuchehr Khosrodad to fly over the demonstration, make a reconnaissance, and report back to him.

The Queen called for her helicopter, too. But rather than fly over the crowds, Farah made the sensational decision to set down among them. Her office contacted Eqbal Hospital, in southern Tehran, and hastily arranged a visit to the facility's cancer ward, so hasty indeed that officials had no time to assemble an official welcoming party or to mobilize crowds of supporters. Nonetheless, word quickly spread that she was en route, and by the time her chopper fluttered down onto the hospital grounds a throng had gathered to cheer the Queen as she made an impromptu walk along Bagher Khan Street. Farah was accompanied by Hushang Nahavandi, who had resigned his post as her private secretary and accepted a cabinet position in the new government. While the Queen toured the wards and spoke to hospital staff and patients, the crowd of admirers grew in number to several thousand. Farah waded into the throng amid cries of "Long live the Shah!," shaking hands, asking questions, and listening to concerns. Journalists on the scene said "the crowd was so large the helicopter pilot had trouble in picking up the Queen on her way out." Her gamble to join the Eid demonstration had paid off. "It was a remarkable, entirely spontaneous demonstration," recalled Nahavandi.

The Shah's distinctive helicopter, with its blue and white markings, flew low over Shah Reza Avenue so that Djahinbini, Badrei, and Khosrodad could provide an accurate assessment of the number of demonstrators. They estimated the crowd at well under half a million people but could still hear the chants of "Down with the Shah!" They returned to Niavaran and presented their findings to the Shah, who until now had convinced himself that popular discontent with the economy, corruption, and repression was not directed at him personally but at the government and bureaucracy. As the father of the nation he believed that he somehow floated above the fray in his role as guide and counselor, and for fifteen years he had flattered himself that he could wield executive power yet escape blame for executive failings. The Day of Eid changed everything. In a single, crushing instant he realized how wrong he had been, and that far from symbolizing unity the throne had become the major source of division in the land. The farr was gone and nothing he could do could bring it back.

By day's end the Shah had reached a momentous decision: he would quit Iran at the earliest possible chance and end his days in exile. He was not about to beg for another chance from an ungrateful people. "He was like a man who had lavished everything for years on a beautiful woman only to find she had been unfaithful to him all along," was how Court Minister Hoveyda described the Shah's mood of self-pity and grief. Yet the Shah's decision to end his mission was also an act of courage and tremendous self-sacrifice. He had never known a life other than public service, and his departure, he hoped, would restore peace and end disunity in Iran. "If my people don't want me," he said, "I will not stay by force."

IN EARLY SEPTEMBER Ardeshir Zahedi was visiting the Texas town of Lubbock, where Crown Prince Reza had begun training as an air force pilot, when Queen Farah called and asked him to telephone the Shah, who felt demoralized and needed encouragement. "The Shah was not in a good way," said Zahedi. Their conversation convinced him to hurry back to Tehran. He was already fielding calls from worried friends asking him to return home. "We need you," they said. "The Shah can't make up his mind and it's like 1953 again."

During a brief stopover in Washington, Zahedi tried to talk with CIA director Stansfield Turner and National Security Adviser Zbigniew Brzezinski, but found they were preoccupied with the Camp David peace talks. The Eid-e Fetr march had dispersed and the streets were quiet when Zahedi's plane landed at Mehrebad Airport late on the night of Monday, September 4. The ambassador was greeted by the Imperial Court's grand master of ceremonies, Amir Aslan Afshar, who briefed him as they drove through the darkened streets. Their car was spotted pulling up outside Saadabad's main entrance shortly before midnight. Queen Farah sent an aide down to Zahedi with a request that he talk to her before seeing her husband. Zahedi refused, insisting that he had come to see the Shah, but before he could make a start for the Shah's suite Farah appeared at the top of the stairs. She came down and pleaded with him to take care: "Don't say anything bad to His Majesty because he may kill himself."

Zahedi ran past her and up the stairs to the Shah's study. The Shah greeted him and brushed aside his offer to return in the morning. "No, we must meet now," he said, and the two men took their seats while tea was served. The ambassador's nerves were so frayed that when at one moment the Shah reached into his jacket pocket, Zahedi lunged—he feared his hand was reaching for a pistol. The Shah gave him a quizzical glance: "Ardeshir, this is a vitamin." But his next remark hinted at the emotional scenes that had preceded Zahedi's arrival. "The Queen is so upset she may jump out the window," he said. Zahedi was nonplussed. "Maybe you should push her out," he snapped. The ambassador blamed the Queen's liberalism for her husband's political collapse. The Imperial Court was in disarray, the generals were circling, and the ministers were unsure what to do. Everyone wanted to be in charge, but no one would make a decision. "If you have too many midwives, the child will be born without a head" was how Zahedi later put it. But Zahedi had also misread the situation. During his years in Washington he had lost touch with events and the street. He knew nothing of the Shah's cancer and like everyone else had been blindsided by the Shah's determination to liberalize his regime, cede power, and introduce genuine democratic reforms.

The next morning Zahedi met in secrecy with a delegation of senior courtiers, generals, senators, and parliamentarians, who begged him to assume a leadership role. "They recalled the crisis in 1963 and how they took their orders from Alam and not the Shah," said one participant. "They were looking desperately for a civilian to step in and tell them what to do. They were waiting for the Shah to act, and they wanted someone who was a hundred percent loyal to him." Zahedi also paid a quiet visit to southern Tehran to meet sympathetic clergy, who were prepared to support an army putsch to prevent Khomeini from seizing power.

Out of these meetings emerged Operation Kach, a top secret plan for a military coup d'état to overthrow Sharif-Emami's flailing government and smash Khomeini's rebellion. Named after a small town deep in Iran's desert interior, Operation Kach relied on the commanders of the three branches of the armed forces to take leadership positions. In phase one of the operation, the Shah and his family would retire to Kish Island, while the army, navy, and air force arrested moderate opposition leaders and detained them at the naval base on Kharg Island. Anyone who came out onto the streets to defy martial law would be rounded up and held in Tehran's Olympic stadium. "The police would have a list and the arrests would be made at the same time," said Zahedi. "We made sure the facilities had enough food, showers and toilets for a long stay." Religious extremists and Mujahedin and Fedayeen guerrilla fighters would be flown to holding pens at Kach, deep in the province of Baluchistan, near the border with Pakistan. The coup planners studied how to keep Iran's cities supplied with food and powered with electricity if workers went out on strike. Strict discipline would be imposed on the army. "Being tough, you have to look to your army," observed Zahedi. "But you have to keep your army off the streets to stop fraternization and not let the soldiers get infected by protests." Once order was restored, only after a suitable cooling-off period would the ruling junta implement far-reaching political reforms to return power to parliament, stamp out corruption, and hold free and fair general elections. The Shah's role would be reduced to that of a constitutional figurehead.

The coup plotters were overtaken by events when on Wednesday, September 6, Mujahedin commandos staged a daring early morning raid on a police barracks in Tehran. Armed with submachine guns, they killed the officer on duty and fled the scene, leaving behind a car bomb that failed to detonate. Fearing the assault was the prelude to an armed uprising, the government announced an immediate ban on all unauthorized rallies. The Islamists responded by staging a show of strength after dark, massing twenty thousand people at the southern end of Pahlavi Avenue and announcing plans to hold a second big rally, at Qeitariyeh field, on Thursday morning. In Shemiran, a Mujahedin terror cell tossed a pipe bomb under a bus taking eighteen British aerospace workers home. Though there were no injuries, news of the ambush spread fear throughout the foreign community. Everyone sensed events were rushing to a climax.

On Thursday morning, September 7, for the second time in three days tens of thousands of Khomeini supporters filled Tehran streets in a defiant show of force. This time they left the flowers at home and came in anger. The men wore white to signify their willingness to die, and the women marched in separate columns clad in black to proclaim their chastity and modesty. They chanted in support of an Islamic republic and cried "Death to the Shah!" The surging crowds alarmed Iranians and Americans alike. Across the road from the Tehran American School, where more than three and a half thousand American children went to class, high school senior Jonathan Kirkendall was taking a nap in his family's apartment when he began "dreaming of an ocean, the murmur of the waves driving themselves onto a sandy beach." He slowly awakened to hear "excited, noisy voices in the living room" and assumed his father, James, had returned home. He was very much mistaken when he realized that "in the distance came another noise. It sounded like the ocean that I had heard in my dreams, a low, ever present murmur, but louder and more rhythmic than the ocean. I got up from bed and went out onto the porch. I could make out a chant. It wasn't an ocean of water, but an ocean of people, and as I was later to see and hear carrying banners and chanting 'Death to the Shah!'" His mother, Libby, looked out the window at the flood of people surging past their home and shook her head in dismay. "The ball has started rolling," she told her son. "Not even the Shah will be able to stop it now."

The Shah stuck to his schedule and held a working lunch with Prime Minister Takeo Fukuda of Japan as though nothing were wrong. In private, however, the reports of mobs out on the streets left him "visibly shaken," reported Newsweek. "Obviously things had gone too far." In the afternoon he received a delegation of senior generals "who argued that the demonstrations were surely eroding his authority—and in turn the army's—and must be stopped." To press home their point the officers raised the specter of civil war. "We told the Shah, as Lincoln once said, a house divided cannot stand," said one participant. One of his fellow generals bluntly told the Shah that he faced an insurrection if he refused to take action: "It is against our military honor to stand the present situation."

Lost in the excitement of the day was the news that Queen Farah had appointed the Islamic scholar Hossein Nasr to replace Hushang Nahavandi as the new head of her Special Bureau. The appointment of such an eminent authority on Islam was hardly a coincidence. Nasr had studied in Qom's seminaries and was well known to the senior ayatollahs. In making the appointment, the Pahlavis wanted to send a signal to Qom that they were serious about reforming their household and Islamizing the monarchy. "Ayatollahs Shariatmadari and Khonsari favored me working with the Queen," said Nasr. "I accepted the position on the condition that there was an expectation on all sides of reform. The reforms included a complete change in the type of personality around the King and Queen. I wanted rid of morally decadent people." Nasr understood that if the Shah faltered then it would be Farah, in her capacity as Regent, who would wield power until Crown Prince Reza came of age. He envisioned his job as building "a bridge between the monarchy and the ulama who wanted to head off the unrest. My office became the center of action." In his talks with the moderate ulama, Nasr drew on the Safavid era for inspiration. "Nasr could be the bridge between the clergy and the Court," said his friend Reza Ghotbi. "He had the idea of an Islamic monarchy, something like in Safavid times. It could have been a good solution, bring back the old-fashioned Safavid-era monarchy."

While Tehran shook, Princess Ashraf boarded a flight from Alma-Ata, the capital of Soviet Kazakhstan, where she had attended a meeting of the World Health Organization. After hearing of the latest unrest she decided to defy her brother's admonition to stay outside the country. On arrival at Mehrebad, the Princess learned that roads to the north were blocked by demonstrations and that Saadabad Palace could be reached only by helicopter. "As I flew over the Shahyad Monument, I saw that one corner was completely dark," she recalled. "A moment later I realized this black mass was a mass of Iranian women, women who had achieved one of the highest levels of emancipation in the Middle East. Here they were in the mournful black chador their grandmothers had worn. My God, I thought, is this how it ends? To me it was a little like seeing a child you had nurtured suddenly sicken and die." Her private secretary noticed the stricken look on her face. "Why aren't we doing anything about it?" she asked him. As soon as they landed she went straight to see her brother, who assured her everything was under control.

Court conservatives were relieved to hear that the Shah's feisty twin sister, who had played an important role in defeating Mossadeq twenty-five years earlier, was back in town. Anxious to gain her support for Operation Kach, a small group came in the evening to Ashraf's residence and petitioned her to support their plan for a crackdown. The men in the room included the commander of the Imperial Guard, General Badrei; courtiers; and an industrialist who offered to raise funds and another who promised to turn out the crowds. Ashraf expressed shock when the plotters suggested her brother should retire to Kish Island and let them get the job done. "His Majesty is in control," she reassured them—he had told her so himself. The men in the room vehemently disagreed. "The situation is getting out of hand," they told her. The conspirators left the Princess without obtaining a firm commitment of support.

Shortly before seven o'clock, Iranian guests attending the Japanese prime minister's cocktail reception froze when Hushang Nahavandi, the only government minister in attendance, was handed a note and abruptly excused himself without explanation. Clutching the piece of paper, he rushed to his car and drove to an emergency meeting of national security advisers who included the prime minister, the cabinet, and generals. Nahavandi arrived to find the group learning details of a plot by Khomeini's agents to seize power in a coup. Apparently emboldened by their show of force on the streets, the Coalition of Islamic Societies had decided to mass their followers in Jaleh Square on Friday morning and stage a march to the Majles. Once there they planned to force their way in, seize the prime minister and members of parliament, and declare an Islamic republic. In the debate that followed, Sharif-Emami sided with conservatives who supported an immediate declaration of martial law in twelve cities. The Shah was dining with Queen Farah and Ardeshir Zahedi when he received a call from the prime minister to ask his opinion. He expressed ambivalence about putting inexperienced army conscripts on the streets—the sight of young soldiers accepting flowers from the crowds on Eid-e

Fetr had raised questions in his mind about their preparedness to open fire on civilians. He asked his dinner companions what they thought. Ardeshir Zahedi made clear that he had no confidence in Sharif-Emami regardless of the decision. The Queen worried that there was not enough time to issue alerts over radio and television to ensure that people did not venture out before the curfew was lifted. The Shah was loath to challenge his prime minister and generals and reluctantly approved the martial law decree.

Reza Ghotbi was finishing up his last day at work as director of National Iranian Radio and Television when he received a telephone call at about 11:00 p.m. Two weeks earlier, Ghotbi had handed in his resignation during the change of government but agreed to stay on an extra two weeks to help with the transition. His deputy and successor, Mahmud Jaafarian, had attended the National Security Council meeting and phoned Ghotbi to brief him about the martial law decision. He said he was worried that with only an hour left before television went off the air they had run out of time to issue news bulletins. "What shall we do?" he asked.

"I will be out of the office in a few minutes," Ghotbi answered. "You will have to decide." He suggested Jaafarian call Minister of State for Executive Affairs Manuchehr Azmun for guidance, and Azmun agreed that to avoid possible confusion and bloodshed it would be better to start the broadcasts as early as possible on Friday morning, starting at six o'clock. Throughout the night, army trucks with loudspeakers moved through the deserted streets urging people to stay off the streets and comply with curfew regulations.

ON FRIDAY MORNING, September 8, Reza Ghotbi was at home when he received another harried call from Mahmud Jaafarian, who begged him to come back into the office. "The streets are filling up with people and crowds are heading for Jaleh Square," he said. "You've been at this organization for twelve years. Come in please." Ghotbi drove in and helped marshal the staff, dispatching reporters and camera crews onto the streets and asking them to radio in eyewitness accounts. He also instructed that a helicopter be readied so his reporters could survey the scene from the air.

Jaleh Square was a misleading name for the modest traffic circle that joined Farahabad Road with Jaleh Road, a narrow carriageway that passed the American Community School in a westerly direction toward the Majles. Overlooking the roundabout, which could be entered from several sides, were low-slung, flat-roofed buildings containing apartments and small businesses. On Friday morning several thousand people converged on a space too congested to accommodate everyone. They ignored warnings from police and army officers to disperse and listened to a fiery speech by Ayatollah Nouri, who led them in chants for Khomeini and an Islamic republic and against the Pahlavi Dynasty and the monarchy. "Death to the Shah!" they cried. The mostly male crowd was comprised of Khomeini supporters, students, and leftists, but also a contingent of PLO-trained Mujahedin guerrillas, who regularly used big crowds as a cover to stage provocations and take control of the streets. A second, less visible armed group was at the scene. They were battle-hardened veterans of seven clandestine militias that reported directly to Khomeini's agents in Najaf and Qom. Their presence exposed the fallacy of Khomeini's public claim that he supported a nonviolent approach to street protests. "Khomeini did not believe in armed struggle but there were armed groups under his observation" was how the young religious revolutionary Ali Hossein cautiously put it. "In some cases there was a need for such groups. For example, if the regime was going to attack demonstrators these groups would support the demonstrators. And in some cases, since the army of the Shah was on the streets there should be power to protect the people [and stage] attacks against the army of the Shah." The Khomeini movement followed its usual practice of placing women, children, and young people at the head of the demonstration to intimidate the security forces and provide cover for their gunmen.

The tension exploded at 9:20 a.m. Reza Ghotbi was at his desk when two eyewitness accounts were radioed in from journalists at Jaleh Square. The first reported seeing and hearing shots fired from apartments overlooking Jaleh Square and people collapsed on the ground. The second journalist stated that shots were being fired from within the square, though apparently over the heads of the crowd. The scene was one of pandemonium and panic.

Exactly who fired first was never conclusively determined, though Reza Ghotbi's correspondent and other eyewitnesses insisted that at least one gunman had opened fire from a high window overlooking the square. If his intention was to shoot into the crowd to cause maximum bedlam and provoke a gun battle, it worked. When the army troop commander saw his men coming under fire he ordered them to lower their weapons, assume combat positions, and fire machine-gun blasts into the crowd.

"According to witnesses, the troops ordered the demonstrators to abandon the demonstration several times, then fired overhead and shot tear gas canisters into the crowd," reported the *Washington Post*'s William Branigan, who wrote one of the most succinct accounts of what happened during those first chaotic moments. "The demonstrators replied by throwing rocks at troops and breaking nearby bank and government office windows, the witnesses said, whereupon the troops opened fire, literally mowing down scores of people." Confirmation of an attack on the soldiers came from the Islamists themselves. "At Jaleh Square there were people among the crowd who used guns," admitted Ali Hossein. "One probability is that both sides shot into each other." An investigation later conducted by the U.S. embassy, which sent a ballistics expert to the scene, concluded that "troops were attacked by a stone-throwing, club-wielding crowd at Jaleh Square, they had had no weapons with which to retaliate other than their rifles. They wore helmets but carried no shields. When their rifle bursts into the air failed to stop the advancing crowd, the resulting slaughter was inevitable."

The crackle of gunfire set off a panicked stampede to safety. Blood-splattered survivors stumbled down side streets. "Shortly after the shooting, demonstrators left the scene with clothes blood-soaked from helping carry away victims," reported the the *Post*'s Branigan. Riots broke out almost immediately as the crowds vented their anger. Bonfires and barricades were set alight, women wept in the streets, and men angrily shouted anti-Shah slogans. One young man tossed a piece of wood and shouted to no one in particular, "We only need guns." Nearby, a woman wearing a chador cursed the Shah's "fascist" government. She cried, "We only want an Islamic government with a religious leader like Khomeini."

CHARLIE NAAS WAS leaving his residence in the American embassy compound when he heard gunfire. "I was outside the bedroom window and my wife was standing on a ledge trying to see over the perimeter wall."

"What's going on?" asked Jean.

"I don't know," said Charlie. "There's a lot of shooting."

Naas ran back to the chancellery, where Ambassador Sullivan was rounding up his staff. "You manage the place," Sullivan told his deputy, "and I'll be the chief political officer." They started phoning their contacts around town to find out what was going on. John Stempel reached one of his sources, Associated Press correspondent Parviz Raein, who said he had been in Jaleh Square standing next to the army's communications gear when the shooting erupted. Raein told Stempel that he "heard the radio announce there had been no more than ninety dead," though he estimated another twenty to thirty killed in the surrounding streets.

ONE OF THE few souls brave enough to head down to Jaleh Square after everyone else had fled was Dr. Fereydoun Ala, director of the national blood bank. He set out in an ambulance with colleagues bound for the city hospital that fell within the army's security cordon and that was also treating most incoming casualties. They drove carefully through Jaleh Square dodging bits of debris that lay scattered on the ground. To their astonishment they were forced to stop and present their papers at street barricades that were manned not by army troops but by swaggering Mujahedin guerrillas sporting Palestinian head scarves. The hospital was a desperate scene. Local residents dragged in mattresses, donated medical supplies, and lined up in their hundreds to donate blood. "The hospital's ramp was spotted with blood and inside frantic nurses tried to cope with the new arrivals," reported the *Guardian*. Relatives of the dead and wounded besieged the hospital gates looking for their loved ones. "Just before 11 a.m., the troops, roaring 'Shah, Shah!' moved in to disperse the increasingly angry crowd. 'We will kill you!' one soldier yelled at foreign journalists who assembled outside. 'Go and hide!' The crowd chanted back, 'Shame on you!' and 'Who pays for you?!' Minutes later the troops fired. They were followed by 14 trucks and there was a heavy silence except for the sporadic bursts of gunfire in the direction of Iran's lower house of Parliament on Baharestan."

BY MIDDAY SMOKE from more than a hundred fires floated above roof-tops in eastern and southern Tehran, and the sound of automatic weapons fire resounded through the streets. Flames engulfed the Armstrong Hotel on Amir Kabur Avenue. Twelve banks, two supermarkets, and the Ramsar Now restaurant were put to the torch, and major boulevards were littered with the burning hulks of tankers, refuse collection trucks, and double-decker buses. In some areas fires raged out of control when emergency crews were caught up in traffic as thousands of residents fled to safer neighborhoods. "South-east Tehran was a scene of destruction tonight," reported the correspondent for the *Times* of London. "I was caught in a taxi on one main square as troops fired to disperse groups of people." The scale of unrest overwhelmed the army, which lacked trained personnel, armor, and rubber bullets. "Unless the government makes a bigger show of force," remarked a European ambassador, "these demonstrations and riots are likely to continue and the Shah may be forced to step aside."

In the early afternoon a devastating rumor took hold that the Shah had been seen in a helicopter hovering over Jaleh Square and that he had not only ordered the massacre but also picked off demonstrators with a rifle, like a big-game hunter on the African veld. Khomeini's men were quick to distribute leaflets alleging that the bloodletting had actually been carried out by Israeli paratroopers disguised as Iranian soldiers. "It's the Israelis!" hysterical mobs bayed in the streets. "Tell the world that the Israelis are killing us!" The revolutionaries also spread the false rumor that Khomeini's close aide Ayatollah Nouri had been murdered by Savak agents. Most effective was their claim that the official death toll of eighty-six was a cover-up. The real number, they insisted, was at least two thousand and most likely three thousand killed. Blared a headline in Britain's *Guardian*, "3,000 DEATHS IN IRAN SAY SHAH'S OPPONENTS." The newspaper's correspondent dismissed the government death toll as "a gross underestimate" and repeated unproven allegations that the registry at Tehran's Beheshtzahra Cemetery showed three thousand bodies buried in a "mass grave." In fact, a drive to the cemetery would have revealed there was no burial site and that the registry showed just forty new bodies. Many years later, the Islamic Republic's Martyrs' Foundation confirmed a death toll of eighty-eight—sixty-four in the square and twenty-four in surrounding streets—or two higher than the original estimate provided by the Shah's government. By then, of course, the damage had already been done, and the Shah was given the moniker "Butcher of Jaleh Square."

The Shah was devastated when he heard that dozens of civilians had been killed on the streets of his capital. Much like Russia's Czar Nicholas II after the 1905 massacre outside the Winter Palace, the King of Iran now occupied a throne stained with the blood of his people. Black Friday was the final confirmation that he had indeed lost the farr. The proud Shah of old was gone and in his place was "an immensely saddened man," reported two Americans who saw him shortly after the tragedy. "It showed in his face, which was grim and gaunt, and in his eyes, which were tired and melancholy. Even his dress, so often elegant, was somber." Ambassador Sullivan cabled Washington that "the Shah looked awful" and described him as "a shattered man who looked to be on the brink of a nervous collapse." He made no attempt to deny rumors that he planned to abdicate the throne in his son's favor. "I would like to wave goodbye but that would be a catastrophe," he admitted. "It is certain that the main program, which is the liberalization and democratization of the country and then real, free elections, will continue. Martial law is for six months, and it will end before the elections start. In the meantime, all aspects of freedom, free speech and everything, will be absolutely carried out. But democracy will take place in the parliament, as in any civilized country. We have not stopped the clock. We will not go back."

On the afternoon of that terrible September day, Princess Ashraf went to the palace to comfort her brother. By her own account, the Princess described him as "completely calm on the surface, but I could see that he was extremely anxious."

"What will you do?" she asked him. "How much danger is there?"

He avoided direct answers to her questions. "It is not wise for you to be here right now," he advised her. "You know how often you are made the object of attacks against the regime. I think you had better leave at once."

"I won't leave you alone," she retorted. "As long as you are here, I'll stay with you."

The Shah "raised his voice" at her for the first time "in our adult lives": "I am telling you that for my peace of mind, you must go."

She left after an hour.

"His Majesty asked me to leave," the chastened Princess told her private secretary. He was shocked at her decision, which he thought was so out of character. "This is not the time to go," Reza Golsorkhi told Ashraf. "We have to put up a fight. Either we all die or we can win."

The Princess was in no mood to argue. "No," she told him. "My brother is in control. And if he wants me to leave then I must go. We will leave."

THE SHOOTINGS AT Jaleh Square finally concentrated American attention on the crisis engulfing its Iranian ally.

On Sunday, September 10, President Carter phoned the Shah to offer his condolences and support. The call from Camp David was placed to Saadabad at 7:56 a.m. and lasted all of six minutes. Gary Sick, who listened in, described the Shah's "flat, almost mechanical voice. . . . [He] sounded stunned and spoke almost by rote, as if going through the motions." The Shah restated his commitment to democratization. "We shall have freedom of speech, freedom of assembly, freedom of demonstration according to the law, freedom of the press," he told the president. "The next elections will be free, there is no other way. The country must be prepared for democracy." He asked Carter to issue a public statement of support as "it would have a good effect. Otherwise, his enemies could take advantage of it." He added that if Carter "wanted a free independent friendly Iran allied to the West, he believed that he would have to come forward very clearly and very frankly. The President said he understood."

THE ISRAELI OFFICIAL responsible for organizing the evacuation of his country's nationals arrived in Tehran. Military attaché Segev and Mossad chief Eliezer Tsafrir took Nahum Navot out onto the streets so he could "smell the burning tires and sense the atmosphere." They told him that Iran's Jewish community was thoroughly panicked at the prospect of a takeover by Muslim fundamentalists, and Navot agreed the evacuation plan should be expanded to include any Iranian Jews who wanted to leave. Within one week the Israeli presence in Iran was reduced by a third, to around a thousand people. Those who chose to stay behind were given detailed instructions on how to conduct themselves during riots and where to go in an emergency. Embassy staff were taught how to defend themselves if the embassy was attacked by mobs, and as a precaution they began burning sensitive documents.

THE ARMY PRESENCE restored calm to the streets of Tehran. "In many parts of the city, martial law had a benign appearance yesterday, with the usual traffic jams clogging the streets and shoppers crowding the stores in the smog-covered central part of the city," reported the *Washington Post*. "No serious incidents were reported yesterday in the capital or in provincial cities, and the government continued to encourage the appearance of a city returned to normalcy following the aberration of social unrest." The weekend after Jaleh Square marked the official end of summer, and forty thousand travelers flocked to Caspian Sea beaches. Football fans had a chance to watch the Valiahd Cup games in Bandar Pahlavi. Hundreds of visitors flocked to Tehran from around the world for the conference of the Association of Girl Guides and Girl Scouts, while corporate executives jetted in for the sixth Tehran International Trade Fair. The underlying mood was skittish. "Traffic was chaotic on many roads and there were also many accidents as residents of the north set out for home around 7 p.m.," reported *Kayhan*. "Those who left it later only just got home in time and in many cases were unable to collect bread and other commodities they needed for their families."

The combined impact of an evening curfew and the new mood of Islamic obeisance dealt another blow to Iranian nightlife, arts, and entertainment. Canceled were the Shiraz Festival of Arts, the Isfahan Festival of Popular Traditions, the Kerman Traditional Music Festival, and the Tehran International Film Festival. Rudaki Hall abruptly pulled its production of *The Merry Widow* and sent the Austrian cast home. The magazine *Rangeen Kaman* was banned "because in its latest issue it printed material contrary to Islamic tenets." The mosques were quiet, too. "Sentries in battle dress were posted on the main avenues around the mosque," reported Joe Alex Morris of the *Los Angeles Times*. He visited the Shah Mosque in downtown Tehran for noontime prayers and found it deserted. "They were reinforced by armored cars and other vehicles at crossroads. The mullahs—Moslem priests—have decided for the moment, to cool it. . . . there were no fiery speeches on Friday. The mullahs asked people to pray at home. Only a few old men prayed in the courtyard, unable to break years of tradition."

Martial law was supposed to instill fear and discourage dissent and lawbreaking, but by the end of the first week Tehranis were back to displaying their usual contempt for authority. "People hardly glanced during the day at the occasional trucks full of soldiers at the ready who were there to remind us of the martial law situation," reported the local press. "The Tehranis' natural sense of humor was more noticeable again, as drivers and shopkeepers exchanged their more usual badinage." Those with money weren't about to wait for the next crisis. Outbound flights were booked up through the rest of the month, and the flow of capital to safe havens abroad picked up. "As previously reported," Ambassador Sullivan wired the State Department, "numerous Iranians readily voice to us their intent to migrate [*sic*] if they become convinced that the future is with conservative Muslims."

21

STATE OF SIEGE

Evil has come to our great house; I weep
That all our foes are wolves, and we are sheep.
—*THE PERSIAN BOOK OF KINGS*

I am fighting for my son.
—QUEEN FARAH

The Shah refused to accept—indeed, he could not accept—that martial law and liberalization were incompatible. He astonished observers when he insisted there was no need to postpone national elections planned for the summer of 1979, then announced new legislation to guarantee freedom of the press and assembly. By now the Imperial Court was in full retreat before the forces of Islam. Another round of concessions followed. The Shah replaced Amir Abbas Hoveyda as his Imperial Court minister with a former foreign minister, Ali Qoli Ardalan, and announced a code of conduct that banned members of the Imperial Family from involvement in state affairs and business deals related to government. He was so anxious to buy peace that he even offered to scrap his beloved social reforms. "We have always thought that our major decisions [for reform] were taken in accordance with the spirit of Islam. If it can be proven that they are against those principles, this is something that can be discussed."

The Shah may have seen these concessions as tactical but to friend and foe alike they amounted to a straightforward policy of appeasement. Prime Minister Sharif-Emami took his cue and proceeded to dismantle the entire edifice of the Pahlavi state on national television. He allowed broadcasters to film live debates from the floor of the Majles, where deputies accused him of graft and incompetence and demanded his resignation. To satisfy the complaints of shopkeepers, he shortened curfew hours. Anxious to placate the ulama, the prime minister quietly suppressed the military investigation into Jaleh Square that revealed evidence of Palestinian involvement. He likewise made no attempt to prosecute several religious fanatics arrested on suspicion of involvement in the Rex Cinema arson. The blizzard of concessions included lifting all restrictions on hajj pilgrimages, freezing electricity and water prices, and extending the national health insurance plan. The prisons became revolving doors, and Sharif-Emami boasted that in the space of two weeks the police had arrested 1,106 people and released 981 of them. Three hundred political prisoners were released in a single day to make room for former government officials and prominent businessmen rounded up as the regime began sacrificing its own to buy time and placate the mobs.

The Shah issued explicit instructions to General Oveissi that there should be no repeat of Jaleh Square. "I don't want any Iranian to even have a bloody nose," he ordered. If the troops had to fire in self-defense or clear the streets, he insisted they first fire rounds in the air and only in extreme situations aim at protesters' legs. "I overheard the Shah say to Oveissi, 'No, no, no one should be hurt,'" recalled one of the Shah's counselors. "I told the Shah, 'We are in a revolution, Your Majesty. People will die.'" Oveissi and the generals felt that the Shah distrusted them and wanted two very different things, ordering them to prevent an insurrection with one arm tied behind their back. "What kind of general was I?" asked Oveissi. "The army had to smile to the people. They shot in the air." But the Shah was insistent. Again and again, courtiers overheard him reminding this general or that colonel to hold fire. "How many times have I said to you?" he told one officer. "No blood from the nose of an Iranian."

The Imperial Family spent September ensconced at Saadabad Palace. Before they returned to their winter residence, Colonel Djahinbini and his security detail swept Niavaran and the offices of both the King and Queen for electronic bugging devices. The escalation of unrest in Tehran over the summer had presented Djahinbini with a new and unnerving set of challenges, not least of which was Khomeini's public call for the Shah's murder. The colonel was aware that members of the Imperial household staff emulated Khomeini as their marja: the women among them had started covering their hair and the men were becoming more withdrawn. "There was a lot of pressure amongst the staff who tended to be religious," said Kambiz Atabai, who managed the household. "They were torn between Khomeini and the family. I could feel and I knew that some of the staff were struggling with their loyalties." In this fraught atmosphere no one could say for sure where the line between religious observance and political fanaticism began and where it ended. Djahinbini also worried that foreign powers were trying to take advantage of the unrest in the streets to step up efforts to infiltrate the palace and eavesdrop on conversations. Starting in the early autumn "we checked His Majesty's office regularly. We were suspicious. There were so many rumors outside the palace and I was not sure where the information was coming from." The Shah and Queen Farah assumed they were under surveillance and made sure to never discuss sensitive matters over the phone. Despite the advent of Xerox machines and the telex, the Shah's preference was to always use back channels and personal envoys to ferry handwritten messages to his interlocutors. His wife followed his example and told her friends to assume that if they phoned the palace their conversations were likely being recorded.

The Queen agreed with her husband's decision to avoid bloodshed at all costs. She also made it clear that her main priority was to stay strong and secure the throne for her son. "She is the one with guts," Hoveyda told Britain's ambassador Parsons. Hoveyda stayed in touch with Farah over the phone, though after his dismissal he was careful not to venture near the palace. In an interview with *Paris Match* magazine shortly after Jaleh Square, Farah said she was "gripped by a deep sadness" at the tragic turn of events. "I think our country is at a crossroads," she said. "Iran has reached one of the most important pages of its history, one of the most important in the past 2,500 years. We are entering a new era. This requires that we gather all our forces to fight and work. As for me, I consider that my first priority is to protect my mental and physical health in order to devote myself to my country, my people and to democracy to which we all aspire."

Farah made no mention of her husband—they both knew he was finished—and focused instead on the Crown Prince and the prospect of her regency. "I am fighting for my son," she said. "The most essential quality he can have is faith. Faith in his country, his people, faith in the task—he has to perform for the good of all. And he will have to remain close to his people. This has never been easy for those who have such heavy responsibilities."

"All observers are struck by one fact," her interviewer pointed out. "While many criticisms are directed at the government and against the Shah, none are aimed at you."

Farah tapped the top of her desk. "Touch wood," she murmured. "I am trying to do everything I can to find a solution to the problems. A whole set of issues have arisen at the same time in our country. We are going through a crisis of growth that is the inevitable price of progress. It is a crisis of culture, society, politics, and spirituality. Iran can be compared to a man of vigor who has been taken ill with a fever. My hope is that the sudden pressure will decrease so we can see more clearly the path to follow." Her greatest source of strength and pride, she said, was "to have won the hearts of a large part of our population." Farah was trying to control her fear and apprehension of the future. "I force myself to overcome my anxiety, to forget my fear. Each mother is preoccupied with the future of her children. This is what I do, too, for my son."

All hope was not lost. The Pahlavis believed they still had one last arrow left in their quiver: they still had Musa Sadr, whose charisma and moderation posed the greatest threat to Khomeini from within the ranks of the senior clergy.

ON MONDAY, SEPTEMBER 11, a Lebanese radio station broadcast a short news item informing listeners that Imam Musa Sadr "had been kidnapped in the Libyan capital of Tripoli." President Elias Sarkis ordered an immediate inquiry and dispatched a team of investigators to Tripoli, Rome, and Paris where the Imam's wife and children had fled to escape the civil war. Interpol issued a worldwide bulletin asking for information about his whereabouts, and governments in the region mobilized their resources. Colonel Gadhafi's government insisted that Musa Sadr had left for Rome on August 31, a claim swiftly refuted by Italian authorities, who checked "hotels, boarding houses and the homes of Lebanese in Rome." Rumors surfaced in the Arab press suggesting that Musa Sadr had secretly returned to Iran to join the fight against the Shah or that he had been kidnapped by Savak. "Certainly he is no friend of the Shah," commented Britain's *Guardian*. The stories were plants and his supporters were quick to rubbish them. "We strongly believe the Imam is still in Libya," declared Lebanon's Shiite Council. "If he really departed from Libya, as Libyan officials claim, then we demand conclusive proof."

Musa Sadr's boyhood friend Dr. Ali Kani was in Tabriz trying to marshal support for the Shah with Ayatollah Seyyed Mohammad Hossein Tabatabai, one of the most prominent Shia clerics, when the King's valet telephoned him at ten thirty at night. "According to Your Majesty," said the caller, "you should return immediately to Tehran." With the curfew in force, Kani telephoned Azerbaijan's governor-general "to send someone to protect me if I ventured outside. I asked him to send me two officers to bring me to the hotel where my pilot was located. We drove to the airport with a military escort."

Early the next morning, Kani drove to Niavaran where he found the Shah "very upset." The Shah got straight to the point: "I ask you to save your friend."

"Majesty, which friend?"

"Your friend Musa Sadr."

Kani felt "quite astonished. I was speechless." What was going on?

The Shah gravely looked at him: "You know, we have discovered that Musa Sadr was not a traitor."

Kani couldn't believe what he was hearing. "I am awfully sorry, Your Majesty, are you joking or pulling my leg?" For the past several years, whenever the Shah had mentioned the Imam in Ali Kani's presence he had described him as a traitor. But now Kani listened in stunned disbelief as the Shah explained that Musa Sadr had not been seen in two weeks and had missed a secret meeting with a palace envoy set for September 5–7 in West Germany. The dates eerily coincided with the crucial end of Ramadan protest marches and street unrest.

The Shah impressed on Ali Kani the importance he placed on locating and rescuing Musa Sadr. "A plane is at your disposal," he instructed. "If to save him you need money, we are okay—there is no limit on the price. And I have arranged a meeting for you with Crown Prince Fahd [of Saudi Arabia]. After Fahd you will see King Hussein [of Jordan]. And then [President] Sadat is waiting for you in Cairo."

In Qom, Grand Ayatollah Shariatmadari called reporters to his home and read out the text of a telegram he had sent to Colonel Gadhafi demanding an explanation: "Islam holds the Libyan government responsible for his disappearance and demands information on his well-being."

THE HAMMER BLOWS kept coming. Iranians were still absorbing the shock of Jaleh Square and the imposition of martial law when the northeast of the country was struck by a devastating earthquake. The ground broke open at the dinner hour on Saturday, September 16, when a temblor measuring 7.7 on the Richter scale tore through Iran's Great Salt Desert. Worst hit was the oasis town of Tabas and forty surrounding villages. "Tabas is a mound of rubble," reported an Iran radio correspondent. "There is nothing standing except the palm trees. All houses have collapsed, burying thousands of people." Picturesque Tabas, the "Gem of Kavir," was one of Iran's most important historic settlements. The King and Queen agreed that he would stay in Tehran to manage the political crisis while she flew to the scene of the disaster, but Prime Minister Sharif-Emami was hesitant to approve Farah's trip. "Mr. Sharif-Emami did not know how I would be received; he doubted how the population would react," she recalled. "The government had in fact lost direction. It was bombarded with differing opinions from politicians, clerics, and the army."

The Queen ignored the prime minister's protests and flew to the disaster zone in the back of a C-130 transport plane. Arriving to scenes of utter devastation, she bore the brunt of angry survivors who demanded faster action from the government. Farah also had to contend with yet another false rumor spread by the mullahs, this one blaming her husband for causing the earthquake by reportedly allowing the American military to conduct a nuclear test in the desert. Once again, Khomeini's men were spreading lies and conspiracy theories. "Dig out the dead!" voices in the crowd called out. "Dig out the dead!" She drove through the wrecked streets of Tabas in an open car to survey the damage and a young man hurled himself forward. "Don't go sightseeing!" he accused her. "Go pull out the bodies of my family!" Onlookers reported that the Queen "sat motionless, looking as if she might burst into tears at any moment." Later, she wept, stunned by the scale of human suffering and distraught at her treatment.

Two days later it was her husband's turn, but as had happened at other critical times in his reign the Shah's mere presence was enough to turn the crowds. "They gave him the sort of treatment that in the West is normally reserved for rock stars," reported one thoroughly impressed British correspondent who accompanied him. Hundreds pressed around him cheering, "Shahanshah!" Survivors broke through the security cordon and threw themselves at his feet, kissing his shoes and hands and beseeching his help. "I do not want anything from you my dear father," wept one woman who had lost her child. "I lost everything I had. But please enlarge the photograph of my eighteen-year-old son Khodabaksh." The most touching scene involved a twelve-year-old boy who had lost his parents and family. He pushed his way through the crowd and begged the Shah to help him continue his studies. "I've always been the top student in my class," he earnestly explained and pulled out his report cards to prove it. The Shah gravely shook his hand, quietly listened to his story, and turning to Khorassan governor-general Seraj Hejazi instructed that the boy be given a scholarship to complete his studies. He asked the authorities to compile a list of all children orphaned by the disaster so they could continue with their schooling. He turned to address the crowd, promising to do his utmost to rebuild their town and passing on the condolences of his son Reza, who was at pilot training school in Texas.

The Shah returned from Tabas to learn that Grand Ayatollah Shariatmadari had publicly declared that he would not negotiate with the Imperial Court or the government over his demand that they move quickly to implement the 1906 Constitution, which guaranteed the ulama veto power over parliamentary legislation. "There is nothing to talk about," he told a small assembly of foreign correspondents who made the trek to Qom. "The government knows our views and our demands. Our demands are simply stated. We want a national government for the nation." He refused to either endorse or oppose the overthrow of the monarchy. "History and the Iranian people alone, not I, will decide. There is fire in the hearts of the people."

Foreign observers interpreted Shariatmadari's threat as a sign that the ulama were united in their opposition to the Shah. But Khomeini despised the 1906 Constitution as a form of liberal mongrelism and had already threatened Shariatmadari for defending it. By declaring that the Constitution was nonnegotiable, Shariatmadari was trying to stay ahead of the crowds while signaling the Shah that there was still time to reach a settlement.

SENIOR ARMY OFFICERS were distraught that their men were under orders to avoid the use of force even though they faced near-constant harassment in the streets. The troops also made a convenient target for professionally trained terrorists. In Tabriz on Friday morning, September 15, three men wearing military uniforms opened fire on an army unit in the Shams Tabrizi district. In the ensuing hour-long gun battle six soldiers, one civilian, and two gunmen were killed. Several civilians were wounded and rushed to area hospitals in the city. The attackers were remarkably confident and brazen. According to eyewitness reports, "after the initial ambush, the terrorists took up position on the corners of Shams Tabrizi and Seqatoleslam Avenues and continued to fire at the patrol."

During this unsettled period, Imperial Court official Kambiz Atabai and his good friend General Manuchehr Khosrodad paid a visit to General Hossein Fardust. Khosrodad was worried about army morale and suggested to Kambiz that they "go and see Fardust for a talk." Atabai did not want to join him. Like many others at court, he considered Fardust to be "not a pleasant man. He used to be invited to all the private parties at the palace. He would speak with very few people. People tended to avoid socializing with him. He had an aura of menace about him and no charisma. He kept to himself." Fardust's behavior over the past twelve months had already raised eyebrows. He no longer held regular audiences with the Shah and the two men corresponded only by briefcase though no one, not even the Queen, knew why. "They did not have face-to-face meetings," Atabai recalled. "This was unusual."

Atabai and Khosrodad arrived at Fardust's office at about five in the afternoon. For the next four hours, Fardust subjected the two younger men to a lecture on the Shah's faults. He said he had disrespected the Constitution and tolerated corruption for too many years. "I've given all the reports [on corruption] to the Shah," he told them, "but it's too late, too late. He cannot hide under the umbrella of the Constitution." Fardust dismissed Sharif-Emami as "the boy." "I have all these files on corruption and I have given them to [Minister of the Interior] General Gharabaghi and said, 'Give them to the boy.'"

Atabai and Khosrodad were shocked by what they heard. "Because when Fardust spoke it was like the Shah spoke. He had a lot of influence with the other generals. We didn't go to the Shah because we knew that if we told him he would call Fardust while we were in the room and say, 'Is it true that you said these things . . .' and he would have never believed them."

ON A STILL warm night in September several men in plainclothes crept quietly through the back streets of Qom until they made their way to the home of Ayatollah Kashani. Their rapping at the door drew the attention of Ali Hossein, who served as the Ayatollah's aide, courier, and organizer in the religious underground. One of the men introduced himself as a general and his friends as midranking officers in the Imperial Army. He asked if they could come inside and talk to Kashani in private. "I was allowed to stay," said Hossein, who witnessed the remarkable exchange that followed.

The men told their story. Following Grand Ayatollah Khomeini's declaration of a fatwa in August calling on army officers to desert, the officers had formed their own revolutionary cell. "We have left [the army] but our friends are still there and they have access to guns and they are under our supervision. What should we do? Should we stay and provide weapons for the revolutionary people or leave?"

Kashani urged them to return to their base. "Leave," he told them. "We have enough weapons now."

"We are ready to join the armed groups," they replied.

"We do not need you yet," said Kashani.

The men explained, "The nation spent too much money on us to train. We want to fight for the nation."

"You will still be martyrs, you are on the right path. We have members of the armed forces in our groups."

The officers returned to the army and began carrying out a sabotage operation. They quietly disobeyed orders and caused the maximum disruption possible to martial law ordinances. They stockpiled weapons and gathered recruits to prepare for the final offensive against the monarchy. Hossein recalled that there were others in government and the military "who had relations with the revolutionary people. We had people inside the army and Savak before the revolution. They were against the Shah and they provided intelligence to the revolutionary cells."

The Imperial Iranian Army was a central pillar of the Pahlavi state. The decision by the officers to commit treason against their commander in chief was the most tangible sign yet that the regime had started to implode. They realized that Jaleh Square had sullied their reputation and compromised their integrity in the eyes of many Iranians, who now viewed them as an occupying force rather than as defenders of the realm.

ALI KANI LISTENED as Saudi Crown Prince Fahd told him what he thought had happened to Musa Sadr in Libya. "Gadhafi arrested him," he explained. "For the sake of [PLO leader] Arafat." The Saudis concluded that Arafat had appealed to Gadhafi to eliminate Musa Sadr because he was hurting the Palestinian cause in Lebanon.

From Riyadh, Kani flew to Jordan, where King Hussein told him the same thing. His final stop on his regional tour was to Egypt. President

Anwar Sadat had wrapped up the Camp David peace talks with a historic peace deal with Israel's prime minister, Menachem Begin. Sadat asked Kani to meet him in Alexandria instead of Cairo. Kani explained "what His Majesty the King of Iran would like to know" about the strange disappearance of Musa Sadr. Did His Excellency have any information?

"You know, Gadhafi is a madman, a criminal, a foolish man," Sadat told his Iranian guest. "That is why we have intelligence in Libya. My agents sent me a secret telegram: 'Gadhafi has killed Musa Sadr.' Yesterday, the chief of [Great Britain's] MI6 visited me for two hours and he told me the same thing."

On hearing this, Kani grasped his head and lurched forward in his chair.

"What is the matter with you?" Sadat asked with sympathy.

"Since childhood I have loved Musa Sadr like a brother," Kani exclaimed.

"I am awfully sorry to give you such bad news," said Sadat. "And you tell my brother in Tehran that unfortunately Musa Sadr no longer exists." The president added the horrific detail that Gadhafi had placed Musa Sadr's body in a box, sealed it in concrete, and dropped it from a helicopter into the Mediterranean.

Ali Kani now had the grim task of returning to Tehran to convey the news of Musa Sadr's death to the Shah, who was anxiously awaiting his report.

When Kani arrived at Niavaran he was ushered straight into the Shah's presence. "When I returned and relayed the news to His Majesty he was very touched," Kani remembered. "He was very, very upset. He sat in his chair for ten minutes."

The Shah was bereft. He had looked to the Imam as his last and best hope for mobilizing the moderate ulama and their followers against the extremist minority who espoused Khomeini's velayat-e faqih and a religious takeover of the state. Grand Ayatollahs Shariatmadari and Khoi had also counted on Musa Sadr to return to Iran, enter the fray, and address public concerns about the need to reconcile faith with modernity. Now Musa Sadr was dead, and the Shah's hope for a moderate religious bloc against Khomeini's power grab collapsed. He faced the deluge alone.

The Shah always operated at two levels, the public and the private, and his next move was characteristic of a ruler whose life had been spent in a veil of intrigue, suspicion, and mistrust. Though in private he accepted that Musa Sadr was dead, to the Iranian media he expressed concern for the cleric's whereabouts and announced he was sending an envoy, Fereydoun Movassaghi, to the region to meet with the king of Jordan and the president of Syria. The Custodian of the Shia Faith explained that he had "every right to interfere in this question as the Imam is an Iranian citizen and the spiritual leader of a million Lebanese Muslims Shiites." The Shah was well aware that Khomeini's agents were behind the smear that *he* was responsible for Musa Sadr's disappearance. By sending Movassaghi to the region he hoped to reassure the ulama in Qom that he was doing everything possible to find Musa Sadr. He also hoped to flush out from the woodwork anyone who might know something about the exact circumstances of Musa Sadr's kidnap and murder.

Grand Ayatollah Shariatmadari refused to accept that Musa Sadr was dead. "We are convinced Gadhafi is holding Imam Sadr," an unnamed "clergy source" presumed to be Iran's senior marja told reporters on September 22. He said he believed Musa Sadr was being held captive in a prison outside Tripoli and added that the behavior of Yasser Arafat was suspect. Investigators from Qom were sent to Libya and Italy to join the hunt.

IN THE AFTERMATH of Jaleh Square, Carter administration officials scrambled to assess the Shah's prospects for survival and build relations with the men trying to depose him. Remarkably, White House officials were still in the dark about Ambassador Sullivan's aggressive yearlong effort to cultivate Mehdi Bazargan and other senior figures in the National Front and Liberation Movement of Iran. The Shah, who *was* aware of the ambassador's overtures, became convinced that the White House was involved in a conspiracy to oust him. Bureaucratic dysfunction extended to intelligence sharing and analysis. Carter's National Security Council was unaware of CIA intelligence that documented the flow of Palestinian and Libyan money and arms to Khomeini. Though Khomeini's anti-American and anti-Jewish tirades were a matter of public record, Sullivan's embassy made no effort to obtain copies of the audiocassettes that were for sale on street corners and in the main bazaar. U.S. officials had still not initiated a study of the role of religion in the unrest or how the mosques and marjas had historically acted as vehicles for protest and change in Iran.

Carter, Secretary of State Vance, and National Security Adviser

Brzezinski still remained focused on the Camp David peace accords. They were presumably assured by the latest State Department intelligence estimate that concluded the Pahlavi regime "has a better than even chance of surviving the present difficulties, and the Shah will probably be able to maintain his position through the early 1980s."

Into the decision-making vacuum stepped lower-tier officials such as Henry Precht, the State Department's Iran desk officer who harbored a visceral dislike for the Shah and the Pahlavi regime. Precht made contact with Ibrahim Yazdi, a Khomeini loyalist, who raised funds, organized anti-Shah student protests, and published human rights propaganda from his medical practice in Texas. Precht's contempt for the Shah influenced the way he drafted reports and even the talking points Carter relied on during his September 8 telephone conversation with the Shah. Though Precht later explained that his actions were motivated by the hope for a "peaceful accommodation between the Shah and his opponents," he conceded that at the time he "did not have a real sense of Khomeini. We knew who Khomeini was. We knew he'd been strongly anti-Shah, but knew nothing about his views." He knew even less about Yazdi. "We didn't really know anything about him. I don't think we knew Yazdi was a US citizen. We had no idea what would happen or who would replace the Shah. We didn't know the Shah was desperately ill. We did no analysis of how the older National Front and Liberation Movement leaders would fill the vacuum. My impression at that time was that Ayatollah Khomeini wanted to set up a secular government, so the front group would be Bazargan, Yazdi, Ghotzbadegh and the clerics would be in the background." Precht believed the successor regime to the Pahlavis would be leftist and nationalist but not overtly Islamic.

U.S. officials were developing policy based on little more than hunches, imperfect intelligence, and their own personal prejudices and grudges. There was especially acute distrust between the State Department and Sullivan's embassy. Officials in Washington complained that diplomats in Tehran were not providing them with accurate reports. Meanwhile, Sullivan's political counselors suspected Henry Precht's intentions. George Lambrakis complained that Precht "may have taken my reporting and embroidered it," and he wondered why key information was not passed from the Iran desk to Gary Sick at the White House. Precht, for his part, considered Lambrakis "astute" but said he "wasn't impressed" with the quality of John Stempel's political reporting. John Stempel recalled that

Secretary Vance "was really pissed off with my reporting" but he saved his biggest criticism for Deputy Secretary of State Warren Christopher, whom he described as a "little creepy son of a bitch." Still, everyone could agree with Lambrakis's assessment of the CIA: "They were of no help at all."

The Shah and his officials were puzzled and alarmed by American behavior. At the opening of the UN General Assembly in New York on Tuesday, October 3, Foreign Minister Amir Khosrow Afshar complained to Secretary of State Cyrus Vance that rumors were circulating in Tehran "of U.S. support for the Iranian opposition. He noted that since the U.S. embassy maintained contacts with the National Front and [former Prime Minister Ali] Amini, there were those who believed the embassy was supporting the opposition."

Vance and his aides finally admitted that U.S. diplomats "did have occasional low-level conversations with certain individuals associated with the opposition, but this did not imply support and it was conducted very discreetly. They were unaware of any contact with Amini."

Afshar warned of "the danger that such meetings might be misinterpreted."

Vance assured the minister that "it was clearly not US policy to support the Shah's opposition and asked if there was anything further we could do to demonstrate support for Iran or to be helpful in these difficult circumstances." The secretary conceded to Afshar that based on his "limited information . . . the degree of organization in recent Iranian demonstrations indicated to us some organizing hand, possibly the Soviets, had played a part."

The Shah's accusations of betrayal so appalled U.S. officials back in Washington that they decided to have their ally evaluated for evidence of emotional problems and possibly a mental disorder. Three years earlier the CIA had concluded that the Shah's refusal to bend on oil prices was probably related to feelings of sexual inadequacy and an inferiority complex toward his father. Now they wondered if his reluctance to call out the army had similar psychosexual roots. Henry Precht informed Embassy Tehran that the CIA's Dr. Jerrold Post, MD, planned to update the agency's psychological profile of the Shah and begin a new study of Crown Prince Reza. Post's task was to answer six key questions. First, were the Shah's "depressive episodes ever so severe as to significantly interfere with his leadership? Did they seem disproportionate to the circumstances or were they rather appropriate discouragement or frustration in the face of severe political problems? What happens to his decision-making at these times—does he ever become paralyzed with indecision, tend to delegate to others decisions he might otherwise make himself?" Second, how did he "pull himself out of these downs"?

Third, the CIA wanted to learn more about Queen Farah's influence "and the degree to which he relies on her." Fourth, the Shah had talked about eventually transferring power to his son. Did he believe he was slipping behind schedule for the handover? Fifth, did he expect external military support, presumably from the United States, "during this period of internal unrest"? Sixth, the Shah's plans to liberalize Iran "have been well delineated for many years" yet he still complained about U.S. pressure to reform: "Please discuss your views of the imbalance between the Shah's own concepts he hopes to implement and reluctant compliance to external pressure."

While the Americans dissected the Shah's childhood and undermined each other, the situation in Iran took an ominous turn for the worse. In the lead-up to the forty-day Rex Cinema mourning observances a rash of strikes erupted in the southern oil fields.

THE SHAH HAD predicted that martial law would only push opposition to his regime underground, leading to terrorism, strikes, and civil disobedience. While Khomeini's followers held back to avoid provoking the army, their putative allies in the Communist Tudeh Party took the lead in organizing strikes designed to force concessions and cripple the economy. On September 24, oil workers in Khuzestan Province walked off the job, demanding higher pay. Drilling operations were suspended, and the workshop at the main Abadan oil refinery was shut down. Strikes quickly spread to the banking and telecommunication sectors.

The strikers were also reacting to reports that the Iraqi government, acting at the behest of Tehran, had placed Grand Ayatollah Khomeini under house arrest. Saddam Hussein had his own reasons for trying to neutralize the Marja, whose crusade to collapse the Pahlavi regime was spreading fear and hope throughout a region riven by religious, sectarian, and ethnic rivalries. Khomeini had emerged as the face of an Islamic resurgence, and young Shia and Sunni alike responded with fervor to his call for a single Islamic state to replace socialist republics, military dictatorships, and conservative monarchies. The Iraqis relented on September 25 in response to a plea from the Shah to lift house arrest but Khomeini refused to accept new rules that placed restrictions on his ability to engage in politics and issue public proclamations. He preferred to leave Iraq but stay in the region and tried to move across the border to Kuwait. Nervous Kuwait authorities blocked his entry and he remained in legal limbo. The drama at the Iraq-Kuwait border plunged his followers in Iran into a frenzy. He returned to Najaf while Abolhassan Banisadr and Sadegh Ghotzbadegh applied for temporary visas for entry into France, where they were based.

Anxious to stop the Khuzestan strike before it led to a shutdown of the entire oil sector, Sharif-Emami's government approved higher salaries and subsidies for workers in the oil, banking, and telecommunication sectors. These concessions inspired a wave of copycat strikes that shut down hospitals, high schools, the postal service, steel plants, and the civil service. "In the spirit of accommodation, the government has speedily given in to almost all economic demands with the result that wages have virtually doubled in many areas and more civil servants are going on strike to get similar benefits," the U.S. embassy reported. "The wage increases to civil servants will likely be followed by increases to employees of private companies." The strategy of the Sharif-Emami government "is to negotiate quietly with the bloc of moderate religious leaders and opposition politicians and meanwhile contain the disturbances in the hope that such a deal will isolate troublemakers who come from more extremist groups. By attempting to placate various segments of the nation with the quick fix— such as the large pay raises, the ill-considered pieces of legislation, etc.— the Government of Iran has unwittingly contributed to stirring up a number of other hornets' nests."

Encouraged by the regime's surrender to labor, and aware that public anger over Rex Cinema and Jaleh Square was still running high, on Sunday, October 1, Khomeini's agents unleashed a new wave of attacks and riots in the cities of Kermanshah, Hamadan, and Daroud and six other towns not covered by the martial law ordinance. By now street marches in cities such as Dezful numbered in the tens of thousands. After months of sitting on the sidelines the Iranian public was stirring but not in the direction the government or the Shah hoped. The strikes had even brought middle-class professionals out onto the streets. This time, emboldened by the experience, their mobilization threatened to collapse another central pillar of support for the Pahlavi regime.

If the Shah was to survive he would have to rally his supporters like

President Charles de Gaulle of France, who had faced down a popular revolt in 1968. De Gaulle had appealed to French patriotism and against the odds managed to turn the tide. The Shah's appearances in recent days at Tabas and Mashad, and the Queen's forays into southern Tehran and the provinces, suggested the Pahlavis could still draw on a deep wellspring of support from key groups, including the military, moderate ulama, middle- and upper-middle-class conservatives, farmers, factory workers, and millions of poorer observant Iranians who did not subscribe to Khomeini's fundamentalist view of Islam and Sharia law. Many liberals and leftists who otherwise opposed the monarchy now trembled at the prospect of rule under the mullahs. If the Shah intended to mobilize these disparate groups he would first have to give them a reason to stay and fight. The message he sent at the state opening of the new parliamentary session on Friday, October 6, was not what they wanted to hear. He continued to insist that more and not less liberalization was the answer to unrest. His own supporters interpreted the speech as a sign of surrender, while intellectuals, students, and the left sneered that the Shah was simply trying to placate the crowds before he launched a bloody crackdown to save his throne. "Whatever the regime said, people believed the opposite," said Ali Hossein. "We saw liberalization as weakness."

The Shah's speech failed to draw the sting. Clashes erupted the next day in the Caspian towns of Babol and Amol, where protesters set fires, attacked banks and public buildings, and battled police and the army. Shots were fired and several people were killed, among them a woman who tried to offer shelter to students fleeing the police. Thoroughly dejected by events, the Shah hinted to his advisers that he was thinking about leaving the country for a while to "recuperate." They had heard the same talk before, in 1953. "I became aware in the second week of October," said Reza Ghotbi. "I went to see [Minister of State for Executive Affairs] Manuchehr Azmun and he said somehow that the King is going to leave, or he suggested maybe if the King left we can bring calm to the country. That afternoon I went to the court to see if the King can receive me for a few minutes. And he did. I told him there was a rumor he was leaving, or a suggestion that if he did it would bring calm. 'Sire, I just met [so-and-so] who told me Your Majesty has probably decided to leave the country. People like me are ready to take up arms to defend you. But if you are not here, I don't know how many of us will defend this building. If you leave it will be the end of Iran. People will defend you but not the government.'"

"It's interesting you say that," replied the Shah, "because just before you General Azhari was here and he said the same thing."

Ghotbi interpreted his response to mean that "he will not leave the country in chaos, but he *will* leave the country when the chaos has ended. Maybe he was trying to comfort me. I think he had given thought that he would leave if he couldn't calm the country. I don't think he had plans at that time to abdicate. He was disillusioned but still engaged."

Lebanon's ambassador Khalil al-Khalil resigned his post. He had long since concluded that the Shah's reluctance to use force meant the Pahlavi Dynasty was finished. Before leaving he paid one final visit to the Shah, at Saadabad. "The Shah hardly spoke," he said. "When I said I hope things would get better he only smiled."

ON SUNDAY, OCTOBER 8, Ambassador William Sullivan sent an urgent classified telegram to Washington warning that Grand Ayatollah Ruhollah Khomeini and his entourage were likely to apply for visas to enter the United States. Two days earlier the Marja had flown to Paris with his son Ahmad after a humiliating twenty-four hours spent in limbo on Iraq's border with Kuwait, where they were denied entry. Thanks to the quick thinking of Abolhassan Banisadr, who lived in Paris, Khomeini secured a three-month visa to enter France. But Khomeini's advisers apparently had their eyes on another destination. "Source with good access to religious circles tells us that a number of people around Ayatollah Khomeini have been urging him to go to U.S. as a way of publicizing opposition cause where it will do even more good than in Paris," said Sullivan. "One reason Khomeini has gone to Paris (apart from presence of many Iranian opposition representatives) is said to be because French government has been 'hard' on Iranian students there. Khomeini is to try to influence parliamentarians and other prominent Frenchmen to go easier on students."

Khomeini spent his first few days in Paris living in Banisadr's apartment before he moved to a more spacious rented home in the suburb of Neauphle-le-Château. Banisadr and two colleagues, the voluble Sadegh Ghotzbadegh, who maintained relations with Gadhafi, Arafat, and the armed groups, and Ibrahim Yazdi, the Houston-based fund-raiser and student organizer, assumed the role of campaign advisers. They screened Khomeini's visitors, handled media requests for interviews, and made sure their "candidate" stayed "on message." The talk of moving to New York was set aside as hundreds of news reporters from around the world and thousands of admirers converged on Khomeini's château. On French soil the Marja, who had lingered in exile for fourteen years, became an international celebrity.

Westerners were fascinated with the mysterious old man, who appeared like a mirage out of the Arabian desert with his flowing beard and black eyes to regale them with tales of the bestial Pahlavis. News reporters hung on Khomeini's every word, though as Banisadr later freely admitted very few of them were actually his own. In his first press interview, Khomeini spoke at length about his idea to turn Iran into a Muslim theocracy and administer Sharia justice. The Frenchman interviewing Khomeini did not speak Persian, and Banisadr deliberately mistranslated to avoid a scandal. When the reporter left he advised Khomeini that "if you don't want to become a permanent exile you have to forget about your book. He accepted that. The proof is what he said in Paris." Khomeini was already an expert dissembler, and he agreed to avoid controversial subjects and follow the talking points provided by Banisadr's committee of public relations experts, which emphasized democracy, elections, and women's rights. When Banisadr asked him, "What is an Islamic republic?" Khomeini carefully replied, "It will be like the French republic." Remarks like this delighted American and European intellectuals who acclaimed Khomeini as an enlightened revolutionary in the tradition of George Washington and Mahatma Gandhi.

While Khomeini settled into his new surroundings in Paris, Banisadr was curious to learn more about Musa Sadr's fate. He phoned Yasser Arafat, and the PLO chief provided him with a new twist on the mystery. According to Arafat, Gadhafi had told him that during their meeting in Tripoli Musa Sadr became so upset during their conversation that he threatened to leave. Gadhafi said he left the room and ordered his security guards to "calm him down" or "do whatever it takes to get him to stop doing whatever he is doing. His idea was that they either bribe him or scare him. But his intelligence people took this as an order to kill him."

When Gadhafi returned he asked after Musa Sadr. His men told him, "He's gone."

"You mean he's left?" asked Gadhafi. "He's gone?"

"No, we killed him," they answered.

According to the version of events propagated by Arafat, the murder of Musa Sadr had been Gadhafi's fault, a terrible mistake, and the result of a simple miscommunication.

22

TEHRAN IS BURNING

There is nothing I or anyone else can do about it.
—THE SHAH

I have the feeling there is no hope anymore.
—QUEEN FARAH

The tempo of unrest picked up again in mid-October with strikes closing schools, the Aryamehr steel mill in Isfahan, the Behshahr industrial complex, and the Sarcheshmeh copper works. Large crowds gathered to challenge martial law. Mujahedin gunmen attacked the Iraqi consulate in the port city of Khorramshahr, in apparent retaliation for Saddam Hussein's decision to expel Khomeini. Tehran's northern hills began emptying out and every day the classified pages in daily newspapers were filled with property listings and fire sales. By late October, capital worth $50 million was leaving Iran each day, a total of $3 billion since Jaleh Square, and the social season consisted of one maudlin farewell party after another as old friends and familiar faces took their leave. In a single week the ambassadors of Austria, Algeria, Japan, and Pakistan departed. Envoys from the Nordic countries stayed on, but sent out their wives and children. The departure of popular television host Richard Mayhew Smith, whose Thursday afternoon program *Window on Iran* had entertained and enlightened for many years, drew a big crowd that included the British and New Zealand ambassadors. Mayhew Smith put on a brave face, blaming his decision to leave on a contractual dispute with his employer and declaring before a skeptical audience that he wouldn't "rule out returning one day." There were emotional scenes at the farewell reception for Jean-Claude Andrieux, the well-liked general manager of the Hilton Hotel. "Thank heavens we're leaving at four in the morning," said his wife, Therese, "otherwise my husband just wouldn't be able to face his colleagues without tears." Longtime Austrian resident Carl Hohenegger was more forthright at his farewell: "Iran isn't the Iran it used to be."

Fearing the collapse of martial law, a shadowy group of military officers and government officials considered scotching Operation Kach in favor of a full-scale coup that would send the Shah, Queen Farah, and their children out of the country and into permanent exile. Their provisional military government then would lead the nation into elections scheduled for 1979. Rather than tolerate an Islamist state, they also decided that if Khomeini's bid for power was successful they would pull the army back to Abadan in the south and if need be let mobs burn Tehran to the ground. The generals would form a rebel military government, seize the southern oil fields to cut fuel supplies and revenues to the capital, and from there fight their way north and launch an assault against Tehran— they preferred civil war to an Islamic state. That these scenarios were under discussion in mid-October showed the level of fear and anxiety within the senior ranks of the armed forces. The panic extended to Qom, where moderate clerics predicted a bloodbath if Khomeini ever returned to Iran. They knew him, they knew his ambitions, and they knew what he was capable of if he ever gained power.

Ambassador Ardeshir Zahedi began shuttling back and forth between Washington and Tehran in an attempt to rally the royalist cause. Late one night he drove down to Qom for a secret rendezvous with Grand Ayatollah Shariatmadari, arriving at about two in the morning to evade Khomeini's agents, who had placed the Marja under surveillance. Shariatmadari was beside himself with worry. "He was nervous and scared of his surroundings," recalled Zahedi. Moderate clerics were subjected to physical assaults and threats from gangs of young Islamist storm troopers. Zahedi told Shariatmadari he needed his help—the Shah was talking about leaving Iran. "Please call the Shah and say, 'Don't leave,'" he pleaded. The next day Shariatmadari phoned the palace and begged the Shah not to leave. Zahedi also reached out to Grand Ayatollah Khoi in Najaf, who sent him a gold ring to give to the Shah with the message, "Have courage."

Shariatmadari urged rebellious oil workers to ignore Khomeini's summons to strike and stay on the job. Unsure which marja to follow, the workers sent a delegation to Qom. Shariatmadari repeated his injunction for the men to remain at their posts. From there they went to the home of Ayatollah Kashani, where they were let in by Ali Hossein. "They asked about the strike and their duty and should they continue," he said. "It was a very important strike. The Shah could not export [oil]. Khomeini had also ordered people not to pay their power and water bills. They wanted to know Khomeini's opinion about the strike. Was it compulsory to strike or not? Shariatmadari had told the workers it was *forbidden* to continue and the strike must stop. Now they wanted to know Khomeini's view."

Ayatollah Kashani opened his remarks by lauding Shariatmadari as a great marja. Then he asked the workers, "Who is the leader of the movement in Iran?"

They responded, "Imam Khomeini."

Kashani asked them a second question. "If there is a movement and there is some effort related to that movement, should you ask the leader or the one who is not the leader? You made a mistake. Shariatmadari is not the leader. You should not refer to him. He has no role. Therefore, the real authority in this struggle is Ayatollah Khomeini and I am going to convey his message to the laborers and engineers: 'It is your *compulsory* duty to continue the strike. And after a while you will become victorious.'" The delegation left and relayed Kashani's message to the striking oil workers. Iranian oil production collapsed by two thirds in the last week of October to less than two million barrels per day, a daily loss of $60 million in oil revenues. "Iran's oil supplies are the regime's jugular vein," observed a senior Western diplomat. "To cut these supplies is to cut the Shah's throat."

WITH HIS KINGDOM in flames, his people in open revolt or headed for the doors, and his generals agitating for a putsch, the Shah saw only a series of trapdoors that led to the basement. On Thursday, October 19, he declared before an audience of senior parliamentarians that he had decided to pave the way for "a natural transfer of power" back to the legislative branch—Iran would continue with or without his hand at the helm. His remarks read like a valedictory and the end of an era. "God willing, our history will never have a finish," he declared in somber tones. "Iran will be everlasting, as long as there is a world."

At Niavaran, the Shah's intimates watched the Shah walk the length of his office, playing with his hair, lost in thought. "I would walk one step behind him, always on his left," recalled Reza Ghotbi. "I remember he turned back, his eyebrows down, and said, 'I'm not a Suharto. A king cannot kill his nation.'" He accepted his fate and hinted at his future intentions during a small private dinner in late October. "The mood was somber," said Maryam Ansary. "It was not the joking, teasing, fun times we used to have." Her brother had recently been injured in a car accident in Milan and she told the Shah she planned to spend three weeks in Italy to help him recover. She was taken aback by his reaction to this news. "Good," he responded. "It is better that you leave now." The dinner table conversation turned to the grim subject of unrest. "Everyone was giving advice," she said. Their bickering drew an unusually sharp response from the top of the table. "Stop it," the Shah interrupted them. "You know something? It's like when you go to the casino. Your number comes up and you're a winner. For fifteen years everything I picked up turned to gold. And now every time I pick up gold it turns to shit. It's the way life is. There is nothing I or anyone else can do about it." His companions were stunned into silence.

Since the end of the summer the Shah had sent his extended family out of the country. Only he remained behind with the Queen, their three youngest children, and Queen Mother Taj ol-Moluk. Prince Gholam Reza's wife, Princess Manigeh, received permission to return for a few days to collect some personal items and check on the family home. "I went back alone in October just to make sure the house was in order and to bring out winter clothes," she said. "In that period I felt that things were not normal. There was a lot of tension and you could feel that. I went to the court and had the chance to visit His Majesty. You could read on his face that he was worried for the country. His Majesty told me that we have to stay outside Iran for the time being." The Princess instructed her husband's staff to temporarily close his office. "I just let them know that we do not know when we will back." She packed suitcases of clothes for the children but left her jewels behind in a safe. Only her husband knew the safe combination and it still hadn't occurred to them that their exile might be permanent. The Princess was so sure they would return she even brought back their summer clothes. "We could never ever believe that events would take this direction and that we could never go back," she said. "I did not bring our photo albums. We left everything behind, even our memories."

The Shah's refusal to save himself meant that ministers, generals, and courtiers directed their petitions to Queen Farah. They bombarded her with ideas to pass on to her husband—he should order a crackdown, hold a rally, make a televised appeal to the nation admitting his mistakes and beg for forgiveness. The dutiful intermediary usually came back with the same answer. "The prime minister was coming to me, and the generals, and others," she recalled. "It was confusing. They wanted us to act stronger because we still had the people with us." Despite their past disagreements on policy matters, husband and wife were united in their belief that violence was not the answer. Unlike the Shah, though, Farah refused to accept that they were finished. She wanted to keep fighting—for Reza, for the dynasty, for the White Revolution, and for the millions of people counting on them, not least the women of Iran who faced subjugation at the hands of the mullahs. She could not stand by and watch the destruction of a half-century legacy of progressive social policy.

The Queen refused to be a prisoner in the palace and held her head high during public appearances. She made a highly publicized trip to open the new training center for nursing and health workers housed at the Society for the Protection of Children, where she was cheered and embraced by the excited students. Farah returned to the palace, pulled the doors closed behind her, and collapsed. "I have the feeling there is no hope anymore," she wrote in a notebook. The Pahlavis threw a small bash to celebrate Farah's fortieth birthday, but their attempt to lift everyone's spirits failed. Elli Antoniades described the atmosphere as "very sad. And after that the social life ended."

In the downstairs dining room where the King and Queen took their evening meals, a piece of paper was found on the table. The handwritten scrawl read, "Death to the Shah."

THE SHAH HAD lost all faith in the technocrats who had been at his side since 1963. He blamed them for covering up mistakes and excesses and lying to protect their prerogatives and privileges—the Persian court mentality had always been to tell the king what he wanted to hear. Ambassador William Sullivan cabled Washington that "the Shah feels himself without any clear plan for the immediate future and without any reliable Iranian advisers from whom he can get objective reactions." For that reason, the Shah began holding regular consultations with the American and British envoys. He held Sullivan and Anthony Parsons in only marginally higher esteem but assumed—naively, as it turned out—that they at least understood the threats he faced from the far right and the far left. He recalled the diplomatic intrigues that had surrounded his accession to the throne in 1941 and recognized that Allied support would be crucial if and when his son took the throne.

Neither envoy was suited to the role of Imperial confidant. Parsons was an inveterate gossip, "the favorite source of all the American correspondents in Tehran," recalled *Chicago Tribune* reporter Ray Moseley, and the ubiquitous "senior Western diplomat" whose patronizing assessments of the Shah convinced officials in Washington and London that Iran's king needed a night nurse and a glass of hot milk to calm his nerves. Indeed, Parsons's self-appointed role as resident sage of the revolution would have been laughable if it weren't so tragic—with the exception of Sullivan, the Briton was one of the most misinformed diplomats in Iran. Foreign correspondents who made the trek to the British chancellery and spotted the "elderly man in rumpled clothing, hair uncombed, tending rose bushes," and usually took him for the gardener, couldn't have found a more highly placed source—or one less knowledgeable about the country where he served.

Sullivan was more problematic. The Shah knew that U.S. embassy officials were holding talks with his opponents inside Iran. But he was unaware that the CIA had successfully intercepted the telephone lines at Neauphle-le-Château, where Khomeini and his supporters were ensconced. The Americans recorded and read incoming and outgoing calls placed from the house, then sent transcripts of the conversations to officials who managed Iranian affairs in the White House, the State Department, and the embassy in Tehran. "We were able to intercept some messages," confirmed Henry Precht, who read them. "They were not intercepted from his residence but from his phone calls," confirmed Charlie Naas. "We had the means to do it. We would discuss them with Sullivan." The ambassador did not share what U.S. intelligence knew about Khomeini with the Shah, and he felt free to offer advice to the Shah even though he knew the CIA had also intercepted Queen Farah's private phone line, sending the transcripts back to the White House, where they were closely studied. They didn't learn much—like Khomeini, Farah knew better than to reveal her true intentions over the phone.

Sullivan and Parsons encouraged the Shah to oppose the generals who pressed him to replace Sharif-Emami with military rule. The ambassadors suspected the officers were unduly pessimistic, "feeding the Shah the darkest possible view of the current situation," and that military rule would only "create worst [sic] pressures which might lead to a real explosion." Sullivan was so opposed to the idea of a military government that he even lobbied Washington against sending over a team of U.S. specialists to train the Iranian Army in riot control and the peaceful dispersal of large crowds of protesters: "He did not want to give the Iranian military the idea that we wanted to help them have the capability of maintaining themselves in power bloodlessly if they took over." Sullivan's policy meant that young Iranian Army recruits were forced to confront large groups of rioters, some infiltrated by professional agitators, with only rifles and live rounds at their disposal, making bloodshed more, not less, likely.

MARTIAL LAW DISINTEGRATED at the end of the month. On October 26 the Shah's formal birthday salaam went ahead in Golestan Palace's Hall of Mirrors, with thousands of spectators lining the streets to watch the Pahlavi motorcade with motorcycle outriders pull up. "There was not the least demonstration—no cheers, no jeers, no whistles—only a heavy silence, both going and coming back," observed Hushang Nahavandi. "This reflected the view mainly taken by the public—amazement and expectancy. People were waiting for an end to events and the winner of the confrontation." The Shah "arrived ashen-faced. . . . He was expecting, perhaps, signs of hostility but not this silence—these questioning looks turned towards him." Before entering the hall he drank a cup of sweet tea. Chief of Protocol Afshar whispered in his ear, "Sire, no one must notice your sadness, especially today—you must inspire confidence." "You're right," he answered. Forcing a smile, he entered the room on his wife's arm.

Away from the capital, tens of thousands of protesters poured into the streets of Khorramabad waving black banners and chanting, "Allah Akbar!" ("God is Great!"). They gave chase to two men they suspected were undercover police agents and stoned one to death. In Isfahan a terrorist died when his bomb prematurely exploded. Mobs launched an assault on the governor's office in Kermanshah. Five people were shot and killed in a small town outside Hamadan. In Mashad an estimated one hundred thousand demonstrators marched through the streets and in

Gorgan a crowd of thirty thousand chanted, "Victory to Khomeini!" and "Victory to Sharia!" Government buildings in Soussangerd were stormed. Rioters burned the center of town in Rasht. In Kermanshah an unveiled woman was pulled from her car, which was then set alight. In the southern city of Jahrom a rooftop sniper took aim at a jeep traveling through town and assassinated the local police chief. The authorities were shocked when the arrested gunman revealed himself to be one of their own soldiers.

Unrest flared in Tehran on Sunday, October 29, when gangs of youths took over city streets, overturning vehicles and building flaming barricades. "The entire capital was plagued by demonstrations and sporadic clashes between students and troops and police in east and west Tehran," reported *Kayhan*. Barricades were thrown up on Shahreza and Shah Avenues to block the progress of army convoys. Thousands of student protesters charged up Sabah Avenue until troops dispersed them with water cannons, tear gas, and rubber bullets. Army helicopters hovered overhead to direct tanks and armored cars to the scene, and troops fired live rounds in the air to drive the crowds back. Traffic came to a halt and motorists were teargassed where they sat in their cars. Sullivan and Parsons were returning to Shemiran after meeting with the prime minister when the Briton's Rolls-Royce came to a halt on a side street. Fifty yards up the road men with clubs and pipes began overturning and setting fire to automobiles. Parsons's driver spun the big car around—no easy maneuver on a crowded side street—and "we shot off down a small alley pursued by some of the club wielders." The ambassadors and their plainclothes police escorts took shelter in a bank, where the manager offered them tea and sympathy.

The Shah's strategy of appeasement had ended in a rout. "The more you feed an alligator, the bigger and hungrier it becomes," observed a senior Iranian military officer. The unrest continued even after the security forces and civil service were purged of hard-liners, an action that effectively decapitated the regime's security and intelligence apparatus. Dozens of high-ranking regime officials, including Parviz Sabeti, were tipped off in advance and fled Iran before they could be jailed. The prison gates were flung open and 1,451 political prisoners, including Communists, convicted terrorists, and religious fanatics, were pardoned and set free. Twenty-five years earlier, Deputy Court Minister Abolfath Atabai had accompanied the Shah and Queen Soraya into exile. He recalled those dark days as he watched the Shah struggle with the decision to use force against his people. He took aside the generals and begged them to proceed with their coup. "My boss cannot make up his mind," he told them. "Go ahead and take action. Put tanks around the palace, cut the phone lines so you won't have anyone in the palace telling you not to act, and do what you need to do to save the country."

On the evening of the last long day of October, the Shah reviewed the deteriorating situation with the two ambassadors. He told Sullivan and Parsons that his generals were losing patience. Earlier in the day the army had marched into Abadan and seized control of the oil refinery and other oil installations along the southern coast. The Shah, said Sullivan, was "sober but controlled and occasionally displaying a rather macabre touch of humor." He repeated his opposition to a military government, which "would at best be a quick fix and in the long run no solution at all." He said he was considering which opposition leaders would make suitable ministers in a coalition government. Almost as an aside, he explained that he expected former prime minister Hoveyda and former Savak chief Nasiri "to go to jail" to satisfy the mobs. It was now that his bleak humor came to the fore. "Finally, the Shah said life was cruel," Sullivan jotted down in his notebook. "His loyal prime minister was at that very moment courageously pleading his heart out in the Majles to obtain a vote of confidence, while he sat plotting with the British and American ambassadors to replace him."

On November 1, the day all domestic air travel was grounded by strike action at the airports, and with tens of thousands protesting in the streets of the capital, the Shah intimated to Sullivan and Parsons for the first time that he might leave the country. His efforts to cajole the leaders of the National Front to join a coalition government had come to naught. He refused their condition to hold a referendum on the future of the monarchy, telling the ambassadors that he would rather "leave the country than submit to that." He knew the Imperial regime "was melting away daily and time was running out; therefore, he had to look at alternatives." The generals were starting to take measures into their own hands. In recent days the palace had been presented with a petition signed by three hundred senior officers urging the monarch to call out the army. The Shah told the ambassadors that he was aware that "many people, including his military probably considered him cowardly or indecisive for failing to take the military course of action. He wondered how history would judge him." Sullivan and Parsons assured him that his stand "was viewed as very prudent and courageous" in Washington and London (Sullivan wrote "Hip Hip Hooray" in the margin of his meeting notes).

The Shah and the ambassadors were still in conference when a call came through from his ambassador to Washington. Ardeshir Zahedi was rumored to be behind a series of recent pro-royalist vigilante-style attacks in Kerman and other provincial towns. In the most dramatic episode, several hundred Baluchi horsemen had stormed the center of Paveh during an opposition rally and killed eleven people. Zahedi was telling friends in Washington that "his advice to the Shah is to bring out progovernment groups to demonstrate and if necessary to do battle even if that means civil war." The Shah would have none of it. Speaking in front of the ambassadors, he "cut [Zahedi] off short with a statement that this was not 1953 and was not even the same situation that existed two weeks ago when [you were] here." He hung up the phone and Sullivan said that he agreed with the Shah's view that "in 1953 the bazaaris and mullahs led mobs in support of the monarchy. In 1978 they are leading mobs against the monarchy. Zahedi cannot switch the bazaaris and mullahs off today. Recourse to mob violence under present conditions would only assist the polarization between the Shah and Khomeini supporters."

Sullivan returned to Roosevelt Avenue and cabled Washington for instructions. He said he needed to know what he should tell the Shah if, as expected, the monarch "reported that none of his efforts or a political situation will work and that he needs to decide whether to abdicate and turn the government over to the military or to impose military government under his continuing rule." He expected that the Shah would inform him that he would stay on as ruler "only if the US and UK say that they will continue to support him."

The ambassador's telegram caused consternation in the White House, which had consistently underestimated the scale of unrest in Iran. On the evening of November 2, President Carter's national security team met to consider their options. They expressed astonishment at the scale and speed of disturbances and decided that Moscow must be involved in trying to upset the balance of power in the Persian Gulf. "The fact is there was some external support for the unrest," said National Security Adviser Zbigniew Brzezinski. Yet U.S. officials were surprised only because they had not been closely following events in Iran over the past year. They lacked any real understanding of Islam and the Shah's preference to avoid bloodshed.

On Friday, November 3, Brzezinski thought he saw his silver lining. "Good news!" he informed President Carter. According to a CIA assessment, issued in August, "Iran is not in a revolutionary or even a 'pre-revolutionary' situation." The intelligence agency reported,

There is dissatisfaction with the Shah's tight control of the political process, but this does not at present threaten the government. Perhaps most important, the military, far from being a hotbed of conspiracies, supports the monarchy. Those who are in opposition, both the violent and the nonviolent, do not have the ability to be more than troublesome in any transition to a new regime.

THE NEXT DAY, Saturday, November 4, all hell broke loose.

Shortly before noon several thousand student protesters gathered outside the main gates of the University of Tehran. A similar disturbance the day before had led to clashes with police. "There were students in Western sports jackets, young women in traditional robes and a contingent of street-wise toughs from the bazaars," reported one observer. This time the students faced off against five hundred troops "with fixed bayonets." The students hurled insults, rocks, and bottles and chanted, "Down with the Shah!" and "Death to the Shah!" The senior army officer ordered them to break into smaller groups, and when they refused to comply tried to disperse them using a water cannon, tear gas, and by firing live rounds over their heads. "They are only firing in the air!" the demonstrators jeered. They set fire to vehicles and used the flaming debris to build a barricade. But when they tried to pull down a statue of the Shah the troops lost patience and sprayed the crowd with automatic weapons fire, killing at least five students.

The students stampeded back onto the grounds of the campus, then poured out onto Shahreza and Kakh Avenues waving blood-soaked shirts and rampaging through the central business district. Banks, restaurants, shops, liquor stores, and buses and trucks were set alight. At the Inter-Continental Hotel hundreds of tourists and businessmen took refuge in the lobby or watched from upper-floor windows as the mob "surged onto the hotel grounds, armed with fists and pockets of rocks taken from the gravel trucks. Within minutes they had broken every ground floor window, invaded the coffee shop where they overturned most of its tables and hurled decorative lamps and vases down the hallway, and demolished the shops that line the ornate arcade." The tourists ran for the stairwells and elevators while security guards formed a chain to unravel high-pressure hoses and "washed the invaders back through the windows." After trashing the hotel's interior the rioters fled the scene "as if by signal. Most of them evaporated down side streets, like troops dispersing after an ambush, but a rear guard of about 50 paused and in a remarkably short time overturned and set fire to three automobiles blocking their retreat."

Iranians in their hundreds of thousands took to the streets to demand Khomeini's return and the Shah's departure. Two hundred thousand marched in Isfahan, two hundred thousand in Qom, two hundred thousand in Ahwaz, twenty thousand in Dezful, and ten thousand in Borazjan. There were vast turnouts in Mashad, Abadan, Bushehr, and a score of other cities and towns. Troops panicked and fired into crowds in Kohdasht in Lorestan Province, killing two people. The town of Paveh remained cut off from the outside world, surrounded by the same vigilante militia that had terrorized residents the week before, denied food and medical supplies. Staff at the Post, Telephones, and Telegraph Department staged a wildcat strike. Iran Air pilots refused to fly. Industrial action shut down the port city of Bandar Abbas. Three dozen oil tankers idled in the waters off Kharg Island, unable to load their fuel shipments. Following several bomb threats, guests at Tehran's Hilton Hotel were served dinner and drinks in their rooms.

Late on Saturday afternoon, the Shah invited Sullivan and Parsons to Niavaran, where they "spent a long prayer session" reviewing the crisis. Sullivan told the Shah that the White House was prepared to support a military government. In response, the Shah "wondered why a military government would be successful. He cited the day's events to demonstrate his own doubts about the military's capability to restore law and order." The troops had stood firm against the demonstrators in the morning, though he "did not yet know if there were any fatalities, but he did know that hit and run demonstrations had then broken out all over town beyond the capability of troops to control." He added that while he appreciated Carter's support "he could not see what the President would actually do in tangible terms . . . the situation was vastly different from 1953 when US assistance had been helpful." His only real hope was for a civilian government that would "accept the Constitution, i.e., the monarchy, and on the other hand have the support of Shariatmadari and the moderate clergy." The problem was that for a coalition to work "Shariatmadari and the

National Front would have to break with Khomeini and come out publicly for a negotiated settlement. If the moderates surrendered to Khomeini's dictates he would likely call for a jihad and there would be a bloodbath. Even some of the military would take their obligations to Islam ahead of their obligations to the Shah."

SUNDAY, NOVEMBER 5, dawned overcast with light drizzle and temperatures predicted in the high fifties by the afternoon. There was nothing at first to suggest that Tehran's simmering unrest would come to a boil, or that by evening residents would be standing on their rooftops watching the town burn from one end to the other. In the morning, staff at the Sheraton Hotel prepared the banquet hall for the annual St. Andrew's Ball, and in Shemiran the Niavaran Cultural Center opened its doors for the visiting Shadow Theater of China. Despite the recent surge of anti-Semitism, the Goldis Cinema was screening *Fiddler on the Roof.* Ambassador William Sullivan started his morning with a visit to Iran's beleaguered prime minister Jafar Sharif-Emami, who told him that "order was rapidly evaporating and that he felt a military government was needed." The prime minister said he doubted that the Shah's strategy of trying to peel away moderate clergy and politicians from the Khomeini movement would succeed because Shariatmadari and the National Front lacked "courage." When Sullivan asked why the army was not doing more to restore lost Iranian oil production, Sharif-Emami pinned the blame on Savak, which he intimated had gone rogue. Sullivan returned to his embassy in time for a luncheon appointment with Ambassador Tony Parsons. As the Briton's Rolls-Royce swung into Roosevelt Avenue, Parsons took note of demonstrators filling the sidewalks and "the feeling of extreme tension was palpable."

For the third day in a row, thousands of young protesters gathered outside the main gates of Tehran University, hurling projectiles and chanting. This time when they surged forward and began attacking a bank across the road the troops "sort of shrugged their shoulders, waved goodbye and were gone." As if by prearranged signal, similar scenes were reported elsewhere in the capital. Trucks filled with army conscripts drove back to base and left the city's flash points exposed to the crowds. Students surged toward the center of town waving staves and hurling rocks and bottles. Mobs from the bazaar joined in and "hijacked buses and lorries and set them on fire. . . . Workers in the Palace of Justice and the Commerce

Ministry tore up pictures of the Shah and tossed them out of the window."

The rioting followed the pattern of earlier insurrections in Tabriz and Isfahan. Buildings associated with foreigners were targeted for destruction, and "carpet stores owned by Jews were attacked, their ornate and priceless carpets dragged into the streets and burnt," reported the correspondent for the *Times* of London. For the first time the students also set their sights on diplomatic missions. Dozens of youths clambered over the gates of the British embassy, overpowered the guards, and destroyed the guardhouse. They poured onto the grounds, ordered all the staff out of the main office block, and set it alight. Only the presence of Iranian Army tanks and troops prevented a second invasion of the U.S. embassy, from where Sullivan and Parsons watched incredulously as buildings to their left and right burst into flames: "One large eleven-story building two streets away became a towering inferno, burning for several hours before it collapsed in a heap of rubble with a resounding swoosh."

Panic took hold in Tehran's commercial district. Foreigners caught up in the riot were chased, abused, and roughed up. Americans Bruce and Eileen Vernor were lunching with friends when their driver ran into the restaurant and told them to quickly get out because "there is a mob coming toward us." Diners grabbed their coats and bags and ran to safety just before the windows were smashed in. American advisers in the Ministry of Labor were "forcibly evicted" from their offices. Two Bell Helicopter employees barely escaped with their lives when their Iranian taxi driver was fatally shot in the head by a sniper while he was ferrying them across town. Fifty-six British stewardesses were trapped on the eleventh floor of the Imperial Hotel. "Below us on the streets rioters were burning pictures of the Shah and lighting massive bonfires," said one woman. "They were smashing everything in sight. It was like a Guy Fawkes night gone mad." An Iranian ran up to a Western journalist and ran his finger across his throat in a slitting motion. "The Shah is finished," he said with a grin. "Write that."

By the time American high school student Jonathan Kirkendall got home from school in the afternoon "smoke [was] rising over the town" and "we could hear guns going off." "The mob spread garbage in the street right in front of our building and lit it on fire so that black columns of smoke were soon going up all around our building," expatriate lawyer John Westberg wrote in his diary. "The rioters then picked up a minibus that was parked directly in front of our building, carried it a short distance around the corner, and laid it on its side squarely in the middle of the street to serve as a barricade to keep the martial law forces from coming through that way." There were fraught scenes at the Tehran American School, where teachers and administrators struggled to safely evacuate thirty-six hundred children from two campuses in different parts of town. Elementary school principal Donna Colquitt, who had children as young as four-year-old kindergarteners to think about, rallied her teachers and administrators and reminded them of the job they had to do. "There will be no hysteria," she instructed. "We will have no tears in front of the children." The staff loaded the children into their minibuses and before each set off Donna climbed aboard and cheerfully told them that "they were playing a new game on the way home, and that they should get down on the floor until each one arrived home." But the ride home was a terrifying ordeal for students whose buses strayed into the riot zone. The children heard rocks glancing off the window grilles and crouched low, saying not a word and hiding their faces in the hope that no one would see they were American.

Out on the streets, paper rained down from office windows like confetti, and buses and cars exploded in flames. The Radio City Cinema burst into flames. Buildings that housed Pan American World Airways, the German automobile manufacturer BMW, and the Irano-British Bank burned out of control. Mobs sacked the ground floor of the luxury Waldorf Hotel and used accelerants to light a fire that quickly spread through the lobby. In scenes straight out of *The Towering Inferno*, seventy-five terrified guests fled to the hotel roof while dozens of others were seen hanging out of upper windows, screaming for help. Two young men working on an adjacent construction site swung into action and pulled off a remarkably daring rescue operation. They attached a building pallet onto the boom of a crane and then lowered it onto the roof. The trapped guests scrambled aboard five at a time, lay down, and were carefully winched to the street below. Shortly after the last guest was lowered to safety the Waldorf went up like a blowtorch. Thick clouds of black smoke from four cinemas and an estimated 400 banks billowed over the Shah's stricken capital. Army troops, police, and the emergency services were conspicuous by their absence. "As slogan-chanting demonstrators surged from neighborhood to neighborhood, breaking banks and igniting buildings— the Information Ministry among them—police, army and firefighting units often were nowhere to be seen," reported the *Los Angeles Times* correspondent at the scene. "Only after a particular area had been hit, sometimes as much as a half-hour, did the troops appear, seemingly indifferent to renewed destruction raging only a block or two away."

Ambassador Parsons decided to make a dash for it. He left his Rolls-Royce at Roosevelt Avenue and accepted Sullivan's offer to drive back in an Iranian-made Peykan. Parsons's plainclothes security detail followed behind in an unmarked police car. "When we emerged into the main street, I found myself faced by a scene such as I had not experienced since the end of the Second World War," Parsons later wrote. "Fires were burning everywhere, furniture and office equipment had been piled in the middle of the street and set alight, burning cars and buses littered the roadway. Young men were dancing around in a frenzy, feeding the flames and plastering the few passing cars with stickers reading 'Death to the Shah.'"

The two cars were edging past flaming debris in Ferdowsi Square when rioters spotted the radio in the police car. Parsons watched as a group of young men "wrenched open the doors and were trying to drag the occupants out. The last I saw of my escort, who eventually found their way back to the American embassy, was the car careering down a side street with three of its doors open and a mob of young men clinging to the sides." Men clung to the roof of his own car and to save himself the British ambassador joined in the chants of "Death to the Shah!" Parsons retreated to the safety of the French embassy and didn't make it back to his own smoldering compound until late afternoon.

Columns of smoke were clearly visible from Niavaran, where courtiers rushed to the windows to watch the city burn. In the late afternoon a large mob was seen advancing up the hill and the Imperial Guard took up defensive positions and moved Chieftain tanks and an antiaircraft battery into place. Barbed wire was strung around the perimeter of the palace grounds, and machine-gun-toting troops stood watch. General Khosrodad and several senior military officials flew over the city in a helicopter to survey the destruction. They were appalled by the scale of the carnage. "This has got to stop," said Khosrodad. "We have to act severely or things will really get out of control."

The generals returned to Niavaran and appealed to Grand Master of Ceremonies Amir Aslan Afshar to talk to the Shah, but the older man was quick to put them in their place. "I am the protocol chief," he reminded them. "You are the generals. Why don't *you* speak with him? You command all the military in Tehran. Why don't you stop this nonsense?" They walked over to the Jahan Nama Palace, and when Afshar saw the Shah at the foot of the stairs he prostrated himself in the traditional manner, kneeling and gripping the monarch's shoes. The generals fell to their knees, too. The Shah, who was embarrassed by their display, tried and failed to pull Afshar to his feet. "What is it?" he asked.

"Your Majesty, the city is on fire," said Afshar. "The banks have been burned. The citizens' possessions have been destroyed. Civil documents have been cast away. No one is safe. It is no longer clear what remains to the people or of the authority they can turn to. Please, Sire, something must be done."

"But the army is attending to the matter," the Shah told them. He was apparently unaware that the decision by the army to pull back earlier in the day had allowed the tide of vandalism to wash unchecked through the streets.

General Khosrodad stood and saluted. Tears ran down his cheeks. "Your Majesty," he begged, "your army has become an object of scorn, contempt, disrespect. They spit on your soldiers. No honor remains to the Imperial forces. Your Majesty must order us to defend you, the country, and ourselves."

The Shah, "visibly shaken" by this display of emotion, offered his assurance that "Of course, we shall take measures." He returned to his office and asked Afshar to send for General Oveissi, which the generals interpreted as a sign that he meant to replace Sharif-Emami with his martial law administrator. The Shah also asked for the American and British ambassadors to join him at Niavaran so he could explain his decision to suspend civilian government.

Sullivan was the first to arrive. Usually when guests arrived at Niavaran they passed through security and were welcomed and announced by an aide-de-camp. This evening, however, the usual guards and courtiers were nowhere to be seen, their absence a sign that the Imperial Court was in a state of complete disarray. "While I was puzzling what to do next, a door from one of the small rooms off the drawing room opened and the Shahbanou came in," said Sullivan. "She was obviously surprised to see me, and I had clearly not expected that she would be the first person I would encounter there." Queen Farah arranged for Sullivan to be escorted to her husband's study, where the Shah explained that he had run out of time and choices—a military government was inevitable. The ambassador responded that rumors were spreading that Savak agents had deliberately lit the fires to justify an army takeover. The Shah sighed and answered, "Who knows? These days I am prepared to believe anything."

At one point the Shah answered a call on his private line. By now Sullivan knew enough Persian to "make out that he was telling [the Queen] of his intention to install a military government and answering some of the reservations she was expressing about such a decision. It was a gentle, patient sort of conversation with nothing peremptory in its tone." Court liberals associated Oveissi with the debacle at Jaleh Square and feared that his appointment would doom any chance of a settlement with moderate clergy. Farah preferred General Gholam Reza Azhari, chief of the supreme commander's staff, "a thinking, cultured man . . . considered a moderate who was open to dialogue." When the call ended the Shah placed one of his own to General Azhari, asking him to come at once to the palace. He told Sullivan he had decided to appoint Azhari and not Oveissi to lead the new military government. The American expressed relief at the Shah's decision to appoint a moderate and graduate of the U.S. Army Command and General Staff College. They were eventually joined by Ambassador Parsons, who arrived at the palace in an armored personnel carrier and in a state of high dudgeon, still furious about the attack earlier in the day on his embassy compound. Unlike Sullivan, who believed the street gossip that Savak was behind the arson attacks, Parsons and his staff had concluded that Mujahedin guerrilla fighters were responsible: the scale and organization behind the violence fit the pattern of unrest seen elsewhere around the country.

Downstairs, courtiers and generals drank tea to celebrate what they assumed was Oveissi's pending appointment to the premiership. Their fear was that the Shah would appoint another in a line of mild-mannered milquetoasts, men who lacked the guts to make the tough decisions. General Azhari, for example, was known in the officer corps as a man who spoke loudly and carried a small stick. He was also seen as too close to U.S. officials, who were known to oppose harsh measures to restore order. The crowd hushed. Sullivan and Parsons appeared at the top of the landing, and the crowd parted to let them walk through the grand lobby. The ambassadors brushed past General Khosrodad and his friend Kambiz Atabai. Atabai could not contain himself and asked Parsons, whom he knew socially, "Mr. Ambassador, who is going to be nominated prime minister?"

Before Parsons had a chance to reply, William Sullivan wheeled around and delivered the smug news everyone dreaded: "A *civilized* general."

Khosrodad and Atabai were crushed by the news. "When we heard that we knew it would be Azhari," said Atabai. "He was a good general for the salons but not a decisive man. And he did not want the job. In that moment I knew it was all over. We were finished."

General Azhari most certainly did not want the job. He arrived as Sullivan and Parsons were on their way out. As he climbed the stairs he looked like a man consigned to the gallows.

ELLI ANTONIADES WAS in Greece when she heard that the Shah had appointed a military government. For the past several weeks daily life had become an ordeal for the Queen's oldest and closest friend, who lived with her mother behind the Russian embassy near Rudaki Hall. Every morning now the two women opened their door to see the familiar refrain "Death to the Shah" painted in large letters. A friend had recently handed Elli a revolver and told her to keep it ready in case "they" came over the wall. She stubbornly refused to submit to the new regime on the streets or wear the obligatory head scarf. "People threw things, they yelled abuse," she said. "A lot of women covered up because they felt threatened."

Before leaving Athens to fly home to Tehran, she called on a friend who worked in the Greek foreign ministry. He asked why she was going back. "Elli," he said. "It's finished. It's over." "It was so difficult," she remembered. "Not to understand, but to accept."

23

SULLIVAN'S FOLLY

How hurriedly we are putting nails to our coffin.

—THE SHAH

*Tell the Shah that it is better that a thousand
Iranians die now than a million people die later.*

—SADDAM HUSSEIN

On Monday, November 6, Iranians awoke to the news that the country was under military rule and a 9:00 p.m. to 5:00 a.m. curfew. For the first time since the unrest began, troop commanders were handed orders to shoot martial law violators on sight. Twenty tanks entered the capital from the west, and tens of thousands of troops took up positions near key installations and trouble spots. There were scattered outbreaks of violence but no major challenges to the army. Troops fired into the air to break up small crowds around Rudaki Hall, Tehran University, and the British embassy, but otherwise the streets were quiet. The threat to shoot curfew violators and rioters was popular among Tehranis still shell-shocked by Sunday's rampages. "A jolly good job, too," an office worker told an American foreign correspondent. "I think shooting is the best thing. These people [the rioters] are mad." "We feel the army will give us protection now," said a construction worker repairing the entryway to the battered Waldorf Hotel. The driver of a pickup truck agreed with that sentiment: "Maybe now we get peace."

This time martial law was backed up by arrests. Leading dissidents and opposition leaders were detained, and censorship was reimposed. Schools and universities were closed for one week and street gatherings of more than two people were banned. Tehranis cautiously ventured into the streets to stock up on food and other essentials. "Long lines of automobiles and people with plastic containers formed at gasoline stations in the capital of the second-largest oil exporting country in the world," reported the *New York Times*. "With almost no bus transportation and relatively few cars on the streets, businesses closed and some food shortages developed. Uncollected garbage piles are rising throughout the city." The country's telex system remained out of order. Credit dried up, investment was frozen, capital flight accelerated, and people rushed to buy foreign exchange. Along with the hardship there was a general sense of relief that the authorities had finally intervened to restore order. With Iran's major cities secure, the battle for Iran's future moved from streets in the north to the oil fields in the south. The intellectuals, students, and leftists weren't about to give up and decided to try to collapse the national economy with the help of striking oil workers. "With the oil workers on our side, we found new confidence," said one protest leader. Skeleton crews kept oil output at 1.2 million barrels a day, barely enough for domestic consumption but far below the usual 6 million barrels required for export. "We were suppressed for so many years," said an oil worker. "We suffered for so long that now we have burst. It was not the Shah who liberalized but we who grasped liberalization from him. We took it."

Reza Ghotbi arrived at Jahan Nama Palace on Monday morning with a television crew in tow. The night before, the Shah had phoned him at home requesting help to write a speech he planned to give to the Iranian people the next day explaining his decision to install a military administration. "Sire, I am not a speechwriter," Ghotbi protested. The silence on the other end of the line convinced him otherwise. "I had the impression he thought or may think I am refusing his request. So I said, 'I will do whatever Your Majesty wants me to do.'" He offered to consult with Hushang Nahavandi and Hossein Nasr in putting together a draft.

"Nasr," said the Shah.

"What does Your Majesty want in the speech?"

"I will bring a patriotic government," explained the voice on the other end of the line, "but because of the turmoil I have to bring in a military government first."

Ghotbi reminded the Shah that "military governments are also patriotic."

"I don't mean patriotic," the Shah said, correcting himself. "I mean democratic. I am going to send you some notes people have written for the speech." He was referring to former prime ministers Ali Amini and Amir Hoveyda who had been asked for their thoughts.

Later that night a court official drove to Ghotbi's house and delivered typed-up notes for the draft. Ghotbi noticed that one phrase in particular was underlined and circled for emphasis: "I have heard the voice of the revolution."

The Shah's hero de Gaulle had expressed similar sentiments to the people of France when he made his dramatic appeal to them in 1968 to rally to his side, and like his hero the Shah wanted to deliver a speech that cloaked him in the mantle of national unity while acknowledging past mistakes. Trying to achieve a balance between strength and contrition would not be easy. "In my mind that was what he wanted," said Ghotbi. "From the notes, and from our conversations, my idea was that the Shah was the Good King, the father of the country." Ghotbi recalled a story the Shah had told him from his youth. During a visit to the provinces an old woman had approached him and said, "You are younger than my son, but you are my father." Her words had stayed with the Shah ever since. "What I thought he wanted to do was say, 'I am the loving father of his nation but at this moment what the nation needs is tough love.'" The Shah made it clear that he wanted Ghotbi to collaborate with Hossein Nasr. "For months, I and Ghotbi would say to the Shah, 'Why don't you talk to the people?'" said Nasr.

On Monday morning, Ghotbi and Nasr went to the Queen's chambers with their speech draft but found her out of sorts. The unrest of the previous day had frayed her nerves. "She came out and said she couldn't read the speech because she had taken a sleeping pill and was not alert," said Ghotbi. Farah read the speech only after it was delivered. "I did not find anything wrong with it," she said. "But I don't know what transpired before. Dr. Nasr says the ideas came from His Majesty. Who was involved in drawing up those ideas I do not know."

The Shah became testy when by late morning he still had not read the speech. "I was asked to see what had happened to the speech," said Amir Afshar. "I was informed that Reza Ghotbi and Hossein Nasr had taken the draft of the speech to the Empress. Once I informed the Shah of this, he became very angry." "Why have they taken the speech to Her Majesty?" demanded the Shah. "Is she the one who reads it on television? Am I not to read it at least once to know what it contains before I deliver it?" Ghotbi and Nasr hurried over. "For the first time, the Shah came to my office, and sat behind my desk," recalled Afshar, who called in two secretaries in case the Shah wanted to make notes and changes. As the Shah read through the speech he expressed concern because he thought it "put him in a position of weakness." "I should not say the things that have been written here for me," he protested.

Ghotbi and Nasr assured him that "if he were to give a speech of this sort, he might as well put himself squarely on the side of the people and say what the people wanted him to say." "Your Majesty, you have to say now what the people want to hear and you have to raise their spirits and change the atmosphere." The Shah threw the speech down on the desk and, followed by Afshar, stalked out. After calming down he made several revisions, but with no time to rehearse before the two o'clock deadline he swallowed his reservations and decided to proceed. "He was not forced or manipulated," said Ghotbi.

Instead of the usual two o'clock national news broadcast, the Iranian people tuned in to watch and listen as the Shah explained his decision to install a military government. He appeared ill at ease, tense, and gaunt. He struggled to read the handheld cue cards from behind his desk. "In the climate of liberalization which began gradually two years ago you arose against oppression and corruption," he began. "The revolution of the Iranian people cannot fail to have my support as the monarch of Iran and as an Iranian." The Shah, who had already surrendered his executive powers, now proceeded to bury his legacy. "I once again repeat my oath to the Iranian nation to undertake not to allow the past mistakes, unlawful acts, oppression and corruption to recur but to make up for them," he mechanically intoned. "I heard the revolutionary message of you the people, the Iranian nation. I am the guardian of the constitutional monarchy which is a God given gift. A gift entrusted to the Shah by the people." It was a phrase that became synonymous with appeasement and surrender.

The Shah's speech evoked not de Gaulle but another French ruler, Louis XVI, sent to the block with his wife, Marie Antoinette, and Nicholas II, the Russian emperor shot and bayoneted with his wife, Empress Alexandra, and their children and servants in a Siberian cellar in 1918. "In this speech, instead of pointing to all the good things done in the country, and all the progress, he only spoke about the failures," observed Amir Afshar. "The speech was a total failure." The servile, apologetic tone caused revulsion among royalists, who could not bear the humiliation of watching the King of Kings debase himself before the mullahs. "The tone was contrite," reported *Time*. "The words were conciliatory. The old imperial arrogance was gone. . . . The speech was unprecedented for Iran's proud autocrat."

Royalists who had not yet left the country began packing their bags: they could tell that the Shah had no fight left in him. Liberals were more hopeful that the speech might appease moderate ulama and persuade the National Front and the Liberation Movement to reach an accommodation with the palace. "People called the court and said they liked the speech," said Ghotbi. "Shariatmadari said he had tears in his eyes." The Shah was polite enough to phone Nasr afterward and thank him for his work. Later, he considered the speech one of his biggest regrets. "I should never have agreed to give this speech," he admitted to Afshar.

In Paris on November 6, Grand Ayatollah Khomeini told a large crowd of journalists gathered at Neauphle-le-Château that he would not relent in his crusade to bring down the monarchy. "In one hand, the Shah held out a letter of repentance for his crimes, but in the other he held out a bayonet and a gun," he jeered. "Until the day an Islamic republic is installed the struggle of our people will continue." He expressed "great bitterness" toward the U.S. government for its continued support for the Shah. "The relationship between the American government and our government that is now like that of a master and a servant should finally cease and a healthy relationship would then replace it." As long as the United States remained "hostile to our Islamic movement our attitude will be negative." Khomeini repeated his earlier call for soldiers in the Iranian army "to join the people" against "the traitor."

In the months since Khomeini's arrival in Paris, Abolhassan Banisadr, Ibrahim Yazdi, and Sadegh Ghotzbadegh had successfully molded his public image in the foreign press as a venerable sage leading an uprising against a corrupt and cruel king. Reporters were required to submit their questions each morning in advance of Khomeini's daily fifteen-minute afternoon press conferences. The several-hours delay gave Banisadr and his media relations committee time to draft replies, which were intended to present Khomeini as a social moderate, respectful of women's rights and human rights, tolerant of different political views, yet a dedicated anti-Communist. They emphasized that Khomeini had no interest in politics and was opposed to only those aspects of the Shah's modernization program that did not help the poor. Banisadr told reporters that Khomeini "rejects the authoritarian models of Islamic republicanism in much of the Arab world. Iran is not an Arab country." After he returned to Iran, he explained, Khomeini would leave politics to the politicians and spend the rest of his days in a seminary in Qom.

Khomeini went along with the game but at times chafed against his handlers' constraints. He could barely contain the hatred he felt for Americans. In his November 6 press conference he insisted that "at least 45,000" American military advisers were in Iran and that the Iranian Army was "totally under their control." This was yet another gross exaggeration: only 5,000 of the approximately 52,000 Americans living in Iran were military personnel. The rest were dependents, civilian professionals, and Americans married to Iranians. Khomeini's condemnation of all Americans living in Iran as "hostile to our Islamic movement" placed everyone, including women and children, in the direct line of fire.

IN WASHINGTON, PRESIDENT Carter's national security team met at 11:00 a.m. on Monday, November 6, to discuss the Tehran riots and their aftermath. If a week was a long time in politics, the seventy-two hours since National Security Adviser Brzezinski had assured Jimmy Carter that Iran was not in the throes of a full-scale revolution was a lifetime. Brzezinski was especially critical of the CIA, which apparently had failed to anticipate the serious nature of unrest, and also of Ambassador Sullivan, who he had learned had been in contact with the revolutionaries.

One of the most pressing questions facing officials was what to do with the large American community residing in Iran. Popular hatred toward the Shah extended to Americans, who were blamed for propping up the regime and profiting from the oil boom. American citizens reported daily harassment in the streets. American homes were firebombed, businesses invaded and sacked, and family pets poisoned. "There has been an increase in number of random telephone threats to foreigners," reported the U.S. embassy. "Many callers know name of recipient and those receiving calls are being advised to leave Iran in 24 hours, two weeks, or by December 2, or be killed." The date marked the start of the Muslim holy month of Muharram. "Absence of newspapers and minimal reporting on radio have left both Iranians and foreigners prey to loosest kind of rumors. Example is story which is untrue, repeat untrue, that three Americans were killed evening November 8 in Tajrish area of north Tehran. It appears opposition is attempting to increase psychological pressure on foreign residents by threats and rumor-mongering." Some companies began pulling out family dependents but most followed official instructions to stay in place and hunker down.

In Washington, officials considered an airlift using wide-bodied jets and aircraft carriers but admitted an evacuation could take nine or ten days, assuming Iranian airports remained open. The other question was how an evacuation would affect the Shah's confidence and army morale. Brzezinski shut down the conversation: "Any discussion of evacuation implies doubts about the Shah and about U.S.-Iranian relations, which can be very damaging."

The Israeli government was not about to wait and see what December would bring. The Shah's November 6 speech to the nation provided a convenient cover for three El Al airliners to leave Iranian airspace on Monday, bound for Tel Aviv. The 365 passengers on board comprised the final airlift of Israeli citizens from Iranian soil. With the exception of Israeli diplomatic staff and their families who stayed behind, everyone else was safely out.

IRANIANS EXPECTED PRIME Minister Azhari to take a no-nonsense approach to unrest and end the strategy of concessions. They were startled when in his first address to the Majles he preached conciliation instead and even recited quotes from the Quran. "We are in office temporarily," he intoned. "Once order is restored, we will hand over power to a truly national government which will organize entirely free elections and which will grant all liberties." Azhari invited the ulama to join new "emergency committees" established by the military to enforce order in riot-torn cities. They rejected the offer, and the National Front called instead for more strikes. But while the opposition rejected Azhari's authority, Niavaran swiftly agreed to his demands to cooperate with an investigation into the finances of all members of the Imperial Family and secure the Shah's authorization to arrest former prime minister Amir Abbas Hoveyda and other former top officials on charges relating to graft, financial mismanagement, and abuse of power. Others prominent on the list included Dariush Homayoun, the former minister of information who back in January had ordered *Ettelaat* to print the defamatory letter against Khomeini that sparked the riots in Qom, and Gholam Reza Nikpey, former mayor of Tehran.

Faced with Azhari's request, the Shah summoned the Queen and their closest advisers to his office to discuss the matter. "I am being pressed to authorize the arrest of Hoveyda, under the powers allowed by martial law, because they say it would pacify public opinion," he said. "Let me ask you to give me your advice on this matter." The consensus among those in the room was that the arrested men would be well looked after by the military and ensured a fair trial. But elderly court minister Ardalan expressed disgust at the idea they should serve up their own to appease the mobs. "I do not understand how you can arrest a former prime minister who was in power for thirteen years," he protested. At one point the Shah's phone rang and the others watched as he listened in silence. He hung up the receiver and told them they had run out of time. Later, he told his wife that Savak chief General Moghadam had informed him that "Mr. Hoveyda's arrest was more important than our daily bread." The group approved the arrests but the Shah balked at phoning Hoveyda as a courtesy to explain his decision. "That would not be easy for me," he said. He turned to the Queen: "You could do it, perhaps."

"Why me?" Farah protested. "He was *your* prime minister, not mine!"

The Shah hurriedly swallowed the pill: "It shall be done." But as the meeting broke up he was heard to say, "How hurriedly we are putting nails to our coffin."

ON ROOSEVELT AVENUE, Ambassador Sullivan decided that the Shah was finished.

The ambassador wrote a lengthy cable to Washington titled "Thinking the Unthinkable," in which he argued that the Shah's basis of support had shrunk to the military, which was unlikely to sanction a bloodbath to keep him in power. The ideal scenario Sullivan laid out was the departure of the Shah and his top generals into exile, followed by an accommodation between younger officers and the opposition. "The religious [people] would find it useful for the military to remain intact because they have no Islamic instruments for maintaining law and order," Sullivan advised. Khomeini "could be expected to return to Iran in triumph and hold a Gandhi-like position in the political constellation." Because Khomeini was likely to choose as his new prime minister a politician like Mehdi

Bazargan, who could work alongside the military, moderates and anti-Communists were likely to win the 1979 elections. It was a gamble, but if the Shah was replaced by Khomeini the Iran of the 1980s would likely assume a less pro-Western posture in international relations but could still be relied on as an important anchor of stability in the Persian Gulf. According to Sullivan's logic, Khomeini was not a threat to U.S. interests. The "Thinking the Unthinkable" telegram became the basis for what Henry Precht later referred to with dry disdain as "Sullivan's grand idea that Khomeini and the military could run the country." In fact, the ideas expressed in the telegram were not those of Sullivan but of Mehdi Bazargan, leader of the Liberation Movement of Iran, which showed the extent to which the ambassador and his diplomats had become influenced by English-speaking, Westernized republican Iranians.

The telegram showed that William Sullivan was at sea in Iran: the complexities of the country's political fabric, its religious traditions, its culture, and the characteristics of its people eluded him. What Sullivan failed so spectacularly to understand was that many Iranians, including most farmers, workers, moderate ulama, and conservatives in the middle and upper-middle classes, still supported the Shah and counted them-selves as royalists. Khomeini was one of only several marjas—and the junior one at that—but Sullivan bestowed on him the title "leader" and inexplicably decided he was a pacifist in the spirit of Gandhi. He was utterly wrong on the question of the military. The Shah's generals, men such as Oveissi, Badrei, and Khosrodad, consummate military profes-sionals and patriots who had sworn their lives to serve crown and king-dom, were not about to voluntarily board planes and hand Iran over to the mullahs. If anything, they were prepared to either stage a coup or retreat to the south and then wage civil war.

Though Sullivan ended his telegram endorsing the current U.S. policy of supporting the Shah and the military, he made it clear to his senior counselors that the telegram should be interpreted as their blueprint for action. "Sullivan had these ideas himself," confirmed George Lambrakis. "And he talked Washington into it. Basically, Sullivan was trying to walk his way through the muck. He was also working closely with Tony Par-sons. We thought the moderates might have enough weight to balance Khomeini. We believed that Khomeini would go to Qom. Khomeini was the big political ayatollah but he was not the main ayatollah. We believed he was isolated and his religious credentials were not of the highest order but his political influence was." Sullivan pursued a self-paralyzing policy. On the one hand, the ambassador pressed the Shah to continue with liberalization and appoint Azhari, a softhearted military prime minister unlikely to crack down hard on dissent. "We didn't want to be responsible for shedding blood or a repeat of 1953," explained Lambrakis. Yet the Shah's refusal to use force made him appear weak in Sullivan's eyes. "When the Shah failed to react strongly after Jaleh Square and November 5, we concluded he was finished," said Stempel. "He was fucked! He would not order the troops to shoot. If he'd come down hard he would have survived." But the Americans also concluded they were powerless. "After November 5 nobody gave a shit what we thought," Stempel admitted. "The U.S. was sidelined."

Through his words and deeds, Ambassador Sullivan sent Mehdi Bazargan the unmistakable signal that he was ready to cut a deal on behalf of the United States, in effect declaring American neutrality and offering Khomeini an assurance that "we were not involved on either side, to let them know that the Americans were perfectly prepared to deal with them." Though the ambassador had not cleared his strategy with the White House, Bazargan naturally assumed from Sullivan's behavior that the Carter administration had withdrawn support from the Shah. In fact, Sullivan's strategy encouraged the Shah's enemies and removed one of the last obstacles to a takeover of Iran by Islamic fundamentalists.

IN LATE NOVEMBER, Queen Farah became involved in two extraordinary initiatives to try to prevent collapse. The first involved Shahpur Bakhtiar, one of the leaders of the National Front and a former cabinet minister in Mohammad Mossadeq's government. Bakhtiar's grandfather had been executed by the Qajars, and his father was jailed and executed under Reza Shah, and as he once told his cousin Reza Ghotbi, "I have blues on my skin from the Shah's jail." Yet Bakhtiar had never walked in lockstep with his allies on the secular left. Though he opposed the Shah's personal rule, he admired the general thrust of his social and economic reforms, and he was appalled that men such as Bazargan were prepared to set aside their own deeply held principles and accept Khomeini's leadership of the anti-Shah forces, whom he regarded as "barbarians." Bakhtiar worried that the extremists could easily overpower the leftists and democrats who lacked their own charismatic leader and were not trained for armed combat.

After Bakhtiar made his concerns clear, former prime minister Jamshid Amuzegar gently steered him toward the Imperial Court. Bakhtiar hoped to enter into a dialogue with the Shah but refused to come to Niavaran until he had a better sense of the monarch's attitude toward political reform. The Queen asked her husband, "Do you want me to go and talk to him and see what his position is?" He agreed, and Farah arranged a clandestine rendezvous at the home of her aunt Louise Ghotbi, Reza's mother. Farah's role as mediator between the Shah and Bakhtiar was carried out with the blessing of both men, though later she was accused by her critics of promoting Bakhtiar to advance her own clan interests. In true Iranian fashion, and although the two had never before met, Farah and Bakhtiar were related. "My mother was the sister of Bakhtiar's mother," said her cousin Reza Ghotbi. "Although we were first cousins I had never met him, though I knew his son, Yves, because Shahpur was much older. My mother didn't like his policies. We had a very large family. I had five uncles and I only met two of them." Farah's critics neglected to point out that Bakhtiar was more closely related to Queen Soraya, who was also a cousin, and that as late as November she still believed Hushang Nahavandi was the best candidate for the premiership.

The Queen's meeting with Bakhtiar took place on a cold, overcast late November day. Louise Ghotbi's house was a two-mile drive from the palace, and Farah set off, with her security detail bringing up the rear. Bakhtiar arrived thirty minutes early and spent the time chatting with Mme Ghotbi. "He told her she looked so much like her sister," said her son Reza, "and that he lost his mother when he was very young and he always wanted to see the aunt who looked like his mother." The Queen arrived and Louise withdrew to leave them alone. After formalities, Bakhtiar began by launching into a litany of complaints. "He made an analysis of the situation. He lamented the past—the Shah had ruled instead of the government—and said the Shah must reign and not rule. If he had done that we wouldn't be here. Everything was going wrong and it all pointed in one direction—to him." Farah listened patiently but felt there was no time to waste. "Look," she said, "the country is in deep trouble. We now must concentrate on saving it rather than harping on the past." Bakhtiar said he agreed with her. He was prepared to meet with the Shah if certain conditions were met. They included the release from jail of opposition leader Karim Sanjabi, who had been detained following his trip to Paris to see Khomeini. Farah returned to Niavaran and briefed her husband on the conversation. They both felt this first contact was promising. Bakhtiar supported the Constitution and the monarchy, and he would not let old grudges get in the way of working for the national interest. His name was put on a short list of names for the position of the next civilian prime minister.

The Queen's second initiative was led by her private secretary Hossein Nasr, who was involved in intense negotiations with moderate ulama. Grand Ayatollah Shariatmadari still had not given up on reaching an accommodation with the Shah, though he was under relentless pressure from Khomeini's agents in Qom, who surrounded his residence and spied on him. "At the height of the revolution Shariatmadari wanted to talk to the Shah," said Nasr. "But there were men downstairs with guns. He said to me, 'I can't call until nine p.m., when the gunmen have gone. I will go to the women's part of the house and call you on my wife's phone.'" The day and time were arranged, and the Shah sat by his phone for two hours, waiting for the Marja's call. But Shariatmadari was unable to get away and the conversation never happened. "I don't know what is happening in Iran," said the Marja. "It is erupting like a volcano, and, like a volcano, after building up pressure for years and years it is impossible to stop."

Next, Nasr set his sights on Grand Ayatollah Abol Qasem Khoi, who lived out of harm's way in Najaf and led the "quietist" school favored by Musa Sadr. Despite the publicity that surrounded Khomeini, Khoi enjoyed the status as paramount marja and boasted the biggest following among the Shia faithful. "Khoi was not siding with the revolutionaries," said Nasr. "And he did not believe this was the role of Shiism. He was the supreme enlightened one, the most emulated by the Shia. I decided to go and visit him." Nasr decided that Queen Farah should accompany him so that she could be seen in the presence of the most influential and popular of the marjas. "It was Dr. Nasr's idea," she recalled. "The idea was that if I go and see Khoi he might say something [in public] to help ease the problems." Her willingness to go, and Khoi's decision to receive her, showed just how desperate the moderates were to try to form a block against Khomeini's ambitions. Farah was escorted by Nasr and accompanied by her mother, Mrs. Diba; her children Farahnaz and Ali Reza; Reza Ghotbi; and two generals.

The Queen and her party flew first to Baghdad on November 18, where they were met at the airport by Iraq's minister of health. When they arrived at their guest villa they learned that Saddam Hussein wished to pay his respects. His motorcade pulled up at four o'clock and he swept in with his entourage. Nasr was impressed with the Iraqi leader's height, dark good looks, and natty dress sense: "He arrived wearing a European suit with an Islamic cloak, an abaya, which fell off when he shrugged his shoulders, and his servants rushed to pick it up." It made for great theater. Farah introduced Hussein to her mother and then to Nasr. He shook everyone's hands and then told Nasr, fluent in Arabic, that he had something to tell the Queen in private.

Saddam Hussein, the Queen, and Nasr moved to a side room, where they shared a small sofa. Nasr sat between them and translated. Hussein had already offered to assassinate Khomeini, whom he worried was stirring grievances and sectarian tensions inside Iraq, which, like Iran, was a Shia-majority society. He preferred a stable, pro-Western Iran under the Shah to a radical theological state that might be tempted to export its revolution throughout the region. The Iraqi turned to Nasr and calmly said, "Tell Her Majesty to tell my brother the Shah to take out his tanks and guns and turn them against the revolutionaries. Tell him it is better that a thousand Iranians die now than a million people die later." Nasr translated this to Farah "and we looked at each other." After Hussein left they agreed that Farah would go back to Niavaran and relay the Iraqi strongman's advice to her husband.

From Baghdad they traveled to Najaf to see Khoi. This was not an easy trip for Farah. Since childhood she had associated the mullahs with bullying and repression. She bitterly resented them for cheering her husband to his face for so many years while plotting behind his back. "All these mullahs would push each other out of the way to have pictures taken with the King," she remembered with distaste. The trip to Najaf made her nervous. "I was uncomfortable. I remember entering the small entrance to his house and everyone was sitting around [looking obsequious]." There was a momentary flash of anger when Khoi's aides told her not to look directly at him. "I was told to look down. It was very difficult. He started talking Turkish with me because he knew my family came from Azerbaijan, but I don't speak Turkish."

Khoi told Farah that he acknowledged the Shah as the true Custodian of the Faith. He said he would pray for her husband, and in keeping with tradition presented her with a gold ring to give him. But he offered no public statement of support that could be used to rally the majority of the Shia people to the Shah's side. He proceeded to lecture the Queen on the state of daily life in a country he had not lived in for decades. "In Iran people are dying of hunger," he said. Farah was indignant. This was like Khomeini telling the world that schoolchildren in Iran ate grass to survive and that a hundred thousand people were behind bars. She wouldn't let these lies go unchallenged. "What hunger?" she retorted. Her decision to talk back struck a nerve. The paramount Marja decided that the Queen of Iran, though a direct relative of the Prophet, still needed to be taken to the woodshed and schooled in how to behave like a good Muslim wife. He regarded Farah as willful and therefore deviant. "At the end," said Queen Farah, "he told me, 'You are a Moslem, your pictures should not be in the newspapers, and you should not shake hands with me.' He lectured me on my clothes and about modesty."

Farah's mission to Najaf ended in failure, but at least an effort had been made. She returned to Niavaran to give her husband Khoi's ring and passed on Saddam Hussein's message to bloody the opposition. As she expected, he dismissed the idea as repellent: "I cannot sully my hands with the blood of my people."

TEHRAN UNDER MARTIAL law was a shadowland of rumor, intrigue, and barely suppressed hysteria. "In the downtown area, barricades have gone up around the ravages of burned-out cinemas and bars, and steel plates have replaced broken windows," reported *Time*. "Not many Iranian women venture out into the streets anymore; those who do shroud themselves in the chador, the long black veil that has become a sort of silent symbol of solidarity with the protest movement. Because everyone has to get home before the 9 p.m. curfew, the cocktail hour begins and ends earlier. Conversation, in more fashionable circles, tends to center on the shortage of butane gas for cooking and whether to stay and support the Shah or get out. Then everyone says their farewells and leaves, only to become ensnarled in a huge traffic jam on their way home. Promptly at 9 the shrill of the traffic gives way to silence and a long low rumble: the Shah's tanks are once again rolling into position."

As the world around them collapsed, Tehranis were prepared to believe the most fantastic and bizarre conspiracy theories. Iran's most persecuted religious minority, the Baha'i, supposedly pulled the strings of revolution. The British government plotted with the Freemasons to divide the Middle East between them. The CIA orchestrated the labor unrest in the southern oil fields. Queen Farah plotted a coup to depose her husband and seize the Peacock Throne. "The condition affects even the most rational and educated of men," the *Los Angeles Times* reported from Abadan. "Many people here and in Tehran are convinced that the Israelis are here helping the Shah put down public unrest. During the recent disturbances in Tehran, one Iranian pointed to troops guarding an intersection and said they were Israelis. When the soldiers were questioned, however, they answered in the everyday Farsi of the average Iranian. But the man still wasn't convinced." The belief that an unseen hand guided events from afar was not new. The Shah himself suspected that the United States, Great Britain, and the Soviet Union schemed to divide Iran among them. The conspiracy theories conveniently relieved Iranians, and middle-class Iranians in particular, of any responsibility for the catastrophe befalling the kingdom.

Middle-class Iran's fatal attraction to Khomeini and fundamentalist Islam revealed itself one night in late November. In recent months the country had been rattled by reports of flying saucers and monsters, and these omens of doom set the scene for the remarkable collective hysteria that gripped Iran on the evening of Monday, November 27. It began, as everything seemed to in those fraught days, with a rumor. Word spread in the mosques that an old lady who lived in Qom had found a stray hair belonging to the Prophet Mohammad in the pages of her Quran. This discovery was accompanied by an apparition who shared the revelation that on the evening of the next full moon Khomeini's face would be visible on its surface only to believers. The rumor held special significance because of the advent of Muharram, the first month in the Islamic calendar, whose tenth day, Ashura, commemorated the slaying of Imam Husayn at the hands of Caliph Yazid in AD 680. For years, Khomeini had compared the Shah to Yazid and criminalized him as an apostate and traitor to the Shia nation. Indeed it was with this in mind that Khomeini's closest aides—Ayatollah Mohammad Beheshti was the likely instigator—fashioned the tale of the old woman, the stray hair, and the man on the moon.

At the appointed hour hundreds of thousands and perhaps millions of Iranians came out onto the streets and crowded rooftops to marvel at the sight of their Marja staring back at them from the face of the moon. The phenomenon affected rich and poor alike. At a dinner party hosted by Gholam Reza Afkhami, who worked on social issues for Queen Farah, some of the most learned men and women in the kingdom "traced Khomeini's face in the moon with their fingers." Even the Shah's valet, Amir Pourshaja, bore witness. "One night we heard the rumor, we went up on the roof to see Khomeini in the moon," he said. "People with us could see his beard." No one wanted to be left out—not even the Tudeh Party. The official organ of Iran's atheistic Communist Party performed the ideological feat of a triple somersault with its gushing account of the big night. "Our toiling masses, fighting against world-devouring Imperialism headed by the blood-sucking United States, have seen the face of their beloved Imam and leader, Khomeini, the Breaker of Idols, in the moon," blustered Tudeh's official organ. "A few pip-squeaks cannot deny what a whole nation has seen with its own eyes."

The Communists may have been taken in by the collective delusion, but Khomeini's fellow marjas scolded him for his shameless trickery and expressed outrage that his agents were prepared to use the Quran to further his political ambitions. One senior ayatollah in Mashad spread a rumor of his own, telling his congregants that he had been visited in his sleep by Imam Reza, who told him that "true Shiites should not oppose a Shah who was named after both the Prophet and the eighth Imam." Sure enough, statues of the Shah that had been pulled down in Mashad were restored to their plinths. Khomeini's agents countered by spreading the lie that "the ayatollah of Mashad suffered periodic moments of hallucination prompted by an upset stomach," and the Shah's statues were pulled down again. The Grand Ayatollah justified the man-in-the-moon story as one of many "spontaneous initiatives of the people."

Khomeini's "moon trick" convinced the Shah that he had utterly failed in his efforts to modernize Iran. Despite the billions he had invested in education, training, and industry, when the Iranian people were faced with a choice between his vision of progress and modernity and Khomeini's face in the moon, they had succumbed to a fairy tale and corner store magic. He felt sickened and embarrassed—his children had let him down. "For me everything is at an end," he lamented. "Even if I return to Iran one day as Shah, nothing will be the same again. It is like a beautiful crystal vase that is broken for good; repair it and it will still show the same cracks." A palace aide remarked that Iran was "returning to the Dark Ages," and the Shah answered him, "I wonder if we ever left them." He mused aloud why he had even bothered. "Why?" he asked his valet. "I worked for thirty-seven years. Why?"

Not so long ago the gates at Niavaran Palace had swung open to welcome presidents and prime ministers, kings and queens, Nobel laureates and Oscar-winning actors. Now the atmosphere at Niavaran resembled a "ghost ship." "Usually there was protocol," said Reza Ghotbi. "But it disappeared." The Shah himself seemed isolated from events. Behind closed doors and in rare interviews he struggled to come to terms with the collapse of his life's work. "His eyes betrayed immense sadness," wrote *Newsweek*'s Arnaud de Borchgrave. "When I asked him what he had felt as rioters tossed pictures of himself and Queen Farah into bonfires, his eyes glistened, but he fought back the tears and remained silent. He wanted to say something, but the words choked his throat." The Shah's bleak mood reflected his physical decline. The weight loss that started over the summer was now plainly, shockingly visible. French physicians Jean Bernard and Georges Flandrin continued to fly into and out of Tehran, monitoring his reaction to the medication and drawing blood samples. Since Alam's death they had lost access to the safe house in northern Tehran and were obliged to stay in tourist hotels that could not guarantee their security or privacy. "The worse events became, the less I wanted to put my nose outside," said Flandrin, "for the demonstrations, the electricity failures, the street demonstrations—sometimes bordering on riots—made even the short visits I had to make to the palace quite a problem." The Shah remained, as ever, patient and courteous, "but the visits were brief and, especially at our last meetings, one could feel that he was extremely tense and preoccupied."

Despite his evident distress, the Shah did not spend his days sitting alone in a corner feeling sorry for himself. He holed up in his office, calling around the country, counseling his generals, and reminding them to avoid bloodshed at all costs. "He was seeing people morning till night," the Queen attested. Former ministers, ambassadors, generals, industrialists, and artists dropped by with suggestions, and he received and listened to them all. Few had any sound or even rational ideas for a way out of the morass. One former government minister recommended that the Shah appease the mobs by hanging a hundred of his closest aides in central Tehran. Others sent advice from afar, not all of it helpful or relevant. The Pahlavis had entertained former California governor Ronald Reagan back in April. "Shoot the first man in front," he advised the Shah, "and the rest will fall into line." Reagan, observed Ardeshir Zahedi, "did not understand how serious the problem was."

Newspaper columnist Joseph Kraft from the *New York Times* visited Niavaran in late November. The Shah, who received him in a second-floor salon, "looked pale, spoke in subdued tones, and seemed dwarfed by the vast expanse of the room, with its huge, ornate chandeliers and heavy Empire furniture. He wore a double-breasted suit whose blackness suggested mourning." Kraft began by pointing out that the Shah still held several advantages over his adversaries. The army was intact, the clergy was divided, and the opposition was not united. Surely, he asked, these groups "could be played off against each other"?

The Shah shrugged his shoulders "in an elaborate show of disbelief." "Possibly," he answered without enthusiasm.

Kraft reminded him that the army was loyal.

"You can't crack down on one block and make the people on the next block behave."

Joseph Kraft was puzzled. This was not the Shah he had known for so many years. Where was the old confidence and hubris? In all their previous encounters he had never seen Iran's king "so sombre." He asked the Shah "when the black mood had begun."

"Sometime in the summer."

"Any special reason?"

"Events."

Kraft said he had heard—most likely from Ambassador Sullivan—that "maybe he was overdoing the blues to elicit sympathy and perhaps support from the United States."

"What could America do?"

The American then inquired what the Shah's advisers "thought was going to happen."

"Many things," the Shah answered with a brittle laugh. He rose from his chair to signal that their audience, like his dream of a new Iran, was over.

24

SWEPT AWAY

They are going to kill us.
—QUEEN FARAH

You don't want to be Marie Antoinette.
—GENERAL FEREYDOUN DJAM

The Muharram religious observances came to a head on Sunday, December 10, and Monday, the eleventh. On Sunday, seven enormous orderly columns numbering somewhere between half a million and a million people set off toward Tehran's Shahyad Monument, modern symbol of Pahlavism. "It was an impressive performance," reported the *Los Angeles Times*. "The tail end of the procession on Shah Reza Ave., which started in east Tehran at 9:00 a.m., had only reached the university by 2:30 a.m. and still had about four miles to go to the Shahyad Monument." Marchers held aloft Khomeini's picture and chanted, "We want Islamic government under Khomeini," and "Khomeini, you are the leader of the free Iranian people." Intense negotiations had preceded the march. Prime Minister Azhari had initially opposed allowing any public processions during Muharram, but he relented to avoid another round of street clashes. The Grand Bazaar's processional organizers, the men who usually organized big religious events, cooperated with the mullahs to impose impressive discipline on the crowds. "The march showed that the feeling against the Shah cuts across Iranian society," observed the *Wall Street Journal*. "Doctors and lawyers, students and raggedly dressed peasants participated in the procession. Thousands of women, hiding their faces behind chadors, or long black veils, walked along with small children in tow. There was a carnival atmosphere, with many marchers chanting joyously and spectators giving them bread and water as they passed."

The floodgates opened the next day on Ashura, the 1,298th anniversary of the Battle of Karbala, when about a million people—a quarter of Tehran's residents—swamped the center of town. Ashura was the deluge the regime had always dreaded, and if Ramadan had battered the pillars of the Pahlavi state, then Muharram tipped them to the point of collapse. The tone of the Ashura march was more explicitly political, aggressive, and xenophobic. "We will kill Iran's dictator!" roared sections of the crowd. "Death to the American establishment!" "The Shah and his family must be killed!" "We will destroy Yankee power in Iran!" "Arms for the people!" "This American king should be hanged!" "Shah, if you don't get the message, you'll get it from the barrel of a machine gun!" The churning black and white tide of mourning garb and chadors swamped the middle-class idealists, who until now had naively assumed that they would inherit the revolution. "We would settle for the 1906 Constitution," said one man. "But they want the end of the monarchy and, as you can see, they are more numerous."

Elsewhere in Iran on Ashura there was an eruption of mob violence in Isfahan, with statues of the Shah toppled, banks set alight, the city's last cinema torched, and five people dying in an assault on the local Savak headquarters. Mujahedin gunmen tried to kill the governor of Hamadan. Rioters in Mashad stormed the Hyatt Hotel and "smashed its ground-floor windows, overturned furniture in the lobby and bar, tore down portraits of the King and Queen, and tried without success to set fire to the hotel nightclub." The most shocking act of violence on Ashura did not occur out on the streets but behind closed doors, at one of the most secure locations in Iran. The headquarters of the Shah's elite palace guard, the Immortals, was at Lavizan, just a short distance from Niavaran. The officers were sitting down to lunch in the mess hall when two men, Private Salamatbakhsh and Corporal Abedi, stood and sprayed the room with semiautomatics, killing twelve officers and wounding another thirty-six. Both assassins were shot on the spot. The attacks horrified the Shah and Queen, and Farah rushed to the hospital to comfort the wounded. "It was deeply distressing," she said. "I cannot forget, in particular, how one of the men looked at me with such loyalty in his eyes as I held his cold hand. He died a few hours later." She was shown a copy of the letter Abedi had left in his jacket pocket for his widow. "I did it on the orders of the Ayatollah Khomeini and I will go to heaven," he wrote. "But don't worry. I will not look at the houris [female agents, virgins]. I will wait for you there."

The bloodshed in the mess hall suggested that military morale and discipline were starting to collapse. After Khomeini called on soldiers in the army to leave their posts on Ashura there were reports of hundreds of troop desertions in Mashad and Qom, and in Tabriz two dozen soldiers were seen waving to the crowds and putting down their weapons. Many senior officers now regarded their own commander in chief as the real obstacle to ending the crisis. "They would be willing to see the Shah go," a U.S. military adviser told the *New York Times*, "if they could take over and do what they think needs to be done: kick the hell out of the protesters."

After Ashura, reported *Time*, "Tehran was like a city that had survived a siege all but unscathed. Shops and schools were reopening, and office workers were returning to their jobs. Chieftain tanks and Russian-built armored cars, which had been in evidence everywhere, were now out of sight. Soldiers ventured into restaurants and parked their automatic weapons in corners as they ate. Locked in a monumental traffic jam, a Western diplomat sighed, 'Things are back to normal in Tehran.'" But as always with Iran, the outward calm was deceptive. After a year of plying heavy seas the Pahlavi ship of state, that modern marvel of social engineering and technical proficiency, suddenly listed to one side and began to settle in the water. The scramble began to get off before it keeled over.

THE NIGHT WIND whipped through the plane trees, bearing ghostly voices that crept in through the windows and kept the children awake in their beds. "We could hear 'Allah Akbar!' every night," said the Queen, who crossed the landing to calm their sobs. "The children heard the chanting at night and we tried to comfort them," she said. Ali Reza and Leila were traumatized by the ceaseless, mechanical intonation of "Allah Akbar!" interspersed with bloodthirsty cries of "Death to the Shah!" They wondered who wanted to kill their father.

Barricaded in the palace behind Chieftain tanks, sandbags, barbed wire, and machine-gun nests, the Pahlavis were hostages to fortune and rulers of a kingdom whose dominion had shrunk to the size of a small municipal park. Many old friends and acquaintances had already fled the country to safety, while others, with an eye to the future, now preferred to keep a discreet distance from Niavaran. The King and Queen had never spent so much time together or in the residence. Though the main house had its own power generator for emergencies, the couple turned out the lights at night to share in the hardships of the people. Their ever-loyal bodyguard Colonel Djahinbini described the atmosphere in Niavaran as "very tense," with everyone waiting for the next crisis. The massacre at Lavizan base meant that no one could be sure when an agitated servant or guard might snap and start shooting. He was also worried about assassins and spies infiltrating the household. "The staff were conflicted by their loyalty to His Majesty," said the valet Amir Pourshaja. "Their Majesties noticed what was going on. They were a little alarmed but they recognized it as private. But they noticed." One of the Shah's attendants, a man named Hassasi, had been wounded when he tried to close the door on the gunman who forced his way into the Marble Palace in 1965 and almost succeeded in wiping out the Imperial Family. During the revolution Hassasi's son, a soldier in the Imperial Guard, "went berserk during lunch" and tried to pull the Shah's picture off the wall. Kambiz Atabai offered his sympathy to Hassasi "and wondered aloud how anyone could think that a man like Khomeini would be able to rule a country like Iran." To Atabai's shock, Hassasi revealed that he, too, emulated Khomeini. "I am devoted to His Majesty," he said, "but I am also a follower of the Imam. I will not have anyone disparage the Imam in my presence." For Hassasi, his son, and millions like him, the Shah might be head of state but the word of their Marja was law.

Long winter evenings were spent in the screening room watching old movies and a French television series "with the intriguing title of *Les rois maudits* (The Cursed Kings)." Eager to escape Niavaran's claustrophobic atmosphere, on December 20 the Shah, Queen Farah, and their two youngest children went skiing for a day in the Alborz Mountains "and stood in line like ordinary folks for the lifts at the fashionable resort of Dizin." Another outing, to Lake Latian for fresh air and a walk in the hills, was not as enjoyable. "Someone wrote 'Death to the Shah' on a wall and the children saw it," said the Queen. This apparently minor incident was the final straw for both parents. "After that we decided the children should leave," she said. "They were suffering too much." The children were at least spared the indignities of the slanders spread by Khomeini's men in the mosques and bazaars. "Farah, where are your gloves?" they jeered. "And where is your pimp of a husband?" "When we have killed the

Shah, Farah will rush into the arms of Carter." The Queen had already accepted that she was unlikely to get out alive. "One day I was looking out the window and I thought, 'They are going to kill us.' After that I was calm. I accepted what would happen."

Resigned to death yet refusing to accept defeat, Farah was prepared to consider every idea and any avenue in a last, desperate attempt to hold back the revolutionary tide and save the throne for her son. Hossein Nasr pursued his concept of an Islamized monarchy based on the Safavid period, and he played to clerical fears of Khomeini's fanaticism and his support from the far left and terrorist groups. "The ulama were negotiating with us right to the end," he said. The tragedy was that the Queen's delicate negotiations with the moderates were undermined by Ambassador William Sullivan's efforts to ingratiate himself with Mehdi Bazargan and Ayatollah Beheshti, who represented Khomeini and the extremists. Nasr was appalled that Sullivan placed so much faith in empty suits such as Bazargan, Tavakoli, and Sanjabi. The Americans, he said, were "fumbling around, not knowing what they were doing." "It is very pleasant to talk politics with them after dinner," he told the ambassador about Bazargan and his ilk, "but they can't tie their own shoelaces."

One remarkable last-minute intervention came from King Hussein of Jordan, who had always looked to the Shah as a mentor, patron, and benefactor. Hussein shared the concerns of Saddam Hussein, the Saudi king, and Persian Gulf monarchs that the overthrow of the Shah would open Pandora's box, destabilize the Middle East, and unleash a wave of religious and political violence for years to come. In December he flew to Tehran to remind the Shah that in 1970 he had almost lost his own kingdom to Yasser Arafat's PLO during the "Black September" uprising. At that time he had unleashed the Jordanian army, and he urged the Shah to do the same now. "Don't listen to the ambassadors," he said, referring to Sullivan and Parsons, and he recommended that the Shah expel them from Iranian soil. As a descendant of the Prophet, Hussein said he was prepared to drive to Qom to make a personal appeal to Shariatmadari and the marjas to back the Shah. Finally, the King of Jordan offered to put on his military tunic and lead the Iranian military into battle against the fanatics and radicals. If the Shah could not issue an order that might result in bloodshed, Hussein offered to do it for him. The Shah listened but turned him down. King Hussein understood that it was over, and he left for Amman convinced that the Pahlavis were finished.

* * *

IN WASHINGTON, U.S. officials were starting to learn more about the leader of the movement to overthrow the Shah. The CIA's National Foreign Assessment Center completed its first major study of Khomeini's political views and the ramifications for U.S. policy in Iran and the region if he deposed the Shah. The outlook did not look good. The CIA observed that compared to the Shah, Khomeini held reactionary social views. He opposed equal rights for women, land reform, and the presence of foreigners in Iran. He stoked popular resentment against Jews, Baha'i, and other religious minorities. Khomeini and his closest aides, including Banisadr and Ghotzbadegh, maintained close ties to terrorist groups "including the Palestinian commandos." Six years earlier Khomeini had called on his followers to donate generously to the Mujahedin, a group that targeted American officials and civilians for assassination: "The money was raised from the ulama and in the bazaars and funneled to Khomeini, who in turn gave it to the terrorists."

Yet the CIA was convinced that Khomeini's vision for an Islamic republic remained just that—a vision. "Khomeini has been vague as to what this would mean in practice," read the agency analysis. "He rejects any comparison with Saudi Arabia or Libya and claims that 'the only reference point [would be] the time of the Prophet Mohammad and the Prophet Ali." Here was the red flag—the agency should have provided the White House with a picture of what living conditions were like in mid-seventh-century Persia. Instead, the White House was assured that Khomeini had "no interest in holding power himself." Remarkably, Central Intelligence still seemed unaware of Khomeini's 1970 velayat-e faqih thesis, even though it was openly for sale on Tehran street corners. The agency was of the view that Khomeini, the most political Shia marja in history, was essentially an apolitical figure, a religious leader who displayed "a lack of interest in a specific political program. For him Shia Islam is a total social/political/economic system that needs no further explanation. In addition, he would risk losing support from some elements of the opposition if he tried to spell out out a detailed program of action. . . . Khomeini promises social equality and political democracy in his new Iran."

Ambassador Sullivan stepped up his efforts to reach an accommodation with Bazargan and the Islamic left. By now Bazargan had shared with Sullivan his blueprint for a post-Shah Iran. His plan called for the Shah to surrender power to a Regency Council dominated by the National Front and the Liberation Movement. The council would appoint Bazargan to the post of prime minister and hold elections for both houses of parliament and also for the Constituent Assembly, which would vote on whether to retain the monarchy. Privately, Bazargan meant to abolish the throne, but to Sullivan he offered the assurance that if the Assembly vote went the other way "Crown Prince Reza would be invited to return to Iran." He cleverly played to American anxieties about the Tudeh Party and Soviet ambitions in the Persian Gulf, pledging that his government "would be friendly to the US [and] anti-Communist . . . and would even continue to sell oil to Israel." The plan also called for an end to martial law, the disbandment of Savak, and freedom of the press. Bazargan assured Sullivan that he had nothing to fear from Khomeini or the mullahs in a future Islamic republic because their political ambitions were limited and they "would not take position of minister in a future cabinet."

Those were the carrots; now for the stick. If the United States wished to maintain any influence in Iran in the future it would have to accept not only the Shah's departure but also the permanent exile of the entire senior command of the Imperial Armed Forces. "Probably 10–15 senior military officers would leave with the Shah," read the copy of Bazargan's plan forwarded to the State Department in Washington. "Most of the purged officers would be ground force [army]. The opposition had already selected military leaders who could assume the loyalty of the army and no serious problem was anticipated. A number of officers had called recently on Shariatmadari and separately on the National Front." If enacted with U.S. support, Bazargan's plan would amount to the systematic decapitation of the entire senior command structure of the Imperial Armed Forces, replacing the generation of senior officers sympathetic to Washington with leftists and Islamists. Sullivan seemed to miss the point entirely and described the concept as "encouraging" because "our interests lay in preserving the integrity of the armed forces."

Sullivan had peered through the looking glass and was in a very strange land indeed. So anxious was the ambassador to gain entrée into Khomeini's inner circle that he allowed Bazargan to lead him to the man who wielded real power in the Islamist movement and ran Khomeini's ground operations in Iran: Ayatollah Beheshti. In his memoir, Sullivan praised Mohammad Beheshti as an erudite anti-Communist who understood that "the prime threat to the future of Iran came from the Soviet Union and that the United States . . . had long been a force for social, economic, and political improvement for the people of Iran." In fact, as the CIA was already aware, Beheshti held virulently anti-American views and had raised the funds that enabled the Mujahedin to assassinate U.S. military officers and American civilians. He had personally played a part in at least two acts of terrorism himself, the assassination of the pro-American prime minister Mansur in 1965 and the recent kidnapping of Imam Musa Sadr. Beheshti's singular goal was to destroy any chance of an accommodation between the Carter White House and religious moderates, who, against overwhelming odds, were still frantically trying to form a block to keep Khomeini from seizing power. Sullivan's meddling undermined this initiative and encouraged the extremists to press forward.

Sullivan's staff also held a lengthy face-to-face meeting with the rabid anti-Semite Ayatollah Yahya Nouri at the home of a prominent bazaari in early December. The Americans and Iranians discussed a scenario under which the Shah would stay on as constitutional monarch but step down as commander in chief of the Imperial Armed Forces. Nouri assured the embassy that once in power Khomeini and his supporters "would want to retain their good relations with the US and the West while keeping their distance from the Soviet Union." Further, Nouri dangled the possibility of fixing oil prices, though "he did not elaborate on this statement." He lamented that the Iranian Army was to blame for recent violence and "suggested that the US use its influence with the Iranian Armed Forces and the Shah to prevent firing on demonstrators." In a year of strange events, perhaps the strangest was the sight of American diplomats receiving two anti-American religious revolutionaries leading a violent revolt against the Shah of Iran, their staunchest ally in the Muslim world.

Sullivan and his men sincerely believed the assurances given to them by Beheshti and Nouri—they had apparently never heard of the Shia concept of taqiya, or lying for self-preservation—and were convinced they had a deal safeguarding a U.S. presence in Iran after the Shah left power. The Americans were sure that Khomeini was a moderating influence over the leftists and radicals in his entourage. Each day the CIA presented the diplomats with transcripts of Khomeini's telephone conversations with his agents inside Iran, including Beheshti. They noted with approval his negative reaction to attacks against Americans in Iran. "Tell the brothers not to use arms," they heard him tell his agents. But the Americans missed the point. The revolutionaries in Paris knew they were under electronic surveillance and made sure Khomeini toned down his rhetoric when issuing instructions to his followers back home. "We knew we were tapped by French intelligence," admitted Abolhassan Banisadr. The plan was always to stockpile weapons and restrain the Mujahedin guerrilla fighters until the Shah left Iran. Only then would they launch the final offensive that would take advantage of the army's disoriented, leaderless state to overthrow the regime.

Sullivan's freelance foreign policy merely took advantage of a crippling decision-making vacuum in the White House. On the one hand, National Security Adviser Brzezinski supported military action to save the Shah and was drawing up a contingency plan to send U.S. Marines into the southern oil fields. But military intervention was firmly opposed by Secretary of State Cyrus Vance, who had served as President Kennedy's army secretary in the early sixties and recoiled at the prospect of a repeat of the 1953 and 1963 crackdowns. Sullivan was disdainful of Vance, whom he regarded as absent and weak, and openly contemptuous of Brzezinski, who shared Ardeshir Zahedi's support for a coup as a last resort. Sullivan was convinced that he alone understood the complexities of the crisis in Iran.

WHILE U.S. OFFICIALS debated their options, Americans living in Iran reached their own conclusions about where the country was headed and quite literally ran for the exits. Frightened by attacks and threats against foreigners, exhausted after weeks of living in barricaded houses without heat and postal delivery, and only intermittent water, electricity, and working telephones, they formed convoys to drive to Mehrebad Airport, where "a great wave of humanity" had congregated. Everyone, it seemed, had the same idea: it was time to get out.

There were tearful, hysterical scenes in the main passenger terminal at Mehrebad Airport, where foreigners watched in horror as Iranians threw toddlers into the air in a desperate attempt to get them to the front of the ticket lines. "We were terrified," said Cyndy McCollough, an American teenager whose father had decided to send his wife and children out. "People were screaming and crying." The McCollough family's flight was so crowded, and it took off so quickly, that people had no time to secure their bags or pets, and "animals were walking up and down the aisles, cats and a rabbit." At one point a stewardess trying to maneuver her beverages cart down the aisle calmly asked, "Can someone please move the animals?" Like the McColloughs, the Kirkendall family was stunned at the chaos that greeted them. "People were screaming to get out," said Jonathan. "There were lost people and lost luggage. The airport was packed, lots of people, lots of noise. My memory of it is that it was dark—though I can't imagine that the lights were out. It just seemed dim, crowded, chaotic, people pushing their way up to the ticket counters, yelling." "When the plane took off there was a round of cheers," said Bruce Vernor, "and when the plane left Iranian airspace there was a roar."

Those who stayed behind bore witness to scenes of bloodlust, savagery, and unbridled anarchy. Paul Grimm, a senior American oil executive working in Ahwaz for the oil consortium, was ambushed on his way to work by Mujahedin gunmen and shot to death. Two Iranian managers for the oil consortium were assassinated on the same day. Rioters surrounded a group of young soldiers and "a colonel was dragged from his tank and axed to death by the mob. His throat was cut and he was disemboweled. His intestines were packed in plastic bags that were delivered back to the army labeled 'executed by the people's court.'" In another episode, a mob attacked the home of a Savak colonel on Bahar Street. "The colonel was taken alive and dismembered by the crowd," said the press, "while his wife and children were burned in the fire which leveled their three-story house." The dead man's corpse was strung up outside the charred ruins of his house as a warning sign to other regime loyalists. Riots erupted in Tabriz, Dezful, and Qazvin, and in Kermanshah the Dariush Hotel and other buildings were destroyed. The Italian expatriate club in Bandar Abbas was leveled, and British Council centers and libraries were attacked and torched by rioters in Mashad, Ahwaz, and Shiraz. Anyone in a uniform became a target. Among thirty troops and police officers butchered in mob attacks was a gendarmerie sergeant dragged from his house and set alight in the street.

On Christmas Eve, high school students rioted in downtown Tehran and ran through the streets chased by army troops wearing gas masks and bearing rifles. One group converged on the U.S. embassy, chanting, "Yankee go home!" and "Death to the Shah!" They forced an American civilian and his driver out of their car at the gate and set the car on fire, then threw rocks and missiles over the fence into the yard. The young Marine guards on duty fired tear gas to discourage anyone from climbing the walls, and Iranian troops rushed to the scene firing shots into the air to clear the streets. One student said he knew his parents hoped "I would rather sit home until it all blows away. Of course, it's not going to blow away, and everything will continue until the Shah leaves or is dead. The fact is most people want that. They don't want him to escape. They don't want him to have exile. They want him to die." Another teenager, a female student clad in her chador, echoed those sentiments when she shrieked, "The Shah will not come out of this alive."

American lawyer John Westberg had lived in Iran since the midsixties. In his diary he tried to reconcile his fondness for the Iranian people with the madness he saw on the streets. "So many Iranians seem to think the problems are attributable to the Shah and once he is gone with his retinue, all will be well," he wrote. "The problems are, of course, older and deeper than that. I do not defend the Shah and I have concluded it is necessary for him to go entirely before anyone can hope for peace and stability here. But the sense of discussions I have with Iranians is that they think only in negative terms, that is they think by being against the Shah and getting rid of him, the problems of the country will be solved. . . . In my view, the central problem is Iran itself, or more cogently, Iranian culture which takes such great pride in its resistance to changes that are imperative if Iran is ever to develop into a just and stable, modern society." The Iranian people, he concluded, "want the benefits of the modern world but they don't want to make the changes in their way of life that are necessary." Christmas 1978 was "the gloomiest I can remember. I fear for this sad country's future and find no reason for hope things are going to straighten out anytime soon. To the contrary, all I can see is more trouble and reason for despair."

EVENTS NOW BEGAN to move very quickly indeed.

Martial law collapsed on Wednesday, December 27, amid scenes of "wild shooting and lawlessness. . . . Trucks and cars burned in the streets of Tehran, soldiers opened fire with automatic weapons on a funeral procession, according to a witness, after they shot their own colonel, and the city became a bellowing sound stage of sirens, gunfire and automobile horns. Tear gas, smoke from pyres set aflame by anti-Government demonstrators, power cuts, stores shutting and merchants piling their stock on the back of trucks—Tehran almost visibly tottered. . . . All schools were closed and the state airline, rail and bus services were not functioning." Oil production collapsed to less than half a million barrels a day, and Iranian petroleum exports halted. Pan Am canceled all flights into and out of Tehran. "We consider it too dangerous to go to the airport," said an airline official. "It is an insane risk just driving through this city."

General Oveissi and General Moghadam drove to Niavaran and begged Queen Farah to tell the Shah that it was time to replace the hapless General Azhari, who had suffered a mild heart attack, with the younger, more dynamic Shahpur Bakhtiar. General Badrei, commander of the Imperial Guard, had already spoken to Bakhtiar and received his pledge that "he would kill if necessary, even if blood rose up to his elbow." The Queen recalled the generals' dramatic intervention. "General Oveissi and General Moghadam came to me and said, 'If His Majesty doesn't choose someone it will cause a problem and the mob will attack the palace.'" She went straight to her husband and he issued the invitation for Bakhtiar to come to the palace the next day. Since Farah's meeting with Bakhtiar one month earlier, the Shah had stayed in touch with the opposition politician with the help of two intermediaries. Bakhtiar offered Reza Ghotbi an assurance that the future of the monarchy would not be put to the popular vote. "Iran is not ready for a republic," he said. "In fifty years, maybe Iran will be ready, but if we have a good constitutional monarchy, why change? We should remain a constitutional monarchy." Ghotbi was reluctant to become more involved in the political negotiations and readily stepped back to allow General Moghadam to assume the role of interlocutor.

Bakhtiar phoned Ghotbi after Christmas to let him know that the Shah had requested a meeting at Niavaran. "I have an audience tomorrow with His Majesty," he said. "And I want you to see me after that." Shortly after his morning appointment with the Shah, Bakhtiar sat down with Ghotbi and briefed him on their discussion. "I went to see His Majesty," said Bakhtiar. "He was very kind to me. He told me that he had not seen me for years, but I did not seem old."

"His Majesty put all the burdens on his shoulders and somehow you've aged while I have stayed young," Bakhtiar said he told the Shah. "We talked about politics, he listened, he was very responsive, and showed lots of interest. He asked what I wanted to drink—I had tea but he did not sip from his cup. He was very happy. It seemed the Shah accepted me."

When their half-hour conversation drew to a close the Shah asked, "And when do we have to leave?"

Bakhtiar was taken aback: "I didn't know what he meant."

"Everyone is telling us to leave the country," the Shah explained.

"I think Your Majesty must stay," said Bakhtiar. "After the government takes power you may leave the country for a short period. You can take a vacation and then return."

Bakhtiar informed the rest of the National Front that he had accepted the Shah's offer to form a government. They were appalled at his decision to break ranks and condemned the Shah's announcement on December 29 that their former colleague had decided to accept the post of prime minister. Ambassador Sullivan and his staff were just as aghast—the stunning news threatened to unravel their own strategy, which depended on Mehdi Bazargan forming a government with Khomeini's support. Even before Bakhtiar was sworn in the Americans decided he was finished. "Everyone knew that he would not survive," said John Stempel, who employed a more choice turn of phrase behind closed doors. "Bakhtiar doesn't have a fucking chance," he lectured his colleagues. The Shah's prime minister-designate, he decided, was a "nonentity."

PERHAPS IT WAS fitting that at this late, desperate hour the Shah received the man who had been at his side during the turmoil that had surrounded his ascension to the Peacock Throne. As a young army officer, Fereydoun Djam had captured the heart of Princess Shams and won the favor of Reza Shah, who looked on him as the son he never had. Widely regarded as a respected and competent officer, Djam had incurred the Shah's wrath in the early seventies with his habit of challenging Imperial decrees. At that time the Shah had removed Djam from his post as army chief and packed him off to Madrid to serve as ambassador. Djam, who by now was living in London, still carried a grudge over the earlier incident.

Though the Shah suspected Djam's ambitions, he called him back to Tehran in January 1979 in deference only to Shahpur Bakhtiar, who wanted to appoint the general to run his war ministry. Djam was a popular figure with the army rank and file and just the sort of strong-willed individual who could boost troop morale and discipline during the decisive days ahead. But the Shah did not hide his unhappiness, and Djam received a cool reception at the palace.

"Bakhtiar asked for you, I didn't," said the Shah.

Djam returned the sentiment when he made it clear he would only cooperate with Bazargan if the Shah relinquished the title he prized most. "Your Majesty," he said, "I have a request."

"What is your request, General?"

"If you are leaving the country, you must give me responsibility as commander in chief."

"General Djam," said the Shah, "I don't think that is necessary."

Djam's bitterness spilled out. He pointedly refused to serve in Bakhtiar's administration and before departing Niavaran warned the Shah that he risked the same fate as Nicholas II of Russia. Farah had her own unhappy run-in with Djam when he called on her and advised her to leave. He scoffed at her pretensions to say behind and lead the resistance. "You don't want to be Marie Antoinette," he lectured the Queen. Farah was outraged by the comparison and appalled that one of the kingdom's most respected senior generals and diplomats would dare encourage the Shah or anyone else to flee during a national crisis. "You don't want to hear this from the person with the sword," said Reza Ghotbi, "the person charged with protecting you." Farah had no intention of leaving Iran and despaired at her husband's choice of exile. "I offered to stay," said Farah, "not to be active, but just as a symbol, for the army and the people. I wouldn't do anything." But her husband wouldn't hear of it and told her, "You don't have to be Joan of Arc." He preferred that she "stay by his side."

In those final days the Shah's face was a mask of exhaustion and grief. "His Majesty was in a very bad state," said Amir Pourshaja. Professor Jean Bernard made a final trip to Iran to treat the Shah and was shocked at his ragged appearance. "On that last occasion," he wrote, "the patient was almost unrecognizable, visibly suffering from apparently dreadful tension. He would not stop listening to the news on the radio while I examined him that Sunday morning."

Everyone felt the end was near. On Friday, December 29, Queen Mother Taj ol-Moluk flew out of Iran aboard an Iranian military aircraft to join her daughter Shams in Los Angeles. "The queen mother was carried off the Boeing 747 on a stretcher to a private ambulance," reported the *Los Angeles Times*. "A convoy of limousines and sedans sped the group out of the airport, losing pursuing newsmen on the San Diego Freeway."

The Shah told his valet to start packing his clothes for a trip. "Don't pack too much because it is just for a short period of time," he assured Amir Pourshaja.

Tehran took on the twilight air of revolutionary-era Petrograd.

Each morning at six o'clock Elli Antoniades waited patiently in line to buy a precious bottle of gasoline. "When the power failed you had to throw out all your food," she said. Every night around midnight she received a phone call from her old friend former prime minister Amir Hoveyda, who was living under house arrest. "He would call to hear a friendly voice," she recalled. He wanted to know, 'How are you? What did you do today?' We didn't discuss politics or what was going on. His phone line was bugged. On New Year's Eve he called to wish me a happy new year. I asked, 'What is so happy about it?'"

Elli's last conversation with the Queen came on Wednesday, January 3, at the end of another day of strikes, power blackouts, and shootings. "I don't know how long I will stay," Farah told her, "but if you have your passport ready it is time to leave." Elli phoned her cousin and asked him to drive her to the airport. They left shortly after curfew lifted in the early hours of Thursday morning. "I took one suitcase. We arrived at the airport and there were already five thousand people there. Americans with their children and dogs. And people like me." She wept at the memory of it. "I went to Swissair. I had no ticket. There were a thousand people in line. I said to the guy behind the desk, 'You know, I have to leave.'"

The strike in the oil fields meant that passenger jets could not take off fully loaded with fuel. The caterers were on strike, too, and so there was no food. Worse, the traffic control tower was not working because the controllers were on strike. This meant that pilots were having to rely on visual signals at one of the world's busiest airports. "We had to carry our own bags out to the plane and there were no stairs so we climbed a ladder. Our flight left at two o'clock. We sat on the plane hungry. And nobody said anything until we reached the frontier and the pilot said, 'We are safe. We are no longer in Iran. We are in Turkey.'" The foreigners cheered and clapped but for many Iranians it was a day of tears—only when they left did it dawn on them they were never going back.

As ROYALISTS AND foreigners fled Iran in their tens of thousands, hundreds of religious extremists, Communists, and anarchists living in exile flocked back to join the revolution. Someone else who returned to Tehran on Sunday, January 4, was General Robert E. Huyser, deputy commander of U.S. ground forces in Europe, and the official who had visited the Shah at Nowshahr to discuss the plan to reform the armed forces' command control system.

This time Huyser had been sent to Tehran at the orders of President Carter to work with the Shah's generals and make sure they did not launch a coup in his absence. The Americans tried to smuggle Huyser into Iran without the Shah's knowledge. "By then we knew he was finished," admitted National Security Adviser Brzezinski. "We knew that sending a senior general to Iran would not be welcomed by the Shah because it harked back to 1953 and he was determined to leave as best he could. My own simple view was that we support a military action to end the unrest and then follow it up with reforms. I conveyed this view to him. But the Shah opposed a crackdown. He told me he did not want to bequeath a bloodied throne to his son and shed the blood of Iranians."

The U.S. decision to try to circumvent the Shah backfired with disastrous consequences for American policy and a near-fatal outcome for the general. The Shah quickly learned about Huyser's arrival and naturally interpreted it as confirmation that Carter was trying to arrange a coup. His generals were so outraged that they offered to put an end to the American game right away. "The generals came to me and offered to shoot Huyser," recalled Ambassador Zahedi. "The fear was that the Americans were about to repeat their involvement in the 1967 coup in Greece against King Constantine." The Shah wouldn't hear of it, but Zahedi was so furious he urged that Huyser be arrested and deported.

THOUSANDS OF MILES away from Iran's death spiral, on Friday, January 5, President Jimmy Carter, Prime Minister James Callaghan of Great Britain, President Valéry Giscard d'Estaing of France, and West Germany's chancellor Helmut Schmidt arrived on the French Caribbean island territory of Guadeloupe for a four-power summit to discuss a host of issues related to the Cold War. Iran was expected to be a major topic of discussion for Western leaders. Arab oil producers led by Saudi Arabia had taken advantage of Iran's political turmoil to push through a double-digit price increase. The Saudi decision combined with Iran's cutoff of oil exports had led to a surge in oil prices that experts compared to a second "oil shock."

The leaders' morning session covered East-West relations. Carter could tell that Schmidt was in a foul, negative mood. The German chancellor was delivering a small lecture on Romania's president, Nicolae Ceauşescu, criticizing his "dangerous and idiotic policy toward the Soviet Union," when he veered off topic to say that "he considered Tehran and Bucharest to be similar. That he had long known the megalomaniac Shah would be brought down." The other leaders let the remark pass and the conversation shifted to Soviet leader Leonid Brezhnev, whom Giscard d'Estaing said was "almost incoherent and approaching senility." The four leaders and their wives enjoyed a pleasant lunch at the Villa Creole. Carter wrote that his daughter, Amy, was "a good swimmer and during the stay in Guadeloupe we thoroughly enjoyed the snorkeling and scuba diving." The evening ended with a barbecue supper, a demonstration of surf sailing, and "a remarkable concert by natives of Guadeloupe playing tuned oil drums where they have a note to the scale very clearly and purely defined by tapping out little sections of the top of an oil drum which they play with xylophone sticks."

CARTER RAISED THE subject of Iran and the Shah's future during the leaders' Saturday morning session. "Found very little support among the other three for the Shah," he wrote in his journal. "They all thought that the civilian government would have to be established. And they agreed with me that the military ought to be kept strong and intact if possible. They were unanimous in saying that the Shah ought to leave as soon as possible." They failed to realize that it was only the Shah's presence in Iran that kept the military cohesive. The British record of their talk provided additional details. "In the course of a general discussion there was general agreement that the Shah would have to leave Iran within the next few days. Nevertheless President Carter thought that the chances of a stable outcome to the crisis were rather better than they had been a fortnight earlier and that General Djam had returned to the country. We had however to face the fact that any future Iranian Government was likely to be less of a moderating influence in Arab councils and would possibly be more friendly to the Soviet Union."

France's Giscard d'Estaing defended his decision to admit Khomeini in the first place and tolerate the political activity and speech making that clearly violated the terms of his visitor's visa. "Valéry reported that he had decided earlier to expel Khomeini from France," wrote Carter, "but the Shah said it would be better to keep him in France instead of letting him go to Iraq or Libya or some other place where he might stir up even more trouble for the Shah. Therefore Valery had decided to keep Khomeini in France." The French president at least acknowledged "the Shah's restraint in not taking ruthless measures when he was in a position to do so but said that politicians would now count for nothing in Iran. The struggle would be between the Army and the religious leaders." After repeatedly imploring the Shah not to crack down, Western leaders now blamed him for being too soft and losing control.

The leaders of the four powers moved on to other matters that at the time appeared at least as pressing as the Shah's political collapse: the price of oil, Israel's refusal to give up the West Bank and Gaza, Turkey's economy, Vietnam's invasion of Cambodia, and unrest in Zaire and white-ruled southern Africa. After a press conference at the Meridian Hotel the four leaders "ate lunch together, with topless women bathers walking down on the beach below us." Callaghan joked that he could not see the action because "his back was turned to the beach!" The sun, surf, and sand put everyone in a good mood. "Jim is one person I enjoy being with," Carter mused. "I promised to send him a book about the 100 most influential people in history." The president returned to his bungalow and asked his Secret Service agents to brief him on "how to use scuba diving equipment." With the business part of the trip out the way, Jimmy Carter could look forward to his winter vacation.

The president arrived back at the White House on Tuesday evening to find Brzezinski's latest update on the situation in Iran on his desk. In addition to outlining what he thought would happen once the Shah left office, the national security adviser had provided his own brutal assessment of the Shah's handling of the crisis. "We are giving up on the Shah only after being forced reluctantly to conclude that he is incapable of decisive action," he reminded Carter. But Brzezinski failed to point out that during the unrest the administration had repeatedly and consistently pressed the Shah not to use force against protesters, even as it denied him the means to purchase antiriot equipment that would have made a nonviolent response work. Carter's neat scrawl lined the edge of the memo: "Zbig—After we make joint decisions deploring them for the record doesn't help me."

FAR FROM WASHINGTON, there were stirrings of life in a Libyan prison cell. According to intelligence that reached the CIA after the revolution, Musa Sadr was alive.

Yasser Arafat had lied when he told Abolhassan Banisadr that the Imam had been killed during a late-night altercation at Colonel Gadhafi's residence. The truth was more diabolical than the crime: Arafat and Gadhafi had agreed with Ayatollah Beheshti that Musa Sadr posed a real threat to their effort to overthrow the Shah, America's closest ally in the Persian Gulf and Israel's firmest friend in the Muslim world. By now Palestinian involvement in the revolution was out in the open. Palestinian arms and gunmen were flooding into Iran, and a senior Palestinian official, claiming to speak on Arafat's behalf, had already declared that "the PLO is proud to be accused of fomenting trouble in Iran."

With victory in sight the revolutionaries were not about to allow anyone, least of all Musa Sadr, the leader of a million Shia, to interfere with their plans. For now—if the CIA's Palestinian source was correct—Musa Sadr would stay where he was: underground.

25

FLIGHT OF THE EAGLE

*We are leaving for a long-needed rest
and shall soon return.*

—THE SHAH

We are leaving. God knows what will happen.

—QUEEN FARAH

The final days were an agony. Following Shahpur Bakhtiar's presentation of his new cabinet at Niavaran on Saturday, January 6, 1979, the Shah confirmed that as soon as his new prime minister won a parliamentary vote of confidence he planned to leave Iran for an indeterminate period of time. "I'm tired," he said. "I need a rest. If this rest takes place in a foreign country, a Regency Council will be created according to the Constitution. More important than this is that the wheels of the economy start turning again and that the economy returns to normal, because if this does not happen, I don't see a good future for the country, I don't forecast a happy future for any Iranian." Grand Ayatollah Khomeini immediately denounced Bakhtiar's government as illegal and declared the formation of a rival shadow cabinet called the Council of the Islamic Revolution. He made it clear that he would hold American citizens responsible if the Iranian military tried to foment a coup when the Shah left. "The influence of the U.S. in the Iranian military is well known," he said. "A military coup will be implemented by the Americans in the eyes of the Iranian people. It is difficult to imagine a coup that could take over without the influence of the Americans."

Ambassador Sullivan was so anxious to prove American goodwill to the revolutionaries that he all but helped walk the Shah to the door. Each time the Shah returned from his audiences with Sullivan, he told Queen Farah that Sullivan pestered him about a departure date. "He keeps asking, 'When are you leaving?'" The ambassador bluntly told the Shah that "it would be best for stability in Iran if he left" and asked if he would like him to secure an invitation to enter the United States. In Sullivan's typically acerbic retelling of their conversation the Shah "leaned forward, almost like a small boy, and said, 'Oh would you?'" Sullivan didn't need to be asked twice. State Department cable traffic reported that at 10:54 a.m. on Friday, January 12, Ambassador Ardeshir Zahedi telephoned Walter Annenberg, the wealthy publisher of *TV Guide* and close friend of Ronald and Nancy Reagan, to let him know that the King and Queen would arrive in Palm Springs the following Thursday or Friday after making a brief stopover for several days in Egypt to visit their friends the Sadats. "Zahedi indicated that he would like the party to arrive at a nearby military base and be helicoptered to Annenberg estate," Secretary of State Vance informed Sullivan. "At our request Annenberg is willing to receive the Shah and party of up to 15 and put them up through the first week in February and he so informed Zahedi." The Shah's initial plan to stay at the Beverley Hills residence of Princess Shams was scotched by security concerns after Iranian student protesters rioted outside the grounds. The Annenberg estate, by contrast, said Vance, was "completely walled and surrounded by barbed wire." He added that State Department officials were working with the office of former vice president Nelson Rockefeller to find a second port of call once the Pahlavis left Palm Springs.

THE SHAH'S DEPARTURE announcement cast a pall over the Imperial Court. Staff and courtiers who had worked for the Pahlavis since the time of Reza Shah reacted with shock, scorn, and grief to the news that the family intended to leave Iran. "They were so upset and disillusioned," said a senior court official. "Their morale was so low." They feared for their livelihoods but also for their lives. At one time the envy of their friends and neighbors, now the palace's cooks, cleaners, stable hands, guards, and gardeners were "insulted, accosted in the streets, and sometimes physically attacked" in their own neighborhoods. They were terrified they would be left to fend for themselves against the revolutionaries. "People were breaking down all over the place in the last week," said Hossein Amir

Sadighi, the son of the Shah's chauffeur. "The Shah was suffering enormously and his aides were useless. Without the Empress it would have been impossible. She was the tower of strength. She ran things in the end."

The Shah withdrew into himself. When he was not in audiences he watched movies, played bridge, and walked around the palace grounds. "Strolling among the larches and pines," reported *Newsweek*, "the Shah at one point bent down and picked up a handful of soil. He would take it with him when he left the country—just as his father had done when he was sent into exile in 1941." Rather than deal with his generals in person, the Shah assigned a sergeant attached to the Imperial Guard the task of conveying his wishes because he could not bear another appeal for a crackdown or petition urging him to stay in Iran. Chief of the General Staff General Abbas Gharabaghi begged Queen Farah to help change her husband's mind. "If His Majesty leaves," he warned, "the army won't hold out." Generals Badrei and Khosrodad urged her to help them persuade the Shah to remove himself to Kish so they could finish the rebellion. "I also received a delegation of members of Parliament who pleaded the same cause," said Farah, who recalled their "panic at the thought of the King's leaving," and raised the idea of forming armed citizens' militias to put down the uprising.

One of Farah's last callers was Mansur Eqbal, one of the nephews of the late former prime minister Manuchehr Eqbal. Eqbal's cousin was married to Princess Ashraf's son Shahriar, who served in the Imperial Navy. The Eqbal family enjoyed close ties to the ulama—Mansur's father, Khosrow, was custodian of the Holy Shrine of Fatima in Qom—and one of his best friends was closely connected to the Khomeini movement. Through his friend the revolutionary, Mansur learned that Khomeini planned to stage a coup with the help of Banisadr, Ghotzbadegh, and Yazdi when he returned to Iran. Eqbal passed on the tip to another cousin serving in the military, who in turn contacted Ardeshir Zahedi. Zahedi arranged for a car and driver to take Eqbal to Niavaran so he could pass on the intelligence to the King in person.

Mansur Eqbal was the Shah's last appointment of the day when he entered his study at ten o'clock. "When I went to Niavaran I saw the guard," he recalled. "I went in and it was empty. I went upstairs to his room and waited for a few minutes. I saw him for twenty minutes. I couldn't take it. How a country could be destroyed like this and to see the face of the Shah, how sad he looked." Eqbal told him about Khomeini's plan to stage a Bolshevik-style armed insurrection once he returned home. He asked the Shah point-blank: "Do you think this is a one-way trip? Your Majesty, why don't you accept the suggestions of Khosrodad and the others and go to Nowshahr and let them take care of this?" The Shah avoided answering his question. Instead, he said he wished Eqbal had come to see him years earlier to talk about his concerns. Why hadn't he done so? Eqbal replied that some time ago he had sent the Shah the university thesis he had written on the problems facing Iran's economy. He had never heard back. Though he didn't tell the Shah, Eqbal suspected that Prime Minister Hoveyda had suppressed his report as he had filed away so many others over the years. Farah also received counselors and friends. Shahin Fatemi visited Niavaran eight times in the final weeks to offer support and to encourage the couple to stay on and fight. He knew Farah did not want to leave. "When I said I thought the Shah should stay, she would say, 'Please tell His Majesty what you tell me.'"

The Shah and Queen were agreed on one thing: they would take their clothes and personal effects with them out of the country but otherwise leave everything else behind. The Shah's decision was fueled by bitterness toward the people he believed had rejected him. Farah recalled her visit to the Kremlin years before and was determined not to give their critics any more ammunition. "I did not want to give them any reason to think that we had left taking our possessions with us," she said. "No, we were leaving with our heads held high, sure of having worked ceaselessly for the benefit of the country." The Shah pointed out a work of art on the wall in the dining room. "You liked this tableau," he said. "I don't want anything," said Farah, who was so determined to prove her point that she even left behind the exquisite private collection of jewels she had purchased with her own funds. They included such treasures as her favorite turquoise tiara set with matching necklace and earrings. In the days leading up to departure loading vans were spotted inside the palace grounds taking valuable works of art and state gifts into storage in the city's museums. Farah invited a group of foreign correspondents to tour and film the interior of the residence. "So no one will accuse us of taking things out," she told Fatemi. He was struck by her naïveté. "You don't know these people," he warned.

On Monday, January 15, an Iranian C-130 military transport left Tehran with Madame Diba, Prince Ali Reza, Princess Leila, Leila's governess, and several court officials and military officers bound for Lubbock, Texas, where the party planned to join Crown Prince Reza. The strike at the airport meant there was no catering for the flight, "no food, no water, nothing," said Amir Pourshaja, who accompanied the party. Another passenger was Deputy Court Minister Abolfath Atabai, who twenty-five years earlier had been one of only two aides to accompany the Shah and Queen Soraya to Rome. For the second time in his life he was headed into exile.

On Monday evening the King and Queen threw a small farewell party for their dwindling circle of friends. The Shah assured everyone they would be back after a few months' rest. Few who were present took him at his word. "On the last night I did not tell him anything," said Reza Ghotbi. "He had decided. I didn't have the heart to go to the airport the next day. I didn't know if he would come back or not but I thought not."

For Shahin Fatemi the Shah's decision to leave Iran "was like a nightmare." "Don't leave, Your Majesty," he pleaded.

"Don't worry," said the Shah. "We will leave and we will come back."

"Not this time, Your Majesty," said Fatemi. He pointed out the window to the plane trees that lined the grounds like sentinels. "If you leave Khomeini will come back and he will pray under these trees."

In the days leading to the Shah's departure, Ambassador Sullivan received crucial intelligence suggesting that he might have backed the wrong horse after all. "Embassy keeps getting reports from various sources that moderate religious leaders are very concerned by situation that is likely to arise when Shah leaves the country," Sullivan informed Washington on Wednesday, January 10, though he curtly dismissed their fears as "not very coherent or well reasoned and the motives involved are not always clear. Religious moderates are angry at Khomeini for putting them in present difficult position but do not know what to do about it." Ayatollah Milani of Mashad, twice jailed under the Shah's regime, still expressed the hope that "the Shah will not leave the country" and tried to open a back channel to Sullivan to beg the Americans to take action. The ambassador also reported that extremist mullahs had surrounded the house of Grand Ayatollah Shariatmadari and that "religious moderates are now scared enough to talk more publicly about their fears."

Four days later Karim Sanjabi, one of the most prominent leaders of the National Front, made a belated admission to George Lambrakis. The revolutionaries had not yet taken power but already splits were developing among the different factions. Ibrahim Yazdi and Sadegh Ghotzbadegh, he explained, were "very angry at [the] National Front. He does not know why." Lambrakis was already aware that Khomeini nursed a deep grudge against Mossadeq's former aides for their failure to oust the Shah in 1953 when they had a chance. "According to this theory," said Lambrakis, "Khomeini has never forgiven Mossadegh for pleading allegiance to the Shah and serving as his prime minister when he was strong enough to oust him." Khomeini blamed "Mossadegh and his people" for flirting with the Tudeh Party, a foolish action that he believed had provoked the United States to stage Operation Ajax. "Khomeini sees no reason to trust power to the National Front again," he advised. Sanjabi also confessed to Lambrakis that he and Bazargan, his putative ally, were neither personally nor professionally close. Finally, Sanjabi revealed that Khomeini planned to purge the military once he returned from exile, though he tried to excuse it away as "some small trials." Lambrakis said he hoped the Islamists were not planning anything on the scale of postwar Germany's Nuremberg trials. He added that he shared Sanjabi's hope that the army would hold and not stage a coup to rescue the monarchy.

American fears of a royalist coup had prompted General Huyser's mission to Tehran, but confusion surrounded his orders. He complained to Washington that his instructions were imprecise and open to different interpretations. In an attempt to seek clarification the general cabled Secretary of Defense Harold Brown and Chairman of the Joint Chiefs of Staff David Jones, asking for guidance. As he understood it his mission was to work with the Shah's generals to persuade them to support Bakhtiar and discourage them from staging a coup. If, however, Bakhtiar's government faltered, and if the Communist Tudeh Party tried to seize power, Huyser was to stand aside while the generals took action. The plan made no mention of the threat from Khomeini or the Islamists, whom the Americans assumed shared their own anti-Communist beliefs. "I have told [the generals] that I consider a military coup as an absolutely last resort," said Huyser. "I have explained to them that there are degrees before that action." First, they should allow Bakhtiar the opportunity to exert his authority. Second, if the internal situation worsened, Bakhtiar could declare martial law and call out the army to restore basic services, such as running the oil fields or maintaining the power grid. Only if the first and second steps failed would the United States endorse an army takeover. Huyser summed up his instructions this way: "I'll do my best to . . . give full support to Bakhtiar, and not jump into a military coup."

The revolutionaries were confident they had neutralized the possibility of U.S. military action to save the Shah. By now Khomeini's shock troops had also eliminated his main rivals. Imam Musa Sadr had disappeared in Tripoli. Grand Ayatollah Kazem Shariatmadari was a prisoner in his own home. Other moderate clerics had been silenced with death threats and intimidation. Khomeini stood on the brink of a clean sweep.

TUESDAY, JANUARY 16, was a day that began like any other. The Shah rose early, perused the morning papers over breakfast, and walked across the lawn to his office at the Jahan Nama Palace trailed by Colonel Djahinbini. He expected the Majles to give Prime Minister Bakhtiar's government a vote of confidence later in the morning. "He really surprised me," said Djahinbini. "He accepted a regular program of audiences. Early in the morning I checked the morning's list of visitors. He left the residence and went to the office as usual. The last name on the list was Deputy Court Minister Baheri at eleven." But his office staff noticed that the Shah was more subdued than usual. "Where is your smile, Your Majesty?" one greeted him. He wearily responded, "I haven't been able to smile much for a long time now."

Queen Farah spent the morning packing up family photo albums, choosing favorite books from her library, and taking souvenirs for the children. "We are leaving," she telephoned her friend Fereydoun Djavadi. "God knows what will happen." Word of the couple's departure quickly spread to the staff, who gathered in small, tearful knots in the grand hall. The atmosphere was one of grief, shock, and despair. "I could feel the distress in the men and women of our staff," said Farah. She came out to greet them and presented each with a small memento or money in the traditional manner. "Around eleven His Majesty came out of his office and walked up to the residence," said Djahinbini. "Her Majesty came out, they talked and stood before the staff and some family friends." The sight of the Shah brought everyone to tears. "They gathered around the King and Queen, shouting and kissing their hands and feet," said Djahinbini. The Shah tried to calm them. "No reason to worry," he said. "We are leaving for a long-needed rest and shall soon return."

Outside the sky darkened, the temperature plummeted, and the wind whipped up. The King and Queen walked out of the residence for the last time accompanied by several hundred men and women who spontaneously lined the driveway leading to the top lawn, where the helicopters were loaded and ready for the short flight to Mehrebad. Men and women who had known the Shah since he was a young boy, or who had been with the Queen since she arrived from Paris as a young bride, fell to their knees and crumpled to the ground. Others stood frozen like stone. The air rang with sobs and shrieks. "Where are you going?" they wept. "When will you be coming back? Why are you leaving us? We feel abandoned like orphans, orphans." The Shah and Queen struggled to contain their own emotions and comforted them. "Please get up," they pleaded. "Trust in God. We will be back. . . . Hands were stretched out to us. I can still see faces twisted with emotion," remembered Farah. The Shah walked toward his helicopter and turned and gave the crowd a final parting wave before boarding the craft with Colonel Djahinbini, General Badrei, and Grand Master of Ceremonies Amir Aslan Afshar. Farah embraced her tearful attendants and took her seat in the second helicopter. The final liftoff was excruciating. "With the sound of the whirring rotors in my ears," said Farah, "I soon saw the palace disappear behind the buildings of Tehran."

For the next ten minutes the choppers and their escorts clattered high above the streets of Tehran, which for a change were quiet. Each passenger was lost in his or her thoughts. "No one said anything," said Djahinbini. They set down alongside Mehrebad Airport's Imperial Pavilion, where only a few months earlier the Pahlavis had welcomed President Scheel of West Germany. The Shah could barely stand the strain and made it clear he was anxious to leave. He asked someone to call the Majles to get a progress report on the parliamentary vote of confidence and was told the phone lines had been cut. The only sound, Farah recalled, "was the whining of the wind coming down from the Alborz Mountains." Djahinbini watched as Chief of the General Staff General Abbas Gharabaghi asked the Shan to sign a decree handing over control of the army while he was out of the country. "His Majesty didn't sign it," said the colonel. "He told Gharabaghi twice—the General tried one more time—that if you want something signed take it to the government. This was highly unusual. It had never happened before. Before, he had always signed such a decree." The Shah told the few journalists at the scene that he was unsure when he would return. "It depends on the status of my health and I cannot define the time." Farah, "trying to keep her emotions under control," added, "I'm sure that the independence and national unity of our country will be preserved. I have faith in the Iranian people and in the culture of Iran. May God bless and preserve the Iranian nation."

After what seemed an interminable wait, Prime Minister Bakhtiar's helicopter came into view. He strode into the pavilion with the news they had been waiting for. The Shah and Bakhtiar conferred in private for a few minutes and then the Shah left the pavilion with his wife on his arm and walked toward the *Shahine*. For the first time in his reign there was no departure ceremony, no diplomatic corps, "no honor guard for him to review, no national anthem to herald his presence." The Shah kept his composure until General Badrei burst into tears and knelt before him and grabbed his shoes, causing him to tearfully try to raise the general off the tarmac. Before boarding the aircraft the Pahlavis walked under a copy of the Quran "with tears in their eyes and kissed the holy book before boarding the royal aircraft."

Prime Minister Bakhtiar joined the couple in their forward compartment for a few last words. "You now have all the power and authority," the Shah told him. "I leave the country in your hands and with God." Bakhtiar kissed his hand and left the aircraft. He stood on the tarmac and watched as the *Shahine* with the Shah at the controls roared down the runway for the last time. At 1:24 p.m. the wheels lifted off and the silver and blue bird set course for Egypt.

On the streets below, American lawyer John Westberg was returning from lunch with a colleague "when we began to hear horns honking and noticed cars putting their lights on. As we walked back to the office, people were coming into the street with big smiles on their faces. One fellow noticing us looking perplexed said: 'Mister, Shah *raft* [is gone]!' So we knew it had happened. Back at the office, everyone was at the windows watching the people in the streets milling around and shouting. Soon cars were honking all over the place and the streets were jammed. People filled the streets on all sides of our building. The celebration was joyous and a little wild. It was a bit frightening."

Grand Master of Ceremonies Amir Afshar summed up the degrading spectacle of the Shah's departure this way: "It needs a Shakespeare to do justice to what the Iranians did to their sovereign on his last day in his country."

THE END CAME quickly in a paroxysm of violence and bloodshed.

Grand Ayatollah Khomeini returned to Tehran on Thursday, February 1, 1979, and was greeted by hundreds of thousands of ecstatic supporters. "Khomeini's flight from Paris to Tehran was for many of his followers like the Prophet Mohammad's flight from Mecca to Medina in AD 622," wrote his biographer Baqer Moin. "In the new vocabulary developed by the Islamists, Khomeini was 'prophet-like,' the man who 'brought to an end the age of ignorance and introduced the light of Islam.'" Teeming crowds jammed the eleven-mile route from the airport into the center of Tehran. Khomeini did not return the sentiment. Asked what emotions he felt on seeing his homeland for the first time in fourteen years, he batted away his questioner with a single word. "None!" he snapped. When he emerged from the Air France flight he did not speak of reconciliation and unity but of revenge and the need for blood. He said he held foreigners and especially Americans responsible for Iran's ills. "Our final victory will come when all foreigners are out of the country," he told his followers. "I beg God to cut off the hands of all evil foreigners and all their helpers."

The very next day, National Security Adviser Brzezinski sought to assure President Carter that the tumult playing out in Iran was an isolated episode. "We should be careful not to over-generalize from the Iranian case," he explained, underlining two sentences for emphasis. "Islamic revivalist movements are not sweeping the Middle East and are not likely to be the wave of the future."

Eight days later, on February 10, the armed coup that Mansur Eqbal had predicted came to pass when young Islamist air force technicians staged a revolt at their base in eastern Tehran and turned their weapons on their comrades and officers. Their rebellion was the signal for the armed insurrection that the Mujahedin and Fedayeen had been planning for the past two years. The machine guns, rifles, and explosives they had stockpiled in mosque basements around Tehran were quickly handed out to militias, whose gunmen turned the streets of Tehran into a free fire zone. The ministries, palaces, and national broadcasting headquarters were quickly seized. The Shah's senior officers held a meeting and debated what to do, but General Gharabaghi vetoed the idea of staging a rebellion when he declared the army's neutrality. Twenty-four hours later, Tehran fell to the revolutionaries, and the revolutionaries declared final victory over the Shah.

RETRIBUTION WAS SWIFT under Iran's new Islamic regime. The names of the many hundreds sent to the firing squads in the first eighteen months of the Islamic republic's existence read like a "who's who" of Imperial

Iran. The rooftop of the school used by Khomeini as a temporary head-quarters doubled as an execution chamber, and the crème of the Shah's officer corps was eliminated, though not in the way William Sullivan had been led to expect. Among the high-ranking former officers and officials sent to the firing squad in the blood-soaked first weeks:

General Nematollah Nasiri, former chief of Savak.

General Manuchehr Khosrodad, commander of the air corps.

General Amir Rahimi, former martial law administrator of Tehran.

General Reza Naji, former military governor of Isfahan.

General Nasser Moghadam, successor to Nasiri as chief of Savak.

General Hassan Pakravan, the former head of Savak who had inter-vened in 1963 to persuade the Shah to spare Khomeini's life. In their last days alive Pakravan and Moghadam shared the same prison cell. Mogha-dam told Pakravan that he was confident he would be spared. He admit-ted that before the Shah left Iran he had reached a secret agreement with Khomeini's men to help neutralize Savak and provide them with inside information, including the names of top clergy who collaborated with the regime. "I am helping them to establish a new intelligence service and nothing will happen to me," he assured Pakravan. "Be careful," the gen-eral told his cellmate. "You don't know the mullahs." The other prisoners told Pakravan he would be spared. "General, you saved the life of Kho-meini," they reminded him. Pakravan knew better. "He will execute me because he knows I know a lot about him." He was right—both men went to their deaths before the firing squad.

General Parviz Amini-Afshar, head of G2 Military Intelligence and commander of the Imperial Chief of Staff.

General Amir-Hossein Rabii, commander of the Imperial Air Force.

General Ali Neshat, commander of the Immortals.

General Nader Djahanbani, deputy commander of the Imperial Air Force, the handsome "blue-eyed general" whose brother Khosrow was married to Princess Shahnaz.

By the time former prime minister Amir Abbas Hoveyda was brought to trial the revolutionaries had abolished the monarchy and established Iran as an Islamic republic. During this time the prisons were packed with thousands of people suspected of ties to the Pahlavi regime. Press reports spoke of upwards of ten thousand who had "disappeared."

Hoveyda was held in brutal conditions and tried for "crimes against the people" in a circus atmosphere that caused widespread outrage inside and outside Iran. Over the protests of Mehdi Bazargan and Karim Sanjabi, the courtly former prime minister and court minister was executed along with six military officers at 6:00 p.m. on April 7 by young volunteers who enthusiastically blasted them with Israeli-made Uzi machine guns.

Other prominent civilian officials put to death included:

Manuchehr Azmun, the former minister of labor and minister of state for executive affairs who oversaw the disastrous handling of September's martial law announcement.

Gholam Reza Nikpey, former mayor of Tehran.

Mahmud Jaafarian, Reza Ghotbi's successor as head of the national broadcasting service.

IMAM MUSA SADR was never seen alive again. According to Palestinian sources who tipped off the CIA, in the spring of 1979 Colonel Gadhafi telephoned Ayatollah Beheshti and asked what he wanted to do with his "guest." Beheshti reportedly told Gadhafi that "Musa Sadr is a threat to Khomeini." The Americans later learned that Musa Sadr and his two traveling companions had been "summarily executed and buried at an unmarked desert gravesite."

Following the overthrow of Colonel Gadhafi in 2011 a former top aide came forward to reveal that the Imam had survived his imprisonment well into the late 1990s. Hopes were briefly raised that Musa Sadr's family and followers would finally learn the truth about his disappearance. Following his election to the Iranian presidency in 2013, Hassan Rouhani pledged to undertake a new investigation to find out the truth about Musa Sadr's disappearance. Libya's descent into civil war soon provided Rouhani with a convenient excuse not to act. If Shia Muslims ever learned the truth about the disappearance of their beloved "Missing Imam"—that he had actually sided with the Shah against Khomeini in 1978 and that the founders of the Islamic republic were complicit in his murder—the tremors would be felt from Najaf to Qom.

GRAND AYATOLLAH MOHAMMAD Kazem Shariatmadari refused to accept his rival Khomeini's claim to rule Iran and denounced velayat-e faqih or "guardianship of the jurists." He opposed the referendum to abolish the monarchy, protested the seizure of U.S. diplomats in November 1979, and bitterly attacked Khomeini's regime as a totalitarian fraud. Khomeini placed him under house arrest, and members of the Marja's family were arrested and tortured by the secret police. These actions led to a brief popular revolt in Tabriz. Shariatmadari was later accused of complicity in an abortive coup attempt and on Khomeini's orders Iran's most senior marja was sensationally stripped of his black turban and beaten by thugs. In a final act of vengeance, Khomeini deprived Shariatmadari of the life-saving drugs he needed to treat cancer. Kazem Shariatmadari was living under house arrest when he died in obscurity in 1986.

ON MARCH 20, 1979, the CIA quietly announced that it had translated and published a seventy-four-page book that it gave the innocuous title *Translations on Near East and North Africa, No. 1897.* Nine years overdue, the agency had finally published *Islamic Government,* Khomeini's blueprint for the establishment of an Islamic republic and the expulsion of U.S. influence from Iran.

GRAND AYATOLLAH RUHOLLAH Khomeini assumed the mantle of Supreme Leader of the Islamic Republic and ruled Iran with an iron fist until his death in 1989. Sharia became the law of the land, tight censorship was imposed, and no independent political activity was tolerated. "Prison life was drastically worse under the Islamic Republic than under the Pahlavis," observed Iranian historian Ervand Abrahamian. "One who survived both writes that four months under [Khomeini] took the toll of four years under Savak. Another writes that one day under the former equaled ten years under the latter. . . . In the prison literature of the Pahlavi period, the recurring words had been 'boredom' and 'monotony.' In that of the Islamic republic they were 'fear,' 'death,' 'terror,' 'horror,' and, most frequent of all, 'nightmare.'"

In a bizarre historical twist, Khomeini and his coterie fulfilled the litany of crimes they had laid at the Shah's feet. Royalists, leftists, liberals, homosexuals, Jews, Baha'i, and Freemasons were severely repressed. An estimated eight thousand Iranians were put to death for political "crimes" during the four-year period from 1981 to 1985, and in total twelve thousand Iranians were reportedly killed by the Islamic republic during Khomeini's decade in power. Under Khomeini, prison space more than doubled and torture practices banned by the Shah were reinstated. The single deadliest atrocity occurred in July 1988, when an estimated three thousand young men and women accused of holding leftist political views were slain in a single week. In the 1990s a number of prominent Iranian intellectuals were murdered in their homes by regime death squads. In 2009 several hundred pro-democracy protesters were massacred and hundreds more tortured when they protested the rigged election that returned Mahmud Ahmadinejad to power. In addition, about a million Iranians and Iraqis perished during the eight-year Iran-Iraq war fought from 1980 to 1988. During the revolution, Saddam Hussein had presciently warned Queen Farah that "it is better that a thousand Iranians die now than a million people die later."

The men who brought Khomeini to power were consumed in the inferno.

Mehdi Bazargan served as Khomeini's first prime minister and resigned in November 1979 to protest the seizure of the American embassy compound in Tehran. Bazargan died in exile in Switzerland in 1995 at age eighty-six.

Abolhassan Banisadr was elected the first president of the Islamic Republic in 1981. He clashed with Khomeini, who suspected his populism and his leftist pretensions. Impeached by the Iranian parliament in 1981, Banisadr made a dramatic escape to France. He lives in exile in France and now resides in a château in Versailles, the seat of the French kings.

Ayatollah Mohammad Beheshti served as chairman of the Assembly of Experts, the body responsible for selecting Khomeini's putative successor, and emerged as kingmaker in the new republic. In June 1981 he was blown up along with seventy-one other senior officials in a blast reportedly carried out by the Mujahedin, which had declared war on the Islamists. To this day many Iranians suspect he was actually assassinated by jealous rivals within the regime.

Sadegh Ghotzbadegh served as Iran's foreign minister and handled the negotiations to release the American diplomats seized when student radicals stormed the U.S. embassy in Tehran in November 1979. In April 1982 he was arrested and accused of plotting a coup to overthrow the Islamic Republic. Imprisoned and tortured, Ghotzbadegh was executed in September 1982.

Ibrahim Yazdi served in Bazargan's government but resigned with him to protest the takeover of the U.S. embassy in November 1979. He assumed the leadership of the Liberation Movement and emerged as a critic of Khomeini and the Islamic Republic. His house was firebombed and he was arrested and rearrested, most recently during the 2009 upheavals.

THE ARCHTRAITOR HOSSEIN Fardust, the Shah's friend and aide since childhood, was one of the few pillars of the ancien régime who stayed in Iran after the revolution and was not consigned to the firing squad. As penance for his service to the Pahlavi Dynasty, Fardust wrote a scurrilous memoir that accused the Shah of corruption, brutality, sexual deviancy, and treasonous dealings with foreign governments. Fardust played to Iranian paranoia about British influence in Iran when he "revealed" that the secret brains behind Savak's special intelligence branch was actually the "satanic" Queen Elizabeth II. The Shah, wrote Fardust, used to meet each day with the head of British intelligence's Tehran office to receive his instructions. It was unclear whether Fardust wrote the book on his own initiative or acted under duress. He died in 1987 shortly after giving his first television interview.

THE FALL OF the Shah led to a great deal of soul-searching and not a little retribution in Washington, where President Carter and his top officials were accused of failing to support an ally in his hour of need. Carter's election defeat in November 1980 was blamed in large part on his handling of the revolution and subsequent hostage crisis. Carter went on to found the Carter Center to advance democracy and human rights and alleviate conflict, poverty, and disease. He was awarded the Nobel Prize for Peace in 2002.

Today, former national security adviser Zbigniew Brzezinski teaches American foreign policy at Johns Hopkins University in Washington, DC, and is a scholar at the Center for Strategic and International Studies in the nation's capital. He continues to speak out on the subject of U.S.-Iran relations and supported the 2015 U.S.-Iran nuclear deal.

Ambassador William Sullivan left Tehran in 1979 and retired from the State Department to accept a post at Columbia University as head of the American Assembly. Sullivan, who died in October 2013 at age ninety, never fully explained the logic behind his support for Khomeini's return, and his memoir Mission to Iran left many unanswered questions.

Charlie Naas, Sullivan's deputy, is today retired and living outside Washington, DC. He still closely follows events in Iran.

Henry Precht was blamed by many White House officials and members of Congress for mishandling the State Department's response to the revolution. Congressional opposition ended his chances of securing an ambassadorship. He remains an unrepentant critic of the Shah.

George Lambrakis is retired and living in Paris.

John Stempel recently retired after twenty-six years as administrator and teacher at the Patterson School of Diplomacy and International Commerce at the University of Kentucky. He recalled the events surrounding the Shah's downfall in his book *Inside the Iranian Revolution*.

THE PAHLAVIS' FRIENDS and courtiers scattered after the revolution.

Elli Antoniades settled in New York, later retired to Athens, Greece, and maintains her close friendship with Queen Farah.

Amir Pourshaja, the late Shah's valet, lives with his family in Maryland.

Reza Ghotbi lives in Maryland and works as an IT consultant.

Seyyed Hossein Nasr is a professor in Islamic Studies at George Washington University in Washington, DC, and has authored and edited fifty books. In later years, Nasr tried to distance himself from Queen Farah and in interviews with the Iranian press expressed regret at his decision to head her office in the final months of 1978. He is the father of Vali Nasr, dean of the Johns Hopkins School of Advanced International Studies and a prominent expert on Iran and U.S.-Iran relations.

Ardeshir Zahedi retired to Switzerland and has completed his volumes of memoirs. He continues to speak out about the Pahlavi era and U.S.-Iran relations.

Parviz Sabeti, who urged the Shah to crack down against Khomeini in the spring of 1978, lives in the United States.

Ali Kani, the friend to Imam Musa Sadr who conveyed Khomeini's *Islamic Government* thesis to the Shah, settled in exile in France.

Colonel Kiomars Djahinbini, the Shah's faithful head of security, lives in Virginia with his family.

Fereydoun Djavadi, friend to Queen Farah, lives in Paris.

OF THE SHAH's surviving brothers and sisters, Princess Ashraf and Prince Gholam Reza moved to France. After the revolution the Princess became a vocal opponent of the Khomeini regime and wrote two books, *Faces in a Mirror* and *Time for Truth*, about her life and the revolution that deposed her beloved brother and destroyed the Pahlavi Dynasty. She died on January 7, 2016.

Pahlavi family matriarch Queen Mother Taj ol-Moluk died of cancer in 1982.

Former Queen Fawzia, the Shah's first wife and the mother of Princess Shahnaz, died in Alexandria, Egypt, on July 2, 2013, at age ninety-one.

Former Queen Soraya, the Shah's second wife and the woman he divorced to sire an heir, died in Paris on September 26, 2001, at age sixty-nine.

Khosrow Djahanbani, scion of the powerful and wealthy Djahanbani Dynasty, whose brother Nader was executed by Khomeini's men, died in 2014. He supported the goals of the revolution to the end and never recanted his support for the man responsible for overthrowing his father-in-law and killing his brother.

Princess Shahnaz followed her husband's lead when after the revolution she took an Islamic name and rejected her Pahlavi heritage. After Khosrow's death, however, Shahnaz insisted on being addressed as the King's daughter and a member of the Imperial House. Now unveiled, she lives quietly in Switzerland.

THE SHAH WAS pursued to the ends of the earth by his mortal enemy Khomeini, who never let him rest. He and the Queen were condemned by the new rulers of the Islamic Republic as the "corrupt on earth," sentenced to death in absentia, and hunted by trained assassins. Gunmen sent from Tehran successfully eliminated the three men considered most capable of leading organized resistance to the Islamist regime. General Oveissi and Prince Shahriar, Princess Ashraf's naval commander son, were both shot in Paris in 1980 in separate attacks. Former prime minister Shahpur Bakhtiar and his assistant had their throats cut by armed intruders who made their way into Bakhtiar's heavily secured Paris apartment.

The Shah, Queen Farah, and their youngest children and entourage left Cairo after a short stay and flew to Morocco as guests of King Hassan. They were in Morocco in February 1979 when the monarchy was finally overthrown. The new Islamic republic promised to cut oil sales and relations with any country that offered them safe haven, and many of the princes, presidents, and prime ministers who once called at Niavaran looking for favors turned their backs on them. Old friends such as Prince Rainier and Princess Grace, and the Dutch, Swedish, and Spanish royal families stayed in touch but lacked the political power to extend practical help. The family moved to the Bahamas and Mexico before President Carter reluctantly allowed the Shah to enter the United States for cancer surgery. His decision prompted the student takeover of the U.S. embassy in Tehran. From New York the Pahlavis spent time in Panama before returning to the Middle East. President Sadat welcomed the Shah back to Egypt, where he died on July 27, 1980.

In the months before he succumbed to lymphoma the Shah spoke more freely than at any time in his life. He held a series of revealing conversations with his wife's friend Fereydoun Djavadi. "Why didn't you go all out against Khomeini?" Djavadi asked him. "Why didn't you finish this?" "I wasn't this man," the Shah answered. "If you wanted someone to kill people you had to find somebody else." Djavadi was perplexed. He reminded the Shah that he had ordered the army crackdown in 1963. "You gave the orders to finish the job," said Djavadi. "It wasn't me," the Shah told him. "It was Alam who gave the orders."

The Shah spoke often about fate and destiny. In the space of a few decades he had transformed a backward, poverty-stricken country into southwestern Asia's most powerful state and the world's second-largest oil producer. The Iran he left behind boasted one of the best-educated workforces in the Middle East and a burgeoning manufacturing and industrial base. Despite the economic dislocations caused by the oil boom, in his last year the economy had finally started to cool off and settle down. Iran under his watch experienced one of the greatest artistic and cultural revivals in its modern history, and the country was on its way to becoming a regional hub for industry, science, and medicine. He had hoped that his farewell gift to Iran would be free elections, a return to democracy, and the handover of the crown to his eldest son. Like his father, Mohammad Reza Shah Pahlavi had simply run out of time and luck. "I hadn't the time," he mused. "If I had five more years everything would be done."

The Shah was in Cairo when Djavadi asked him to describe his feelings about Iran and the Iranian people. "Your Majesty, you're in love with Iran," said Djavadi. "Can you define what is Iran?"

The Shah, for whom nationalism was like a religion, paused to consider his answer. "Iran is Iran," he soberly replied. There followed a minute's silence. "It's land, people, and history," he added. Another minute passed. "Every Iranian has to love it." He repeated over and over: "Iran is Iran. Iran is Iran."

Shortly thereafter he slipped into unconsciousness and passed away. He was sixty years old, an age when many statesmen in Western countries were winning their first elections to national office.

One thing he knew for sure. Though the glory days of empire might be over, the claim to past greatness ran through the land and the people like a pulse.

NOTES

INTRODUCTION: Back to Cairo

3   *"I turn to right and left"*: Abolqasem Ferdowsi, *Shahnameh: The Persian Book of Kings,* trans. Dick Davis (New York: Penguin, 2006), p. 764. p. 273.

3   *"Ingratitude is the prerogative of the people"*: Author interview with Bob Armao, October 20, 2014. The Shah made his comment to Armao shortly before he left Iran in January 1979.

5   *"I didn't want to come on the anniversary"*: Author interview with Farah Pahlavi, February 15, 2015.

8   *"It will be back up soon enough"*: Author interview with Amir Pourshaja, March 16, 2013.

8   *"Ingratitude is the prerogative of the people"*: Author interview with Bob Armao, October 20, 2014.

9   *"protecting Adolf Eichmann"*: "Buttoning Andy Young's Lip," *Newsweek*, November 26, 1979, p. 33.

9   *"a saint"*: "Mr. Ambassador," *Newsweek*, August 27, 1979, p. 17.

10   *$25 billion*: "Nobody Influences Me!" *Time*, December 10, 1979, p. 34.

10   *"No, I wouldn't deny it"*: Oriana Fallaci, *Interviews with History and Conversations with Power* (New York: Rizzoli, 2011), p. 158.

10   *casualty estimates*: See later chapters of this book and also http://www.emadbaghi.com/en/archives /000592.php#more.

10   *3,164 names*: See http://www.emadbaghi.com/en/archives/000592.php#more.

10   *"The problem here"*: Ali Ansary, *The Politics of Nationalism in Modern Iran* (New York: Cambridge University Press, 2012), p. 226.

11   *Chile, casualty figures*: For more information on Chile during the dictatorship of Augusto Pinochet, see *The Report of the Chilean National Commission on Truth and Reconciliation,* http://www.usip.org /sites/default/files/resources/collections/truth_commissions/Chile90-Report/Chile90-Report.pdf.

11   *Argentina, casualty figures*: For more information on Argentina in the 1970s, see Paul H. Lewis, *Guerrillas and Generals: The "Dirty War" in Argentina* (Westport, CT: Praeger, 2002).

11   *Iraq*: John F. Burns, "How Many People Has Hussein Killed?" *New York Times*, January 26, 2003.

11   *Syria*: To learn more about events in Syria in 1982, see the *Guardian* newspaper's coverage, http:// www.theguardian.com/theguardian/from-the-archive-blog/2011/aug/01/hama-syria-massacre -1982-archive.

12   *"Green what?"*: Author interview with Zbigniew Brzezinski, September 4, 2015.

13   *"Everyone is a psychologist, you know?"*: Author interview with Farah Pahlavi, March 24, 2013.

15   *"Blunt histories do not always meet"*: Margaret MacMillan, *Dangerous Games* (New York: Modern Library, 2009), p. 41.

15   *"Historians, of course, do not own the past"*: Ibid., p. 43.

16   *"When did you reveal yourself"*: The author was witness to the dinner table conversation.

1. THE SHAH

19   *"A country's king can never be at peace"*: Abolqasem Ferdowsi, *Shahnameh: The Persian Book of Kings,* trans. Dick Davis (New York: Penguin, 2006), p. 764.

19 *"I want my son to inherit not dreams"*: John B. Oakes, "Shah Is Offering New Plan to Aid Developing Nations," *New York Times*, September 24, 1975.

19 *His day began*: Author interview with Amir Pourshaja, March 16, 2013. Details in this chapter about the Shah's daily routine, except where indicated, are taken from this interview session.

19 *sensitive stomach, food allergies*: Ibid. Author interview with Fereydoun Djavadi, July 13, 2013.

19 *larger than Great Britain*: Edward J. Linehan, "Old-New Iran, Next Door to Russia," *National Geographic* 199, no. 1 (January 1961): 47.

20 *thirty-five million subjects*: James O. Jackson, "Shah: Dedicated, Dominant, Distrustful," *Chicago Tribune*, January 8, 1978.

20 *twenty-one*: The number of dams built under the Shah was provided by Dr. Iradj Vahidi, former minister of water and power, via an e-mail exchange with Abdol Reza Ansari, former minister of the interior, April 15, 2015. Under the Shah a total of twenty-one dams were constructed. Fifteen were water storage dams and six were diversionary dams. The storage dams were: Karaj, Sepeed-Rood, Dez, Latian, Karoon, Mehhabad, Golpayegan, Shah-Abbas, Arras, Zarrineh-Rood, Gheshlaagh, Meenaab, Doroodzan, Gorgan, and Shahnaz. The diversion dams were: Karkheh, Shabankaareh, Kahhak, Zahhak, Shaour, and Bampour.

20 *during the rainy season*: Author interview with Kambiz Atabai, October 25, 2015.

20 *One day at the Caspian*: Author interview with Fereydoun Djavadi, July 13, 2013.

20 *"What is he doing?"*: Ibid.

21 *"a feeling of déjà vu"*: Farah Pahlavi, *An Enduring Love: My Life with the Shah* (New York: Miramax, 2004), p. 245.

21 *"We are delighted to salute"*: "Who Else Would Have Done It?," *Kayhan International*, October 27, 1967.

21 *second largest oil exporter*: "Troops Guard Oil," *Kayhan International*, November 1, 1978.

21 *education statistics*: Jagdish Sharma, "Student Unrest Stems from Just Grievances," *Kayhan International*, October 9, 1978.

22 *17 percent to more than 50 percent*: Joe Alex Morris, "Iran's Future Grows Less and Less Certain," *Los Angeles Times*, May 21, 1978.

22 *"Nobody can dictate to us"*: "Shah Rejects Bid by Ford for Cut in Prices of Oil," *New York Times*, September 27, 1974.

22 *"to a threshold of grandeur"*: "Oil, Grandeur, and a Challenge to the West," *Time*, November 4, 1974, p. 28.

22 *"Boom?"*: "Iran's Race for Riches," *Newsweek*, March 24, 1975, p. 38.

22 *"living better than most"*: Jackson, "Shah: Dedicated, Dominant, Distrustful."

22 *423-fold*: Ibid.

22 *14-fold*: Ibid.

22 *"The Shah's power is virtually total"*: Ibid.

22 *"one of the most pervasive"*: Ibid.

22 *10 percent*: "Oil, Grandeur, and a Challenge to the West."

22 *40 percent of the wealth*: Ibid.

22 *sixty-one thousand villages*: Richard T. Sale, "Iran, the New Persian Empire: Shah's Vision of Progress Clashes with Iranian Reality," *Washington Post*, May 8, 1977.

22 *"piped water, sanitation, doctors"*: Ibid.

22 *"People hunt for undigested oats"*: Ibid.

23 *"It's all skin deep"*: Ibid.

23 *"It's all fake pretension"*: Ibid.

23 *fifth-strongest nation*: "Expert Puts Iran up with World Big Guns," *Kayhan International*, December 6, 1977.

23 *5.9 billion rials*: Changiz Pezeshkpur, "Stock Volume Hits 5.9b. Rials," *Kayhan International*, January 1, 1978.

23 *380,000 tourists*: "Foreign Tourism Still Rising," *Kayhan International*, July 5, 1978.

23 *100,000 foreign residents*: "Riots 'Don't Alarm' Foreign Community," *Kayhan International*, September 7, 1978.

23 *52,000 Americans*: Author interview with Henry Precht, June 4, 2009.

23 *expatriate communities in Iran*: "Riots 'Don't Alarm' Foreign Community."

23 *"Look at them"*: "Iran's Race for Riches," *Newsweek*, March 24, 1975, p. 38.

23 *defended by a crack professional fighting force*: Figures and quotes (unless otherwise indicated) describing the size of the different branches of the Imperial Armed Forces come from a White House document titled "Iran's Petroleum Vulnerabilities," February 21, 1978, Jimmy Carter Presidential Library.

23 *pledge to defend "God, Shah, and Fatherland"*: "An Army with Two Missions," *Time*, November 27, 1978, p. 29.

24 *"His is a formidable personality"*: "Memorandum: Nothing Succeeds Like a Successful Shah," Central Intelligence Agency Office of National Estimate, October 8, 1971, *Iran: The Making of US Policy, 1977–80*, National Security Archive (Alexandria, VA: Chadwyck-Healey, 1990), document 00757.

25 *"My Quran, I forgot it! I have to go back!"*: Two former palace aides relayed this story to the author. The Shah's staff never understood the accusations made by opposition groups that the King did not take his devotions or religion seriously.

25 *stayed at his side for the rest of the day*: Author interview with Colonel Kiomars Djahinbini, March 25, 2013.

25 *"I remember him coming down the stairs"*: Author interview with Reza Pahlavi, March 26, 2013.

25 *worked without air-conditioning*: Author interviews with Farah Pahlavi, March 23–25, 2013, and Fereydoun Djavadi, July 13, 2013.

26 *"We start getting work"*: Jackson, "Shah: Dedicated, Dominant, Distrustful."

26 *"Often I order minor officials"*: Ibid.

26 *"I barely had time"*: Ibid.

26 *"I not only make the decisions"*: Lewis M. Simons, "Shah's Dreams Are Outpacing Iran's Economic Boom," *Washington Post*, May 26, 1974.

26 *approved salary increases, etc.*: Khosrow Fatemi, "Leadership by Distrust: The Shah's Modus Operandi," *Middle East Journal* 36, no. 1 (Winter 1982): 54.

26 *No military plane took off or landed*: Ibid., p. 48.

26 *above the rank of lieutenant colonel*: Confirmed by Kambiz Atabai, October 24, 2015.

26 *itineraries were sent to the Shah*: Jackson, "Shah: Dedicated, Dominant, Distrustful."

26 *"Copies of every story"*: Ibid.

27 *"He only wanted to get things done"*: Author interview with Dr. Parviz Mina, September 11, 2014.

27 *"He would let you explain yourself"*: Author interview with Abdol Reza Ansari, September 12, 2014.

27 *"He asks very, very sharp questions"*: Jackson, "Shah: Dedicated, Dominant, Distrustful."

27 *"He was familiar with everything"*: Foundation for Iranian Studies oral history interview with Armin Meyer by William Burr, Washington, DC, March 29, 1985, pp. 1–18.

27 *"Once you lost his goodwill"*: Habib Ladjevardi, director, interview with Denis Wright, Harvard University Center for Middle East Studies, Iranian Oral History Project, October 10, 1984, tape 3, p. 5.

27 *Once a week*: Confirmed by Kambiz Atabai, October 24, 2015.

27 *padlocked to the wrist*: Asadollah Alam, *The Shah and I: The Confidential Diary of Iran's Royal Court, 1969–77*, introduced and edited by Alinaghi Alikhani (New York: St. Martin's Press, 1991), p. 159. Confirmed by Ardeshir Zahedi, who served as Iranian foreign minister from 1966 to 1973, in author interviews, October 27–28, 2012.

28 *"My voice is heard everywhere"*: Margaret Laing, *The Shah* (London: Sidgwick & Jackson, 1977), p. 225.

28 *"some enormous earth slide"*: "Iran: Desert Miracle," *National Geographic* 147, no. 1 (January 1975): 6.

28 *inaugurated the soaring Shahyad Monument*: Amir Taheri, "Tehran's Ctesiphon: Shahyad Inaugurated," *Kayhan International*, October 17, 1971.

28 *Construction on an underground metro*: "Work Gets Started on City Metro," *Kayhan International*, November 14, 1977.

28 *forested green belt*: "Forest Belt Around Tehran," *Kayhan International*, November 14, 1977.

29 *"stern, icily correct"*: Jackson, "Shah: Dedicated, Dominant, Distrustful."

29 *"Some found him a little humorless"*: Cynthia Helms, *An Ambassador's Wife in Tehran* (New York: Dodd, Mead, 1981), p. 92.

29 *"rather a bore"*: Habib Ladjevardi, director, interview with Denis Wright, Harvard University Center for Middle East Studies, Iranian Oral History Project, October 10, 1984, tape 4, p. 7.

29 *"found the Shah heavy going"*: Ibid., p. 8.

30 *play with a loose strand of hair*: Author interviews with Farah Pahlavi, March 23–25, 2013.

30 *"The expression in his face never changed"*: Author interview with Khalil al-Khalil, June 21, 2013.

30 *"As serious as a mullah"*: Princess Soraya Esfandiary Bakhtiary, in collaboration with Louis Valentin, *Palace of Solitude*, trans. Hubert Gibbs (London: Quartet Books, 1992), p. 80.

30 *the formal Persian word for "you"*: Ibid., p. 67.

30 *"He had really great self-control"*: Author interviews with Farah Pahlavi, March 23–25, 2013.

30 *"Not so fast! Not so fast!"*: Ibid.

30 *"The missile was fired from six miles away"*: Author interview with Lieutenant General Mohammad Hossein Mehrmand, January 13, 2015.

31 *"On a one-to-one, eyeball-to-eyeball basis"*: Don A. Schanche, "Contradictions Shadow Image of Shah," *Los Angeles Times*, November 12, 1978.

31 *"He was exactly the opposite"*: Author interview with Mahnaz Afkhami, August 16, 2013.

31 *"My father was shy"*: Author interview with Reza Pahlavi, March 26, 2013.

32 *"If I take a liking to someone"*: Jackson, "Shah: Dominant, Dedicated, Distrustful."

32 *he was careful*: Author interview with Fereydoun Djavadi, July 13, 2013.

32 *"stiffly seated"*: Donnie Radcliffe and Jacqueline Trescott, "Back-Door Diplomacy at the White House," *Washington Post*, November 16, 1977, p. 129.

32 *the false rumor spread*: Ibid.

32 *"He was so shy"*: Author interview with Parvine Farmanfarmaian, February 16, 2015.

32 *"There was a gentleman"*: Author interview with Farah Pahlavi, November 13, 2014.

33 *made sure thank-you gifts*: Author interview with Elli Antoniades, April 3, 2013.

33 *paid the medical expenses*: Ibid.

33 *"I can't allow this"*: Ibid.

33 *the wrong medication*: Alam (1991), p. 479.

33 *"I am sorry I was too busy"*: http://www.freerepublic.com/focus/f-news/1031880/posts.

33 *"Pull this fellow's ears"*: Ibid.

34 *"Dangerous"*: Edward J. Linehan, "Old-New Iran, Next Door to Russia," *National Geographic* 199, no. 1 (January 1961): 84.

34 *"And do you know how many died"*: Author interview with Robert Armao, October 20, 2014.

34 *fell "into such prolonged laughter"*: Alam, (1991), p. 503.

34 *presented him with checks*: Author interview with Robert Armao, October 20, 2014.

34 *"a fantastic tailor"*: Author interview with Maryam Ansary, April 17, 2013.

34 *"You can't throw a stone"*: Jackson, "Shah: Dominant, Dedicated, Distrustful."

35 *"Isn't there any other news"*: Author interview with Reza Ghotbi, March 25, 2013.

35 *"Let me tell you quite bluntly"*: Max Frankel, "'This King Business,' a Headache to Shah," *New York Times*, April 14, 1962.

35 *"It is hardly a pleasant job"*: E. A. Bayne, *Persian Kingship in Transition* (New York: American Universities Field Staff, 1968), p. 38.

35 *"children"*: Various associates and acquaintances of the Shah confirmed to the author that the Shah often affectionately referred to the Iranian people as his "children."

35 *"You Westerners simply don't understand"*: Jackson, "Shah: Dominant, Dedicated, Distrustful."

35 *the farr*: To read more about the farr see Bayne (1968), p. 67; Homa Katouzian, *State and Society in Iran: The Eclipse of the Qajars and the Emergence of the Pahlavis* (London: I. B. Taurus, 2006), p. 5; and Abolala Soudavar, *The Aura of Kings: Legitimacy and Divine Sanction in Iranian Kingship* (Costa Mesa, CA: Mazda Publishers, 2003).

36 *"love me and will never forsake me"*: Alam (1991), p. 177.

36 *"A real king in Iran"*: "It Began with the King of Kings," *Kayhan International*, October 14, 1971.

36 *"I am not Suharto"*: Author interview with Parviz Sabeti, May 10, 2014. This catchphrase was the Shah's mantra during the year of revolution.

37 *"a lamb in lion's clothing"*: Author interview with Dr. Parviz Mina, September 11, 2014.

37 *"In the afternoon His Imperial Majesty"*: Alam (1991), p. 511.

37 *"95 percent of the population"*: Charles Douglas-Hume, "State Intent on Staying in Power Despite Violence," *Times* (London), November 23, 1978.

37 *"You can see by the look in their eyes"*: Eric Pace, "Shah Courting Popular Support," *New York Times*, May 13, 1975.

37 *"This is not a new idea"*: "Shahanshah Ponders Abdication," *Kayhan International*, October 19, 1971. In 1976 the Shah explained similar plans to abdicate to the author Margaret Laing. See Laing (1977), p. 184. He suggested he needed another dozen years in power to consolidate his achievements.

38 *"The time of Reza"*: Author interview with Fereydoun Djavadi, July 13, 2013.

38 *"nothing can threaten it"*: Oakes, "Shah Is Offering New Plan to Aid Developing Nations."

39 *kalleh pacheh or boiled mutton's head and foot*: Gholam Reza Afkhami, *The Life and Times of the Shah* (Berkeley: University of California Press, 2009), p. 43.

40 *in a special drawer*: Author interview with Amir Pourshaja, March 16, 2013.

2. CROWN AND KINGDOM

41 *"I wish you life and long prosperity"*: Abolqasem Ferdowsi, *Shahnameh: The Persian Book of Kings*, trans. Dick Davis (New York: Penguin, 2006), p. 332.

41 *"I found myself plunged into a sea of trouble"*: Mohammad Reza Pahlavi, *Mission for My Country* (New York: McGraw-Hill, 1961), p. 75.

41 *ranking brigadier*: Reza Khan commanded the Hamadan Brigade. Gholam Reza Afkhami, *The Life and Times of the Shah* (Berkeley: University of California Press, 2009), p. 16.

41 *stood smoking . . . anxiously awaiting*: Ashraf Pahlavi, *Faces in a Mirror: Memoirs from Exile* (Englewood Cliffs, NJ: Prentice-Hall, 1980), p. 1.

41 *"It's a boy!"*: Ibid.

41 *"There is another child"*: Ibid.

42 *"O God, I place my son in your care"*: Afkhami (2009), p. 10.

42 *"To say that I was unwanted might be harsh"*: A. Pahlavi (1980), p. 1.

42 *Land of the Lion and the Sun*: To learn more about the history of pre-Islamic Persia the following titles are helpful: Michael Axworthy, *Empire of the Mind: A History of Iran* (New York: Basic Books, 2008); Gene R. Garthwaite, *The Persians* (Oxford: Blackwell Publishing, 2007); Gene Gurney, *Kingdoms of Asia, the Middle East, and Africa: An Illustrated Encyclopedia of Ruling Monarchs from Ancient Times to the Present* (New York: Crown, 1986); Homa Katouzian, *The Persians: Ancient, Medieval, and Modern Iran* (New Haven, CT: Yale University Press, 2009); and A. T. Olmstead, *History of the Persian Empire* (Chicago: University of Chicago Press, 1948).

42 *"first sole superpower"*: Arnold Toynbee, "The First Iranian Empire," *Kayhan International*, October 14, 1971.

42 *"The establishment of the largest empire"*: Touraj Daryaee, ed., *The Oxford Handbook of Iranian History* (New York: Oxford University Press, 2012), p. 3.

42 *"all men the freedom to worship"*: "Cyrus: The Anointed One," *Kayhan International*, October 14, 1971.

43 *"the camp of the Persians"*: Ibid.

43 *"storm from the east"*: Daryaee (2012), p. 243.

43 *"as a child"*: Amir Taheri, *The Unknown Life of the Shah* (London: Hutchinson, 1991), p. 218.

43 *The Pahlavi Dynasty emerged*: To learn more about the decline of Qajar rule in the late nineteenth and early twentieth centuries, and the rise of Reza Khan and the Pahlavis, the following titles are recommended: Ervand Abrahamian, *A History of Modern Iran* (Cambridge, UK: Cambridge University Press, 2008); Homa Katouzian, *State and Society in Iran: The Eclipse of the Qajars and the Emergence of the Pahlavis* (London: I. B. Taurus, 2006); and Nikkie R. Keddie, *Qajar Iran and the Rise of Reza Khan, 1796–1925* (Costa Mesta, CA: Mazda Publishers, 1999).

44 *The Constitutional Revolution*: To read more on Iran's Constitutional Revolution see Abrahamian (2008), 34–62; Said Amir Arjomand, *The Turban for the Crown: The Islamic Revolution in Iran* (Oxford: Oxford University Press, 1986), pp. 34–58; Katouzian (2006), pp. 25–87; and Keddie (1999), pp. 44–64.

45 *"was gentle, reserved, and almost painfully shy"*: A. Pahlavi (1980), p. 15.

45 *"must have gotten"*: Ibid.

45 *"a straightforward kind of man"*: E. A. Bayne, *Persian Kingship in Transition* (New York: American Universities Field Staff, 1968), p. 58.

46 *"physical presence"*: A. Pahlavi (1980), p. 9.

46 *"Despite all the independence"*: Her Imperial Highness Princess Soraya Esfandiary Bakhtiary, in collaboration with Louis Valentin, *Palace of Solitude*, trans. Hubert Gibbs (London: Quartet Books, 1992), p. 70.

46 *"I was never afraid"*: Author interview with Fereydoun Djavadi, July 13, 2013. See also Afkhami (2009), p. 24.

46 *"his father's love"*: Afkhami (2009), p. 24.

46 *climb on his father's back*: Author interview with Fereydoun Djavadi, July 13, 2013.

46 *"Oh! yes"*: R. K. Karanjia, *The Mind of a Monarch* (London: George Allen & Unwin, 1977), p. 32.

46 *instructed his other children*: A. Pahlavi (1980), p. 12.

46 *"a very dictatorial woman"*: James O. Jackson, "Shah: Dedicated, Dominant, Distrustful," *Chicago Tribune*, January 8, 1978.

46 *"In his early days as Shah"*: Directorate of Intelligence, Intelligence Report: "Centers of Power in Iran," May 1972, No. 2035/72, *U.S. State Department Office of the Historian, Foreign Relations of the United States RUS 1969–76*, vol. E-4.

47 *"woman of the harem"*: Bakhtiary (1992), p. 71.

47   *"Although polygamy was commonly practiced"*: A. Pahlavi (1980), p. 10.
47   *agreed to live separate lives*: Ibid.
47   *"No, I was not considered strong at all"*: Karanjia (1977), p. 44.
47   *"manly education"*: M. R. Pahlavi (1961), p. 52.
47   *enthralled her young charge*: Afkhami (2009), p. 29.
48   *"the virtues of democracy"*: Ibid.
48   *"To her I owe the advantage"*: M. R. Pahlavi (1961), p. 52.
48   *"Water is the chief concern"*: F. L. Bird, "Modern Persia and Its Capital: And an Account of an Ascent of Mount Demavend, the Persian Olympus," *National Geographic* 39, no. 4 (April 1921): 357.
48   *"magnificent plateau"*: The Baroness Ravensdale, "Old and New in Persia: In This Ancient Land Now Called Iran a Modern Sugar Factory Rears Its Head Near the Palace of Darius the Great," *National Geographic* 76, no. 3 (September 1939): 325.
48   *"the great lifeless desert"*: Bird, "Modern Persia," p. 361.
49   *a shepherd and his flock of sheep*: Edward J. Linehan, "Old-New Iran, Next Door to Russia," *National Geographic* 199, no. 1 (January 1961): 59.
49   *"Some sections in their utter bleakness"*: George W. Long, "Journey into Troubled Iran," *National Geographic*, vol. C, no. 4 (October 1951): p. 441.
49   *"an oasis situated on a high plateau"*: Parisa Parsi, "Shiraz: All Love and Poetry," *Kayhan International*, October 12, 1971.
50   *trebled Iran's oil production*: Gregory Lima, "Crowding the Persian Gulf," *Kayhan International*, October 14, 1971.
50   *"Iran's entry into the Persian Gulf would affect"*: Amir Taheri, "We Stand on Our Own Feet," *Kayhan International*, October 19, 1971.
51   *"Iran is a country of walls and mirrors"*: Frances Fitzgerald, "Giving the Shah Everything He Wants," *Harper's* 249, no. 1494 (November 1974): 55.
51   *typhoid*: M. R. Pahlavi (1961), p. 55.
51   *While he drifted into and out*: Karanjia (1977), p. 174.
51   *After the Crown Prince fell*: Ibid., p. 54.
52   *"a man with a halo"*: Ibid.
53   *"the vehicle for expressing public opinion"*: Amir Taheri, "Return of the Mosque," *Kayhan International*, October 21, 1978.
53   *"A fine system of mutual checks and balances"*: Ibid.
53   *"the social and political conditions"*: Ibid.
54   *"did not particularly like Fardust"*: Afkhami (2009), p. 28.
54   *"His entourage consisted of a chauffeur"*: Frederick Jacobi Jr., "New Boy," *New Yorker*, February 26, 1949, pp. 52–53.
55   *"I was determined that later when"*: M. R. Pahlavi (1961), p. 62.
55   *prayed five times a day*: Afkhami (2009), p. 33.
55   *"public complaints" box*: M. R. Pahlavi (1961), p. 63.
55   *The Shah nursed the ambitions*: To learn more about Reza Shah's efforts to reform Iran in the 1930s the following texts provide a wealth of detail: Abrahamian (2008), pp. 63–96; Ervand Abrahamian, *Iran: Between Two Revolutions* (Princeton, NJ: Princeton University Press, 1982), pp. 118–168; Afkhami (2009), pp. 1–41; Arjomand (1986), pp. 59–68; Amin Saikal, *The Rise and Fall of the Shah: Iran from Autocracy to Religious Rule* (Princeton, NJ: Princeton University Press, 1980), pp. 19–24.
56   *"The hallmark of the era"*: Abrahamian (2008), p. 65.
56   *In a letter dated February 1, 1936*: Letter From Reza Shah to Mohammad Reza Pahlavi, February 1, 1936, shared with the author by Farah Pahlavi.
57   *"standing alone, watching"*: Afkhami (2009), p. 34.
57   *shook hands, exchanged a hug*: Ibid.
57   *"happy and healthy"*: A. Pahlavi (1980), p. 22.
57   *"a different country. I recognized nothing"*: Mohammad Reza Pahlavi, *Answer to History* (New York: Stein & Day, 1980), p. 65.
57   *"as an Iranian version of the south of France"*: Ravensdale, "Old and New in Persia."
57   *Dodge motorcars*: Ibid.
57   *"huge new hotels pushing their heads into the air"*: The April 1921 edition of *National Geographic* was devoted in its entirety to Persia. It included a colorful account of travel into and around the Kingdom of Persia. See. Bird, "Modern Persia and Its Capital."
57   *travel to Tehran*: Ibid.

58 *"the superb Chalus road"*: Ibid.
58 *"elaborate wayside hotels"*: Ibid.
58 *tossing flowers and bouquets*: M. R. Pahlavi (1980), p. 65.
58 *"so much in awe"*: M. R. Pahlavi (1961), p. 64.
58 *"I advanced my views"*: Ibid., pp. 64–65.
58 *"he concentrated buying"*: M. R. Pahlavi (1980), p. 65.
59 *would live to regret*: Afkhami (2009), p. 113.
60 *"So I was married"*: M. R. Pahlavi (1980), p. 30.
60 *"With his characteristic forthrightness"*: M. R. Pahlavi (1961), p. 218.
60 *"For reasons still obscure to medical science"*: Ibid., p. 219.
60 *"The Allies have invaded"*: A. Pahlavi (1980), p. 40.
61 *"Ashraf, keep this gun with you"*: Ibid., p. 41.
61 *"I would love to have you with me"*: Ibid., p. 43.
61 *"You might say that Reza Shah"*: M. R. Pahlavi (1961), p. 75.
62 *"it seemed a curious situation"*: Ibid., p. 79.
62 *"plunged into a sea of trouble"*: Ibid., p. 75.
62 *"no solid power base and no political machine"*: Malcolm Byrne, ed., "The Battle for Iran," National Security Archive, Electronic Briefing Book 476.
62 *"I inherited a crown"*: Franc Shor, "Iran's Shah Crowns Himself and His Empress," *National Geographic*, 133, no. 3 (March 1968): 302.
62 *"I told them that we must establish"*: "Reformer in Sako," *Time*, September 12, 1960, p. 31.
63 *"People must not remain silent"*: Abbas Milani, *The Persian Sphinx: Amir Abbas Hoveyda and the Riddle of the Iranian Revolution* (Washington, DC: Mage, 2004), p. 85.

3. THE OLD LION

64 *"I will never start anything against [him]"*: Her Imperial Highness Princess Soraya Esfandiary Bakhtiary, in collaboration with Louis Valentin, *Palace of Solitude*, trans. Hubert Gibbs (London: Quartet Books, 1992).
64 *"Has there ever been a monarch"*: Ibid., p. 96.
64 *"passed through my military cap"*: Mohammad Reza Pahlavi, *Mission for My Country* (New York: McGraw-Hill, 1961), p. 57.
65 *"We had to make a forced landing"*: Ibid., p. 56.
66 *"Iran's chief city"*: George W. Long, "Journey into Troubled Iran," *National Geographic*, vol. C, no. 4 (October 1951): 432.
67 *"It was a sort of rupture"*: Bakhtiary (1992), p. 9.
67 *"If he doesn't like me"*: Ibid., p. 31.
67 *celluloid dreams*: Ibid.
67 *"imposing, magnificent"*: Ibid., p. 38.
68 *Soraya's legs gave out*: Ibid., p. 61.
68 *"In spite of a first marriage"*: Ibid., p. 45.
68 *"He can put his bed over there!"*: Author interview with Maryam Ansary, March 13, 2014.
68 *by picking up a vase*: Ibid.
68 *"the German woman"*: Ibid.
68 *During a state visit to India*: Habib Ladjevardi, ed., *Memoirs of Fatemeh Pakravan*, Iranian Oral History Project, Center for Middle Eastern Studies (Cambridge, MA: Harvard University, 1998), pp. 82–83.
68 *"Well, I'm very lucky"*: Ibid., p. 84.
69 *"threw an embarrassing temper tantrum"*: Abbas Milani, *The Shah* (New York: Palgrave Macmillan, 2011), p. 200.
69 *"wasn't very kind to [the princess]"*: Ladjevardi (1998), p. 85.
69 *Ayatollah Abul-Qasem Kashani*: For a short biography see Abbas Milani, *Eminent Persians: The Men and Women Who Made Modern Iran 1941–79*, vol. 1 (Syracuse, NY: Syracuse University Press, 2008), 343–349.
70 *"I will never forget"*: Bakhtiary (1992), p. 96.
70 *Prime Minister Mohammad Mossadeq*: To learn more about Mossadeq see Christopher de Bellaigue, *Patriot of Persia: Muhammad Mossadegh and a Tragic Anglo-American Coup* (New York: Harper-Collins, 2012).
70 *85 percent of its fuel*: Ervand Abrahamian, *The Coup: 1953, the CIA, and the Roots of Modern-Iranian Relations* (New York: New Press, 2013), p. 12.

70 *faced national bankruptcy*: Telegram, Secretary of State to the Department of State, November 10, 1951, U.S. Department of State, Office of the Historian, *Foreign Relations of the United States 1952–1954*, vol. X, Iran, 1951–1954, document 129.

71 *"The cardinal policy"*: Ibid.

71 *"But Mossadeq was frail"*: Author interview with Reza Ghotbi, May 9, 2013.

72 *he probably knew in advance of the plot*: De Bellaigue (2012), p. 152.

72 *"saved the National Front in its infancy"*: Ibid., p. 153.

72 *"Had the British sent in the paratroops"*: Malcolm Byrne, ed., "The Battle for Iran," *National Security Archive*, Electronic Briefing Book 476.

73 *"make political friends"*: Ashraf Pahlavi, *Faces in a Mirror: Memoirs from Exile* (Englewood Cliffs, NJ: Prentice-Hall, 1980), p. 76.

73 *"I have lost my status"*: Bakhtiary (1992), p. 92.

73 *"feared complete nervous breakdown"*: Milani (2008), p. 164.

73 *have emergency surgery*: Ibid., p. 157.

73 *"wild with anxiety"*: Bakhtiary (1992), p. 82.

73 *succumbed to anorexia*: Ibid.

74 *dispatched an intermediary*: Ibid., p. 83.

74 *"I promise you that I will stay in Tehran!"*: Ibid., p. 94.

74 *"take leadership in overthrowing Mossadeq"*: Byrne, ed., "The Battle for Iran."

74 *"If the Shah fails to go along"*: Darioush Bayandor, *Iran and the CIA: The Fall of Mossadeq Revisited* (London: Palgrave Macmillan, 2010), p. 93.

74 *"unless extreme pressure was exerted"*: Byrne, ed., "The Battle for Iran."

75 *"I could no longer bear"*: Bakhtiary (1992), p. 96.

75 *"Only a coup against Mossadeq"*: Ibid.

75 *on August 3, 1953*: Byrne, ed., "The Battle for Iran."

76 *"When can I act?"*: Bakhtiary (1992), p. 98.

76 *"Don't do anything against Mossadeq"*: Ibid.

76 *"I will sign a decree"*: Ibid.

76 *changed beds and rooms*: Ibid., p. 99.

77 *"I found the Shah worn"*: Byrne, ed., "The Battle for Iran."

77 *"He just took off"*: Ibid.

77 *"O traitor Shah, you shameless person"*: Ibid.

77 *"tearing down statues"*: Ibid.

77 *200 tomans ($26.65)*: Ibid.

78 *"Sensing that the army was with them"*: Ibid.

78 *forty-three deaths*: Ibid.

78 "MOSSADEQ OVERTHROWN": Bakhtiary (1992), p. 107.

78 *"Can it be true?"*: Stephen Kinzer, *All the Shah's Men: An American Coup and the Roots of Middle East Terror* (Hoboken, NJ: Wiley, 2003), p. 184.

78 *"How exciting"*: Ibid.

78 *"I hope the well-augured return"*: Bayandor (2010), p. 154.

79 *"counterrevolution had been scheduled"*: E. A. Bayne, *Persian Kingship in Transition* (New York: American Universities Field Staff, Inc., 1968), p. 163.

79 *"Ah, but the people called for me to return"*: Asadollah Alam, *The Shah and I: The Confidential Diary of Iran's Royal Court, 1969–77*, introduced and edited by Alinaghi Alikhani (New York: St. Martin's Press, 1991), p. 177.

80 *eighty Iranian Army soldiers*: "The Shah of Iran—Will His Land Have a Revolution from Above?," *Newsweek*, June 26, 1961, p. 46.

80 *"the boy"*: Author interview with Maryam Ansary, January 7, 2014.

80 *"So when are you going to give my son a boy?"*: Bakhtiary (1992), p. 71.

80 *"Nobody was entitled to forget"*: Ibid.

80 *"It is good that we are going"*: Ardeshir Zahedi as told to Ahmad Ahrar, English translation by Farhang Jahanpour, *The Memoirs of Ardeshir Zahedi*, vol. 1: *From Childhood to the End of My Father's Premiership (1928–1954)* (Bethesda, MD: Ibex, 2012), p. 258.

80 *"Why did you kick me?!"*: Ibid.

81 *"If you are directly involved in the talks"*: Ibid., p. 272.

81 *"Rule, your country needs it!"*: Bayne (1968), p. 149.

81 *"You know, there is no more lonely"*: Ibid.

81 *"was afraid of General Zahedi's huge popularity"*: Bakhtiary (1992), p. 131.

82 *"If I have a son"*: Ardeshir Zahedi, English translation by Farhang Jahanpour, *The Memoirs of Ardeshir Zahedi*, vol. 2: *Love, Marriage, Ambassador to the U.S. and the U.K. (1955–1966)* (Bethesda, MD: Ibex, 2014), p. 122.

82 *Princess Ashraf was likely behind*: Ibid., p. 114. Zahedi told the author in an interview that he and Ashraf were sworn enemies, to the point he suspected she wanted him dead. He emphasized that they had since patched up their differences. Author interview, October 27, 2012.

82 *exchanged insults and stormed out*: Ibid., pp. 116–117.

82 *a senior clergyman*: Ibid., p. 117.

83 *"How could you envisage such a thing?"*: Bakhtiary (1992), p. 136.

83 *Hossein Ala made it clear*: Ibid., p. 140.

83 *his voice barely audible*: Ibid.

4. FARAH DIBA

84 *"She was the woman I had been waiting for so long"*: Lesley Blanch, *Farah, Shahbanou of Iran* (Tehran: Tajerzadeh, 1978), p. 49.

84 *"But he was my king"*: Ibid.

84 *$40 million loan*: "Shah Grieves for Ex-Wife," *Chicago Tribune*, July 4, 1958.

84 *"the hardest decision I have ever taken"*: Ibid.

85 *sent word to General Zahedi*: Ardeshir Zahedi, English translation by Farhang Jahanpour, *The Memoirs of Ardeshir Zahedi*, vol. 2: *Love, Marriage, Ambassador to the U.S. and the U.K. (1955–1966)* (Bethesda, MD: Ibex, 2014), p. 130.

85 *"He said he would accept personal responsibility"*: Ibid.

85 *$500 million*: Edward J. Linehan, "Old-New Iran, Next Door to Russia," *National Geographic* 119, no. 1 (January 1961): 62.

86 *"His Imperial Majesty is above everything"*: "Reformer in Shako," *Time*, September 12, 1960, p. 31.

86 *"The Shah used the military"*: Ervand Abrahamian, *A History of Modern Iran* (Cambridge, UK: Cambridge University Press, 2008), p. 128.

86 *"Even yet, the Iranian economy remains"*: "Reformer in Shako," p. 32.

86 *"cold-war criminal"*: Ibid., p. 33.

86 *"Should the Shah lose his fight"*: Ibid.

87 *"military strength alone"*: Dana Adams Schmidt, "Arms Alone Will Not Ensure Security, Eisenhower Tells Iran," *New York Times*, December 15, 1959.

87 *"I hope this rumor"*: Zahedi (2014), p. 148.

87 *"If His Majesty were to go ahead"*: Ibid.

87 *observed that her choice of profession*: Farah Pahlavi, *My Thousand and One Days: The Autobiography of Farah, Shabanou of Iran* (London: W. H. Allen, 1978), p. 39.

87 *"sad eyes"*: Ibid., p. 40.

87 *The name Farah*: Details of the Queen's biography were gathered from sources including the author's interviews with Farah Pahlavi and her friends and associates; newspaper and magazine articles from the period; a biography: Blanch, *Farah, Shahbanou of Iran*; and two autobiographies: *My Thousand and One Days* and Farah Pahlavi, *An Enduring Love: My Life with the Shah* (New York: Miramax Books, 2004).

88 *"To whom shall we give this girl?"*: F. Pahlavi (1978), p. 9.

88 *"considered one of the prettiest"*: Blanch (1978), p. 38.

88 *"I don't usually talk about this"*: Sally Quinn, "It Isn't Easy Being the Empress of Iran," *Washington Post*, October 8, 1971.

88 *"The days were entirely given up"*: F. Pahlavi (1978), p. 12.

88 *"I would not say"*: Blanch (1978), p. 39.

89 *"A pall of melancholy"*: F. Pahlavi (2004), p. 29.

89 *not until the day she left for Paris*: F. Pahlavi (1978), p. 15, and Blanch (1978), p. 40.

89 *"Look, there's Farah!"*: Blanch (1978), p. 44.

89 *"learned to read the [Quran]"*: F. Pahlavi (2004), p. 22.

89 *unpleasant childhood encounter*: Ibid., p. 23.

89 *"Architecture is an act of creation"*: Blanch (1978), p. 45.

90 *drew the attention of a KGB agent*: This episode in Farah Pahlavi's life is covered in Christopher Andrew and Vasili Mitrokhin, *The KGB and the World: The Mitrokhin Archive II* (New York: Penguin, 2005), pp. 171–173.

90 *The mystery man*: F. Pahlavi (2004), p. 68.

90 *"misplaced"*: Andrew and Mitrokhin (2005), p. 172.

90   *"a hard worker"*: Blanch (1978), p. 46.
90   *"And why shouldn't the Shah marry you?"*: F. Pahlavi (2004), p. 64.
91   *"Farah Diba=Farah Pahlavi"*: F. Pahlavi (1978), p. 37.
91   *"his niece had all the requisite qualifications"*: Zahedi (2014), p. 153. He confirmed this to the author in our interview of October 27, 2012.
91   *behind a sliding glass door*: Zahedi (2014), p. 153.
91   *"Good Lord!"*: F. Pahlavi (2004), p. 74.
91   *"I think I knew, directly I saw her"*: Blanch (1978), p. 49.
91   *"I did not treat my daughter"*: Zahedi (2014), p. 156.
91   *"This time I had an inkling"*: F. Pahlavi (2004), p. 75.
91   *"The undercarriage wouldn't come down"*: Ibid., p. 78.
91   *"It is certain that on that day"*: Ibid., p. 83.
91   *"unfair to hold that against her"*: Author interview with Ardeshir Zahedi, October 27, 2012.
93   *Madame Diba could not hide her anxiety*: F. Pahlavi (1978), p. 42.
93   *"I saw, stretching ahead for her"*: Blanch (1978), p. 50.
93   *"He was the figure-head"*: Ibid., p. 49.
93   *mobbed at the airport*: F. Pahlavi (1978), p. 46.
93   *"I was screaming"*: F. Pahlavi (2004), p. 89.
93   *"shone like the sun"*: "Shah Announces Troth," *New York Times*, November 24, 1959.
93   *a blue case*: "Shah Gives Farah Dazzling Jewels," *Washington Post*, November 30, 1959.
94   *"She said she knew"*: "Farah Diba Would Give the Shah a Trio," *Washington Post*, November 12, 1959.
94   *"We were the only two girls"*: Author interview with Elli Antoniades, April 3, 2013.
94   *thirty-three pounds*: "Farah Diba's Dress Weighs 33 Pounds," *Washington Post*, December 21, 1959.
94   *"She wore a matching veil"*: "Shah Weds Again as Iran Calls for a Prince," *New York Times*, December 22, 1959.
94   *ritually slaughtering*: "Iran's Shah to Marry Farah Today," *Washington Post*, December 21, 1959.
95   *"By the end of the day"*: Author interview with Elli Antoniades, April 3, 2013.
95   *assigned Amir Pourshaja*: Author interview with Amir Pourshaja, March 16, 2013.
95   *"Her Majesty could fall back on her friends"*: Author interview with Elli Antoniades, April 3, 2013.
95   *"Ostentatiously, he collected identity cards"*: "Reformer in Shako," p. 34.
95   *"May Allah grant you"*: "It's Queen Farah of Iran as Shah Takes Third Bride," *Washington Post*, December 22, 1959.
95   *"rather too much anesthetic"*: F. Pahlavi (1978), p. 52.
95   *"In the rejoicings, I think I was almost forgotten"*: Ibid.
95   *tapping her on the cheek*: Ibid.
95   *"I burst into tears"*: Ibid.
96   *"such an outpouring of universal joy and warmth"*: F. Pahlavi (2004), p. 109.
96   *President John F. Kennedy*: The following scholarly articles offer analyses of Kennedy-Shah relations in the early 1960s: James Goode, "Reforming Iran During the Kennedy Years," *Diplomatic History* 15, no. 1; April R. Summitt, "For a White Revolution: John F. Kennedy and the Shah of Iran," *Middle East Journal* 58, no. 4 (Autumn 2004): 560–575.
96   *"I talked to Jack"*: Abbas Milani, *The Shah* (New York: Palgrave Macmillan, 2011), p. 304.
96   *"I just think it is going to be a miracle"*: Senators Frank Church and Hubert Humphrey quoted in James A. Bill, *The Eagle and the Lion: The Tragedy of American-Iranian Relations* (New Haven, CT: Yale University Press, 1988), p. 136.
97   *half a million acres*: Franc Shor, "Iran's Shah Crowns Himself and His Empress," *National Geographic* 133, no. 3 (March 1968): 306.
97   *"Four thousand schoolteachers"*: "The Shah of Iran—Will His Land Have a Revolution from Above?," *Newsweek*, June 26, 1961, p. 42.
97   *no further aid to Iran would be forthcoming*: In November 1977 the Shah ordered the Iranian press to recount this episode in U.S.-Iran relations on the eve of his state visit to Washington. See Dusko Doder, "Shah Says President Kennedy Influenced Naming of Premier," *Washington Post*, October 23, 1977.
97   *"I must either rule or leave"*: Summitt, "For a White Revolution," p. 567.
98   *"hang Amini"*: "The Shah of Iran—Will His Land Have a Revolution?," p. 46.
98   *"We do not consider religion"*: H. E. Chehabi, *Iranian Politics and Religious Modernism: The Liberation Movement of Iran Under the Shah and Khomeini* (Ithaca, NY: Cornell University Press, 1990), p. 158.

98   *Mehdi Bazargan*: To learn more about Mehdi Bazargan's personal religious and philosophical beliefs see Hamid Dabashi, *Theology of Discontent: The Ideological Foundation of the Islamic Revolution in Iran* (New Brunswick, NJ: Transaction, 2008), pp. 324–366.

98   *"His father's personal integrity"*: Chehabi (1990), p. 107.

98   *"You must be wondering"*: Ibid.

98   *struck by the ease with which*: Ibid., p. 109.

98   *"The French had voluntary associations"*: Ibid.

99   *"What the Iranian nation wants is just one word"*: Dabashi (2008), p. 336.

99   *"This is one of our wonderful spring days"*: Carroll Kilpatrick, "Kennedy Greets Shah, Notes Similarity of Aims," *Washington Post*, April 12, 1962.

100 *"After that, it was a matter"*: Maxine Cheshire, "Sneakers Were Vying for Diadems," *Washington Post*, April 13, 1962.

100 *"Actually, I preferred Mrs. Kennedy's"*: Author interview with Farah Pahlavi, November 13, 2014.

100 *"The Shah and I both have something in common"*: Cheshive, "Sneakers Were Vying for Diadems."

100 *"this king business"*: "'This King Business': A Headache to the Shah," *New York Times*, April 14, 1962.

100 *"In addition to giving children"*: Farnsworth Fowle, "Shah Depicts Aim of Modern Iran," *New York Times*, April 17, 1962.

101 *"If I go there to be insulted again"*: F. Pahlavi (2004), p. 119.

101 *During their talks in the Oval Office*: For a summary of the Shah-Kennedy talks see Department of State Memorandum, United States–Iran Relations, the President, the Shah of Iran et al., April 13, 1964, and Eric Hogland, project ed., *Iran: The Making of US Policy, 1977–80*, National Security Archive (Alexandria, VA: Chadwyck-Healey, 1990), document 450.

5. THE AYATOLLAH

103 *"I am going to go faster"*: "The Emperor Who Died an Exile," *Time*, August 4, 1980, p. 36.

103 *"I can summon a million martyrs to any cause"*: Margaret Laing, *The Shah* (London: Sidgwick & Jackson, 1977), p. 168.

103 *The chief beneficiary*: The standard English-language biography of Ayatollah Ruhollah Khomeini is still Baqer Moin's *Khomeini: Life of the Ayatollah* (London: I. B. Taurus, 1999). Given the factual discrepancies and varying interpretations that surround Khomeini's early years and rise to power, I hewed closely to Moin's book and cross-referenced with other sources, including newspaper and magazine articles, and also Said Amir Arjomand, *The Turban for the Crown: The Islamic Revolution in Iran* (New York: Oxford University Press, 1988); James Buchan, *Days of God: The Revolution in Iran and Its Consequences* (London: Murray, 2012); and Amir Taheri, *The Spirit of Allah: Khomeini and the Islamic Revolution* (Bethesda, MD: Adler & Adler, 1986).

103 *"He was a particularly striking"*: Moin (1999), p. 2.

103 *"Even as a youngster"*: Ibid., p. 2.

104 *"The qualities of autocracy"*: Ibid., p. 37.

104 *"pledging allegiance to the Shah"*: Confidential cable from George Lambrakis, Embassy Tehran, State Department, January 14, 1979; Eric Hogland, project ed., *Iran: The Making of US Policy, 1977–80*, National Security Archive (Alexandria, VA: Chadwyck-Healey, 1990), document 02086.

104 *"I can't be completely sure"*: Author interview with Ardeshir Zahedi, October 27, 2012. In 1953 Zahedi was the nineteen-year-old son of General Fazlollah Zahedi, the general who led the royalist forces against Mossadeq. He told me that he distinctly recalled walking into the house of Ayatollah Kashani, Khomeini's mentor and an ally of the coup plotters. The memory stuck in his mind when Khomeini rose to prominence in the early 1960s.

105 *"There are, of course, no bars or liquor shops"*: Martin Woollacott, "The Holy City of Iran Where the Shah Takes Second Place," *Guardian*, June 26, 1978.

105 *"everything goes on"*: Ibid.

106 *the apex of the clerical pyramid*: An understanding of the role of marja is essential to understanding not only Shiism but also the dynamics of the Iranian revolution. The author's description is based on his reading but also on interviews with practitioners and scholars of Iranian Shiism in Qom in 2013; with Dr. Farhad Daftary, codirector of the Ismaili Center based in London, September 4, 2014; and with Hassan Shariatmadari, the son of Grand Ayatollah Kazem Shariatmadari, based in Hamburg, September 21, 2014. Linda S. Walbridge wrote perhaps the definitive text in the English language on the role of marjas in Shiism; see her book *The Thread of Mu'awiya: The Making of a Marja Taqlid* (Bloomington, IN: Ramsay Press: 2014).

106 *"Of the money and goods donated"*: Nicholas Gage, "For Iranians, the Mullah's Orders Are Law," *New York Times*, December 9, 1978.

107 *"If there is to be a revolution in this country"*: John K. Cooley, "Prosperity, Vitality Mark Iran's 2,500th Year," *Christian Science Monitor*, October 15, 1971.

107 *"I concluded that my destiny"*: James O. Jackson, "Shah: Dedicated, Dominant, Distrustful," *Chicago Tribune*, January 8, 1978.

107 *"I am going to show"*: "A Revolutionary on the Throne," *Kayhan International*, October 29, 1967.

107 *"I am going to go faster"*: "The Emperor Who Died an Exile," p. 36.

109 *"The son of Reza Khan"*: Moin (1999), p. 75.

109 *"If you give the order"*: Ibid., p. 80.

109 *Coalition of Islamic Societies*: Buchan (2012), p. 121.

110 *"Even in the womb"*: Author interview with Abolhassan Banisadr, July 11, 2013. The former president also provided the following details about his life story. Details of his conversations with Khomeini were provided in the same interview. See also Hamid Dabashi, *Theology of Discontent: The Ideological Foundation of the Islamic Republic of Iran* (New Brunswick, NJ: Transaction, 2006), pp. 367–408.

112 *"stupid and reactionary bunch"*: Buchan (2012), p. 122, and Moin (1999), p. 88.

112 *"sordid and vile elements"*: Moin (1999), p. 89.

112 *stormed through the Feiziyah*: The violence at the seminary school is recalled in Buchan (2012), p. 123, and Moin (1999), pp. 92–94. In July 2013 the author visited the Feiziyah to study the school's physical layout. The school is adjacent to the Holy Shrine of Fatima in Qom and opens onto a large public square. Entry to the school is through a narrow alleyway and then into an interior courtyard enclosed by classrooms and bedrooms. Modernity and convenience have arrived at the Feiziyah: the complex now boasts at least one cash-dispensing ATM machine.

112 *"With this crime"*: Moin (1999), p. 195.

112 *"I can summon a million martyrs to any cause"*: Laing (1977), p. 168.

112 *"We did consider the possibility of violence"*: Author interview with Parviz Sabeti, May 10, 2014.

113 *"Let me give you some advice, Mr. Shah!"*: Accounts of the "Second Ashura" speech are provided by Buchan (2012), pp. 124–125, and Moin (1999), pp. 102–104.

113 *swept into the streets*: The unrest of June 3–5, 1963, is provided by Moin (1999), pp. 107–118.

113 *"The tension was evident"*: Farah Pahlavi, *An Enduring Love: My Life with the Shah* (New York: Miramax Books, 2004), p. 130.

114 *"Tomorrow is going to be very crucial"*: Author interview with Kambiz Atabai, February 13, 2013. Atabai was in the room during this conversation and witnessed the exchange between Prime Minister Alam and the senior generals.

114 *"He was panicking"*: Author interview with Parviz Sabeti, May 10, 2014.

114 *"I had to"*: Anthony Parsons, *The Pride and the Fall: Iran 1974–79* (London: Jonathan Cape, 1984), p. 27.

114 *"I was determined to make a stand"*: Author interview with Kambiz Atabai, February 13, 2013.

115 *"His Majesty was as a rock"*: Laing (1977), p. 168.

115 *"They had no plan [as such] to take over"*: Author interview with Parviz Sabeti, May 10, 2014.

115 *one-fifth that number*: Ibid.

115 *"My stomach was upset"*: Author interview with Kambiz Atabai, February 13, 2013.

115 *"In the Ministry of Justice, files were burned"*: Confidential: Memorandum of Conversation, Dr. Hussein Mahdavy and William Green Miller, Dr. Mahdavy's home, Evening—June 5, 1963, "Tehran Riots of June 5, 1963," United States–Iran Relations, the President, the Shah of Iran et al., April 13, 1964; Hogland, project ed., *Iran: The Making of US Policy, 1977–80*, document 481.

116 *"Eat shit!"*: Author interview with Kambiz Atabai, February 13, 2013.

116 *"Who has the guns?"*: Ibid.

116 *troops phoned General Nasiri*: Author interview with Parviz Sabeti, May 10, 2014.

116 *thousands killed*: Reza Baraheni, in his polemic *The Crowned Cannibals: Writings on Repression in Iran* (New York: Vintage, 1977), claimed a staggering 6,000 people were killed by the security forces during the June 5–6, 1963, crackdown; see p. 7 of his book. By contrast, when the Islamic Republic commissioned historian Emad al-Din Baghi to conduct a head count of the number of people who died in 1963 he could come up with only 32 names. The Alam government admitted to 120 deaths, a number the Shah apparently believed himself. See Abbas Milani, *The Shah* (New York: Palgrave Macmillan, 2011), p. 299.

116 *"It was not an easy decision for me"*: E. A. Bayne, *Persian Kingship in Transition* (New York: American Universities Field Staff, Inc., 1968), p. 54.

116 *"a man of great culture"*: F. Pahlavi (2004), p. 131.

116 *"He said he knew that"*: Habib Ladjevardi, ed., *Memoirs of Fatemeh Pakravan*, Iranian Oral History Project, Center for Middle Eastern Studies (Cambridge, MA: Harvard University, 1998), p. 39.

117 *"If it was discussed I didn't hear about it"*: Author interview with Parviz Sabeti, May 10, 2014.

117 *"Khomeini is a grand ayatollah like us"*: Author interview with Hassan Shariatmadari, son of Grand Ayatollah Shariatmadari, September 21, 2014. He confirmed the details of his father's decisive intervention. Important to remember is that Shariatmadari used the title "grand ayatollah" to refer to Khomeini and not "marja." It would have been impossible for any single member of the ulama, no matter how senior, to anoint another as a "marja." The honorific of "marja" came from the people and could not be bestowed.

118 *"their appeals . . . should be disregarded"*: Milani (2011), p. 298.

118 *"He is very handsome"*: Ladjevardi, ed., (1998), p. 39.

118 *"I felt like a helpless wave"*: Taheri (1986), p. 145.

118 *"Khomeini is now an important"*: Department of State Bureau of Intelligence and Research, Research Memorandum, June 26, 1963, "The Iranian Riots and Their Aftermath," to the Acting Secretary from George C. Demney Jr., United States–Iran Relations, the President, the Shah of Iran et al., April 13, 1964; Eric Hogland, project ed., *Iran: The Making of US Policy, 1977–80*, 1990) document 483.

118 *"greatly underestimated"*: Confidential: Memorandum of Conversation, document 481.

118 *"I had a phone call from [Khomeini's eldest son]"*: Author interview with Abolhassan Banisadr, July 11, 2013.

119 *"Finally I became so exasperated"*: Laing (1977), p. 217.

119 *"Having successfully stripped"*: Department of State Bureau of Intelligence and Research, document 483.

119 convened a meeting of grandees: According to legend, the elder statesmen of the Pahlavi Court confronted the Shah, who told them he would "flush them down the toilet." But Dr. Fereydoun Ala, son of former prime minister Hossein Ala, firmly disputes this version of events as a myth. Although the Shah fired the officials after he learned of their discussion, neither he nor they actually met in person to discuss the matter. The Shah recoiled from personal confrontations. Author interview with Fereydoun Ala, May 8, 2013.

120 *"I urged His Majesty to reign and not rule"*: Author interview with Ardeshir Zahedi, October 27, 2012.

120 *"They have reduced the Iranian people"*: The account of the October 1964 speech is provided by Moin (1999), pp. 121–128.

121 a Royal Iranian Air Force Hercules: Ibid., p. 128.

121 *"But when he left Turkey"*: Ibid., p. 136.

6. "JAVID SHAH!"

122 *"Shah is a kind of magic word with the Persian people"*: Eric Pace, "Oil Boom Is Aiding Reform Plans of Shah of Iran," *New York Times*, September 25, 1967.

122 *"Now I could do more than sympathize"*: Farah Pahlavi, *An Enduring Love: My Life with the Shah* (New York: Miramax, 2004), p. 141.

122 small M3 machine gun: Author interview with Colonel Kiomars Djahinbini, March 25, 2013.

122 *"As soon as [the guman]"*: Ibid.

122 *"Oh, my God, Farah, darling!"*: F. Pahlavi (2004), p. 135.

123 *"I continued putting on my makeup"*: Ibid.

123 *"Four times in my reign"*: E. A. Bayne, *Persian Kingship in Transition* (New York: American Universities Field Staff, 1968), p. 38.

123 *"After that the system was changed"*: Author interview with Colonel Kiomars Djahinbini, March 25, 2013.

124 *"Once we were driving back to Saadabad"*: Ibid.

125 *"I want to build a government"*: Bayne (1968), p. 59.

125 *"a copy of the Quran and a picture of Ruhollah Khomeini"*: Abbas Milani, *The Persian Sphinx: Amir Abbas Hoveyda and the Riddle of the Iranian Revolution* (Washington, DC: Mage, 2004), p. 171.

125 One of the judges: Amir Taheri, *The Spirit of Allah: Khomeini and the Islamic Revolution* (Bethesda, MD: Adler & Adler, 1986), p. 156.

125 Khomeini approved the fatwa: Ibid., p. 156.

125 handed the gunman his weapon: James Buchan, *Days of God: The Revolution in Iran and Its Consequences* (London: Murray, 2012), p. 133.

126 Mansur had tried to persuade: Abbas Milani, *The Shah* (New York: Palgrave Macmillan, 2011), p. 173.

126 Farah collapsed: Farah Pahlavi, *My Thousand and One Days: The Autobiography of Farah, Shabanou of Iran* (London: W. H. Allen, 1978), p. 59.

126 *"I was filled with sadness"*: Ibid.
126 *"When I was first married"*: Sally Quinn, "Why Iranian Monarchy Is Different," *Kayhan International*, October 13, 1971.
126 *"I had nothing to do"*: Amir Taheri, *The Unknown Life of the Shah* (London: Hutchinson, 1991), p. 182.
126 *"sticking my nose"*: Ibid.
127 *"I remember in the Golestan Palace"*: Author interviews with Farah Pahlavi, March 23–25, 2013.
127 *"For the first time I saw"*: F. Pahlavi (2004), p. 141.
127 *"all the facilities, schools"*: Author interviews with Farah Pahlavi, March 23–25, 2013.
128 *"Now I could do more than sympathize"*: F. Pahlavi (2004), p. 141.
128 *photographed donating blood*: Author interview with Dr. Fereydoun Ala, May 8, 2013.
128 *"We built libraries in public places"*: Author interviews with Farah Pahlavi, March 23–25, 2013.
128 *28 children's libraries*: Lesley Blanch, *Farah, Shahbanou of Iran* (Tehran: Tajerzadeh, 1978), p. 76.
128 *118 mobile libraries*: Ibid.
128 *2,400 villages*: Ibid.
128 *success in reducing illiteracy*: In the short space of fifteen years Iran's rate of literacy climbed to 50 percent from just 17 percent. Amir Taheri, "New Frame for a New Picture," *Kayhan International*, June 10, 1978.
128 *received a phone call from the Queen*: Author interview with Elli Antoniades, April 3, 2013.
129 *"His Majesty was always asking me about my day"*: Author interviews with Farah Pahlavi, March 23–25, 2013.
129 *"a sprawling city of one- and two-story buildings"*: Franc Shor, "Iran's Shah Crowns Himself and His Empress," *National Geographic* 133, no. 3 (March 1968): 302.
129 *"The beaches bounce"*: "Revolution from the Throne," *Time*, October 6, 1967, p. 32.
129 *10 percent annual growth spurt*: "US Asks Shah's Aid in Mideast," *Christian Science Monitor*, August 24, 1967.
130 *$130*: "Revolution from the Throne," p. 32.
130 *$250*: Pace, "Oil Boom."
130 *$700 million*: Ibid.
130 *75 percent*: "Revolution from the Throne," p. 32.
130 *26 million subjects*: Pace, "Oil Boom."
130 *98 percent*: "Revolution from the Throne," p. 32.
130 *"Iran must first become"*: Author interview with Reza Ghotbi, May 9, 2013.
130 *"Shah is a kind of magic word"*: Pace, "Oil Boom."
130 *"When everybody in Iran"*: Bayne (1968), p. 73.
130 *"If you don't say to the Iranians"*: Author interview with Fereydoun Djavadi, July 13, 2013.
130 *"always ridiculous reasons"*: Bayne (1968), p. 233.
131 *"One village elder"*: "Revolution from the Throne," p. 32.
131 *"by the year 2000 the world would be divided"*: Bayne (1968), p. 233.
131 *"the realities of the future"*: Eric Hogland, project ed., *Iran: The Making of US Policy, 1977–80*, National Security Archive (Alexandria, VA: Chadwyck-Healey, 1990), "Political/Intelligence Issues: The Strength and Durability of the Shah's Regime—Assessments of the Bureau of Intelligence and Research (INR)," p. 3.
131 *"uses [parliament] mostly for window-dressing"*: "Revolution from the Throne," p. 33.
132 *"that our independent policy"*: Eric Pace, "Shah of Iran Says He Hopes World Will 'Do Without' Military Alliances," *New York Times*, September 14, 1967.
132 *"beckons all the Middle East"*: "LBJ Calls Iran's Progress a Lesson 'Others Have to Learn,'" *Washington Post*, August 23, 1967.
132 *advanced fighter jets*: "US Asks Shah's Aid in Mideast."
132 *"It is not a source of pride or satisfaction"*: "A Revolutionary on the Throne," *Kayhan International*, October 29, 1967.
132 *"Daddy, it's time to come!"*: Bayne (1968), p. 33.
133 *"This month, Iran will hold a blowout"*: "Revolution from the Throne," p. 32.
133 *"hospitals all over Iran"*: Ibid., p. 34.
133 *"God bless His Majesty"*: "Iran: Crowns Himself—and His Queen," *Time*, November 6, 1967, p. 47.
133 *Tehran's stock exchange*: "Hoveyda Opens Stock Exchange," *Kayhan International*, October 24, 1967.
133 *The barbaric practice of hanging criminals*: Pace, "Oil Boom."
133 *pardoned by the Shah*: "Royal Pardon for Convicts," *Kayhan International*, October 26, 1967.
133 *men who had planned*: "Monarch Pardons Marble Palace Conspirators," *Kayhan International*, October 29, 1967.

133   *arts festivals*: Karim Emami, "Empress Opens Arts Festival at Shiraz," *Kayhan International*, September 12, 1967.
133   *270 million television viewers*: "270 Million People See Eurovision Telecast," *Kayhan International*, October 28, 1967.
134   *"box of jewels"*: "Tehran 'Like a Box of Jewels' from the Sky," *Kayhan International*, October 24, 1967.
134   *"I told the Shah it was foolish"*: Author interview with Ardeshir Zahedi, October 27, 2012.
134   *approved the change*: "Assembly Names Empress Regent," *Kayhan International*, September 9, 1967.
134   *"Long may her influence"*: Asadollah Alam, *The Shah and I: The Confidential Diary of Iran's Royal Court, 1969–77*, introduced and edited by Alinaghi Alikhani (New York: St. Martin's Press, 1991), p. 171.
135   *"This could have been a ceremony"*: Patrick O'Donovan, "Shah's Byzantine Rite," *Washington Post*, October 27, 1967.
135   *"The Shah and Queen remained"*: Eric Pace, "Coronation of a Modern Monarch and His Queen in Iran Is Marked by Pomp of Old Persia," *New York Times*, October 27, 1967.
136   *"shaped rather like a wastepaper basket"*: O'Donovan, "Shah's Byzantine Rite."
136   *"as spectacular as a city in flames"*: Ibid.
136   *Struggling to hold back tears*: "Empress Had to Fight Back Tears," *Kayhan International*, November 5, 1967.
136   *"It was the Queen and her son"*: Nicholas Herbert, "The Shah Crowns Himself at Brilliant Tehran Ceremony," *Times* (London), October 27, 1967.
136   *"guns fired, bells rang, trumpets sounded"*: O'Donovan, "Shah's Byzantine Rite."
136   *"ignoring the bows and curtsies"*: Ibid.
136   *"The King of Kings is wearing the crown"*: Pace, "Coronation of a Modern Monarch."
137   *17,532 roses*: "Crowning the Shadow of God," *Time*, November 3, 1967.
137   *one for every day of the Shah's life*: Ibid.
137   *"The crowds were enormous"*: O'Donovan, "Shah's Byzantine Rite."
137   *"the sleepless population"*: "The Night of Nights in Tehran," *Kayhan International*, October 28, 1967.
137   *"He launched a revolution"*: "Iran: A King Crowns Himself—and His Queen," p. 47.
137   *"It had been a dignified, rich and popular coronation"*: Herbert, "The Shah Crowns Himself."
137   *"It was a morning of dazzling jewels"*: O'Donovan, "Shah's Byzantine Rite."

7. ROYALS AND REBELS

139   *"Wake up!"*: Imam Khomeini, *Islamic Government: Governance of the Jurist* (Tehran: International Affairs Department, The Institute for Compilation and Publication of Imam Khomeini's Works, 2008), p. 131.
139   *"I always had in mind the Romanovs"*: Author interview with Farah Pahlavi, March 26, 2013.
139   *up before dawn*: Author interview with one of Grand Ayatollah Khomeini's former bodyguards, July 2013.
139   *set their watches by his daily walk*: Ibid.
139   *"Even we were affected by his discipline"*: Ibid.
139   *"In private meetings"*: Ibid.
140   *"I do not know what sin I have committed"*: Baqer Moin, *Khomeini: Life of the Ayatollah* (London: I. B. Taurus, 1999), p. 147.
140   *"this old man who is spending"*: Ibid.
140   *infiltrated his household with informers*: Author interview with Parviz Sabeti, May 10, 2014.
140   *"the old shark has had his fangs pulled out"*: Amir Taheri, *The Spirit of Allah: Khomeini and the Islamic Revolution* (Bethesda, MD: Adler & Adler, 1986), p. 155.
140   *"Najaf, like Qom and Mashad"*: Moin (1999), p. 147.
140   *"If we staged an uprising"*: Ibid., p. 142.
141   *"full of crazy ideas"*: Asadollah Alam, *The Shah and I: The Confidential Diary of Iran's Royal Court, 1969–77*, introduced and edited by Alinaghi Alikhani (New York: St. Martin's Press, 1991), p. 42.
142   *On the evening of August 5*: Ibid., p. 81.
142   *"to abandon his hippyfied ways"*: Ibid., p. 83.
143   *"Where on earth"*: Ibid., p. 93.
143   *forty-day ski vacation*: Alam (1991), p. 121.
143   *thirteen lectures*: The lectures can be read in English in Khomeini, *Islamic Government*.
143   *"remain in abeyance"*: Ibid., p. 21.
143   *"We have in reality, then, no choice"*: Ibid., p. 29.

144   *"pseudo saints"*: Ibid., p. 131.
144   *"negligent, lazy, idle and apathetic people"*: Ibid., p. 129.
144   *"Wake up!"*: Ibid., p. 131.
144   *"is the religion of militant individuals"*: Ibid., p. 2.
144   *"[The ulama] must be exposed and disgraced"*: Ibid., p. 134.
144   *54 percent or 14.5 million Iranians*: Department of State Airgram, "Youth in Iran: Assessment by Embassy Youth Committee," American Embassy Tehran, February 22, 1971, *U.S. Department of State, Foreign Relations 1969–76*, vol. E-4, Documents on Iran and Iraq 1969–72.
145   *Ali Shariati*: To learn more about the life and work of Ali Shariati see Al Rahnema, *An Islamic Utopia: A Political Biography of Ali Shariati* (New York: I. B. Taurus, 2000), and Ali Shariati, *On the Sociology of Islam: Lectures by Ali Shariati*, trans. Hamid Algar (Berkeley, CA: Mizan Press, 1979).
145   *$50 million*: E. A. Bayne, *Persian Kingship in Transition* (New York: American Universities Field Staff, 1968), p. 80.
145   *"The liberal states of Western Europe"*: Department of State Airgram.
146   *"a terrible character"*: Count Alexandre de Marenches interviewed by Christine Ockrent, *Dans le secret des princes* (Paris: Stock, 1986), p. 245; translation by Roger McKeon.
146   *"medieval tyrant"*: Ibid.
146   *"One day, a child of his family"*: Ibid.
146   *Parviz Sabeti*: Parviz Sabeti provided the author with details of his biography in a series of telephone and in-person interviews.
146   *"Our task was not only to fight"*: Author interview with Parviz Sabeti, May 10, 2014.
146   *an Israeli recommendation*: Ibid.
147   *infiltrating his household with informers*: Ibid.
147   *"I often used to see the Shah"*: Ibid.
147   *General Nasiri*: To learn more about his life see Abbas Milani, *Eminent Persians: The Men and Women Who Made Modern Iran, 1941–79*, vol. 1 (Syracuse, NY: Syracuse University Press, 2008), pp. 468–473.
148   *"He parlayed his power into wealth"*: Ibid., p. 471.
148   *"Any time I wrote reports"*: Author interview with Parviz Sabeti, May 10, 2014.
148   *Hossein Fardust*: To learn more about his life see Milani (2008), pp. 438–444.
148   *"eyes and ears"*: Ibid., p. 438.
148   *"the ultimate 'clearinghouse' for all reports"*: Ibid., p. 442.
149   *"notorious for wearing the same shirt"*: Ibid., p. 443.
149   *"They can't even let me have one friend"*: Ibid., p. 442.
149   *he told his wife to consult him*: Author interviews with Farah Pahlavi, March 23–25, 2013.
149   *The Queen was aware*: Ibid.
149   *"He grew to despise all those whose birthrights"*: Milani (2008), p. 440.
149   *as a boy on the tennis court*: Ibid., p. 441.
150   *"Why is Savak pushing so much negativity?"*: Author interview with Parviz Sabeti, May 10, 2014.
150   *"I didn't blame His Majesty but Fardust"*: Ibid.
150   *edit his intelligence reports*: Ibid.
150   *met each other on only one occasion*: Ibid.
151   *"Farah knew me from television"*: Ibid.
151   *"He is very, very independent"*: Margaret Laing, *The Shah* (London: Sidgwick & Jackson, 1977), p. 21.
151   *"In general I get the impression"*: Alam (1991), p. 150.
151   *"young people in Iran"*: Central Intelligence Agency, Research Study: "Elites and the Distribution of Power in Iran," February 1976; Eric Hogland, project ed., *Iran: The Making of US Policy, 1977–80*, National Security Archive (Alexandria, VA: Chadwyck-Healey, 1990), document 01012.
152   *"The Shah had too many brothers and sisters"*: Habib Ladjevardi, ed., *Memoirs of Fatemeh Pakravan*, Iranian Oral History Project Center for Middle Eastern Studies (Cambridge, MA: Harvard University, 1998), p. 85.
152   *"We never spoke politics in family gatherings"*: Author interview with Prince Gholam Reza, December 7, 2014. The author's questions were forwarded to the Prince who then dictated his replies and e-mailed them back through an associate.
153   *"most ambitious supporters"*: Central Intelligence Agency, document 01012, p. 65.
153   *"a wheeler-dealer"*: Ibid., p. 66.
153   *"quasi-legal business ventures"*: Ibid.
153   *"most flagrant act of irresponsibility"*: Ibid.
154   *"I always had in mind the Romanovs"*: Author interview with Farah Pahlavi, March 26, 2013.
155   *"She was obsessed with corruption"*: Author interview with Parviz Sabeti, May 10, 2014.
155   *"I spoke against corrupt courtiers"*: Ibid.

155 "'How can my son become king'": Ibid.

155 "It took three days to write": Ibid.

156 "Mr. Sabeti, the report you": Ibid.

156 "As her father I may be able to forgive": Alam (1991), p. 105.

157 "an unexpected growth of interest in religion": Department of State Airgram, "Youth in Iran."

157 "The banning of political parties": Amir Taheri, "Return of the Mosque," *Kayhan International*, October 21, 1978.

157 "conservative, inward looking": Department of State Airgram, "Youth in Iran."

8. THE CAMP OF GOLD CLOTH

159 "We stand on our own feet": "We Stand on Our Own Feet," *Kayhan International*, October 19, 1971.

159 "Ah yes, Khomeini": Carole Jerome, *The Man in the Mirror* (Toronto: Key Porter, 1986), p. 84.

159 "Let's go and visit the halls": Hushang Nahavandi, *The Last Shah of Iran*, trans. Steve Reed (London: Aquilion, 2005), p. 39.

159 *two thousand schools*: Sally Quinn, "A Sumptuous Party of Parties by the King of Kings," *Washington Post*, October 11, 1971.

159 "What status does this library": Nahavandi (2005), p. 43.

160 "Of course my life is better": John K. Cooley, "Prosperity, Vitality Mark Iran's 2,500th Year," *Christian Science Monitor*, October 15, 1971.

160 *Sixty thousand had recently turned out*: Asadollah Alam, *The Shah and I: The Confidential Diary of Iran's Royal Court, 1969–77*, introduced and edited by Alinaghi Alikhani (New York: St. Martin's Press, 1991), p. 64.

160 "a worthy successor to earlier monarchs": "Memorandum: Nothing Succeeds Like a Successful Shah," Central Intelligence Agency Office of National Estimate, October 8, 1971, National Security Archive.

161 "the foreseeable future": Ibid.

161 "obviously happy, almost radiant": Nahavandi (2005), p. 39.

161 "modern, but so suited": Ibid.

163 *the inspiration of Shojaeddin Shafa*: Cyrus Kadiver, "We Are Awake: 2,500-Year Celebrations Revisited," http://iranian.com/CyrusKadivar/2002/January/2500/index.html, January 25, 2002.

163 "the most wonderful thing": "Iran: The Show of Shows," *Time*, October 25, 1971.

163 "rewaken the people": William McWhirter, "We All Meet at the Club for Lunch," *Life*, October 29, 1971, p. 22.

163 *blanched at the cost*: Alam (1991), p. 143.

163 *on his own initiative*: Ibid., p. 166. Alam's diary makes clear that he had already signed the contracts with Jansen before the Queen accepted patronage of the Celebrations Council.

163 "to prove that the times we are living in now": Farah Pahlavi, *An Enduring Love: My Life with the Shah* (New York: Miramax Books, 2004), p. 216.

163 "whatever was European was good, noble": Charlotte Curtis, "Tent City Awaits Celebration: Shah's Greatest Show," *New York Times*, October 12, 1971.

163 "Of all the tasks that fell to me": F. Pahlavi (2004), p. 217.

164 *$100 million*: Quinn, "A Sumptuous Party of Parties."

164 *$22 million*: Kadiver, "We Are Awake."

164 *$300 million*: Ibid.

164 "Why are we reproached": Curtis, "Tent City Awaits Celebration."

164 *eighty thousand Iranian mothers and children*: Quinn, "A Sumptuous Party of Parties."

164 *one-third of children admitted to hospitals*: Ibid.

164 *Hamid Ashraf*: To learn more about his life see Abbas Milani, *Eminent Persians: The Men and Women Who Made Modern Iran, 1941–79*, vol. 1 (Syracuse, NY: Syracuse University Press: 2008), pp. 96–102.

165 "Theoretically the guerrillas must have hoped": Jonathan Randal, "The Shah's Iran: Arms, Debt and Repression Are the Price of Progress," *Washington Post*, October 10, 1971.

165 *established the Anti-Terrorist Joint Committee*: Author interview with Parviz Sabeti, September 21, 2013.

165 *special holding facility at the national police headquarters*: Ibid.

165 "kept a retinue of cannibals": "Cruelty No Stranger in Persia's History," *Chicago Tribune*, January 10, 1978.

166 *the male population blinded*: Ibid.

166 "God shall torture in the next world": Ervand Abrahamian, *Tortured Confessions: Prisons and Public Recantations in Modern Iran* (Berkeley: University of California Press, 1999), p. 18.

166 "an array of corporal punishments": Ibid., p. 17.

166 *the prisons of Reza Shah*: Abrahamian notes that when Qasr Prison was opened in the 1920s "the first transfers from the Central Jail were impressed by its cleanliness, sunlit windows, wide corridors, spacious courtyards, flowered gardens, and, most of all, running water and shower rooms." Ibid., p. 27.

To learn more about prison conditions and detention of political prisoners during the reign of Reza Shah see ibid., pp. 17–72.

166 *thrown young Ardeshir Zahedi in prison*: Author interview with Ardeshir Zahedi, October 27, 2012.

166 *Though the Shah was not aware*: No evidence has emerged to suggest the Shah was aware of the details of interrogation techniques applied by the security forces to political detainees. In exile, he spoke at length on the subject to television interviewer David Frost and admitted that he first learned of torture practices used inside Iran from external sources, presumably the Red Cross task force he invited to travel to Iran in 1976 to investigate prison conditions and recommend reforms. See Gholam Reza Afkhami, *The Life and Times of the Shah* (Berkeley: University of California Press, 2009), pp. 385–388. In his book, Afkhami provides a detailed account of the Shah's relationship with Savak.

166 *the boom of a 101-gun salute*: Karen Schickedanz, "Iran Opens Lavish Celebration, Marks 2,500 Years as Empire," *Chicago Tribune*, October 13, 1971.

167 *"O Cyrus"*: "The Torch Has Never Died," *Kayhan International*, October 13, 1971.

167 *"With that . . . a huge sand storm"*: Sally Quinn, "Splendor in the Dust," *Washington Post*, October 13, 1971.

167 *Cigarettes and tranquilizers*: Farah Pahlavi, *My Thousand and One Days: The Autobiography of Farah, Shabanou of Iran* (London: W. H. Allen, 1978), p. 91.

167 *"quite thin, drawn and tired"*: Sally Quinn, "It Isn't Easy Being Empress of Iran," *Washington Post*, October 8, 1971.

168 *saw crowds gathered*: "Sovereign, Empress Meet People of Shiraz," *Kayhan International*, October 13, 1971.

168 *"This is a fine place for a murder"*: Quinn, "Splendor in the Dust."

168 *"Little by little, the guests"*: Ibid.

168 *"a regime founded on oppression"*: Imam Khomeini, *Islam and Revolution: Writings and Declarations of Imam Khomeini (1941–80)*, trans. Hamid Algar (Berkeley, CA: Mizan Press, 1981), p. 200.

169 *"And then, of course, everyone meets informally"*: McWhirter, "We All Meet at the Club," p. 30.

169 *"Calling cards and small gifts"*: Ibid.

170 *"If I did go"*: "Iran: The Show of Shows."

170 *"The Queen does not go on international jamborees"*: Habib Ladjevardi, director, interview with Peter Ramsbotham, Harvard University Center for Middle East Studies, Iranian Oral History Project, October 18, 1985, tape 1, p. 23.

170 *"Why should we, having all this abuse hurled at us"*: Habib Ladjevardi, director, interview with Denis Wright, Harvard University Center for Middle East Studies, Iranian Oral History Project, October 10, 1984, tape 4, p. 5.

170 *"What's the panic?"*: Sally Quinn, "The Party's Over," *Washington Post*, October 16, 1971.

170 *fifteen hundred imported Cyprus trees*: John I. Hess, "Made in France—Persia's Splendorous Anniversary Celebration," *New York Times*, October 5, 1971.

170 *fifty thousand carnations*: Ibid.

170 *"acres of other floodlit flora"*: Ibid.

170 *"The entire area looks like the Berlin Wall"*: Quinn, "A Sumptuous Party of Parties."

170 *seventy miles*: "Iran: The Show of Shows."

170 *poisonous snakes, scorpions, and lizards*: Kadiver, "We Are Awake."

170 *"The entire tented city"*: Randal, "The Shah's Iran."

171 *"pissing on the Shah's party"*: Author interview with Jonathan Randal, September 14, 2014.

171 *"All the butter, cream, eggs"*: "Iran: The Show of Shows."

171 *literally bumped heads*: McWhirter, "We All Meet at the Club," p. 30.

171 *"a rather dowdy man"*: Ibid.

171 *shuffled around in his suspenders*: Ibid.

171 *"the Shah's revenge"*: Quinn, "The Party's Over."

171 *"Does anyone know where the hell I have to go?!"*: McWhirter, "We All Meet at the Club," p. 30.

171 *"The reception room for the arrivals"*: Sally Quinn, "A Tent Full of Royalty," *Washington Post*, October 13, 1971.

172 *"At last, a woman in a decent dress"*: Cynthia Greinier. "Iran: Catching a Bite to Eat at Anniversary Celebration," *Los Angeles Times*, October 17, 1971.

172 *"Kind of swimsuit halter top"*: Ibid.

172 *"Most [guests] had remarkably little to say"*: Quinn, "The Party's Over."

172 *When Marie Antoinette said, 'Let them eat cake'"*: Loren Jenkins, "Iran's Birthday Party," *Newsweek*, 25, 1971, p. 59.

172 *"The conspicuous consumption of this thing"*: Ibid.

172 *"Whose foolish idea was it"*: Author interview with Kambiz Atabai, August 15, 2014.

173 *twenty water buffalo*: Quinn, "A Sumptuous Party of Parties."

173 *"The setting was spectacular"*: Charlotte Curtis, "Neighbors Go Visiting in Iran's Tent City," *Kayhan International*, October 16, 1971.

173 *"After 25 centuries"*: Ibid.

173 *"crimes, Iran's poverty, the wide chasm separating the economic classes"*: Afkhami (2009), p. 413.

174 *"the many buildings, hotels, roads"*: "We Stand on Our Own Feet."

174 *"We stand on our own feet"*: Ibid.

174 *"For goodness sake"*: Alam (1991), p. 246.

174 *Imam Musa Sadr*: To learn more about the life of Imam Musa Sadr the following publications are helpful. The most detailed text, and the one that perhaps best reflects the complexity of the man and his times, is Majed Halawi, *A Lebanon Defied: Musa al-Sadr and the Shia Community* (Boulder, CO: Westview, 1992). Fouad Ajami wrote a well-received biography of Musa Sadr in the 1980s that the Imam's family has since disavowed: Foaud Ajami, *The Vanished Imam: Musa al-Sadr and the Shia of Lebanon* (Ithaca, NY: Cornell University Press, 1986). An essential scholarly text is H. E. Chehabi, ed., *Distant Relations: Iran and Lebanon in the Last 500 Years* (London: Centre for Lebanese Studies in association with I. B. Taurus, 2006). Considering the controversy surrounding the life and disappearance of Imam Musa Sadr, the author hewed closely to the Halawi book and two chapters in *Distant Relations* by H. E. Chehabi and Majid Tafresjhi (chapter 6) and by W. A. Samii (chapter 7). The interviews in this book offer important new revelations about the personal struggles of Imam Musa Sadr, one of the most compelling figures in the modern history of Shia Islam.

176 *"[He was] tall, very tall"*: Halawi (1992), p. 127.

176 *"an exquisite slightly self-disparaging"*: Ibid.

176 *"He was different, he was open"*: Author interview with Khalil al-Khalil, June 21–24, 2013.

177 *$30 million*: Chehabi (2006), p. 176.

177 *"Ah yes, Khomeini"*: Jerome (1986), p. 84.

177 *"We had a mutual friend"*: Author interview with Parviz Sabeti, September 21, 2013.

177 *Djahinbini insisted*: Author interview with Kiomars Djahinbini, March 25, 2013.

177 *"This undoubtedly happened"*: Author interview with Kambiz Atabai, June 18, 2013.

177 *"He was very happy"*: Author interview with Parviz Sabeti, September 21, 2013.

177 *"charismatic, a smart man, but not principled"*: Ibid.

9. THE PAHLAVI PROGRESS

178 *"Our lives pass from us"*: Abolqasem Ferdowsi, *Shahnameh: The Persian Book of Kings*, trans. Dick Davis (New York: Penguin, 2006), p. 764.

178 *"They told me it was treatable"*: Author interview with Robert Armao, October 20, 2014.

178 *"four-square, lofty white cube"*: Lesley Blanch, *Farah, Shahbanou of Iran* (Tehran: Tajerzadeh, 1978), p. 85.

179 *drop peanuts . . . on the heads of guests*: Author interviews with Farah Pahlavi, March 23–25, 2013.

179 *"In this vast, bright room"*: Farah Pahlavi, *An Enduring Love: My Life with the Shah* (New York: Miramax Books, 2004), p. 163.

179 *"We put restrictions"*: Author interview with Kiomars Djahinbini, March 15, 2013.

179 *Djahinbini's fear*: Author interview with Kiomars Djahinbini, March 25, 2013.

180 *intercepted his telephone conversations*: Ibid.

180 *"We had electronic devices"*: Ibid.

180 *spent a month in the Élysée Palace*: Ibid.

180 *"It was very important"*: Author interview with Kambiz Atabai, February 8, 2013.

181 *"There was always great excitement"*: Ibid.

181 *Farah placed a bet*: Author interview with Farah Pahlavi, April 19, 2013.

181 *"I'm not there"*: Ibid.

181 *"the security, Iranian and Swiss"*: Ibid.

182 *"Mashad is like nowhere else"*: Blanch (1978), p. 129.

182 *new Islamic university*: Author interview with Hossein Nasr, August 21, 2013.

182 *"dark and gloomy"*: F. Pahlavi (2004), p. 162.

182 *"That was the time"*: Author interviews with Farah Pahlavi, March 23–25, 2013.

182 *"We arrived at 9 a.m."*: Author interview with Fereydoun Djavadi, July 13, 2013.

183 *"In the first year our bed was on a tilt"*: Author interviews with Farah Pahlavi, March 23–25, 2013.

183 *"It was very casual"*: Ibid.

183 *"hanging from parachutes"*: F. Pahlavi (2004), p. 188.

183 *"Why are you taking it down?"*: As witnessed by Mahnaz Zahedi, the Shah's granddaughter, during her vacations to Nowshahr. Author interview with Mahnaz Zahedi, November 4, 2014.

184 *Mahnaz returned to Iran*: Ibid.

184 *five palaces and twelve hundred staff*: Author interview with Kambiz Atabai, February 8, 2013.

185 *"Often I have instructed the staff"*: "My Lifetime Goal Is to Serve the Nation," *Kayhan International*, October 15, 1977.

185 *"The rumors were that my mother"*: Author interview with Reza Pahlavi, March 26, 2013.

185 *hands that resembled duck feet*: Habib Ladjevardi, ed., *Memoirs of Fatemeh Pakravan*, Iranian Oral History Project, Center for Middle Eastern Studies (Cambridge, MA: Harvard University, 1998), pp. 97–98.

185 *rumors of muteness*: Author interview with Kambiz Atabai, August 16, 2014.

185 *"They said absolutely anything"*: Ladjevardi, *Memoirs of Fatemeh Pakravan*, pp. 97–98.

185 *"Do you know how many miles"*: Author interview with Reza Pahlavi, March 26, 2013.

185 *"In another life"*: Ibid.

186 *"I was far more scrutinized"*: Ibid.

186 *Farah bit her lip*: F. Pahlavi (2004), p. 191.

186 *barely concealed satisfaction*: Ibid.

186 *sped off in his Mini Cooper*: Author interview with Reza Pahlavi, March 26, 2013.

186 *covered over the dozen security cameras*: Ibid.

186 *in the music stores*: Ibid. The Prince told me that among his favorite haunts were the music stores along Pahlavi Avenue.

186 *"She was a real tomboy"*: Author interview with Farah Pahlavi, November 13, 2014.

186 *keen interest in the lives*: F. Pahlavi (2004), p. 194.

187 *"If she came across people"*: Ibid.

187 *standing at the palace gates*: Author interview with Farah Pahlavi, November 13, 2014.

187 *spending time with her father*: Ibid.

187 *flung bread pellets*: Ibid.

187 *jumped into a barrel of tar*: Ibid.

187 *"He was so naughty"*: Ibid.

187 *his first day at nursery school*: F. Pahlavi (2004), p. 159.

187 *"People will say"*: Author interview with Farah Pahlavi, November 13, 2014.

187 *"free love"*: F. Pahlavi (2004), p. 159.

187 *"Pray for rain, Leila joune"*: Ibid., p. 161.

187 *"I like it when the sky is gray"*: Ibid.

187 *"Her father has passed on his love"*: Ibid.

188 *"I physically didn't see"*: Author interview with Reza Pahlavi, March 26, 2013.

188 *"Basically, we were never able"*: F. Pahlavi (2004), p. 186.

188 *"Behind me, in class"*: Farah Pahlavi, *My Thousand and One Days: The Autobiography of Farah, Sha-banou of Iran* (London: W. H. Allen, 1978), p. 135.

188 *"Is it true that you bathe in milk"*: Ibid.

188 *"I am never photographed"*: Ibid., p. 139.

189 *"Flatterers everywhere!"*: Asadollah Alam, *The Shah and I: The Confidential Diary of Iran's Royal Court, 1969–77*, introduced and edited by Alinaghi Alikhani (New York: St. Martin's Press, 1991), p. 472.

189 *"had done nothing"*: Ibid., p. 244.

189 *"His Majesty and I"*: Ibid., p. 246.

189 *"For example"*: Author interviews with Farah Pahlavi, March 23–25, 2013.

190 *"His Majesty banished it from the residence"*: Ibid.

190 *"It's very difficult for me"*: "My Lifetime Goal."

190 *"I have watched her dash out"*: Blanch (1978), pp. 84–85.

191 *"Farah and the Shah"*: Gholam Reza Afkhami, *The Life and Times of the Shah* (Berkeley: University of California Press, 2009), p. 53.

191 *clientele*: William Stadiem, "Behind Claude's Doors," *Vanity Fair*, September 2014, p. 310. Author William Shawcross wrote about the Shah's affairs in *The Shah's Last Ride: The Fate of an Ally* (New York: Simon & Schuster, 1988), pp. 339–341.

191 *"Often a conversation"*: Afkhami (2009), p. 53.

191 *"If I don't have this recreation"*: Abbas Milani, *The Shah* (New York: Palgrave Macmillan, 2011), p. 315.

191 *"At times she would grumble or cry"*: Afkhami (2009), p. 53.

192 *welcome divorce*: Author interview with Ardeshir Zahedi, October 27, 2012.

192 *"divorce insurance"*: Laurie Johnston, "Feminism and Empress Farah Diba of Iran," *New York Times*, May 20, 1975.

192 *"to have some security"*: Ibid.

192 *Empress Farah Foundation*: Information on the activities of the foundation comes from Abdolmajid Majidi, "A Brief Overview of the Empress Farah Foundation," trans. Dariosh Afskar, *Rahavard Quarterly Persian Journal*, issue 98 (Spring 2012).

193 *"They told me it was treatable"*: Author interview with Robert Armao, October 20, 2014.

10. EMPEROR OF OIL

194 *"My problem"*: Farah Pahlavi, *An Enduring Love: My Life with the Shah* (New York: Miramax, 2004), p. 266.

194 *"This is the juice of a sick mind"*: Author interview with Ali Kani, February 23, 2013.

194 *"Ten years before the revolution"*: Author interview with Abolhassan Banisadr, July 11, 2013.

195 *"The way we looked at Khomeini"*: Ibid.

195 *"You do not know these people"*: Ibid.

197 *agreed to Ghotzbadegh's request*: Author interview with Jonathan Randal, September 14, 2014.

197 *"to discuss certain related"*: Imam Khomeini, *Governance of the Jurist: Islamic Government* (Tehran: Institute for Compilation and Publication of Imam Khomeini's Words, 2008), p. 1.

197 *Gestetner photostat machine*: Amir Taheri, *The Spirit of Allah: Khomeini and the Islamic Revolution* (Bethesda, MD: Adler & Adler, 1986), p. 159.

197 *five hundred mutjahid*: Said Amir Arjomand, *The Turban for the Crown: The Islamic Revolution in Iran* (New York: Oxford University Press, 1988), p. 98.

197 *twelve thousand religious students*: Ibid.

198 *"The Persian Gulf delivers"*: "A False Sense of Security Will Destroy You," *U.S. News & World Report*, March 22, 1976, p. 57.

198 *"But I like him, I like him"*: "Conversation Among President Nixon, Ambassador Douglas MacArthur II, and General Alexander Haig, Washington, April 8, 1971, 3:56–4:21 PM," *Foreign Relations of the United States 1969–76*, vol. E-4.

198 *"Our economic progress"*: Frances Fitzgerald, "Giving the Shah Everything He Wants," *Harper's* 249, no. 1494 (November 1974): 77.

199 *every cannon fired*: Asadollah Alam, *The Shah and I: The Confidential Diary of Iran's Inner Court, 1969–77*, introduced and edited by Alinaghi Alikhani (New York: St. Martin's Press, 1991), p. 290.

199 *"These are the people"*: Ibid.

199 *"What a farce"*: Ibid., p. 250.

199 *capsules of Valium*: Author interview with Colonel Kiomars Djahinbini, March 25, 2013.

199 *insomnia*: Alam (1991), p. 250.

199 *"I believe that the peasantry are with me"*: E. A. Bayne, *Persian Kingship in Transition* (New York: American Universities Field Staff, 1968), p. 52.

199 *"reform popular attitudes"*: Alam (1991), p. 341.

200 *Amir Abbas Hoveyda*: To learn more about his life see Abbas Milani, *Eminent Persians: The Men and Women Who Made Modern Iran, 1941–79*, vol. 1 (Syracuse, NY: Syracuse University Press, 2008), pp. 193–204, and Abbas Milani, *The Persian Sphinx: Amir Abbas Hoveyda and the Riddle of the Iranian Revolution* (Washington, DC: Mage, 2004).

200 *"old Quasimodo"*: Alam (1991), p. 246.

200 *related to senior religious figures*: Taheri (1986), p. 159.

200 *requested a whiskey*: Author interview with Kambiz Atabai, February 15, 2013.

200 *"They shared a love"*: Milani (2008), p. 198.

200 *"The Shah is the Chairman"*: Anthony Parsons, *The Pride and the Fall: Iran 1974–79* (London: Jonathan Cape, 1984), p. 30.

200 *"Well Tony"*: Ibid., p. 62.

200 *"Hoveyda was a very good friend"*: Author interview with Mahnaz Afkhami, August 16, 2013.

201 *"Amir, are you drunk already?"*: Author interview with Ardeshir Zahedi, October 27, 2012.

201 *"I was usually frank and ruthless"*: Milani (2004), p. 26.

202 *"should be so negligent"*: Alam (1991), p. 315.

202 *"a growing sense of alienation"*: Ibid., p. 221.

202 *"There is considerable anxiety"*: Telegram 2488 from the Embassy in Tehran to the Department of State, May 1, 1972, *FRUS*, vol. E-4, documents on Iran and Iraq, 1969–72, document 182.

203 *"Iran was in the category of states"*: Author interview with Dr. Zbigniew Brzezinski, September 4, 2015.

203 *$4.6 billion in 1973–1974*: Hossein Razavi and Firouz Vakil, *The Political Environment of Economic Planning in Iran, 1971–83: From Monarchy to Islamic Republic* (Boulder, CO: Westview, 1984), p. 63.

203 *"Iran is not a volcano now"*: Mohamed Heikal, *The Return of the Ayatollah: The Iranian Revolution from Mossadeq to Khomeini* (London: Andrew Deutsch, 1981), p. 104.

204 *"Once dismissed by Western diplomats"*: "Oil, Grandeur and a Challenge to the West," *Time*, November 4, 1974, p. 28.

204 *33 percent*: Andrew Scott Cooper, *The Oil Kings: How the U.S., Iran and Saudi Arabia Changed the Balance of Power in the Middle East* (New York: Simon & Schuster, 2011), p. 212.

204 *40 percent*: Ibid.
204 *"We have no real limit on money"*: Ibid., p. 182.
204 *25 percent stake*: "Oil, Grandeur," p. 28.
204 *"on projects ranging from schools to hospitals"*: Ibid.
204 *$700 million*: Ibid.
204 *$1 million*: Ibid.
204 *"He was our baby"*: Cooper (2011), p. 212.
204 *Dr. Ali Kani stopped off in Beirut*: Author interview with Ali Kani, February 23, 2013. Dr. Kani provided the details of his encounter with Musa Sadr in the same interview.
207 *"I want them finished in my lifetime"*: Alam (1991), p. 363.
208 *they not mention the word "cancer"*: F. Pahlavi (2004), p. 246.
208 *formal diagnosis of "Waldenstrom's disease"*: Ibid., p. 247.
208 *He and Alam had both expressed admiration*: Cooper (2011), p. 165.
209 *Flandrin watched in horror*: F. Pahlavi (2004), p. 253.
209 *told the French president*: Ibid., p. 266.
209 *$5 million*: "Farah: Working Empress," *Time*, November 4, 1974, p. 36.
209 *forty office workers*: Ibid.
209 *twenty-six patronages*: Ibid.
209 *fifty thousand letters*: Ibid.
209 *"We will have to continue"*: Ibid.
209 *"Many problems touch me"*: Ibid.
209 *"My husband is interested in Iran's GNP. I am interested in its GNH—Gross National Happiness"*: Ibid.
209 *"The only beautiful thing"*: Author interviews with Farah Pahlavi, March 23–25, 2013.
209 *"I didn't want to repeat"*: Author interview with Farah Pahlavi, November 13, 2014.
210 *wrote him a letter*: Author interviews with Farah Pahlavi, March 23–25, 2013.
210 *opposed construction*: Ibid.
210 *preserve the ancient bazaar*: Ibid.
210 *"He was very hardworking"*: Ibid.
210 *Reza Ghotbi*: Biography based on author interviews with Reza Ghotbi, March 25, 2013, and May 9, 2013.
210 *Seyyed Hossein Nasr*: Biography based on author interviews with Hossein Nasr, August 21, 2014, and November 18, 2014.
210 *"I met her and she became very interested"*: Ibid.
211 *"The Queen was always the person"*: Author interviews with Reza Ghotbi, March 25, 2013, and May 9, 2013.
211 *"They once arrested a man"*: Author interview with Farah Pahlavi, November 13, 2014.
211 *"Furious, I spoke"*: F. Pahlavi (2004), p. 236.
211 *demanded the man leave his office*: Author interview with Fereydoun Djavadi, July 13, 2013.
211 *"Why do you hire so many leftists?"*: Author interviews with Ardeshir Zahedi, October 27–28, 2012.
212 *"I saw the Empress"*: Parsons, *The Pride and the Fall*, p. 25.

11. THE TURNING

213 *"Right across Islam, the mullahs are doomed"*: Asadollah Alam, *The Shah and I: The Confidential Diary of Iran's Royal Court, 1969-77*, introduced and edited by Alinaghi Alikhani (New York: St. Martin's Press, 1991), p. 480.
213 *"People are turning to Islam"*: "Religious Revival: Islamic Conservatives, Increasingly Militant, Stir Worries in the West," *Wall Street Journal*, August 15, 1978.
213 *"simple, sharply angled, steeply gabled"*: Lesley Blanch, *Farah, Shahbanou of Iran* (Tehran: Tajerzadeh, 1978), p. 137.
213 *"Kish was fantastic"*: Author interviews with Farah Pahlavi, March 23–25, 2013.
214 *establishing a committee of experts*: Martin Woollacott, "The Shah Shoves Iran Towards Freedom," *Guardian*, July 8, 1978.
214 *"The bazaar is not just a collection of shops"*: Amir Taheri, "The Bazaar," *Kayhan International*, October 2, 1978.
215 *80 percent*: Ibid.
215 *five thousand agents*: Ibid.
215 *"the religious processions"*: Ibid.
215 *"Politically, it is the bazaar"*: Ibid.
215 *"The Iranian government"*: Ibid.
216 *"government is best that governs least"*: Ibid.

216 *"The cost of living in Iran"*: James F. Clarity, "Iran's Flood of Oil Money Aggravates Her Inflation," *New York Times*, October 7, 1974.

216 *"There's something a little desperate in the air"*: "Iran's Race for Riches," *Newsweek*, March 24, 1975, p. 43.

216 *"was to raise Iran's standard of living"*: Ibid.

216 *"I genuinely fear"*: Alam (1991), p. 464.

217 *declared a one-party state*: To learn more about the Shah's decision to declare a one-party state in Iran in March 1975 and his views on democracy and pluralism, the following references are helpful: Ervand Abrahamian, *Tortured Confessions: Prisons and Public Recantations in Modern Iran* (Berkeley: University of California Press, 1999), pp. 149–154; Gholam Reza Afkhami, *The Life and Times of the Shah* (Berkeley: University of California Press, 2009), pp. 423–440; Ali M. Ansari, *Modern Iran Since 1921: The Pahlavis and After* (London: Longman, 2003), pp. 185–187; Abbas Milani, *The Persian Sphinx: Amir Abbas Hoveyda and the Riddle of the Iranian Revolution* (Washington, DC: Mage, 2004), pp. 274–280; Amin Saikal, *The Rise and Fall of the Shah: Iran from Autocracy to Religious Rule* (Princeton, NJ: Princeton University Press, 1980), pp. 188–191.

218 *"My motto is: ask the advice of the technocrats"*: "We Cannot Take Chances," *Newsweek*, March 1, 1976, pp. 20–21.

218 *"I not only make the decisions, I do the thinking"*: Lewis M. Simons, "Shah's Dreams Are Outpacing Iran's Economic Boom," *Washington Post*, May 26, 1974.

218 *"was taking on too much"*: Habib Ladjevardi, director, interview with Denis Wright, Harvard University Center for Middle East Studies, Iranian Oral History Project, October 10, 1984, tape 3, p. 9.

218 *"People are turning to Islam"*: "Religious Revival."

218 *1.6 million*: Mohammad Abdul-Rauf, "Pilgrimage to Mecca," *National Geographic* 154, no. 5 (November 1978): 582.

219 *"like a harlot"*: Andrew Borowiec, "Moslem Fundamentalists Fight Shah's Reforms," *Washington Post*, June 24, 1975.

219 *"the unholy alliance of black reactionist[s]"*: Charles Kurzman, *The Unthinkable Revolution in Iran* (Cambridge, MA: Harvard University Press, 2004), p. 289.

219 *"Khomeini?" he asked*: Amir Taheri, *The Spirit of Allah: Khomeini and the Islamic Revolution* (Bethesda, MD: Adler & Adler, 1986), p. 169.

219 *"Right across Islam"*: Alam (1991), p. 480.

219 *"rather alarmed"*: Ibid., p. 483.

219 *"There seems to be a need for religion"*: Marvine Howe, "Iranian Women Return to Veil in a Resurgence of Spirituality," *New York Times*, July 30, 1977.

219 *"Do they suppose the military"*: Alam (1991), p. 516.

220 *"Young professional people want to escape"*: Joseph Kraft, "Letter from Iran," *New Yorker*, December 18, 1978, p. 144.

220 *Prince Patrick Ali*: The most detailed public source available on Patrick Ali's life can be found on his Facebook page. The author e-mailed Patrick Ali Pahlavi at the Gmail account published on the writers.net site but did not receive a response.

221 *"psychologically tortured"*: http://www.writers.net/writers/72914.

221 *"would like to lead a revolution"*: Eric Hogland, project ed., *Iran: The Making of US Policy, 1977–80*, National Security Archive (Alexandria, VA: Chadwyck-Healey, 1990), "Research Study: Elites and the Distribution of Power in Iran," February 1976, document 01012, p. 66.

221 *over "the recent outrages"*: Alam (1991), p. 428.

222 *"It is human nature"*: "Revolutionary Goals Will Remain Constant," *Kayhan International*, September 13, 1977.

223 *crammed with so many potions, pills, and creams*: Several of the Shah's inner circle raised their eyebrows at the suggestion that General Ayadi was a doctor in the truest medical sense of the word. Dr. Flandrin wryly observed that Ayadi was "a great purveyor of a variety of drugs." See Farah Pahlavi, *An Enduring Love: My Life with the Shah* (New York: Miramax, 2004), p. 257.

223 *Flandrin's schedule rarely varied*: Flandrin's schedule was described in self-penned letters to Jean Bernard and published in F. Pahlavi (2004), pp. 254–255.

223 *At the bottom of the gangway*: The Shah's chief of personal security and bodyguard, Colonel Kiomars Djahanbini, explained the logistics of the comings and goings of the French doctors. Author interview with Colonel Kiomars Djahanbini, March 25, 2013.

223 *"I knew they were doctors"*: Ibid.

224 *"Each bottle lasted five days"*: Author interview with Amir Pourshaja, March 16, 2013.

224 *accidentally refilled the Shah's bottles*: F. Pahlavi (2004), pp. 256–257.

224 *was swollen*: Ibid, p. 257.

224 *"Secondary school"*: "We Cannot Take Chances," *Newsweek*, March 1, 1976, pp. 20–21.

225 *"a sudden icy wind"*: F. Pahlavi (2004), p. 261.

225 *lost interest in the monarchy*: Alam (1991), p. 494.

225 *"The internal situation is sound"*: Ibid., p. 524.

225 *"I saw the problems"*: Amir Taheri, *The Unknown Life of the Shah* (London: Hutchinson, 1991), p. 218.

226 *"the rate of migration"*: Eric Pace, "Teheran Projects Face Challenges," *New York Times*, June 6, 1978.

226 *"What had happened"*: Author interviews with Farah Pahlavi, March 23–25, 2013.

226 *The group's report*: F. Pahlavi (2004), p. 258.

227 *"would have alerted"*: Ibid., p. 259.

227 *"I am very sorry"*: Eric Pace, "Corruption and Mistrust of Officials Continuing to Plague Iranian Government," *New York Times*, February 22, 1976.

228 *$100 million*: Alam (1991), p. 460.

228 *"to recommend changes"*: Woollacott, "The Shah Shoves Iran Towards Freedom."

229 *"Everything is okay with the Shah"*: Author interview with Henry Precht, March 13, 2013.

229 *regular meetings*: John Stempel wrote transcripts of their conversations, which were captured by the Iranian students who seized the U.S. embassy in Tehran in November 1979. The documents were later published in Hogland, project ed., *Iran: The Making of US Policy, 1977–80*.

229 *"whether we had any recent difficulties"*: Ibid., document 0145, April 14, 1976.

229 *"about the future"*: Ibid., document 01048, April 28, 1976.

12. THIRSTY FOR MARTYRDOM

231 *"Something is in the air"*: Ashraf Pahlavi, *Time for Truth* (N.p.: In Print Publishing, 1995), p. 11.

231 *"I wonder when we're going"*: Author interview with Hossein Nasr, August 21, 2013.

231 *38 percent*: "How the Opec Fight Will Be Won," *Economist*, January 15, 1977.

231 *two million barrels a day*: "Iran Reports Exports of Oil Decline 34.7%," *New York Times*, January 12, 1977.

231 *"We're broke"*: Asadollah Alam, *The Shah and I: The Confidential Diary of Iran's Royal Court, 1969–77*, introduced and edited by Alinaghi Alikhani (New York: St. Martin's Press, 1991), p. 535.

232 *50 percent*: Joe Alex Morris Jr., "Is It for Real?: New Broom Stirs Lots of Dust in Iran," *Los Angeles Times*, October 7, 1977.

232 *"Government officials must walk up"*: Marvine Howe, "Iran Fights Power Shortage, Threat to Development," *New York Times*, July 11, 1977.

232 *"we are now in dire"*: Alam (1991), p. 537.

232 *"People were flocking to town"*: Interview with William Lehfeldt by William Burr, Foundation for Iranian Studies, Washington, DC, April 29, 1987, February 9 and April 19, 1988, pp. 3–167.

232 *"we have more students"*: Author interview with Parviz Sabeti, September 21, 2013.

233 *"Sabeti sees everything as black"*: Ibid.

234 *"feeds and encourages the opposition"*: A. Pahlavi (1995), p. 11.

234 *"People were telling me things were bad"*: Author interview with Ardeshir Zahedi, October 27, 2012.

234 *"try feeding them cake"*: William Branigan, "William H. Sullivan Dies at 90: Veteran Diplomat Was Last U.S. Ambassador to Iran," *Washington Post*, October 22, 2013.

235 *"The nearest I had been"*: William H. Sullivan, *Mission to Iran: The Last U.S. Ambassador* (New York: Norton, 1981), p. 12.

235 *between twenty-five thousand and a hundred thousand*: Amnesty International Briefing, November 1, 1976, MDE 13/001/1976, p. 6.

235 *"unprecedented"*: "Torture as Policy," *Time*, August 16, 1976, p. 32.

235 *"Thousands of men and women"*: Reza Baraheni, *The Crowned Cannibals: Writings on Repression in Iran* (New York: Vintage, 1977), p. 6.

236 *"largely self-sufficient and comparatively wealthy"*: "Torture as Policy," p. 34.

236 *"a bunch of Clockwork Orangers"*: "Oil, Grandeur and a Challenge to the West," *Time*, November 4, 1974, p. 38.

236 *"There has been enough of this preaching"*: U.S. Embassy cable to Secretary of State, "Subject: Shah Comments on Human Rights and Student Dissidents," February 24, 1977, JCL, NLC-21-44-4-15-0.

236 *described as "petty"*: Gholam Reza Afkhami, *The Life and Times of the Shah* (Berkeley: University of California Press, 2009), p. 387.

237 *met with Martin Ennals*: See Laurence Marks, "Shah Puts Carter's Principles to the Test," *Guardian*, November 20, 1977, and also William J. Butler, Chairman, Executive Committee, International Commission of Jurists, "Aide Memoire: Summary of Discussions Between His Imperial Majesty the Shahanshah Aryamehr and William J. Butler at Shiraz on May 2, 1978," to His Excellency Amir Abbas Hoveyda, Minister of Court, Imperial Court, Tehran, Iran, June 8, 1978, *Iran: The Making of*

US Policy, 1977–80, National Security Archive (Alexandria, VA: Chadwyck-Healey, 1990), document 01414. Although Butler's letter to Hoveyda is dated June 8, 1978, it includes reference to his first meeting with the Shah, on May 30, 1977.

237 *"pure fabrication"*: H. D. S. Greenway, "Secret Police of Iran Call Image Unfair," *Washington Post*, September 3, 1976.

237 *3087 political prisoners*: From the start, confusion surrounded the number of prisoners held in detention, tortured, and executed during the 1971–76 "dirty war" period. Consider the numbers alleged to be imprisoned. Whereas Amnesty International stated as many as a hundred thousand prisoners, the U.S. State Department estimated that the number of political prisoners jailed in Iran actually peaked at 3,700 in early 1976. See Jonathan Steele, "Iran Rights Improve," *Guardian*, October 27, 1977. One year earlier, the Shah had provided *Time* magazine with a general estimate of between 3,400 and 3,500 detainees, though his numbers were given no credence in the Western press or by Western human rights organizations. See his interview in "Torture as Policy: The Network of Evil," *Time*, August 16, 1976, p. 32. Savak's Parviz Sabeti provided a still lower figure of 3,200 in his interview with the author of September 21, 2013. Ironically, Sabeti's lower estimate was confirmed to the author by an Iranian government official during the author's July 2013 visit to the Center for the Study of the Islamic Revolution in Tehran. In reviewing the available sources, the number of political prisoners held in detention in Iran in the midseventies most likely ranged from a low of 3,200 to a high of 3,700. An earlier estimate of 7,500 provided by Iranian-born historian Ervand Abrahamian in his book *Tortured Confessions: Prisoners and Public Recantations in Modern Iran* (Berkeley: University of California Press, 1999), p. 108, should now be regarded as too high.

237 *386 and as few as 312*: Similar controversy involved the numbers of prisoners executed and tortured while in detention. While the Shah was in power he was accused of ordering the executions of thousands of dissidents. After the revolution, the Center for the Study of the Islamic Revolution commissioned Emad al-Din Baghi to conduct a new investigation. He was able to verify 386 deaths. See http://www.emadbaghi.com/en/archives/000592.php#more. His final report caused a sensation because until then the Islamic Republic had blamed the Shah for between 60,000 and 70,000 deaths. Baghi's final toll was still too high, according to Savak's Parviz Sabeti who told the author in their September 13, 2013, interview that the real number of deaths in custody was 312. Separately, historian Ervand Abrahamian provided a slightly higher figure of 368 in his book *Tortured Confessions*, p. 103. Citing Iranian sources, he claimed 93 executions with an additional 45 tortured to death, 9 suicides, and 197 guerrillas dead in gun battles with the Iranian security forces in the 1970s. Regardless of the different estimates, no more than 400 people died during the "dirty war" waged between antiregime terrorists and the Pahlavi regime in the 1970s.

238 *"During the past year"*: "Progress on Human Rights in Iran," U.S. State Department Bureau of Intelligence and Research, *JCL*, NLC-31-38-3-2-1.

238 *"assist needy families"*: Ibid.

238 *"The human rights situation"*: "Memorandum of the U.S. Stand on Human Rights," Central Intelligence Agency Directorate of Intelligence, *JCL*, NCL-28-22-8-1-8.

238 *five thousand office workers*: Author interview with Parviz Sabeti, September 21, 2013.

238 *twenty thousand claimed by critics*: "Torture as Policy," p. 32.

238 *Ten thousand additional names*: Author interview with Parvez Sabeti, September 21, 2013.

238 *fifty conversations at a time*: Author interview with a former Savak officer, July 2013.

238 *"People worried about Savak"*: Author interview with Martin Woollacott, September 3, 2014.

239 *"like a hotel"*: Author interview with Parviz Sabeti, September 21, 2013.

239 *"No one dared talk among the prisoners"*: A fact confirmed by the author's interview with Grand Ayatollah Mohammad Ali Gerami in Qom, Iran, July 3, 2013. Gerami was subjected to confinement, whether under house arrest or imprisonment, for most of the period 1965–1978. He told the author that he was tortured by Savak. He explained that in 1976 prison conditions markedly improved as a result of the decision to allow Red Cross inspection teams into Evin. This led to great excitement among the inmates, who assumed the incoming Carter administration had withdrawn its support from the Shah.

240 *"Once inside, he unhitched his tunic"*: Sullivan (1981), p. 84.

240 *"Everyone buckled up"*: Author interview with Maryam Ansary, April 17, 2013.

240 *"Be careful. Sullivan is trouble"*: Author interviews with Farah Pahlavi, March 23–25, 2013.

241 *"I was quite surprised"*: Author interview with Farhad Massoudi, April 11, 2015.

241 *"I wonder when we're going to have a revolution in Iran"*: Author interview with Hossein Nasr, August 21, 2013.

241 *Ali Hossein*: "Ali Hossein" is the pseudonym for an Iranian clergyman living in Iran and who does not wish to be publicly identified. The author interviewed him in 2013.

243   *60,000 "undergraduates"*: Amir Taheri, "Return of the Mosque," *Kayhan International*, October 21, 1978.

243   *300 religious schools*: Ibid.

243   *180,000 mullahs*: Ibid.

245   *"The young had absolutely no interest in religion"*: Joseph Kraft, "Letter from Iran," *New Yorker*, December 18, 1978, pp. 146–147.

245   *"[Marx] exposes the imperialists"*: Ibid., p. 149.

245   *"More and more women"*: Marvine Howe, "Iranian Women Return to Veil in a Resurgence of Spirituality," *New York Times*, July 30, 1977.

246   *second-best-selling book*: Said Amir Arjomand, *The Turban for the Crown: The Islamic Revolution in Iran* (New York: Oxford University Press, 1988), p. 93.

246   *"thousands of women wearing the veil"*: Alam (1991), p. 543.

246   *"We don't want your civilization!"*: Ray Vicker, "Religious Revival: Islamic Conservatives, Increasingly Militant, Stir Worries in the West," *Wall Street Journal*, August 15, 1978.

246   *"Afterwards, we found out"*: Author interviews with Farah Pahlavi, March 23–25, 2013.

247   *"medieval" ways*: "Revolutionary Goals Will Remain Constant," *Kayhan International*, September 13, 1977.

247   *to build a new Islamic university*: "Teachers' Bank, Islamic University in Spotlight," *Kayhan International*, October 26, 1978.

248   *invited Nasr to enter politics*: Author interview with Hossein Nasr, November 18, 2013.

248   *"We have not been allowed"*: "The Shah's Divided Land," *Time*, September 18, 1978, p. 35.

249   *"Something is in the air"*: A. Pahlavi (1995), p. 11.

249   *She was puzzled to see*: Farah Pahlavi, *An Enduring Love: My Life with the Shah* (New York: Miramax Books, 2004), pp. 264–265.

249   *"And so I asked"*: Ibid., p. 271.

249   *handed a cryptic note*: Author interview with Hossein Nasr, August 21, 2013.

249   *"I have to stay on an extra day"*: Ibid.

249   *"chronic but serious"*: F. Pahlavi (2004), p. 264.

250   *"I thought that was the end"*: Amir Taheri, *The Unknown Life of the Shah* (London: Hutchinson, 1991), p. 287.

250   *July 16*: Queen Farah remembered the date of her return to Tehran from the United States as June 1977; see F. Pahlavi (2004), p. 265. Hossein Nasr told the author that he accompanied her on her tour of the United States, which took place in the first two weeks of July 1977. He said he was with her on the trip to Paris when she received a note asking to stay behind one day. According to a twelve-month time line constructed by the *Kayhan* newspaper, Queen Farah returned to Tehran on July 16, 1977. Amir Ali Afshar, "Twelve Months of Transition," *Kayhan International*, March 20, 1978.

250   *"We would move in groups"*: Quotes attributed to Ali Hossein come from the author's interviews with him in 2013.

250   *"fanatic religious conservatives"*: "Secret: A Comment on Terrorism in a Revolutionary Situation," February 2, 1979, *Iran: The Making of US Policy, 1977–80*, document 02353. This remarkable document, captured and published by Iranian revolutionaries in 1980, offers an important insight into what U.S. diplomats and intelligence officials stationed in Iran knew about the capabilities of anti-Shah terror groups.

251   *"the duty of all good Muslims"*: Ibid.

251   *"as clergymen"*: "The Shah's Divided Land," *Time*, September 18, 1978, p. 35.

251   *"The quantity and sophistication of weapons available"*: "The Terrorist Threat Against Americans in Iran," September 30, 1977, Jimmy Carter Presidential Library, NLC-25-33-9-7-2.

251   *"siphoned off a portion and gave the rest"*: "Secret: A Comment on Terrorism."

251   *infiltrated Ambassador Sullivan's embassy*: Ibid.

251   *in terrorist camps*: Ibid.

251   *explosives, machine pistols, revolvers*: Ibid.

252   *$400,000 each year*: Ibid.

252   *"Most people had still not heard his name"*: Author interview with Hassan Shariatmadari, September 21, 2014.

252   *"rabidly anti-Shah"*: "Intelligence Memorandum: Khomeini's Lieutenants in Iran," Central Intelligence Agency National Foreign Assessment Center, Jimmy Carter Presidential Library, January 10, 1979.

253   *$285,000 or 2 million tomans*: Ibid.

253   *"Beheshti also functions"*: Ibid.

253   *"The level of organization"*: Author interview with Ali Hossein, 2013.

253   *"there are still between"*: "Revolutionary Goals Will Remain Constant."

253 *"We totally destroyed them"*: Author interview with Parviz Sabeti, June 17, 2013.
253 *"On the basis of fragmentary information"*: "Iran's Petroleum Vulnerabilities," February 21, 1978, Jimmy Carter Presidential Library, NLC-132-93-1-5-6.
254 *"have the expertise to assemble"*: Ibid.
254 *monitor Savak's*: "Secret: A Comment on Terrorism."
254 *"We knew firepower was coming in"*: Author interview with John Stempel, February 20, 2013.
254 *flew to his rented villa in the south of France*: Alam (1991), p. 555.
255 *"His Majesty is not thinking clearly"*: Author interview with Maryam Ansary, December 5, 2014.
255 *"The country is lost"*: Ibid.

13. LAST DAYS OF POMPEII

256 *"Stop it when gets into the streets"*: Author interview with Parviz Sabeti, September 21, 2013.
256 *"This time either Islam triumphs"*: Amir Taheri, *The Spirit of Allah: Khomeini and the Islamic Revolution* (Bethesda, MD: Adler & Adler, 1986), p. 181.
257 *Shiraz-Persepolis Festival of Arts*: Mahasti Afshar, "Festival of Arts, Shiraz-Persepolis: Or You Better Believe in as Many as Six Impossible Things Before Breakfast," unpublished manuscript, October 2013.
257 Pig, Child, Fire!: Ibid., p. 14.
257 *Princess Mahnaz chanced upon the scene*: Author interview with Mahnaz Zahedi, December 13, 2014.
257 *"indecent acts"*: Afshar (2013), p. 14.
257 *"speak out and protest"*: Ibid.
258 *"plots to create campus unrest"*: "Students Blast Campus Plotters," *Kayhan International*, September 24, 1977.
258 *"to become acquainted"*: Ibid.
258 *"we could become more and more active"*: Author interview with Ali Hossein, 2013.
259 *On Sunday, October 9, 1977*: A detailed account of the disturbance was published in the *Kayhan* newspaper, whose English-language edition republished the report. "Women to Fight Campus Bigotry," *Kayhan International*, October 12, 1977.
259 *"Warning to the Elements of Corruption"*: Ibid.
259 *"revolting attempt"*: Ibid.
259 *worst display of violence*: "Foreign Agitators 'Incited Campus Segregation Bid,'" *Kayhan International*, October 15, 1977.
259 *appealed to the anonymous*: "Students Blast Campus 'Reactionary Extremists,'" *Kayhan International*, October 13, 1977.
259 *efforts of student leaders to rouse their peers*: Ibid.
260 *self-service cafeteria was segregated*: Ibid.
260 *bus drivers refused to drive onto campus grounds*: Ibid.
260 *"The only negative article written about me"*: Author interview with Mahnaz Afkhami, August 16, 2013.
260 *the streets of Rey*: Liz Thurgood, "Shah Says Student Rioters Are Traitors," *Guardian*, October 17, 1977.
260 *"All these developments"*: "Monarch Lashes Traitorous Acts," *Kayhan International*, October 16, 1977.
260 *"They want to set the country back"*: Ibid.
260 *poetry readings*: Liz Thurgood, "The Shah Finds a Vocal—but Loyal—Opposition," *Guardian*, October 26, 1977.
261 *"It was absolutely unbelievable"*: James O. Jackson, "Torture Banned in Iran—or Is It?" *Chicago Tribune*, January 10, 1978.
261 *"His people were well organized"*: "Memorandum of Conversation Between Hedayatollah Matin-Daftari, Prominent Dissident and Lawyer (and Grandson of Former Prime Minister Mohammad Mossadeq) and George Lambrakis, Political Counselor, American Embassy Tehran, December 12, 1977," *Iran: The Making of US Policy, 1977–80*, National Security Archive (Alexandria, VA: Chadwyck-Healey, 1990), document 1253. The figure of twenty thousand at the religious demonstration in Tehran was also provided in Thurgood, "Shah Finds a Vocal—but Loyal—Opposition."
261 *hundreds of local development initiatives*: "Iran Celebrates Birthday of Empress Farah," *Kayhan International*, October 15, 1977.
261 *handing out awards*: Ibid.
261 *"A huge filmy sky sculpture"*: "Ambitious Addition to Tehran's Art World," *Kayhan International*, October 15, 1977.
261 *"A lot of Iranians"*: Ibid.
262 *the first Festival of Popular Traditions*: "Empress Opens Iran's First Traditions Festival," *Kayhan International*, October 13, 1977.

262 *she flew to Kerman*: "Empress to Open Museum in Kerman," *Kayhan International*, October 15, 1977.
262 *to devote more resources*: "Empress Urges More Aid for Deaf," *Kayhan International*, November 6, 1977.
262 *Eleven of the twelve imams*: Sayyed Mohamad Rizvi, *Islam: Faith, Practice, and History* (Qom: Ansariyam Publications, 2010). The imams are listed by name and cause of death on pages 126 and 127. I included the first imam whose sword wound was infected with poison.
262 *"God's hidden providence"*: Baqer Moin, *Khomeini: Life of the Ayatollah* (London: I. B. Taurus, 1999), p. 185.
262 *Parviz Sabeti suspected*: Author interview with Parviz Sabeti, September 21, 2013.
262 *"Stop it when it gets into the streets"*: Ibid.
263 *"our one and only leader"*: Taheri (1986), p. 183.
263 *"thunderous cries of 'Allah Akbar' "*: Ibid., p. 183.
263 *"And it spread"*: Author interview with Parviz Sabeti, September 21, 2013.
263 *"that unfit element"*: Taheri (1986), p. 184.
263 *an anonymous caller*: "Bomb Found in Cinema Screening 'Porno' Film," *Kayhan International*, November 6, 1977.
263 *Isolated acts of violence*: "Warrants to Arrest Agitators," *Kayhan International*, November 27, 1977.
264 *pro-Khomeini militants rioted*: "Protests Reported in Shiraz, Isfahan," *Kayhan International*, November 29, 1977.
264 *main synagogue*: Ibid.
264 *"There was a lot of panic"*: Author interview with Mahnaz Afkhami, August 21, 2013.
264 *leftists broke windows*: "Ten Students Held After Campus Clash," *Kayhan International*, December 7, 1977.
264 *college wrestling team*: "Anti-American Demonstration," *Kayhan International*, December 10, 1977.
264 *"Tens of thousands"*: Jackson, "Torture Banned in Iran—or Is It?"
264 *"I never had any political experience before now"*: Author interview with Parviz Sabeti, May 10, 2014.
265 *"I thought party members would talk"*: Ibid.
265 *the commission released reports*: "Imperial Commission Submits Reports to Monarch: Delay in Supplies Hits Rail Line Network; Imperial Orders to Speed Up Work on Roads, Ports," *Kayhan International*, November 13, 1977.
265 *"incompetence and negligence"*: "Moinian Lashes Executive Incompetence, Negligence," *Kayhan International*, November 13, 1977.
266 *who assured them*: "Memorandum of Conversation Between Hedayatollah Matin-Daftari, Prominent Dissident and Lawyer (and Grandson of Former Prime Minister Mohammad Mossadeq) and George Lambrakis, Political Counselor, American Embassy Tehran, December 12, 1977," *Iran: The Making of us Policy, 1977–80*, document 1253.
266 *met privately*: Their conversation, in quotes and summarized, is referenced to "Cable from American Embassy Tehran to Secretary of State, Subject: Student Unrest, December 8, 1977," *Iran: The Making of US Policy, 1977–80*, document 01374. The cable is included in a pouch of documents dated April 26, 1978.
267 *"Patience is the imperative"*: "Don't Overreact to Minor Unrest: Majidi," *Kayhan International*, December 14, 1977.
268 *"I was aware of it"*: Author interview with Hassan Ali Mehran, January 13, 2015.
268 *$100 million*: Ibid. In his memoir, former British ambassador Anthony Parsons wrote that his embassy put the value of monthly capital outflow at $1 billion each month, starting in 1976. This figure was considerably overblown.
268 *number of Iranians seeking visas*: "Secret: Consulate Principal Officers Conference," June 5, 1978, *Iran: The Making of US Policy, 1977–80*, document 1438.
268 *"buying up the place"*: "Iranians 'Buying Up' the Place," *Kayhan International*, February 11, 1978.
268 *"pouring"*: "Iranian Pioneers Flood into South California," *Kayhan International*, May 9, 1978.
268 *"saw the writing on the wall"*: Oral history interview with William Lehfeldt, by William Burr, Foundation for Iranian Studies, Washington, DC, April 29, 1987, February 9 and April 19, 1988, pp. 3–167.
268 *"there are things that are happening"*: Ibid.
268 *"The men seemed even more hostile"*: Notes on life in Pahlavi-era Iran dated May 20, 1982, provided to the author by Chris Westberg in 2013.
269 *issued a public fatwa*: Taheri (1986), p. 170.
269 *"a strange handwritten"*: Ibid.
269 *"deposed the Shah"*: Ibid., p. 171.
269 *"still angry enough"*: Ibid., p. 173.

270 *established a special committee*: Amir Taheri described the inner workings of the secret committee. See ibid., p. 200.

270 *"The Shah must go"*: Ibid., p. 171.

270 *Iranian embassy in Denmark*: "Iranians Jailed for Attack on Embassy," *Kayhan International*, December 17, 1977.

270 *banks and businesses*: "Hooligans in Publishing House Attack," *Kayhan International*, December 22, 1977.

271 *exploded in the washroom*: "The Bomb Damages IAS Center," *Kayhan International*, December 31, 1977.

271 *"Although it was a clear day"*: Jimmy Carter, *White House Diary* (New York: Picador, 2010), p. 156.

272 *ski fields at Dizin*: "Come on Up, the Snow's Fine!" *Kayhan International*, December 5, 1977.

272 *northern cities*: "Snow Covers North Iran as Cold Wave Sweeps In," *Kayhan International*, December 15, 1977.

272 *the Kharkeh River*: "River Floods Farmland in Khuzestan," *Kayhan International*, December 19, 1977, and "Nation Reels Under Impact of Floods and Foul Weather," *Kayhan International*, December 23, 1977.

272 *water supply of Ahwaz*: "Ahwaz Water Supply Probe," *Kayhan International*, December 22, 1977.

272 *victory over Australia*: Hushang Nemazee, "Historic Berth," *Kayhan International*, November 26, 1977.

272 *A team of Iranian mountaineers*: "Iran, China in Joint Effort to Scale Everest," *Kayhan International*, December 17, 1978.

272 *temblor in Kerman*: "521 Die as 'Quake Rocks Kerman Villages," *Kayhan International*, December 22, 1977.

272 *broadcast in color*: "TV to Go Color by Next Summer," *Kayhan International*, September 20, 1977.

272 *Marcel Marceau*: "Marcel's Loved the World Over," *Kayhan International*, April 6, 1978.

272 *Joe Dassin*: "France's Heartthrob Brings Down the House," *Kayhan International*, February 26, 1978.

272 *Birgit Nilsson*: "Nilsson to Sing 'Tristan' in New Rudaki Season," *Kayhan International*, September 18, 1977.

272 *Museum of Contemporary Art*: "Ambitious Addition to Tehran's Art World," *Kayhan International*, October 15, 1977.

272 *exhibition of African art*: "Royal Couple Inaugurates Exhibition of African Art," *Kayhan International*, November 2, 1977.

272 *Tenth Festival of Arts and Culture*: *Kayhan International*, October 26, 1978.

272 *Shahpur Gharib*: "Iran Wins Top Film Festival Prize," *Kayhan International*, November 8, 1977.

272 Caravans: "Jennifer O'Neill Finds Love and Happiness in Isfahan," *Kayhan International*, December 4, 1977.

272 *announced her engagement*: Ibid.

272 *Alex Haley*: Maryam Kharazmi, "'Roots' Author Praises Baghe Ferdows Show," *Kayhan International*, November 6, 1977.

272 *Tehran International Film Festival*: "Feast of Foreign Movies at This Winter's Festival," *Kayhan International*, November 3, 1977.

273 Dick Whittington: Amir Ali Afshar, "Dick Whittington—Crown Players Pantomime," *Kayhan International*, January 5, 1978.

273 *2,500 to 3,000 rials*: Ali Hosseinzadeh, "Fresh Fish Due to Flood Tehran's Food Markets," *Kayhan International*, December 18, 1977.

273 *nylon bags half filled with sand*: "Mysterious Shortages Hit City Groceries," *Kayhan International*, November 3, 1977.

273 *"Get your milk and yogurt"*: "Milk Products Scarce," *Kayhan International*, April 17, 1978.

273 *36 percent in just twelve months*: Ibid.

273 *two thousand tons of eggs*: "Eggs from Overseas," *Kayhan International*, January 25, 1978.

273 *rose 10 percent in price*: "Prices for Local Beer Allowed to Rise 10 pc," *Kayhan International*, April 17, 1978.

273 *eighty-five-mile-square radius*: William Graves, "Iran, Desert Miracle," *National Geographic* 147, no. 1 (January 1975): 6.

273 *"Private cars, taxis, minibuses"*: "Cold Wind, Hot Soup Greet the Early Birds," *Kayhan International*, January 24, 1978.

274 *1,200 traffic police*: "78 km of Roads for Tehran to Cost 830b Rials," *Kayhan International*, June 14, 1978.

274 *12,000 roads*: Ibid.
274 *109 filling stations*: "Four New Stations to Cut Down City Petrol Queues," *Kayhan International*, November 1, 1977.
274 *almost 1.5 million cars*: "78 km of Roads for Tehran."
274 *rates of fatalities involving children*: "'Children at Risk' in City," *Kayhan International*, November 9, 1977.
274 *Crown Prince Reza made front-page news*: "A Royal Poser on Mayor's Phone-In," *Kayhan International*, October 29, 1977.
274 *700,000*: James G. Scoville, "The Labor Market in Prerevolutionary Iran," *Economic Development and Cultural Change*, 34, no. 1 (October 1985): p. 151.
274 *"sewage wells"*: "Villagers Should Be Sent Home," *Kayhan International*, June 20, 1978.
274 *one street cleaner per sixty*: "N. Tehran 'Favored in Budget'—Councillor," *Kayhan International*, March 6, 1978.
274 *one worker for every 540 residents*: Ibid.
274 *five-year roadworks plan*: "Mayor Presents Five-Year Plan for Tehran Traffic," *Kayhan International*, November 14, 1977.
274 *2.8-mile tunnel*: "Work Gets Started on City Metro," *Kayhan International*, November 14, 1977.
274 *bomb shelters*: "Air Raid Shelters to Be Built in Iran Cities," *Kayhan International*, February 9, 1978.
275 *nineteen miles south*: "Work to Start on New City Airport," *Kayhan International*, December 5, 1977.
275 *forested green belt*: "Forest Belt Around Tehran," *Kayhan International*, November 14, 1977.
275 *installation of new equipment*: "NIOC Acts to Save Capital from Pollution," *Kayhan International*, February 12, 1978.
275 *20-billion-rial sewage treatment plant*: "Sewage Unit to Be Located in S. Tehran," *Kayhan International*, January 12, 1978.
275 *forty-two battery-run cars*: Ralph Joseph, "Tehran Drivers Give 'Car of the Future' the Cold Shoulder," *Kayhan International*, December 25, 1977.

14. LIGHTS OVER NIAVARAN

279 *"Caesar, I never stood on ceremonies"*: William Shakespeare, edited by Jonathan Bate and Eric Rasmussen, *The RSC Shakespeare: Julius Caesar* (New York: Modern Library, 2011), p. 37.
279 *"All the elements of trouble"*: "Monarch Uneasy on Palestinian State," *Kayhan International*, January 4, 1978.
279 *at the home of John Hoyer*: "Bloody Mary Stars at Embassy Brunch," *Kayhan International*, January 3, 1978.
280 *"busy hive of activity"*: "Zahedi Pays a Visit Home," *Kayhan International*, December 31, 1977.
280 *Tehran's hotels anticipated a busy night*: The list of New Year's events at hotels around Tehran was published in "Hotels Promise a Lively New Year's Eve," *Kayhan International*, December 29, 1977.
280 *Abba's "Name of the Game"*: The list of the most popular music tracks of December 1977 was published in "Top of the Pops: Nothing to Stop Soaring Wings," *Kayhan International*, December 4, 1977.
280 *After-dinner entertainment*: "Hotels Promise a Lively New Year's Eve," *Kayhan International*, December 29, 1977.
280 *$50,000 to disrobe*: This report, which first appeared in the Iranian press, was repeated to U.S. diplomats by Iran's former ambassador to the United States Mahmoud Foroughi as an example of the widening gap in Iran between the "haves" and "have-nots." "Country Team Minutes," *Iran: The Making of US Policy, 1977–80*, National Security Archive (Alexandria, VA: Chadwyck-Healey, 1990), February 22, 1978, document 01312.
280 *"belly dancers, strip teasers"*: Advertisement for Vanak nightclub, *Kayhan International*, March 2, 1978.
280 *blacklisted by Hollywood studios*: Hollywood's boycott of Iran in the mid-1970s is explained in volume two of Hamid Naficy's four-volume history of Iranian cinema. Hamid Naficy, *A Social History of Iranian Cinema*, vol. 2, *The Industrializing Years, 1941–78* (Durham NC: Duke University Press, 2011), pp. 423–426.
280 Towering Inferno: "Film Guide," *Kayhan International*, November 8, 1977.
280 Earthquake: Ibid., January 21, 1978.
281 Jaws: Ibid., August 2, 1978.
281 *slim pickings on New Year's Eve*: For the New Year's Eve cinema listings see "Film Guide," *Kayhan International*, December 31, 1977.
281 *regular nighttime lineup*: To learn more about NIRT's schedule for the 1977–1978 year see Amir Ali Afshar, "NIRT International Looks Ahead to Its Second Year," *Kayhan International*, October 26, 1978.
281 The Pendulum: "Teleguide," *Kayhan International*, December 31, 1977.

281 *"a fascist movie"*: Roger Ebert, review of *Pendulum,* February 10, 1969, http://www.rogerebert.com/reviews/pendulum-1969.

281 *shortly after ten o'clock*: The Daily Diary of President Jimmy Carter, December 31, 1977, http://www.jimmycarterlibrary.gov/documents/diary/1977/d123177t.pdf.

281 *"I looked at his pale face"*: Ashraf Pahlavi, *Faces in a Mirror: Memoirs from Exile* (Englewood Cliffs, NJ: Prentice-Hall, 1980).

281 *"The situation in Iran was already bad"*: Author interview with Elli Antoniades, October 4, 2013.

282 *habit of laying it on thick*: Haynes Johnson, "A Few Ideas for the Next Journey from a Fellow Traveler," *Washington Post,* January 8, 1978.

282 *their two countries shared similar values*: Paul Eidelberg, "Mr. Carter and the Praise of Tyrants," *Jerusalem Post,* April 10, 1978.

282 *"I wish you'd quit saying"*: Johnson, "A Few Ideas."

282 *"delightful"*: Toast by President [Carter] at a State Dinner, Tehran, December 31, 1977, *Iran: The Making of US Policy, 1977–80,* document 01261.

282 *"'With whom would you like to spend New Year's Eve?'"*: Ibid.

282 *"Iran, because of the great leadership of the Shah"*: Eric Hogland, project ed., *Iran: The Making of US Policy, 1977–80,* document 01261.

282 *"throwing away all the material"*: An interview with Jack Shellenberger, April 21, May 12 and July 12, 1990, conducted by Lew Schmidt, The Ability Group, pp. 55–56.

282 *White House speechwriter James Fallows*: Mr. Fallows confirmed to this author that he wrote Carter's speech and also penned the celebrated phrase "island of stability." Author e-mail exchange with James Fallows, October 2, 2013: "I was indeed the only speechwriter on that trip with Carter, and thus had the memorable responsibility for that quote. I didn't know then (and don't know now) the exact lineage of that phrase. But in all matters of foreign policy, the speechwriters would take their guidance from the actual experts."

282 *loaded history of "island of stability"*: Memorandum from the President's Assistant for National Security Affairs (Kissinger) to President Nixon, Washington, April 16, 1970, *FRUS 1969–77,* vol. E-4.

282 *for a private conference*: "Carter Will Meet Sadat to Discuss Talks on Mideast," *Washington Post,* January 1, 1978.

283 *the Queen prevailed on them*: William H. Sullivan, *Mission to Iran: The Last U.S. Ambassador* (New York: Norton, 1981), p. 134.

283 *"I have a happy memory"*: Farah Pahlavi, *An Enduring Love: My Life with the Shah* (New York: Miramax Books, 2004), p. 273.

283 *practiced their dance moves*: William Shawcross, *The Shah's Last Ride: The Fate of an Ally* (New York: Simon & Schuster, 1988), p. 131.

283 *Their father grimaced*: Ibid.

283 *"I went to the InterContinental"*: Author interview with Ali Hussein, 2013.

283 *"I wish you were coming with me"*: "I Wish You Were Coming Too—Carter," *Kayhan International,* January 2, 1978.

283 *"We admired the Shah"*: Author interview with Bruce Vernor, March 12, 2013.

284 *"You Americans are really very nice people"*: Sullivan (1981), p. 136.

284 *"Period of Trepidation"*: "Period of Trepidation Ahead Says the Zodiac Calendar," *Kayhan International,* January 1, 1978.

284 *"the past we are condemned to relive"*: Gwynne Dyer, "Wild Cards," *Jerusalem Post,* January 2, 1978.

285 *"written itself off"*: "Arafat Says Bye-Bye to the U.S. in Mideast," *Kayhan International,* January 2, 1978.

285 *"It's not bye-bye PLO, Mr. Brzezinski"*: Ibid.

285 *"But the destructive, negative elements"*: "Monarch Uneasy on Palestinian State," *Kayhan International,* January 4, 1978.

286 *Crown Players' production*: "Tehran Diary," *Kayhan International,* January 7, 1978.

286 *Eugene O'Neill's*: Ibid.

286 *staged a fashion show*: "Dior Comes to Kish Island," *Kayhan International,* January 4, 1978.

286 *"The new, mechanized way of life"*: "Capital City 'One of World's Safest,'" *Kayhan International,* January 2, 1978.

286 *6.4 million barrels*: "December Oil Output at Highest for 1977," *Kayhan International,* January 8, 1978.

286 *arrived in Bangkok*: "Crown Prince Arrives in Bangkok," *Kayhan International,* January 5, 1978.

286 *"hunting for pleasure"*: "Monarch Urges Criteria for Protection of Wildlife," *Kayhan International,* January 7, 1978.

286 *global hub for science*: "Iran's Medical Challenge," *Kayhan International,* January 8, 1978.

286 *three hundred computers*: "New Uses Are Urged for Iran's Idle Computers," *Kayhan International,* June 4, 1978.

286   *300 percent*: Ibid.
286   *$500 million*: "Iran Computer Market to Hit Record $500M Mark," *Kayhan International*, July 24, 1978.
286   *This at a time*: "New Uses Are Urged."
287   *computerized ticketing center*: "Iran Air to Boost Flights," *Kayhan International*, January 14, 1978.
287   *Concorde flying to Kish*: "December Paris–Kish Debut for Concorde," *Kayhan International*, November 24, 1977.
287   *"subversive intrigues"*: "Monarch Stresses Need for Political Education," *Kayhan International*, January 5, 1978.
287   *"red and black reactionaries"*: "Amouzegar Slams Vicious Conspiracy by Colonialists," *Kayhan International*, January 5, 1978.
287   *"a few innocent deceived youths"*: Ibid.
287   *Damavand College*: To learn more about this Iranian institution for women's learning see D. Ray Heisey, "Reflections on a Persian Jewel: Damavand College, Tehran," *Journal of Middle Eastern and Islamic Studies (in Asia)* 5, no. 1 (2011): 19–44.
287   *"a great deal to prepare"*: Maria Khonsary, "Ceremony at Damavand Recalls Lifting of the Veil," *Kayhan International*, January 8, 1978.
287   *"Iranian women were hidden"*: Ibid.
288   *a third of all university students*: Marvine Howe, "Iranian Women Return to Veil in a Resurgence of Spirituality," *New York Times*, July 30, 1977.
288   *half of all medical school applicants*: Ibid.
288   *twenty female members of parliament*: Ibid.
288   *four hundred female city councillors*: Ibid.
288   *Iran Air appointed*: "Computers Keep Iran Air in Vanguard of Progress," *Kayhan International*, January 15, 1978.
288   *singer Aki Banai*: "Aki Banai Takes States by Storm," *Kayhan International*, January 15, 1978.
288   *first hair salon*: Ali Hosseinzadeh, "Stylist with a Difference Keeps Tehran Men Trim," *Kayhan International*, January 1, 1978.
288   *one hundred women*: "'Bring Back Veil' Protest in Mashad," *Kayhan International*, January 9, 1978.
288   *protested in Isfahan and Mashad*: From Ambassador Sullivan to Secretary of State Vance, January 11, 1978, cable 1300Z, *Iran: The Making of US Policy, 1977–80*, document 01277.
288   *"Their demonstration was in effect"*: "Female Emancipation," *Kayhan International*, January 9, 1978.
289   *"There is nothing to be afraid of"*: "Kayhan Photo Prompts Threat," *Kayhan International*, January 17, 1978.
289   *"IRAN AND RED-AND-BLACK COLONIALISM"*: James Buchan, *Days of God: The Revolution in Iran and Its Consequences* (London: Murray, 2012), p. 198.
290   *"Hoveyda wrote the letter"*: Author interview with Ardeshir Zahedi, October 27, 2012.
290   *"Homayoun was leaving the conference hall"*: Author interview with Farhad Massoudi, April 11, 2015.
290   *"Writing such an article"*: Author interview with Ali Hossein, 2013.
290   *setting fire to Ettelaat's newsstands*: Amir Taheri, *The Spirit of Allah: Khomeini and the Islamic Revolution* (Bethesda, MD: Adler & Adler, 1986), p. 201.
291   *the Shah was in Aswan*: "Ball in Israel's Court: Monarch," *Kayhan International*, January 11, 1978.
291   *Queen Farah was en route to Paris*: "Empress Trip," *Kayhan International*, January 12, 1978.
291   *"banks, government offices, girls' schools"*: Taheri (1986), p. 201.
291   *twenty thousand*: Ibid.
291   *"Death to the Shah!"*: Ibid.
291   *Police Station Number One*: "Six Killed as Qom Mob Turns Violent," *Kayhan International*, January 11, 1978.
291   *killing six people*: "6 Killed as Iranian Police Quell Moslem Dissidents," *Washington Post*, January 11, 1978.
291   *crushed underfoot*: Ibid.
291   *evening reception*: Telegram from Embassy Tehran to Secretary of State, Washington, DC, "Serious Religious Dissidence in Qom," January 11, 1978, *Iran: The Making of US Policy, 1977–80*, document 01277.
291   *six visiting American senators*: The six senators were Harrison A. Williams Jr., Ted Stevens, Howard Cannon, Abraham Ribicoff, Ernest F. Hollings, and Jacob K. Javits. Letter from Jack C. Miklos, Deputy Chief of Mission, to Aslan Afshar, January 5, 1978, *Iran: The Making of US Policy, 1977–80*, document 01267.

291 *Hoveyda took aside*: Telegram from Embassy Tehran to Secretary of State, Washington, DC, "Serious Religious Dissidence in Qom."

291 *seventy religious students*: William Branigan, "Iran's Most Powerful Moslem Leaders Angry at Government," *Washington Post*, January 20, 1978.

291 *"stones, iron bars, and wooden staves"*: Telegram from Embassy Tehran to Secretary of State, Washington, DC, "Serious Religious Dissidence in Qom."

291 *scattered outbreaks of violence and strikes*: See, for example, "6 Killed as Iranian Police Quell Moslem Dissidents"; Branigan, "Iran's Powerful Moslem Leaders Angry at Government"; "Religious Rites Incite Attack on Cinema," *Kayhan International*, January 15, 1978; "Two Held in After-Sermon Vandalism," *Kayhan International*, January 15, 1978; and Telegram from Embassy Tehran to Secretary of State, Washington, DC, "Dissidence: Qom Aftermath and Other Events," January 16, 1978, *Iran: The Making of US Policy, 1977–80*, document 01282.

291 *Arya Cinema*: "Religious Riots Incite Attack on Cinema," *Kayhan International*, January 15, 1978.

291 *hurled rocks at police*: "Two Held in After-Sermon Vandalism," *Kayhan International*, January 15, 1978.

292 *protest marches reported*: Telegram from Embassy Tehran to Secretary of State, Washington, DC, "Dissidence: Qom Aftermath and Other Events."

292 *stage a large progovernment*: "Qom Protest Condemns 'Return to Stone Age,'" *Kayhan International*, January 16, 1978.

292 *The Princess phoned Parviz Sabeti*: Author interview with Parviz Sabeti, September 21, 2013.

292 *"I counted the crisis"*: Author interview with George Lambrakis, September 13, 2014.

293 *"in most serious incident"*: Telegram from Embassy Tehran to Secretary of State, Washington, DC, "Serious Religious Dissidence in Qom."

293 *"fundamentalist religious leaders"*: Telegram from Embassy Tehran to Secretary of State, Washington, DC, January 26, 1978, "Religion and Politics: Qom and Its Aftermath," *Iran: The Making of US Policy, 1977–80*, document 01291.

293 *follow-up airgram*: Airgram, from American Embassy Tehran to Department of State, "The Iranian Opposition," February 1, 1978, *Iran: The Making of US Policy, 1977–80*, document 01296.

293 *"At the present time"*: Ibid.

294 *"The true leader of the Shia faithful"*: Ibid.

294 *waving female undergarments*: Author interview with Parviz Sabeti, September 21, 2013.

294 *$35 million*: Taheri (1986), p. 214.

294 *"Austerity during liberalization"*: Author interview with Parviz Sabeti, May 10, 2014.

295 *"The sudden cut"*: Taheri (1986), p. 214.

295 *"un-Islamic and inhumane"*: Branigan, "Iran's Most Powerful Moslem Leaders Angry at Government."

295 *"The Shah is the son-in-law of the Ayatollah"*: Author interview with Reza Ghotbi, May 9, 2013.

295 *"Do you mean that you want to run the state?"*: Ibid.

296 *Mustafa Chamran*: To read more about Mustafa Chamran and his role in the anti-Shah opposition movement in Lebanon see H. E. Chahabi, ed., *Distant Relations: Iran and Lebanon in the Last 500 Years* (London: Centre for Lebanese Studies in association with I. B. Tauris, 2006), pp. 137–200.

296 *He bitterly complained*: Musa Sadr's efforts to repair his relations with the Shah were confirmed in author interviews with Ali Kani, February 12, 2013; with Ambassador Khalil al-Khalil, June 21–24, 2013; and with Ambassador Abbas Nayeri, July 12, 2013.

297 *"Ahmad was someone thinking"*: Author interview with Abolhassan Banisadr, July 11, 2013.

297 *"Many Iranians appear to have ceased"*: Telegram from Embassy Tehran to Secretary of State, Washington, DC, "Religion and Politics: Qom and Its Aftermath."

297 *"raged for hours"*: "Bowling Club Fire," *Kayhan International*, January 21, 1978.

297 *three-story Sabouri furniture store*: "Furniture Shop Goes Up in Flames After Bog Blast," *Kayhan International*, January 29, 1978.

298 *a run on Iran's largest private commercial bank*: Jonathan Randal, "Post-Riot Tabriz Retreats into a World of Rumors," *Washington Post*, March 5, 1978.

298 *largest private commercial bank*: Author interview with Hassan Ali Mehran, January 13, 2015.

298 *three thousand branches*: Ibid.

298 *"the southern end of the city"*: "Colored UFO Seen over City," *Kayhan International*, January 29, 1978.

298 *"extraterrestrial being"*: "Girl Says She Met 'a Being from Space,'" *Kayhan International*, January 8, 1978. UFO sightings and end times have often been connected in the popular mind. "This pattern extends back through the Middle Ages and back to Biblical times," noted Curtis Peebles. "Ezkiel's Wheel is often

described by believers as a UFO. What is left out is the social situation of 592 BC—the people of Israel had been defeated, the Babylonians had taken Jerusalem and the Israelites had been reduced to slavery. Their society was spiritually and politically bankrupt. Then, as now, people looked to the skies, seeking salvation and escape from dark and threatening forces." See Curtis Peebles, *Watch the Skies: A Chronicle of the Flying Saucer Myth* (Washington, DC: Smithsonian Institution Press, 1994), p. 286.

298 *The most notorious incident*: The author's account of this dramatic episode is taken from his interview with Lieutenant General Mohammad Hossein Mehrmand, January 13, 2015, the Hamadan base commander at the time.

299 *"Yes," he said, "for sure there was something out there"*: Ibid.

15. THE CARAVAN PASSES

300 *"Death to the Shah!"*: Imam Khomeini, *Islam and Revolution: Writings and Declarations of Imam Khomeini (1941–80)*, trans. Hamid Algar (Berkeley, CA: Mizan Press, 1981), p. 230.

300 *"Khomeini has to be assassinated"*: Author interview with Parviz Sabeti, September 21, 2013.

300 *"satellite summit"*: "Satellite Summit," *Kayhan International*, February 2, 1978.

300 *"Year of the Microchip"*: "The Computer Society," *Time*, February 20, 1978.

300 *"was solid proof"*: "Satellite Summit."

300 *"about a prince"*: Ibid.

301 *spoke out forcefully*: "Sadat Must Succeed," *Kayhan International*, February 5, 1978.

301 *"we [Iranians] were civilized"*: Ibid.

301 *gala celebrations*: Maryam Kharazmi, "Carpet Industry Will Thrive, Says Monarch," *Kayhan International*, February 12, 1978.

301 *"a giant-size nomadic tent"*: Taruneh Gharagoziou, "Tradition Woven into a Modern Setting," *Kayhan International*, February 21, 1978.

301 *"used a great deal in mosques"*: Ibid.

301 *"a pond and bubbling fountain"*: Ibid.

301 *"turn Tehran into an international"*: Kharazmi, "Carpet Industry Will Thrive."

302 *"What do you think?"*: Author interviews with Farah Pahlavi, March 23–25, 2013. See also Farah Pahlavi, *An Enduring Love: My Life with the Shah* (New York: Miramax, 2004), p. 265.

302 *"We talked a great deal"*: Amir Taheri, *The Unknown Shah* (London: Hutchinson, 1991), pp. 286–287.

302 *"I am only asking you"*: F. Pahlavi (2004), p. 266.

303 *"somewhat dingy" city of eight hundred thousand*: Jonathan Randal, "Post-Riot Tabriz Retreats into a World of Rumors," *Washington Post*, March 5, 1978.

303 *refuse to sell imported meat*: "Tabrizis Say No to Foreign Meat," *Kayhan International*, February 11, 1978.

303 *"it is not comfortable"*: Randal, "Post-Riot Tabriz Retreats."

303 *"plastered with signs"*: Ibid.

303 *"People in charge of the movement"*: Author interview with Ali Hossein, 2013.

303 *On the morning of February 18*: Details of the collapse of law and order in Tabriz on February 18, 1978, are taken mainly from dispatches filed by American and British foreign correspondents who traveled to the city in the weeks following the unrest. Their reports can be considered unbiased and straightforward. Perhaps surprisingly, the Iranian newspaper *Kayhan*, which was operating under mild censorship, also provided its readers with a fairly detailed account of the time line of the day's events.

303 *government offices, schools*: Paul Hoffman, "Behind Iranian Riots, a Web of Discontent," *New York Times*, March 5, 1978.

304 *gates of the Masjed-e-Jomeh Mosque*: Jonathan Randal, "Shah Moves to Defuse Iranian Dissent," *Washington Post*, March 4, 1978.

304 *setting fire to a traffic kiosk*: "Tabriz After the Mob," *Kayhan International*, February 20, 1978.

304 *"Death to the Shah!"*: Liz Thurgood, "Shah Seeking a Period of Calm," *Guardian*, March 3, 1978.

304 *134 blazes*: "6 Killed, 125 Hurt in Riots in Northern Iranian City," *Washington Post*, February 20, 1978.

304 *"was dragged from her car"*: Memorandum of Conversation: M. Henri Marchal, director, French Cultural Center, Tabriz, and David C. McGaffey, American consul, Isfahan, February 23, 1978, "Subject: Tabriz Riots of February 18, 1978," *Iran: The Making of US Policy, 1977–80*, National Security Archive (Alexandria, VA: Chadwyck-Healey, 1990), document 1322.

304 *"more than twenty girls at the Parvin School"*: Ibid.

304 *"people in the mob"*: "Monarch Orders Tabriz Flareup Inquiry," *Kayhan International*, February 21, 1978.

305 *12 dead and 125 seriously injured*: Statistics are taken from "Tabriz After the Mob," *Kayhan International*, February 20, 1978.
305 *"Banks and trading companies"*: "Monarch Orders Tabriz Flareup Inquiry."
305 *"imported incendiary bombs"*: Ibid.
305 *"who had passed through Palestinian training camps"*: Hushang Nahavandi, *The Last Shah of Iran* (London: Aquilion, 2005), p. 86.
305 *"The attacks seemed extraordinarily well planned"*: Hoffman, "Behind Iranian Riots."
305 *"It is rare now"*: Ibid.
306 *"Death to the Shah!"*: Khomeini (1981), p. 230.
306 *"We shall continue with our liberalization policy"*: Vida Moattar, "Abuses 'Will Not Stop Liberalization,'" *Kayhan International*, February 28, 1978.
307 *recalled the governor of Eastern Azerbaijan*: "Tabriz Governor Finishes Term of Office," *Kayhan International*, March 2, 1978.
307 *"I am not going"*: Jonathan Randal, "Iranian Oil Embargo Hinted," *Washington Post*, March 6, 1978.
308 *the kidnapping and murder*: "Kidnap Boy's Body Found," *Kayhan International*, March 9, 1978.
308 *"Those with younger children"*: "Taking No Chances," *Kayhan International*, April 23, 1978.
308 *"a young couple who fall in love"*: "Showbiz Makes Gougoush Sick," *Kayhan International*, March 14, 1978.
309 *"If only I could have a simple, normal life"*: Ibid.
309 *"But I am pretty certain"*: Kiumars Mehr-Ayin, "After London, Where Next for Iranians?" *Kayhan International*, April 10, 1978.
309 *"since foreign tourists"*: Ibid.
309 *traffic jams starting at four*: "Road Jams as Millions Begin Now Ruz Rush," *Kayhan International*, March 20, 1978.
310 *"Hang in there"*: "Gregory Lima, "Hang in There for the Year of the Horse," *Kayhan International*, March 20, 1978.
310 *"no increase in sales"*: "The Now Ruz Spree Is Over Before It Began," *Kayhan International*, March 13, 1978.
310 *"its busiest period so far"*: "Over 20,000 to Holiday Abroad," *Kayhan International*, January 25, 1978.
310 *twenty thousand*: Ibid.
310 *the Leningrad Ballet*: "Leningrad Ballet Brings Eager Crowds Rushing," *Kayhan International*, March 30, 1978.
310 *Swedish opera diva Birgit Nilsson*: Terry Graham, "Rudaki Thrills to Nilsson," *Kayhan International*, March 6, 1978.
310 *The trial was under way of Maryam*: "Acid-Thrower Is in Prison Again," *Kayhan International*, March 5, 1978.
310 *Broadway star Pearl Bailey*: "Empress and Prince Reza Meet Pearl," *Kayhan International*, March 5, 1978.
310 *"I am always moved"*: "Pearl Is Moved by Iranian Hospitality," *Kayhan International*, March 5, 1978.
310 *"new international economic order"*: "Monarch Renews Call for New World Order," *Kayhan International*, March 25, 1978.
311 *prefer the respondent to be of Iranian origin*: Author interview with Maryam Ansary, March 2, 2014.
311 *turned sweet sixteen*: "Royal Birthday," *Kayhan International*, March 12, 1978.
311 *learning to play the guitar*: Mansureh Pirnia, "My Lifetime Goal Is to Serve the Nation," *Kayhan International*, October 15, 1977.
311 *"In Kish I presented an assessment"*: Author interview with Reza Ghotbi, March 25, 2013.
311 *reported they were coming under attack*: Author interview with Mahnaz Afkhami, August 16, 2013.
312 *"Several foreign companies"*: Liz Thurgood, "Iranian Government Censured Over Riot," *Guardian*, March 17, 1978.
312 *"People around us were shocked"*: Author interview with Mahnaz Afkhami, August 16, 2013.
312 *on pilgrimage to Mecca and Medina*: "Princess Ashraf on Pilgrimage," *Kayhan International*, March 25, 1978.
312 *"I spoke to His Majesty"*: Author interview with Mahnaz Afkhami, August 16, 2013.
312 *sixty thousand to seventy thousand*: Geoffrey Wigoder, "A Visit to the Tomb of Esther," *Jerusalem Post*, March 2, 1978.
312 *"Anti-Jewish books"*: Ibid.
312 *half of the fifty thousand Jews*: Ibid.
312 *20 percent*: Ibid.
312 *30 percent*: Ibid.

313   *Fifteen hundred Israeli citizens*: Uri-Bar Joseph, "Forecasting a Hurricane: Israeli and American Estimates of the Khomeini Revolution," *Journal of Strategic Studies* 36, issue 5 (2013): 5.

313   *$210 million*: Jonathan Broder, "Israel, Iran Maintain Quiet, Closely Guarded Ties," *Chicago Tribune*, February 26, 1978.

313   *six weekly flights*: Ibid.

313   *"The Jews have every confidence in the Shah"*: Wigoder, "A Visit to the Tomb."

313   *enjoyed a close working relationship*: Joseph, "Forecasting a Hurricane," p. 6.

313   *shocked at the speed*: Ibid., p. 11.

313   *"the Shah was finished and his days were numbered"*: Ibid.

313   *secretly visited the Shah on Kish Island*: Ibid., p. 12.

313   *"is rapidly taking on"*: Confidential Memorandum of Conversation: Hedayat Eslaminia, Leila (translator), George B. Lambrakis, John D. Stempel, "Subject: Internal Politics and Religion," May 23, 1978, *Iran: The Making of US Policy, 1977–80*, document 01397.

313   *"concluded that the combination"*: Joseph, "Forecasting a Hurricane," p. 12.

313   *"the main challenge"*: Ibid.

314   *tempo of unrest flared*: For example, see "Textile Plant Gutted in Fire," *Kayhan International*, March 25, 1978, and "Bank Offices Come Under Violent Attack," *Kayhan International*, March 29, 1978.

314   *bomb threat had been called in*: "Confidential: Country Team Minutes," March 29, 1978, *Iran: The Making of US Policy, 1977–80*, National Security Archive, document 01351.

314   *thirty-five shops along Shohoda Street*: "Mysterious Fire Destroys 35 Shops," *Kayhan International*, March 30, 1978.

314   *shoot-out that left one gunman dead*: "Terrorist Killed in Qazvin Encounter," *Kayhan International*, April 1, 1978.

314   *Bands of rioters*: "Several Cities Hit by Violent Anti-State Riots," *Kayhan International*, April 1, 1978.

314   *weekend of Friday, March 31, to Saturday, April 1*: The list of incidents was reported in "Rioters Stage Sneak Attacks on Banks," *Kayhan International*, April 3, 1978.

314   *gruesome crime scene*: "Foreigner Killed," *Kayhan International*, April 3, 1978.

315   *"I drove down at night with a security car in the rear"*: Author interview with Parviz Sabeti, September 21, 2013.

16. FIVE DAYS IN MAY

316   *"My headstrong lord, consider now and say"*: Abolqasem Ferdowsi, *Shahnameh: The Persian Book of Kings*, trans. Dick Davis (New York: Penguin, 2006), p. 502.

316   *"The Americans want to eliminate me"*: Author interview with Reza Ghotbi, March 25, 2013.

316   *Downtown, tens of thousands of picnickers*: "Tehranis Rush to Enjoy the 13th," *Kayhan International*, April 3, 1978.

316   *"There were only a few cases"*: Ibid.

316   *fresh snowfall in northeastern Iran*: "Tehran 'Won't Be Windy Long,'" *Kayhan International*, April 12, 1978.

316   *drenched by heavy rains*: Ibid.

316   *"raised the dust and scattered garbage"*: Ibid.

317   *"Foreign trade delegations"*: Anthony Parsons, *The Pride and the Fall: Iran 1974–79* (London: Jonathan Cape, 1984), p. 64.

317   *Formal state visits*: President and Mrs. Scheel of West Germany arrived in Tehran on April 21, 1978. See "Scheels Arrive for State Visit," *Kayhan International*, April 22, 1978. President and Mrs. Senghor of Senegal arrived in Tehran on April 24, 1977. See "Senghor Visit," *Kayhan International*, April 25, 1978.

317   *commander of the Indian Navy*: "The Shahanshah Receives the Commander of the Indian Navy," *Kayhan International*, April 26, 1978.

317   *American feminist leaders*: "Empress Farah Received a Delegation of American Feminists," *Kayhan International*, April 20, 1978.

317   *"Ron and Nancy stayed in my house"*: Author interview with Ardeshir Zahedi, October 27, 2012.

317   *"Isfahan was full of European"*: Parsons (1984), p. 65.

317   *escorted into his office*: The Shah received Thatcher and Bush on April 29, 1978. See "Niavaran Audiences," *Kayhan International*, April 30, 1978.

317   *attracted a steady trade*: Irene Sarshar, "Lalezar: Still a Bustling Appeal to the Senses," *Kayhan International*, March 15, 1978.

317   *looking for a shady lunch spot*: Irene Sarshar, "Avenue Kakh is a Nostalgic Backwater," *Kayhan International*, April 17, 1978.

317   *"The parks are immaculate"*: Iran's Affluent, Indebted to the Shah, Give Him Little Support in Crisis," *New York Times*, November 18, 1978.

318 *five dead and ninety-eight injured*: William Branigan, "Shah Maintains Firm Control Despite New Wave of Protests," *Washington Post*, April 7, 1978.

318 *"Mohammad Reza Pahlavi is beset"*: Jonathan Randal, "Shah's Economic Project Hits Snags, Periling His Regime," *Washington Post*, April 2, 1978.

318 *"A year ago you"*: William Branigan, "Little Joy Greets the Shah's Anniversary," *Washington Post*, August 20, 1977.

318 *from $10 to $7*: Ibid.

318 *"The only way out for him now"*: Randal, "Shah's Economic Project."

318 *returned from their Kish vacation*: "Monarch, Empress Return from Kish," *Kayhan International*, April 4, 1978.

318 *rushed to the Takht-e Jamshid movie theater*: "Riots, Sabotage Continue to Hit Several Cities," *Kayhan International*, April 5, 1978.

318 *In Zarand*: "Rioters Stage Sneak Attacks on Banks," *Kayhan International*, April 3, 1978.

318 *"was suddenly engulfed in flames"*: "Riots, Sabotage Continue."

318 *plant on Karaj Road*: "Fires Strike Village, Manufacturing Plant," *Kayhan International*, April 9, 1978.

318 *a bus depot in the town of Shushtar*: "Riots, Sabotage Continue."

318 *the Physical Culture Organization building*: Ibid.

318 *The Youth Hostel in Kermanshah*: Ibid.

319 *A policeman was blinded*: Ibid.

319 *"These groups have obviously"*: "The Barren Womb of Red and Black Reaction," *Kayhan International*, April 12, 1978.

319 *"mostly drawn from the marginal strata"*: Ibid.

320 *"The Americans want to eliminate me"*: Author interview with Reza Ghotbi, March 25, 2013.

320 *Pakravan explained*: Memorandum of Conversation, "Home of General Hassan Pakravan, Niavaran, Tehran," April 19, 1978, *Iran: The Making of US Policy, 1977–80*, National Security Archive (Alexandria, VA: Chadwyck-Healey, 1990), document 1362.

321 *the death five days earlier*: "Elder Statesman Alam Dies After Long Illness," *Kayhan International*, April 15, 1978.

321 *Over the Nowruz holiday*: Ibid.; author interview with Parviz Sabeti, May 10, 2014.

321 *Sabeti agreed to write the report*: Ibid.

321 *"brutally frank"*: Nahavandi provided an account of his meeting with Moghadam in Hushang Nahavandi, *The Last Shah of Iran* (London: Aquilion, 2005), pp. 109–111.

321 *"dramatic measures"*: Author interview with Parviz Sabeti, May 10, 2014.

321 *"nonsense"*: Author interviews with Farah Pahlavi, March 23–25, 2013.

322 *"Eyewitness said he saw"*: Telegram: Embassy Tehran to Secretary of State, "GOI Breaks Up Student Demonstration Roughly," April 24, 1978, *Iran: The Making of US Policy, 1977–80*, document 1366.

322 *"brownshirt tactics"*: Telegram from Embassy Tehran to Secretary of State, Subject: "GOI Discouragement of Dissident Political Action," April 25, 1978, *Iran: The Making of US Policy, 1977–80*, document 01374.

322 *They got into a "big fight"*: Author interview with Parviz Sabeti, September 21, 2013.

323 *the latest CIA review*: Central Intelligence Agency, "Iran in the 1980s," August 1977, *Iran: The Making of US Policy, 1977–80*, document 1210.

323 *the Shah enjoyed "good health"*: Ibid., p. 49.

323 *"no radical change"*: Ibid., p. iii.

323 *"The Shah could die suddenly"*: Ibid., p. iv.

324 *"on the verge of panic"*: Airgram from U.S. Consul David McGaffey to Department of State, "Disturbances in Isfahan," May 6, 1978, *Iran: The Making of US Policy, 1977–80*, document 01382.

324 *"strength and growing violence"*: Ibid.

325 *"I talked with people"*: "South 'Becoming a Powerhouse,'" *Kayhan International*, May 7, 1978.

325 *"Over the last three months"*: "The Rule of Law Must Prevail During This Time of Liberalization," *Kayhan International*, May 6, 1978.

326 *"a lavish cocktail and dinner"*: "Town Talk by Konjav: Tehran Gives U.S. Travel Agents a Warm Welcome," *Kayhan International*, May 8, 1978.

326 *first shots were fired in Tabriz*: "Rioters Attack Public Property in Many Cities," *Kayhan International*, May 11, 1978.

326 *mourners destroyed three hundred vehicles*: Ibid.

326 *more than a thousand rioted in Kerman*: Ibid.

326 *he had drawn up a contingency plan*: Author interview with Parviz Sabeti, June 15, 2013.

327 *"We had the names of five thousand people"*: Ibid.

327 *"Now we have to do our job"*: Author interview with Parviz Sabeti, September 21, 2013.

328 *"simply went from door to door"*: "Empress Farah Talking with a Woman," *Kayhan International*, May 11, 1978.

328 *"I went to try to find out"*: Author interview with Farah Pahlavi, July 15, 2013.

329 *"Such large demonstrations"*: Tehran Police Fire Shots to Disperse Demonstrators," *Los Angeles Times*, May 11, 1978.

329 *British and American schools*: "Iran Firms Restrict Employee Travel," *Guardian*, May 15, 1978.

329 *The Shah rearranged his schedule*: "Iran Riots Spread to Tehran," *Times* (London), May 12, 1978.

329 *Beside the names of the five groups*: Author interview with Parviz Sabeti, September 21, 2013

329 *"collective arrests"*: Ibid.

330 *"in the end he only approved three hundred arrests"*: Ibid.

330 *"We are going the wrong way"*: Author interview with Parviz Sabeti, June 15, 2013.

330 *On the evening of Friday, May 12*: Memorandum of Conversation, "Subject: Religious Situation, Hedayat Eslaminia, Simin Hedayat, George B. Lambrakis, John D. Stempel."

330 *"He was a Savak agent"*: Author interview with Parviz Sabeti, September 21, 2013.

330 *"foreshadowed a gigantic explosion"*: Memorandum of Conversation, "Subject: Religious Situation, Hedayat Eslaminia, Simin Hedayat, George B. Lambrakis, John D. Stempel."

331 *On Saturday, May 13*: An account of the meeting of the Shah's security chiefs is found ibid.

332 *"These people are politically bankrupt cases"*: "Anti-Government Groups 'Seek Iran's Partition,'" *Kayhan International*, May 14, 1978.

332 *looked and sounded "like a man in retreat"*: Memorandum of Conversation, Rahmatolah Moghadam Maregheh, George Lambrakis, June 12, 1978, *Iran: The Making of US Policy, 1977–80*, document 01417.

332 *cheered and applauded by friendly crowds*: Nahavandi (2005), p. 93.

333 *"expounded at great length"*: Memorandum of Conversation, "Armenian Leader's Views on Iranian Political Stability," Diyair Paessian, Der Hounessian, Michael J. Metrinko, May 20, 1978, *Iran: The Making of US Policy, 1977–80*, document 01392.

333 *The Queen had done the honors*: Author interview with Farah Pahlavi, November 12, 2014.

333 *Crown Prince Reza raised cheers*: "Prince's First Solo," *Kayhan International*, May 27, 1978.

333 *standing in the back of an open car*: "Warm Welcome Given to Shah, Empress," *Hartford Courant*, May 29, 1978. See also "Royal Tour of Khorassan Underlines Ties to Islam," *Kayhan International*, June 1, 1978.

333 *"Greetings to the king of kings"*: "Warm Welcome Given to Shah, Empress."

334 *"You know about my faith in Islam"*: "Mashad Fetes Royal Couple: Monarch Warns Clergy of Threat to Islam," *Kayhan International*, May 29, 1978.

334 *"sufficient understanding of the true principles"*: Ibid.

334 *The Queen made spontaneous walkabouts*: "Royal Tour of Khorassan Underlines Ties to Islam."

334 *"If the principles of the [White] Revolution"*: "Workers 'Are the Builders of Revolution,'" *Kayhan International*, May 30, 1978.

335 *"why some Iranians felt scared"*: "Patriots Will Save Us from Communism," *Kayhan International*, June 1, 1978.

335 *"What point is there in living abroad"*: Ibid.

335 *"My God, we would like a decent opposition"*: Colin Smith, "Mullahs' Mobs Fight Shah," *Observer*, May 28, 1978.

335 *"much of the [religious] protest movement"*: Ibid.

335 *throwing acid in the faces of women*: Ibid.

336 *"Bankers suggest that wealthy"*: Jonathan Randal, "Iran's Slow-Motion Crisis Triggers Fears About Future," *Washington Post*, May 29, 1978.

336 *"will play itself out"*: Nicholas Gage, "Shah of Iran Faces Challenge Headed by Muslim Clergy," *New York Times*, June 4, 1978.

336 *"Many Iranians are not so sure"*: Ibid.

17. INTO THE STORM

337 *"Nobody can overthrow me"*: "Nobody Can Overthrow Me—I Have the Power," *U.S. News & World Report*, June 26, 1978.

337 *"The Shah will be gone before I leave"*: Author interview with Charlie Naas, March 14, 2013.

337 *"Rumors and alarmist reports notwithstanding"*: "Yesterday's Quiet Non-Event Shows Lack of Support for Intimidation," *Kayhan International*, June 6, 1978.

337 *"Political sources said the surprise dismissal"*: "Shah of Iran Fires Feared Security Chief," *Washington Post*, June 7, 1978.

338 *"I'm sure you know your job"*: Hushang Nahavandi, *The Last Shah of Iran* (London: Aquilion, 2005).

338 *"Well, I hope you're satisfied"*: Ibid., p. 114.

338 *"Who says the intellectuals don't like us?"*: Ibid.

338 *"the stability and unity of Iran"*: Ibid., p. 115.

339 *"gratified to see you here again"*: Ibid.

339 *"Eighteen months ago"*: Amir Taheri, "Why the Shahanshah Has Endorsed Liberalization: New Frame for a New Picture," *Kayhan International*, June 10, 1978.

339 *"This was the first time"*: Ibid.

340 *"unthinkable in a totalitarian system"*: "Dissent 'Proves Liberalization Is a Success,'" *Kayhan International*, May 2, 1978.

341 *"Many feel that an accelerated process"*: Uri-Bar Joseph, "Forecasting a Hurricane: Israeli and American Estimates of the Khomeini Revolution," *Journal of Strategic Studies* 36, issue 5 (2013): 13.

341 *"out of the woods"*: Airgram, Ambassador Sullivan to Secretary of State, "Subject: Why the Sudden Quiet?" May 28, 1978, *Iran: The Making of US Policy, 1977–80*, National Security Archive (Alexandria, VA: Chadwyck-Healey, 1990), document 01401.

341 *Sullivan played tennis on Tuesdays*: Author interview with Hossein Nasr, August 21, 2013.

341 *"began to pester me"*: Ibid.

341 *Stempel was introduced to Bazargan*: Memorandum of Conversation, "Liberation Movement of Iran (LMI)—Views on Politics in Iran," Engineer Mehdi Bazargan, Dr. Yadollah Sahabi, Mohammad Tavakoli, John Stempel, May 25, 1978, *Iran: The Making of US Policy, 1977–80*, document 01399.

342 *"looked forward to a dialogue"*: Ibid.

342 *"indicating the LMI"*: Ibid.

342 *"The fix is in"*: Author interview with Henry Precht, March 13, 2013.

342 *Deputy Chief of Mission Charlie Naas*: Details of Charlie Naas's biography taken from his interview with the author, March 14, 2013.

342 *"raised the question whether [he]"*: Secret: Consulate Principal Officers' Conference, June 5, 1978, *Iran: The Making of US Policy, 1977–80*, document 1438. Note: Document is dated June 5, but actual date of conference was July 5, 1978.

343 *"fall guy for Iran's problems"*: Ibid.

343 *"What do you think, Mike?"*: Author interview with Charlie Naas, March 14, 2013.

344 *124-degree Fahrenheit*: "Eight Dead in Abadan's Unprecedented Heatwave," *Kayhan International*, June 11, 1978.

344 *40-mile-per-hour wind gusts*: "Ahwaz Brought to Standstill by Heatwave," *Kayhan International*, June 12, 1978.

344 *burning freshwater melons*: Ibid.

344 *Television antennae*: Ibid.

344 *"the city was left in total silence"*: Ibid.

344 *eight hours a day*: "Eight Dead in Abadan's Unprecedented Heatwave."

344 *"to see if there is enough water"*: "No Power or Water Cuts, City Promised," *Kayhan International*, February 6, 1978.

344 *"The national power network"*: "Electricity Cuts Unlikely—'but No Promises,'" *Kayhan International*, March 16, 1978.

344 *"forced to shut down"*: "Ahwaz Brought to Standstill by Heatwave."

344 *ten heat-related deaths*: Ibid.

344 *numerous cases of food poisoning*: "Eight Dead in Abadan's Unprecedented Heatwave."

344 *thousands of residents*: "Ahwaz Brought to Standstill by Heatwave."

345 *"a shortage of drinking water"*: Ibid.

345 *the United Nations warned Iran*: "Locust Plague Threatens Iran," *Kayhan International*, June 13, 1978.

345 *Observation posts were erected*: "Full Alert Against Locusts Ordered," *Kayhan International*, June 24, 1978.

345 *seventeen hundred staff laid off*: "Job Cuts at Customs," *Kayhan International*, March 11, 1978.

345 *eight hundred employees retired*: Ibid.

345 *"trucks importing materials for a firm"*: "Newsbriefs," *Kayhan International*, June 27, 1978.

345 *"There were no controls"*: Author interview with former Savak agent, July 2013.

346 *tax burden would increase*: "New Air-Tight System to Catch Tax Dodgers," *Kayhan International*, June 11, 1978.

346 *"hunt down" tax cheats*: Ibid.

346 *a traveler who paid $30*: Gregory Lima, "Iranians Go Further Afield in Search of Big Bargain," *Kayhan International*, July 6, 1978.

346 *the most punitive in the world*: Ibid.

346 *"The further abroad you go"*: Ibid.

346 *Shah sent several intermediaries*: Details of the Shah's efforts to forge common ground with moderate ulama during June and July can be gleaned from U.S. embassy documents. See, for example, Memorandum of Conversation, Hedayat Eslaminia and George Lambrakis, June 21, 1978, *Iran: The Making of US Policy, 1977–80*, document 1427, and Memorandum of Conversation Between Mehdi Bazargan, Mohammad Tavakoli, Yadollah Sahebi, and John Stempel, "Liberation Movement of Iran (LMI)—Uncertainty over Iranian Politics, Reticence in American Contact," ibid., July 18, 1978, document 1442.

347 *shocked his own rank and file*: Author interview with Parviz Sabeti, May 10, 2014.

347 *"When he came back"*: Ibid.

347 *"His Majesty said this is wrong"*: Ibid.

347 *"I control this city"*: "Peaceful Iran Protest Breaks Six-Month Cycle of Violence," *Washington Post*, June 18, 1978.

347 *demonstrations were reported in Isfahan*: Ibid.

347 *saboteurs attacked Ferdowsi University*: "Attackers Kill Guard at Mashad University," *Kayhan International*, June 19, 1978.

348 *incinerated one guard*: "Guard Dies," *Kayhan International*, June 25, 1978.

348 *fire quickly spread from the basement*: "Cinema Blaze," *Kayhan International*, June 20, 1978.

348 *meant "no new 'martyrs' "*: "Peaceful Iran Protest Breaks Six-Month Cycle of Violence."

348 *"This morning I had an audience"*: Author interview with Kambiz Atabai, February 15, 2013.

348 *"The liberalization will continue"*: "Nobody Can Overthrow Me—I Have the Power."

349 *"escorted to the Imperial Stand"*: Soumaya Saikali, "Fourth Tus Festival Opened by Empress," *Kayhan International*, July 8, 1978.

349 *bearing a secret communication from Musa Sadr*: Author interview with Khalil al-Khalil, April 8, 2013. Al-Khalil's account was backed up by Parviz Sabeti in the author's interview of June 15, 2013.

349 *"In the letter, Musa Sadr offered to help the Shah"*: Author interview with Parviz Sabeti, June 15, 2013.

349 *250,000 Shia villagers*: John K. Cooley, "Shah Promotes Security in Lebanon," *Christian Science Monitor*, April 19, 1978.

349 *The Shah condemned the Israeli action*: "Lebanon Grateful for Prompt Iranian Aid," *Kayhan International*, March 25, 1978.

350 *"By responding quickly to the material needs"*: Cooley, "Shah Promotes Security in Lebanon."

350 *Savak agents who operated under cover*: Ibid.

350 *"plans to end if he can"*: Ibid.

350 *"Musa Sadr was not considered as someone"*: Author interview with Abolhassan Banisadr, July 11, 2013.

350 *"[Musa Sadr] promised Gadhafi to take action"*: Author interview with Khalil al-Khalil, April 8, 2013.

350 *Gadhafi offered to broker*: Kai Bird, *The Good Spy: The Life and Death of Robert Ames* (New York: Crown, 2014), p. 205.

351 *"He actually had a great ambition"*: Author interview with Khalil al-Khalil, April 8, 2013.

351 *At his farewell luncheon*: Author interviews with Khalil al-Khalil, June 21–24, 2013.

351 *"He wants to improve relations"*: Ibid.

351 *"I am ready to help you"*: Author interview with Ali Reza Nourizadeh, May 1, 2015. Nourizadeh was briefed on the contents of the secret message by the Savak agent who carried it from Beirut to Tehran.

352 *"And why not?"*: Author interviews with Khalil al-Khalil, June 21–24, 2013.

352 *knew of the message but not the conditions*: Author interview with Ali Reza Nourizadeh, May 1, 2015.

352 *"The holidays of the summer of 1978"*: Nahavandi (2005), p. 131.

352 *"He would work until one o'clock"*: Author interview with Elli Antoniades, April 3, 2013.

352 *"the elder folk would play cards"*: Nahavandi (2005), p. 131.

352 *"awash with rumors of the Shah's health"*: Telegram, Embassy Tehran to Secretary of State, July 26, 1978, *Iran: The Making of US Policy, 1977–80*, document 01449. Alteration to the Shah's official schedule was announced by the Imperial Court and published on the front page of *Kayhan International* on July 4, 1978.

352 *"At every social occasion embassy officers"*: Telegram, Embassy Tehran to Secretary of State, July 26, 1978.

352 *escorted Lady Bird Johnson*: Lady Bird visited visited Niavaran on Saturday, July 1, 1978. A photograph of her meeting with the Shah and Queen was published the following day on the front page of *Kayhan International*.

353 *"to see if the rumors were true"*: Author interview with Amir Pourshaja, March 16, 2013.
353 *"We sent Charlie up to see the Shah"*: Author interview with John Stempel, February 20, 2013.
353 *six hundred to seven hundred nonimmigrant visas*: "Country Team Minutes: July 19, 1978," *Iran: The Making of US Policy, 1977–80*, document 01488.
354 *inflation fell to 12 percent*: "Iran Slashed Inflation by Two-Thirds—Yeganeh," *Kayhan International*, June 25, 1978.
354 *2.4 percent increase*: "GNP growth 2.4 pc, CBI Reports," *Kayhan International*, June 28, 1978.
354 *a million people flocked to beaches*: "Over a Million Flock Back to Seaside 'Joys,'" *Kayhan International*, July 9, 1978.
354 *granted favorable trade status*: "EC Aide Raises Hopes of Special Status for Iran," *Kayhan International*, June 26, 1978.
354 *"advanced technologies"*: "Irano-German Technology Pact," *Kayhan International*, June 15, 1978.
354 *$12 million date processing plant*: "Hungary Gets Iran Deal," *Kayhan International*, June 18, 1978.
354 *Tehran's underground metro*: "Metro Digs Slowly Under the Capital's Traffic Chaos," *Kayhan International*, June 20, 1978.
354 *the Trans-Iranian Gas Pipeline*: "Prague Set for a Big Iran Gas Role," *Kayhan International*, June 26, 1978. The Shah had mentioned the pipeline to President Nixon during their July 1973 discussions in Washington, DC. See Memorandum of Conversation, Meeting with His Imperial Majesty Mohammad Reza Shah Pahlavi, Shahanshah of Iran on Tuesday, the 24th of July, 1973 at 10:43 a.m.–12:35 p.m., in the Oval Office, National Security Archive.
354 *transit rights of $100 million*: "Prague Set for a Big Iran Gas Role."
354 *four nuclear power plants*: "Iran Agrees to Buy French Nuclear Plants," *Wall Street Journal*, June 27, 1978.
354 *"has been running into increasing financial difficulties"*: Ibid.
354 Close Encounters of the Third Kind: "Film Guide," *Kayhan International*, August 2, 1978.
354 *"Suddenly, we spotted something flashing"*: "UFO . . . or Goofo?" *Kayhan International*, July 26, 1978.
354 *"We think Ali and Amir are having us on"*: Ibid.
355 *duty officers in the control tower*: "Newsbriefs," *Kayhan International*, July 18, 1978.
355 *"pleading a return from vacation"*: Memorandum of Conversation, John Stempel and Guennady Kazankin, July 18, 1978, *Iran: The Making of US Policy, 1977–80*, document 1443.

18. RAMADAN RISING

356 *"What do you think is going on?"*: Author interview with Elli Antoniades, April 4, 2013.
356 *"Iran is not in a revolutionary"*: Memorandum for the President from Zbigniew Brzezinski, NSC Weekly Report 78, November 3, 1978, Jimmy Carter Presidential Library.
356 *fatal car crash*: "Policeman Killed in Mashad Funeral Riot," *Kayhan International*, July 26, 1978.
357 *Sheikh Kafi's funeral procession*: Ibid.
357 *mourners in southern Tehran*: "Tear Gas Used to Quell Demonstrations," *Kayhan International*, July 31, 1978.
357 *buses ferrying American workers*: Charles Ismail Semkus, *The Fall of Iran 1978–79: An Historical Anthology* (New York: Copen, 1979), 46.
357 *teargassed demonstrators*: "Tear Gas Used to Quell Demonstrations."
357 *a police officer was blown up*: Ibid.
357 *Rioters in Shiraz*: Ibid.
357 *six deaths and three hundred arrests*: "Six Deaths, 300 Arrests Reported in Riots," *Kayhan International*, August 1, 1978.
357 *"The relative calm"*: Prepared by Major Don Adamick, "Intelligence Appraisal: Renewal of Civil Disturbances," August 16, 1978, *Iran: The Making of US Policy, 1977–80*, National Security Archive, (Alexandria, VA: Chadwyck-Healey, 1990), document 1472, p. 3.
358 *"The preachers took advantage"*: Author interview with Ali Hossein, 2013.
358 *"Oh, that old man!"*: Hushang Nahavandi, *The Last Shah of Iran* (London: Aquilion, 2005), p. 131.
359 *"Within [the] past few days"*: Telegram from U.S. Embassy to Secretary of State, "Increase in Religious Pressure on Government," August 17, 1978, *Iran: The Making of US Policy, 1977–80*, document 01474.
359 *"Source who has been involved"*: William Branigan, "Thousands Demand Shah End the Exile of Moslem Leader," *Washington Post*, September 5, 1978.
359 *"My father was not pro-monarchy"*: Author interview with Hassan Shariatmadari, September 21, 2014.
359 *"I can't just ring him up"*: Nahavandi (2005), p. 134.
359 *"Shariatmadari was very weak"*: Author interview with Ali Kani, February 23, 2013.
360 *"The failure of the Shah"*: Author interview with Hassan Shariatmadari, September 21, 2014.

360   *the situation in Iran*: "Confidential: Conversation with Iranians Dissident," July 17, 1978, *Iran: The Making of US Policy, 1977–80*, document 1439.

360   *"We have a constitution"*: Nahavandi (2005), p. 140.

360   *"to come to some sort of"*: Cable from Embassy Tehran to Secretary of State, "Implications of Iran's Religious Unrest," August, 2, 1978, *Iran: The Making of US Policy, 1977–80*, document 01460.

360   *"The paradigm we were working under"*: Author interview with John Stempel, February 20, 2013.

360   *"Still one finds [Prime Minister Amuzegar] to be relaxed"*: Ray Vicker, "The Opposition in Iran," *Wall Street Journal*, August 3, 1978.

361   *disappearance of Ayatollah Jalal Al-Din Taheri*: Cable from Embassy Tehran to Secretary of State, "Implications of Iran's Religious Unrest."

361   *seized control of the streets*: Author e-mail exchange with Hassan Shariatmadari, March 29, 2015.

361   *"one child was hit"*: "Country Team Minutes," August 2, 1978, *Iran: The Making of US Policy, 1977–80*, document 01461.

361   *American Club was firebombed*: Ibid.

361   *"Every day His Majesty"*: Author interview with Amir Pourshaja, March 16, 2013.

362   *Reza Ghotbi flew to Nowshahr*: Author interview with Reza Ghotbi, May 9, 2013.

362   *"He talked about when he and his father"*: Ibid.

362   *"is serious about opening up"*: Cable from Embassy Tehran to Secretary of State, "Shah's Constitution Day Speech Calls for Full Political Liberalization, Free Elections," August 7, 1978, *Iran: The Making of US Policy, 1977–80*, document 1464.

362   *"in terms of political liberties"*: Ibid.

362   *"They are glad the Shah"*: Ibid.

363   *fanned out from Pahlavi Square*: "Ayatollah's Isfahan Home Cordoned Off," *Kayhan International*, August 14, 1978.

363   *"proceeded to pour benzene"*: Ibid.

363   *Amid scenes of complete anarchy*: Ibid.

363   *running gun battles*: "Riots Situation 'Under Control,'" *Kayhan International*, August 15, 1978.

363   *Five police officers died*: "Martial Law, Curfew Follow Isfahan Riots," *Kayhan International*, August 12, 1978.

363   *At 8:00 p.m. on Friday evening*: Ibid.

363   *outside the New Mosque*: "Background to Days of Violence," *Kayhan International*, August 14, 1978.

363   *ramming them through police lines*: Ibid.

363   *"a number of deaths"*: Ibid.

364   *"that said someone had thrown"*: Author interview with Bruce Vernor, March 12, 2013.

364   *"In Babol on the Caspian Sea"*: "After the Abadan Fire," *Time*, September 4, 1978.

364   *a man carrying a black bag*: "Blast Victims Describe Horror," *Kayhan International*, August 15, 1978.

364   *"While I was going to help the injured"*: Ibid.

364   *"the heads of two of them"*: Ibid.

365   *"August was the crucial time"*: Author interview with Fereydoun Ala, May 8, 2013.

365   *"Rhetoric and crowd activity"*: Telegram from U.S. Embassy to Secretary of State, "Increase in Religious Pressure on Government."

365   *"Even before the inception of Zionism"*: Cable from U.S. Embassy to Secretary of State, "Anti-Semitic Campaign by Religious Fundamentalists, Iran: Where Are We Now and Where Are We Going?," August 16, 1978, *Iran: The Making of US Policy, 1977–80*, document 01471.

365   *"People would break their fast"*: Author interview with Reza Ghotbi, May 9, 2013.

366   *"Things are terrible"*: Author interview with Mahnaz Afkhami, August 16, 2013.

366   *Brzezinski received a written report*: Memorandum for the President from Zbigniew Brzezinski, NSC Weekly Report 70, August 11, 1978, Jimmy Carter Presidential Library.

366   *"On balance, I should think"*: Ibid.

367   *"On the one hand"*: Author interview with Zbigniew Brzezinski, September 4, 2015.

367   *"Iran is not in a revolutionary"*: Memorandum for the President from Zbigniew Brzezinski, NSC Weekly Report 78.

368   *"The people will not rest"*: Telegram from U.S. Embassy to Secretary of State, "Increase in Religious Pressure on Government."

368   *"Do your duty by Islam"*: Liz Thurgood, "Iran Dissidents Seek Army Revolt," *Guardian*, August 23, 1978.

368   *"Death to the Shah is an Islamic slogan"*: "Iraq Embarrassed by Iranian Exile," *Guardian*, August 26, 1978.

368 *Soldiers who disobeyed Khomeini's fatwa*: Author interview with Ali Hossein, 2013.

368 *sent General Moghadam*: Telegram from U.S. Embassy to Secretary of State, "Increase in Religious Pressure on Government."

368 *received Charlie Naas*: "Country Team Minutes," August 16, 1978, *Iran: The Making of US Policy, 1977–80*, document 01473.

369 *"recent vandalism"*: Ibid.

369 *"predicted this development"*: General Robert E. Huyser, *Mission to Tehran: The Fall of the Shah and the Rise of Khomeini—Recounted by the U.S. General Who Was Secretly Sent at the Last Minute to Prevent It* (New York: Harper & Row, 1986), p. 11.

369 *"what do you think is going on in my country?"*: Author interview with Charlie Naas, March 14, 2013.

369 *"The Shah was asking"*: Author interview with Elli Antoniades, April 4, 2013.

370 *"We offer the people the Great Civilization"*: Raji Samghabadi, "Communists 'Stirred Up Wave of Riots,'" *Kayhan International*, August 19, 1978.

370 *"Press noted this could mean change"*: Telegram from U.S. Embassy to Secretary of State, "Shah Gives Warning and Promises to Dissidents," August 21, 1978, *Iran: The Making of US Policy, 1977–80*, document 01479.

371 *"The press conference went badly"*: Author interview with Mahnaz Afkhami, August 16, 2013.

371 *"somebody with [the] confidence"*: Telegram from U.S. Embassy to Secretary of State, "Increase in Religious Pressure on Government."

371 *"because he is a religious man himself"*: Ibid.

371 *"When the revolution began"*: Author interview with Hossein Nasr, August 21, 2013.

372 *"I have heard [the ulama] believed"*: Author interview with Hassan Shariatmadari, September 21, 2014.

372 *"Musa Sadr was a threat"*: Author interview with Ali Kani, February 23, 2013.

372 *hosted an old friend*: Author interview with Ali Reza Nourizadeh, May 1, 2015.

372 *"You don't know Khomeini"*: Ibid.

372 *"crazy"*: Author interview with Parviz Sabeti, June 15, 2013.

372 *"Our ambassador in Syria"*: Ibid.

372 *"in a virtual state of war"*: "Reform-Minded Opposition Must Join the War Against Subversion," *Kayhan International*, August 19, 1978.

373 *"The Shah is on a tight rope"*: Telegram from U.S. Embassy to Secretary of State, "Iran: Where Are We Now and Where Are We Going?," August 17, 1978, *Iran: The Making of US Policy, 1977–80*, document 01474.

373 *"Goose-stepping Iranian soldiers"*: William Branigan, "Little Joy Greets Shah's Anniversary," *Washington Post*, August 20, 1978.

373 *"More than half the doctors"*: "Newsbriefs," *Kayhan International*, July 29, 1978.

373 *"The cinema is on fire!"*: James Buchan, *Days of God: The Revolution in Iran and Its Consequences* (London: Murray, 2012), p. 213.

19. THE GREAT TERROR

374 *"What did I do to them?"*: Author interview with Reza Ghotbi, May 9, 2013.

374 *"He will lead us straight into the abyss"*: Hushang Nahavandi, *The Last Shah of Iran* (London: Aquilion, 2005), p. 124.

374 *"In total darkness"*: "Survivors Describe Panic-Filled Scene," *Kayhan International*, August 21, 1978.

374 *"It began at the corner"*: Ibid.

374 *"The cries for help"*: Ibid.

374 *The first fire crew*: "Inquiry Rules Arson, Blasts Fire Service," *Kayhan International*, August 27, 1978.

375 *"The cinema was engulfed"*: "Survivors Describe Panic-Filled Scene."

375 *"Several rescuers collapsed"*: "Holocaust," *Kayhan International*, August 21, 1978.

375 *One of the few survivors*: Arsonist Hossein Takbalizadeh was eventually tried and convicted of murder by an Iranian court after the revolution. This author's account of his personal background and subsequent involvement in the Rex Cinema fire hews to that provided by James Buchan in *Days of God: The Revolution in Iran and Its Consequences* (London: Murray, 2012), pp. 210–213.

375 *affiliated with the local chapter*: Author interview with Assdollah Nasr, October 10, 2014.

376 *at least 430*: "Iran Theater Fire Death Toll Rises to 430," *Los Angeles Times*, August 21, 1978.

376 *"The holocaust stunned Iranians"*: "Holocaust."

376 *cinemas closed their doors*: "Cinemas Closing to Mark Tragedy," *Kayhan International*, August 22, 1978.

376 *"echo with scores"*: "Abadan Still in Shock," *Kayhan International*, August 22, 1978.

376 *draped in black*: Ibid.

376   *treated hundreds of people for shock*: Ibid.

376   *ran out of tranquilizers*: Ibid.

376   *gathered in town squares*: Ibid.

376   *twenty-nine cinemas*: "Cinemas, Restaurants Hit by Wave of Arson Bids," *Kayhan International*, August 21, 1978.

376   *"The Khomeini people selected August 19"*: Author interview with Assdollah Nasr, October 10, 2014.

376   *123 bombs*: "Premier Unveils Marxist Plot," *Kayhan International*, September 17, 1978.

376   *set fire to a cinema in Mashad*: "Cinemas, Restaurants Hit by Wave of Arson Bids."

376   *cinema fire in Shiraz*: Ibid.

376   *Hatam Restaurant, on Pahlavi Avenue*: Ibid.

376   *the Baccara, the capital's biggest nightclub*: Ibid.

377   *plant explosives on the roofs*: "30 Shops Gutted in South Tehran." *Kayhan International*, August 24, 1978.

377   *Southern Tehran's vegetable market*: Ibid.

377   *three children were injured*: Ibid.

377   *arsonists destroyed a brewery*: Tony Allaway, "Iran Police Protected from Mourners," *Times* (London), August 23, 1978.

377   *a mob threw rocks at a school*: Ibid.

377   *the Darvish nightclub was bombed*: "Demonstrations, Riots Continue in Abadan," *Kayhan International*, August 27, 1978.

377   *a large blaze*: Tony Allaway, "Iran Shuts All Cinemas as Abadan Toll Reaches 430," *Times* (London), August 22, 1978.

377   *restaurant was bombed in Yazd*: "Demonstrations, Riots Continue in Abadan."

377   *private construction company*: Ibid.

377   *"There is no question now"*: "We Must All Join Up to Stop This Madness," *Kayhan International*, August 21, 1978.

377   *"who have urged people"*: "Holocaust."

377   *"hot-headed people"*: "Nation Is Stunned by Tragedy," *Kayhan International*, August 21, 1978.

377   *"Such a crime"*: "Fascists Behind Fire," *Kayhan International*, August 28, 1978.

378   *"As always, the reception was sumptuous"*: Nahavandi (2005), p. 151.

378   *"mingled with the guests"*: Ibid.

378   *"Usually when there was a tragedy"*: Author interviews with Farah Pahlavi, March 23–25, 2013.

378   *"This heart-rending tragedy"*: Imam Khomeini, *Islam and Revolution: Writings and Declarations of Imam Khomeini (1941–1980)*, trans. Hamid Algar (Berkeley, CA: Mizan, 1981), pp. 231–232.

378   *"the burning of human life"*: "Shariatmadari Leads Clergy Condemnation," *Kayhan International*, August 22, 1978.

378   *a crowd of thirty thousand*: Allaway, "Iran Police Protected from Mourners."

379   *ten thousand mourners*: "Wild Scenes at Mass Funeral," *Kayhan International*, August 23, 1978.

379   *"Men, women and children"*: Ibid.

379   *Boy Scouts, who sobbed*: Ibid.

379   *beaten and bloodied*: Ibid.

379   *Mourners rioted*: Author interview with Assdollah Nasr, October 10, 2014.

379   *the Shah telephoned Khuzestan governor*: Ibid.

379   *bag checks*: "Nation Steps Up Security," *Kayhan International*, August 24, 1978.

379   *waving black flags*: "Demonstrations, Riots Continue in Abadan."

379   *police were ambushed*: Ibid.

379   *rioted outside a mosque*: Ibid.

379   *set fire to a branch of Bank Saderat*: Ibid.

379   *In nearby Karaj*: "Two Killed in Qom as Rioting Spreads," *Kayhan International*, August 29, 1978.

380   *burned the grand bazaar*: "Abadan, Qom Hit by Continued Riot Wave," *Kayhan International*, August 28, 1978.

380   *"I cut my stay short"*: Author interview with Reza Ghotbi, March 25, 2013.

380   *"We were not panicking in August"*: Author interview with Charlie Naas, March 14, 2013.

381   *"While You Were Away"*: Memorandum for Ambassador Sullivan from John Stempel, "While You Were Away . . . the Place Didn't Turn to Crap, but It Might Have Looked Like It," August 22, 1978, *Iran: The Making of US Policy, 1977–80*, National Security Archive (Alexandria, VA: Chadwyck-Healey, 1990), document 1483.

381   *start drawing up*: Uri-Bar Joseph, "Forecasting a Hurricane: Israeli and American Estimates of the Khomeini Revolution," *Journal of Strategic Studies* 36, issue 5 (2013): 14.

381   *"Some of the slogans say 'Jews out of Iran'"*: "Anti-Jewish Slogans Surface in Iran," *Jerusalem Post*, August 25, 1978.

381   *"calling on Iranian oil workers"*: Ibid.

381   *"Many of those who have already left"*: Ibid.

381   *"expressed concern that Jews"*: Author interview with Charlie Naas, March 14, 2013.

381   *"When the King came back"*: Author interview with Reza Ghotbi, May 9, 2013.

382   *"What did I do to them?"*: Ibid.

382   *"If the people are so ungrateful"*: Author interview with Parviz Sabeti, June 15, 2013.

382   *"In the past few days"*: NSC Evening Report, August 29, 1978, Jimmy Carter Presidential Library.

383   *canceled the controversial deal*: Bijan Mossavar-Rahmani, "Iran Drops Plan to Store Austrian Nuclear Wastes," *Kayhan International*, August 23, 1978.

383   *sent his brothers and sisters*: Author interview with Gholam Reza Pahlavi, conducted via e-mail, December 4, 2014.

383   *On the morning of Thursday, August 24*: Nahavandi (2005), p. 161.

383   *"I permit myself to intercede"*: Ibid., p. 162.

384   *"I thought Nahavandi should be prime minister"*: Author interviews with Farah Pahlavi, March 23–25, 2013.

384   *"I proposed Nahavandi"*: Author interview with Reza Ghotbi, May 9, 2013.

384   *the palace confirmed*: "Change of Government: Sharif-Emami Will Head New Cabinet," *Kayhan International*, August 27, 1978.

384   *"I thought it was a joke"*: Author interviews with Ardeshir Zahedi, October 27–28, 2012.

384   *was "astonished at the choice"*: Ashraf Pahlavi, *Faces in a Mirror* (Englewood Cliffs, NJ: Prentice-Hall, 1980), p. 201.

384   *"for us—and by us I mean the Pahlavis"*: Parviz C. Radji, *In the Service of the Peacock Throne: The Diaries of the Shah's Last Ambassador to London* (London: Hamish Hamilton, 1983), p. 224.

385   *"had been too rapid"*: "'Save Iran from Edge of Abyss,'" *Kayhan International*, August 28, 1978.

385   *the Pahlavi state was in full retreat*: "Major Concessions to Clergy, Opposition," *Kayhan International*, August 28, 1978.

385   *"The Club Discotheque"*: "After the Abadan Fire," *Time*, September 4, 1978.

385   *Imam Musa Sadr had arrived in Tripoli*: The Sadr family has produced a time line of events documenting what they know to be true in relation to the disappearance of Imam Musa Sadr in Libya in August 1978. The undated document is titled "The Disappearance of Imam Mussa al Sadr, Sheikh Mohammad Ya'cub and Mr. Abbas Badreddin in Libya."

385   *"The Call of the Prophets"*: Imam Musa Sadr, president of the Higher Shiite Islamic Council, "The Call of the Prophets," *Le Monde*, August 23, 1978.

386   *"Arriving at the Tripoli airport"*: Kai Bird, *The Good Spy: The Life and Death of Robert Ames* (New York: Crown, 2014), p. 205.

387   *one of the Imam's friends*: Author interview with Ali Reza Nourizadeh, May 1, 2015.

387   *Security was so tight*: William Branigan, "Unrest, Soviet Shadow Upstaged Hua in Iran," *Washington Post*, September 2, 1978.

387   *"Security around Hua's Golestan Palace"*: Ibid.

387   *An evening rally*: Ibid.; "183 Detained as Rioters Take to Tehran Streets," *Kayhan International*, August 31, 1978.

387   *the King was approached by an aide*: This account of the Shah's discussion with Saddam Hussein concerning Khomeini was provided by Ahmad Ahrar in a letter dated October 24, 2015. Ahrar was personally briefed on the contents of the discussion the next day by Prime Minister Sharif-Emami.

388   *recommended that his government*: Joseph, "Forecasting a Hurricane," p. 14.

388   *"flooding back into town from Europe"*: Konjkav, "Talk of the Town," *Kayhan International*, September 2, 1978.

388   *new Hyatt Crown Tehran*: Ruth Iravani, ed., *Iran Scene* (Tehran: Iran Scene International, 1978), p. 5.

388   *The Merry Widow*: "Tehran Diary," *Kayhan International*, September 6, 1978.

388   *works by Corelli and Tchaikovsky*: Iravani, "Iran Scene Calendar," *Iran Scene*, pp. 6–7.

388   *Museum of Contemporary Art*: Ibid.

388   *Shahin Farhat at the City Theater*: Ibid.

388   *final weekend of water skiing*: Iravani, "Leisure Time Activities," *Iran Scene*, pp. 18–19.

388   *Mini-City amusement park*: Ibid.

389   *One wealthy couple*: This story was told to the author by an Iranian living in the United States who wished to remain anonymous.

389   *"the windows of their homes broken"*: Amir Taheri, *The Spirit of Allah: Khomeini and the Islamic Revolution* (Bethesda, MD: Adler & Adler, 1986, p. 216.

389   *"Death to the Shah!"*: Author interview with Elli Antoniades, April 3, 2013.

389   *"There was usually dinner for forty people"*: Ibid.

20. BLACK FRIDAY

390   *"By saying this he lost God's farr"*: Abolqasem Ferdowsi, *Shahnameh: The Persian Book of Kings,* trans. Dick Davis (New York: Penguin, 2006), p. 8.

390   *"If my people don't want me"*: Author interview with Reza Ghotbi, March 25, 2013.

390   *fifteen thousand people*: Most estimates of the Qeitariyeh crowd settled on a figure of fourteen thousand to fifteen thousand. William Branigan, "Thousands Demand Shah End Exile of Muslim Leader," *Washington Post,* September 5, 1978.

390   *"long march"*: "Massive March for Peace," *Kayhan International,* September 5, 1978.

390   *"Motorcyclists for Allah"*: Charles Kurzman, *The Unthinkable Revolution in Iran* (Cambridge, MA: Harvard University Press, 2004), p. 63.

390   *"Iran is our country!"*: Branigan, "Thousands Demand Shah."

390   *"At one point"*: "Massive March for Peace."

391   *pitchers of water*: Charles Ismail Semkus, *The Fall of Iran 1978-79: An Historical Anthology* (New York: Copen, 1979), p. 119.

391   *"clearly frightened by the size"*: Ibid.

391   *two hundred thousand*: Estimates of the crowd's size ranged from a hundred thousand to a million. Most observers settled on a figure of between two hundred thousand and a quarter million. See Kurzman (2004), p. 63.

391   *"I was in the middle of the crowd"*: Ibid.

391   *"The never before sighted"*: "Massive March for Peace."

391   *reported violent clashes*: "Clashes in Provincial Cities Claim Ten Lives," *Kayhan International,* September 6, 1978.

391   *"the meeting would be similar"*: The deception is detailed in Kurzman (2004), pp. 62–63.

392   *"These groups and 'parties'"*: Amir Taheri, "Liberalization or Iron Fist?," *Kayhan International,* September 13, 1978.

392   *asked his bodyguard Colonel Djahinbini*: Author interview with Kiomars Djahinbini, May 13, 2015. Almost every account of that day has the Shah flying over the crowd; not so. According to Colonel Djahinbini, who never left his side, at no time did the Shah fly over street protests in 1978. But the sight of the Imperial helicopter flown by others created the legend that he did. In Mohammad Heikal's *The Return of the Ayatollah: The Iranian Revolution from Mossadeq to Khomeini* (London: Deutsch, 1981), p. 152, the Shah is quoted as asking his pilot, "Are all these people demonstrating against me?" The conversation never happened. In Gholam Reza Afkhami's *The Life and Times of the Shah* (Berkeley: University of California Press, 2009), p. 462, the Shah is said to have listened to a tape recording of the demonstrators calling for his downfall. In fact, the Shah received a verbal account of the chants from the three officials who made the helicopter reconnaissance at his request.

392   *hastily arranged a visit*: "Surprise Empress Tour Draws Crowd," *Kayhan International,* September 5, 1978.

393   *several thousand*: Hushang Nahavandi, *The Last Shah of Iran* (London: Aquilion, 2005), p. 185.

393   *"Long live the Shah!"*: Ibid.

393   *said "the crowd was so large"*: "Surprise Empress Tour Draws Crowd."

393   *"It was a remarkable"*: Nahavandi (2005), p. 185.

393   *They estimated the crowd*: Author interview with Kiomars Djahinbini, May 13, 2015.

393   *"He was like a man"*: Anthony Parsons, *The Pride and the Fall: Iran 1974-1979* (London: Cape, 1984), p. 77.

393   *"If my people don't want me"*: Author interview with Reza Ghotbi, March 25, 2013.

394   *"The Shah was not in a good way"*: Author interviews with Ardeshir Zahedi, October 27-28, 2012.

394   *Zahedi tried to talk*: Ibid.

394   *picked up at the airport*: Ibid.

394   *"Don't say anything bad"*: Ibid. Zahedi has told the story of his dramatic late-night encounters with the Shah and Queen Farah on September 4, 1978, on at least two separate occasions. The version he told this author in 2012 was virtually identical to the one he relayed to Mike Evans, author of *Jimmy Carter: The Liberal Left and World Chaos* (Phoenix: Time Worthy Books, 2009), pp. 143–44.

394   *"If you have too many midwives"*: Ibid.

395   *"They recalled the crisis in 1963"*: Author interview with Kambiz Atabai, May 17, 2013.

395   *quiet visit to southern Tehran*: Ibid.

395 *Operation Kach*: Ibid. Details of the plan were confirmed by Parviz Sabeti and Kambiz Atabai to the author.

395 *"The police would have a list"*: Author interviews with Ardeshir Zahedi, October 27–28, 2013.

395 *raid on a police barracks*: Tony Allaway, "Terror Raid on Tehran Police Post," *Times* (London), September 7, 1978, and "Public Meetings Curbed by Iran," *Washington Post*, September 7, 1978.

396 *ban on all unauthorized rallies*: "Unauthorized Rallies Banned," *Kayhan International*, September 7, 1978.

396 *twenty thousand people*: Ibid.

396 *tossed a pipe bomb under a bus*: "Bomb Hurled at Bus with 18 Britons," *Kayhan International*, September 7, 1978.

396 *tens of thousands*: Though most accounts agreed on a figure of a hundred thousand protesters ("The Shah's Divided Land," *Time*, September 18, 1978, p. 32), French diplomats in Tehran put the number much lower, at fifty thousand. See Memorandum of Conversation: "Internal Situation," September 15, 1978, *Iran: The Making of US Policy, 1977–80*, National Security Archive (Alexandria, VA: Chadwyck-Healey, 1990), document 1523.

396 *"Death to the Shah!"*: "Iran Explodes," *Newsweek*, September 18, 1978, p. 41.

396 *"dreaming of an ocean"*: Jonathan Kirkendall, personal scrapbook: "A Senior and a Revolution," May 1979.

396 *"The ball has started rolling"*: Ibid.

396 *held a working lunch*: "Shahanshah, Japan PM Hold Talks over Lunch," *Kayhan International*, September 9, 1978.

396 *"visibly shaken"*: "Iran Explodes," p. 41.

396 *"who argued that the demonstrations"*: "The Shah's Divided Land," p. 32.

397 *appointed the Islamic scholar Hossein Nasr*: "Empress Bureau Chief Introduced to Monarch," *Kayhan International*, September 9, 1978.

397 *"Ayatollahs Shariatmadari and Khonsari"*: Author interview with Hossein Nasr, August 21, 2013.

397 *"As I flew over the Shahyad Monument"*: Ashraf Pahlavi, *Faces in a Mirror* (Englewood Cliffs, NJ: Prentice-Hall, 1980), p. 205.

398 *"Why aren't we doing anything about it?"*: Author interview with Reza Golsorkhi, May 13, 2013.

398 *a small group came to Ashraf's residence*: Ibid.

398 *"His Majesty is in control"*: Ibid.

398 *Iranian guests attending*: "Missing Party Guest Has Everyone in a Dither," *Kayhan International*, September 9, 1978.

398 *handed a note*: Nahavandi (2005), p. 188.

398 *plot by Khomeini's agents*: Joe Alex Morris Jr., "Iran in Turmoil as Shah Begins 38th Year of Rule," *Los Angeles Times*, September 17, 1978.

398 *In the debate that followed*: Accounts of the cabinet meeting appear in Afkhami (2009), p. 464; Nahavandi (2005), pp. 189–190; and Telegram from Ambassador Sullivan to Secretary of State, "Situation in Iran," September 10, 1978, *Iran: The Making of US Policy, 1977–80*, document 1507.

398 *He expressed ambivalence*: Nahavandi (2005), p. 190.

399 *Ardeshir Zahedi made clear*: Author interviews with Ardeshir Zahedi, October 27–28, 2013.

399 *The Queen worried*: Author interviews with Farah Pahlavi, March 23–25, 2013.

399 *finishing up his last day at work*: Author interview with Reza Ghotbi, March 25, 2013.

399 *received another harried call*: Ibid.

399 *instructed that a helicopter be readied*: Author interview with Reza Ghotbi, March 25, 2013.

399 *the modest traffic circle*: During his 2013 visit to Iran the author walked through Jaleh Square to gain a sense of its size and proportions.

400 *several thousand people converged*: William Branigan, "Iranian Troops Fire on Crowds; Scores Killed," *Washington Post*, September 9, 1978.

400 *"Khomeini did not believe in armed struggle"*: Author interview with Ali Hossein, 2013.

401 *"According to witnesses"*: Branigan, "Iranian Troops Fire." The author reviewed every available account he could and found Branigan's to be the most immediate and dispassionate of those filed by reporters from the scene.

401 *"At Jaleh Square there were people"*: Author interview with Ali Hossein, 2013.

401 *sent a ballistics expert*: Author interview with Bruce Vernor, March 12, 2013.

401 *"troops were attacked"*: Telegram from Ambassador Sullivan to Secretary of State, "Crowd Control Equipment in Iran," September 14, 1978, *Iran: The Making of US Policy, 1977–80*, document 01521.

401 *"Shortly after the shooting"*: Branigan, "Iranian Troops Fire."

401 *"angrily shouted anti-Shah slogans"*: Ibid.

401 *Charlie Naas was leaving*: Author interview with Charlie Naas, March 14, 2013.

402 *"heard the radio announce"*: Memorandum for the Files, "Dinner Conversation at DCM's Residence," October 16, 1978, *Iran: The Making of US Policy, 1977–80*, document 01612.

402 *He set out in an ambulance*: Author interview with Fereydoun Ala, May 8, 2013.

402 *dragged in mattresses*: Ibid.

402 *"The hospital's ramp"*: Liz Thurgood, "Shah's Men Turn Guns on Crowds," *Guardian*, September 9, 1978.

402 *more than a hundred fires*: "100 Fires Set During Friday Disturbances," *Kayhan International*, September 10, 1978.

402 *Flames engulfed the Armstrong Hotel*: Ibid.

402 *Twelve banks, two supermarkets, etc.*: Ibid.

402 *"South-east Tehran"*: Tony Allaway, "Protesters Shot Down as Iran Imposes Martial Law in 12 Cities," *Times* (London), September 9, 1978.

403 *"Unless the government makes a bigger show of force"*: Branigan, "Iranian Troops Fire."

403 *Khomeini's men were quick*: Thurgood, "Shah's Men Turn Guns on Crowds," and Branigan, "Iranian Troops Fire."

403 *"It's the Israelis!"*: Liz Thurgood, "Shah's Men Turn Guns on Crowds."

403 *Ayatollah Nouri had been murdered*: Liz Thurgood, "The Shah Goes Back to Rule by the Bullet," *Guardian*, September 11, 1978.

403 *eighty-six deaths*: "Tehran Calm as Toll Hits 86 Dead," *Kayhan International*, September 10, 1978.

403 *three thousand killed*: Liz Thurgood, "3,000 Deaths in Iran Say Shah's Opponents," *Guardian*, September 13, 1978.

403 *"3,000 DEATHS IN IRAN"*: Ibid.

403 *"a gross underestimate"*: Thurgood, "The Shah Goes Back."

403 *three thousand bodies buried in a "mass grave"*: Thurgood, "3,000 Deaths."

403 *forty new bodies*: Kurzman (2004), p. 75.

403 *eighty-eight*: http://www.emadbaghi.com/en/archives/000592.php#more.

403 *"an immensely saddened man"*: "An Interview with the Shah," *Time*, September 18, 1979.

403 *"the Shah looked awful"*: Evening Report, National Security Council, September 10, 1978, Jimmy Carter Presidential Library.

404 *"I would like to wave goodbye"*: Ibid.

404 *Princess Ashraf went to see her brother*: Author interview with Reza Golsorkhi, May 13, 2013.

404 *"completely calm on the surface"*: A. Pahlavi (1980), p. 205.

404 *"What will you do?"*: Ibid.

404 *"His Majesty has asked me to leave"*: Author interview with Reza Golsorkhi, May 13, 2013.

404 *The call from Camp David*: President Carter Telephone Conversation with the Shah, National Security Council, September 10, 1978, Jimmy Carter Presidential Library.

404 *"flat, almost mechanical voice"*: Gary Sick, *All Fall Down: America's Tragic Encounter with Iran* (New York: Random House, 1985), p. 51.

405 *"smell the burning tires"*: Uri-Bar Joseph, "Forecasting a Hurricane: Israeli and American Estimates of the Khomeini Revolution," *Journal of Strategic Studies* 36, issue 5 (2013): 15.

405 *reduced by a third*: Ibid., p. 16.

405 *"In many parts of the city"*: William Claiborne, "Army Intensifies Patrols in Tehran," *Washington Post*, September 12, 1978.

405 *forty thousand travelers*: "Tourists Flock to Caspian Beaches," *Kayhan International*, September 17, 1978.

405 *Valiahd Cup*: Ibid.

405 *Association of Girl Guides*: "Global Gathering of Guides Gets to Grips with Important Agenda," *Kayhan International*, September 12, 1978.

405 *"Traffic was chaotic"*: James Underwood, "Curfew Hits Shops, Restaurants," *Kayhan International*, September 14, 1978.

406 *"because in its latest issue"*: "Magazine Ban," *Kayhan International*, September 18, 1978.

406 *"Sentries in battle dress"*: Joe Alex Morris, "Iran's Capital Quiet Under Martial Law," *Los Angeles Times*, September 16, 1978.

406 *"People hardly glanced"*: Underwood, "Curfew Hits Shops, Restaurants."

406 *Outbound flights were booked up*: Parviz C. Radji, *In the Service of the Peacock Throne: The Diaries of the Shah's Last Ambassador to London* (London: Hamish Hamilton, 1983), p. 227.

406 *flow of capital to safe havens*: Telegram from Ambassador Sullivan to Secretary of State, "Economic Impact of Iran's Political Upheaval," September 13, 1978, *Iran: The Making of US Policy, 1977–80*, document 01515.

406 *"As previously reported"*: Ibid.

21. STATE OF SIEGE

407 *"Evil has come to our great house"*: Abolqasem Ferdowsi, *Shahnameh: The Persian Book of Kings*, trans. Dick Davis (New York: Penguin, 2006), p. 798.

407 *"I am fighting for my son"*: "Je Me Force a Oublier la Peur," *Paris Match*, September 22, 1978, p. 57.

407 *replaced Amir Abbas Hoveyda*: "Thousands of Iran Troops, Tanks Enforce Martial Law," *Los Angeles Times*, September 10, 1978.

407 *Ali Qoli Ardalan*: "Statesman Ardalan New Court Minister," *Kayhan International*, September 27, 1978.

407 *code of conduct*: "Shahanshah Bans Royal Influence-Peddling," *Kayhan International*, September 27, 1978. See also "Shah Tells Family to End Ties with Public Bodies," *Washington Post*, September 27, 1978.

407 *"We have always thought"*: John K. Cooley, "Shah of Iran Voices Liberalization Goal," *Christian Science Monitor*, September 19, 1978.

407 *allowed broadcasters to film*: "Uproar in Majlis," *Kayhan International*, September 14, 1978.

408 *shortened curfew hours*: "Curfew Reduced," *Kayhan International*, September 18, 1978.

408 *suppressed the military investigation*: Hushang Nahavandi, *The Last Shah of Iran* (London: Aquilion, 2005), p. 195.

408 *hajj pilgrimages*: "Haj Controls to be Abandoned," *Kayhan International*, September 20, 1978.

408 *electricity and water prices*: "Water and Power Prices to be Frozen," *Kayhan International*, September 21, 1978.

408 *national health insurance*: Vida Moattar, "Full Health Insurance October 23—Minister," *Kayhan International*, September 26, 1978.

408 *arrested 1,106 people*: "Martial Law to be Lifted 'Soon as Possible'," *Kayhan International*, September 25, 1978.

408 *"I don't want any Iranian"*: Author interview with Fereydoun Djavadi, July 13, 2013.

408 *"I overheard the Shah say to Oveissi"*: Author interview with Shahin Fatemi, July 16, 2013.

408 *"What kind of general was I?"*: Ibid.

408 *"How many times have I said to you"*: Ibid.

408 *"There was a lot of pressure"*: Author interview with Kambiz Atabai, February 15, 2013.

409 *"we checked His Majesty's office"*: Author interview with Kiomars Djahinbini, March 25, 2013.

409 *"She is the one with guts"*: Anthony Parsons, *The Pride and the Fall: Iran 1974–1979* (London: Jonathan Cape, 1984), p. 75.

409 *"gripped by a deep sadness"*: "Je Me Force a Oublier la Peur," p. 57.

410 *"had been kidnapped"*: "Shiite Chiefs Kidnap Fear," *Kayhan International*, September 12, 1978.

410 *dispatched a team of investigators*: "Beirut Team Off to Libya to Find Sadr," *Kayhan International*, September 14, 1978.

410 *Interpol issued a worldwide bulletin*: Ibid.

410 *insisted that Musa Sadr had left*: Ibid.

410 *"hotels, boarding houses"*: "An Imam Is Missing," *Time*, October 9, 1978.

410 *Rumors surfaced*: Ibid. See also "Beirut Team Off to Libya to Find Sadr."

410 *"Certainly he is no friend of the Shah"*: Colin Smith, "Mystery of the Missing Imam," *Guardian*, October 1, 1978.

410 *"We strongly believe"*: "Beirut Team Off to Libya to Find Sadr."

411 *"According to Your Majesty"*: Author interview with Ali Kani, February 12, 2013.

411 *"Islam holds the Libyan government"*: "Qom Concern over Sadr," *Kayhan International*, September 17, 1978.

412 *measuring 7.7 on the Richter scale*: "Killer Quake," *Kayhan International*, September 18, 1978. See also "The Town That Disappeared," *Time*, October 2, 1978.

412 *"nothing standing except the palm trees"*: "11,000 Killed in Iran Earthquake," *Times* (London), September 18, 1978.

412 *"Mr. Sharif-Emami did not know"*: Farah Pahlavi, *An Enduring Love: My Life with the Shah* (New York: Miramax, 2004), p. 283.

412 *conduct a nuclear test in the desert*: Curiously, rumors that a Soviet nuclear test had triggered the quake did not cause a similar amount of outrage in Tabas. See "Experts Deny Soviet Quake Link," *Kayhan International*, September 21, 1978.

412 *"Dig out the dead!"*: "Pleas Deluge Iran Empress in Quake Region," *Los Angeles Times*, September 18, 1978.

412 *"Don't go sightseeing!"*: Ibid.

412 *"sat motionless"*: Ibid.

412 *"They gave him the sort of treatment"*: Colin Smith, "When Even the King of Kings Can't Help," *Guardian*, September 24, 1978.

412 *"I do not want anything"*: "Monarch Gives Tabas Hope," *Kayhan International*, September 21, 1978.

413 *"I've always been the top student"*: Ibid.

413 *"There is nothing to talk about"*: John K. Cooley, "Shia Moslem Foes Reject Sitting Down with Shah," *Christian Science Monitor*, September 29, 1978.

413 *"after the initial ambush"*: "Nine Killed in Ambush on Tabriz Patrol," *Kayhan International*, September 17, 1978.

414 *"go and see Fardust for a talk"*: Author interview with Kambiz Atabai, February 15, 2013.

414 *several men in plainclothes*: Author interview with Ali Hossein, 2013.

414 *"I was allowed to stay"*: Ibid.

415 *"Gadhafi arrested him"*: Author interview with Ali Kani, February 12, 2013.

417 *"every right to interfere"*: "Monarch Concerned at Fate of Imam," *Kayhan International*, September 23, 1978.

417 *"We are convinced"* "Iran Clergy Join Hunt for Sadr," *Kayhan International*, September 23, 1978.

418 *"has a better than even chance"*: Uri-Bar Joseph, "Forecasting a Hurricane: Israeli and American Estimates of the Khomeini Revolution," *Journal of Strategic Studies* 36, issue 5 (2013): 16.

418 *Precht made contact with Ibrahim Yazdi*: Author interview with Henry Precht, March 13, 2013.

418 *drafted reports and even talking points*: Ibid.

418 *"peaceful accommodation"*: Ibid.

418 *"may have taken my reporting"*: Author interview with George Lambrakis, September 13, 2014.

418 *"astute"*: Author interview with Henry Precht, March 13, 2013.

419 *"was really pissed off"*: Author interview with John Stempel, February 20, 2013.

419 *"They were of no help at all"*: Author interview with George Lambrakis, September 13, 2014.

419 *"of U.S. support for the Iranian opposition"*: Ibid.

419 *"did have occasional low-level"*: Ibid.

419 *"depressive episodes ever so severe"*: Letter from Henry Precht to Ambassador Sullivan, October 10, 1978, *Iran: The Making of US Policy, 1977–80*, National Security Archive (Alexandria, VA: Chadwyck-Healey, 1990), document 01576.

420 *under house arrest*: "Protests to Iraq Against Khomeini's House Arrest," *Kayhan International*, September 30, 1978. See also Liz Thurgood, "Iraq Backs Silencing of Shah's Critic," *Guardian*, September 27, 1978.

420 *relented on September 25*: "Iraq Lists Restrictions on Shia Leader," *Times* (London), September 26, 1978.

421 *blocked his entry*: Baqer Moin, *Khomeini: Life of the Ayatollah* (London: I. B. Taurus, 1999), p. 189.

421 *approved higher salaries*: Tony Allaway, "Iran Strikers' Demands to be Met," *Times* (London), October 4, 1978. See also "NIOC, Bank Strikes End, *Kayhan International*, October 4, 1978.

421 *"In the spirit of accommodation"*: Telegram, Ambassador Sullivan to Secretary of State, "The Sharif-Emami Government: An Analysis and Projection," October 16, 1978, *Iran: The Making of US Policy, 1977–80*, document 01593.

422 *He continued to insist*: "Shahanshah Urges 'Unity and Oneness,'" *Kayhan International*, October 7, 1978.

422 *"Whatever the regime said"*: Author interview with Ali Hossein, 2013.

422 *the Caspian towns of Babol and Amol*: "Four Die in Caspian Towns as Demonstrations Continue," *Kayhan International*, October 10, 1978.

422 *"I became aware in the second week"*: Author interview with Reza Ghotbi, May 9, 2013.

423 *"The Shah hardly spoke"*: Author interviews with Khalil al-Khalil, June 21–24, 2013.

423 *"Source with good access"*: Telegram from Ambassador Sullivan to Secretary of State, "Ayatollah Khomeini's Plans," October 8, 1978, *Iran: The Making of US Policy, 1977–80*, document 01577.

423 *screened Khomeini's visitors, handled media requests*: Author interview with Abolhassan Banisadr, July 11, 2013.

424 *In his first press interview*: Ibid.

424 *deliberately mistranslated*: Ibid.

424 *"if you don't want to become"*: Ibid.

424 *"What is an Islamic republic?"*: Ibid.

424 *"calm him down"*: Ibid.

22. TEHRAN IS BURNING

425 *"There is nothing"*: Author interview with Maryam Ansary, April 17, 2013.

425 *"I have the feeling there is no hope anymore"*: Farah Pahlavi, *An Enduring Love: My Life with the Shah* (New York: Miramax, 2004), p. 285.

425 *strikes closing*: "Over 2,000 Workers at Sarcheshmeh Join Strike," *Kayhan International*, October 11, 1978.

425   *attacked the Iraqi consulate*: "Gunmen Hit Iraq Mission in South," *Kayhan International*, October 11, 1978.

425   *$50 million a day*: "The Shah's Fight for Survival," *Time*, November 20, 1978, p. 53.

425   *$3 billion since Jaleh Square*: Ibid., p. 52.

425   *the ambassadors*: Konjkav, "Town Talk—Envoy Bids Farewell to Second Home," *Kayhan International*, October 22, 1978.

425   *sent their families out*: "Premier Mobbed by Pressmen," *Kayhan International*, October 5, 1978.

426   *"rule out returning one day"*: Konjkav, "Town Talk—Ramazan Doesn't Believe in Beating About Bush," *Kayhan International*, October 19, 1978.

426   *"Thank heavens we're leaving"*: "Premier Mobbed by Pressmen."

426   *"Iran isn't the Iran it used to be"*: Konjkav, "Town Talk—Austrian Farewell Party More Nostalgic Than Usual," *Kayhan International*, October 21, 1978.

426   *a shadowy group*: The secret plan to oust the King and Queen, and the military contingency plan to withdraw the army south of Tehran to fight a civil war, was described in detail to the author by someone involved in the planning discussions.

426   *"He was nervous and scared"*: Author interviews with Ardeshir Zahedi, October 27–28, 2012.

426   *"Please call the Shah"*: Ibid.

426   *"Have courage"*: Ibid.

427   *"They asked about the strike"*: Author interview with Ali Hossein, 2013.

427   *collapsed by two thirds*: "Iran: At the Brink?" *Newsweek*, November 13, 1978, p. 79.

427   *$60 million*: Jonathan Kandell, "Iran's Oil Workers Told to End Strike or Face Discharge," *New York Times*, November 13, 1978.

427   *"Iran's oil supplies are the regime's jugular vein"*: "Iran: At the Brink?," p. 79.

427   *"a natural transfer of power"*: "Transfer of Power Must Be Natural," *Kayhan International*, October 21, 1978.

428   *"I would walk one step"*: Author interview with Reza Ghotbi, May 9, 2013.

428   *"The mood was somber"*: Author interview with Maryam Ansary, April 17, 2013.

428   *"I went back alone in October"*: Author interview with Princess Manigeh. The Princess responded to written questions with a statement dated November 5, 2014, and e-mailed the same day.

429   *make a televised appeal*: The idea of a televised address was suggested as early as October 21 by Khosrow Eqbal, brother of the late prime minister. Crucially, Eqbal believed the Shah should express sorrow "for some mistakes but he is trying hard and pleads for unity in the future. Iranians will easily forgive somebody who asks their forgiveness." Memorandum of Conversation: Khosrow Eqbal and George Lambrakis, "Internal Situation," October 21, 1978, *Iran: The Making of US Policy, 1977–80*, National Security Archive (Alexandria, VA: Chadwyck-Healey, 1990), document 01607.

429   *"The prime minister was coming to me"*: Author interviews with Farah Pahlavi, March 23–25, 2013.

429   *she was cheered and embraced*: Konjkav, "Town Talk—Ramazan Doesn't Believe in Beating About Bush."

429   *"I have the feeling there is no hope anymore"*: F. Pahlavi (2004), p. 285.

429   *"very sad"*: Author interview with Elli Antoniades, April 3, 2013.

429   *"Death to the Shah"*: Author interview with Kambiz Atabai, June 5, 2015.

429   *"the Shah feels himself"*: NSC Evening Report, October 24, 1978, Jimmy Carter Presidential Library.

430   *"the favorite source"*: Ray Moseley, *In Foreign Fields* (London: Moseley, 2010), p. 133.

430   *"elderly man in rumpled clothing"*: Ibid.

430   *"We were able to intercept some messages"*: Author interview with Henry Precht, March 13, 2013.

430   *"We had the means to do it"*: Author interview with Charlie Naas, March 3, 2014.

430   *the CIA had also intercepted*: Author interview with a former U.S. official who was among those reading transcripts of the Queen's telephone conversations.

431   *"feeding the Shah"*: NSC Evening Report, October 24, 1978.

431   *"He did not want to give"*: NSC Evening Report, October 27, 1978, Jimmy Carter Presidential Library.

431   *"There was not the least demonstration"*: Hushang Nahavandi, *The Last Shah of Iran* (London: Aquilion, 2005), p. 295.

431   *"Sire, no one must notice"*: Ibid.

431   *tens of thousands*: "Four Dead as Rioting Continues," *Kayhan International*, October 26, 1978.

431   *stoned one to death*: Ibid.

431   *terrorist died*: Ibid.

431   *governor's office*: "Gendarmes Fire on Crowd Near Hamadan, 5 Dead," *Kayhan International*, October 28, 1978.

431   *Five people were shot and killed*: Ibid.

431   *hundred thousand*: "Unrest Enters Fifth Week," *Kayhan International*, October 29, 1978.

432 *thirty thousand turned out in Gorgan*: Ibid.
432 *Government buildings*: Ibid.
432 *Rioters burned the center of town in Rasht*: "Now Violence Sweeps Rasht," *Kayhan International*, October 29, 1978.
432 *pulled from her car*: "Gendarmes Fire on Crowd Near Hamadan, 5 Dead."
432 *assassinated the local police chief*: "Soldier Held for Jahrom Shooting," *Kayhan International*, October 29, 1978.
432 *"The entire capital was plagued"*: "Student Defiance in Tehran," *Kayhan International*, October 29, 1978.
432 *"we shot off down a small alley"*: Anthony Parsons, *The Pride and the Fall: Iran 1974–79* (London: Jonathan Cape, 1984), p. 81.
432 *"The more you feed an alligator"*: "The Shah's Fight for Survival," *Time*, November 20, 1978, p. 50.
432 *purged of hard-liners*: "Purge of Savak," *Kayhan International*, October 30, 1978.
432 *1,451 political prisoners*: Tony Allaway, "Shah Frees 1,451 Prisoners as Gesture of Conciliation Towards Opposition Critics," *Times* (London), October 24, 1978.
433 *"My boss cannot make up his mind"*: Author interview with Kambiz Atabai, February 15, 2013.
433 *the army had marched into Abadan*: "Troops Guard Oil," *Kayhan International*, November 1, 1978.
433 *"sober but controlled"*: NSC Evening Report, November 1, 1978, Jimmy Carter Presidential Library.
433 *"leave the country than submit to that"*: Ibid.
433 *three hundred senior officers*: "Iran: At the Brink?"
434 *Baluchi horsemen*: "Horsemen Attack Western Town Leaving Huge Toll," *Kayhan International*, October 31, 1978.
434 *that "his advice to the Shah"*: NSC Evening Report, November 1, 1978.
434 *"reported that none of his efforts"*: Cable from Ambassador Sullivan to Secretary Vance and Dr. Brzezinski, November 1, 1978, Jimmy Carter Presidential Library.
434 *"The fact is there was some"*: Author interview with Zbigniew Brzezinski, September 4, 2015.
435 *"Good news!"*: Memorandum for the President from Zbigniew Brzezinski, NSC Weekly Report 78, November 3, 1978, Jimmy Carter Presidential Library.
435 *"There were students in Western sports jackets"*: "Iran: At the Brink?," p. 78.
435 *"with fixed bayonets"*: Ibid.
435 *"They are only firing in the air!"*: "Mobs Run Wild," *Kayhan International*, November 5, 1978.
435 *five students*: Ibid.
435 *rampaging through the central business district*: Dan Schanche, "Core of Tehran No Longer Safe from Mob Violence," *Los Angeles Times*, November 5, 1978.
435 *"surged onto the hotel grounds"*: Ibid.
436 *"as if by signal"*: Ibid.
436 *Two hundred thousand marched in Isfahan, etc.*: "Two Killed in a Continuing Wave of Provincial Protests," *Kayhan International*, November 5, 1978.
436 *fired into crowds in Kohdasht*: Ibid.
436 *The town of Paveh remained cut off*: "Armed Men Cut Off All Links with Town," *Kayhan International*, November 5, 1978.
436 *Staff at the Post, Telephones, and Telegraph*: "PTT Strike," *Kayhan International*, November 5, 1978.
436 *Iran Air pilots refused to fly*: Ibid.
436 *the port city of Bandar Abbas*: "Transport Grinds to a Halt in Ports," *Kayhan International*, November 5, 1978.
436 *several bomb threats*: "Hilton Bomb Threat Scare," *Kayhan International*, November 5, 1978.
436 *"spent a long prayer session"*: NSC Evening Report, November 4, 1978, Jimmy Carter Presidential Library.
437 *dawned overcast with light drizzle*: "Weather Watch," *Kayhan International*, November 5, 1978.
437 *prepared the banquet hall*: "Tehran Diary," *Kayhan International*, November 5, 1978.
437 *Shadow Theater of China*: Ibid.
437 Fiddler on the Roof: Ibid.
437 *"order was rapidly evaporating"*: NSC Evening Report, November 5, 1978, Jimmy Carter Presidential Library.
437 *"the feeling of extreme tension was palpable"*: Parsons (1984) p. 93.
437 *gathered outside the main gates*: Tony Allaway, "Tehran Burns as Anti-Shah Rioters Go on Rampage," *Times* (London), November 6, 1978.
437 *"sort of shrugged their shoulders"*: Ibid.
437 *"hijacked buses and lorries"*: Ibid.
438 *"carpet stores owned by Jews"*: Ibid.

438   *"One large eleven-story building"*: William H. Sullivan, *Mission to Iran: The US Ambassador* (New York: Norton, 1981), p. 177.

438   *"there is a mob coming toward us"*: Author interview with Bruce Vernor, March 12, 2013.

438   *"forcibly evicted"*: NSC Evening Report, November 5, 1978.

438   *fatally shot in the head*: Barry Came, "Yonky, Go Home," *Newsweek*, November 20, 1978, p. 67.

438   *"Below us on the streets rioters"*: Tony Allaway, "Former Ministers Arrested as Shah Purges Old Regime," *Times* (London), November 8, 1978.

438   *"The Shah is finished"*: William Claiborne, "Government Falls as Iranians Riot," *Washington Post*, November 6, 1978.

438   *"smoke [was] rising over the town"*: Author interview with James and Libby Kirkendall, May 7, 2013.

438   *"The mob spread garbage in the street"*: John Westberg, "We Experience the Gathering Storm of Revolution," personal diaries (1978–79).

439   *"There will be no hysteria"*: Author interview with Roy Colquitt, January 21, 2014.

439   *"they were playing a new game"*: Ibid.

439   *the ride home was a terrifying ordeal*: Author e-mail exchange with Cyndy McCollough, a student whose bus was stoned by rioters, June 3, 2015.

439   *Mobs sacked the ground floor*: Claiborne, "Government Falls." See also Don A. Schanche, "Shah Puts Iran Under Rule of Military Regime," *Los Angeles Times*, November 7, 1978.

439   *seventy-five terrified guests*: Claiborne, "Government Falls."

439   *Two young men working on an adjacent construction site*: Schanche, "Shah Puts Iran Under Rule."

439   *400 banks*: "An End to Iranian Dreams," *Time*, December 4, 1978, p. 66.

439   *"As slogan-chanting demonstrators surged"*: Schanche, "Shah Puts Iran Under Rule."

440   *"When we emerged into the main street"*: Parsons (1984), p. 94.

440   *a large mob was seen advancing*: Allaway, "Tehran Burns."

440   *"This has got to stop"*: Author interview with Kambiz Atabai, June 8, 2013.

441   *"I am the protocol chief"*: Gholam Reza Afkhami, *The Life and Times of the Shah* (Berkeley: University of California Press, 2009), p. 472.

441   *"visibly shaken"*: Ibid.

441   *"While I was puzzling what to do next"*: Sullivan (1981), p. 178.

442   *"make out that he was telling [the Queen] of his intention"*: Ibid., p. 179.

442   *"a thinking, cultured man"*: F. Pahlavi (2004), p. 287.

442   *in a state of high dudgeon*: Parsons (1984), p. 96.

442   *that Mujahedin guerrilla fighters were responsible*: Ibid., p. 99.

443   *"Mr. Ambassador, who is going to be"*: Author interview with Kambiz Atabai, June 8, 2013.

443   *"People threw things"*: Author interview with Elli Antoniades, April 3, 2013.

23. SULLIVAN'S FOLLY

444   *"How hurriedly we are putting nails to our coffin"*: Gholam Reza Afkhami, *The Life and Times of the Shah* (Berkeley: University of California Press, 2009), p. 486.

444   *"Tell the Shah that it is better"*: Author interview with Hossein Nasr, November 18, 2013.

444   *Twenty tanks entered the capital*: Jonathan Kandell, "Iran Arrests Head of Secret Police, Other Officials and Businessmen," *New York Times*, November 8, 1978.

444   *Troops fired into the air*: Ray Vicker, "As Tension Lingers in Iran, Shah Faces Problem of Maintaining Control While Bringing Reforms," *Wall Street Journal*, November 10, 1978.

444   *"A jolly good job, too"*: Tony Allaway, "Tank Watchers in Tehran Await Back-to-Work Day," *Christian Science Monitor*, November 10, 1978.

444   *"We feel the army will give us protection now"*: Vicker, "As Tension Lingers in Iran."

444   *"Maybe now we get peace"*: Ibid.

445   *"Long lines of automobiles and people"*: Ibid.

445   *telex system remained out of order*: William Claiborne, "Former Prime Minister Jailed in Iranian Anticorruption Drive," *Washington Post*, November 9, 1978.

445   *Credit dried up*: "An End to Iranian Dreams," *Time*, December 4, 1978, p. 66.

445   *"With the oil workers on our side"*: "The Shah's Fight for Survival," *Time*, November 20, 1978.

445   *1.2 million barrels a day*: James Tanner, "World Oil Output Is Said to Be Surging as Interruptions in Iran Enter 10th Day," *Wall Street Journal*, November 9, 1978.

445   *"We were suppressed for so many years"*: Jonathan Randal, "No Quick End Seen to Petroleum Strike," *Washington Post*, November 10, 1978.

445   *the Shah had phoned him*: Author interview with Reza Ghotbi, March 25, 2013.

445   *"Sire, I am not a speechwriter"*: Ibid.

446   *"For months, I and Ghotbi"*: Author interview with Hossein Nasr, November 18, 2013.

446 *"She came out"*: Author interviews with Reza Ghotbi, May 9, 2013.

446 *"did not find anything wrong with it"*: Author interviews with Farah Pahlavi, March 23–25, 2013.

446 *"I was asked to see what had happened"*: Statement provided to the author by Dr. Amir Aslan Afshar, former grand master of ceremonies to the Shah of Iran, Walchsee, Austria, August 21, 2015. Dr. Afshar's statement described the events surrounding the Shah's decision to deliver his November 6, 1978, speech to the nation.

446 *"Why have they taken the speech to Her Majesty?"*: Afkhami (2009), p. 479.

447 *"For the first time, the Shah came to my office"*: Afshar, statement, August 21, 2015.

447 *"put him in a position of weakness"*: Author interview with Reza Ghotbi, March 25, 2013.

447 *"I should not say the things"*: Afshar, statement, August 21, 2015.

447 *"if he were to give a speech of this sort"*: Afkhami (2009), p. 479.

447 *threw the speech down*: Afshar, statement, August 21, 2015.

447 *he made several revisions*: Author interview with Reza Ghotbi, March 25, 2013.

447 *"He was not forced or manipulated"*: Ibid.

447 *"In the climate of liberalization"*: NSC Evening Report, November 6, 1978, Jimmy Carter Presidential Library.

447 *"In this speech"*: Afshar, statement, August 21, 2015.

448 *"The tone was contrite"*: "The Shah's Fight for Survival," *Time*, November 20, 1978.

448 *"People called the court"*: Author interview with Reza Ghotbi, March 25, 2013.

448 *phone Nasr afterward*: Ibid. See also Afkhami (2009), p. 480.

448 *"I should never have agreed"*: Afshar, statement, August 21, 2015.

448 *"In one hand, the Shah held out"* "The Shah's Fight for Survival," p. 50.

448 *"Until the day an Islamic republic"*: Ronald Koven, "Military Cracks Down on Rebels in Iran," *Washington Post*, November 7, 1978.

448 *Reporters were required to submit their questions*: Ibid.

448 *present Khomeini as a social moderate*: Author interview with Abolhassan Banisadr, July 11, 2013.

449 *"rejects the authoritarian models"*: Koven, "Military Cracks Down."

449 *"at least 45,000"*: Ibid.

449 *5,000*: Barry Came, "Yonky, Go Home," *Newsweek*, November 20, 1978, p. 67.

449 *met at 11:00 a.m. on Monday, November 6*: Policy review Committee Meeting, White House Situation Room, 11:00 a.m.–12:12 p.m., November 6, 1978, Jimmy Carter Presidential Library.

449 *"There has been an increase"*: Telegram from Ambassador Sullivan to Secretary of State, "Political/Security Report November 9," November 9, 1978, *Iran: The Making of US Policy, 1977–80*, National Security Archive (Alexandria, VA: Chadwyck-Healey, 1990), document 01709.

450 *The 365 passengers on board*: Uri-Bar Joseph, "Forecasting a Hurricane: Israeli and American Estimates of the Khomeini Revolution," *Journal of Strategic Studies* 36, issue 5 (2013): 18.

450 *"We are in office temporarily"*: "Shah Appoints Military Government to Halt Riots," *Times* (London), November 7, 1978.

450 *new "emergency committees"*: Tony Allaway, "Iran Plea to Muslim Leaders to Help in Halting Violence," *Times* (London), November 10, 1978.

451 *"I am being pressed to authorize"*: Hushang Nahavandi, *The Last Shah of Iran* (London: Aquilion, 2005), pp. 321–322.

451 *"I do not understand how you can arrest"*: Ibid., p. 323.

451 *"Mr. Hoveyda's arrest"*: Farah Pahlavi, *An Enduring Love: My Life with the Shah* (New York: Miramax, 2004), p. 288.

451 *"That would not be easy for me"*: Navahandi (2005), p. 323.

451 *"The religious [people] would find"*: NSC Evening Report, November 9, 1978, Jimmy Carter Presidential Library.

452 *"Sullivan's grand idea"*: Author interview with Henry Precht, March 13, 2013.

452 *"Sullivan had these ideas himself"*: Author interview with George Lambrakis, September 13, 2014.

453 *"We didn't want to be responsible"*: Ibid.

453 *"When the Shah failed to react"*: Author interview with John Stempel, February 20, 2013.

453 *"we were not involved on either side"*: Ibid.

453 *"I have blues on my skin from the Shah's jail"*: Author interview with Reza Ghotbi, May 9, 2013.

453 *"barbarians"*: Afkhami (2009), p. 496.

454 *refused to come to Niavaran*: Author interviews with Farah Pahlavi, March 23–25, 2013.

454 *"Do you want me to go and talk to him"*: Ibid.

454 *"My mother was the sister"*: Author interview with Reza Ghotbi, May 9, 2013.

454 *November day*: There is some confusion among the principals as to the exact date of Farah Pahlavi's

first meeting with Bakhtiar. In the final weeks of November and December 1978 the rapidly changing situation and numerous breaking crises meant that dates and events became telescoped. In separate interviews with the author, Farah Pahlavi and Reza Ghotbi agreed that her first meeting with Bakhtiar likely occurred in the latter part of November, certainly after the November 5 riots but before opposition leader Karim Sanjabi's release from prison in early December (his release was one of the conditions Bakhtiar had stipulated during their first meeting). In her autobiography *An Enduring Love*, the Queen apparently conflated two separate events that actually occurred five to six weeks apart: her meeting with Bakhtiar and her discussion with Generals Moghadam and Oveissi, who urged her to talk to her husband about appointing Bakhtiar to the premiership (see pp. 291–292). The conversation with the generals actually occurred in late December, at about the time the Shah was trying to persuade another statesman, Gholam Hossein Sadiqi, to accept the post of prime minister. The author's conclusion based on research and interviews is that Farah's introductory meeting with Shahpur Bakhtiar took place between November 25 and 30, 1978.

454 *Bakhtiar arrived thirty minutes early*: Author interview with Reza Ghotbi, May 9, 2013.
454 *"He told her she looked"*: Ibid.
454 *"He made an analysis of the situation"*: Ibid. See also Afkhami (2009), p. 496.
454 *"Look," she said*: Afkhami (2009), p. 496.
455 *"At the height of the revolution"*: Author interview with Hossein Nasr, November 18, 2013.
455 *"I don't know what is happening in Iran"*: Joseph Kraft, "Letter from Iran," *New Yorker*, December 11, 1978, p. 135.
455 *"Khoi was not siding with the revolutionaries"*: Author interview with Hossein Nasr, November 18, 2013.
455 *"It was Dr. Nasr's idea"*: Author interview with Farah Pahlavi, July 15, 2013.
455 *met at the airport by Iraq's minister of health*: Author interview with Hossein Nasr, November 18, 2013.
456 *"He arrived wearing a European suit"*: Ibid.
456 *Farah introduced Hussain to her mother*: Ibid.
456 *"Tell Her Majesty to tell my brother"*: Ibid.
456 *"All these mullahs would push each other"*: Author interview with Farah Pahlavi, July 15, 2013.
456 *"I was told to look down"*: Author interviews with Farah Pahlavi March 23–25, 2013.
456 *Khoi told Farah*: Author interview with Farah Pahlavi, July 15, 2013.
457 *"In Iran people are dying of hunger"*: Ibid.
457 *"At the end," said Queen Farah*: Ibid.
457 *"I cannot sully my hands"*: Author interview with Hossein Nasr, November 18, 2013.
457 *"In the downtown area"*: "The Military Is in Charge," *Time*, November 27, 1978, p. 35.
458 *"The condition affects even the most rational"*: Joe Alex Morris Jr., "In the Confusion, Rumors and 'Plots' Plague Iran," *Los Angeles Times*, November 19, 1978.
458 *an old lady in Qom*: The story of Khomeini's face appearing on the moon is told in Amir Taheri, *The Spirit of Allah: Khomeini and the Islamic Revolution* (Bethesda, MD: Adler & Adler, 1986), p. 238.
458 *Ayatollah Mohammad Beheshti*: Ibid. The author agrees with Amir Taheri that the genius behind the tale was most likely Beheshti.
458 *"traced Khomeini's face in the moon"*: Author interview with Gholam Reza Afkhami, March 11, 2013.
458 *"One night we heard the rumor"*: Author interview with Amir Pourshaja, March 16, 2013.
458 *"Our toiling masses"*: Taheri (1986), p. 238.
459 *"true Shiites should not oppose"*: Ibid., p. 239.
459 *"the ayatollah of Mashad"*: Ibid.
459 *"moon trick"*: Ibid., p. 238.
459 *"For me everything is at an end"*: Amir Taheri, *The Unknown Life of the Shah* (London: Hutchinson, 1991), p. 289.
459 *"returning to the Dark Ages"*: Ibid.
459 *"Why? I worked for thirty-seven years. Why?"*: Author interview with Amir Pourshaja, March 16, 2013.
460 *"ghost ship"*: Author interview with Reza Ghotbi, May 9, 2013.
460 *"Usually there was protocol"*: Ibid.
460 *"His eyes betrayed immense sadness"*: Arnaud de Borchgrave, "Tea with the Shah," *Newsweek*, November 20, 1978, p. 65.
460 *"The worse events became"*: F. Pahlavi (2004), p. 294.
460 *"He was seeing people morning till night"*: Author interviews with Farah Pahlavi, March 23–25, 2013.
460 *hanging a hundred of his closest aides*: Author interview with Kambiz Atabai, March 10, 2013.
460 *"Shoot the first man in front"*: Author interviews with Ardeshir Zahedi, October 27–28, 2012.
460 *"looked pale, spoke in subdued tones"*: Kraft, "Letter from Iran," p. 134.

24. SWEPT AWAY

462 *"They are going to kill us"*: Author interviews with Farah Pahlavi, March 23–25, 2013.

462 *"You don't want to be Marie Antoinette"*: Author interview with Reza Ghotbi, May 9, 2013.

462 *"It was an impressive performance"*: Joe Alex Morris Jr., "Masses Protest Shah's Rule," *Los Angeles Times*, December 11, 1978.

462 *"We want Islamic government under Khomeini"*: Ibid.

462 *"The march showed that the feeling"*: Bill Paul, "Mammoth Peaceful March Against Shah Seen Increasing Pressure on Iran Regime," *Wall Street Journal*, December 11, 1978.

463 *"We will kill Iran's dictator!"*: Joe Alex Morris Jr., "Iran Demonstrators Openly Urge Death of the Shah," *Los Angeles Times*, December 12, 1978.

463 *"The Shah and his family must be killed!"*: Nicholas Gage, "Protesters March for 2nd Day in Iran; Violence Is Limited," *New York Times*, December 12, 1978.

463 *"We would settle for the 1906 Constitution"*: Jonathan Randal, "Iranians Harden Protest Tone," *Washington Post*, December 12, 1978.

463 *mob violence in Isfahan*: William Branigan, "Mob in Isfahan Pulls Down 4 Statues of Shah," *Washington Post*, December 12, 1978.

463 *five people dying*: James Allan, "5 Shot in Attack on Savak HQ," *Daily Telegraph*, December 12, 1978.

463 *tried to kill the governor of Hamadan*: Gage, "Protesters March."

463 *"smashed its ground-floor windows"*: Allan, "5 Shot in Attack on Savak HQ."

463 *sprayed the room with semiautomatics*: "Hard Choices in Tehran," *Time*, December 25, 1978, p. 22.

463 *"I cannot forget, in particular"*: Farah Pahlavi, *An Enduring Love: My Life with the Shah* (Miramax: New York 2004), p. 289.

464 *"I did it on the orders of the Ayatollah Khomeini"*: Ibid.

464 *hundreds of troop desertions*: R. W. Apple Jr., "Shah's Army Is Showing Stress," *New York Times*, December 19, 1978.

464 *seen waving to the crowds*: Ibid.

464 *"They would be willing to see the Shah go"*: Ibid.

464 *"Tehran was like a city that had survived a siege"*: "Hard Choices," p. 22.

464 *"We could hear 'Allah Akbar!' every night"*: Author interviews with Farah Pahlavi, March 23–25, 2013.

465 *"very tense"*: Author interview with Kiomars Djahinbini, March 25, 2013.

465 *"The staff were conflicted"*: Author interview with Amir Pourshaja, March 16, 2013.

465 *"went berserk during lunch"*: Gholam Reza Afkhami, *The Life and Times of the Shah* (Berkeley: University of California Press, 2009), p. 526.

465 *"with the intriguing title"*: Amir Taheri, *The Unknown Life of the Shah* (London: Hutchinson, 1991), p. 272.

465 *"and stood in line like ordinary folks"*: R. W. Apple Jr., "Iran Lull Reflects Confused Situation," *New York Times*, December 21, 1978.

465 *"Someone wrote 'Death to the Shah'"*: Author interviews with Farah Pahlavi, March 23–25, 2013.

465 *"Farah, where are your gloves?"*: Amir Taheri, *The Spirit of Allah: Khomeini and the Islamic Revolution* (Bethesda, MD: Adler & Adler, 1986), p. 200.

466 *"One day I was looking out the window"*: Author interviews with Farah Pahlavi, March 23–25, 2013.

466 *"The ulama were negotiating"*: Author interview with Hossein Nasr, November 18, 2013.

466 *In December he flew to Tehran*: Ibid.

466 *"Don't listen to the ambassadors"*: Ibid.

467 *"including the Palestinian commandos"*: Central Intelligence Agency, National Foreign Assessment Center, "Intelligence Memorandum: The Politics of Ayatollah Ruhollah Khomeini," November 20, 1978, Jimmy Carter Presidential Library.

467 *"Khomeini has been vague"*: Ibid.

467 *shared with Sullivan his blueprint*: Telegram from Deputy Secretary of State Warren Christopher to Ambassador Sullivan, "Approach [to the] National Front," December 15, 1978, *Iran: The Making of US Policy, 1977–80*, National Security Archive (Alexandria, VA: Chadwyck-Healey, 1990), document 01929.

468 *"Crown Prince Reza would be invited to return to Iran"*: Ibid.

468 *"Probably 10–15 senior military officers"*: Ibid.

468 *"the prime threat"*: William H. Sullivan, *Mission to Iran: The Last Ambassador* (New York: Norton, 1981), p. 200.

469 *"would want to retain their good relations"*: "Confidential Telegram: Conversation with Ayatollah Nouri," December 8, 1978, *Iran: The Making of US Policy, 1977–80*, document 01882.

469 *"Tell the brothers not to use arms"*: Author interview with Henry Precht, March 13, 2013.

470 *"We knew we were tapped"*: Author interview with Abolhassan Banisadr, July 11, 2013.

470 *"a great wave of humanity"*: Author interview with Cyndy McCollough, August 21, 2013.

470 *"People were screaming and crying"*: Author interview with Jonathan Kirkendall, August 21, 2013.

471 *"When the plane took off"*: Author interview with Bruce Vernor, March 12, 2013.

471 *ambushed on his way to work*: John Vinocur, "Gunmen in Iran Ambush and Kill Two Oil Officials, One from US," *New York Times*, December 24, 1978.

471 *"a colonel was dragged from his tank"*: Thomas Lippman, "Population Takes Over Battered Iranian City," *Washington Post*, January 4, 1979.

471 *"The colonel was taken alive"*: Telegram from Embassy Tehran to Secretary of State, "Bazaari Views on Bakhtiar Candidacy and on Continuing Confrontation," January 3, 1979, *Iran: The Making of US Policy, 1977–80*, document 02007.

471 *high school students rioted*: John Vinocur, "US Embassy Guards in Iran Fire Tear Gas at Student Protesters," *New York Times*, December 25, 1978.

471 *converged on the U.S. embassy*: Ibid.

471 *"I would rather sit home"*: Ibid.

472 *"The Shah will not come out of this alive"*: Ibid.

472 *"So many Iranians seem to think the problems"*: John Westberg, "We Experience the Gathering Storm of Revolution," personal diaries (1978–79).

472 *"wild shooting and lawlessness"*: John Vinocur, "Daylong Violence Cripples Tehran; Iran to Ration Oil," *New York Times*, December 28, 1978.

472 *half a million barrels a day*: Ibid.

472 *"We consider it too dangerous"*: James Allen, "Fuel Ration Imposed in Persia," *Daily Telegraph*, December 28, 1978.

473 *"he would kill if necessary"*: Afkhami (2009), p. 497.

473 *"General Oveissi and General Moghadam"*: Author interviews with Farah Pahlavi, March 23–25, 2013.

473 *"Iran is not ready for a republic"*: Author interview with Reza Ghotbi, May 9, 2013.

473 *"I have an audience tomorrow"*: Ibid.

474 *"Everyone knew that he would not survive"*: Author interview with John Stempel, February 20, 2013.

474 *"Bakhtiar doesn't have a fucking chance"*: Author interview with Charlie Naas, March 14, 2013.

474 *"Bakhtiar asked for you, I didn't"*: Author interview with Kambiz Atabai, May 17, 2013.

475 *"You don't want to be Marie Antoinette"*: Author interview with Reza Ghotbi, May 9, 2013.

475 *"You don't want to hear this"*: Ibid.

475 *"I offered to stay"*: F. Pahlavi (2004), p. 295.

475 *"His Majesty was in a very bad state"*: Author interview with Amir Pourshaja, March 16, 2013.

475 *"The queen mother was carried"*: "Shah's Ailing Mother Flown to LA from Iran," *Los Angeles Times*, December 30, 1978.

475 *"Don't pack too much"*: Author interview with Amir Pourshaja, March 16, 2013.

475 *Each morning at six o'clock*: Author interview with Elli Antoniades, April 3, 2013.

475 *"When the power failed"*: Ibid.

476 *"I don't know how long I will stay"*: Ibid.

476 *"By then we knew he was finished"*: Author interview with Zbigniew Brzezinski, September 4, 2014.

477 *"The generals came to me and offered to shoot Huyser"*: Author interview with Ardeshir Zahedi, October 27, 28, 2012.

477 *"dangerous and idiotic policy"*: President Carter's notes on Guadeloupe Four Power Summit, January 5, 1979, Jimmy Carter Presidential Library.

478 *"a good swimmer"*: Ibid.

478 *"Found very little support"*: Ibid.

478 *"In the course of a general discussion"*: "Four Power Discussion in Guadeloupe 5/6 January 1979: Third Session on Saturday 6 January 1979 at 0900," British National Archives.

478 *"Valéry reported"*: President Carter's notes on Guadeloupe Four Power Summit, January 5, 1979.

479 *"the Shah's restraint in not taking ruthless measures"*: Ibid.

479 *"ate lunch together"*: President Carter's notes on Guadeloupe Four Power Summit, January 6, 1979.

479 *"We are giving up on the Shah"*: NSC Weekly Report #84, January 12, 1979, Jimmy Carter Presidential Library.

479 *Musa Sadr was alive*: Following the overthrow of Colonel Gadhafi's regime former officials came forward to attest that Musa Sadr was kept alive for a period ranging from months to years. In 2014 author Kai Bird revealed in his biography of CIA operative Robert C. Ames that the American was secretly tipped off in 1979 that Musa Sadr had been disposed of after Khomeini came to power. The account provided by Hassan Salameh, PLO leader Yasser Arafat's chief of operations, holds special

credence because of its detailed nature. See Kai Bird, *The Good Spy: The Life and Death of Robert Ames* (New York: Crown, 2014), p. 206.

480 *"the PLO is proud"*: "PLO Pledges Support to Iran people," *Kayhan International*, October 25, 1978.

25. FLIGHT OF THE EAGLE

481 *"We are leaving for a long-needed rest"*: Author interview with Kiomars Djahinbini, March 15, 2013.

481 *"We are leaving"*: Author interview with Fereydoun Djavadi, July 13, 2013.

481 *"I'm tired"*: Nicholas Gage, "Bakhtiar Installed and Shah Declares He'll 'Take a Rest,'" *New York Times*, January 7, 1979.

481 *"The influence of the U.S."*: Don Cook, "US Accused of Planning Coup in Iran," *Los Angeles Times*, January 15, 1979.

482 *"He keeps asking, 'When are you leaving?'"*: Author interview with Farah Pahlavi, August 30, 2015.

482 *"it would be best for stability in Iran if he left"*: Bernard Gwertzman, "Stresses a Trip Would Be Temporary, but Return Is Viewed as Difficult," *New York Times*, January 9, 1979.

482 *"leaned forward, almost like a small boy"*: William H. Sullivan, *Mission to Iran: The Last Ambassador* (New York: Norton, 1981), p. 231.

482 *at 10:54 a.m. on Friday, January 12*: Telegram from Secretary of State to Embassy Tehran, January 12, 1979, "Departure of Shah," *Iran: The Making of US Policy, 1977–80*, National Security Archive (Alexandria, VA: Chadwyck-Healey, 1990), document 02072.

482 *"Zahedi indicated that he would like"*: Ibid.

482 *"They were so upset and disillusioned"*: Author interview with Kambiz Atabai, March 10, 2013.

482 *"insulted, accosted in the streets"*: Gholam Reza Afkhami, *The Life and Times of the Shah* (Berkeley: University of California Press, 2009), p. 525.

482 *"People were breaking down all over the place"*: "Empress Took Over—Shah's Last Days: Bridge and Movies," *Los Angeles Times*, January 17, 1979.

483 *"Strolling among the larches and pines"*: "The Shah's Final Days," *Newsweek*, January 29, 1979, p. 18.

483 *conveying his wishes*: Afkhami (2009), p. 526.

483 *"If His Majesty leaves"*: Farah Pahlavi, *An Enduring Love: My Life with the Shah* (New York: Miramax, 2004), p. 293.

483 *"I also received a delegation"*: Ibid.

483 *Through his friend . . . Mansur learned*: Author interview with Mansur Eqbal, November 17, 2014.

483 *"When I went to Niavaran I saw the guard"*: Ibid.

484 *"When I said I thought the Shah should stay"*: Author interview with Shahin Fatemi, July 16, 2013.

484 *"I did not want to give them"*: F. Pahlavi (2004), p. 4.

484 *"You liked this tableau"*: Author interview with Fereydoun Djavadi, July 13, 2013.

484 *left behind her private jewelry collection*: Author interviews with Farah Pahlavi, March 23–25, 2013.

484 *"So no one will accuse us of taking things out"*: Author interview with Shahin Fatemi, July 16, 2013.

485 *"no food, no water, nothing"*: Author interview with Amir Pourshaja, March 16, 2013.

485 *"On the last night I did not tell him anything"*: Author interview with Reza Ghotbi, May 9, 2013.

485 *"was like a nightmare"*: Author interview with Shahin Fatemi, July 16, 2013.

485 *"Embassy keeps getting reports"*: Telegram from Ambassador Sullivan to Secretary of State, "Religious Leaders Fear Departure of Shah," January 10, 1979, *Iran: The Making of US Policy, 1977–80*, document 02048.

485 *"not very coherent"*: Ibid.

486 *"very angry at [the] National Front"*: Telegram from Ambassador Sullivan to Secretary of State, "First Meeting with National Front Leader Karim Sanjabi," January 14, 1979, *Iran: The Making of US Policy, 1977–80*, document 02086.

486 *"According to this theory"*: Ibid.

486 *As he understood it his mission*: Cable from General Huyser to Secretary Brown and General Jones, January 12, 1979, Jimmy Carter Presidential Library, NLC-25-41-3-2-4.

486 *"I have told [the generals] that I consider a military coup"*: Ibid.

487 *"He really surprised me"*: Author interview with Kiomars Djahinbini, March 15, 2013.

487 *"Where is your smile, Your Majesty?"*: "Empress Took Over: Shah's Last Days."

487 *spent the morning packing*: F. Pahlavi (2004), p. 4.

487 *"We are leaving"*: Author interview with Fereydoun Djavadi, July 13, 2013.

487 *"I could feel the distress"*: F. Pahlavi (2004), p. 6.

487 *"Around eleven His Majesty"*: Author interview with Kiomars Djahinbini, March 15, 2013.

487 *"Where are you going?"*: F. Pahlavi (2004), p. 10.

487 *"With the sound of the whirring rotors in my ears"*: Ibid.

487 *"No one said anything"*: Author interview with Kiomars Djahinbini, March 15, 2013.

487 *"was the whining"*: F. Pahlavi (2004), p. 7.

487 *"His Majesty didn't sign it"*: Author interview with Kiomars Djahinbini, March 15, 2013.

488 *"It depends on the status of my health"*: Nicholas Gage, "Ruler Goes to Egypt," *New York Times*, January 17, 1979.

489 *"no honor guard for him"*: Afkhami (2009), p. 527.

489 *"with tears in their eyes"*: William Branigan, "Iranians Jubilant as Shah Departs," *New York Times*, January 17, 1979.

489 *"when we began to hear horns honking"*: John Westberg, "We Experience the Gathering Storm of Revolution," personal diaries (1978–79).

489 *"It needs a Shakespeare"*: Afkhami (2009), p. 528.

489 *"Khomeini's flight from Paris"*: Baqer Moin, *Khomeini: Life of the Ayatollah* (London: I. B. Tauris, 1999), p. 202.

490 *"None!"*: Ibid., p. 199.

490 *"Our final victory will come"*: R. W. Apple Jr., "Khomeini Arrives in Tehran; Urges Ouster of Foreigners; Millions Rally to Greet Him," *New York Times*, February 1, 1979.

490 *"We should be careful"*: Memorandum for the President from Zbigniew Brzezinski, NSC Weekly Report 87, February 2, 1979, Jimmy Carter Presidential Library.

491 *"I am helping them"*: Author interview with Kiomars Djahinbini, March 15, 2013. Colonel Djahinbini's father-in-law was in jail with Moghadam and witnessed the former Savak chief's conversations with Pakravan.

491 *upwards of ten thousand who had "disappeared"*: Youssef Ibrahim, "Hoveida Believed Doomed in Iran; 6 More Die in Renewed Executions," *New York Times*, April 7, 1979.

493 *translated and published*: "Text Tied to Khomeini Published by the CIA," *New York Times*, March 21, 1979.

498 *"Why didn't you go all out against Khomeini?"*: Author interview with Fereydoun Djavadi, July 13, 2013.

498 *"You gave the orders to finish the job"*: Ibid.

498 *"I hadn't the time"*: Ibid.

498 *"Your Majesty, you're in love with Iran"*: Ibid.

BIBLIOGRAPHY

BOOKS

Abrahamian, Ervand. *The Coup: 1953, the CIA, and the Roots of Modern US-Iranian Relations*. New York: New Press, 2013.

——. *A History of Modern Iran*. Cambridge, UK: Cambridge University Press, 2008.

——. *Tortured Confessions: Prisons and Public Recantations in Modern Iran*. Berkeley: University of California Press, 1999.

——. *Khomeinism: Essays on the Islamic Republic*. Berkeley: University of California Press, 1993.

——. *The Iranian Mojahedin*. New Haven, CT: Yale University Press, 1989.

——. *Iran Between Two Revolutions*. Princeton, NJ: Princeton University Press, 1982.

Afkhami, Gholam Reza. *The Life and Times of the Shah*. Berkeley: University of California Press, 2009.

Ajami, Fouad. *The Vanished Imam: Musa al Sadr and the Shi'a of Lebanon*. Ithaca, NY: Cornell University Press, 1986.

Alam, Asadollah. *The Shah and I: The Confidential Diary of Iran's Royal Court, 1969–1977*. New York: St. Martin's Press, 1991.

Alvandi, Roham. *Nixon, Kissinger, and the Shah: The United States and Iran in the Cold War*. Oxford, UK: Oxford University Press, 2014.

Amuzegar, Jahingir. *The Dynamics of the Iranian Revolution: The Pahlavis' Triumph and Tragedy*. Albany: State University of New York Press, 1991.

——. *Iran: An Economic Profile*. Washington, DC: Middle East Institute, 1977.

Ansari, Ali M. *The Politics of Nationalism in Modern Iran*. Cambridge, UK: Cambridge University Press, 2012.

——. *Modern Iran Since 1921: The Pahlavis and After*. London: Longman, 2003.

Arjomand, Said Amir. *The Turban for the Crown: The Islamic Revolution in Iran*. Oxford, UK: Oxford University Press, 1986.

Avery, Peter, Gavin Hambly, and Charles Melville (eds.), *The Cambridge History of Iran in Seven Volumes*. Cambridge, UK: Cambridge University Press, 1991.

Axworthy, Michael. *Empire of the Mind: A History of Iran*. New York: Basic Books, 2008.

Bakhtiary, Princess Soraya Esfandiary. *Palace of Solitude*. London: Quartet Books, 1992.

Banisadr, Abolhassan. *My Turn to Speak: Iran, the Revolution, and the Secret Deals with the US*. New York: Brassey's US, 1991.

Bayandor, Darioush. *Iran and the CIA: The Fall of Mossadeq Revisited*. London: Palgrave Macmillan, 2010.

Bayne, E. A. *Persian Kingship in Transition: Conversations with a Monarch Whose Office Is Traditional and Whose Goal Is Modernization*. New York: American Universities Field Staff, 1968.

Bill, James A. *The Eagle and the Lion: The Tragedy of American-Iranian Relations*. New Haven, CT: Yale University Press, 1988.

Bird, Kai. *The Good Spy: The Life and Death of Robert Ames*. New York: Crown, 2014.

Blanch, Lesley. *Farah: Shahbanou of Iran*. Tehran: Tajerzadeh, 1978.

Brzezinski, Zbigniew. *Power and Principle: Memoirs of the National Security Adviser, 1977–1981*. New York: Farrar, Straus & Giroux, 1983.

Buchan, James. *Days of God: The Revolution in Iran and Its Consequences*. London: Murray, 2012.

Carter, Jimmy. *White House Diary*. New York: Picador, 2010.

——. *Keeping Faith: Memoirs of a President*. New York: Bantam Books, 1982.

Chehabi, H. E. *Iranian Politics and Religious Modernism: The Liberation Movement of Iran Under the Shah and Khomeini*. Ithaca, NY: Cornell University Press, 1990.

——, ed. *Distant Relations: Iran and Lebanon in the Last 500 Years*. London: Centre for Lebanese Studies in association with I. B. Tauris, 2006.

Cobban, Helena. *The Making of Modern Lebanon*. Boulder, CO: Westview, 1985.

——. *The Palestinian Liberation Organization: People, Power, and Politics*. Cambridge, UK: Cambridge University Press, 1984.

Cooper, Andrew Scott. *The Oil Kings: How the U.S., Iran, and Saudi Arabia Changed the Balance of Power in the Middle East*. New York: Simon & Schuster, 2011.

Dabashi, Hamid. *Theology of Discontent: The Ideological Foundation of the Islamic Revolution of Iran*. New Brunswick, NJ: Transaction, 2008.

Daftary, Farhad. *A History of Shi'i Islam*. New York: I. B. Tauris, 2013.

Daryaee, Touraj, ed. *The Oxford Handbook of Iranian History*. Oxford, UK: Oxford University Press, 2012.

de Bellaigue, Christopher. *Patriot of Persia: Mohammad Mossadegh and a Tragic Anglo-American Coup*. New York: HarperCollins, 2012.

de Villiers, Gerard. *The Imperial Shah: An Informal Biography*. Boston: Little, Brown, 1976.

Esposito, John L., ed. *The Oxford History of Islam*. Oxford, UK: Oxford University Press, 1999.

Evans, Mike. *Jimmy Carter: The Liberal Left and World Chaos*. Phoenix: Timeworthy Books, 2009.

Ferdowsi, Abolqasem. *Shahnameh: The Persian Book of Kings*. New York: Penguin, 2006.

Fischer, Michael M. J. *Iran: From Religious Dispute to Revolution*. Madison: University of Wisconsin Press, 1980.

Foran, John, ed. *A Century of Revolution: Social Movements in Iran*. Minneapolis: University of Minnesota Press, 1994.

Gangi, Manouchehr. *Defying the Revolution: From a Minister to the Shah to a Leader of Resistance*. Westport, CT: Praeger, 2002.

Gasiorwski, Mark J., and Malcolm Byrne, eds. *Mohammad Mossadeq and the 1953 Coup in Iran*. Syracuse, NY: Syracuse University Press, 2004.

Graham, Robert. *Iran: The Illusion of Power*. London: Croom Helm, 1979.

Halawi, Majed. *A Lebanon Defied: Musa al-Sadr and the Shi'a Community*. Boulder, CO: Westview, 1982.

Heikal, Mohamed. *The Return of the Ayatollah*. London: Deutsch, 1981.

Helms, Cynthia. *An Ambassador's Wife in Iran*. New York: Dodd, Mead, 1981.

Helms, Richard, with William Hood. *A Look over My Shoulder: A Life in the Central Intelligence Agency*. New York: Ballantine, 2003.

Hussein, Asaf. *Islamic Iran: Revolution and Counter Revolution*. New York: St. Martin's Press, 1995.

Huyser, General Robert E. *Mission to Tehran*. New York: Harper & Row, 1986.

Jacqz, Jane W., ed. *Iran: Past, Present, and Future*. New York: Aspen Institute for Humanistic Studies, 1976.

Jalali, Ali Hussein. *Karbala and Ashura*. Qom: Ansariyan, 2007.

Jerome, Carole. *The Man in the Mirror: A True Story of Love, Revolution, and Treachery in Iran*. Toronto: Key Porter Books, 1987.

Jervis, Robert. *Why Intelligence Fails: Lessons from the Iranian Revolution and the Iraq War*. Ithaca, NY: Cornell University Press, 2010.

Karanjia, R. K. *The Mind of a Monarch*. London: George Allen & Unwin, 1977.

Keddie, Nikki R., with a Section by Yann Richard. *Roots of Revolution: An Interpretive History of Modern Iran*. New Haven, CT: Yale University Press, 1981.

Keshavarzian, Arang. *Bazaar and State in Iran: The Politics of the Tehran Marketplace*. Cambridge, UK: Cambridge University Press, 2007.

Khomeini, Iman. *Islam and Revolution: Writings and Declarations of Imam Khomeini (1941–1980)*. Trans. Hamid Algar. Berkeley, CA: Mizan Press, 1981.

——. *Islamic Government: Governance of the Jurist*. Tehran: International Affairs Department, The Institute for Compilation and Publication of Imam Khomeini's Works, 2008.

Kinzer, Stephen. *All the Shah's Men: An American Coup and the Roots of Middle East Terror*. Hoboken, NJ: Wiley, 2003.

Kurzman, Charles. *The Unthinkable Revolution in Iran*. Cambridge, MA: Harvard University Press, 2005.

Ladjevardi, Habib, ed. *Memoirs of Fatemeh Pakravan*. Cambridge, MA: Iranian Oral History Project, Center for Middle Eastern Studies, Harvard University, 1998.

Laing, Margaret. *The Shah*. London: Sidgwick & Jackson, 1977.

Ledeen, Michael, and William Lewis. *Debacle: The American Failure in Iran*. New York: Knopf, 1981.

Lenczowski, George, ed. *Iran Under the Pahlavis*. Stanford, CA: Hoover Institution Press, 1978.

Milani, Abbas. *The Shah*. New York: Palgrave Macmillan, 2011.

———. *Eminent Persians: The Men and Women Who Made Modern Iran, 1941–1979*. Syracuse, NY: Syracuse University Press, 2008.

———. *The Persian Sphinx: Amir Abbas Hoveyda and the Riddle of the Iranian Revolution*. Washington, DC: Mage, 2004.

Milani, Mohsen M. *The Making of Iran's Islamic Revolution: From Monarchy to Republic*. Boulder, CO: Westview, 1994.

Moin, Baqer. *Khomeini: Life of the Ayatollah*. London: I. B. Tauris, 1999.

Naficy, Hamid. *A Social History of Iranian Cinema*. Vol. 2, *The Industrializing Years, 1941–1978*. Durham, NC: Duke University Press, 2011.

Nahavandi, Hushang. *Iran: The Clash of Ambitions*. London: Aquilion, 2006.

———. *The Last Shah*. Berkshire, UK: Aquilion, 2005.

Nasr, Seyyed Hossein. *Islam in the Modern World: Challenged by the West, Threatened by Fundamentalism, Keeping Faith with Tradition*. San Francisco: HarperOne, 2011.

Olmstead, Michael B. *History of the Persian Empire*. Chicago: University of Chicago Press, 1948.

Pahlavi, Ashraf. *Time for Truth*. N.p.: In Print Publishing, 1995.

———. *Faces in a Mirror*. Englewood Cliffs, NJ: Prentice-Hall, 1980.

Pahlavi, Farah. *An Enduring Love: My Life with the Shah*. New York: Miramax, 2004.

———. *My Thousand and One Days: The Autobiography of Farah, Shabanou of Iran*. London: W. H. Allen, 1978.

Pahlavi, Mohammad Reza. *Answer to History*. New York: Stein & Day, 1980.

———. *Mission for My Country*. New York: McGraw-Hill, 1961.

Pakravan, Saideh. *The Arrest of Hoveyda: Stories of the Iranian Revolution*. Costa Mesa, CA: Mazda, 1998.

Parsa, Misagh. *Social Origins of the Iranian Revolution*. New Brunswick, NJ: Rutgers University Press, 1989.

Parsons, Anthony. *The Pride and the Fall: Iran 1974–79*. London: Jonathan Cape, 1984.

Potter, Lawrence G., ed. *The Persian Gulf in History*. New York: Palgrave Macmillan, 2009.

Radji, Parviz C. *In the Service of the Peacock Throne: The Diaries of the Shah's Last Ambassador to London*. London: Hamish Hamilton, 1983.

Rahnema, Ali. *Superstition as Ideology in Iranian Politics from Majlesi to Ahmadinejad*. Cambridge, UK: Cambridge University Press, 2011.

———. *An Islamic Utopian: A Political Biography of Ali Shari'ati*. London: I. B. Tauris, 1998.

Razavi, Hossein, and Firouz Vakil. *The Political Environment of Economic Planning in Iran, 1971–1983: From Monarchy to Islamic Republic*. Boulder, CO: Westview, 1984.

Rizvi, Sayyid Muhammad. *Islam: Faith, Practice, and History*. Qom: Ansariyan, 2010.

Saikal, Amin. *The Rise and Fall of the Shah: Iran from Autocracy to Religious Rule*. Princeton, NJ: Princeton University Press, 1980.

Semkus, Charles Ismail. *The Fall of Iran 1978–1979: An Historical Anthology*. New York: Copen Press, 1979.

Shakerin, Hamid-Reza. *Forty Questions on Islamic State: A Collection of Students Queries on Political Thought*. Qom: Ansariyan, n.d.

Shanahan, Rodger. *The Shi'a of Lebanon: Clans, Parties, and Clerics*. London: I. B. Tauris, 2011.

Shariati, Ali. *On the Sociology of Islam: Lectures by Ali Shariati*. Berkeley, CA: Mizan, 1979.

Shawcross, William. *The Shah's Last Ride: The Fate of an Ally*. New York: Simon & Schuster, 1988.

Sick, Gary. *October Surprise: America's Hostages in Iran and the Election of Ronald Reagan*. New York: Random House, 1992.

———. *All Fall Down: America's Tragic Encounter with Iran*. New York: Random House, 1985.

Smith, Luise J., and David H. Herschuler, eds., and David S. Patterson, gen. ed. *Foreign Relations of the United States, 1969–1976*. Vol. 1, *Foundations of Foreign Policy, 1969–1972*. Washington, DC: US Government Printing Office, 2003.

Sobhani, Ayatollah Ja'far. *Doctrines of Shi'i Islam: A Compendium of Imami Beliefs and Practices*. Qom: Imam Sadeq Institute, 2012.

Stuckey, Mary E. *Jimmy Carter, Human Rights, and the National Agenda*. College Station: Texas A&M University Press, 2008.

Sullivan, William H. *Mission to Iran: The Last Ambassador*. New York: Norton, 1981.

Syed, S. Z. H. *Introduction to Islam*. Qom: Al-Hadal, 2006.

Taheri, Amir. *The Unknown Life of the Shah*. London: Hutchinson, 1991.

———. *The Spirit of Allah: Khomeini and the Islamic Revolution*. Bethesda, MD: Adler & Adler, 1986.
Vance, Cyrus. *Hard Choices: Critical Years in America's Foreign Policy*. New York: Simon & Schuster, 1983.
Walbridge, Linda S. *The Thread of Mu'awiya: The Making of a Marja' Taqlid*. Bloomington, IN: Ramsay Press, 2014.
Ward, Steven R. *Immortal: A Military History of Iran and Its Armed Forces*. Washington, DC: Georgetown University Press, 2009.
Zahedi, Ardeshir. *The Memoirs of Ardeshir Zahedi*. Vol. 2, *Love, Marriage, Ambassador to the US and UK (1954–66)*. Bethesda, MD: Ibex, 2010.
———. *The Memoirs of Ardeshir Zahedi*. Vol. 1, *From Childhood to the End of My Father's Premiership*. Bethesda, MD: Ibex, 2006.
Zonis, Marvin. *Majestic Failure: The Fall of the Shah*. Chicago: University of Chicago Press, 1991.
———. *The Political Elite of Iran*. Princeton, NJ: Princeton University Press, 1971.

ARTICLES
Abrahamian, Ervand. "The Guerrilla Movement in Iran, 1963–77." *MERIP Reports* 86, "The Left Forces in Iran" (Mar.–Apr. 1980).
———. "Iran in Revolution: The Opposition Forces." *MERIP Reports* 75/76 (Mar.–Apr. 1979).
———. "Iran: The Political Crisis Intensifies." *MERIP Reports* 71 (Oct. 1978).
———. "Iran: The Political Challenge." *MERIP Reports* 69 (Jul.–Aug. 1978).
Amini, Parvin Merat. "A Single Party State in Iran, 1975–78: The Rastakhiz Party: The Final Attempt by the Shah to Consolidate His Political Base." *Middle Eastern Studies* 38, no. 1 (Jan. 2002).
Ansari, Ali M. "The Myth of the White Revolution: Mohammad Reza Shah, 'Modernization,' and the Consolidation of Power." *Middle Eastern Studies* 37, no. 3 (Jul. 2001).
Ashraf, Ahmad, "Pahlavi—Mohammad Reza." *Encyclopedia of the Modern Middle East*. New York: Macmillan, 2006.
Bar-Joseph, Uri. "Forecasting a Hurricane: Israeli and American Estimates of the Khomeini Revolution." *Journal of Strategic Studies* 36, issue 5 (Feb. 2013).
Brun, Thierry, and Rene Dumont. "Iran: Imperial Pretensions and Agricultural Dependence." *MERIP Reports* 71 (Oct. 1978).
Faghfoory, Mohammad H. "The Dynamics of the Iranian Revolution: The Pahlavis' Triumph and Tragedy." *Middle East Journal* 47, no. 1 (Winter 1993).
———. "Iran—Iranian Politics and Religious Modernism: The Liberation Movement of Iran Under the Shah and Khomeini." *Middle East Journal* 45, no. 3 (Summer 1991).
Fatemi, Khosrow. "Leadership by Distrust: The Shah's Modus Operandi." *Middle East Journal* 36, no. 1 (Winter 1982).
Frings-Hessami, Khadiji. "Resistance to the Shah: Landowners and Ulama in Iran." *Middle Eastern Studies* 37, no. 3 (Jul. 2001).
Goode, James. "Reforming Iran During the Kennedy Years." *Diplomatic History* 15, issue 1 (Jun. 2007).
Halliday, Fred. "Iran: Trade Unions and the Working Class Opposition," *MERIP Reports* 71 (Oct. 1978).
Heisey, D. Ray. "Reflections of a Persian Jewel: Damavand College, Tehran." *Journal of Middle Eastern and Islamic Studies (in Asia)* 5, no. 1 (2001).
Kazemi, Farhad. "Urban Migrants and the Revolution." *Iranian Studies* 13, no. 1/4, "Iranian Revolution in Perspective" (1980).
Keddie, Nikkie. "Iranian Revolutions in Comparative Perspective." *American Historical Review* 88, no. 3 (Jun. 1983).
———. "The Midas Touch: Black Gold, Economics, and Politics in Iran Today." *Iranian Studies* 10, no. 4 (Autumn 1977).
Kurzman, Charles. "The Qum Protests and the Coming of the Iranian Revolution." *Social Science History* 27, no. 3 (Fall 2003).
Ladjevardi, Habib. "The Origins of U.S. Support for an Autocratic Iran." *International Journal of Middle East Studies* 15, no. 2 (May 1983).
Lytle, Mark. "Tragedy or Farce? America's Troubled Relations with Iran." *Diplomatic History* 14, no. 3 (July 1990).
McFarland, Stephen L. "A Peripheral View of the Origins of the Cold War: The Crises in Iran, 1941–47." *Diplomatic History* 4, no. 4 (Oct. 1980).
Moens, Alexander. "President Carter's Advisers and the Fall of the Shah." *Political Science Quarterly* 106, no. 2 (Summer 1991).
Moran, Theodore H. "Iranian Defense Expenditures and the Social Crisis." *International Security* 3, no. 3 (Winter 1978–1979).

Precht, Henry. "The Iranian Revolution: An Oral History with Henry Precht, Then State Department Desk Officer." *Middle East Journal* 58, no. 1 (Winter 2004): 9–31.
Richards, Helmut. "Land Reform and Agribusiness in Iran." *MERIP Reports* 43 (Dec. 1975).
———. "America's Shah, Shahanshah's Iran." *MERIP Reports* 40 (Sept. 1975).
Ricks, Thomas. "U.S. Military Missions to Iran, 1943–78: The Political Economy of Military Assistance." *Iranian Studies* 12, no. 3/4 (Summer–Autumn 1979).
Samii, Abbas William. "The Shah's Lebanon Policy: The Role of SAVAK." *Middle Eastern Studies* 33, no. 1 (Jan. 1997).
Scoville, James G. "The Labor Market in Prerevolutionary Iran." *Economic Development and Cultural Change* 34, no. 1 (Oct. 1985).
Summitt, April R. "For a White Revolution: John F. Kennedy and the Shah of Iran." *Middle East Journal* 58, no. 4 (Autumn 2004).
Zirinsky, Michael P. "Modern History and Politics—U.S. Foreign Policy and the Shah: Building a Client State in Iran." *Middle East Journal* 46, no. 2 (Spring 1992).

RESEARCH INSTITUTES AND LIBRARIES

UNITED STATES
Harvard University Center for Middle Eastern Studies Iranian Oral History Project, Boston, MA
Columbia University Center for Iranian Studies, New York, NY
National Security Archive, Washington, DC
Jimmy Carter Presidential Library and Museum, Atlanta, GA
Gerald Ford Presidential Library and Museum, Ann Arbor, MI
Ronald Reagan Presidential Foundation and Library, Simi Valley, CA
New York Public Library, New York, NY

ISLAMIC REPUBLIC OF IRAN
Center for Documentation on the Iranian Revolution, Tehran
University of al-Mustafa, Institute of Short Term Education & Sabbatical Leaves, Qom

ACKNOWLEDGMENTS

Researching and writing this book was a journey and a great adventure that took me to many places, including Iran, where I studied Shia Islam and toured the Pahlavi palaces, and also to Tyre in southern Lebanon where I walked in Musa Sadr's footsteps. In Paris, I interviewed former ambassadors, ministers, and members of the Pahlavi family, then traveled the short distance to Versailles, the seat of the French kings, to interview Abolhassan Banisadr, the revolutionary who deposed them and went on to become the first elected president of the Islamic Republic of Iran. In Cairo, I viewed the Shah's resting place, and in New York and Washington I met with former U.S. government officials and diplomats. Throughout my travels, I was extended a warm welcome and helping hand from Iranians who were happy to help with my investigation and eager to find out what I had learned. Almost all my interviewees, Iranian or American, royalist or revolutionary, understood that the time was right for a fresh perspective on the dramatic events of 1977–1979.

I would like to thank everyone who helped me in any way over the past four years. Due to privacy and safety concerns I can't name you all. Some Iranian interviewees, usually those with family members living inside Iran, preferred to talk to me on background or off-the-record to avoid repercussions for their loved ones back in Iran. Others sat for hours, and in some cases days, reminiscing, while still others volunteered to place phone calls, write e-mails, and tap into their networks to locate interviewees and unpublished documents. As a historian, although I felt uncomfortable writing a book that included anonymous or unnamed sources, I felt compelled in this case to made exceptions. The religious revolutionary "Ali Hossein," for example, is the pseudonym for someone who lives in Iran. Not knowing how the final book would be received inside Iran, I thought it best not to identify him. To provide balance, on the other hand, I respected the wishes of two former Savak officers who asked that they not be identified. To them, and to everyone who cooperated, I would like to extend a heartfelt thanks. I should add that any mistakes contained in this manuscript are my responsibility and not theirs.

From the very beginning, members of the Pahlavi family gave generously of their time and made themselves available for interviews and requests. Empress Farah Pahlavi and her private secretary Kambiz Atabai not only encouraged my research, but placed calls on my behalf and encouraged longtime friends and acquaintances to meet with me. Prince Reza Pahlavi reminisced about his childhood growing up at Niavaran. I am appreciative to the Shah's surviving brother, Prince Gholam Reza, and his wife, Princess Manigeh, for answering questions and helping with illustrations.

Those who sat for formal interviews or provided statements *and* were prepared to be publicly acknowledged included Gholam Reza Afkhami, Mahnaz Afkhami, Amir Aslan Afshar, Ahmad Ahrar, Faoud Ajami, Fereydoun Ala, Parviz Alam, Iraj Amini, Abdul-Reza Ansari, Maryam Ansary, Elli Antoniades, Robert Armao, Ahmad Ashraf, Abolhassan Banisadr, Zbigniew Brzezinski, Roy Colquitt, Farhad Daftary, Layla Diba, Kiomars Djahinbini, Fereydoun Djavadi, Mansur Eqbal, Parvine Farmanfarmaian, Shahin Fatemi, Abdulwahab Forati, Reza Ghotbi, Reza Golsorkhi, Hekmat Hormoz, Ali Kani, Khalil al-Khalil, James Kirkendall, Jonathan Kirkendall, Libby Kirkendall, George Lambrakis, Javad Mansuri, Farhad Massoudi, Cyndy McCollough, Hassan Ali Mehran, Mohammad Hossein Mehrman, Parviz Mina, Ray Moseley, Mortaza Mousavi, Charlie Naas, Assdollah Nasr, Hossein Nasr, Abbas Nayeri, Karen Oliver, Katie Oliver, Saideh Pakravan, Amir Pourshaja, Henry Precht, Jonathan Randal, Parviz Sabeti, Saeed Sanjabi, Hassan Shahidi, Hossein Shariatmadari, Gary Sick, John Stempel, Yakub Tavakoli, Bruce Vernor, Barbara Walters, Chris Westberg, Martin Woollacott, Ardeshir Zahedi, and Mahnaz Zahedi.

This book is dedicated to my friends and for good reason. The many individual contributions that made *The Fall of Heaven* possible were remarkable and selfless. During the writing of this book I lived in the wonderful Brooklyn home of Judy Popkin whose hospitality, patience, and sense of adventure are legend. The same is true of Jonnet and Pater Abeles who managed the singular feat of helping me in a thousand different ways during my winter stay on Shelter Island and also in New York City. Thanking them for everything they did and continue to do seems somehow inadequate.

During my many back-and-forth trips to Washington, DC, I stayed with my great friends Steve Parker and Jennifer and Michael Oko who now know more about the ins and out of late Pahlavi-era Iran than they could ever have imagined.

A new friend, Dariosh Afshar, who lives in Great Britain, translated Persian documents into English, while simultaneously translating *The Oil Kings* into Persian for my Iranian readers.

Translation of articles from the French to English was done by Roger McKeon, one of the many friends who helped out on Shelter Island. To him, and to them, I am thankful for the words of encouragement, for the hot meals, and for car rides to the supermarket during more ice storms than I thought possible in a single winter season.

Photographer Hali Helfgott, my very talented Columbia Journalism School classmate, gave generously of her time and talents to snap my jacket portrait.

Historians owe a debt of gratitude to the academic institutions and libraries that are designed with our special needs in mind. Everyone who writes about United States foreign policy owes a big thank you to the men and women who staff America's presidential libraries and the National Archives. Without them, and without the resources put at their disposal by the federal government, books like this could not be written.

I owe a special thank you to my friends and colleagues at the University of al-Mustafa's Institute of Short Term Education & Sabbatical Leaves in Qom, where I was welcomed with such kindness and interest. It is my hope that as international tensions ease there will be many more cultural and educational exchanges allowing students and scholars to see and experience Iran, and vice versa.

My editors at Henry Holt, Gillian Blake and Caroline Zancan, understood from the beginning that *The Fall of Heaven* was a special book that, especially in the current overseas climate, deserved the widest possible readership. Holt's editorial and design staff did a wonderful job in bringing my dream to fruition.

My literary agent, Sandra Dijkstra, and her wonderful team were always there to cheer me on and provide guidance whenever I needed it. I still find it hard to believe that together we have produced two books in the past seven years.

My family in New Zealand endured yet another long absence, but I think we agree that the wait was worth it.

As with *The Oil Kings*, it is my hope that *The Fall of Heaven* will inspire young people everywhere to read history books and take an active interest in the world around them. More than ever, recent events have shown how important it is for all of us, wherever we live, to develop that critical faculty we call historical awareness.

INDEX

ABOUT THE AUTHOR

ANDREW SCOTT COOPER is the author of *The Oil Kings: How the U.S., Iran, and Saudi Arabia Changed the Balance of Power in the Middle East* and an adjunct assistant professor at Columbia University. He is a regular commentator on U.S.-Iran relations and the oil markets, and his research has appeared in many news outlets including *The New York Times* and *The Guardian*. He holds a PhD in the history of U.S.-Iran relations and lives in New York City.